BRITISH ENVOYS TO GERMANY
1816–1866

VOLUME II: 1830–1847

BRITISH ENVOYS TO GERMANY
1816–1866

VOLUME II: 1830–1847

edited by

MARKUS MÖSSLANG, SABINE FREITAG
and PETER WENDE

CAMDEN FIFTH SERIES
Volume 21

CAMBRIDGE
UNIVERSITY PRESS

FOR THE ROYAL HISTORICAL SOCIETY IN ASSOCIATION
WITH THE GERMAN HISTORICAL INSTITUTE LONDON
2002

Published by the Press Syndicate of the University of Cambridge
The Edinburgh Building, Cambridge CB2 2RU, United Kingdom
40 West 20th Street, New York, NY 1011–4211, USA
477 Williamstown Road, Port Melbourne, VIC 3207, Australia

First published 2002

A catalogue record for this book is available from the British Library

Library of Congress Cataloging-in-Publication Data applied for

ISBN 0 521 81868 0 hardback

SUBSCRIPTIONS. The serial publications of the Royal Historical Society, *Royal Historical Society Transactions* (ISSN 0080–4401) and Camden Fifth Series (ISSN 0960–1163), volumes may be purchased together on annual subscription. The 2002 subscription price (which includes postage but not VAT is £63 (US$102 in the USA, Canada and Mexico) and includes Camden Fifth Series, volumes 19, 20 and 21 (published in July and December) and Transactions Sixth Series, volume 12 (published in December). Japanese prices are available from Kinokuniya Company Ltd, P.O. Box 55, Chitose, Tokyo 156, Japan. EU subscribers (outside the UK) who are not registered for VAT should add VAT at their country's rate. VAT registered subscribers should provide their VAT registration number. Prices include delivery by air.

Subscription orders, which must be accompanied by payment, may be sent to a bookseller, subscription agent or direct to the publisher: Cambridge University Press, The Edinburgh Building, Shaftesbury Road, Cambridge CB2 2RU, UK; or in the USA, Canada and Mexico; Cambridge University Press, Journals Fulfillment Department, 110 Midland Avenue, Port Chester, NY 10573–4930, USA.

SINGLE VOLUMES AND BACK VOLUMES. A list of Royal Historical Society volumes available from Cambridge University Press may be obtained from the Humanities Marketing Department at the address above.

Printed and bound in the United Kingdom by Butler & Tanner Ltd, Frome and London

CONTENTS

ACKNOWLEDGEMENTS

For a number of reasons it is a great pleasure for me to present the second volume of the series 'British Envoys to Germany' only two years after the appearance of the first. And this is due to the unflagging enthusiasm of the persons engaged in the project and the unwavering support of the institutions involved.

As, at the same time, this is the last volume to which I had the chance to add my personal share of advice and work, I am especially grateful to my successor, Professor Hagen Schulze, for not only allowing the project to be continued but even planning to extend its range.

The editors would not have been able to complete their work without the support of the British Public Record Office and thus my thanks go to its Keeper, Sara Tyacke, and her staff as well as to the Royal Historical Society for again allowing this volume to be published as part of the Camden Series.

Many people contributed to the considerable workload involved in the preparation of this volume: Andreas Fahrmeir was the first to sift through the mass of reports from the early 1830s; Hilary Canavan took over the task of checking the final transcripts against the originals; Stefan Petzold and Eva Maria Hundsnurscher meticulously researched details for the annotations and Annika Mombauer this time prepared the index.

Again the editors are indebted to Angela Davies and Jane Rafferty who provided the English translations whenever necessary.

Finally, I still remember numerous sessions with my co-editors, Sabine Freitag and Markus Mösslang, when – confronted with a huge mass of source material – we discussed the criteria for selecting those reports to be published. My last word of gratitude is to both of them whose dedication to the project has been characterized by indefatigable efficiency and untiring care.

Frankfurt am Main, June 2002   Peter Wende

INTRODUCTION

The reports of British envoys in Germany from 1830 to 1847 which have been selected for inclusion in this volume convey a changed and more dynamic picture of the states of the German Confederation and of British policy for Germany than the first volume of this edition (1816–1829). One reason is that this period was much more turbulent and eventful in the states of the German Confederation than the 1820s had been. Another is that the policies of the Foreign Office itself had changed. Two political events in the German Confederation were mainly responsible for Britain abandoning the foreign policy restraint which it had previously practised. The first was the passing of the Six Articles by the Federal Diet in 1832 in reaction to the revolutionary unrest which had been precipitated in Germany by the revolution of July 1830 in Paris, and which culminated in the Hambach Festival two years later. The second event was the occupation of Frankfurt by federal troops after the Storming of the Frankfurt Guard House in 1833. Both measures provoked the British Foreign Office to express objections directly in the form of circular dispatches and verbal notes.

The British Foreign Secretary, Palmerston, had been shaped by the experience of domestic reform under the Whig administration in the early 1830s. He did not consider the anti-liberal policies initiated by Austria, but also supported by Prussia, as an adequate means of calming down the tense political situation in Germany. On the contrary, he feared that these policies would exacerbate the tensions, and perhaps encourage people in the constitutional states, who feared that their established rights would now be curtailed, to turn more strongly towards France. He even believed that French intervention was possible. For reasons of security, Palmerston was greatly interested in maintaining the federal structures intact as a crucial guarantee for the internal stability of Germany. He believed that a stable German Confederation as a buffer zone between France and Russia would have a positive impact on the balance of the European system of states as a whole.

Palmerston's views were not changed by the reports submitted by some of his accredited diplomats in the German Confederation, who attempted to defend the Confederation's policies in the context of the existing situation. Unlike Frederick Lamb, who had been British ambassador to Vienna since 1831, and had initially supported the line taken by the Austrian Chancellor, Metternich, defending the Confederation's repressive measures, the British Foreign Secretary wrote in a private letter: 'I am afraid Metternich is going to play the Devil in Germany with his Six Resolutions for the Diet. If he tries to carry them & succeeds, he will set all the Constitutional Sovereigns by the Ears with their Subjects, & then he will march in so many thousand Austrian Policemen to keep order, but this system cannot last, & must break down under him; and whenever it does there will be a crash [...]. Now I see no reason why Mett.[ernich] should sally forth like another Mahomet with the Koran of Vienna in one hand and martial law in the other, to dragoon all Europe into passive submission [...]. Divide et imperia should be the maxims of government in these Times. Separate by reasonable Concessions the moderate from the exaggerated, content the former by fair concessions and get them to assist in resisting the insatiable Demands of the latter. This is the only way to govern nowadays [...]. But this German Plan frightens me.'[1]

In recommending the principle of *divide et imperia*, Palmerston was, in his foreign policy, advocating a course that had proved to be highly effective domestically at precisely the same time – namely, defusing a critical situation at home by calculated flexibility and granting concessions in time; in short, avoiding revolution by conceding reform. His recommendation for the German Confederation was to encourage and secure reforms at home by limiting the exercise of autocratic power and strengthening the constitutional element. In achieving a balance between the interests of rulers and ruled, which Palmerston regarded as necessary, it was important that constitutions which had already been introduced in individual states of the German Confederation should not be repealed or substantially cut back. Palmerston saw the passing of the Six Articles in 1832 as an instance of the Confederation exceeding its powers and infringing the sovereignty of individual states. This, he believed, would not only exacerbate the quarrel between the Confederation and the constitutional states, but also make conflict inevitable between the rulers of constitutional states and their people.

The British envoy to the German Confederation in Frankfurt, Sir Thomas Cartwright, also believed that repressive policies could encourage political radicalization. Although, like Palmerston, basically conservative in his political opinions, Cartwright felt his opinions had been vindicated after the Storming of the Frankfurt Guard House in April 1833. He saw the incident as a direct attack on the German Confederation, and regarded it as a failure of the politics of repression practised since the passing of the Six Articles: 'We have now had

---

[1] Viscount Palmerston to Frederick Lamb, Private, Foreign Office, London, 30 June 1832, quoted in Günther Heydemann, *Konstitution gegen Revolution: Die britische Deutschland- und Italienpolitik 1815–1848*, Publications of the German Historical Institute London, 36 (Göttingen and Zürich, 1995), p. 228.

speaking evidence that the Decrees of the Diet of last year, which were to have suppressed all political irritation and which according to the language of the Members of the Diet had indeed restored tranquillity, have been no remedy at all. They have in many States augmented the ranks of the enemies of the Governments. They have in some of the Representative Chambers increased the existing spirit of hostility to the Government[.] [...] The measures of the Diet therefore have failed in their effect[.]'[2]

Even if the Storming of the Frankfurt Guard House had been the act only of a few radical fanatics, the event itself was a revealing of the extent to which Germany had been radicalized. The deputies to the Federal Diet felt threatened, and inadequately protected by the state's forces for order, yet the immediate occupation of the city by federal troops, ordered by the Federal Diet, represented a formal legal infringement of the Federal Act of 1815. As the Free City of Frankfurt had not, itself, at any point asked the Confederation for help, the Confederation's intervention lacked legal legitimacy.

Not immediately, but only after the conflict between the Frankfurt Senate and the Federal Diet had escalated again, Palmerston intervened, arguing that to maintain the independence 'even of the smallest State of Europe' was in Britain's interests.[3] Once again, different interpretations of the rights and duties of the German Confederation and its member states lay at the heart of the quarrel about the legality of the measures taken by the Confederation. The Confederation, argued Palmerston, could not interfere arbitrarily with the sovereign rights of individual states. In this case, as in his criticism of the passing of the Six Articles, Palmerston derived Britain's right to object from the guarantee undertaken by the European Great Powers in 1815. In the British view – and the French government expressed a similar one through its envoy to the German Confederation – the powers that had signed the Treaties of Vienna had undertaken to guarantee the sovereignty and autonomy of the German states. But as in the autumn of 1832, the Confederation, and, in particular, the Austrian and Prussian government, rejected this. On 18 September 1834, the Federal Diet deprived the powers that had signed the Act of the Vienna Congress of 1815 of the right to guarantee the independence of federal states and the right to monitor the resolutions of the Confederation. The relevant resolution evoked the following cynical commentary from Cartwright: 'This document is a most extraordinary production, and is more

---

[2] FO 30/43: Thomas Cartwright to Viscount Palmerston, No. 54, Confidential, Frankfurt, 20 April 1833.

[3] FO 30/48: To Thomas Cartwright, Foreign Office, No. 24, London, 15 May 1834 (draft); not included in this volume.

remarkable for its abuse and a display of rancorous feeling than of argument and reason [...]. There is but little argument in it, and what little there is, is all distorted.'[4]

The fact that the British envoys in Frankfurt were not permitted to see the Federal Diet's confidential minutes was a measure of how unwanted Britain's interference was. They obtained information about the contents only by co-operating with the Hanoverian envoys to the Federal Diet, as the Britons had no legal right to this information. And in 1834 a similar thing happened again at the Vienna Conferences. Here too, strict confidentiality excluded any official flow of information, which meant that the British diplomats were able to obtain information about the negotiations and resolutions of the Vienna Conferences only informally. Yet the difficulty of obtaining information did not prevent the diplomats from clearly expressing their own assessment of the political situation. Thus, all British envoys harboured considerable doubts that the articles agreed upon confidentially in Vienna and passed as a number of laws in October and November 1834 by the Federal Diet in Frankfurt would be efficiently translated into reality. Ralph Abercromby, accredited to the Prussian court in Berlin, summed up the scepticism of all the British envoys: 'So many decrees and regulations have already been issued by the Diet, for the internal regulation of Germany, and for its preservation against the Contamination of Revolutionary Principles, – all of which nearly have proved ineffectual from the impossibility of fully executing them, that it is by no means improbable that a similar fate may attend the results of the late deliberations of Vienna.'[5] The fact that they criticized the politics of the German Confederation, however, by no means meant that the British envoys therefore automatically supported the radical democratic forces in the German Confederation. Their idea of a politically moderate preservation or restoration of orderly conditions – still dictated by an elitist claim to leadership – involved a controlled liberalization of conditions, for example, by the German chambers changing their functions to become legislative rather than advisory organs. This would involve a limited redistribution of political power in favour of broader sections of the population, and included the view that subversive forces had to be dealt with firmly. Thus, the envoy John Ralph Milbanke had initially attributed the spread of the revolutionary mood in Germany in September 1830 mainly to the lack of decisive measures taken by the individual German states. '[T]he rapid progress', he reported to London, 'which it has made, is to be mainly attributed to the absence

---

[4] FO 30/53: Thomas Cartwright to Viscount Palmerston, No. 111, Frankfurt, 1 October 1834.

[5] FO 64/196: Ralph Abercromby to Viscount Palmerston, No. 1, Berlin, 2 July 1834.

of energetick measures on the part of most of the Governments where it has manifested itself.'[6]

Despite such clear statements, Palmerston did not allow the reports of his envoys to influence him unduly in a political sense. In any case, the question of how much real influence the envoys had on the foreign policy of their home country cannot be answered unequivocally. Palmerston received quite different reports from the various German states concerning the situation in the German Confederation. While Lord Erskine in Munich, and the otherwise conservative Sir Thomas Cartwright in Frankfurt sharply criticized the infringement of the sovereign rights of the constitutional states, Palmerston's close friend Frederick Lamb in Vienna and Lord Minto in Berlin initially defended the Confederation's actions, and emphasized the radical tendencies of the conspiracies which made a harsh response necessary. The envoys' reports confirm once again how much their reportage depended on where they were accredited, for they were still bound by the rule that said their first concern should be to make the motives and interests of their respective host governments clear and comprehensible, while exercising restraint in expressing their personal opinions. Palmerston, whose main goal was to secure British interests, pursued his course without letting the assessments of his diplomats confuse him; indeed, he sometimes diametrically opposed their views.

British diplomats observed and described the process of transformation that was taking place at different speeds in the various German states more clearly and perceptively than most German contemporaries, in particular, the force that emanated from the latent fear of revolution that was present during the *Vormärz* period. This fear of revolution, a perceptible 'sensitivity', takes many different shapes in the reports. Reports about excesses, unrest and protests (in Hesse-Kassel, Hesse-Darmstadt, Brunswick, Dresden, Karlsruhe, Hanau, Schwerin, Hanover, Bavaria, and the Rhineland Palatinate, among others) can be found throughout all the years covered in the present volume, but are especially frequent in the period after the revolution of July 1830 in Paris, and again from the mid 1840s. After the Rhine crisis of 1840, political consciousness becomes noticeably more nationalized. Further, the envoys' reports demonstrate that individual conflicts were noted and discussed far beyond the borders of the individual German states. The crises of the years after 1830 were diverse in political, economic and social terms, and their character was thus assessed very differently by the British envoys. Sometimes economic factors, such as rising prices

---

[6] FO 30/32: John Ralph Milbanke to Earl of Aberdeen, No. 25, Frankfurt, 29 September 1830.

for bread and beer in consequence of bad harvests, were seen as setting them off; at other times, the inappropriate raising of taxes was seen as responsible; at times, unrest was explained by specific local conditions; at others, just a few confused fanatics seemed to be at work; sometimes, with a glance at the student population, the education system was blamed; at other times the inappropriate authoritarian leadership style of certain small German princes was seen as having provoked a popular oppositional movement, which was prepared to extend the struggle to a bureaucracy unwilling to reform. Most envoys avoided monocausal explanations, and thus clearly distanced themselves from the official pronouncements in Germany, in particular of Austria and Prussia, which, as a rule, assumed far-reaching conspiracies and targeted campaigns, and tended to see every incident as a sign of imminent revolution. George William Chad, in any case, was of the opinion 'that these accounts, if not entirely false, are much exaggerated'.[7] Sir John Ralph Milbanke, too, was personally convinced 'that in many cases the accounts are much exaggerated', but did not dispute that 'it would be useless to deny that a very strong revolutionary spirit appears at this moment to pervade many of [the German States]'.[8] Precisely because the envoys were aware of the diversity of causes for the unrest and revolts, they did not see intervention by the Confederation, whether military, with the aid of federal troops, or legislative, through the passing of repressive resolutions, as an appropriate means to create permanent peace and order. In their eyes, permanent success could be achieved only by addressing the underlying causes through reform, for example, by decreasing the tax burden, introducing constitutions, or making further constitutional concessions.

Well versed, from their experience at home, in the conditions and rules governing a constitutional monarchy, the British envoys proved to be particularly astute in describing the real conflict at the heart of the German Confederation. This was the outcome of struggles between the supporters of constitutional reform and the defenders of autocratic rule. Two zones of conflict were thus created. The first concerned the influence of the Federal Diet on the internal conditions of the constitutional states, and the second related to tensions between the territorial princes and the diets in the constitutional states, which, as a rule, had the people on their side. The British observers were well aware of the possible consequences of the constitutional struggles: '[M]atters can only terminate in the total overthrow of one of the two

[7] FO 30/31: George William Chad to Earl of Aberdeen, No. 47, Frankfurt, 11 September 1830.

[8] FO 30/32: John Ralph Milbanke to Earl of Aberdeen, No. 25, Frankfurt, 29 September 1830.

Systems: either the Absolute System will come out of this struggle triumphant, overturning every thing opposed to it, or its Antagonists will gain a solid footing and the Diet lose its paramount Authority.'[9]

The conflict between the German Confederation and the constitutional states was crucially shaped by the Great Powers, Austria and Prussia. The politics of both states were diametrically opposed to developments in those German states in which the drive towards constitutionalism had been given an extra boost by the revolution of July 1830 in France. The two Great Powers were able to influence the internal politics of individual states through the Federal Diet, and they intervened on constitutional questions in particular. In several cases, the rights of the Confederation conflicted with those of individual states, for example, in connection with the highly contentious issue of press censorship, which soon became a symbol for the repressive policies of the Confederation as a whole. Thus the envoys often mention these disputes in their reports, not least also because its Personal Union with the Kingdom of Hanover, meant that Britain was directly involved in the constitutional struggles of the incipient *Vormärz*, precipitated by the Revolution of July 1830 in Paris. William IV's moderate policies and the granting of a constitution in 1833 initially calmed down the domestic situation in the Kingdom of Hanover. However, when Ernst August came to the throne in 1837, his decidedly anti-constitutional policies gave rise to new constitutional struggles which British diplomats and London were actively involved in settling.

Prussia also paid great attention to the open question of a constitution for the whole state. Since Friedrich Wilhelm III had promised a constitution in May 1815, the internal discussion about convoking a parliament for the whole of Prussia had not stopped. On Friedrich Wilhelm IV's accession in 1840, this became one of the topics dominating Prussian domestic politics. In 1847, when the issue of financing a railway to East Prussia suddenly made convoking an assembly to represent the whole state an urgent matter, Prussia was one of only four German states, including Austria, which did not yet have a constitution for the whole state.

The reports of the British envoys on constitutional realities in the individual constitutional states were much more specific than the diplomatic reports on the constitutional situation in Prussia, which was largely dictated by matters of principle until 1847. Accounts of the periodic diets and assemblies of the Estates frequently mention conflicts with princely governments. There is no doubt that the British diplomats were especially interested in developments in the constitutional states.

[9] FO 30/45: Thomas Cartwright to Viscount Palmerston, No. 54, Confidential, Frankfurt, 20 April 1833.

The smaller German states were coming to grips with a political system that was not so different from Britain's. In many constitutional states – and especially in those which had early gained a constitution, such as Baden, Bavaria and Württemberg – the people had become so accustomed to their constitutional arrangements that it seemed quite impossible that the rights of the chambers should be curtailed. Their work had long become a fixed component of the everyday political life of the German Confederation, and British diplomats were convinced that their further development could not be blocked by power political means, especially as most of the diets had managed to acquire more and more rights. Monarchy as the sole principle legitimizing political rule had thus been considerably restricted. And as reports of events in Hesse-Kassel, Brunswick, and Hanover, where there was less and less will to accept a traditional autocratic style of rule show, the monarchical principle had also forfeited significance among the people of constitutional states. Yet given the chance to push the conflict so far that the Federal Diet was provoked into intervening, most people, as Cartwright reported in 1833 about the conflict in Hesse-Kassel, chose to put their own home in order in order to prevent external interference: 'The Government is dissatisfied with the States, and the States are displeased with the Government. [...] [B]ut both the Government and the States feel that it is their common interest to avoid any act which through its consequences may call down upon them the interference of the Diet, and they therefore refrain from carrying their hostility to too great an extent.'[10]

Whereas the debates in the Federal Diet reflected the attitudes of the individual governments, debates in the diets reflected the mood in the territories. There, an effective liberal opposition could make its voice heard through a number of talented deputies, some of whom were extremely popular. All the envoys distinguished in their reports between the 'revolutionary party', which, in their opinion, was not influential, mostly worked outside parliament, and aimed for the total overthrow of existing conditions, and progressive liberal forces 'among the really respectable Classes',[11] whose supporters were often to be found in the second chambers of the diets. But the British envoys found it extraordinarily difficult to describe the admittedly highly diverse elements of German liberalism more precisely. One reason was that the social composition of the German liberal reform movement clearly differed from that of its aristocratically tinged Whig counterpart in

---

[10] FO 30/45: Thomas Cartwright to Viscount Palmerston, No. 176, Frankfurt, 19 December 1833.

[11] FO 30/38: Thomas Cartwright to Viscount Palmerston, No. 73, Frankfurt, 25 June 1832.

Britain. In Germany, its members were drawn predominantly from the academic intelligentsia; they were professors, writers, reformed civil servants, journalists, and lawyers. German liberalism was largely a bourgeois movement. This also applied to its radical republican variant, whose representatives were also to be found in the diets, and did not restrict their political agitation to the oppositional press which was so highly regarded by the British envoys. Nor could they be subsumed under the rather vaguely named 'revolutionary party'. But an understanding of nuances and details among most British envoys did not go further than this. With the menacing image of Chartism at home before them, British observers saw the subversive 'revolutionary party' in the German Confederation as an indefinable force 'from below'. In any case, it was something whose spread had to be stopped at all costs because it represented a latent anarchist threat to established conditions. For most British envoys, who had attentively followed the conflicts of the 1830s, it came as no surprise that similar conflicts, which had never been satisfactorily resolved, flared up again in the 1840s, aggravated by social unrest and economic crises. This time the crucial debates took place in the diets of the several constitutional states, not in the Federal Diet. In the constitutional states, growing self-confidence led to a determination not to allow Austrian or Prussian objections to curtail their rights, and even in Prussia demands for a constitution for the whole state, as has already been mentioned, became increasingly loud. In general, the government's unpopular measures hit a more sensitized public which, for its part, did not hesitate to criticize. The escalating political conflict, which some envoys had predicted in the 1830s and which was increasingly feared in the 1840s, was to become a reality in the revolutions of 1848–1849.

The trading policies of the German states and the creation of the German Customs Union (*Zollverein*) were observed and described quite separately from developments in domestic politics. Dispatches on economic issues also play a prominent part in this second volume of the planned series. The rapid succession of agreements which Prussia concluded with Hesse-Darmstadt, Bavaria, Württemberg, and the Central German Trade Association caused consternation in Britain. Yet neither Britain nor Austria could do anything effective to prevent the foundation of the German Customs Union in 1833 – it officially came into being on 1 January 1834. The envoys' reports are strikingly unanimous in suggesting that Prussia stood to gain most, perhaps not so much in economic as in political terms. Thus Thomas Cartwright in Frankfurt pointed out, as early as 1836, that 'the Customs Union gives the real power in Germany to Prussia. Every thing tends to prove that assertion, and if no unforeseen event, such as a war in Germany should occur, which in the confusion which it would bring with it would break up the Union, I am fully persuaded that all great questions affecting the peace, prosperity and mutual interests of Germany will in point of fact be henceforward decided at Berlin and not at Vienna.'[12] Although Britain had grave reservations in respect of trade policy, for most of the envoys a stronger Prussia as a buffer zone in the middle of Europe was not unwelcome. Lord Minto in Berlin believed that Prussia, as the weakest European Great Power, had no extra-territorial ambitions: 'Prussia, unlike Russia and Austria, has no external objects of ambition beyond the frontiers of Germany; whatever encroachments she may contemplate, are within these limits, and she is very conscious that amongst the Great European States her power is purely defensive.'[13] As Prussia's purposeful and systematic development of the Customs Union also involved expanding its influence in the German Con-federation at Austria's expense, the British side hoped that Prussia might display a greater readiness for compromise at home. If Prussia wanted as many states as possible to join the future Customs Union, it could not jeopardize this goal by pursuing decidedly anti-liberal policies. Austria's attempts to persuade Bavaria and Württemberg to join its side on matters of customs policy had failed; Prussia would have to practise more restraint than Austria in imposing unpopular measures: 'Prussia [...] is very loath to involve herself too openly in transactions which may have a detrimental influence on her grand project, and she is well aware that by taking too deep or forward a part, or appearing too ostensibly as a Principal in any coercive measures directed against the constitutional States, or the liberal System, she might bring upon her the hostility of the liberal Leaders in the Chambers of those States with whom she wishes to form this close commercial connexion [...]. It is then self-interest which makes Prussia so backward in entering fully into the Austrian views for the present, rather than a repugnance to interfere against the Liberals.'[14]

Britain did not, at first, perceive Prussia's expansion via the Customs Union as a political threat. Yet, in economic and trade terms, it had serious misgivings because the path Prussia had embarked upon with the Customs Union was quite clearly contrary to British economic interests. Britain feared the loss of its dominant position as an exporter to Germany. Opinions differed about the extent of the impact on the British economy; none of the envoys could make definitive projections.

[12] FO 30/61: Thomas Cartwright to Viscount Palmerston, No. 36, Frankfurt, 14 May 1836.
[13] FO 64/190: Lord Minto to Viscount Palmerston, No. 88, Berlin, 18 December 1833, not included in this volume.
[14] FO 30/35: Thomas Cartwright to Viscount Palmerston, No. 143, Confidential, Frankfurt, 23 November 1831.

What Britain's attitude should be was not clear. Thus an attempt was initially made to keep the Free City of Frankfurt, an important centre for foreign trade, out of the Customs Union by means of a treaty with Britain.[15] Soon thereafter, however, the opinion gained currency that Frankfurt's entry to the Customs Union was entirely compatible with British interests.[16] Once Britain had agreed to abrogate the trade treaty concluded in 1832, Frankfurt joined the Customs Union in 1836.

An economically backward Austria also had to submit to Prussia's trade policy ambitions. Although the Austrian government and Metternich, in particular, tended to see things differently, for most British diplomats Prussia's rise and increase in power was combined with a simultaneous Austrian decline and a decrease of influence within the German Confederation. Having criticized Austria's pioneering role in the passing of the Six Articles, many envoys now could not understand its passive behaviour in allowing Prussia to expand. 'The influence of Austria', Thomas Cartwright reported to the Foreign Office only two years after the establishment of the Customs Union, 'may be considered to be already undermined and it is perfectly immaterial to Prussia what endeavours she may make now to resume the ascendancy she was formerly wont to exercise in Germany. The Prussian System has already been carried too far to allow of a Collision with Austria upon the subject [occupation of Frankfurt] leading to any other result than the discomfiture of the latter and hastening the Crisis which must inevitably sooner or latter ensue.'[17]

In this context, it is obvious that over time, a number of envoys expressed the conjecture that in the short or long term, Austria would withdraw from the German Confederation. As matters pertaining to each state were discussed in its respective diet, the Federal Diet in Frankfurt became less important anyway. Thus, in 1846 William Fox-Strangways reported to the Foreign Office from Frankfurt that the Federal Diet had not assembled 'literally from the total absence of business. The gradual decline of business before the Diet, and the growing insignificance of that Body, are becoming subjects of general remark. Many reasons may be assigned for this decline: the inattention of Austria to any but the greatest questions in Germany; the increasing activity of Prussia; the very frequent declarations of its own incompetency which the Diet does not shrink from giving when questions of

[15] Cf. FO 30/35: To Thomas Cartwright, Foreign Office, No. 9, London, 25 November 1831 (draft); FO 30/37: Thomas Cartwright to Viscount Palmerston, No. 2, Frankfurt, 6 January 1832; not included in this volume.
[16] FO 30/50: Thomas Cartwright to Viscount Palmerston, No. 51, Frankfurt, 12 April 1834; not included in this volume.
[17] FO 30/61: Thomas Cartwright to Viscount Palmerston, No. 36, Frankfurt, 14 May 1836.

even small difficulty are referred to it; the growing tendency to confer
on, and to treat all the great matters in which Germany is interested,
at other places than Francfort; and above all the unwillingness to
enforce Decrees of the Diet on any Member of the Confederation who
may be inclined to resist them, are causes in themselves quite sufficient
to account for the diminishing importance and utility of this August
Body."[18]

Prussia was clearly taking the lead in the struggle for economic
supremacy in Germany, but forces were not so clearly distributed when
it came to religious policy. Bavaria, in particular, with its Catholic,
conservative government, toed the Austrian line. The Kingdom of
Saxony, where a Catholic ruling house confronted a predominantly
Protestant population, was in a special position. Given this background,
it is not surprising that religious questions were particularly significant
in Saxony. Controversies concerning religious policy fill much space in
the correspondence of all the British envoys accredited in the state of
the German Confederation.
    British diplomats, sensitized by the Irish Question, were always aware
that religion could not be separated from politics. The debate on mixed
marriages in the late 1830s can be seen as a precursor of the *Kulturkampf*,
the struggle which broke out between state and church in the 1870s.
Many British diplomats regarded the Prussian government's suspension
from office of the Archbishop of Cologne as a serious political mistake.
This step had been provoked by the argument concerning how children
of marriages between Catholics and Protestants were to be brought up.
Considering the Catholic population in the Rhine provinces and the
Catholic states in the German Confederation, the envoys concurred in
the view that Prussia had thereby done itself a disservice and unnecessarily damaged its reputation.
    The close connection between religion and politics in the years
before 1848 was also clearly revealed in other developments. The
movement for religious renewal in the 1840s, the rise of religious
sects, and especially the phenomenon of the *Deutschkatholiken* (German
Catholics) reveal how much the process of social transformation
extended to religious life in the first half of the nineteenth century. The
German Catholics' declaration of independence from church and state
institutions made church and state leaders fear for their authority.
Francis George Molyneux saw them as a religious movement of
world historical significance: 'Many well informed persons indeed
consider it as the fore-runner of great religious changes, and as the

---

[18] FO 30/95: William Thomas Horner Fox-Strangways to Earl of Aberdeen, No. 13,
Frankfurt, 17 February 1846.

commencement of an Epoch hardly inferior in magnitude to the Reformation itself."[19]

British envoys were also interested in many other subjects, often from motives related to their own domestic political concerns. Some of their reports on social legislation or penal reform, railway building or state encouragement of industry were in response to questions from the Foreign Office. The number of reports on the cholera epidemic that threatened Germany and the whole of Europe during the 1830s is striking. The frequency with which the cholera is mentioned in the British reports contrasts with the reassuring tone of the official pronouncements by German governments. The class-conscious British diplomats were particularly annoyed by the fact that the epidemic swept through all social classes, and was not restricted to the poorer sections of the population, who lived in unhygienic conditions. The death from cholera of the philosopher Hegel was immediately mentioned in the British reports as the most prominent example. Unfortunately, space does not permit the inclusion in this volume of many of the vivid reports of conditions in numerous towns and regions in the German Confederation. The same applies to reports on the state of agriculture, and accounts of general conditions in the economy and society of individual states. The envoys' reports leave no doubt that most German states had to deal with considerable economic and social problems during early industrialization. The depiction of social questions was not a priority in diplomatic dispatches, which were dominated by the politics of the German Confederation, the domestic politics of individual German states, and general foreign policy aspects, which are treated in passing in the present volume. Yet the picture of Germany between 1830 and 1847 which the reports of British envoys convey reflects the complexity and heterogeneity of the states within the German Confederation. Thus while these envoys' reports can be read as a prehistory to the 1848 revolution, they also testify to the significance of the years 1830 to 1847 as an important period of German history in its own right.

[19] FO 30/91: Francis George Molyneux to Earl of Aberdeen, No. 30, Frankfurt, 9 June 1845.

EDITORIAL PRINCIPLES AND TECHNICAL DETAILS

This second volume comprises a selection of official reports sent by the British envoys in Germany to the Foreign Office between 1830 and 1847. Since there was far more original material in the Public Record Office than for the years covered by the first volume (1816–1829) the selection process had to be even more rigorous. Due to limited space there are also more omissions in the texts selected than in the first volume. In general, however, the editorial principles in the first volume have been retained (cf. vol. 1, xviii–xxi).

From 1838 onwards the six familiar legations were joined by the new legation of Hanover. Until 1837 Hanover had a chancellery in London headed by a minister with cabinet rank, which dealt with all affairs directly on the spot. This chancellery was disbanded when the personal union between England and Hanover ended with the death of William IV in 1837. It was not until then, when Ernst August had come to power in Hanover, that a British legation was established and continued to exist until 1866. A selection of its correspondence has been included in the second volume.

The correspondence of the British consulate for the Hansa towns of Hamburg, Bremen, and Lübeck is not included, even though this consulate, based in Hamburg, acquired legation status after 1837 and retained it until relations were broken off in 1870. Even after this change in status the correspondence remained essentially that of a consulate, for two reasons. Firstly, there was no change in personnel: Consul-General Henry Canning, who had been in office since 1823, continued to be in charge after 1837 until he handed over to Sir George Floyd Hodges in 1841. Secondly, Britain's relations with the Hansa towns were mainly economic rather than political, and were therefore very different from the relations maintained with the individual German states via envoys at the courts. Had reports from Hamburg been included, this would have altered the character of the reports considered for this volume, even though certain reports from the Hamburg legation are not without interest, for example those by Sir George Floyd Hodges on the great fire in Hamburg in 1842.[20]

---

[20] Cf. FO 33/92: Sir George Floyd Hodges to Earl of Aberdeen, unnumbered, Hamburg, 6 May 1842; FO 33/92: Sir George Floyd Hodges to Earl of Aberdeen, No. 7, 10 May 1842; neither of these despatches included in this volume.

The reports by the British envoys to the states of the German Confederation are not always confined to one particular state as envoys were often accredited to several courts at the same time and therefore had to report on events in different states. It should be borne in mind that from 1836 onwards the envoys accredited to the Württemberg court at Stuttgart were simultaneously accredited to the Grand Duchy of Baden. From the 1840s onwards the British envoys to the Prussian court in Berlin were also accredited to Anhalt-Dessau, Mecklenburg-Schwerin and Mecklenburg-Strelitz. The envoys to Saxony with residence in Dresden were simultaneously accredited to Saxe-Altenburg, Saxe-Coburg-Gotha, Saxe-Meiningen and Saxe-Weimar-Eisenach; and the envoys to the German Confederation with its permanent representative Diet assembled in Frankfurt were simultaneously accredited to Hesse-Kassel, Hesse-Darmstadt and the Duchy of Nassau.

DIET OF THE GERMAN CONFEDERATION

(FRANKFURT)

FRANKFURT

FO 30/31: George William Chad to Earl of Aberdeen, No 10, Frankfurt, 28 May 1830

Duke of Brunswick's declaration; response of different ministers; question of England's attitude

I found on arriving here the general opinion to be that the Declaration of the Duke of Brunswick, although tardy and ungracious, and although couched in such obscure terms as to be hardly intelligible, would nevertheless be accepted.[1] The Hanoverian Minister[2] spoke to me in this sense, and the Committee which is to report to the Diet on the Declaration and which consists of the President, the Prussian, the Bavarian, the Saxon, and the Baden Ministers,[3] has determined by three against two to recommend that the satisfaction be deemed sufficient. The minority, however, (Prussia and Baden) are very strong in their sense of the insufficiency of the atonement, and I was informed last night by the Hanoverian Minister that he had received fresh instructions directing him to require a more complete and less exceptionable submission on the part of the Duke of Brunswick to the sentence of the Diet.[4] Before my conversation with Baron Stralenheim had ended, we were joined by the Baden Minister who expressed strongly his opinion of the insufficiency of the satisfaction, and stated his intention and that of more who thought with him to urge their view of the subject on the Diet. He ended by saying: 'We are now going to put ourselves forward in opposition to Austria and to draw

---

[1] In the Declaration of 22 April 1830, to which this dispatch refers, Duke Karl II revoked a patent which he had issued on 10 May 1827. In this patent he had declared invalid all the resolutions and decrees issued during the period of his minority until 1832. The Declaration of 22 April, however, did not establish whether the 1820 constitution was valid or invalid, and this was the subject of a dispute with the Brunswick diet. This issue was never finally clarified by the Federal Diet because the Brunswick diet revolted, and Duke Karl was deposed in September 1830.

[2] Karl Friedrich Freiherr von Stralenheim.

[3] President: Joachim Graf von Münch-Bellinghausen; Prussian minister: Karl Ferdinand Friedrich von Nagler; Bavarian minister: Maximilian Freiherr von Lerchenfeld; Saxon minister: Georg August Ernst Freiherr von Manteuffel; Baden minister: Friedrich Landolin Karl Freiherr von Blittersdorf.

[4] Resolution of the Confederation, 20 August 1829, which had forced Duke Karl II to revoke the patent of 10 May 1827.

upon ourselves her ill will for you and for your cause. Will your Government support us and see us through?'

I replied 'I am in this affair the Auxiliary of the Hanoverian Minister, and therefore to him I must refer you.'[5]

'But that is not sufficient for us. When Baron Stralenheim speaks, we look upon him as the organ of Count Münster; but if you come forward we consider ourselves as backed by Lord Aberdeen and by the Government of England. The one offers the support of Hanover (a small State like ourselves, and therefore insufficient), the other would give us the protection of England, and that is what we want.' –

My answer was –

'I am bound by duty and inclination to support the Hanoverian Minister, but I cannot put myself in the foreground. The King of England is not a Member of the Germanick Confederation.[6] I am not a member of the Diet, and it would not therefore become me to assume the character or the language of a Principal in the matter.'

FO 30/31: George William Chad to Earl of Aberdeen, No 13, Frankfurt, 4 June 1830

Treaty of Einbeck as an early stage of the North German Tax Association

I have the honor to inclose to Your Lordship the Copy of a commercial Treaty concluded at Einbeck on the 27th of March last between Hanover, Electoral Hesse, Oldenbourg, and Brunswick.[7]

By this Treaty the four Contracting Powers agree

to establish in their Dominions a uniform system of indirect taxes, to abolish all Custom Houses and all Export and import Duties between their respective Dominions, and in lieu thereof to draw

---

[5] The British envoys to Frankfurt were in a special position because George IV acted as regent during the minority of Duke Karl II from 1815 to 1823. George regarded the revocation in 1827 of the constitution promulgated in 1820 as a contempt of his regency, and this led to the quarrel between Brunswick and Hanover at the Federal Diet which is the subject of this dispatch.

[6] As King of Hanover, William IV was a member of the German Confederation. Britain's representation at the German Confederation through the legation in Frankfurt was strictly separated, formally and in terms of staff, from Hanover's.

[7] The Treaty of Einbeck was an attempt by the contracting states, which had already come together to form the Central German Trade Association in 1828, to develop their own, independent, customs area in opposition to Prussia's attempts to expand its customs policy. The treaty did not come into force because of the lack of an implementing regulation. However, the Treaty of Einbeck was an early stage of the North German Tax Association which was founded in 1834; cf. p. 277 in Hanover Section.

round the totality of the territory of the four Contracting Powers a general exterior line of Custom Houses,

to allow perfect freedom of commerce in the interior for every commodity except Salt used for domestick purposes, and Cards,

to establish common uniform regulations respecting prohibitions with regard to foreign States,

to conclude no Treaties with foreign States which may affect the produce of the import or Export-duties, but with common consent,

to divide the whole produce of the indirect taxes, (after deducting the expense of levying the same,) amongst the four contracting States, in proportion of their respective populations. The population of the 1st of January 1830 to be taken as the basis of this calculation, which calculation is however to be revised every 6 years,

to allow the subjects of each of the contracting Parties, in the dominions of each and every one of the States, all immunities for trade enjoyed by Natives.

to consider the Treaty as lasting till the end of the year 1841, unless in the meanwhile all the States of the Germanick Confederation should unite in a common System of Indirect Taxes.

The Tariff of the rate of duties to be levied under this Treaty is to be agreed upon by Commissioners, who are to meet at Hanover for the determination of this the most important point of the question.

The system of amalgamating the indirect taxes of different States, and of dividing at the end of the year the common produce, after deducting the expence of collection, is gaining ground in Germany. It appears calculated to augment the influence of the large States at the expense of the small Powers, who are however induced to accede to it by the opinion that it will tend to increase their revenues.

As to the present Treaty, the advantage is supposed to be on the side of Hesse, whose peasants, poor and frugal, subsist chiefly on food which pays nothing to the excise or Customs; whereas the Hanoverian farmers, particularly those in the neighbourhood of the Elbe, consume annually a considerable quantity of excisable articles.

FO 30/31: George William Chad to Earl of Aberdeen, No 16, Frankfurt, 25 June 1830

Acceptance of Duke of Brunswick's atonement; question of whether Federal Diet has gained 'character' and power by handling this affair

The decision of the Diet in respect to the sufficiency of the satisfaction given by the Duke of Brunswick was, as I have had the honor to inform

Your Lordship in my N° 11, put off until the 24th of this month in order that the Ministers might be enabled to receive in the meanwhile specifick Instructions from their respective Governments.[8]

The Sitting was opened yesterday by the President[9] who voted that the satisfaction should be accepted. His example was followed by all the members of the Diet, except the Ministers of Hanover, Prussia, and Baden.[10] The two Lippes[11] also voted with the Minority, but as these Princes together form only the quarter of a Vote, and as the remaining three quarters were with the majority, the collective Vote was against us.

The Question was carried by a large majority, and the Duke of Brunswick's atonement is therefore accepted. The Vote of the Minority expressed that it was not consistent with the dignity of the Diet to accept such an incomplete submission as that offered by His Highness. [...]

The Affair may now be considered as at an end, except as to such matters of detail as the wording of the Protocol to which I have already alluded. Although the result is not entirely satisfactory, yet I think it cannot be doubted that the Diet has gained in character by the Question. It had become a sort of fashion to revile this Body and to look upon it as incapable of either decision or vigour. The many cases in which an appeal to its Authority elicited no Sentence & was only followed by mutual compromises between the contending Parties, have been cited as failures on the part of the Diet instead of being considered evidences of the useful effect of this Body in preventing, hostile collision in the case of equal Adversaries, or unmitigated oppression in the case of unequal ones.

Now however it has been proved that the Diet has a power of acting, and may be brought to bear in extreme cases such as that of the Duke of Brunswick, and it may be fairly expected that the consequences of this conviction will be favorable to the authority of the Diet and the tranquillity of Germany. [...]

---

[8] For the constitutional struggle in Brunswick and Duke Karl II's proclamation cf. p. 3 in this section.

[9] Joachim Graf von Münch-Bellinghausen.

[10] Karl Friedrich Freiherr von Stralenheim, Karl Ferdinand Friedrich von Nagler, Friedrich Landolin Karl Freiherr von Blittersdorf. These envoys put forward formal reasons against accepting the Duke of Brunswick's explanation.

[11] Lippe-Schaumburg and Lippe-Detmold. The two Lippes, plus Hohenzollern, Liechtenstein, Neuß and Waldeck made up one vote between them in the Federal Diet.

FO 30/31: George William Chad to Earl of Aberdeen, No 44, Frankfurt, 9 September 1830

Disturbances in Hesse-Cassel; reasons for them; expected disturbances in Hesse-Darmstadt

Some slight disturbances have taken place at Hesse-Cassel, but the populace immediately on the appearance of the Troops called out upon the occasion gave way and dispersed.

The sudden and general rise in the price of bread, which the apprehension of war has occasioned, caused lately a riot at Mayence. The people endeavored to prevent some Vessels conveying Corn from leaving the Town, and succeeded, I understand, in getting possession of one boat laden with flour. The disturbance was however immediately put down, and all mention of it in the publick papers has been prevented.

It is probable that the Grand Duchy of Darmstadt will not long remain quiet, as the people are disgusted with the Prussian System of Excise and Customs which has lately been introduced there,[12] and are moreover at present much excited by the discussions in the Chambers respecting the payment of the Debts of the Grand Duke[13] and the settlement of the Civil List.

FO 30/31: George William Chad to Earl of Aberdeen, No 47, Frankfurt, 11 September 1830

Insurrection in Brunswick; reports probably exaggerated; possible causes of the incident

Accounts have been received from Brunswick, that an insurrection has taken place in that Capital: that the Mob repulsed the Troops which the Duke directed against them and finally set fire to the Ducal Palace, from which His Serene Highness[14] escaped not without having been exposed to some danger.[15]

I find, that these accounts, if not entirely false, are much exaggerated. It is true, that a mob did break some windows and destroyed a Carriage

---

[12] Hesse-Darmstadt joined the Prussian customs union on 25 August 1831.
[13] Ludwig II.
[14] Karl II.
[15] Duke Karl II's refusal to convene the Estates set off the unrest in Brunswick. Initial disturbances took place on 6 September, and on 7 September the ducal palace was stormed. After Karl had fled, his brother Wilhelm assumed the regency in September 1830.

belonging to the Duke, and that a deputation represented to His Serene Highness, that it was the prayer of his Subjects, that his reported intention of leaving Brunswick should be changed, and, that H.S.H. should reside in his States and take measures for employing the working classes. The Duke replied that he would take the subject into consideration.

Some excitement has taken place even at Frankfort. Inflammatory handbills have been pasted up in the streets containing threats of popular commotion in case the price of bread, which has experienced a sudden and considerable rise, should continue to augment.

FO 30/31: George William Chad to Earl of Aberdeen, Frankfurt, No 56, 22 September 1830

Disturbances at Carlsruhe because of Baden's accession to the Prussian commercial system; hostility to the Jews

Disturbances have broken out at Carlsruhe: the Populace, excited by the accession of the Government of Baden to the Prussian Commercial System,[16] assembled tumultuously crying: 'Down with Custom-Houses! No Custom-House Officers!'

The Great majority of the Inhabitants of the Grand Duchy are hostile to this commercial System, and there is a hope that the determination of the Government may be shaken by this burst of popular feeling.

The enmity to the Jews which pervades many Towns in Germany, shewed itself on this occasion, and the cry of Hep ! Hep! (the signal for attacking them)[17] was heard.

This hostility, for which no rational, or at least sufficient cause can be assigned, exists to a certain degree here at Frankfort and is not entirely confined to the very lowest dregs of Society. Measures of precaution have however been taken, which I think will be effectual in preventing any disturbance of this place.

[16] Chad here refers to the discussion about Baden entering the Prussian customs system. Baden did not join the *Zollverein* until 12 May 1835.

[17] The battle cry '*Hep-Hep, Jud verreck*' (Hep-Hep, Jews die), which was heard among the urban underclasses and in some artisan circles in a number of towns in 1830, had already been a feature of the Germany-wide pogroms as early as 1819. The 'Hep-Hep riots', which were repeated in 1834 in the Rhineland, interrupted the process of Jewish emancipation in Germany.

FO 30/32: John Ralph Milbanke to Earl of Aberdeen, No 25, Frankfurt, 29 September 1830

State of revolt in the Electorate of Hesse; government paralysed; revolutionary spirit in Belgium

The insurrectionary spirit which has lately manifested itself in the Electorate of Hesse, is daily assuming a more serious character.[18] The Country from Hanau to Fulda is in a complete state of revolt, and every day brings the news of some fresh excess on the part of the people, whose attacks are no longer confined to the Custom-Houses, but are apparently destined to involve in one common destruction every species of property both publick and private.

Several Noblemen's houses have been already pillaged and burnt to the ground, and as these proceedings are carried on with impunity, it is impossible to foresee where they will end.

The Troops have positively declared that they will not interfere, and the Government seems paralysed and fast approaching to dissolution. The person of the Elector[19] is, I am informed, scarcely treated with common respect.

In the mean time the States General, which are assembled at Cassel, are occupied in composing a Constitution, in doing which they have taken the last French one for a model.[20]

A circumstance worthy of remark is, that the actors in these disturbances are well supplied with money, which is furnished from some unknown source. It is said, I know not with what degree of truth, that some of the Inhabitants of this Town are not altogether strangers to the destruction of the Custom-Houses in the Electorate.

The Grand Duchy of Hesse is comparatively tranquil; and it is principally to the good conduct of the Troops, who were compelled in one or two instances to fire upon the populace, that this return to order is to be ascribed.

[18] After his return from Vienna, Prince Elector Wilhelm II was forced by increasing public pressure to convene the Estates in September 1830 and to recognize the citizens' guards formed in the towns. These successes encouraged large sections of the population to join the revolutionary movement in Electoral Hesse in order to pursue their own economic and social goals.

[19] Wilhelm II.

[20] The main feature of the constitution of Electoral Hesse, which was promulgated in January 1831, was the unicameral system modelled on the French one. A long list of basic rights and the far-reaching rights of the *Landtag* (full legislative powers, the right to grant the budget and taxes, the right to accept petitions and pass them on, and the right to impeach ministers) made the constitution of Electoral Hesse the most radical in the German Confederation so far.

These events, combined with what is now taking place at Brussels,[21] have produced a general consternation amongst the German States; and, although I am persuaded that in many cases the accounts are much exaggerated, it would be useless to deny that a very strong revolutionary spirit appears at this moment to pervade many of them. I am however of opinion that the rapid progress which it has made, is to be mainly attributed to the absence of energetick measures on the part of most of the Governments where it has manifested itself. [...]

FO 30/33: Thomas Cartwright to Viscount Palmerston, No 13, Frankfurt, 16 January 1831

Revolutionary uprising in Göttingen; civil and military measures taken by the government

Monsieur de Stralenheim this morning received advices from Hanover dated the 12th Inst[t] from which it appears the Insurrection at Göttingen was not then suppressed.

These official accounts mention, that the movement at Osterode[22] was soon got under, and that the Ringleaders[23] were arrested, but that on the 8th Inst[t] a rising took place at Göttingen.[24] Several Attorneys and private teachers, uniting with a part of the Inhabitants, formed a Common Council and organised a National Guard. They declared their object to be to petition His Majesty for the grant of a free Constitution and universal Representation. A Magistrate[25] has been sent to endeavour to prevail by persuasion upon the misguided people to return to their obedience to the laws, but at the same time the necessary steps have been taken for suppressing the Insurrection by force of arms, should other means fail.

[21] Inspired by the French revolution of July, the Belgian revolution took place on 25 August 1830. It resulted in Belgium seceding from the Netherlands. From 23 to 26 September fierce fighting, in which 1,200 people were killed, took place between the Dutch crown and the Belgian revolutionaries in Brussels.

[22] On 5 January a revolutionary common council and a citizens' guard were formed in the town of Osterode. The aim of this movement was to strengthen the rights of the urban middle classes vis-à-vis the government of Hanover. Intervention by the police and the army quickly put down this movement in Osterode.

[23] The ringleaders were Gustav König and August Freitag. The latter, however, evaded arrest.

[24] Three university teachers, Heinrich Ahrens, Ernst Johann von Rauschenplatt, and Theodor Schuster, led an assault on the Göttingen town hall on 8 January 1831, forcing the army to withdraw. Until the Hanoverian army intervened and took Göttingen without a struggle on 16 January, a common council and national guard drawn from the ranks of the rebels had control of Göttingen.

[25] Name not traceable.

The attempts which have been made to raise the Country have not yet met with success.

The University by a Decree of that day's date (the 12th) was declared shut till Easter. The Students have been ordered to quit the Town; and, in case of disobedience to this order, those who are Hanoverian Subjects have been threatened to be held incapable of ever obtaining employment in the Service.

The Hanoverian Government is desirous that the Students, subjects of the other States of the Confederation, should receive similar orders from their respective Sovereigns.

In addition to the above details I can add, that a Force of from five to six thousand men was collecting at Nordheim under General Busche[26] to act against Göttingen.

The Students have not generally taken part in this Affair, and those the most active are principally Hanoverian Subjects. The Town is barricaded in several parts, and the Gates are shut.

FO 30/33: Thomas Cartwright to Viscount Palmerston, No 24, Frankfurt, 17 February 1831

Disappointment of the ultra liberal party in Bavaria at limited changes made by the Bavarian King; critical attitude of the press

Considerable anxiety is entertained respecting the state of Bavaria, where in different parts disenchantment and political irritation exist in a very high degree.[27]

The Ultra liberal Party has been for some time much disappointed at the policy of the King, who has set such limits to the extent of his liberalism as do not at all satisfy the expectations it had formed at the outset of His Reign; and at this moment it is exerting itself to the utmost to excite a spirit of hostility throughout the Country to The King and Government.

The King, when Prince Royal, was well known to be one of the warmest advocates of the Constitutional Form of Government established in Bavaria, and he even gave such proofs of his opinions on that head as to draw upon Himself the animadversion and ill will of some of the Members of the Confederation. Since His accession to the Throne, though on some occasions acts certainly have emanated directly from His Majesty which may not be strictly in accordance with the Powers of a Constitutional Monarch, the Policy of His Majesty's

[26] Friedrich August Philipp Freiherr von dem Bussche-Ippenburg.
[27] Cf. pp. 407–409 in Bavaria section.

Government has generally borne the character of a rationally liberal System. Many ancient abuses have been reformed and various measures adopted which tended to the general Welfare of the Community, such, for instance, as the establishment of the Provincial States.

Since the French Revolution[28] in July last His Majesty has thought fit to take certain precautionary measures[29] to prevent the discontented from fomenting disturbances in His Dominions, and a fortnight since He issued an Edict regulating the Press (which I have the honor to inclose)[30] which naturally increased the dissatisfaction already existing amongst the Liberals, and they have now come to an open breach with The King. [...]

A periodical Newspaper[31] has been established at Würzbourg, edited ostensibly by an Individual named Eisenmann; but Monsieur Behr is the principal Contributor to its Columns. It appears occasionally as matter is furnished for publication, and one of its recent numbers contained an Article of the most inflammatory nature entitled 'Ordonnances' which referred to the transactions in France in July, and as far as I can learn preached in the most open terms the necessity of offering resistance to the Government. The Number has been suppressed as much as possible, but I hope still to obtain a Copy for Your Lordship's Information.

Würzbourg is considered to be the centre of the disaffected, but the spirit of discontentment is spreading every where, and is very likely to give considerable trouble to the Government during the ensuing Session. Monsieur de Münch has expressed to me great uneasiness at the general state of the publick feeling in Bavaria.

---

[28] The conflict between the Bourbon royal house and the liberal majority in the chamber climaxed in a revolt by the people of Paris from 27 to 29 July 1830. The revolution led to the abdication of Charles X and the installation of Louis Philippe, Duke of Orleans, as 'King of the French'. In the aftermath of the revolution there were revolutionary risings and constitutional demands all over Europe.

[29] The measures taken by Ludwig I included reducing the price of bread in order to pacify the population in September 1830, dealt firmly with the students of the university of Munich, and banning students' associations in December 1830.

[30] Enclosures: 1. Edict issued by The King of Bavaria on 28 January relative to the regulation of the Press; 2. Petition addressed by the Citizens of Würzbourg to The King of Bavaria, praying for the admission of the Burgomaster Behr in to the Assembly of States; 3. Answer of The King of Bavaria to the Petition addressed to His Majesty by the Citizens of Würzbourg; 4. Answer of The King of Bavaria to a Petition addressed to His Majesty by the Citizens of Bamberg.

[31] The *Bayerisches Volksblatt*, founded in 1828 by Gottfried Eisenmann, was a forum for patriotic liberalism and constitutionalism. This typically southern German political movement was more interested in progress for Bavaria than in German national unity. The *Volksblatt* was banned in 1832.

FO 30/33: Thomas Cartwright to Viscount Palmerston, No 70, Frankfurt, 30 April 1831

Reports on the state of Hesse Cassel; animosity of the inhabitants towards the Elector, Electoral Prince and their mistresses; restoration of tranquillity in Dresden; unrest in the Duchy of Nassau; dispute respecting the Duke's right to the propriety of the Domains

[...] The state of Hesse Cassel is very unsettled. The Elector[32] for the last two months has been nominally established at a Bath called Wilhelmsbad in the environs of Hanau; but he has in fact been principally passing his time with Madame de Reichenbach, who took a house in this town on being obliged to make her precipitate retreat from the neighbourhood of Cassel in January last.

The States were opened at Cassel by Commission about three weeks since, but His Royal Highness does not evince any disposition to return to His Capital to facilitate the march of business and is fitting up a Summer Palace which belongs to Him near Hanau in a manner which would lead to the belief He has the intention of establishing Himself there altogether.

His apparent determination certainly is to abandon the Capital for the purpose of living with His Mistress, who is held in detestation by His Subjects; and this circumstance has unfortunately increased the aversion which His Subjects have shewn towards His person on many occasions. The Inhabitants of Cassel are particularly indignant at His Royal Highness's proceedings, and have now presented an Address to the States, signed by 17,000 of the Burghers of the Town, requesting them to invite His Royal Highness to return forthwith to Cassel to bear His share in their deliberations, and in case of the Elector's refusal to do so, to propose the Appointment of a Regency.

I am afraid that the people will not stop here, for the animosity to the Elector is so violent that the necessity of declaring His Royal Highness's déchéance is openly canvassed throughout the whole Country. Unfortunately the Electoral Prince[33] is not formed to arrest the evils which may occur, from the nullity of his character. He is held in infinitely greater detestation than the Elector himself, and he does not give a thought to any other subject than his Mistress[34] with whom he is living publickly in this Town under the very eyes of his Father, who so far, may certainly be said to set him the example. He is so totally lost in the estimation of the Inhabitants of the Electorate, that even if the Elector were to separate Himself from Madame de Reichenbach, return to Cassel, and regain the affections of His Subjects,

[32] Wilhelm II.
[33] Friedrich Wilhelm.
[34] Gertrude Falkenstein.

there is little probability of a like proceeding on the part of the Electoral Prince having a like effect.

The irritation therefore that prevails in the Electorate of Hesse Cassel is at such a height that unless the Elector by His personal conduct may allay it immediately, consequences of serious importance may be expected shortly to result from it.

In Dresden tranquillity appears to have been restored by the strenuous measures resorted to by the Government on the 18th and 19th Instant.

The Saxon Minister[35] tells me that his accounts from thence represent the attempts of the discontented to have been entirely thwarted and their plans discovered. A project for the establishment of a Republick was found among the papers of the Ringleaders.[36]

But in the Duchy of Nassau, which of all the States of Germany is perhaps that where there ought to be least cause for complaint, it may be singular to say fermentation reigns in as high a degree as in any other.

A dispute has been for some time going on between the Duke[37] and the States respecting His Highness's Right to the propriety of the Domains. When the Constitution was proclaimed about 10 years since[38] he secured to himself the Domains as his own property; and if he had been mediatised, as other Sovereign Princes were in 1803,[39] I believe there is no doubt but his Right to have preserved them as his own property would never have been contested. At each Meeting of the States the Second Chamber regularly entered its protest against His Highness's Right to these Domains, as it considered them to belong to the State; but in the actual Session for the first time the Chamber instead of contenting itself with its usual protest, has required the Duke to cede the Domains and receive in lieu thereof a Civil List. The Duke regards these Domains as his own property and resists this demand, while the Chamber refuses to vote the Budget for the exigencies of the State unless His Highness consents to give them up. Both Parties hitherto maintain their ground, but a few days must bring this contest to a termination, either by the Duke acceding to the proposed Arrangement, or His Highness dissolving the Chamber.

In the mean time the dispute has created considerable irritation and

---

[35] Georg August Ernst von Manteuffel.

[36] Cf. p. 300 in Saxony section.

[37] Wilhelm.

[38] The constitution of Hesse Nassau was drawn up in 1814. However, the two chambers of the *Landtag* were not convened until 1819.

[39] In the period 1803 to 1806 many of the numerous smaller rulers in the German empire were subordinated to the larger territories. The majority of the imperial towns plus the duchy of Arenberg and the principalities of Salm, Isenburg, Leyen und Fürstenberg were mediatized. Although the Congress of Vienna conceded the mediatized princes a number of privileges in 1815, they were unable to regain their old positions.

excitement throughout the Duchy, and the Inhabitants of all Classes seem inclined to support warmly the views of the Second Chamber, so that unless the Duke yields, it is feared the Affair will not terminate without an ebullition of popular feeling.

FO 30/35: Thomas Cartwright to Viscount Palmerston, Secret, No 133, Frankfurt, 22 October 1831

Alleged project for the dissolution of the Confederation; Austria's declining influence in Germany

Monsieur Sieveking, the Minister of the Hanse Towns in the Diet, came to me this morning to inquire in confidence if I had any information of a project which was supposed to be on foot for the dissolution of the Confederation. –

I told him that I had not heard a syllable on such a subject. He then gave me all the information he possessed, which is contained in the inclosed Extract[40] of a Letter from Berlin, and which I presume has been forwarded to him by his Government at Hamburgh to enable him to try and follow up the thread of the mystery. The letter itself he informs me is from a person who generally gives very accurate information.

Not a word has transpired here of any such plan being in contemplation; but as the assertions in this letter are made very positively, I mentioned them as a rumour to the Saxon Minister, who was very much struck with the supposed transaction, and did not seem to think that it was so improbable. Upon consideration it appears very possible that Austria may have brought forward some such scheme.

The project appears to be, to extend to the Minor German States the system of Neutrality which has been acknowledged in Belgium;[41] and if the Confederation were to be dissolved under such circumstances, the defensive position of Austria with respect to France would only be strengthened by the interposition of Bavaria, Wirtemberg and Baden as neutral Powers between them.

There may be many reasons why Austria may desire the dissolution of the Confederation.

Your Lordship will remark that the Confederation has been found

---

[40] Enclosure: Translation. Extract from a letter dated Berlin 8 October 1831.
[41] In the London Protocol of 21 January 1831 Austria, Prussia, Russia, Britain, and France recognized Belgium's independence from the Netherlands. 'Neutrality in perpetuity', modelled on that of Switzerland, was imposed on the new state.

to work ill in the Luxembourg Question.[42] Difficulties occurred at each moment in completing the Army of Occupation: each Power whose Contingent was called for had some excuse to make and some reason to put forward to prevent its marching; all which circumstances brought to light the faulty System of the Confederation and created doubts of the possibility of its ever being made efficient.

Austria must have observed at the period when Her troops entered the Papal territories,[43] that there was a decided repugnance on the part of many of the German States to support Her in any quarrels She might have in Italy, and She must then have become aware that She could never expect to derive any great advantage from Her connection with the Confederation in the event of a future war in that Country.

She has also had many proofs during the present year that Her influence in Germany is on the decline.– She is jealous of the growing power of Prussia. She is annoyed at the success of the Prussian Commercial Union, which by drawing closer the ties of the Prussian Government with the other German States, must henceforward give it greater weight and political influence in the Confederation. She also reproaches Prussia with leaving Her always to take the lead in unpopular and disagreeable questions, and if in addition to this, Prussia should now be found hesitating to unite with Austria in enforcing some measures to restrain the spirit of liberalism in the constitutional States of the Confederation, (and, it is said that, though not averse to interfere, She desires to abstain from doing so until She shall have completed her Commercial Union with the other States), it appears not so impossible that Austria may be willing to retire from the Confederation altogether under stipulations which She may turn to her advantage.

It is very probable that the Hanse Towns may be alarmed at the possibility of there being any truth in this project; for as Monsieur Sieveking appears to feel certain, Prussia would never consent to the neutrality of the Northern States of Germany, though She might to those in the South of Germany, which would be sufficient for the views of Austria, the North of Germany would consequently be at the mercy

---

[42] The Grand Duchy of Luxemburg was bound to the Netherlands in a personal union and was a member of the German Confederation. The Belgian revolution of 1830 (cf. p. 10 in this section), also affected Luxemburg. After the Netherlands had appealed in vain to the German Confederation for help, the Five-Power Conference in London on 15 October 1831 resolved to divide Luxemburg into a Walloon western part and a German eastern part which, including the town and the fortress, would continue to be the property of the Dutch crown. The quarrel about this act of separation, which was the subject of a complaint by the Netherlands to the German Confederation, was not settled until the London Conference of April 1839.

[43] In the years 1830–1831 Austria saw its dominant position in Italy threatened by the revolutionary crisis. Pope Gregory XVI's request for assistance gave Austria a pretext for military intervention in Italy in March 1831.

of Prussia, and the Hanse Towns might greatly suffer in their commercial relations.

Monsieur Sieveking has begged that his name might not be put forward as my Informant, because he is afraid of standing committed with the Prussian Government; and I therefore hope Your Lordship will not name him in any conversation you may have with Baron Bulow.

FO 30/35: Thomas Cartwright to Viscount Palmerston, No 137, Frankfurt, 7 November 1831

Restoration of tranquillity in Frankfurt; speculations on the origins of the disturbances; precautionary measures taken by the Frankfurt magistrates and their effects

Since the scenes which passed on the 24th and 25th the tranquillity of Frankfort has not been disturbed. Some fifty Artificers, not Natives of Frankfort, employed in different Establishments, who had taken an active part in the tumults, have been sent away from the Town, and several Individuals, concerned as Ringleaders, have been arrested; among others those persons who so dastardly fired without any provocation on the Guard at the Gate of the Town and killed two Soldiers.

It has been rumoured that these disturbances had a political Origin, but I firmly believe that they arose solely from the incidental circumstances[44] mentioned in my Dispatch N° 134, and might have been effectively prevented altogether by a little more foresight on the part of the Magistrates. Nevertheless as the Senate is very unpopular with a large portion of the Inhabitants, it is very possible that, when the Town was in an uproar, some of the discontented Burghers took advantage of the moment to excite the populace and embarrass the Authorities, and it is also possible that secret Agents took their share in fomenting the disturbances when once in force; but I cannot find any evidence of the late disorders having been solely the work of political Intrigue or Secret Agents, with a view to bring the Free Towns into discredit with the Confederation.

From the precautionary measures which have been continued every night until within these few days, the Magistrates appear to have barely recovered from their alarm, and in their zeal to avert a recurrence of the tumults they have unfortunately been led into the adoption of some

[44] The events were triggered by the fact that the city gates had been closed early on 24 October, the first day of the festivities held to celebrate the end of the grape harvest in the area around Frankfurt. On the following evening, several hundred people gathered at the *Allerheiligentor* to protest against this. After fire had been exchanged with the units on watch, the military was called in to restore the peace.

steps which have only served to increase their unpopularity. An Order of the Police for instance was published on the 28th, three days after all riot had ceased, by which it was notified to the Inhabitants that every person who appeared in the streets after 10 o'clock, without he was provided with a lantern, would be arrested.

The natural consequence of so vexatious and useless a Regulation was, that the first evening at the stated hour, several hundred persons paraded the streets very peaceably with lanterns of all sizes and shapes and turned the Police Regulation into ridicule, and after this ambulant Illumination had been repeated two or three nights to the amusement of the townspeople and the annoyance of the Authorities, the Senate was glad to find a pretext to rescind the Regulation. [...]

FO 30/35: Thomas Cartwright to Viscount Palmerston, Confidential, No 143, Frankfurt, 23 November 1831

Prussia's and Austria's attempt to weaken liberal influence in Germany by close cooperation in the Federal Diet; reflections on the meaning of the word 'revolutionary'; measures against the press; Prussia's primary interest in embracing the whole of Germany in one unified Commercial Union

It becomes daily more evident that the two leading Powers of the Confederation are bent upon weakening the influence of the Liberals in Germany and are busily employed in devising the best means of checking the ascendancy they are gaining in the constitutional States. –

They appear to have determined to commence operations by acting with great severity against the Press, which they consider as a most dangerous weapon in the hands of the liberal Party; for the Count de Münch in the Sitting of the Diet on the 10th Inst reminded that Assembly that by the federal Law of 1819 (which Your Lordship may remember emanated from the Conferences of Carlsbad and Vienna)[45] each Member of the Confederation was under an obligation to watch strictly over the Press and prevent all abuse of it in his Dominions, that nevertheless several Newspapers were published in Germany which most artfully disseminated seditious and revolutionary principles, and it was necessary therefore for him to bring to the notice of the Diet the violent language and dangerous doctrines which were to be found in their columns, in order to direct to the subject the serious attention of those Governments in whose States they were printed, and he particularly instanced the Paper called the 'Deutsche Tribune' which

---

[45] Carlsbad Conferences, 6–31 August 1819; Vienna Conferences of Ministers, 25 November 1819 – 24 May 1820, cf. vol. I, pp. 113–123, 493–499.

appears at Munich, the 'Hoch-Wächter' at Stuttgard, and the 'Ver-fassungsfreund' at Carlsruhe.[46]

He then went on to expatiate on the danger which was to be apprehended by the States of Germany from allowing the circulation with impunity of Publications which advocated seditious and revolutionary doctrines, and pointed out a Paper called 'das constitutionelle Deutschland'[47] printed in German at Strasbourg in the sense of the Ultra-Liberals as coming under that description, and proposed to the Diet to prohibit forthwith its further circulation in the States of the Confederation. [...]

It is very difficult to determine what is exactly meant by the word 'revolutionary' in the mouths of the Members of the Diet. By most of them it is often applied to every opinion indiscriminately which is not strictly in unison with what they term the monarchical principle, – which may here be interpreted – the Austrian System, and if the Diet is now going to enforce the Regulations of the Federal Laws against all the Revolutionary Papers in the wide sense that term is usually employed, it will perhaps go further than either reason or necessity require. It is however hardly to be doubted that Austria and Prussia have resolved to suppress all the Ultra-liberal Papers one after another by Decrees of the Diet, and if it is the determination that a publication should be suppressed, it is full as well the blow should come from the Diet, in preference to coming from the Government in whose States it is printed, as by such means that Government would be saved from much of the odium and unpopularity resulting from the exercise of such a stretch of authority. [...]

But to whatever extent the Diet may be inclined to enforce its decrees against the Press, these measures only form a part of the grand plan of operations which it is in the contemplation of Austria and Prussia to direct against the constitutional States.

I mentioned to Your Lordship in a former Dispatch that Austria was

[46] *Deutsche Tribüne*, founded on 1 July 1831 by Johann Georg August Wirth in Munich, is an early example of the German party press. It belonged to the decidedly liberal opposition. In order to avoid censorship, from January 1832 the *Deutsche Tribüne* was published in Homburg, in the Bavarian Rhine Palatinate. Even before the publication of its final issue on 21 March 1832, the *Deutsche Tribüne* had been banned by a resolution of the German Confederation dated 2 March 1832. The *Hochwächter, Volksblatt für Stuttgart und Württemberg* was founded in 1830 in Stuttgart as the daily newspaper of the democratic movement; from 16 January 1833 it appeared as *Der Beobachter*. The newspaper *Der Verfassungsfreund, eine Wochenschrift für Staats- und Volksleben*, which had grown out of the *Hessische Blätter für Stadt und Land* in 1831, was published in Kassel, not Karlsruhe. This weekly paper ceased publication in 1834.

[47] *Constitutionelles Deutschland* was initially a supplement to the Strasburg paper *Niederrheinscher Courier*; from May 1831 it was published independently. On 19 November 1831 its distribution on the territory of the German Confederation was prohibited.

confidentially combining with the Prussian Government some plan for restricting the power of the legislative Bodies in the States Members of the Confederation.

The Austrian Government wished in the first instance to establish Conferences on German Affairs after the manner of those of Carlsbad and Vienna, at which it was hoped that constitutional Governments might be persuaded to go pari passu with Austria and Prussia and adopt some modifications in the Federal Laws which would define very nicely the duties of the legislative Bodies in States Members of the Confederation, as well as set distinct limits within which their deliberations should be confined.

It is now not well understood at Frankfort whether the project of Conferences still exists, but it is known that Austria has not yet been able to come to an understanding with Prussia upon all the points of the project She brought forward, or on the exact mode of proceeding. Prussia indeed manifests considerable hesitation to pronounce herself positively and is unwilling to take as forward and open a part as it is the desire of Austria she should do. This backwardness of Prussia has been imagined to proceed from an apprehension that by taking too prominent a part against the Liberals, she might rouse their animosity and kindle germs of discord in her own Dominions; but though such a reason may also have its weight, the more probable cause of this unwillingness to accede to the Austrian Propositions is to be found in more interested motives.

Prussia is so wrapped up in her plan for embracing the whole of Germany in one Grand Commercial Union under her protection, from which System she flatters herself she shall derive immense advantage and political importance, she is very loath to involve herself too openly in transactions which may have a detrimental influence on her grand project, and she is well aware that by taking too deep or forward a part, or appearing too ostensibly as a Principal in any coercive measures directed against the constitutional States, or the liberal System, she might bring upon her the hostility of the liberal Leaders in the Chambers of those States with whom she wishes to form this close commercial connexion. Therefore She is unwilling to act too openly against the Liberals from fear of the consequences which may ensue to her commercial Union; for were they to declare themselves enemies to her project, they might throw impediments in the way of its accomplishment, which would expose it to some severe checks, if not to total failure.

It is then self-interest which makes Prussia so backward in entering fully into the Austrian views for the present, rather than a repugnance to interfere against the Liberals.

From the notion which is entertained at Frankfort of the real sentiments of Prussia, there is no reason to suppose her to be more favorably disposed towards a liberal system than Austria. Such an idea has got abroad, but it appears founded in error. The Instructions received by the Prussian Minister[48] in the Diet are all conceived in as decided and anti-liberal a sense as Austria could desire. The Prussian Minister on all occasions is ready to support any proposition of an arbitrary tendency, come from what quarter it may, and on any Resolution of that nature he is always ready with a declaration more pronounced than those of his Colleagues; but no proposition of an anti-liberal drift ever originates with him alone. [...]

FO 30/38: Thomas Cartwright to Viscount Palmerston, No 48, Frankfurt, 25 May 1832

Press primary topic of the Federal Diet; effects of the measures taken by this institution; Bavaria's refusal to recognize the authority of the Federal Diet; Liberals gaining strength; unclear position of the Federal Diet; impact of the Hambach Festival

[...] The Press is now the topick which almost wholly engrosses the attention of the Diet, as it is considered the primary cause of all the excitement and revolutionary spirit with which the South of Germany is overrun.

The effect produced by the Decree of the Diet of the 2nd of March last, directing the suppression of the Journals published in the Bavarian Rhenish Provinces, has fallen far short of what was expected, and that measure has indeed been a total failure.

Instead of cutting short the career of the two Editors of those mischievous Papers[49] and intimidating others from following a similar course, as was the intention of the Diet, it has done little else than exasperate the liberal Party and bring to light the want of unanimity among the Powers of the Confederation on the question of the right of the Diet to interfere in the internal affairs of the different States.

The conduct of the Bavarian Government has given great umbrage to the Diet, and it is certain that it has inflicted a blow on the Authority of that assembly which will with difficulty be repaired.

The Bavarian Government has refused to recognize the Authority of the Diet, and until She retracts and is brought to acknowledge her

---

[48] Ferdinand Friedrich von Nagler.

[49] Johann Georg August Wirth, editor of *Deutsche Tribüne* (cf. n. 46 in this section) and Philipp Jakob Siebenpfeiffer, editor of the daily *Der Westbote*, which had been published since April 1831. The Federal Diet's decree of 2 March 1832 affected both papers as well as the *Neue Zeitschwingen*. Wirth und Siebenpfeiffer were banned from working for five years.

error, the whole force of the Diet is paralised; for with what justice can it now call upon any other State to execute its Decrees if it allows Bavaria to refuse to do so with impunity?

It is evident that a Government not disposed to submit to the Dictates of the Diet may now rest its case upon the example set by Bavaria and without any apprehension of the consequences refuse to execute the Ordinances of that Assembly. It is the Argument the Baden Minister[50] is now holding on the question of the repeal of the Baden Law of the Press.[51] He says that until Bavaria executes the Decree of the 2nd of March, it cannot be expected that Baden will repeal that Law at the demand of the Diet, and unless the Confederation is prepared to act with energy and Decision to put an end to this ambiguous state of things, its Authority will soon be annihilated.

The Liberals so well feel the force and truth of their position and the actual impotency of the Diet, that they are straining every nerve in all parts of the Country to turn to good account the schism and discord which they presume prevails among the Powers of the Confederation, and if they are left to themselves much longer, they will certainly give the Confederation much trouble.

They are redoubling their attacks on the Diet and the Absolute Governments, and since the abortive attempt to silence M.M. Siebenpfeiffer and Wirth, new Journals are springing up in such numbers on all sides that even if the Decrees of suppression attained their end, the Diet could never by such means keep pace with the publications with which this Country is now inundated.

From the Inclosure in this Dispatch Your Lordship will observe that M. Siebenpfeiffer, though prohibited by the Diet from editing any Newspaper for Five years, has continued his 'Western Messenger' under the title of 'Deutschland'[52] at Manheim, and when the Diet shall have prohibited that Paper he will go elsewhere with his Press and reproduce his publication under some other title.

The case of M. Siebenpfeiffer is that of Wirth, and will be that of every other Editor whose Paper is suppressed by the Diet, and better evidence can hardly be adduced to shew the utter impossibility, in the present state of opinion, of subduing the Press by the work of suppression, unless all the Governments are decided to exert that arbitrary mode of proceeding to its utmost extent and with the utmost severity. [...]

---

[50] Friedrich Landolin Karl von Blittersdorf.

[51] The Press Law of 28 December 1831 fundamentally abolished censorship in Baden; it was in future to apply only to reports concerning the business of the Confederation and other German states.

[52] The journal *Deutschland* was the continuation of the newspaper *Rheinbayern*, which had been edited in Zweibrücken by Phillipp Jakob Siebenpfeiffer since October 1830, and not of the *Westbote*.

FO 30/38: Thomas Cartwright to Viscount Palmerston, No 54, Frankfurt, 2 June 1832

Hambach Festival; demands of the directing committee; no participation of influential members of the liberal opposition; establishment of a propaganda society; reflections on the political disposition of a large part of the German population; alleged close connection between French and German propaganda

The meeting at Hambach[53] terminated without tumult or any violation of the publick tranquillity; but though the apprehensions that were entertained on that head proved unfounded, the result of the proceedings at Hambach have left the Members of the Diet little room for satisfaction, since the revolutionary sentiments, views, and intentions declared in the most undisguised and unreserved terms by all who were present, combined with the enthusiasm with which those declarations were received and the unanimity of opinion which prevailed there, have imprinted upon that Meeting a character of dangerous political importance which must exert a most pernicious influence in Germany. [...]

There were certainly from 20,000 to 30,000 persons assembled. The Bavarian Government, after having prohibited Foreigners from resorting to the Meeting and after having entreated the German Governments to refuse Passports for Hambach and take every means of preventing those who were not Bavarian Subjects from repairing there, suddenly retracted that Prohibition a few days previous to the 27th and granted full permission to all who chose to do so, to proceed to the Fête without difficulty.

The impediment therefore to the reception of Foreigners at Hambach having been removed, Individuals flocked there from all parts of the South-West of Germany. The patriotick Associations, which now are organized in almost all the most considerable Towns, sent their deputations, and there were also present many Poles and French, and among the latter were several Members of the Society entitled 'Les amis du peuple',[54] who came from Strasbourg.

After having assembled at Neustadt, those who took an active part in this Meeting, wearing the German Tricolor Cockade, and with the tricolor banners unfurled, marched in procession to the Castle of Hambach, where a Banquet was prepared for about 1300 persons, and during, and after, that repast the Leaders on this occasion delivered

[53] The Hambach Festival described here took place from 27 to 30 May 1832. It was held on the Hambacher Schlossberg near Neustadt in the Bavarian Palatinate.

[54] The Strasburg delegates from *La Société des amis du peuple* brought an address of greeting and solidarity to participants in the Hambach Festival. It was read out on 27 May by Lucien Rey, an advocate from Alsace.

various Speeches, which for violence and sedition are universally allowed to have surpassed all that has ever been addressed to the people of Germany since the commencement of the actual agitation. These Addresses were in fact the real business of the day, and until nightfall oration succeeded oration, the one outshining the other in seditious attacks upon the Sovereigns of Germany, the Confederation, and the whole existing System.

On the 28th there was a repetition of this scene, though the Meeting was less numerous, and it was only the 29th that the different Parties finally separated, but not before they had concerted their future plan of operations and laid the foundation of a political Union having ramifications over the whole face of Germany, by which they hope successfully to combat and annihilate the Power of the Confederation.

It is this circumstance which has given so truly dangerous a complexion to the result of the Meeting at Hambach, for there were there collected persons from all parts animated with the same sentiments and brought together for the same object, the effecting a total revolution in the actual order of things. They there had an opportunity of discussing and defining a vast plan for furthering the attainment of that object and establishing a concert of action among themselves, and it is no secret that the 29th was wholly appropriated to the consideration of those topicks.

I am informed on the very best authority that a Directing Committee was instituted, which portioned Germany out into different Districts, and for each District selected Agents to direct the movement of the Party in such District. Thus three Individuals have been appointed to superintend the Revolutionary Interests in Frankfort and the Duchy of Nassau, – viz – a certain M. Henkel, a Wine Merchant of considerable wealth, who is the most respectable of the three, 2dly a Monsr Sauerwein, a theological Student, and 3rdly a Bookseller named Meidinger.

Their Instructions, the same as are given to the Agents for the other Districts of Germany, are to take advantage of every opportunity to promote the attainment of the following three points:

1. Complete Liberty of the Press,
2. Unrestricted Right of Petition,
3. Unrestricted Right of the people to assemble together.

and they are directed to put in practise without hesitation whatever they may consider conducive to the accomplishment of that object.

Your Lordship will observe that of those persons who took a lead at Hambach there was no one remarkable for his station in Society or for property or influence in the Country. Those who did take the lead were chiefly political Traders and Editors of revolutionary Papers, as M.M. Wirth, Siebenpfeiffer, Hepp (Burgomaster of Neustadt) and others of the same stamp; but, saving Monsr de Itzstein, none of the influential liberal Leaders either of the Chambers of Carlsruhe or Cassel were present. M. de Rotteck excused himself as soon as he heard of the prohibition issued by the Bavarian Government against the reception of Foreigners, and he did not think fit to alter his plan when that prohibition was revoked. It is not however to be supposed that because M.M. Rotteck, Jordan, Pfeiffer, and the other violent Leaders at Carlsruhe and Cassel were absent from Hambach, they disapproved the Meeting or are not in close connexion with the Party which did repair there. The fact is very different. They are known to be intimately connected with the actors at Hambach, but are too shrewd and careful openly to commit themselves to any extent till the work on the anvil has assumed a certain consistency which may offer them a fair chance of success. Whenever that period does arrive it is not doubted they will then throw off the reserve and caution with which they now act, and will identify themselves with the violent revolutionary Party.

It is evident from what I have the honor to report to Your Lordship, that a well-organized Propaganda Society[55] is established throughout the whole of Germany; and though, according to the particulars I have received, its views are apparently confined for the present to the three points I have mentioned, they are only to be viewed as the primary step towards the accomplishment of the great plan this Party has in contemplation – distant and difficult as that accomplishment must be to all reflecting minds, the Unity of Germany with republican Institutions.

The eagerness with which persons from all parts flocked to Hambach and the satisfaction with which they there listened to the most seditious and inflammatory discourses into which was infused every topick calculated to excite the mind, are circumstances of no mean importance, as they infallibly attest a strong disposition on the part of the population of a large portion of Germany to participate in the cry raised by the disaffected, and these very circumstances indeed give much uneasiness to the Diet, as proving that the revolutionary doctrines so sedulously preached by a portion of the German Press have already worked on the population.

There is of course at Frankfort a great inclination to blame the Bavarian Government for having tolerated the Meeting at Hambach.

[55] The *Press- und Vaterlandsverein*, founded on 29 January 1832 on the initiative of Philipp Jakop Siebenpfeiffer and Johann Georg August Wirth in the Bavarian Palatinate on the left bank of the Rhine. Within a short time it was joined by a large number of local associations which called for individual liberties and freedom of the press in the whole of Germany. After it was banned in 1832 the *Pressverein* was continued clandestinely.

An Austrian Agent[56] who was sent there to observe what passed has represented that the Bavarian Government might with ease (had it been willing to do so) have prevented the Meeting taking place, that of the persons assembled there were but about 2000 who were real actors, that the rest were only the population of the surrounding country, ready to applaud what they heard but who would without difficulty have dispersed on the first summons, and that if the Bavarian Government had even been obliged to have recourse to force, a very small one would have been ample to have carried the orders of the Government into execution.

As the case now stands it is argued that an example has been given to the rest of Germany which must find imitation. –

A popular Meeting has been held in open day under the Symbol of Revolution, unimpeded by the legitimate Government of the Country, and must bear its fruits.

One circumstance has been brought to light by these occurrences to which I must intreat Your Lordship's attention. The close connexion between the French and German Propaganda has been ascertained fully to exist. It was known that a Monsr Savoye, an Attorney of DeuxPonts,[57] was sent to Paris two months ago to establish an Union between the two Propaganda; and though it was never doubted that he succeeded, the result of his efforts is now evident. On the very day the Hambach Fête was celebrated, a Banquet was held at Paris for the same object, at which General Lafayette presided; and the same German Tricolor Banners and Cockades were displayed in both places.

In conclusion it only remains for me to give Your Lordship the explanation of the Colours which have been selected for the German Tricolor Cockade. The red stripe represents Blood, the black stripe Death, and the golden stripe Liberty. The signification: By blood and death comes golden Liberty; – ('Durch Blut und Todt die goldene Freiheit'–), which is the Motto of the famous Society existing at the Universities, so well known under its denomination 'the Burschenschaft' or 'Germania'.[58]

The Colours and Motto of this Burschenschaft have been adopted on this occasion, and – what is more remarkable – apparently at the instigation of Monsieur Wirth; for in his Paper, 'the German Tribune',[59] some months ago the adoption of a national Cockade was first recommended, and the very Colours now selected were those then pointed out by him.

[56] Not traceable.

[57] Zweibrücken.

[58] The colours black-red-gold were first used by Lützow's volunteer corps in the wars of liberation of 1813–1814. *Germania* was the name of a student group which operated clandestinely after the *Burschenschaft* (student movement) was banned in 1819.

[59] *Deutsche Tribüne*, cf. n. 46 in this section.

FO 30/38: Thomas Cartwright to Viscount Palmerston, Secret, No 57, Frankfurt, 6 June 1832

Federal Diet's reaction to the Hambach Festival; role of Poles who participated in the festival; reflections on 'reading rooms'

I have ascertained that there was much conversation in the Diet on the 30th Ult° on the subject of the Hambach Meeting,[60] and M. de Nagler and M. de Marschall severally communicated various particulars of what had passed there, which they had received from Confidential Agents who had been present on the spot.

The open assumption of the Tricolor Colours[61] on that occasion seems to have made a deep impression on the Diet as giving a positive revolutionary character to a Meeting held for the ostensible purpose of celebrating the Anniversary of the Bavarian Constitution,[62] which the speeches delivered there did not at all contradict.

It was unanimously agreed that means should be taken to prevent a Cockade, which was regarded every where as the Symbol of Revolution, from being openly displayed in Germany, and a Resolution was therefore drawn up prohibiting those Colours from being hoisted or worn in the States of the Confederation.

This was the only Resolution which I believe will be recorded in the Protocol, but it was further determined verbally among the Members of the Diet that the different German Governments should order all the Poles[63] who are now scattered over the face of Germany to quit their States, and should prevent the establishment of Reading Rooms for the lower Classes.

It appears that at Hambach the few Poles present were very active, and that two or three of the most violent speeches on that occasion came from them; but it is asserted that wherever they are found they are always at work exciting the Inhabitants and inflaming their minds against their legitimate Governments, and that from the sympathy felt for them and hospitality with which they are received, they have the means of influencing the population and greatly annoying the different Governments.

The Reading Rooms I have mentioned are some Establishments

---

[60] Cf. pp. 23–26 in this section.

[61] Cf. n. 58 in this section.

[62] The Bavarian constitution had been ratified on 26 May 1818.

[63] After the Warsaw Rising was put down in 1831 about 10,000 Poles fled abroad. Most of the refugees crossed the states of the German Confederation en route to France. The south-west of Germany, in particular, became a temporary gathering point. German opposition circles provided material and moral support for the Polish freedom fighters there. The Hambach Festival in 1832, in which about twenty Poles participated, marked the climax of the German liberals' enthusiasm for things Polish.

denominated 'Cabinets de Lecture' which have been latterly set up by the funds, and under the auspices, of the patriotick Associations, with the express view of corrupting the minds of the Middling and Lower Classes, and all persons may resort to them on the most trifling conditions.

The Diet seems to consider the presence of the Poles in Germany, and these establishments, both dangerous to the tranquillity of the Country, and they are not to be tolerated.

The Governor of Mayence[64] has already closed a Reading Room of this description which had been recently opened within the walls of that Fortress.

FO 30/38: Thomas Cartwright to Viscount Palmerston, Confidential, No 59, Frankfurt, 7 June 1832

Six Articles; details of the 4th Article concerning the establishment of a federal Tribunal; increasing power of the Federal Diet and its present policies; differences between laws passed by constitutional states and Federal Diet; tensions arising out of that conflict

I have the honor to transmit to Your Lordship a Copy, together with a translation, of the six Articles the Count de Münch is to propose in the Diet immediately after his return to Frankfort.[65]

They are the measures which the Courts of Vienna and Berlin have resolved to bring forward to meet the present Crisis in which German Affairs are involved, and their immediate object is to give additional force to the federal Authority, to strengthen the Power of the Constitutional Sovereigns and afford them the means of resisting the encroachments of the Chambers, and to compel the legislative Bodies in States Members of the Confederation to restrict their deliberations to topicks which do not clash with the Federal Legislation.

These Articles, with the exception of the fourth, contain little more than what is already to be found in the meaning and spirit of the fundamental Act of the Confederation and the Final Act of Vienna; but they put a more defined and precise interpretation on various

---

[64] Ferdinand von Würtemberg.
[65] Enclosures: 1. Translation. Six articles to be proposed in the Diet; 2. Translation. Extract of a Protocol of the Diet of 26 April 1832 'Introduction of general Regulations with respect to the Press'.

Articles of those Acts, in order to render them more efficient.[66]

The fourth Article however introduces a totally new topick, and one of immense importance, for it goes to establish a federal Tribunal with power to controul the legislative Bodies in the constitutional States of the Confederation.[67]

The immense power this article places in the hands of the Diet will not fail forcibly to strike Your Lordship; for as by it the Diet is to have the Right to determine what propositions and resolutions made and adopted in the Chambers are, and what are not, at variance with the existing federal obligations, or with the Sovereign Rights as guaranteed by the federal Compacts and Treaties, so on the Diet will devolve the power of refusing to the Chambers the Right of deliberating on any subject it may choose to consider as coming under that category.

This Article at one stroke appears to give the Diet more pretence for interference, and more power to interfere in the internal Affairs of the Minor States of the Confederation, than it derives from the whole of the federal Laws now in vigor; and it is not surprising that such secrecy has been observed on the subject of these Articles.

It is hardly possible to conceive that a State like Bavaria, jealous of its independence, will subscribe to the contents of the fourth Article as it is actually framed, but nevertheless it is, I understand, stated in the Austrian Memoir which accompanies these Articles (but of which I have never been able to obtain a sight) that both Bavaria and Wurtemberg, the Powers from whom the most difficulties were apprehended, have acceded to it.

Nevertheless very great suspicions are entertained here that such will not prove to be the case. They may, when sounded by Austria, have approved its principle; but that they actually signified their willingness to adopt the fourth Article is doubted, and it is certain that the Bavarian and Wurtemberg Ministers[68] at the Diet are still without any Instructions how to act.

New federal Laws, to have force, must be adopted with unanimity

---

[66] Article 1 of the Six Articles confirmed the sovereignty of the monarchs vis-à-vis the *Landtage* with reference to Article 57 of the Vienna Final Act of 1820. Article 2 limited the rights of the *Landtage* to control budgets while also expanding the Confederation's right to intervene, as provided for in Articles 25, 26 and 58 of the Vienna Final Act. Article 3 restricted the legislative powers of the *Landtage* with reference to Article 2 of the Act of the Confederation of 1815 and Article 1 of the Vienna Final Act. Article 5, building on Article 59 of the Vienna Final Act, restricted the parliamentary freedom of opinion and report by obliging state governments to prevent any attacks on the Confederation in their *Landtage*. In Article 6, finally, with reference to Article 17 of the Vienna Final Act, the *Landtage* were deprived of the right independently to interpret the laws of the Confederation.

[67] For the Confederation's control commission cf. pp. 38–39 in this section.

[68] Maximillian Freiherr von Lerchenfeld and Friedrich Landolin Karl von Blittersdorf.

in the Diet; but in the present instance it is pretended that unanimity is unnecessary, since the six Articles are only modifications or amendments of the existing Laws. Their adoption therefore by a majority will suffice.

But unless they are adopted with unanimity no benefit can ensue from their introduction into the federal Code, since the Powers which disapprove them will necessarily refuse to be bound by them.

The Diet will therefore after all find itself in much the same position it is in at present, and the whole Affair seems to depend upon the solution of the grave Question which has often been raised lately, whether, or not, the Leading Powers are prepared to employ force to cause the federal Laws to be enforced and respected.

In a conversation I had but a few days ago with the Baden Minister on these very Articles, he said that Austria and Prussia might propose measures upon measures, all that the Diet might do would lead to no result, and that unless the Count de Münch returned with Powers in his pocket to employ 200,000 Austrians and Prussians in support of the Diet, the dissolution of the Confederation was as good as decreed.

Though M. de Blittersdorff is a most violent Absolutist and may be biassed by his opinions, nevertheless there is much truth in his observation; for as Bavaria has openly refused to acknowledge the Supremacy of the Diet,[69] and the Chambers in Baden and Hesse-Cassel have been passing Laws[70] one after another totally contrary to the Laws of the Confederation, if, with these facts before them, Austria and Prussia are not prepared to push matters to extremities, all the new measures they may propose will not render the Power of the Diet more respected or more efficient.

I can observe however that an opinion is gaining ground, that Austria and Prussia are now resolved to interfere in good earnest, and that after M. de Münch's return Affairs will take a very decided and serious turn whether Bavaria is ready, or not, to cooperate with good will. [...]

---

[69] Bavaria's insistence on its sovereignty in relation to the decisions of the German Confederation is illustrated in, among other things, Bavarian press policy. Thus in March 1832, Bavaria on principle delayed implementing the publication bans imposed by the Confederation. Bavaria gave in to pressure exerted by Austria and Prussia and dealt more severely with the press only after the Hambach Festival of May 1832 (cf. pp. 23–26 in this section).

[70] That is, the Baden press law of 28 December 1831 (cf. n. 51 in this section) and the constitution of Electoral Hesse, 5 January 1831 (cf. n. 20 in this section). On the basis of the constitution of Electoral Hesse, the *Landtag* of Electoral Hesse also drafted a press law in April 1832, but it was never passed.

FO 30/38: Thomas Cartwright to Viscount Palmerston, No 73, Frankfurt, 25 June 1832

Weak Federal Diet and Constitutional governments enable rise of a revolutionary party; its support in the different German states; intended action of M. Münch and question of whether the measures supported by the Federal Diet will be sufficient; measures of the Bavarian government; good prospect of repressing of the revolutionary party at this moment; concessions made by constitutional states to the Federal Diet; necessity of reconciling conflicting interests between Federal Diet's and states' legislation

As the Diet will soon be occupied in important deliberations upon the Affairs of Germany, I think it incumbent on me to offer a few observations on the position in which the Count de Münch finds matters on the resumption of his functions, though they are involved in such confusion as to render it difficult to give Your Lordship any clear idea of them.

I have already pointed out to Your Lordship in my correspondence, that from the combination of a variety of causes the internal affairs of the Confederation were gradually becoming very complicated, that from the differences which had arisen between the Diet and the constitutional States on many points of the federal Legislation, the principal of which were the extent of the Supreme Authority of the Diet, the Liberty of the Press, and the Attributes of the Legislative Bodies in States Members of the Confederation, the Power of the Diet had been shaken and rendered inefficient, that from the inactivity of the Diet arising from those causes as well as from the weakness of the Constitutional Governments and the efforts of a seditious Press, a Party, which aimed at Revolution and not at the introduction solely of liberal Institutions, had been able to push its schemes to an extent which threatened to disturb the tranquillity of some parts of Germany, and therefore that if some remedy was not soon applied to this state of things, the power and welfare of the Confederation might both be seriously compromised.

There are then two grand points to which M. de Münch's attention will be directed: the suppression of the disaffected or revolutionary Party, a Party which must not be confounded with the Advocates of a liberal System, and the adjustment of the differences between the Diet and the Constitutional States, and it is expected that he will immediately submit to the consideration of the Diet a series of measures calculated to meet these ends.

It is supposed he will first call the attention of the different Governments to the absolute necessity of repressing the revolutionary Party in Germany, and as all those Governments have a common interest in putting down a Party whose extravagant doctrines threaten to involve them in Anarchy and confusion, it can hardly be doubted that he will find all the Members of the Diet ready to accede to his proposition.

But there may be some difference of opinion as to the measures to be enforced for that purpose.

Some persons seem to think that Monsieur de Münch has only to make a Declaration in the Diet that Austria and Prussia have 100,000 men at the disposal of any Government who may reclaim their aid to act against the Revolutionists, and the revolutionary excitement will subside of itself, the popular Meetings cease, and the Leaders disappear; but, though I am far from thinking that the revolutionary Party has as yet taken sufficient root to render it very formidable, I cannot believe that with numerous Adherents spread over the whole of so wide a tract as the South West of Germany that Party will be intimidated into submission by a simple declaration of that nature.

Matters are gone too far to admit of that Party being repressed but by energetick measures, and the very fact of the Bavarian Government having found it necessary to send a considerable body of troops at this moment into the Rhenish Provinces is proof that in that Country at least it has gained a head which force alone can subdue.

Since the Festival at Hambach[71] the Diet seems alive to the danger of allowing the Revolutionists to disseminate their principles unimpeded by means of popular Meetings. They are therefore to be prohibited. Not that the popular Meetings which are now so prevalent are considered to offer any thing positively dangerous: but if they are tacitly tolerated they may become dangerous by affording Demagogues the means of demoralizing the population, and it is on that account the Diet thinks they should be prevented.

Excepting in Hesse-Cassel, Baden, and the Bavarian Rhenish Provinces, the revolutionary Party is not strong, and has no partisans among the really respectable Classes. Hesse-Cassel seems to be the Country in which it has the greatest hold, for there almost every Inhabitant is infected. Among the Clergy and the Individuals employed in the subordinate Offices of the State, (and it is said even in the Army), it has many Adherents; but nowhere has any person of mark or influence identified himself with it, and the Leaders in all parts have been confined to Attorney's [!], Professors, Students, Physicians, and persons of a similar stamp, who however seem to have exerted considerable influence on the minds of many of the middling and lower Classes.

In Bavaria propria,[72] and Wirtemberg, the extravagant doctrine of the Unity of Germany under republican Institutions has not made much way, except perhaps in Franconia.

---

[71] Cf. pp. 23–26 in this section.
[72] Bavaria minus the parts of the Palatinate on the left bank of the Rhine, which were territorially separate.

I feel therefore very certain that if all the Governments are united in the determination to extinguish the revolutionary flame, it can easily be done at this moment, though it may happen that in the attempt some partial disturbances may ensue in those Districts in which the minds of the Inhabitants have been most worked upon, as in Hesse-Cassel and parts of Baden.

The revolutionary Party in fact never could have made any way if it had not been for the peculiar circumstances[73] in which the Diet has latterly been placed, and it is to be presumed that it will now be put down; but admitting that that point is set at rest, there still will remain to be settled the Affair of the differences between the Diet and the Constitutional States, which is of far greater moment. It involves indeed a grand Constitutional Question, with the solution of which the very existence of the Confederation is nearly connected.

It must now be the object of the Courts of Vienna and Berlin to find some mode of adjustment which may restore to the Diet that absolute Authority, or if that be impossible, that efficient Authority is originally exercised in the Affairs of Germany.

To attain this end Monsieur de Münch must devise some mode of approximating the views of the Constitutional States to those of the Absolute States upon the Liberty of the Press, upon the Powers of the legislative Chambers, upon the extent of the Authority of the Diet, its Right to interfere in the internal Affairs of the different States, and upon the obligation of all the States equally to execute the Decrees of the Diet: in short he must manage to place the Supremacy of the Diet beyond all dispute.

Of the measures which M. de Münch is to propose in the Diet in order to carry the Confederation through the dilemma in which it finds itself, nothing has yet transpired beyond the six Articles I transmitted to Your Lordship in my Dispatch N° 59, nor is it yet known whether he is in possession of the support and assent of the Constitutional States.

The Bavarian Minister[74] has not yet received one syllable from his Government for the guidance of his conduct, and if the Articles Monsʳ de Münch has to propose are not adopted unanimously, if indeed the whole of the measures now to be discussed are not approved by every State of the Confederation, Austria will only be creating fresh difficulties, not getting out of those with which the Diet is already surrounded.

Bavaria and the Constitutional States have been unwilling to

[73] Cartwright refers to the tardy implementation of the Confederation's resolution against the liberal press in the southern German states, and Bavaria's inadequate (from Austria's and Prussia's point of view) response to the Hambach Festival; cf. pp. 23–26 in this section.

[74] Maximilian Freiherr von Lerchenfeld.

recognize in the Diet the arbitrary Right of interfering beyond a given point in their internal Affairs, and Austria will not be mending matters by carrying through the Diet by a simple Majority a string of Resolutions to increase that arbitrary Power which those States already view with jealousy. If She does resort to such a course the Dissenting States will assuredly not feel themselves bound by Articles to which they refused to accede, and the application and the execution of those Articles can only be enforced by compulsion. The Diet therefore will not find Affairs advanced one iota by the adoption of any measures to which Bavaria and the other Constitutional States are not Parties; on the contrary the difficulties of its actual position will only be aggravated; and if M. de Münch has not the approbation of all the States to the mode of adjusting the existing differences which he is to bring forward, the Affairs of the Confederation will soon become very intricate and perplexed. Under such circumstances but one of two courses would apparently remain at the option of the Diet:

1st Either to compel the refractory States (by refractory I mean those States which now are in collision with the Diet upon different points of their federal engagements) to submit to the will of the Diet, to acknowledge the Supremacy of that Assembly and the existing federal Legislation,

or

2^{ndly} to meet the constitutional States half way by remodelling certain parts of the federal fundamental Act in such a spirit as might enable to Constitutional States to subscribe to every part of the federal Legislation without infringing on their own liberal Institutions.

Your Lordship may suppose that nothing but the most imperious necessity would ever induce Austria and Prussia to take the latter course, for it would at once be introducing into the Confederation a commencement of a liberal System to which they are diametrically opposed.

But if they do not take that course they must then adopt the former if the power of the Confederation is to be maintained; and even then the States forced into submission would never after be willing and efficient Members of a Confederation to which they would then belong by compulsion.

Your Lordship will observe that the repression of the Revolutionary Party is an Affair of itself and must be separated from the more weighty Question of the arrangement of the differences with the Constitutional States, though there is a strong connexion between them, since the former has grown out of the latter.

They are however totally distinct, but the Absolutists in the Diet will not see that there is such a distinction, and they class the whole under one head. Every thing is revolutionary which is not in accordance with their idea of what ought to be the conduct of a federal State. Therefore they make no difference between the views of the Party at Hambach[75] and the opposition raised by Bavaria to the federal Decrees which are not compatible with her own Legislation. Both are revolutionary.

Your Lordship will collect from the statement I have now the honor to make that German Affairs are involved in the greatest confusion, that there are many vital points on which the Diet and the Constitutional States are at issue, and that if Monsieur de Münch has not brought with him the means of reconciling conflicting Interests and adjusting very serious differences, the Power of the Confederation as it has hitherto been exercised is likely to receive a severe check.

A few weeks will suffice to indicate the turn things are likely to take upon these important Questions. It is sincerely to be desired that the means of an adjustment may be found, for if Austria and Prussia should have it in contemplation to compel all the States of the Confederation fully to conform to the will of the Diet without any reference to their own Legislation, it is much to be apprehended a state of things may ensue which will lead to a great convulsion in Germany, for the people of Bavaria, Wirtemberg, and Baden are attached to their Institutions. There is a spirit of independence awakened in those States which must not be overlooked, and any attempt to force them into a course which they are repugnant to as incompatible with those Institutions and that Independence will infallibly involve Germany in trouble and confusion, and perhaps terminate in a Revolution of a far different kind than could ever be effected by Demagogues.

FO 30/39: Thomas Cartwright to Viscount Palmerston, No 86, Frankfurt, 16 July 1832

General acceptance of the Six Articles; expected consequences; no allusion made to the maintenance of independence of the German states; growing power of Austria and Prussia; effects on constitutional states; question of the binding nature of the articles and power of execution

[...] The Protocol of the 28th will and must be regarded as a Manifesto declaratory of the principles by which the Diet is henceforth to govern Germany, and it will undoubtedly create immense sensation.[76] But it

---

[75] Cf. pp. 23–26 in this section.
[76] The Six Articles (cf. n. 66 in this section) were unanimously accepted by the Federal Diet on 28 June 1832 in the Resolution of the Confederation Concerning Measures for the Re-establishment of Legal Order and Tranquillity in Germany.

will be especially against the Governments of the Constitutional States that the resentment and ill will to which these measures may give rise will be directed. The liberal Party will accuse them of having betrayed the Interest of their Countries, and in the next ensuing Session of the different Chambers the reaction of popular feeling against those Governments will render their position extremely difficult.

Your Lordship is well aware that it has been often thought that Austria and Prussia desired nothing better than a fair and favorable pretext for overthrowing the Constitutions altogether. This idea will be revived and it will be inferred that the late proceedings in the Diet are only the prelude to other measures tending to bring about that result.

I therefore wish to call Your Lordship's attention to a circumstance connected with this observation which I have no doubt will be fastened on by those who are inclined to attribute such sinister motives to Austria and Prussia, and on which great stress is likely to be laid.

Hitherto in all the acts promulgated relating to the federal Legislation, allusion has always been made to the principles on which the Confederation was founded.

The 54th Article of the Treaty of Vienna[77] of 1815 states as follows:

'Le but de cette Confédération est le maintien de la sûreté extérieure et intérieure de l'Allemagne, de l'indépendance et de l'inviolabilité des Etats confédérés.'

This article is repeated word for word in the federal Compact of 1815, of which Act it forms the second Article.[78]

When the Final Act of Vienna[79] was drawn up, so necessary was it then thought that the same principles should be proclaimed as forming the basis of the federal Union, that this Article was again repeated, but with this alteration: the sentence alluding to the independence and inviolability of the States was transposed and placed in the first line, leaving the inference that peculiar importance was attached to its insertion.

The first Article of that Act therefore states:

'La Confédération Germanique est &c &c formée pour le maintien de l'indépendance et de l'inviolabilité des Etats qui y sont compris, ainsi que pour la sûreté intérieure et extérieure de l'Allemagne en général.'

Your Lordship will therefore observe that on all these occasions the

---

[77] Act of the Congress of Vienna, 9 June 1815.

[78] The Act of the German Confederation of 8 June 1815 was formally a part of the Act of the Congress of Vienna, 9 June 1815.

[79] Vienna Final Act of 1820.

four points, the independence and inviolability of the federal States, and the internal and external security of Germany, have never been separated.

In the Protocol of the 28th however, which is to every intent a Supplement to those Acts, no allusion whatever has been made to the independence and inviolability of the States. The sentence is omitted altogether, and Your Lordship will observe that at the commencement of the Austrian and Prussian Declaration it is only stated that the Confederation was formed to guarantee the internal and external security of Germany.

It is possible that the measures which have been adopted, having reference solely to the internal security of the Confederation, in the preamble of the Protocol they are called 'measures for the reestablishment of legal order and tranquillity in Germany', it was thought unnecessary to insert the remaining points of the original basis of the federal Compact in the Austrian and Prussian Declaration, but the omission of all allusion to the independence and inviolability of the German States in the present instance is unfortunate and will be interpreted to the disadvantage of those Powers. Coupled with the general spirit of the six Articles and the pretext, if not the Right, which the fourth Article in particular may be interpreted to give the Diet of meddling in the internal Affairs of the Constitutional States, it will furnish ample matter for attributing to Austria and Prussia latent intentions, such as I am unwilling to suppose to be in their contemplation.

I cannot believe there is any plan for overturning the Constitutions. There may possibly be desire to recommend some ameliorations in those Constitutions which are held to be too democratick, such as that of Hesse Cassel;[80] but I have already stated that I look upon the principal object of Austria and Prussia to be to aid the Sovereigns of Germany in resisting the inroads of the Libérals, to place the Diet in the position in which it originally stood when the federal Compact was instituted, and to guard against any further encroachments upon the Monarchical Principle which is viewed as the ground work of the Confederation. However as in the furtherance of this object it is impossible for human foresight to predict into what measures the Diet may not be carried, I have thought it my duty to advert to a circumstance which I view as particularly ill judged in the actual state of political controversy in Germany.– For if the Diet should at any future period be drawn into a struggle with one of the Constitutional States on account of the anti-federal conduct of the Chambers in that State, it may be hurried in support of its prerogatives from one act into

---

[80] For the constitution of Electoral Hesse cf. n. 20 in this section.

another, until, without having entertained any such intention at the outset, it may be forced to arrive at a conclusion which may be viewed as a virtual attack upon the constitutional Rights of that State, and then, notwithstanding such an event may have solely grown out of that struggle, the remarkable omission I have pointed out in the citation of the basis of the federal Compact will infallibly be referred to as evidence of the violation of those Institutions having been a long concerted project. I therefore think it a great misfortune no allusion was made to the maintenance of the independence and inviolability of the German States in the recent Act of the Diet, for the insertion of the 54th Article of the Treaty of Vienna word for word would have at once removed all room for speculation or pretext for misrepresentations.

The natural effect of the six Articles certainly will be to throw immense power into the hands of Austria and Prussia so long as unanimity prevails in the Diet, for as they must draw the ties closer between Austria and Prussia and the other German States, they will place a formidable force at their disposal and fortify their influence in Germany.

But the Protocol of the 28th will be productive of a different effect upon the mass of the Inhabitants in the Constitutional States.

Finding their own Governments lending themselves to measures having for their object the restriction of their liberal Institutions to which they are attached, the Inhabitants of the Constitutional States will turn to France for protection, and a strong French Party may be created in the heart of Germany which may ultimately produce a material change in the political relations of the Country.

M. de Münch proclaimed on his return to Frankfort that the past was to be consigned to oblivion, that perfect union prevailed among the federal Powers, and that a new era was to commence. Whether that era will be of long duration is very problematical, but it is not to be doubted that Austria and Prussia are resolved to reestablish the supreme Authority of the Diet and compel refractory States to obey its mandates. The language of the Protocol is sufficiently explicit on this head, – but much – indeed every thing – must depend on the line the Constitutional Sovereigns will pursue upon the application and execution of the Articles which have now been adopted.

Experience has proved that the letter of the federal Law has not always found ready obedience on the part of the Constitutional States in cases which were considered to be at variance with the Legislation of those States, that the Decrees of the Diet which have trenched too directly upon their constitutional Institutions have not always been executed without hesitation and repugnance, and it is by no means clear that the Diet may not encounter similar difficulties should it find indispensable to put the stipulations of the fourth additional Article into execution.

That Article states in substance that a Committee of the Diet shall be appointed for the express purpose of watching over the deliberations of the legislative Chambers, that that Committee shall call the attention of the Diet to any proposition or Resolution which it may consider to be at variance either with the obligations of the States towards the Confederation or with the Sovereign Rights guaranteed by the federal Compacts and Treaties, and that then the Diet if it conceives the case to require it, shall enter into further communication upon it with the Government concerned.

If then the Government to which the Diet should address itself under this Article should acknowledge that the Diet had just reason to complain of the proceedings of the Chambers, that Government must put itself forward supported by the Diet to check these proceedings, and it will in so doing infallibly draw upon itself the hostility of that Chamber and consequently involve itself in endless disputes with the constitutional Organ of the State.

But if on the other hand the Government refuses to listen to the remonstrances of the Diet, resists its pretensions to interfere with the deliberations of the Chambers, the Diet will then be brought into instant collision with that Government, and nothing but the employment of force will be left to carry the will of the Diet into execution.

Thus it is by no means so evident that the future era will be void of difficulties, though from the accession of the constitutional Sovereigns to the six Articles it is certainly to be presumed that as long as unanimity prevails in the Diet the Governments will control the legislative Chambers and use extraordinary means for that purpose if they should evince any disposition to pass the limits which the Diet chooses to prescribe to them; but should that unanimity be once interrupted or any difference of opinion arise as to the extent of the Power given to the Diet by the 4th and 6th Articles,[81] dissentions must follow between the constitutional States and the Diet of a very serious character for the well-being of the Confederation.

FO 30/40: Thomas Cartwright to Viscount Palmerston, Secret and Confidential, No 123, Frankfurt, 3 October 1832

Remarks on Palmerston's reply to the Six Articles; interpretation of the word 'Landstände' in the 13th Article and its effect on German constitutions

[...] There was another remark M. de Münch then made, which I think merits some attention from its being now very generally brought

---

[81] For Article 6 of the Six Articles cf. n. 66 in this section.

forward by all the Members of the Diet. He said that he was afraid there was one great error in the position assumed by the Government of His Majesty[82] on the Affairs of Germany, that it was conceived the Assemblies of States had the Right of participating in Acts connected with the positive Government of the Country, as in France and England. He denied that Right, and said that at the period the States were originally instituted the privilege of deliberating upon the details of the internal Administration of the Country was alone conferred upon them; that they possessed no other prerogative and never had the Right to participate in any political Act connected with the Government of the Country itself; that they had no power to interfere with the machine of Government, and that in cases where they had done so, the States had overstepped the just limits of their prerogatives and had encroached upon the Sovereign's Rights. He said that a great misconception of the real attributes of the States appeared universally to prevail upon this head, which was one of immense importance and ought to be clearly understood.

Now I wish to remark that the Members of the Diet are beginning to lay great stress upon the difference between Assemblies denominated States and Representative Chambers, and M. de Münch on this occasion adverted to the States and avoided all mention of Representative Chambers.

By a reference to the federal Act of 1815 it will be found that in the 13th Article the word 'Landstände' is made use of in the German Copy, and is translated in the French Copy by the term 'Assemblées d'Etats'.[83]

Now it is argued that the stipulations of that Article were never intended to relate to Representative Constitutions in the usual sense affixed to those Institutions, but that they simply referred to the ancient German Assemblies of the States, which were Institutions much more restricted in their attributes and power than the Representative Chambers of the present day. It is asserted that the real intentions of all Parties at the Congress of Vienna were limited solely to the reestablishment of those ancient Institutions, and that consequently in Countries where Representative Constitutions had been conferred, those Grants were gratuitous Acts of the Sovereigns which exceeded the obligations to which they were bound by the 13th Article of the Federal Act.

---

[82] In conversation with Cartwright, Joachim Graf von Münch-Bellinghausen referred to Palmerston's dispatches to Frederick Lamb and the Earl of Minto; pp. 123–128 in Prussia section.

[83] Article 13 of the Act of the German Confederation reads: 'All states of the Confederation will have a constitution based on the provincial Estates'. The 1815 Act of the German Confederation does not go beyond this vague statement to specify the type of provincial Estates to be set up, or to set a date by which the states were to have implemented a constitution.

By setting up this Argument it is attempted to demonstrate firstly, that the Grant of Representative Assemblies was never obligatory upon the Members of the Confederation, and secondly, that Representative Chambers, wherever they exist in Germany, have not, strictly speaking, a Right to pretend to a further exercise of Authority in political Acts or in the direction of the Government than would have belonged to the Assemblies of the States, for which they have in fact been substituted.

As the Confederation was originally founded on principles which required that the sole political Authority of Government should be concentrated in the hands of the Sovereign, it was not legally possible, it is maintained, for a Sovereign to confer on a Representative Assembly the Right to interfere with any direct Act of Government, for it was a Power of which he was bound not to divest himself by his federal engagements.

Such, My Lord, is the species of reasoning which is brought forward to refute the assertion that Representative Constitutions were promised by the 13th Article of the federal Act of 1815, and great stress is certainly laid upon the necessity of establishing the fact.

But nevertheless there is much greater disposition towards moderation manifested by the Members of the Diet at this moment than has ever been the case since the adoption of the Resolutions of the 28th of June.[84] They all profess to see the expediency of proceeding with the utmost caution and temper. [...]

FO 30/43: Thomas Cartwright to Viscount Palmerston, No 42, Frankfurt, 5 April 1833

'Frankfurter Wachensturm' (Storming of the Frankfurt Guard House) and its aftermath

I regret to state that this Town was, the night before last, the scene of some disturbances of a very serious character, and I therefore feel it necessary to address Your Lordship at some length upon the subject.

In the course of the morning of the 3rd Inst a very respectable Individual,[85] a native of Franconia, called upon the Bavarian Minister and warned him that during the evening an attempt would be made by a party of Revolutionists to overturn the existing order of things here.[86] He gave him an account of their plans as he understood them, and Monsr de Lerchenfeld, after his conversation with this person

---

[84] Cf. pp. 28–30 in this section.

[85] Johann von Seuffert.

[86] The initially successful attack on the Frankfurt main guard means that the attempted putsch described here is well known as the Storming of the Frankfurt Guard House.

became so convinced of the reality of his assertions, that he instantly communicated to Monsr de Guaita, the first Burgomaster, the particulars with which he had been made acquainted and begged him to take every precaution to preserve the publick tranquillity.

Mr de Guaita had hardly quitted Monsr de Lechenfeld before the very individual who had been with the latter came also to him and recapitulated all the details which he had related to the Bavarian Minister.

Monsr de Guaita pressed him very much upon the point of how he came by his information, when he persisted in stating that he had no personal knowledge of the machinations he denounced, but that, having been himself warned by a friend, he had felt it his duty to give timely notice to the Authorities of what he understood to be in agitation.

Mr de Guaita however obtained from this person the name of the informant[87] from whom he had received his particulars, and sent for that individual without loss of time.

When he arrived he was closely interrogated by the Burgomaster; but he would only admit that his knowledge of the plot proceeded from an anonymous letter which had been sent to him and which stated all the details already denounced by his friend, and those were, that at half after nine that night bands of armed men were to attack and overpower the guards at the two chief Guardhouses situated in the very Centre of the Town and adjoining to which are the Prisons, that they were to liberate and arm the prisoners, that the Tocsin was to be sounded at the same moment to give a signal to other partisans without the town to join them, and that after having made themselves masters of the Town the plan then was to seize the treasure of the Diet and establish a Provisional Central Government for Germany.

This individual, who I am assured was a Burgher of the town,[88] denied having any other knowledge of these particulars than through the anonymous communication he had mentioned, and though he received every assurance of secrecy and protection would not make any more positive denunciation.

From what has subsequently occurred it is not doubted that he was intimately acquainted with the proceedings of these people but was afraid of avowing his connexion with them and therefore invented this story of an anonymous letter to screen himself from any consequences.

It appears that the Burgomasters[89] are in the habit of receiving daily letters of this description, and that Mr de Guaita, putting too much faith in the assertion that it was solely from an anonymous letter that

---

[87] Andreas Quante.

[88] Andreas Quante was not a burgher of Frankfurt, but a travelling salesman from Würzburg.

[89] Friedrich von Guaita und Johann Kappes.

this Individual had acquired a knowledge of the plot which his friend had revealed to Mr de Lerchenfeld, did not pay so much attention to the story as he would have done under other circumstances.

Nevertheless he and the directing Members of the Senate thought it advisable to take some precautions, but as they had not much expectation of so daring a Conspiracy being really in agitation, they confined their measures to those usually enforced on occasions of expected tumult. The two Chief Guards were reinforced by a few additional men each, and a Battalion of the troops of the line was held in readiness within the Barracks to act at a moment's notice. A few Police men were also placed at the Door of the Cathedral.

At the very moment, half after nine, which had been announced as that at which the Guard Houses were to be assailed by these unknown Conspirators, the principal Guard House was attacked and soon carried by a Band of Armed Men, who surprised and shot the Sentinel on duty, entered the Building in which most, if not all, of the Soldiers were assembled, forced open the Prisons, and in a few minutes had effected their object without more than five or six shots having been fired.

While this was passing at the Chief Guard House, another attack was made on another Guard stationed at the extremity of the longest street in Frankfort. The Assailants there carried their purpose and forced the Prisons; but the resistance offered to them was more resolute than at the other point, and there were several killed and wounded.

Simultaneously with these attacks the door of the Cathedral was forced by another Party, the few Police men who had been stationed there having been easily routed, and the tocsin gave the signal to the Neighborhood. In short the commencement tallied exactly with the notice which had been given to the Burgomaster.

But the success of the Assailants did not have any further result, for the troops from the Barracks soon reached the points already mentioned and the drums beat to arms in the different quarters of the Town, upon which the disturbers of the publick peace, finding that their projects were known and that they were not joined by the generality of the Townspeople, retreated, or rather disappeared, in an instant, leaving but two of their party on the spot badly wounded, and the rest of the night passed quietly. [...]^{90}

In the course of the night of the 3^{r}d Instan^t several Strangers, principally Students, who were found in the Inns, and many persons Inhabitants of the town known for their subversive opinions and their connexion with secret Societies, were arrested. Several persons supposed to be implicated are also missing.

As every thing which occurred tallied with the previous account

---

^{90} Enclosure: extract from the *Journal de Francfort*, 4 April 1833.

given to Mr de Guaita it is not to be doubted that their further intentions were such as his Informant represented them to be. Every hour indeed furnishes evidence of this extraordinary transaction having been the work of some exaggerated political fanaticks who really contemplated the establishment at Frankfort of a Republican Central Government for Germany, and that the blow attempted to be struck at Frankfort was only part of a grand plan which has vast ramifications in various parts of the Country.

The Chiefs concerned were principally Students from Würzbourg, Heidelberg, and other Universities with some Frenchmen, and they were aided by a Party in the Town.[91] Their measures were well combined and boldly executed, and if it had not been for the notice which had been given to the Burgomasters in the course of the morning of what was to be expected, there is no telling what confusion might not have followed; for the Town taken unawares would have fallen an easy prey to these daring persons and with the support they looked to from without they might have maintained themselves till a good Force from Mayence could have been brought against them.

At the moment the two parties attacked the Guard Houses it is now ascertained that there were Agents in various Quarters trying to excite the Inhabitants to rise and offering Arms to all who would take them.

Outside the Gates which were closed as soon as the tumult commenced, there were collected bands of peasants and country people who were waiting for the signal to join the Assailants, and there have been found in the Town and the Gardens about it a quantity of muskets, cartridges and Rockets which were to have been let off to give notice of their success to their Adherents at a distance.

On the same evening and almost at the same hour the Hessian Customhouse at Preungesheim, about a league from Frankfort, was attacked, part of it set on fire, and the papers were destroyed.

All these facts are evidence of this Affair being a well and deeply organised plot which was connected with the discontented in the Country, and though a party of students were the principal actors within the Town, there were others not less concerned nor less active who were natives of the Place.

The most extraordinary fact connected with this proceeding is the way in which this tumult terminated; for these Assailants and the

---

[91] Fifty participants were known by name. In addition to students from Heidelberg, Erlangen, Würzburg and Göttingen, all of whom were members of the clandestine student movement (*Burschenschaft*), there were a number of older academics who had been involved in earlier unrest and attempted revolutions in Brunswick, Hanover, and Electoral Hesse, and some Polish emigrés. The ringleaders were Rauschenplatt, a former lecturer at the University of Göttingen, Gustav Körner, a lawyer, and Gustaf Bunsen, a doctor from Frankfurt.

different persons connected with them disappeared almost by magick the instant the reinforcements arrived from the barracks. It is believed that they had carriages waiting at different spots without the Town, and that the moment they saw the Authorities were prepared for them, they escaped over the walls, which is very practicable, carrying their wounded with them.

Great blame is attached by the Members of the Diet to the Burgomasters and the Authorities for not having taken better measures of precaution, and they are very loud in their complaints of the incapacity of these Magistrates.

The fact of two Guard Houses with a detachment of fifty men each having been surprised and carried in a few minutes, in one case with hardly any resistance being offered, shews that there was great culpability some where, and it is a fact that the Officers commanding the Guards received no orders to be on the alert and considered the additional force of their detachment as the usual augmentation which is regularly resorted to at the period of the Fair.

But though there is some truth in the accusation brought against the Magistrates, that their measures of precaution were badly taken and that their orders were not sufficiently explicit, still it is very harsh to blame them unconditionally for not having totally prevented the execution of Acts which were planned with such hardihood and secrecy that they might to a certain extent have succeeded even at Berlin and Vienna.

The Diet wishes to force the Town to receive an Austrian Garrison for their protection, which the Magistrates are unwilling to do.

The Members of the Diet assembled in consequence of these outrages and applied to know if the Authorities wished for the aid of an Austrian Force from Mayence, which has been declined; but the Diet on its own impulse has requested the Governor of Mayence to hold a Force in readiness to march to Frankfort at a moment's notice.

I see no reason to apprehend any necessity of any such Force, for the blow having been attempted and having failed, the Authorities will probably gain such a clew to the machinations of those concerned in these transactions as will render a renewal of these scenes impracticable.

FO 30/43: Thomas Cartwright to Viscount Palmerston, Confidential, No 48, Frankfurt, 16 April 1833

Military measures in response to the Storming of the Frankfurt Guard House; Cartwright's doubts as whether they are necessary and right; responsibility rests with the Federal Diet

It cannot be denied that the Military Measures which have been adopted by the Diet, however urgent the motives may have been which induced that Assembly to call for their immediate execution, are of a nature to wound the independence of a free State, and I did not conceal from Baron Manteuffel, when he communicated to me the decision of the Diet, that I regretted for this very reason the determination to send for troops from Mayence.[92]

He assured me, that he had agreed to the measure in question, with the greatest caution and reluctance, and that nothing but the most absolute necessity would ever have induced the Diet to have had recourse to such a step that it had only been adopted after the most mature deliberation, and upon the express declaration of the Military Commission,[93] that the means at the disposal of the Frankfort Authorities were inadequate for the protection and service of the Town, and that if the prisoners were not to be transported to Mayence, the Military force at Frankfort should be instantaneously augmented. He told me that it was this latter circumstance which had had great weight with him in coming to a decision, for that he would certainly have waited for advices from Vienna, had not the report of the Military Commission spoken so positively as to the inefficiency of the then existing measures of protection.

I mentioned to Baron Manteuffel, that necessary as the introduction of an Austrian and Prussian Corps into Frankfort might be in the eyes of the Diet, I understood that the Frankfort Authorities considered such a measure quite uncalled for, and that I, therefore, thought it was a very unfortunate necessity which required their presence, contrary to the wishes of those Authorities.

Baron Manteuffel endeavoured during his conversation with me, to impress on me that these measures where not contrary to the inclinations of the Frankfort Authorities, but I was subsequently informed by M. de Guaita, in strict confidence, that the town had certainly never given its assent to their adoption, and he even told me, that after my interview with Baron Manteuffel, he had declared to him that though the town submitted to the decision of the Diet, the call for the troops from Mayence was contrary to the wishes and without the assent of the Authorities, and that the town would not bear any share of the expences attendant upon its execution.

M. de Manteuffel had indeed informed me that the Diet was to defray the whole of the expences.

[92] In response to the Storming of the Frankfurt Guard House on 3 April 1833 (cf. pp. 41–45 in this section) the Federal Diet resolved to station confederal troops in Frankfurt on 12 April. The occupation of Frankfurt lasted from 15 April 1833 to 1 September 1842, when it was lifted by a decree of the Confederation.

[93] The Federal Diet's resolution of 12 April to occupy Frankfurt with confederal troops was based on the Military Commisson's declaration.

If I had not received this Assurance confidentially from M. de Guaita, the tenor of the proclamation of which I forwarded a copy in my despatch N° 47 would have furnished ample evidence, as it has done to the publick, of this measure having been forced upon the town.[94]

The Members of the Diet are very much displeased at this proclamation, and are particularly annoyed at the last sentence, which expresses the hope that the independence of the town will remain intact.

It is obvious that they disapprove this proclamation, because it throws all the odium of an unpopular act upon their shoulders, and they accordingly abuse the Magistrates for having issued such a document.

But they abuse them very unjustly, for the Diet should recollect that the Magistrates have a duty to perform towards their fellow burghers and inhabitants, as well as towards the Confederation, that they are responsible to their fellow citizens for an upright discharge of those duties which, for the time being, have been confided to their trust, and that the inhabitants had a right to look to them for some explanation of such an Act as the introduction of an Austrian and Prussian Corps into Frankfort. Under such circumstances, the Magistrates cannot be blamed, if being no parties to the measure in question, they gave the publick to understand that it did not proceed from them.

Since this proclamation has appeared, some of the Members of the Diet seem anxious to screen themselves from the responsibility of this measure, by pretending that it was only adopted in deference to the advice of the Military Commission.

The Members of the Military Commission, on the other hand, declare that the questions submitted to their consideration were military questions, which they were bound to examine with the eyes of Military men, that the political question was not of their province, and that they had no choice but to report that the Military force was insufficient for the duty of so populous a town.

There can be no doubt, however, that the whole responsibility rests with the Diet, and the question which is to be solved to justify the Diet, is whether the circumstances were really such as rendered it indispensable that federal Troops should be forced upon the town.

The Diet maintains, that the measure was an absolute necessity, while the Authorities who are full as much interested in the security and welfare of the town as the Diet itself, declare that they think their own resources were sufficient to meet all contingencies. [...]

[94] In the proclamation of 13 April, the Senate communicated the Federal Diet's decision of 12 April to the Free City of Frankfurt, and made it clear that Frankfurt had been occupied against the Senate's wishes. The proclamation ended by declaring that 'the Senate hopes the present misfortune will pass over and that the Free City of Frankfurt will maintain itself'.

Upon the whole, therefore, I am inclined to think that the absolute necessity of the measure which has been decided by the Diet has been overrated. It is certainly a measure of compulsion, but it is one intended for the protection of the inhabitants, and though it in some degree interferes with the sovereign rights of a small State, and may wound its pride and dignity, it is but just to add, that it was far from the intention of the Diet in resorting to it, to attack the independence of Frankfort.

As the Senate and Legislative body were disinclined to accept foreign aid, I cannot but think that it would have been better, had they accepted the proposal to send the prisoners to Mayence, coupled as it was with the condition that the Frankfort Authorities might send a commission to that place to follow up the judicial inquiry, if by so doing, they could have avoided the arrival of a foreign force they were unwilling to receive.

It is impossible as yet to conjecture what final arrangement will be determined on, for that which has been enforced, is only a temporary measure; I am inclined to think, however, that one of two things will occur – either that the Diet will remove to some other town, and abandon Frankfort; or an arrangement will be made for the permanent establishment of a federal force here for the protection of that Assembly.

FO 30/43: Thomas Cartwright to Viscount Palmerston, Confidential, No 54, Frankfurt, 20 April 1833

Particulars on the Storming of the Frankfurt Guard House; introduction of new measures and question of whether they will be able to restore tranquillity; predicted new turbulences; future of the Federal Diet

I today send Your Lordship all the particulars I have been able to collect on the subject of the disturbances which have occurred at Frankfort.[95]

From what has transpired and from the information which daily pours in here, it seems as if there really was a vast plan on foot for revolutionising Germany, which has taken deeper root than the Diet was aware of.

It is quite ascertained that the events of the 3rd Inst^t were not the result of some wild projects of a handful of political fanaticks, but were the work of a Party having extensive ramifications, whose object was to revolutionise this Country.

[95] Cf. pp. 41–45 in this section.

This affair therefore wears a very serious aspect and must lead to important consequences.

We have now had speaking evidence that the Decrees of the Diet[96] of last year, which were to have suppressed all political irritation and which according to the language of the Members of the Diet had indeed restored tranquillity, have been no remedy at all. They have in many States augmented the ranks of the enemies of the Governments. They have in some of the Representative Chambers increased the existing spirit of hostility to the Governments and led to serious disputes and misunderstandings between them, and now a Party has been discovered bent on Revolution which has not been deterred by those measures from pursuing its projects, and which, if it existed previously to their promulgation, did not at that period reckon so many adherents in its ranks.

The measures of the Diet therefore have failed in their effect, but that will not prevent that Assembly from pursuing the same System, and after what has just passed we may expect that more Ordinances will be launched incroaching still more upon the general liberties of Germany.

It is for this reason that the culpable attempts of this revolutionary Party will prove most unfortunate for the interests of the real Constitutionalists, for the Diet will not allow to slip through its hands so fair a pretext for making further inroads upon those institutions whose spirit is opposed to the System advocated by that Assembly.

Thus the Constitutionalists will be the real sufferers for Acts and deeds in which they had no participation and which they most probably condemn as deeply as the most rigid Absolutist.

It is going too far to attribute solely to the Decrees of the Diet the cause of the late events at Frankfort, because the origin of the Party which was concerned in them is of no recent date; but that these events have been a consequence of those Decrees is too probable, since those Acts undoubtedly influenced the direction which has been given to the projects of that Party.

The question why the first and principal blow of this revolutionary Party was to be aimed at the Diet almost answers itself. It was because that Party regarded the Diet as being bent upon the total destruction of the liberties of Germany, and as being the source of all the measures which in late times have been directed by the different Governments against the liberal institutions in their Countries.

Let the Diet now take what further measures it will, – however

[96] The Six Articles of 28 June 1832 (cf. n. 66 in this section) and the Ten Articles promulgated on 5 July 1832 (Measures for the Re-establishment of Legal Order and Tranquillity in Germany), which further limited the freedom of the press, freedom of association, and freedom of assembly. In addition, a number of oppositional newspapers and journals were suppressed in 1832, and their editors banned from working.

severe and however arbitrary, – it is evident that there are too many conflicting interests alive to allow of its being able to restore by its acts alone any lasting quiet and tranquillity to Germany. It may apply some violent remedy to the evil, but the only effect will be to defer the same battle to be fought over again at some future period.

There can be no illusion now as to the state of Germany. The Youth of the whole Country has imbibed at the Universities sentiments and principles which are totally at variance with those the Diet would wish to see predominate, and in many instances indeed most extravagant and unfortunate doctrines.

The rising generation is thus inoculated and that deeply with a spirit which no Diet on earth will be able to stifle or control, and if to this element of trouble be added the ordinary and constitutional hostility to the Diet and the discontent which is known to prevail in many districts, future prospects are of no very consoling character.

Under such circumstances the Diet will find itself in a more embarrassing position than it ever has yet been placed in, and I see more reason than ever to apprehend, what I have often before asserted to Your Lordship, that matters can only terminate in the total overthrow of one of the two Systems: either the Absolute System will come out of this struggle triumphant, overturning every thing opposed to it, or its Antagonist will gain a solid footing and the Diet lose its paramount Authority. There will be no settled tranquillity short of this result, and it is to me evident that things can never return to the state they were in previous to the existing political fermentation and to which the Diet would willingly conduct them.

This struggle will probably last for years; for as the Diet has the ascendancy and the power, it will continue to launch Decrees to keep its Opponents under its control as long as it can hold that power in its hands.

FO 30/43: Thomas Cartwright to Viscount Palmerston, No 64, Frankfurt, 7 May 1833

Austria's response to Magistrates' proclamation; animosity of Frankfurt's inhabitants against the Federal Diet; misconduct of members of the Federal Diet; no withdrawal of the troops expected

Monsr de Handel, the Austrian Minister accredited to the Free Town of Frankfort, has recently received a Dispatch from Prince Metternich on the Affairs of Frankfort which deals very severely indeed with the Magistrates for having issued the Proclamation of the 13th Ult.^{o}.[97]

It is stated in this Dispatch that the Emperor was extremely dissatisfied

[97] Cf. n. 94 in this section.

at the whole tenor of the Proclamation, but particularly at the concluding paragraph which implied a doubt as to whether the Independence of Frankfort was not menaced by the Diet; that the
Magistrates should have remembered that it was principally owing to
the Emperor's influence Frankfort had regained its Independence and
that His Imperial Majesty had always been its chief Protector,[98] that
therefore they ought not to have misconstrued an act which was
considered necessary by the Diet for the general well-being of Germany;
and it further added that if in the sequel any one of His Imperial
Majesty's Soldiers should fall a victim to the outrages growing out of
the irritation which the terms of this Proclamation were calculated to
produce, the consequences for the Town of Frankfort should be very
serious.

Monsr de Handel was directed to communicate the contents of
this Dispatch to the Burgomasters,[99] and they have been very much
intimidated by it. They are so uneasy at the tone taken by France on
the one side and the Diet on the other that they have expressed to me
the hope that the question of this military occupation would not be
further canvassed by either France or England,[100] for that it was best
for the interests of Frankfort that things should take their course.

Things are by no means in a satisfactory state here. With the
exception of Mr Rothschild and a dozen or two of the chief bankers
and merchants who have great sums in their houses and have been so
alarmed by the cry of an approaching Revolution and general pillage
that they hardly know what to believe, there is not one individual
Inhabitant of Frankfort that is not discontented and highly incensed
against the Diet, and the discontent and irritation which prevail are
not likely to diminish while the cause which produces them remains.
The Members of the Diet too are personally taking a very ill-judged
line, of which the following instance will give Your Lordship some idea.

Since the arrival of the Austrian and Prussian troops the Members
of the Diet have by turns been giving entertainments to the Officers,
and two days ago Monsr de Pechlin gave a ball in their honor. To this
ball he did not invite one single Inhabitant of Frankfort properly so
called, not even the Burgomaster, but confined his invitations to the
Circle of the Diet, and the Minister[101] of the Free Towns refused to be
present.

---

[98] Frankfurt owed its independent status as a Free City to Prussia and Austria, which
had prevented the Kingdom of Bavaria from incorporating Frankfurt during the territorial
reorganization of Germany in 1813–1816.

[99] Friedrich von Guaita und Johann Kappes.

[100] For Britain's and France's intervention against the occupation of the Free City of
Frankfurt by confederal troops cf. pp. 133–135 in Prussia section.

[101] Johann Smidt.

During the whole night strong detachments of Austrian troops patrolled all the streets about Monsr de Pechlin's house in different directions.

These particulars will prove how things stand, and that instead of endeavoring to allay the irritation, the Members of the Diet are doing all they can to augment it.

The animosity against the Diet is in fact so great that it is really to be feared that when the troops are withdrawn, if that period is ever to come, some demonstration of popular feeling will be evinced, and the Diet will in such a case have contrived to produce more evil than good by its measures for preserving the tranquillity of Frankfort.

I do not however suppose that there is any idea of withdrawing the troops. The Diet having once called them in for its protection, I do not see how it will ever again do without them; and the opinion is very general that it has long been the object of the Diet to fix a federal Garrison in Frankfort. [...]

Now the Detachment stationed at Sachsenhausen[102] consists of 700 men, and this Force is within the walls of the Town and in very compact quarters, so that it would be attacking what there would be the least chance of carrying.

But from whence the attack was to come, or who were to conduct it, or how he knew that such an attack was in contemplation he either could, or would not inform me.

I still remain of the same opinion that, though the occurrences of the 3rd Ult° were very serious and though the ranks of the discontented have since been augmented by the late proceedings, no real danger is to be apprehended unless there is a general rising throughout the Country, and in such a case the Austrian Force now at Frankfort would prove perhaps as insufficient as the Frankfort Force would have been to stem such a torrent.

FO 30/44: Thomas Cartwright to Viscount Palmerston, Separate, Frankfurt, 14 June 1833

Regulations respecting passports of British subjects in Germany; resulting confusions

Since the occurrences at Frankfort on the 3rd of April[103] some very strict regulations have been enforced in all the German States respecting the granting and countersigning passports. Many travellers have been subjected to great inconvenience, and I have today to report to Your

---

[102] A part of Frankfurt on the south side of the river Main.
[103] Cf. pp. 41–45 in this section.

Lordship a case which is apparently one of great injustice and vexation.

Mr Mackenna, a Subject of His Britannick Majesty, applied to me for a passport for Dresden. On arriving at Aschaffenburg he was not allowed to enter the Bavarian territory, because the passport had not been countersigned by the Bavarian Minister at Frankfort.

He in consequence returned to Frankfort to obtain the Signature which was wanting, and a day or two afterwards recommenced his journey with his passport perfectly in order and countersigned by the Bavarian and Saxon Ministers at this place. He then passed the Bavarian frontier without difficulty and proceeded as far as Würzburg without any interruption. The Authorities at that place even signed his passport for Bamberg, but two hours after that form had been gone through, Mr Mackenna was arrested by the Police, his effects searched, and was himself informed he was not to be allowed to proceed further on his journey. In fact he was immediately delivered over to some Gensd'armes and was escorted by them to the frontier on his way back to Frankfort.

I inclose a copy of the Protocol which the Commissary[104] at Würzburg drew up and required Mr Mackenna to sign, and I have to point out that no explicit motive is assigned in this document for this proceeding.

It is stated therein that the fact of Mr Mackenna's passport containing neither his character nor the object of his journey, and 'other motives' have induced the Authorities to send him back; but these 'other motives' are not specified and great explanation is wanting.

I can assure Your Lordship that no passport was ever issued from my Chancery more in order than that given to Mr Mackenna.

What Mr Mackenna complains of, and what he has some right to complain of, is that he was not informed by the Bavarian Mission here that there were obstacles to his journey before he set out, and that his passport having been countersigned at the Bavarian Mission and being perfectly regular, he was allowed to reach the heart of the Country, and was then arrested, and transported back to the frontier under the escort of an armed Police as if he had been a criminal.

I have made strong representations to the Bavarian Mission here on this proceeding and have insisted on being informed what were the 'motives' for the treatment Mr Mackenna met with. [...][105]

---

[104] Anton Wiesend.
[105] Enclosures: 1. Translation. Protocol, Würtzburg, 6 June 1932; 2. Copy of a Letter addressed by Mr Mackenna to Lord Erskine, 9 June 1833.

FO 30/44: Thomas Cartwright to Viscount Palmerston, No 98, Frankfurt, 4 July 1833

Workings of the Central Authority for Political Investigation; tensions with other institutions of a similar kind; predicted unwillingness to co-operate

[...] This Commission[106] is therefore a milder Institution than that which preceded it in 1819, but nevertheless I cannot think it has been judiciously combined, and I doubt very much whether it can ever be made to work to the extent which certainly is the intention of its framers.

By the Articles regulating its powers Your Lordship will perceive that its labors must entirely depend upon the nature and extent of the information which the German Governments choose to lay before it.

If therefore in the course of time any one of the Governments should take umbrage at this Institution or at the manner in which the inquisitorial functions of its Members are exercised, that Government will have nothing to do but withhold from it all materials for further inquiry, and the Commission is at once deprived of all power of proceeding.

Again if the Ordinary Tribunals, and this is a point which is very likely to occur, from jealousy of the inquisitorial character of this Commission, or from a conscientious feeling that it would be contrary to the judiciary organisation to allow this Commission to take cognizance of their acts, refuse to furnish Acts of accusation or any other documents which the Commission may call for, conflicts without end must ensue between these Bodies all tending to paralise the action of the Central Commission.

But the most injudicious and impolitick point connected with this Institution is contained in the 6th Article, by which this Central Commission is empowered to depute one of its Members to any place in which a legal inquiry is going on to look into the acts and be present at the Trials, though only as a silent observer.

I do not believe in the present times that any one Tribunal in Germany will willingly admit the presence of this mute Inquisitor, and I think that many will openly resist any attempt to introduce this Deputy from the Diet. It will not be a matter of astonishment if the assumption of this power by the Commission is protested against by every Tribunal in Germany as a direct infringement on the Inde-

---

[106] On 20 June 1833 the Federal Diet set up a Central Authority for Political Investigations whose purpose was to pursue the political opposition. This central commission, which existed until 1842, was based in Frankfurt. A comparable institution had existed in Mayence from 1819 to 1828.

pendence of a judicial Court and an interference with the administration of Justice.

It is therefore very evident that a very little will suffice to render this Commission inefficient and even powerless. [...]

FO 30/45: Thomas Cartwright to Viscount Palmerston, No 168, Frankfurt, 10 November 1833

Reasons for the dissolution of the Hesse-Darmstadt second chamber; tensions between government and second chamber

The States of Hesse-Darmstadt were dissolved on the 2nd Inst^t.

The Darmstadt Government had long been dissatisfied with the proceedings of the Second Chamber, and an intention having been manifested by the latter to question the legality of certain Decrees which had been issued by the Grand Duke[107] without the participation of the States, the Government determined to dissolve the Chamber forthwith.

The facts which immediately led to the dissolution are as follow:

In the course of last year, at a time when the States were not assembled, the Grand Duke issued various Ordinances, directing the suppression of some Newspapers and publications and forbidding the circulation of others, prohibiting popular Meetings and political Associations, and enforcing other measures the execution of all of which had been required by the Resolutions of the Diet of July 12th 1832.[108]

The Second Chamber raised a question as to whether the executive power vested in the Grand Duke by the letter of the Constitution was sufficiently extensive to justify his proceeding on his own sole authority, without the sanction of the States, to issue Decrees enforcing measures of so trenching a description, and a Committee was appointed to examine the case, which reported unfavorably to the pretensions assumed by the Grand Duke.

It appears that in this Report the conduct of the Government was handled very severely and that numerous accusations were brought against it of being generally inclined to anti-constitutional practices.

In that part of the Report which treated of the restrictions put by the Government upon the Press and the persecutions directed against the liberal publications, whole Extracts from the 'Tribune'[109] and other suppressed Papers were quoted, which contained precisely those

---

[107] Ludwig II.
[108] Cartwright refers here to the Ten Articles of 5 July 1832, cf. n. 96 in this section.
[109] *Deutsche Tribüne;* cf. n. 46 in this section.

obnoxious and violent Articles which had induced the Diet to insist on their suppression.

It is said that this circumstance gave great offence to the Government, for it saw, or fancied that it saw, in the insertion of these Extracts in this Document a manœuvre on the part of the Chamber to distribute and circulate throughout the Country, under the title of a Report of a Committee, all the most inflammatory Articles from the prohibited Ultra Liberal Papers.

Whether this was or was not the real fact which turned the balance in favor of interference, it is certain that as soon as the Government had acquired a correct knowledge of the contents of this Report, it immediately intimated to the Chamber that if it did not instantly abandon every intention of further discussing this question respecting the legality of the Decrees issued by the Grand Duke, a Dissolution would ensue.

The Chamber showed no disposition to submit to a stretch of Authority which assumed a Right to control its deliberations; and the Government, finding it had no chance of gaining its Point by intimidation, carried its threat into execution and dissolved the Assembly on the 2nd Inst^{t}.

Although these are the facts which were the immediate and ostensible cause of this sudden dissolution, it is understood that the Government had long been secretly determined to seize the first plausible pretext for dismissing a Chamber with which it could not come to any agreement.

The Chamber had been sitting for eleven months, and during that period it had confined its labors almost exclusively to the consideration of a series of Motions and propositions[110] totally at variance with the known System followed by the Government, and had wholly neglected the principal object of deliberation, the Budget, the discussion on which had not even commenced at the moment the Chamber separated.

The Government thinks therefore that it has some grounds for complaint against the Chamber. It accuses the Chamber of having deliberately pursued an unusually harsh and vexing line, and in the Edict I have the honor to inclose,[111] which has been published by the Government to justify its having had recourse to an extreme measure, Your Lordship will find all those complaints enumerated with much

---

[110] On pain of withholding the budget, the *Landtag* demanded a judiciary that was independent of the government, universal and free suffrage, greater local self-administration, and complete freedom of the press and of petition.

[111] Enclosure: copy of an Edict issued by the Grand Duke of Hesse-Darmstadt in original: *Edit concernant la dissolution de l'assemble des Etats et les disposition relatives á de novelles élections pour la deuxième Chambre des Etats*, 2 November 1833; *Publication relative à la dissolution de l'assemblée des Etats*, 3 November 1833.

perspicuity, though perhaps with somewhat of a too dark coloring.

If the Government conceives that it has some motives for accusing the Chamber of carrying hostility beyond all reasonable limits in having wilfully wasted the Session in discussions of no real advantage to the Country and in having intentionally kept back the Budget to obtain concessions on other points, the Chamber on the contrary may accuse the Government of being secretly swayed by an anti-constitutional influence from without, of being determined to resist and refuse all demands for a change of System, and may point out to it that its own Acts and measures have been the origin of those tacticks which have been followed by the Majority.

The Chamber will no doubt make out a Counter-Statement, and one of the first points it will bring forward will be the very last act which preceded the Dissolution, I mean the attempt made by the Government to interfere with and control the discussions in the Chamber.

The Government will probably refer to the famous Articles of the 28th of June 1832[112] to justify its proceedings; but it has decidedly overstepped the natural powers it derived from the Constitution. If it was dissatisfied with the Chamber, it ought to have proceeded to a Dissolution without further hesitation; but it had no right to prescribe to the Chamber any particular course, and it cannot be matter of astonishment that the Chamber should have refused to recognize any such pretensions.

Things are now at this stage in Darmstadt. The States have been dissolved in consequence of having questioned the legality of certain acts of the Government. No Budget has been voted, and a new Chamber is to be elected.

The Government is not yet placed in any particular embarrassment because by the letter of the Constitution, if a Dissolution occurs before the new Budget has been voted, the old Budget is to remain in force for six months after the Dissolution.

It is expected that the new elections will not produce a chamber more favorable to the Government than the late one, and if the Government remains firm in the line it seems to have traced for itself, the same constitutional battle will therefore have to be fought over again.

This contest must however lead to some consequences, for it is impossible that this system of alternately convening and dissolving the Chamber without any Budget having been voted, can be carried on eternally, and I think it looks very much as if the Darmstadt States, should they persist in their opposition to the Government, were likely

---

[112] Cf. pp. 28–30 in this section.

to bring down upon themselves the interference of the Diet in some shape or other.

Either modifications in the Constitution will be insisted on, or the deliberative powers of the Chambers will be restricted: in short the Government or the Chamber must yield, and looking to the feeble resources of a Darmstadt Chamber in opposition to a Government supported by the Diet, the result can hardly be doubtful. [...]

FO 30/45: Thomas Cartwright to Viscount Palmerston, No 176, Frankfurt, 19 December 1833

State of things in Hesse-Cassel; common interest of government and Landtag to avoid interference of the Federal Diet

My enquiries into the state of things and Parties at Cassel have convinced me that though the political irritation in the Electorate[113] seems latterly to have subsided, and though the proceedings during the last Session in the States were ostensibly conducted with more good will towards the Government, there is still much discontent and dissatisfaction prevailing in that Country.

The Government is dissatisfied with the States, and the States are as displeased with the Government.

The Ultra-Liberal Party is said to have a Majority in that Chamber and is accused of a design to force the Prince Regent[114] to form a Government upon those principles, and the Government is accused of a tendency to disrespect the Constitution and return to an arbitrary and absolute system: but both the Government and the States feel that it is their common interest to avoid any act which through its consequences may call down upon them the interference of the Diet, and they therefore refrain from carrying their hostility to too great an extent.

This is the secret of the apparent good understanding which prevailed between the States and the Government during the late Session, which in fact only was produced by the unwillingness of the States to embarrass

[113] Political conflicts in Electoral Hesse started in May 1832, when an ultra-conservative, Ludwig Hassenpflug, was appointed head of the government. Under Hassenpflug, the government took rigorous action against the liberal majority in the *Landtag* of Electoral Hesse. Although the *Landtag* was dissolved twice, on 26 July 1832 and again on 18 March 1833, this did not have the calming effect that the government had hoped for.

[114] The Prince Elector was Wilhelm II; his son Friedrich Wilhelm was co-regent from 1831 to 1847.

the Government too much, from the fear that they would give the Diet a pretext for meddling with the Constitution.[115]

The finances are wretchedly conducted. Hesse Cassel is not a rich country, but is without a Debt and with a Capital in its favor of about 15,000,000 of Crowns.

Notwithstanding these advantages the Revenues are insufficient for the expences, and there is an annual deficit of about 120,000 Crowns, while in Hesse Darmstadt, a Country with about the same population and resources, and a Debt of about fifteen millions of Florins, the income of the State is equal to cover all the expenditure.

The cause of this deficit is attributed solely to bad management.

The expense of the Hessian Army is bitterly complained of. The Force on active Service does not exceed in amount the Contingent Hesse Cassel is bound to maintain as a State of the Confederation; but this little Army is overburthened with Officers of High Rank and Salary. For six thousand men there are thirteen Generals, and the number of Officers of other ranks is in a similar proportion.

M. de Motz, the Minister of Finance, is universally decried as a financier; but he was the instrument made use of by the Prussian Government to carry its views into execution when Hesse Cassel was inveigled into the Prussian Union,[116] and is consequently supported by the interest of that Power. He is both unpopular and inefficient.

The Minister with the most capacity in Cassel is M. de Hassenpflug, the Minister of the Interior, who is now accused by the States of having directly and intentionally violated various Articles of the Constitution. He is detested in the Country, and if the High Court of Appeal should decide that the accusation preferred against him by the Chamber is well founded, he must retire to avoid more serious consequences.

I believe I may safely sum up this brief account of the state of things in Cassel by quoting the words of M. de Cabre to me, who is well acquainted with the Country having resided there eleven years: 'Hesse Cassel is now little better than a Prussian Province, governed by M. de Hassenpflug, who is in his turn directed by his intimate friend M. de Canitz.'

---

[115] For the constitution of Electoral Hesse cf. n. 20 in this section.
[116] Since the Tariff Agreement of 25 August 1831, Electoral Hesse had been a member of the Prussian Customs Union.

FO 30/50: Thomas Cartwright to Viscount Palmerston, No 51, Frankfurt, 12 April 1834

Question of whether Frankfurt's accession to the Prussian Customs Union is in the real interests of Great Britain

[...] The accession of Frankfort to the Prussian Union is now inevitable. Such being the case, the question which I have to submit to your Lordship's consideration is whether it is not for the real interests of Great Britain that She should facilitate that measure by every means in her power.

The object of Frankfort in concluding the Treaty with Great Britain was to obtain support against the Prussian System to enable her to resist it to the last.[117]

The little inclination manifested by other German States to unite with her in opposing the Prussian views, and the rapidity with which Prussia realized her schemes, and in particular her junction with Bavaria, Wirtemberg, and Saxony, have much altered the position of Frankfort.[118]

That position has been rendered latterly still more critical by the known fact that the accession of Baden is a thing determined and that the Duke of Nassau[119] is anxious to conclude a similar arrangement for his Duchy.[120] Frankfort would then stand alone, and would be exposed to such vexations, that its Commerce might be almost annihilated. The Trade with the Interior of Germany would be lost, and though that with Switzerland would remain open, the facility with which Prussia might impede the Transit Trade and commercial intercourse with that Country would leave that Market very uncertain.

Frankfort therefore, abandoned by the rest of Germany, must yield; and it is better that She should do so with a good grace, than hold out till it will be too late for her to obtain favorable terms.

The remarks I am now submitting to Your Lordship's notice are the result of my inquiries into some of the best mercantile opinions in Frankfort. Almost all the Houses dealing with British Goods are convinced that matters have attained a pitch which render it essential for our Interests that Frankfort should unite. I cite particularly the

[117] On 13 August 1832 Frankfurt had concluded a Treaty of Commerce and Navigation with Britain for a period of ten years which, under the terms of international law, made it impossible for Frankfurt to join the *Zollverein* without cancelling the treaty.

[118] Bavaria and Württemberg joined the *Zollverein* on 22 March 1833, Saxony on 30 March 1833.

[119] Wilhelm.

[120] Baden joined the Customs Union on 12 May 1835. Nassau, which had been one of the most obstinate opponents of the Prussian trade system, joined the Customs Union on 10 December 1835 after its trade alliance with France was dissolved.

Houses of Kessler & Co and Dufay, Bernus & Co,[121] which are connected with Manchester and carry on immense business. The Heads of these Houses have always been opposed and still are opposed in principle to the Prussian System; but they now admit that there is no choice. They say that of two evils they must choose the least; that either way British Trade must suffer, but that the loss will be less by the accession of Frankfort to the Union.

The object is to preserve the Market as advantageous as possible. Without the Union it is apprehended that the German Market will be lost altogether for Frankfort; while through the Union the British Merchants hope to preserve the chain of their commercial connexions with the Interior of Germany.

The Fair which is now terminating has not been a bad Fair; but it is principally owing to people having come from Baden to purchase largely to lay in a provision of Goods previously to the accession of Baden to the commercial Union. This cause will not occur a second time.

On the other hand many of the British Houses have found that their Customers from the States within the Union have diminished in number. Many persons from Bavaria and Wirtemberg, who formerly made large purchases here, came to them and represented that as they could not afford to pay down the high duties on British Goods, which must be effected on the Goods passing the line of the frontier, and that as the Prussian Custom House would not allow them Credit, they had purchased Saxon Goods at Offenbach in lieu thereof; but they all said that if Frankfort was once within the line of Customs, they would return to their ancient habit of taking British Goods, provided the Houses would give them Credit for a certain period.

Now the British merchants are afraid that if Frankfort does not unite, many of their Customers will in this way open a new channel and break off their old connexions altogether, to the great injury of British Trade. They think that if the Union is speedily effected they shall be able to induce those Customers to take from them at least a portion of the Mass they may wish to buy, and that by giving Credit they may keep up all their old connexions. [...]

It appears therefore that the best course Frankfort can follow is to negotiate as speedily as possible. The chief condition which is sought for is the right of Entrepôt,[122] as it has been granted to Leipsick; and Frankfort has every right to expect it. At Leipsick the principal

---

[121] These were among the oldest and most established trading and banking families in Frankfurt.

[122] A port, city, or other centre to which goods are brought for import and export, and for collection and distribution.

Merchants have the privilege of keeping an account with the Custom House. They only pay duty upon the Goods they sell in the States of the Union; but upon those they send to Switzerland or other Countries beyond the frontiers, no duty is exacted.

If Frankfort accedes with this condition, I do not myself think that British Trade will in the end be so much injured. The British Merchants here certainly are very fearful that the high rate of the Prussian Tariff will impede the sale of British Goods. Some commodities may not find a Market, such as the low priced Cottons, because the Saxon Cottons will be preferred; but the high priced Cottons and woollen Goods will find a Sale, if the accounts received from Leipsick of what has been done there since the accession of Saxony to the Prussian Union, are correct.[123]

FO 30/51: Thomas Cartwright to Viscount Palmerston, No 61, Frankfurt, 5 May 1834

New disturbances in Frankfurt; attempted escapes by people involved in the Storming of the Frankfurt Guard House; irritation and hostility of the population towards the billeted soldiers and the city authorities

I regret to state that in the evening of the 2nd Inst^t Frankfort was again the scene of some disturbances which have led to the loss of life and have produced considerable fermentation among the lower Orders. [...]

There certainly has been a very deep laid scheme on foot for liberating the persons confined for being implicated in the events of the 3rd of April 1833,[124] but the contrivers of it have been frustrated in their designs.

About 10 o'clock on the night of the 2nd Inst^t the attempt was made to carry it into execution.

The first notice of what was in agitation seems to have proceeded from a Sentinel on duty in front of the Prisons. He was abruptly accosted by another Soldier, a comrade, who told him that the prisoners were about to escape and that he was not to take any notice of what he was about to see. The Sentinel, instead of taking this hint and lending himself to the transaction, immediately gave the alarm. The whole of the Force on duty was on the alert in a moment. Patrols were sent out to reconnoitre the neighborhood of the Prison in all directions and disperse a Crowd of persons which began to form in front of the

---

[123] Enclosure: Translation. Reflexion upon the position of the Free City of Frankfurt with reference to its accession to the German commercial Union.

[124] Cf. pp. 41–45 in this section.

Building. At this moment one or two shots were suddenly fired by some persons in the Crowd, it is asserted at the Soldiers, and at the same instant five of the prisoners descended into the Street by ropes from the windows of the Cells in which they were confined. The Soldiers who had been, or fancied they had been fired on, immediately discharged their muskets on the persons collected in front of the prisons, and the greatest confusion seems to have then ensued. Several shots were fired, five persons were killed and many wounded, but of the five Students who endeavoured to escape, four were retaken, one of whom has since died from having fractured his skull in falling into the Street.[125]

It was immediately said that the troops fired without having received any provocation, and the people have ever since been in a state of extreme exasperation at the circumstance.

That the Affair commenced by one or two shots being fired by some persons among the Crowd appears certain; but whether they were discharged at the Soldiers or merely as Signals to the prisoners to descend from their cells, is, and probably will remain unexplained. [...]

Your Lordship may well suppose that this incident has created great sensation here and that the Members of the Diet consider it as conclusive proof of the necessity of the military measures and regulations they wish to enforce.[126]

Most undoubtedly it is a very unfortunate occurrence for the Authorities particularly in the present stage of the discussions upon the Affairs of the Town. It is now undeniable that there is much to condemn in the Administration of the Police and in the superintendence of the Prisons, and it is inconceivable and unpardonable that the Authorities, after the warning they received by the events of last year, should not have taken better measures of precaution. That their Agents are remiss in the execution of their duties is now not to be disputed, and they have undoubtedly exposed themselves to much censure from the Diet for their carelessness.

But the chief circumstance connected with this Affair of which it is impossible as yet to calculate the consequences is, that the people in the Town are exasperated beyond measure at the conduct of the Soldiers on this occasion, who they are firmly convinced fired wantonly upon the lookers on without any provocation.

The irritation and hostility towards the Rifle Company, of which the Guard was composed, is such that the excesses are apprehended; and if this feeling is not soon allayed, serious quarrels between the Frankfort Military and the People may very possibly ensue.

[125] The students were Eimer, Obermüller, Handschuh, Alban and Rubner. Rubner died during his escape attempt.

[126] After confederal troops were stationed in Frankfurt on 15 April 1833, the Federal

Upon the whole then this incident in its effects is likely to be very injurious to the Authorities, for it will be very difficult for them to eradicate the notions which the people have imbibed and allay the animosity now prevailing against themselves and their own Military Force for the severity with which the troops conducted themselves on the 2nd Inst^t, while on the other hand it will be still more difficult for them to persuade the Diet that there is no necessity for the presence of the Austrian Corps, or that the entire military Authority in Frankfort ought not to be permanently vested in the hands of the Austrian General.[127]

I transmit a Copy of this Dispatch to His Majesty's Ambassador at Vienna.[128]

FO 30/52: Thomas Cartwright to Viscount Palmerston, No 72, Frankfurt, 2 June 1834

Right of the German Confederation to intervene in the affairs of a member state; resistance of the Frankfurt government concerning the internal affairs of the city

I have the honor to acknowledge the receipt of Your Lordship's Dispatch N° 25.

With reference to its contents it is incumbent on me to observe, that throughout the proceedings relating to Frankfort the Diet seems to have laid more stress upon the 28th than upon any other Article of the Final Act,[129] and to have taken it for the basis of its operation.[130]

The 28th Article states 'that if publick tranquillity and legal order shall be menaced in several of the federal States by dangerous plots and associations, and if it is only possible to enforce efficient measures against them by the joint cooperation of the whole Body, the Diet is authorised and is bound to deliberate and decide upon such measures <u>after previous concert with the Governments more immediately exposed to danger.</u>'

The Government of Frankfort certainly will not admit that the first part of this Article is applicable to the state of things here; but admitting for the sake of argument that publick tranquillity is menaced in a way

---

Diet resolved on 3 April 1834 to place the troops of the City of Frankfurt under the command of the Confederation as an additional security measure.

[127] Ludwig Freiherr von Piret de Bihain.

[128] Enclosure: newspaper clipping from *Journal de Francfort*, no date.

[129] Vienna Final Act of 1820.

[130] Despite the City of Frankfurt's resistance, the Federal Diet's resolution of 12 April 1834 (cf. n. 93 in this section) was implemented. The troops of the City of Frankfurt were forcibly integrated into the Confederal Security Corps.

to call for the direct interference of the Diet, it is evident that whatever measures that Body chooses to decide upon, can under the above Article only be enforced after previous concert with the Frankfort Government.

The Diet has been in communication with the Senate from the commencement upon the subject of these proceedings; but the Frankfort Government has all along been averse to the measures the Diet has thought fit to propose and to enforce, and therefore it cannot be maintained that the 28th Article is more to the point than either the 25th, 26th, 32nd, or 33rd Articles.[131]

On the other hand the 15th Article states 'that in cases relating to individual Rights, – jura singulorum,[132] in which the federal Members consequently appear as individual and independent States, and not as Members of the Union, and moreover in all cases in which individual federal Members may be called upon to perform acts or furnish contributions towards the Confederation which are not comprised in their common obligations, no Resolution can be made binding without the free consent of those specially interested.'

It is upon this Article that the Town rests its case, and unless it can be shewn that the internal Administration of a State does not come under the head of Jura singulorum, it is obvious, that by its stipulations all the measures which have been adopted by the Diet never ought to have been carried into execution without the free consent of the Frankfort Government. Speaking strictly therefore, this Article has been violated.

But I feel it my duty to submit to Your Lordship's consideration whether Great Britain, as a Party to the Treaty of Vienna, can admit of any Article of the Final Act being brought forward in justification of measures which do not accord with the fundamental principle of the federal Act of 1815.[133]

The Final Act can only be regarded as the interpretation given to the federal Act of 1815 by the German Governments. It is an Act purely German, emanating solely from the united Councils of the German States, and its stipulations therefore cannot invalidate or annul a prior Treaty to which the principal Powers of Europe are parties. But the Diet by the line it is taking seems disposed to make the Final

[131] The articles of the Vienna Final Act of 1820 listed here regulated the right of the German Confederation to intervene in the affairs of a member state. Article 28, which specified when the Confederation could intervene, was especially significant as its general provisions could be interpreted in different ways and gave the Confederation far-reaching rights vis-à-vis the respective individual states.

[132] The term for the law of a sovereign state, which came into force when the relevant state was acting independently and not in its capacity as a member of the Confederation.

[133] Act of the German Confederation, 8 June 1815.

Act the instrument by which it means to undermine the principal Article of the Federal Act, which establishes the inviolability and independence of the German States, and to consider that its own Resolutions are to supersede a great European Compact.

FO 30/48: To Thomas Cartwright, Foreign Office, No 30, signed by Palmerston, London, 13 July 1834 (Draft)[134]

H.M's. Government's reply to the president of the Federal Diet concerning the military occupation of Frankfurt

H.M's. Government have had under their consideration your Desp[h] N° 82, enclosing the Note Verbale delivered to you by The President[135] of the Diet, in answer to yours of the 24th of May, on the Subject of the Military occupation of the free City of Frankfort; and you are instructed to make to The President of the Diet the following reply.

You will state that H.M's Gov[t] regret very much to perceive, from an Expression in M. de Nagler's Note, that the communication which you were instructed to make to The Diet, upon the subject of the Military occupation of Frankfort, has been considered by The Diet as not having been couched in language sufficiently friendly.

It was far from the intention of H.M's Gov[t] to give any thing like an unfriendly character to the Expressions of that communication; and, with regard to its substance, they are of opinion that there is nothing inconsistent with the Offices of friendship in timely remonstrance, between Contracting Parties, against an apprehended departure from the stipulations of a Treaty.

M. de Nagler's Note claims for the Confederation a right to regulate its internal affairs without any Foreign Interference; and asserts that the Confederation was established for the express purpose of maintaining the Independence of each, and every of the German States of which it is composed.

To neither of these propositions have His Majesty's Gov[t] any objection to offer: Great Britain has no wish to interfere with the purely internal Affairs of the Confederation; and far from denying that one of the principal and avowed objects of the Establishment of the Confederation was the maintenance of the Independence of each of the Confederate States, it is precisely upon the assertion of that fact, that H.M's

---

[134] Original in FO 208/20.
[135] During the absence of Joachim Graf von Münch-Bellinghausen, the Prussian envoy, Karl Ferdinand Friedrich von Nagler, was acting president.

Government have founded their right of remonstrance upon the present occasion.

Great Britain having been a Party to the Treaty of Vienna, is entitled to object to any infringement of the stipulations of that Treaty.[136]

The Germanick Confederation was created by The Treaty of Vienna; and, as regards its relations with other States, the rights of the Confederation, its powers, its duties, are to be sought for in the stipulations of that Treaty, and in those stipulations alone.

The Confederate States are undoubtedly at liberty to make among each other such regulations as they may think fit, with respect to their purely internal affairs; and no other Power has any right to meddle with those regulations, so long as they are not at variance with the stipulations of the Treaty, by which the Confederation itself has acquired an acknowledged existence in Europe. But 'the preservation of the <u>Independence</u> and of the <u>Inviolability</u> of each of the Confederate States', was solemnly recorded in the Treaty of Vienna, as one of the main objects for which the Confederation was established; and The Diet can never imagine that those Powers of Europe,[137] who were Parties to that Treaty, and who, from general principles or from particular interests, deem it important that national independence should be respected, even in the case of the smallest of States; The Diet can surely not imagine that such Powers can ever admit it, that, under the pretext of regulating internal Affairs, the Majority of the States of which the Confederation is composed should be entitled to overturn the Independence, and to destroy the Inviolability, of their Associates; and thus to convert that Confederacy, which was created as a shield for the weak, into an instrument of oppression for the Strong.

His Majesty's Gov^t wish to rest their protest on the present occasion upon general principles & notorious facts; they take their stand upon the Treaty of Vienna, and cannot admit that any subsequent acts of the Diet, unsanctioned by the Powers who were Contracting Parties to that Treaty, could abrogate its stipulations or invalidate its principles. But it would be easy to prove, by reference to many acts & resolutions of the Diet, which have at different times been published to the world, and among others by the Acts: 25–26 & 32 of the final act of 1820,[138]

---

[136] The Act of the German Confederation of 8 June 1815, which was signed by the member states of the German Confederation, was integrated into the Act of the Vienna Congress of 9 June 1815. The issue in the present case was what consequences the contractual linking of the two documents had under international law.

[137] Contracting partners to the Act of the Vienna Congress of 9 June 1815 were the eight Congress powers: Austria, Prussia, Britain, France, Portugal, Russia, Sweden, and Spain.

[138] Articles 25, 26 and 32 of the Vienna Final Act of 1820 stipulated regulations governing exceptional cases in which the Confederation had the right to intervene in an individual state. The Free City of Frankfurt did not constitute such a case.

that the proceedings which form the subject of the present Note, are as much at variance with the principles laid down at former periods by the Diet itself, as they are in opposition to the letter of the Treaty of Vienna.

M. de Nagler in the conclusion of his Note, declares that the Confederation will never claim a right to interfere with the measures which Foreign States may think proper to take, for the prevention or for the repression of disturbance within the limits of their own Territories. If this declaration is meant, as it appears to be, less as an announcement of the course which the Diet intends to pursue, than as an indirect imputation upon the Course which has been pursued by Great Britain, H.M's Gov^t feel themselves called upon to assert that the imputation is destitute of foundation.

H.M's Gov^t have never assumed to themselves a right to interfere with the measures which any Independent State might think fit to take for the maintenance of order within the limits of its own Territory; but H.M's Gov^t, while they repudiate that right for Great Britain, cannot concede it to other Powers. It is strictly upon a denial of such a right that this communication and your note of the 24th of May are founded. The Confederation is not a state possessing any territory, or invested with any Sovereign rights, it is a league formed between independent States, each possessing separate territories, and each exercising within its own territory, its own Sovereign rights.

The extent to which the independent action of each Gov^t has, by the formation of the Confederacy, been rendered subordinate to the general will of the rest, is defined by the Treaty of Vienna. Beyond that extent any interference of one or more Members of the Confederation in the internal affairs of another is a violation of the principle of national independence. And if the overbearing force of a powerful majority shall compel a reluctant and protesting State to submit to the military occupation of its territory by troops not acknowledging its authority, and to the transfer of its own regiments to the Command of a General who obeys the orders of another Sovereign; such a result may indeed demonstrate the ascendancy of numerical superiority, but cannot alter the injustice of the principle upon which such proceedings are founded.

P.S. You will present a Note to the President of the Diet in the words of this Dispatch.

FO 30/53: Thomas Cartwright to Viscount Palmerston, No 111, Frankfurt, 1 October 1834

Reflections on the declaration made during the 34th sitting of the Federal Diet

[...] I have received the Protocol of the 34th Sitting of the Diet, and I am now enabled to transmit to Your Lordship a Copy of the statement made to the Diet by the President,[139] on proposing the adoption of the Decree[140] which I inclosed in my Dispatch N° 109.[141]

This document is a most extraordinary production, and is more remarkable for its abuse and a display of rancorous feeling than of argument and reason.

Your Lordship cannot better judge of the irritation which has been produced by the opposition which England and France[142] have offered to the principle of the measure of the occupation of Frankfort than by the tone of this declaration which comes from Vienna. There is but little argument in it, and what little there is, is all distorted.

After proclaiming, that the Germanick Confederation owes its existence to itself, and to no other source, it proceeds to establish in a summary way, that no Foreign Powers have any right to superintend the application of the principles recorded in the Federal Act,[143] and it asserts, that Germany exists by its own means, 'and is so perfectly organised both for internal and external objects and so firmly grounded upon its own materials, that, as the keystone to the European Body of States, it possesses all the necessary means of guaranteeing, without foreign cooperation, its internal tranquillity as well as the inviolable security and Independence of the sovereign Princes and Free Cities united in the Confederation'.

From this preface it would be conceived, that the Independence of one of the German [States] was menaced from without, and the subsequent paragraphs all lean towards this supposition.

[139] Joachim Graf von Münch-Bellinghausen.

[140] Resolution of the German Confederation Concerning the Inadmissibility of Intervention by Foreign Powers in the Internal Affairs of the German Confederation, 18 September 1834. In this Declaration by the president, Britain's and France's intervention against the Confederation's actions in Frankfurt were decisively rejected. The right of objection that Britain and France claimed as signatory powers of the Act of the Congress of Vienna of 1815, and which encompassed the Act of the German Confederation, was not recognized by the German Confederation.

[141] Not included in this volume.

[142] On 21 and 24 May 1834 respectively, the French envoy, Baron Alleye, and Cartwright had expressed their concerns to the German Confederation about what had happened in the Free City of Frankfurt in the form of a *note verbale*. When the Federal Diet rejected these objections, France and Britain responded by sending detailed notes of protest on 30 June and 13 July respectively (cf. p. 68 in this section).

[143] Act of the German Confederation, 8 June 1815.

Now it is notorious, that the present discussion has not been produced by an attack having been made upon the Independence of one of the German States by a Foreign Power, but that on the contrary it has arisen out of the circumstance of the Independence of one of those States having been violated by the Confederation itself.

Therefore, all Articles which have been quoted to shew what is the real constitution of the Germanick Confederation, as it is interpreted by the Diet, will not, taken collectively, go to exonerate the Diet and settle this discussion in its favor, unless it can be shown, that they confer upon it a right to infringe in a given case the Independence of a Confederate State.

The chief argument of the Diet is, that the Confederation may alter or remodel its Laws as it chooses, and it is evidently intended by establishing this theory as Law, to overturn the main argument of England and France, that the Laws of the Confederation are all subservient to the one great basis in the maintenance of which they have a direct interest.

It is asserted, that the 58th Article of the Act of the Congress[144] gives this power to the Confederation, and it is asked: 'how can the assertion of England, that the Resolutions of the Diet must be in unison with the fundamental principles of the Federal Act, agree with the provisions of the 58th Article, or with the 62nd Article, according to which the organick arrangements of the Confederation with respect to its military, internal, and foreign relations are especially reserved for the decision of the Diet and of the Diet alone?'

Now to borrow an expression from this Declaration it is 'clear as the sun' that the power given by the 58th Article to alter the fundamental Laws, is only meant to be used in a given sense; for if otherwise, what could prevent the Diet from annulling the whole Federal Act and establishing a new Code of Federal Laws on a totally different principle from that established by the 54th Article[145] of the same Treaty.

The Confederation exists solely in virtue of an European Agreement, and it is absurd to maintain, that any Article drawn up for the purpose of giving to the Diet the power to regulate some points of details in its Constitution confers upon it the power of overturning the Act which called it into existence. And yet the argument used in the Declaration

---

[144] Article 58 of the Act of the Congress of Vienna of 9 June 1815 (corresponds to article 6 of the Act of the German Confederation of 8 June 1815) specifies the conditions regulating the drafting and changing of the Basic Laws of the German Confederation.

[145] Article 54 of the Act of the Congress of Vienna of 9 June 1815 (corresponds to article 2 of the Act of the German Confederation of 8 June 1815) defines the purpose of the German Confederation as to maintain the external and internal security of Germany, and the independence and invoilability of the individual German states.

of the President,[146] if it means anything, goes this length; for the moment it is admitted, that the Diet may alter the fundamental Laws as it chooses, and it is this right it now claims, it may also alter the basis of its Constitution.

Your Lordship will not fail to be struck with the ebullition of bitter feeling which pervades the whole of this curious paper.[147] [...]

FO 30/53: Thomas Cartwright to Viscount Palmerston, No 112, Frankfurt, 10 October 1834

On German political refugees in Switzerland and their influence on the German homeland; proposed resolutions of the Federal Diet

In the 32nd Sitting of the Diet on the 28th of August last, the President[148] called the attention of that Assembly to the attempts which he affirmed the revolutionary Party in Switzerland were making to corrupt and gain over by bribery and bad precepts that useful class of persons, the German travelling apprentices ('Handwerks-Gesellen').

He represented that this subject was one of the highest importance, and he proposed that a Committee of the Diet should report without delay upon the measures which it might deem expedient for the German Governments to enforce in order to prevent any evils arising from that circumstance.

In the following Sitting the Report of this Committee was laid before the Diet. It stated that the Committee has ascertained from minute enquires which had been set on foot, that the most notorious German Refugees[149] in Switzerland (notwithstanding the satisfactory assurances which had repeatedly been given by the Swiss Vorort),[150] were still prosecuting their revolutionary schemes in the most open manner in that Country, and has succeeded in forming Clubs or Assemblies among

---

[146] Declaration of the president, 18 September 1834 (cf. n. 140 in this section). The president, Joachim Graf von Münch-Bellinghausen, was replaced by the Prussian envoy, Karl Ferdinand Friedrich von Nagler.

[147] Enclosure: Extract of the 34th Protocol of the Diet of the 18th of September 1834, § 455.

[148] Joachim Graf von Münch-Bellinghausen, replaced by the Prussian envoy, Karl Ferdinand Friedrich von Nagler.

[149] The refugees included were oppositional journalists and writers, members of the banned student movements (*Burschenschaften*) and participants in the revolutionary uprisings of 1830–1831, the Hambach Festival of 1832 and the Storming of the Frankfurt Guard House.

[150] Name of the alternative site for meetings of the *Tagessatzung*, at which deputies from the Swiss Cantons conferred on the concerns of the Swiss Confederation.

the travelling Apprentices,[151] who appeared to be extremely excited and to be indulging in great excesses; that similar scenes had some time ago occurred in Belgium and France, and that the Governments of those Countries had paid but little attention to the circumstance; that the established custom which required that the Apprentices, Subjects of the German States, should travel for a certain number of years before they could be admitted to practise their craft in their native towns, afforded the German Revolutionists abroad a good opportunity for increasing their ranks and extending the ramifications of their schemes without exposing themselves to danger; that they sought to establish Societies amongst the Apprentices upon revolutionary principles in order that on their return to their homes they might disseminate those doctrines and opinions amongst their friends and companions, from which circumstance the utmost danger might ensue; and that, 'as it was for the interest of the Germanick Confederation that the travelling Apprentices should be prevented from taking part in any Associations calculated to endanger or interrupt publick tranquillity either abroad or in Germany', the Committee considered that the Diet should adopt the Following Resolutions:

Proposed Resolutions
1. All Apprentices, Subjects of the German federal States, shall be prohibited from proceeding to France, Belgium, and Switzerland, until the end of 1836.
2. The Right to admit of certain exceptions to this prohibition shall be reserved to the federal Governments.
3. With respect to the recall of such of the German Apprentices as may be sojourning in the three specified Countries, and to the superintendence ('surveillance') of them on their return to their respective homes, the adoption of appropriate measures shall be left to the judgment of the several federal Governments.
4. Such of the German Apprentices as may be travelling at present in Germany shall be under the strict superintendence of the Police, especially as regards the Associations in which they may be implicated.
5. The different Governments are requested to notify to the High Diet the measures which they may enforce for the aforesaid object.

These Resolutions have not yet been adopted, but the Members are to obtain Instructions to vote upon them in the course of this month.

[151] From 1833, German travelling apprentices held regular meetings and set up associations in Biel, Zurich, Geneva, Berne, Lausanne, and St Gallen. These were closely allied with the clandestine organization *Junges Deutschland* (Young Germany), which was established in 1834 by German exiles as a branch of the Young Europe, led by the Italian revolutionary Giuseppe Mazzini.

FO 30/53: Thomas Cartwright to Viscount Palmerston, No 128, Frankfurt, 15 November 1834

Outline of the composition of a tribunal ('Schieds-Gericht') created for the settlement of differences between Federal Diet and representative chambers of the different German states

I have the honor to transmit to your Lordship a French translation of a Protocol which has been published by the Diet announcing the creation of a Tribunal for the settlement of differences between the Sovereigns Members of the Germanick Confederation and the Representative Chambers.

A reference to the twelve Articles of the Protocol[152] will give Your Lordship a correct notion of the composition and the attributes of this Tribunal, which, as it is given out, is henceforward to stifle all dissention between the Governments and the Chambers, and prevent every chance of collision and revolution.

The title given to this Tribunal is 'Schieds-Gericht' (Court of Arbitration), and not 'Compromiss-Gericht' as I have been given to understand.

Each of the 17 Votes in the Diet[153] is to name two persons to act as Arbiters as they may be required. Whenever a case is referred to the Schieds-Gericht, six Members are to be selected from among the thirty four: three by each of the contending Parties; and these six are together to choose another Colleague to themselves from among the remaining number, in order to prevent an equal division of Votes in the Court, it being always understood that the two Members originally named to act as Arbiters by the Sovereign who is a party interested cannot be comprised among the seven. If the six Members neglect to name, or cannot agree upon the seventh Member, the Diet is to appoint him; and the Tribunal thus constituted is to pronounce upon differences submitted to its arbitration.

This outline of the composition of this Tribunal will suffice to shew Your Lordship that no very impartial spirit presided at its organization. All the Advantage is on one side. The Sovereigns name in the first instance the persons from whom the States are forced to select their Arbiters; and in doubtful cases, or as a last resource, it is always the Diet that is to interpret and decide. The Sovereigns will go before such a Tribunal with perfect security and satisfaction, while the States will

---

[152] Federal law of 30 October 1834; concurring with articles 3–14 of the Sixty Articles of the Vienna Conference of Ministers of 12 June 1834, cf. pp. 136–137 in Prussia section.

[153] In the assemblies of the Confederation, the larger German states (Austria, Prussia, Bavaria, Saxony, Hanover, Württemberg, Baden, Electoral Hesse, the Grand Duchy of Hesse, Holstein, and the Grand Duchy of Luxemburg) had one vote each. The rest of members (in 1817 this was thirty sovereign states) shared a total of six votes.

have to defend their cause before a Body of men selected by their Adversaries for the avowed purpose of putting a stop to the exigences of the Chambers, and consequently without any chance of an impartial hearing.

There is nevertheless a shew of concession to the States in the creation of this Tribunal. Hitherto the Diet has always claimed the right to decide peremptorily upon these matters. The famous Articles from 1832[154] were framed to bridle the Chambers, and one of them went to name a Committee whose express object was to watch and report upon the proceedings of the Representative Assemblies. Therefore to admit that any differences between a Sovereign and the Chamber may now be referred to a Court of Arbitration, is a concession; but it is only a concession in name, and not in reality, because when a question is once referred to this Tribunal, it is in fact in the hands of the Diet.

It has evidently been intended that this Tribunal should be an instrument by which the Sovereigns might curb the Chambers and crush all opposition to their views. Whenever a Chamber wishes to curtail a Budget, or insists on measures to which the Sovereign is averse, he may now threaten to appeal to the 'Schieds-Gericht', and by such means endeavor to render the Chambers perfectly subservient to his will. And this may be supposed to have been the chief object of the framers of this measure; for if the Sovereigns do not reap some advantage from it as an instrument of intimidation, they are not likely to derive much essential benefit from it when set in motion.[155] [...]

FO 30/55: Thomas Cartwright to Duke of Wellington, No 14, Frankfurt, 25 February 1835

Negotiations relative to the accession of Frankfurt to the Prussian Commercial Union

I am informed by Mr Burgomaster Thomas that the Negotiations at Berlin relative to the accession of Frankfort to the Prussian Commercial Union have now actually commenced.

M. de Guatia has given in to the Prussian Government a Memoir specifying the terms on which Frankfort is willing to become a Member of the Union, and this step is considered to constitute the opening of the Negotiation.

Frankfort seems more desirous to do away with privileges granted to

---

[154] Cf. pp. 28–30 in this section.
[155] Enclosure: *Supplément au N° 313 du Journal de Francfort.*

other Towns within the Union than to stipulate for extraordinary advantages for herself.

It appears that as the different States joined the Union, each stipulated for some particular benefit for some Town, Port, or Fair within its territories as suited its local position. Saxony, for instance, made terms for the Fair of Leipsick; Bavaria insisted on certain concessions for its commerce with Switzerland; Prussia granted certain privileges to the Fair of Frankfort on the Oder; and thus each State, as the price of its accession, endeavored to do the best for its local interests. But in this way certain monopolies have in fact been established, which must, if they are maintained, bear very prejudicially on the Trade of such a Town as Frankfort on the Maine. The privileges which Prussia has granted to Cologne and Magdeburg will draw all the Commerce of the Rhine and the Elbe to those places and make of them the two great Entrepôts[156] for those Rivers. Prussia, it appears, remits to all Boats which come to Cologne to discharge their cargoes – under whatever Flag they may navigate – the Prussian dues payable for navigation, which advantage must induce merchants to establish their great Warehouses at that Place; and this arrangement will make of Cologne the great Entrepôt of this part of Germany. The same privilege has been granted to Magdeburg for the Elbe.

The Trade which has hitherto been carried on through Frankfort must be materially injured by this arrangement, and one of the principal points on which Frankfort insists in this Negotiation is, that Prussia should renounce granting this advantage for boats discharging at Cologne.

This is considered here a very important point, and Frankfort expects to find support from other Members of the Union in urging the abolition of this practice.

I understand that the other points set forth in this Memoir are as I have already stated them to be in my former Dispatches: 1.) that the conditions granted to Leipsick for the warehousing of Goods, commonly known in the commercial world by the term the 'Entrepôt fictif'[157] be extended to Frankfort; 2.) that Frankfort shall hold an entire Vote in the Council of the States of the Union; and 3.) that the portion of the receipts accruing to Frankfort shall be taken after a different standard than the actual population of this State.

I understand that before M. de Guatia delivered in his Memoir, he had some preliminary conversations with M.M. Ancillon and Eichhorn, and that he expresses himself satisfied with the general dispositions evinced by them.

---

[156] Cf. n. 122 in this section.
[157] Cf. pp. 61–62 in this section.

FO 30/60: Thomas Cartwright to Viscount Palmerston, No 3, Frankfurt, 16 January 1836

'Junges Deutschland' (Young Germany) and the effects of its publications; Federal Diet's interference

So many works have latterly been published in Germany of an irreligious and immoral tendency, that the Diet has thought it advisable to interfere.

These publications are principally the productions of some talented young men who have long made themselves conspicuous by the eccentricity of their opinions upon all subjects, and who now form a literary School, which has been designated 'Young Germany'.[158]

Count Münch first called the attention of the Diet to this subject upon the 29th of October last, and a Committee was then appointed to examine these Works and report upon the measures to be enforced with a view to put a stop to their further publication and sale.

The Committee has not yet made its Report; but as in the mean time the evil continued to gain ground, Count Münch upon the 10th of December last came forward with a separate proposition on the part of Austria which was immediately adopted and amounts in point of fact to the general prohibition and suppression of all publications of this description.[159]

I have the honor to inclose the statement he made upon that occasion (which I have reason to believe was drawn up by M. Jarke at Vienna), the Resolutions which were adopted, and two confidential declarations which had been previously communicated to the Diet by the Prussian and Baden Ministers, giving some details respecting the proceedings of some of the Members of this literary Association, and making known the steps which had been taken by their Governments against them.

By the Resolutions which have been adopted at the instigation of Austria, the federal Governments have been called upon to use all the means in their power to prevent the sale of publications emanating from this School of Literature, the Bookseller in Germany have been warned not to publish or sell these works, and the Government of Hamburg has been called upon particularly to admonish the Booksellers

---

[158] The literary movement *Junges Deutschland* (Young Germany), which had come into being in 1830, aimed to overcome classicism in German literature. Politically, its adherents supported anti-feudal and social ideas, and aspired to a republican German nation-state. *Junges Deutschland* bore no direct relation to the secret society of the same name established in Switzerland in 1834. Its main members were, in addition to the writers named in this dispatch, Christian Dietrich Grabbe, Heinrich Heine, Theodor Mundt, and Ludwig Börne.

[159] Resolution of the German Confederation of 10 December 1835 (Prohibition of the Writings of *Junges Deutschland*).

Hoffman and Campe,[160] from whose Press the principal publications of this Class have been given to the World.

These works are in most instances blasphemous and immoral in the highest degree and replete with doctrines subversive of every received notion of Religion and social order.

In a Volume by M. Wienbarg[161] that Author has endeavoured to prove that the World would have been much happier had nothing ever been taught respecting the existence of God; and in a Novel by M. Gutzkow entitled 'Wally, or the Sceptick',[162] a character is introduced ridiculing the idea of the Divinity of Our Saviour.

Your Lordship will perceive from the Baden Declaration inclosed in this Dispatch, that legal proceedings were instituted against M. Gutzkow at Manheim for the publication of this book. The trial has just terminated. He has been acquitted of blasphemy, but has at the same time been found guilty of an intentional attack upon the established Religion in the Grand Duchy, which judgment most persons conceive to contain in itself a strange contradiction, and has been sentenced to ten weeks imprisonment and the payment one third of the costs.

No one can possibly undertake the defence of such works as these; but there is a difference of opinion with respect to the policy of the interference of the Diet, and it is thought by many persons that it would have been better to have left the different Governments to take their own steps to put down this Association.[163]

FO 30/60: Thomas Cartwright to Viscount Palmerston, No 5, Frankfurt, 16 January 1836

Blittersdorff's political career and his intended policy

M. de Blittersdorff came to Frankfort last week to make the necessary arrangements for the removal of his family to Carlsruhe which the suddenness of his nomination to the Post in the Baden Government[164] he now holds did not leave him time to do, when he was summoned

---

[160] This Hamburg publishing and bookselling company, founded in 1808 and directed by Julius Campe since 1823, published the works of Heinrich Heine and Ludwig Börne among others. The resolution of the German Confederation of 10 December instructed the City of Hamburg to warn the publisher.

[161] *Aestetische Feldzüge* (Esthetical Campaigns, 1834). Printed version of a series of twenty-four lectures given by Wienbarg as a *Privatdozent* at the University of Kiel from 1833.

[162] *Wally, die Zweiflerein* (1835); banned by the Prussian censor in the summer of 1835.

[163] Enclosures: Translation. Extract of the 30th Protocol of the Diet of the 3rd of December 1835; Extract of the 31st Protocol of the Diet of the 10th of December 1835.

[164] Friedrich Landolin Karl Freiherr von Blittersdorf had been Baden's foreign secretary since October 1835.

to that Capital in November last. He only remained here a few days and returned to Carlsruhe on the 23rd Inst^{t}.

During his stay M. de Blittersdorff conversed freely with some of his former Colleagues upon his present position and professed to be quite satisfied that he should be able to maintain himself against all the intrigues and attacks of his enemies. He said that he was now on terms of very good understanding with the Grand Duke. His Royal Highness formerly had great dislike to M. de Blittersdorff. They studied at the University together, and the Grand Duke's prejudice against him seems to have dated from those times, but according to M. de Blittersdorff, that feeling has entirely worn away, and His Royal Highness is now as conciliatory and friendly towards him as he could possibly expect.

But nevertheless the stability of his office seems to most other persons to be very problematical. The difficulties he will have to contend with are of his own creation, and will only come into play upon the meeting of the States which will not take place before next Winter.

There is a numerous party in the Grand Duchy of which M.M. Rotteck and Welker are the leaders, which has long held M. de Blittersdorff in detestation on account of the share he has borne in certain transactions of the Diet.[165] This Party has always looked upon him as an Agent of Russia,[166] as having no sympathy whatever for the Government of which he is the servant, and as having been one of the chief instigators of the repressive and anti-constitutional measures which have emanated from the Diet of late years.

He is himself well aware of the unfriendly dispositions of this Party and is evidently uneasy upon the subject and very anxious to find some means of averting its hostility. But to effect this, is precisely his greatest dilemma.

M. de Blittersdorff's best mode would perhaps be to throw the whole responsibility of the Diet's unpopular measures upon Austria, to shew that they never had had his approbation, and that for Baden to have opposed them would have been useless and even hurtful for the interests of the Grand Duchy, as such opposition would have drawn upon her the ill will of all the other States of the Confederation. He cannot however take this course. He knows that he was himself the great promoter and supporter of those measures, and so committed is he by his previous political career that he now says that he finds it impossible for him to make any concession to gain the good will of M. Rotteck and his partisans.

---

[165] Blittersdorf had taken a leading part in framing the resolution of the German Confederation which, in July 1832, declared invalid the Baden press law which Welcker and Rotteck had initiated (cf. n. 51 in this section).

[166] Blittersdorf had been *chargé d'affaires* at the Baden legation in St Petersburg in 1818.

From M. de Blittersdorff's language however it seems to enter into his ideas that he will be able to disarm his enemies by following a bold national policy, if I may so term the line pursued by the Baden Government. With this view he will extend and protect in every way the essential interests of the Grand Duchy without any reference to his former acts, and will have as little to do with the Diet as possible. He has already given proof of this in having consented to the construction of two new Bridges over the Upper Rhine to facilitate the intercourse with France, much to the astonishment and dissatisfaction of all his former Colleagues in the Diet, and he will continue to follow as independent a system as he can, in the hopes of creating an impression in his favor throughout the Grand Duchy.

There was a very observable tendency in all M. de Blittersdorff said to lean towards Prussia, and I have no doubt he will henceforward seek to side with that State in the Diet in preference to Austria.

In short his language was so striking during his stay here that more than one person remarked to me that he was already become the very opposite of what he was while he sat in the Diet.

FO 30/61: Thomas Cartwright to Viscount Palmerston, No 36, Frankfurt, 14 May 1836

Observation on how the Prussian commercial system affects British interests; commercial and political questions involved; Austria's declining influence

The Prussian Commercial System occupies so prominent a place in German Affairs and has become a matter of such moment for manufacturing and commercial nations, that I think it my duty to submit a few observations to Your Lordship upon the way in which that System is likely to affect British Interests.

The Prussian System comprises within itself two distinct questions – the one commercial – the other political.

It is notorious that for several years all the efforts of Prussia have been directed towards the completion of an Union of the whole of the States of the Germanick Confederation, exclusive of Austria, in one common commercial System, under her own control and protection. By the accession of Baden, Nassau, and lastly of Frankfort to that Union,[167] She has carried her project as far as it is open to her to reach at the present moment, since the States which have not yet joined the Commercial Confederation as Luxemburg, Hanover, Brunswick,

---

[167] Baden joined the *Zollverein* on 12 May 1835, Nassau on 10 December 1835 and Frankfurt on 2 January 1836.

Oldenburg, Mecklenburg, &c are by their political ties, particular interests and geographical position, still so separated from Prussia upon this question, that she cannot hope, for some time forward, to gain them over to her views. If the Union maintains itself their accession will probably follow of itself some years hence, but as circumstances do not admit of the possibility of their uniting at this period, Prussia has in fact embraced in her system all the States it is practicable for her to obtain, and may therefore be fairly said to have realised her object and to have brought the commercial Question to its conclusion.

The result of the success which has attended her efforts, is, that a German population of about 25,000,000, souls is now united in one common commercial Confederation under the control and influence of Prussia, 21,752,153, of which belong to some of the Federal States of Germany, the remainder are made up by the Grand Duchy of Posen and the Prussian Provinces which are not comprised in the Germanick Confederation.[168]

An idea prevails in many countries that the fundamental principle of the Prussian System is prohibitory: This is a great error – it's merely protective. There is no one article except Salt which is prohibited, and Salt is a monopoly in the hands of the Governments. But although the System is not prohibitory, in principle, it is nevertheless true that the protecting duties are in some instances so high that they operate as a prohibition upon many goods of inferior & heavy quality. This result arises from weight having been adopted as the basis of the Tariff. The duties are not raised ad valorem, but are throughout laid upon the hundred weight without reference to quality, so that whenever prohibition occurs it is more the effect of the method which was followed in framing the Tariff, than of a positive intention of Prussia to introduce a prohibitive System. I am the more inclined to this opinion because in as far as the Tariff acts prohibitorily upon British goods, it happens most to affect some of the low Cottons, which were but little known in the German Market when the Prussian System first took root, and against which therefore it could not have been originally directed.

These protecting duties certainly in several instances are equivalent to prohibition upon many British Articles, and they bear so hard upon others, that their sale has considerably diminished and will fall off in a still greater degree: Shirtings, Beaverteens, Satin Tops, Cotton Drills, Common Cambrics, common Prints, Woollen Coatings; and in Hardwares, Buttons; & silver Plated Articles, suffer most, and some are quite lost to the Market. [...]

---

[168] Only those areas of Prussia which had previously been part of the German Empire belonged to the German Confederation; that is, the provinces of Posen, and East and West Prussia were excluded.

The Political Question interwoven with the Prussian System is not less important than the Commercial Question, although it may be, as yet, less apparent in its bearings. A Commercial Confederacy reposing upon a common basis cannot exist long without the interests of all the Members of that Confederacy becoming completely identified upon all questions of National Policy. The one result is the natural consequence of the other, and this will be the case with the Prussian Union.

As the commercial intercourse increases between Prussia and the States which have united with her, and as National Industry advances, a fusion of interests must take place over the whole surface within the limits of the Union, which will in the end essentially make the Cause of Prussia that of the Mass of the Population.

The commercial tie between these States and Prussia already exists. In a few years hence, one of the natural consequences of that tie will be the introduction of the Prussian Coin in most of the States of the Union. This charge will probably ensue of itself. It will be found very inconvenient to levy the duties after two different Standards, in florins in the one Country, in Dollars in the other, and as it is not probable that Prussia will adopt the florin currency, it is to be foreseen that the Prussian Money will soon be the currency in many of the States in which the florin is now the Standard Coin.[169]

The Prussian System of indirect Taxes will then follow. As things stand at present the excise[170] and other duties vary so much in the different States that they are a subject of constant inconvenience to the trader in Articles of consumption. As an example of what I mean I will take Wine. In some of the States of the Union there is an excise duty on Wine, – in others none at all – therefore Wine grown, I will say, in Hesse Darmstadt and having the right, in virtue of the Custom's Union, to be exported to Prussia without being subjected to any Customs Duty, must, if sold in Prussia pay the excise duty, or the Darmstadt Wine grower would have a great advantage over the Prussian. Taking the reverse, other Articles produced in Prussia not subjected to an excise duty in that country may find a heavy duty operating against their sale in Darmstadt, so that altogether these duties clash with the interests of the trader in many of the States and create much inconvenience and confusion. There is already a very pronounced opinion that the excise System should be assimilated to that of Prussia. In Hesse Darmstadt there is a large party in favor of such a measure in the second chamber,

---

[169] Since 1815 Germany had been divided into two currency zones, one based on the *Taler* (north Germany and Prussia) and the other on the *Florin* or *Gulden* (south Germany and Austria). The Dresden Coinage Convention of 1838 (cf. pp. 315–316 in Saxony section) simplified payment transactions between the two zones for the states of the Customs Union by fixing exchange rates.

[170] The *Akzise* was an indirect consumption tax levied in the larger Prussian towns.

and it may be fully expected that in a short time this result must ensue.

Then will come the Military System, and different modifications in the Civil Administration. These Changes may be more distant, but when Prussia has attained a certain ascendancy they will be comparatively easy for her to accomplish.

It has been remarked that if Prussia had possessed a statesman of transcendent Abilities, capable of giving an impulse to the advantages of the position she has created for Herself she might now command in Germany, and take a very prominent part in European Questions, but it is perhaps precisely because she has not proceeded so quickly that she is the more likely to attain her end.

If Prussia had attempted too soon to manifest ambitious views of Political ascendancy, She might have roused the jealous fears of Bavaria & Wirtemberg and afforded Austria an opportunity of overturning her projects, but she is carefully avoiding any fault of the kind. She is playing a cautious and prudent game and quietly laying the sure foundations of future power.

The influence of Austria may be considered to be already undermined and it is perfectly immaterial to Prussia what endeavours she may make now to resume the ascendancy she was formerly wont to exercise in Germany. The Prussian System has already been carried too far to allow of a Collision with Austria upon the subject leading to any other result than the discomfiture of the latter and hastening the Crisis which must inevitably sooner or latter ensue.

It is also very questionable whether, besides laying the foundation of Political Power, Prussia by her Custom's Union has not sown the seeds of future territorial aggrandizement. She has, by putting herself forward in support of the Commercial and Manufacturing interests taught the whole population of Germany to look up to her as possessing both the power and the will to protect and forward the well being of the German Nation. Her conduct in this respect is contrasted with that of Austria who is reproached with having done nothing since 1814[171] to ameliorate the condition of Germany, and it is impossible to say what may be the consequences of the prevalence of such a feeling. It has occurred to me more than once to hear several persons, above the middle Classes in life, having possessions not under Prussian Rule, openly declare that they looked up to Prussia, As the future Benefactor of Germany, and that they would gladly find themselves placed under Her Government.

I therefore, My Lord, cannot but think that the Customs Union gives the real Power in Germany to Prussia. Every thing tends to prove that assertion, and if no unforeseen event, such as a war in Germany

---

[171] This statement refers to Austria's leading role in the reordering of Europe and Germany at the Congress of Vienna (18 September 1814 to 19 June 1815).

should occur, which in the confusion which it would bring with it would break up the Union, I am fully persuaded that all great questions affecting the peace, prosperity and mutual interests of Germany will in point of fact be henceforward decided at Berlin and not at Vienna.

I have the honor to inclose a table of the population of the German Confederation shewing the amount of that portion which is comprised in the Prussian Union.[172]

FO 30/63: Thomas Cartwright to Viscount Palmerston, No 77, Frankfurt, 23 October 1836

Sentences passed upon prisoners involved in the Storming of the Frankfurt Guard House; judicial procedures

Sentence has at length been pronounced upon the prisoners implicated in the events of the 3rd of April 1833.[173]

The Judgments were received upon the 18th Inst^t from Tubingen, the Law Faculty of which University had been called upon to act in this instance,[174] and the Frankfort Tribunal made them known upon the following day.

The paper which I have the honor to inclose contains a statement of the Sentence pronounced upon each individual. The ten who are most culpable have been condemned to imprisonment for life.[175]

Your Lordship will perceive from this result that the reproach which has so often been thrown out against this System of Judicature, viz that the Law Faculties were so imbued with democratick and revolutionary doctrines, no case of a political nature, however aggravated it might be, would ever be treated severely, has upon this occasion proved totally unmerited.

The affair, however, cannot yet be considered at an end, because the prisoners have still the right to appeal against this Judgment, and it is probable that they will avail themselves of it.

[172] Enclosures: 1. Copy, *Observations relatives au commerce des produits de Manufactures Ablaises en Allemagne*, January 1836; 2. Copy, *Return of the population of the States composing the Prussian Commercial Union and of the other States of Germany*.

[173] For the Storming of the Frankfurt Guard House cf. pp. 41–45. in this section.

[174] In Frankfurt, as in numerous other smaller states of the German Confederation, it was the usual practice to call upon the law faculty of a German university to act in judicial proceedings. As in this case, the court of the first instance as a rule accepted its judgement.

[175] The ten condemned to life imprisonment were the students Heinrich Joseph Freund, Ignatz Satori, Wilhelm Zehler, Herrmann Friedrich Handschuh, Eduard Fries, Ernst Matthiae, Hermann Friedrich Moré, Heinrich Eimer, August Ludwig von Rochau, and Wilhelm Obermüller.

The High Court of Appeals for the Free Towns collectively sits at Lübeck, and to that Court the case will be transferred; so that a space of nine months or a year may therefore still elapse before this prosecution is brought to a close.

One of the Prisoners condemned to confinement for life, named Rochow,[176] contrived to escape, I believe the very night of the day upon which the Sentences were proclaimed. No blame, however, can be imputed to the Authorities for this circumstance. Rochow had for some time feigned illness and kept his bed. A Physician was employed by the Government to visit him, and he reported that he believed Rochow to be so unwell that it was absolutely necessary that he should be removed to a more airy building. Upon this representation therefore he was transferred to another Prison which had that advantage, but which was infinitely less secure, and a turnkey was ordered to remain constantly in his room. Upon the night in question, however, both Prisoner and turnkey decamped.[177]

FO 30/65: Francis George Molyneux to Viscount Palmerston, No 1, Frankfurt, 11 January 1837

Escape of six prisoners who had taken part in the Storming of the Frankfurt Guard House; expected impact on military measures

I have the honor to inform Your Lordship that six of the prisoners confined in the jails of this Town for having taken part in the disturbances of the 3rd of April 1833 effected their escape yesterday evening.[178] One of the jailors[179] assisted and accompanied them in their flight. It appears that taking advantage of the carelessness of some of the chief officers of the Establishment and of some favorable circumstances, such as the principal door of the prison having been left open to admit a supply of wood, and the guards having retired within their sentry boxes owing to a violent storm, he effected his escape with his six companions without their absence being discovered for some hours.

[176] August Ludwig von Rochau.
[177] Enclosure: Sentences pronounced by the Court of Appeals in the Free City of Frankfurt on the 19th of October 1836, after previous concert with the Law Faculty, against the individuals who on the 3rd of April 1833 took part in the Storming of the Frankfurt Guard House .
[178] Those who escaped were the students Eduard Fries, Herrmann Friedrich Handschuh, Ernst Matthiae, Wilhelm Obermüller, Ignatz Satori, and Wilhelm Zehler. For the events of 3 April 1833 cf. pp. 41–45 in this section.
[179] Johann Geiger.

It is imagined that they are still in the Town, and the Gates are kept shut and the Guards are doubled.

This is an unfortunate circumstance, considering that the Government of Frankfort have so lately boasted that their prisons had been rendered more secure, that their troops were better disciplined and their Police rendered perfectly effective.

It is to be feared that this contradiction to their assurances may be used as a pretext for prolonging the stay of the Austrian Troops here.[180]

FO 30/68: Thomas Cartwright to Viscount Palmerston, No 43, Frankfurt, 28 May 1838

Osnabrück petition; considerations on the competency of the Federal Diet

The consideration of the Osnabrück Petition is likely soon to come before the Diet, and may possibly lead to the discussion of the whole Hanoverian Question.[181]

The Committee to which the Petition has been referred has chosen M. de Mieg for its reporter, which circumstance is of itself a sufficient guarantee, that in the Committee at least, the rights of each Party will be fairly treated, and that no undue influence will be there exerted to stifle a just examination of the question. But it is impossible to say what may not be done in the Diet upon the Report being brought up for discussion, if Austria and Prussia are determined to side with The King of Hanover.

I understand that the Report is ready, but M. de Strahlenheim in the last Sitting of the Diet put in a fresh Declaration disputing the competency of the Diet to entertain the question upon the demand solely of the City of Osnabrück[182] which may render some alterations and additions necessary, so that its presentation may still be delayed for a time.

I believe that in the history of the proceedings of the Diet there are three cases to which reference may be made in the way of precedent.

First in order of date is that of the States of Schleswig Holstein composed of the Clergy and Nobles who applied in 1823 for the interference of the Diet to obtain for them from The King of Denmark

---

[180] For the military occupation cf. pp. 45–48 in this section.
[181] For the constitutional conflict in Hanover cf. dispatches in the Hanover section for the years 1838 to 1840.
[182] For the Osnabrück petition cf. pp. 253–254 in Hanover section.

the revival of some ancient constitutional privileges to which they laid claim.[183]

The second is that of the Complaint preferred by the States of Brunswick in 1830 against Duke Charles for refusing to recognize the modifications which had been introduced into the Constitution of the Country, with the consent of those States, by King George the Fourth as Guardian during the Minority of the Duke,[184] and the third is that of the States of Waldeck who represented to the Diet in 1836 that the Government of the Principality had for some years been in the habit of encroaching upon their constitutional Privileges and requested that the Diet would interfere for the maintenance of their Rights.[185]

In the first and third cases the Diet decided against the complaining Parties. It rejected the demand of the States of Holstein, because it was proved that the ancient Rights to which they laid claim had not been in vigor for upwards of a Century, and consequently the 56th Article of the Final Act, which says that 'all existing Constitutions in acknowledged activity can only be changed by constitutional means', could not be said to apply to them; and It dismissed the claim of the States of Waldeck, because, after the facts had been examined into, it was found that the accusations brought by the Waldeck Government rested upon no good grounds.

The second case was however decided in favor of the States of Brunswick, and against the Duke. The Diet declared that whatever changes Duke Charles, the then reigning Sovereign, wished to introduce into the Constitution could only be brought about by the regular 'constitutional course'.

The Constitution in defence of which the States of Brunswick appealed to the Diet was, like the Hanoverian Constitution of 1837, a modification of the ancient Constitution which had previously been in vigor in the Country.

When the matter was before the Diet, the Party at that day most

---

[183] The conflict was the result of the wish expressed by the Chambers of the Duchies of Schleswig and Holstein for a joint *Landtag* to be convened and for their old constitution, which had never formally been revoked, to be reinstated or updated. Both demands were rejected by the Danish King, Frederik VI, who was also Duke of Schleswig and of Holstein. His intention to prepare a constitution for Holstein alone was interpreted by Schleswig and Holstein as violating the indivisibility of the two duchies, which had been guaranteed in the Ripen Treaty of 1460, and as pointing to the future integration of Schleswig into a Danish state.

[184] For the Brunswick constitutional conflict cf. p. 3 in this section.

[185] The conflict in the principality of Waldeck, which had been gathering pace since 1834, climaxed in the petition to the Federal Diet. Citing numerous examples, the Estates, in their petition to the German Confederation, accused the government of having disregarded their rights of participation. They argued that as the government did not react to the petition, Waldeck's 1816 constitution was de facto invalid.

vehement against Duke Charles was Hanover. She then stood forward as the Champion of those constitutional Rights and of the Constitution which had been called into existence under Her auspices. Her position is now just reversed. She is now, in Her own case, to defend Herself from the very charge which She may be said at a former period to have brought against Duke Charles of Brunswick: that of illegally suppressing a Constitution; and the consequence is, that the Declarations She put in in 1830 in support of the doctrine She then held, that Duke Charles could not possibly have a legal right to refuse to recognize the Constitution which was called into activity during His Minority by His Guardian King George the Fourth with the consent of the States, are now so many arms which She has placed in the hands of Her opponents to be directed against herself upon Her own question.

The Hanoverian Vote upon the Brunswick case of 1830 is a most curious document when applied to present circumstances, and I have the honor to inclose an Extract of it herewith for Your Lordship's information.[186] The Arguments in it against the Right of a Successor to a Crown to overturn the Constitution which he may find in vigor upon assuming the reins of Government are so pointed and searching, that it is exactly as if it had been drawn up to meet the case of the King of Hanover, and the most violent opponent of His Hanoverian Majesty could not possibly do better than adopt it in extenso upon the present occasion and combat Hanover in the Diet with Her own logick.

But besides placing Hanover in the disagreeable predicament of being forced to refute now the doctrine She then was the foremost to uphold, the Brunswick case of 1830 is a most awkward precedent for Her, because it establishes the fact that in the only question which has ever yet been brought before the Diet at all similar to that now under consideration, a decision was come to directly condemnatory of the course which has been pursued by His Hanoverian Majesty.

If the Hanoverian Question is now regularly gone into, it will be very difficult, with such a decision recorded in its Acts, for the Diet to come to a different conclusion in the present instance without exposing itself to the reproach of having been swayed by unjust and unworthy motive.

The Diet can hardly declare that to be legal in 1838 which stands recorded as having been declared by it to be unconstitutional and inadmissible in 1830, and I therefore think that if there is an inclination on the part of the two Great Powers[187] of Germany to support The

---

[186] Enclosure: extract from the Hanoverian Vote on the subject of the complaint of the States of the Duchy of Brunswick respecting the constitutional Charter of 1820.

[187] Austria and Prussia.

King of Hanover (and I believe such an inclination to exist), those Powers will endeavor to avoid these difficulties by preventing the question from being entertained at all, and that with this view whenever the Report of the Committee upon the Osnabrück Petition shall be brought up, and whatever may be the opinion set forth in it, they will urge that it is contrary to the forms and powers of the Diet to take a question of such magnitude into consideration upon the mere demand of one complaining City, and will on these grounds move its rejection. They will probably attempt in this way to stifle the question in the outset, but if they take this course, I do not believe that they will succeed, without encountering much opposition from some of the Ministers of the Constitutional States who feel that by doing that which may bear the interpretation of a direct step in favor of the cause of the King of Hanover, the character of the Diet, as the natural Guardian of the Constitutional Rights in the German States, will materially suffer, that such a mode of blinking the question will be in itself an unjust proceeding, that it will bring the Diet into disrepute and that it will place the constitutional Governments in an odious and false light and in a very disadvantageous and embarrassing position before the Representative Chambers in their respective Countries.

FO 30/69: Henry George Kuper to Viscount Palmerston, Confidential, No 7, Frankfurt, 11 December 1838

Arrest of the Archbishop of Cologne by Prussian authorities because of his attitude towards the issue of mixed marriages; impact on the Catholic population of the German Confederation

According to the intelligence received here from all quarters it is evident, that the excitement which was caused amongst the Roman Catholicks in the Prussian Rhenish Provinces by the arrest of the Archbishop of Cologne,[188] far from having subsided, is at this moment greater than ever, and that the baneful effects of that proceeding have been felt in a greater or less degree in most of the States of the Germanick Confederation.

It is notorious that the Inhabitants of the Rhenish Provinces have at all times been distinguished for their bigotry and attachment to the priesthood, and it cannot therefore afford matter of surprise, that the arrest and imprisonment of so high a Dignitary as an Archbishop of

---

[188] The Archbishop of Cologne, Clemens August Freiherr von Droste zu Vischering, was removed from office on 15 November 1837. Ordered to leave the diocese, he was first placed under house arrest in Minden on 22 November and then, on 31 December 1837, taken to the fortress in Magdeburg.

Cologne by protestant Authorities, who moreover was a man very popular and renowned for his benevolence, should have produced a most deplorable feeling of resentment and bitterness, and that the excited Roman Catholick population should regard their aged friend and benefactor, the Archbishop, now closely confined within a Fortress, in the light of a Martyr.

The chief point on which the Archbishop refused to conform to the Prussian Legislation was that relative to mixed marriages, between Protestants and Catholicks.

The Prussian Law of the 17th of August 1825 decreed, that all the children issuing from a mixed marriage in the Rhenish Provinces and in Westphalia should be brought up in the religion of their father, and that the Roman Catholick Priests should on no account be at liberty to exact from the bridegroom a written Certificate pledging himself to educate all his children in the Roman Catholick Faith.

The policy of this Law will be easily accounted for, if it be considered how anxiously the Prussian Government has invariably sought to amalgamate the Rhenish Provinces with Prussia Proper, and that in order the more effectively to attain that object, it has done all in its power to promote matrimonial alliances between the respective natives of both portions of the Kingdom. With this view it has been the practise of Prussia to appoint to the different branches of the administration in the Rhenish Provinces none but natives of Prussia Proper,[189] hoping that circumstances would enable the young Civilians and Officers to intermarry with the daughters of the wealthy Inhabitants of those Provinces, whereby the union between both portions of the Kingdom would of course be very materially cemented.

The state of uncertainty and confusion which now prevails in the Rhenish Provinces on this head, owing to the difference of opinion which still exists on the subject between the Pope and the Prussian Government,[190] together with the general dissatisfaction felt in consequence of the alleged violation of the Rights of the Roman Catholick Church, is attended with the most deplorable results, giving rise to increasing collisions and almost daily acts of violence and insubordination in the Provinces, and principally in the great Towns.

In the mean time the flame of discord and schism is kept up in most parts of Germany by the unwearied exertions of the Press. The most

---

[189] 'Prussia Proper' denoted those contiguous provinces which, unlike the Rhine Province and the Province of Westphalia, formed Prussia's integral territory.

[190] The question of mixed marriages was the subject of protracted negotiations between Prussia and the Vatican lasting from 1828 to the compromise achieved by the Berlin Convention of 1834. In 1836, one year after Clemens August Freiherr von Droste zu Vischering became Archbishop of Cologne, the conflict flared up again because Droste disregarded the convention.

violent and intolerant pamphlets appear in rapid succession, and receive an extensive circulation, whilst many of the most talented writers on theological matters are engaged in vehement, and in many cases unbridled, controversy.

All parties agree in deploring the step taken by Prussia and in blaming her strongly for the impolicy of drawing upon herself the displeasure not only of her own Roman Catholick Subjects, but of many German States in which the Court and the Majority of the Inhabitants profess that Faith. It is confidently asserted that Austria has felt deeply wounded in consequence of the violence offered to one of the high Dignitaries of the Roman Church; and the King of Bavaria, between whom and the Prussian Cabinet much angry discussion has lately taken place in consequence of the proceedings of Prussia, appears to have been greatly influenced by the prominent part so openly taken by the latter as the avowed Champion of Protestantism in Germany, in the efforts which His Majesty is evidently making to restore the priesthood in His dominions to the state of ascendancy which they enjoyed in the middle ages. This is apparent from the restoration of so many Convents and Monasteries, the marked partiality with which the Government favors all monastick Institutions, and chiefly from the late systematick restoration of Colleges for the Jesuits.[191]

It has also been observed to me, that Bavaria may possibly go so far in her resentment as to secede from the Prussian commercial Union at the expiration of the term for which the Treaties were concluded in the first instance. That term will expire on the 1st of January 1842.

On the other hand it is satisfactory to observe that the Government of the Protestant States of the Confederation (and more especially those of Wirtemberg and Baden) are using every effort to promote a feeling of forbearance and good will amongst their protestant Subjects.

I am assured by those who have lately visited the Rhenish Provinces, that the state of publick feeling is violent in the extreme, and that such is the discontent and irritation manifested openly by the Inhabitants, that, unless the Government speedily devises some plan for soothing the minds of the people, who, as it is, have never evinced any very sincere partiality for the Prussian Government, being not only essentially imbued with an attachment to constitutional forms, but also professing a different Religion and being governed according to a different Code of Laws,[192] they will by degrees entirely alienate themselves from their

[191] During Ludwig I's reign, about eighty new monastic institutions had been set up by 1837. However, contrary to what is suggested in the dispatch, none of them were Jesuit colleges. Unlike his interior minister Abel, Ludwig opposed any such plan.

[192] The Rhine Province and the Province of Westphalia were still under the *Code Civil* (French Civil Code). This had been introduced in most of the German states of the Confederation of the Rhine between 1806 and 1808 as an expression of French hegemony.

present Rulers, and thus at once defeat the great object for the attainment of which the Prussian Government has for the last three and twenty years made such vast efforts, – viz – that of winning over the affections of the population by means of a conciliatory line of policy.

On one point all observers appear to agree: that, in the event of a War, a French Army entering the Rhenish Provinces would, under existing circumstances, be greeted with enthusiasm.

FO 30/69: Henry George Kuper to Viscount Palmerston, Confidential, No 14, Frankfurt, 29 December 1838

Public attention paid to the 'Hanoverian Question'; approaches by different groups

The question relative to the Hanoverian Constitution still continues to engross publick attention in Germany in a high degree, and all thinking men agree in deploring the irritation which has been caused amongst the great mass of the Subjects of the Germanick Confederation by the unbending pertinacity with which the Hanoverian Government perseveres in that course which it originally traced out for itself on the accession of His Hanoverian Majesty.[193]

The Ultra Liberals, who are still very numerous in Germany, are of course more impetuous than the moderate Party in their loud condemnation of the state of things in Hanover, and although they are less clamorous and openly active than during the years 1831, 1832, and 1833,[194] they continue to harbor violent feelings of dissatisfaction and resentment at what they designate as the present deplorable state of Government and publick Right throughout Germany. It is also well known that they are secretly engaged in active machinations with a view to make a forcible demonstration at the first favorable moment which may present itself.

On the other hand, in all the constitutional States of Germany, even the moderate friends and advocates of a representative form of Government regard the differences now pending between the Hanoverian Government and the States with much anxiety, and even conceive that they are of a nature to endanger the maintenance of their own constitutional Rights. They do not hesitate to proclaim aloud

---

[193] For the Hanoverian constitutional conflict cf. the dispatches in Hanover section for the years 1838 to 1840.

[194] Following the French revolution of July 1830 there had been open conflicts between the liberal opposition and the governments in many German states. After a number of successes in individual states, such as the introduction of a constitution in Hanover in 1833, the conservative governments became increasingly hostile to the liberal movement.

their conviction that if the Sovereign of a German federal State is allowed to overthrow or to modify an existing Constitution at his own exclusive will and pleasure, without the Diet's interfering promptly and energetically to prevent such an arbitrary course, that state of things will tend to open the way to the gradual annihilation of constitutional institutions throughout Germany, for that if the provisions of the 13th Article of the Federal Act[195] are thus left disregarded, that Article is a dead letter and not calculated to afford them any guarantee for the stability of their Constitutions, notwithstanding that such was the especial object of its stipulations.

The Hanoverian Question has also attracted the attention of the Representative Assemblies in several States of the Confederation. Thus in the Grand Duchy of Hesse a motion was lately made and carried in the Chamber, recommending that the Government should be petitioned to use its best efforts with the Diet in order to induce that Assembly to bring about the restoration of the Hanoverian Constitution of 1833; and it is not doubted that a similar step will be taken by the Chambers in many of the other German constitutional States. [...]

I have just been informed confidentially, that since the last Sitting of the Diet on the 29th Ult°, in which the Hanoverian Minister presented to his Colleagues individually a Copy of the Declaration on the part of his Government in reply to the Resolution of the Diet of the 6th of September last,[196] hoping by that course to remove the discussion upon the Hanoverian question altogether from the Diet, those Governments which voted in favor of the Osnabruck Petitioners have been engaged in deep consultation as to what line it would be best to pursue in order to counteract that intention and to render it impossible for the Diet, notwithstanding its last Resolution on the subject, to shrink from a further and more minute investigation of the matter.

Those Governments are principally Bavaria, Saxony, Wirtemberg, Baden, and Hesse Darmstadt, and I am assured that in the very next Sitting of the Diet they will come forward with a forcible Declaration, expressive of the insufficient and unsatisfactory nature of the explanations offered by the Hanoverian Government in its late confidential communication to the German Sovereigns,[197] and urging the Diet to

[195] Cf. n. 83 in this section.

[196] On 6 September the Federal Diet rejected the constitutional complaint lodged by the city of Osnabrück in March 1838. In its petition, Osnabrück had argued that the abrogation of the constitution of 1833 by Ernst August in 1837 was illegal. On the petition of the city of Osnabrück cf. pp. 253–254 in Hanover section, and pp. 85–88 in this section.

[197] On the instructions of the Federal Diet, the Hanoverian embassy to the German Confederation sent a letter, dated 29 October 1838, to all the other embassies to the German Confederation reaffirming Ernst August's actions without bringing forward any new arguments.

call upon that Government to come to a satisfactory arrangement with the Assembly of the States convened according to the Constitution of 1833, and to declare that, in the event of its not bringing about that desired result, the question will be submitted for decision to the federal Court of Arbitration.[198]

FO 30/72: Francis George Molyneux to Viscount Palmerston, Confidential, No 32, Frankfurt, 29 April 1839

Bavaria's attitude towards the 'Hanoverian Question'

At the Sitting of The Diet Friday last, the Bavarian Minister[199] laid before that Body the opinion and declaration of His Majesty The King of Bavaria with regard to the existing differences between The Sovereign of Hanover and the Legislative Chamber of that Kingdom.[200]

His Bavarian Majesty distinctly declares the course that has been followed by The King of Hanover to be highly unconstitutional; that it is in direct opposition to the Federal Act[201] of the German Confederation; that the line which His Hanoverian Majesty has hitherto adopted is calculated to destroy the confidence of the People of Germany in their respective Governments; and that such a state of things, if permitted to continue, must in the end be productive of the most prejudicial consequences to the whole of Germany.

The Declaration of His Bavarian Majesty concludes by a proposition to the effect, that it is necessary to call upon His Majesty The King of Hanover to return within the limits of the Constitution, and to adhere for the future to the Stipulations of the Federal Act, upon the faithful execution of which the safety and tranquillity of Germany depends.

To this declaration the Plenipotentiaries of Wirtemberg, Baden, and the Grand Duchy of Hesse have already adhered,[202] and a similar declaration is momentarily expected on the part of Saxony.

The proposition of Bavaria is to be referred to a Committee of five Members of the Diet, but that Commission has not yet been named.

---

[198] On the Court of Arbitration cf. pp. 73–74 in this section, and pp. 136–137 in Prussia section.

[199] Arnold von Mieg.

[200] On the Hanoverian constitutional conflict, which Bavaria and Baden called on the Federal Diet to deal with in the sitting of 26 April, cf. the dispatches in Hanover section for the years 1838 to 1840.

[201] Act of the German Confederation of 8 June 1815.

[202] Württemberg's envoy was August Heinrich Freiherr von Trott zu Solz; Baden's envoy was Alexander von Dusch; Hesse-Darmstadt's envoy was Peter Joseph Freiherr von Gruben.

In the meantime I am given to understand that a communication is to be made to The King of Hanover of the nature of the late proceedings of the Diet, and a term of from three to four weeks has been allowed for His Majesty to return to reply.

I am told that the communication made by the Bavarian Pleni-potentiaries was directly in the name of his Sovereign, a course not usually followed, and therefore marking still stronger the importance that His Bavarian Majesty attaches to the interference of the Diet in this question.

The feeling entertained by His Bavarian Majesty is, that unless a speedy stop is put to the unconstitutional proceedings of The King of Hanover, all confidence in the good faith of the German Governments will be destroyed, and that should the Diet submit to the infraction of its fundamental Laws, without repelling the attack, the people of Germany will perceive that all control over the conduct of those Sovereigns who may endeavor to subvert the constitutions established in their States, is at an end.

FO 30/74: Ralph Abercromby to Viscount Palmerston, Confidential, No 86, Frankfurt, 28 August 1839

Arbitrary dealings with petitions to the Federal Diet

Enclosed herewith I have the honor to forward to Your Lordship the translations of two extracts from the Geschäftsordnungen[203] of the Diet relative to the course to be followed and the forms to be complied with on the presentation of Petitions to that Assembly.

The first of these Extracts is from a Geschäftsordnung of the 14th November 1816, the second from a similar resolution dated the 29th April 1819.[204] From both these Extracts it will be seen that all petitions addressed to the Diet, whether admissible or inadmissible from the nature of their Contents, must be received and laid before The Committee of Petitions for the time being and duly noticed and registered among the proceedings of The Diet.

I have deemed it my Duty to refer to these Resolutions of the Diet in consequence of the extraordinary course that has been of late pursued by the President with regard to several Petitions forwarded

---

[203] Rules of procedure.

[204] Enclosure: Translation. Regulations respecting the presentation of petitions to the Diet (*Geschäftsordnung vom 14. November 1816*; *Geschäftsordnung vom 29. April 1819*).

from the Kingdom of Hanover to the Diet relative to the differences existing in that Kingdom.[205]

The President, Count Munch, upon receiving them and becoming acquainted with their contents, of his own authority returned them to the parties from whom they had been sent, without even mentioning to the Assembly over which he presides, and to which these Petitions were addressed, that such had been the line he had followed.

A measure so arbitrary in itself, so directly in opposition to the resolutions and forms of the Diet; and which if allowed to become the practice, so evidently tended to withhold from that Body, the knowledge of facts which it might be essential for it to be made acquainted with, as involving principles and interests connected with the welfare of Germany, could not be silently passed over, and the Saxon Plenipotentiary[206] therefore deemed it to be his Duty at the last sitting of the Diet, to bring this Question under discussion.

The President attempted to defend the measure he had adopted, by asserting that the Petitions in question contained matter improper for communication to the Diet, but so unable was he to adduce any plausible reason for this proceeding, that he sought relief from the awkwardness of his position by abruptly leaving the Sitting of the Diet. He has I am informed mentioned privately to several of the Plenipotentiaries his regret at having adopted a course which he now finds to have been in opposition to the opinions of his Colleagues, and he has given private assurances likewise, that for the future all Petitions shall be received and disposed of according to the forms prescribed by the Geschäftsordnung.

The President will, however, before this subject is dropped, be called upon to make a similar official declaration to the Diet when in Assembly.

The suppression by The President of these Petitions is another proof of the partiality that has been shewn towards The King of Hanover in his disputes with his subjects, and how anxiously every opportunity is seized on to prevent the Diet from interfering in this Question.

Had this proceeding been quietly passed over Austria, or the President[207] for the time being, would have acquired the power of allowing only such information and facts to reach The Diet, as tended to assist the political views of the presiding Plenipotentiary, and the Diet must from henceforth have become a blind agent without influence, and deprived of the confidence of the people.

The rejection of these petitions, which I am informed were drawn

---

[205] For the petitions to the Federal Diet cf. pp. 253–254 in Hanover section, and pp. 85–88 in this section.

[206] Georg August Ernst Freiherr von Manteufel.

[207] Joachim Graf von Münch-Bellinghausen.

up in respectful though decided terms, cannot but produce a most hurtful impression towards the Diet throughout all Germany.

The Petitioners must see, in this denial of being heard in defence of their opinions, a predetermination to place them in the wrong, and to protect as far as possible the King of Hanover in the unconstitutional course he has been following.

The publick of Germany must perceive from this measure how completely The Austrian influence prevails in the proceedings of The Diet, and how prejudicially that influence is exercised for the interests and preservations of Constitutional Rights within the Confederation. The result of such observation is manifest and fear that a blow has been struck by the course that has been followed throughout the discussion upon these Hanoverian Questions from which it will be extremely difficult for the Diet to recover.

FO 30/76: Francis George Molyneux to Viscount Palmerston, No 23, Frankfurt, 11 April 1840

Consideration of the policies of strengthening the frontier of Germany along the Upper Rhine because of alleged French aspirations to regain the boundary of the Rhine

I am informed that one of the subjects which will be shortly discussed in the Diet, will be the policy of immediately strengthening the Frontier of Germany along the Upper Rhine.

This topic has often been brought under consideration, but hitherto the sum of twenty millions[208] voted for this purpose has remained untouched, the interest alone having been expended in repairs and additions to the fortresses at Coblentz and Mayence and the construction of a 'tête de point' and other works at Germersheim.

The Governments of Wirtemberg and Baden have always been desirous that the town of Rastadt should be fortified, which the influence of Bavaria has always been employed to uphold the policy of making Ulm the third fortress of the Confederation.[209]

A proposal will now be made and probably carried into effect to take immediate steps to fortify both theses places, making Ulm a fortress of first rate importance, and erecting works of considerable strength at Rastadt, some measures will also be taken at the same time to strengthen the Frontier towards Switzerland, which will then it is conceived render

---

[208] The sum of 20 million Francs was part of the reparations for which France was liable under the terms of the Second Peace of Paris, 15 November 1815.

[209] For the discussion concerning the building of a fortress for the Confederation cf. pp. 377–379 in the Württemberg section.

the whole of that line secure from any aggression on the part of France, or at least make the Frontier of the Upper Rhine as well guarded as that of the Lower.

These plans will be put into execution as soon as possible as the idea gains ground daily, that at some period, more or less distant, an effort will be made by the French to regain the boundaries of the Rhine and that it behoves the Confederation to be armed at all points to repel such an attempt.

The French press has lately so openly encouraged this idea and it is becoming daily so popular in France, and in times of agitation it would afford such sure means of drawing off public attention that perhaps theses measures of safety are not uncalled for.[210]

Several influential Members of the Diet have asked me if England would interfere to prevent such attempts of aggrandizement on the part of France to which I replied that they might feel assured that England would always make every effort in her power to preserve the peace of Europe and that such attempts could not be made without a serious conflict which it would always be the interest of England to prevent.

This question in all probability will not be agitated before Count Munch-Bellinghausen is able to resume the Presidency of the Diet and as yet His Excellency has fixed no period for his return.

FO 30/76: William Thomas Horner Fox-Strangways to Viscount Palmerston, No 21, Frankfurt, 20 December 1840

Unanimity among the members of the diet regarding a possible address to the French government

I am informed by Members of the Diet, that the Governments of Austria and Prussia have addressed Notes to the French Government desiring an explanation of the encrease of armaments lately set on foot by France.[211]

Your Lordship is probably aware of this circumstance: but I think it right to report that my informant states, that, should the answer of the French Government to the Notes above mentioned, not prove satisfactory, the Diet will then, in its own name address a note to that Government upon the same subject. I find it to be matter of

---

[210] In 1840, after the diplomatic defeat of France's Middle Eastern policy, the French people and French foreign policy focused more on reconquering the Rhine frontier, which had been lost in the territorial reorganisation of 1814–1815. The Rhine frontier became a matter of national prestige for France also because weakness in foreign policy was directly linked to France's domestic stagnation.

[211] For the Rhine crisis cf. n. 210 in this section, and pp. 192–193 in Prussia section.

congratulation among the Members of the Diet, that this resolution has so speedily been adopted, it being one which they say would formerly have required a negociation of many months, but which owing to this prompt and early understanding may now be acted upon without delay.

This is a good proof of the unanimity that prevails at present among the German States, but it is also a proof that such unanimity was, but a short time ago, hardly to be expected from them.

FO 30/78: William Thomas Horner Fox-Strangways to Viscount Palmerston, No 34, Frankfurt, 30 August 1841

Passport questions concerning alleged English subjects working in Germany

I am exposed to daily annoyance from persons who profess to be English Subjects, but who state themselves to have lost their Passports, and who can bring no reference as to their being entitled to a new one. They frequently offer to make oath that they are British Subjects; but I cannot take upon myself to admit that mode of proof without express permission from Your Lordship, upon which point I beg to be instructed.

Some of these persons are employed upon railroads and other mechanical establishments in various parts of Germany, and have families settled where their work is. The Agents of the Governments in whose Dominions they can prove themselves to be domiciliated by their occupation, and upon whom therefore I conceive they have a prima facie claim, universally reject them and throw them upon the British Legation, if they have the appearance of being Englishmen.

I was informed the other day by the Secretary of one of the Legations here, that there are several adventurers going about, who have three or four passports of different sorts. Now as old passports ought to be given up when new ones are granted, it is only by pretending to have none, that such accumulations of passports can be obtained; and it is to check the practice, that I refuse (in the absence of an official Regulation) to grant new passports without a satisfactory reference.

FO 30/80: Henry George Kuper to Earl of Aberdeen, No 30, Frankfurt, 1 October 1842

End of Frankfurt's military occupation

I have the honor to inform Your Lordship, that the remainder of the Austrian Troops stationed at Frankfort and Sachsenhausen since the month of April 1833,[212] marched out of the town this morning, and were conveyed to Mayence by the Railroad.

The Frankfort troops of the line were drawn up in front of the Station House to receive the Austrians; the men presenting arms, and the band playing the Austrian national Hymn.

It has been justly observed, that nothing could have excelled the good conduct and discipline of those federal troops during their long sojourn at Frankfort.

FO 30/82: Henry George Kuper to Earl of Aberdeen, No 3, Frankfurt, 27 January 1843

New debates on censorship in the Federal Diet because of growing liberty of the press; financial considerations of Hesse-Cassel and Saxony concerning censorship

The licentious state of the public Press in several States of the Germanic Confederation has for some time past been such as to claim the particular attention of the Members of the Diet; and I am informed that one of the first acts of the present Session of that Assembly will consist in a thorough revision of the federal Law which was adopted by the Diet in 1832 on the subject of Censorship.[213]

The public feeling in Germany has undoubtedly undergone a remarkable change during the last two or three years. In Prussia the public voice is clamorous in its demand for a representative Constitution and for various changes in the organization and administration of the State. The first decided impulse given by the Press to a systematic censure of the existing order of things in Prussia, and to an abusive style of argument in discussing the general politics of Germany, was given by the Königsberg Journal.[214]

This paper found numerous admirers, and its outrageous sentiments were soon echoed in other German Newspapers, particularly in the

---

[212] For the occupation of the Free City of Frankfurt by confederal troops cf. pp. 45–48 in this section.

[213] Article 1 of the Ten Articles of 1832 (cf. n. 96 in this section) made the federal Press Law of 1819 more stringent by subjecting the German-language press abroad to the need for a licence. After consultation on measures to be taken against German-language publications in France and Switzerland, the Federal Diet re-endorsed the 1832 regulations on 18 January 1844.

[214] *Königsberger Zeitung* (*Königlich Preussische Staats-, Kriegs- und Friedenszeitung*). As Königsberg was not on the territory of the German Confederation, the strict censorship laws did not apply there. The content and orientation of the Königsberg newspapers was connected with the political life emerging in the town in the 1840s.

Leipsic Universal Gazette,[215] which has lately been prohibited in Prussia, chiefly on account of its having inserted in its columns the poet Herwegh's letter[216] to the King of Prussia, in which he had presumed to complain of His Majesty's Ministers.

Another Journal, the 'Rheinishe Zeitung',[217] published at Cologne, exceeded those above-mentioned in violence, its columns being exclusively devoted to every species of unbridled invective against the Government and the general state of things in Prussia and other German States; and intelligence of its suppression by the Prussian Government has this day been received at Frankfort.

The Ministers in the Diet complain unreservedly of the licentiousness of the Press more especially in Prussia, in which State a number of books have lately been, and are still published, of a blasphemous and revolutionary tendency.[218] Anonymous pamphlets on the same subjects, and others replete with violent attacks upon the German Sovereigns, their Governments, and the individuals in their Service, all advocating revolutionary doctrines, are now inundating Germany, having for the most part been printed in Switzerland, or, surreptitiously, in the very German States themselves.

That the opinions of the great mass of the populations of the German States should have become more or less contaminated by the perusal of such publications, is not to be wondered at; and the effects of their baneful influence even upon the minds of the intelligent portion of the German community is in some degree perceptible in the conversation of many, and even in the debates which are now carried on in the representative Chambers at Dresden, Cassel, and elsewhere.

The Government of Hesse Cassel having laid before the Chamber on the 17th Inst[t] an estimate of the various items of the Budget for the current year, a violent debate arose upon the subject of the usual allowance of a salary to the Servant of the Government charged with the disagreeable office of Censor of Press, the result of which was, that the allowance was refused by a large Majority of the Chamber.

---

[215] The *Leipziger Allgemeine Zeitung* had been published since 1837. Its liberal orientation ensured that it was disseminated throughout Germany, but it was suppressed in Bavaria in 1842 and in Prussia in 1843.

[216] For Herwegh's letter to the Prussian king cf. pp. 204–205 in Prussia section.

[217] The first issue of the *Rheinische Zeitung für Handel, Politik und Gewerbe* came out on 1 January 1842. From September 1842, Karl Marx was its editor-in-chief. The staff included important members of the German opposition movement such as Friedrich List and Georg Herwegh. On 31 March 1843 the *Rheinische Zeitung* was suppressed because of its radical politics.

[218] Cf. pp. 76–77 in this section.

At Dresden, the Saxon Government having submitted to the Chamber an amended Code of Criminal Laws to be introduced into the Kingdom, and having stated that the previous system of 'official inquisition' and exclusion of publicity would be adhered to as the basis of the new Code, the Chamber, on the 23rd Inst^t, decided by a very large majority against that system, and in favor of public Law pleadings; and I am informed that the Government of The King of Saxony will adopt the innovation which has been recommended by so large a Majority.[219]

In both those debates, especially at Cassel, it was felt, that the reckless and extravagant views and doctrines advocated by many of the speakers were such as had never until then been heard in those respective Chambers.

FO 30/85: William Thomas Horner Fox-Strangways to Earl of Aberdeen, No 26, Frankfurt, 16 May 1844

Reactions to the assumption of new titles by several German sovereigns

The assumption of new Titles or Predicates by several of the Sovereigns of Germany has been variously judged by the Members of the Diet.[220]

In general the representatives of the greater Courts disapprove of the steps which have been taken, and consider it an infraction of the state of things established by various Congresses. They also consider that the haste with which some of the Sovereigns in question have notified their adoption of a new Title to Foreign Courts, before having done so to the Diet or to the rest of the Confederation, was improper in an affair so peculiarly and exclusively German.

The Sovereigns who have, or are now supposed to have taken steps for the acknowledgment of a higher Title or Predicate are, the Ducal Families of Saxony, the Ducal Families of Anhalt, the Landgrave of Hesse Homburg, the Duke of Brunswick, the Duke of Nassau and the Princely Families of Schwarzburg and Reuss.

But I have been informed that some of the Courts have sent Protests against these measures to their Ministers here, to be eventually presented to the Diet; and that among the number are the Courts of Hesse-Cassel and Hesse-Darmstadt.

---

[219] Cf. pp. 324–325 in Saxony section.

[220] The princes named in the dispatch had expressed a desire for their formal titles to be *Hoheit* (Highness), rather than *Durchlaucht* (Serene Highness)..

FO 30/91: Francis George Molyneux to Earl of Aberdeen, No 30, Frankfurt, 9 June 1845

Emergence and development of a new religious sect called 'German Catholics' (Deutschkatholiken); articles of faith

The subject of the new Religious Sect styled 'German Catholics' is daily assuming greater importance in the eyes of all classes of society.

Many well informed persons indeed consider it as the fore-runner of great religious changes, and as the commencement of an Epoch hardly inferior in magnitude to the Reformation itself.

Without attaching so much consequence to the present movement, I may perhaps be permitted to state to Your Lordship, the actual state of the question, even at the risk of mentioning what is already well known.

For a length of time in various parts of Germany, there have existed a number of persons, who, altho' professing the Roman Catholic faith, have nevertheless, from different causes, seen reason to be discontented with the doctrines on the dominion of the Church of Rome; amongst the most prominent of these, appeared a Roman Catholic priest of the name of Ronge. Born in 1813, he was educated for the priesthood, and for some time fulfilled the duties of that office. Disgusted however with many of the doctrines which he had originally received with doubt, and which he was now compelled to teach against the dictates of his maturer judgment, he seized the first opportunity of giving vent to the feelings he had long harboured, and taking up the subject of the Papal nomination to the See of Breslau in 1842, he published an Article, in the newspapers called the 'Sachsischen Vaterlands Blättern',[221] headed 'Rome and the Cathedral of Breslau' which produced at the time considerable sensation. Ronge was suspended shortly afterwards, and published several other articles in the same paper aimed at the supremacy of the Church of Rome.[222]

Last year as Your Lordship is aware, a circumstance occurred which gave additional cause for these attacks.

The Bishop of Treves, Dr Arnoldi, by a Pastoral Letter of July 1844, announced that the miraculous garment of Our Saviour would be

---

[221] The liberal and patriotic newspaper *Sächsische Vaterlandsblätter* was published in Leipzig under the direction of Robert Blum. In 1845–1846 it was banned by the Saxon government.

[222] In his article 'Rome and the Cathedral of Breslau', Ronge criticized the resignation of the Prince Bishop of Breslau in 1840, which had been forced by the Curia. The background to the resignation was the conflict about the issue of mixed marriages (cf. p. 89 in this section). As a result of his article, Ronge was suspended from the priesthood on 31 January 1843. His open letter to Arnoldi, Bishop of Trier, published in October 1844, led to his excommunication.

exhibited for the space of seven weeks in the Cathedral of that City.[223] This exhibition and the scenes which ensued during the time that the Town of Treves was thronged by a crowd of credulous pilgrims from all parts of Germany, drew forth that indignant letter from Ronge which created such a sensation throughout Europe. From this time many persons enlisted themselves under his banner. Amongst the foremost of his followers, were the members of the congregation of a place called Schneidemühl, who with their pastor Czerski, seceded from the Church of Rome, and formed themselves into a separate and independant congregation under the name of 'German Catholics' or 'Catholic Christians'. They proceeded to publish 9 Articles of Faith.[224] By which 1st, they renounced the doctrine that the Priest alone could partake of both elements in the holy sacrament;

2[dly] They rejected the canonization of Saints;

3[rdly] The invocation of Saints;

4[thly] The power of Priests to remit sins, and of the Church to grant indulgence;

5[thly] They denied the necessity of fasting;

6[thly] They declared that the Mass or Service should no longer be said in Latin;

7[thly] Priests were permitted to marry;

8[thly] They declared it to be no sin for Protestants and Catholics to intermarry; and finally 9[thly] They rejected the Doctrine that Christ must be visibly represented on earth.

Ronge, shortly afterwards, transferred his labours to Breslau where he made many converts, and at Berlin, Leipsic, Offenbach, and a great number of other places large congregations were quickly formed.

In order to produce a still more uniform and complete system of religion, these various congregations sent delegates to a general Meeting to be held at Leipsic,[225] in order to draw up and adopt a further series of Articles of Religion, founded on those at Schneidemühl, but capable of so wide an interpretation, that all denominations of Christians should be able to embrace them. This task the meeting appears to have accomplished with considerable success, avoiding all critical points of doctrine, and leaving the field as open as possible. The effect of this has been to increase still further the number of proselytes.

The week before last a meeting for the performance of public worship

---

[223] About 1 million believers took part in the pilgrimage to see the relic of the 'seamless Holy Garment'. This pilgrimage was perceived as a symbol of a renewal of German Catholicism.

[224] *Offenes Glaubensbekenntnis in ihren Unterscheidungslehren der roemisch-katholischen Kirche das heisst der Hierarchie*, 1844.

[225] Leipzig Council, 23–26 March 1845, cf. pp. 328–331 in Saxony section.

according to the new form, was announced at the neighbouring town of Offenbach, and one of the Churches had been lent for the purpose, a few hours however before the time appointed, the Government interfered and forbid the use of the Church. An empty warehouse was hastily fitted up in a suitable manner, and Divine Service was performed in the presence of upwards of 2000 people.

Last week a meeting of the principal leaders of this new Sect was held in this City, and permission has been demanded and obtained to celebrate their worship in the reformed Church here, which is the private property of the Calvinistic Congregation.

As yet this Sect has not been publicly acknowledged by any of the Governments of Germany. Prussia is supposed secretly to favour their establishment, and she is certainly the party most interested in so doing, as anything which would tend to diminish or overthrow the Papal influence in her Catholic provinces, cannot fail to be welcome to her.

On the other hand, Bavaria and Austria oppose this Anti-Catholic movement by all the means at their disposal; the opposition so suddenly encountered at Offenbach, was supposed to come from the Austrian Embassy here. A report also has been industriously circulated, that under the mask of religion, the professors of these new doctrines are occupied with political intrigues of a revolutionary character. This charge I understand is wholly without foundation, and has only been put about in order to throw discredit upon this widely spreading secession from Rome.

At the present moment however, I do not foresee any immediate Changes of a vast or a permanent nature, the leaders of the new Sect are perhaps wanting in those requisites which ought to characterize the leaders of a second Reformation, but amongst the numbers of enlightened persons who are joining the seceders, if one should be found of sufficient talent and energy to take a more decided part, the present state of things may eventually lead to most important and remarkable events.

FO 30/95: William Thomas Horner Fox-Strangways to Earl of Aberdeen, No 13, Frankfurt, 17 February 1846

Absence of business before the Diet

The Hessian Minister[226] informs me that on Thursday last, the 12th instant, the Diet did not hold its usual sitting, literally from the total absence of business.

[226] Peter Joseph Freiherr von Gruben (Grand Duchy of Hesse).

The gradual decline of business before the Diet, and the growing insignificance of that Body, are becoming subjects of general remark. Many reasons may be assigned for this decline: the inattention of Austria to any but the greatest questions in Germany; the increasing activity of Prussia; the very frequent declarations of its own incompetency which the Diet does not shrink from giving when questions of even small difficulty are referred to it; the growing tendency to confer on, and to treat all the great matters in which Germany is interested, at other places than Frankfort; and above all the unwillingness to enforce the Decrees of the Diet on any Member of the Confederation who may be inclined to resist them, are causes in themselves quite sufficient to account for the diminishing importance and utility of this August Body. Still its mere existence, with the care of the Fortresses,[227] and of the Federal Constitution such as it is, may keep the Diet alive for useful purposes hereafter.

FO 30/95: William Thomas Horner Fox-Strangways to Viscount Palmerston, No 75, Frankfurt, 19 November 1846

'Schleswig Holstein question'

Although the Diet by its late Resolution, has for the present closed all discussion with regard to the affairs of Holstein[228] as to the question of succession, it appears that fresh difficulties are likely to arise in that quarter on different grounds.

Your Lordship is aware of the peculiar circumstances of the Duchy of Schleswig, a Danish province without a Danish population – a German population, yet not belonging to Germany

  – a part of Denmark, though administratively unconnected with it
  – financially and provincially united with Holstein, although independent of the great European Confederation of which Holstein is a member,

[227] The fortresses were the permanent military installations of the German Confederation. They were located in Mainz, Luxemburg, Landau, Ulm, and Rastatt.

[228] Since the accession of Christian VIII in 1839, the issue of the succession had dominated the Duchies of Schleswig and Holstein. As Christian's son Frederik (VII) was childless, and there were two different laws of succession in Holstein and Schleswig, the guaranteed indivisibility of the two duchies, which had been in force since 1460, was in doubt. The German side upheld this guarantee (principle of undivided succession), which would have separated Schleswig and Holstein from the Danish crown. When Christian VIII rejected this interpretation, the Holstein Estates made a complaint to the Federal Diet in August 1846. The German Confederation was reticent in its resolution of 17 September 1846, and tried to mediate with the Danish King.

– this Duchy, growing daily more German in language, manners, and interests, is desirous of adding itself to the German Confederation, whatever be the ultimate solution of the question of succession to the Sovereignty.

In consequence, the Diet is threatened with a petition, next Session, from the States of the Duchy of Schleswig, praying to be received as an integral Member of the Germanic Body, a prayer to which the public opinion in Germany is ready to respond, and which is said to be viewed with favour by the collateral branches of the Danish Royal Family, who claim to stand in the separate, or male line of succession to the Duchy.

On my asking the President[229] whether a Petition of this nature could be received, and the question of the union of a new Federal State, rather than Province, be entertained by the Diet, His Excellency replied that the Diet was certainly competent to admit a new Member, provided the request to that effect was made by the proper authority, namely the Sovereign; but that no such Petition from the States, or People, of what must be called a Foreign Country, could be taken into consideration. I asked him whether any Sovereign already Member of the Confederation, could in this manner add a province to the Federal Body, as Galicia[230] for example. He said yes, provided it was a German Province, or if not, one that had formerly belonged to the Empire, as Bohemia.[231] These conditions, however, would exclude Galicia, though they would allow not only Austria, but Prussia, Denmark and perhaps the Netherlands to add considerable districts to their Federal Provinces.

FO 30/95: William Thomas Horner Fox-Strangways to Viscount Palmerston, No 76, Frankfurt, 20 November 1846

On the transaction of Cracow; doubts as to whether it can be called 'legal'

Public attention has been much excited in this Free City, by the announcement of the late change in the political condition of the

---

[229] Joachim Graf von Münch-Bellinghausen.
[230] The Kingdom of Galicia had belonged to the Austrian Empire since 1815, but it was not a member of the German Confederation. Its population was predominantly Polish.
[231] The Kingdom of Bohemia, which was bound to the Austrian Empire by a shared ruler, was part of the German Confederation.

hitherto Free City and State of Cracow,[232] which has appeared in the Newspapers. It is argued that if so great and arbitrary an infraction of the Treaty of Vienna', a Treaty guaranteed by all the Great Powers of Europe, can be thus perpetrated by Three of them, acting alone, there is no longer any security for the other provisions of that Treaty, except in so far as power or opportunity are wanting to those greater States which may be inclined to aggrandize themselves at the expense of the smaller. The fact of the two most powerful German States[233] being Parties to the present transaction concerning Cracow, is a most discouraging and ill-omened circumstance in the eyes of the citizens of this, and other Free Cities of Germany, as it proves that, the case occurring, there is little to be hoped for from those from whom with justice they might expect protection. The views of Bavaria upon Frankfort are not forgotten here, and those supposed to be entertained by Prussia upon Lubeck would meet with but too specious an example in the present destruction of the liberties of Cracow.[234]

One Minister here has told me that he did not think this measure would have been taken against Cracow, had it not been for the tempting opportunity afforded by the supposed misunderstanding between England & France;[235] and another, considered to be well versed in Public Law, laid it down that the consent of all the Powers was required to undo that which the consent of the same Powers had previously done.

Although the German Free Cities have no Protecting or rather Directing Powers as was the case of Cracow, the fear of their powerful neighbours is nevertheless so strong as to cause the effect of the present proceeding against Cracow to be looked for with great anxiety.

[232] The Free Republic of Cracow had been created at the Congress of Vienna by the treaty of 3 May 1815, and was placed under the protection of three powers, Austria, Russia, and Prussia. After a revolt, which occupying Austrian troops finally put down in March 1846, the three protective powers agreed to implement a secret agreement which had been reached as long ago as 1835. Under the terms of the Protocol of 6 November 1846, Cracow lost its sovereignty and was integrated into the Austrian monarchy as part of the Kingdom of Galicia.

[233] Austria and Prussia.

[234] The Kingdom of Bavaria wanted to integrate Frankfurt into its territory within the framework of the territorial reorganisation of Germany which took place in 1814–1816. Denmark had similar plans vis-à-vis the Hanseatic towns of Lübeck and Hamburg.

[235] The Anglo-French relationship was burdened by the rivalry of the two countries in the western Mediterranean. In October 1846 the marriages of the Spanish Queen and the Spanish Infanta to two members of the French royal house led to a break between Britain and France.

FO 30/99: Francis George Molyneux to Viscount Palmerston, No 18, Frankfurt, 12 March 1847

Considerations concerning the publication of the decrees of the Federal Diet

The Wirtemberg Minister[236] in the Diet received instructions from his Government in the early part of the present year to bring under the consideration of his colleagues the propriety of publishing from time to time the Decrees of the Diet.

It was formerly the rule to publish the resolutions of the Diet except any which it was deemed advisable to withhold; Count Münch in assuming the Presidency gradually reversed this plan and published nothing except in very rare instances, the Austrian Government with its characteristic caution avoiding as much as possible anything which could give rise to discussion.

It has long been felt desirable that the public should be in possession of the Decrees and judgments pronounced by so high a tribunal, in order that they might serve as legal precedents and form part of the International Law of Germany.

I understand however that this proposition has not been favorably received at Vienna, and that through the interference of Austria, the King of Wirtemberg has now instructed his Minister in the Diet to postpone the introduction of this subject for the present, and that it is not to be renewed until after the return of the President to Frankfort.

FO 30/99: William Thomas Horner Fox-Strangways to Viscount Palmerston, No 16, Frankfurt, 21 June 1847

Project of a German colony in Texas

There has lately been a Conference of the Princes and other Proprietors interested in the German Colony in Texas,[237] held at Wiesbaden under the auspices of the Duke of Nassau.[238] It was attended by the Duke of

---

[236] Ludwig August Freiherr von Blomberg zu Sylbach.

[237] The Texas Company (*Texasverein*) was founded in 1842 by members of the German nobility. From 1844 German emigrants were sent to settle in Texas in order to earn long-term profits for the company's members and shareholders (in particular, by the proceeds of mining). However, organizational mistakes and a lack of funds, which was the subject of the meeting described here, meant that the Texas Company was dissolved in 1847, and re-founded under the new name of German Colonization Company (*Deutsche Colonisationsgesellschaft*) in 1848.

[238] Adolf.

Saxe Coburg,[239] the Prince of Leiningen,[240] and by Baron Fritsch, Minister of the Duke of Saxe Meiningen[241] in the Diet, on the part of that Sovereign.

I understand that the account of the German Colony in Texas have not of late been very favorable, which is partly attributed to the unsettled state of things in that part of America, and partly to the mismanagement of certain Agents that have been sent out there by the Company.

Your Lordship is probably aware that this Colony has been founded on a principle totally unconnected with the Emigration that goes on so extensively from all the West of Germany, especially from Hesse.

It originated in the desire naturally felt by some of the smaller Sovereigns and greater Nobility of Germany to secure some source of property which might not be exposed to the chances of European Revolutions, from which experience has shown that they could not defend themselves; while at the same time the decreasing importance of the Mediatised Princes and Counts, however supported for the present by High Rank and Illustrious Alliances, makes them feel that they cannot look forward to maintaining their position independently of their resources as Proprietors. They hope therefore to preserve the dignity of their families in Germany by means of wealth to be drawn from America: a doubtful experiment, upon the success of which it would be hazardous to express an opinion.

FO 30/100: William Thomas Horner Fox-Strangways to Viscount Palmerston, No 49, Frankfurt, 18 September 1847

First number of Karl Marx's, 'Kommunistische Zeitschrift' reaches Frankfurt from London

In case it may be unknown to Her Majesty's Government I think it worth while to mention to Your Lordship that there is now in preparation in London, a strongly Republican and Communist Journal, written in German, of which the first Number printed has been sent over to Frankfort.[242]

---

[239] Ernst II.
[240] Victor von Leiningen-Westerburg.
[241] Bernhard II.
[242] This was the pilot issue of a journal which, for financial reasons, was never established. It was edited by the *Bildungsverein für Arbeiter*, a workers' educational association founded in London in 1840 by German emigrants and artisans which later became the Communist Workers' Educational Association. The motto: 'Workers of the world unite' was first published here.

This Journal is in the form of a small Pamphlet and bears the following Title:

Kommunistische Zeitschrift
N° 1 London September 1847
Preis 2^{d}
London 8 Maryleborne 1st Quadrant
191 Drury Lane
Printed by Meldola & Cahn, 18 St Mary Axe

It is sufficient to say that this Journal advocates the most violent opinions, denounces all Governments, calls upon the Proletaires of all countries to rise, and to recover the rights of which they have been deprived: with much more of the same nature.

I have had but a slight view of this production, but enough to shew that it is calculated for extensive circulation among the lower orders of Germany and Switzerland.

PRUSSIA
(BERLIN)

BERLIN

FO 64/163: Brook Taylor to Earl of Aberdeen, No 86, Berlin, 21 September 1830

Disturbances in Berlin; precautionary measures taken by the magistrate; no danger expected from the 'destructive spirit' in neighbouring countries

Reports may possibly reach Your Lordship of disturbances in this Capital, and as more importance may be attached to them than they deserve, I beg leave to enclose the Berlin State Gazette of the 19th Instant from which you will find that the little that has passed here has arisen principally from the misconduct of a Police Officer upon the occasion of a trifling quarrel between some of the lower Classes in the neighbourhood of the Royal Palace in the evening of the 16th.[1] A report was spread on the following day that the Palace would be attacked by the Populace in consequence of which a crowd collected before dark in that quarter but from its general description evidently more from motives of curiosity than from any other. Half the Garrison was however immediately ordered out, the crowd increased, and in the confusion and attempts of the Soldiers to disperse the People several well dressed Persons received Sabre and bayonet wounds. No Symptoms of disaffection were shewn except a few hisses from boys and some of the lower Classes, twenty or thirty of whom were arrested. After eleven O'Clock not a soul was seen in the streets except the Military.

Precautions have since been taken by the Magistracy for the tranquillity of the Town, such as forbidding the assemblage of more than five Persons together in the streets and recommending to the inhabitants not to quit their homes after dark. Patrols of Cavalry and Infantry have continued to parade the streets ever since and a greater part of the Garrison remain under arms during the night.

These proceedings would no doubt have created less alarm at any other moment. I am however persuaded that no danger is to be apprehended in Berlin from the example of the spirit of insubordination and destruction which has been manifested in Neighbouring Countries.[2] That great wretchedness is to be found among the poorer Classes is

---

[1] The disturbances were unleashed by the unjustified arrest of various apprentice cobblers who had gathered in public. The policeman responsible (name not traceable) was suspended from duty on 18 September.

[2] Cf. pp. 7–11 in Frankfurt section.

certain – but whatever grievances they may have – the more respectable inhabitants may justly be considered as devoted to their beloved Monarch, and independent of this consideration, none of them would be disposed to rise against a military force of above 12000 men forming the Garrison of Berlin which would immediately be opposed to them.[3]

FO 64/173: George William Chad to Viscount Palmerston, No 304, Berlin, 24 July 1831

Cholera outbreak in Posen; question of sanitary precautions

Count Bernstorff[4] states that the Cholera which has broken out at Posen was brought thither by a Jew who stole across the Frontiers, and thus evaded the Sanitary Precautions.

One of my acquaintances has received this morning a letter from Posen which describes the people as being in a state of great excitement there on the subject of this disease, and says that force is often necessary to compel them to submit either to measures of precaution, or to medical assistance, which they are convinced are equally unavailing.

Should the disease reach such Capitals as London or Paris, it may be doubted whether in such circumstances force would prevail.

FO 64/174: George William Chad to Viscount Palmerston, No 374, Berlin, 11 September 1831

Expected death rate from cholera; the lower classes suspicious of the disease; King of Prussia orders remuneration for doctors

D[r] Krajewski a Polish Physician who has had some success in treating the Cholera has been sent for by order of the King, and has inspected the hospitals and visited the Patients at this place.

He is of opinion, I hear, that the disease has as yet not got hold of the population, but judging from his experience in other places, and from the appearances here, he expects that about the 19th the number of deaths at Berlin will be from 200 to 250 daily.

Accounts from different parts of the Country where the Cholera reigns agree in one point – viz. that there is amongst the lowest Classes a fixed belief that no such disease exists – that the deaths ascribed to

---

[3] Enclosures: 1. Transmitting article from Berlin State Gazette relative to disturbances in the Capital (*Beilage zur Allgemeinen Preußischen Staatszeitung*, No. 260); 2. Translation.

[4] Christian Günther Graf von Bernstorff.

that malady are produced by poison administered by the Doctors, who
are employed and bribed for that purpose.

'The Rich', say these deluded people, 'find that the poor are
becoming too numerous to be conveniently governed, and therefore
this plan of thinning the population has been adopted – it having been
employed with success by the English in India'.

The foreign Doctors, who have been sent to Russia, Poland, and
Prussia to observe the disease, are according to this Hypothesis, the
Delegates of a Central Committee consisting of 100 Members formed
in London, and who direct the whole proceeding.

The King of Prussia having humanely ordered that a daily remuneration should be given to Doctors who devote themselves to the
Treatment of Cholera-Patients, this fact has been distorted by these
ignorant people into a bribe of 2, or according to some of 3 Thalers a
head to each Doctor for every death caused by these means.

I have not heard this account from one or from two persons nor
does it apply to one or two districts. The statement is generally made
by those who are conversant with the matter, and it applies to nearly
all the Country-places where the Cholera reigns, and to some of the
Towns.

The Cholera-Bulletin of this morning is as follows – '11 September
to 8 A.M. 152 sick – 7 cured – 113 dead.[']

FO 64/174: George William Chad to Viscount Palmerston, No 382,
Berlin, 17 September 1831

*Cholera in Berlin; employment for some of the deprived lower classes; effect of cholera on
trade and the industrious poor; multiple quarantine measures and resulting complications*

Dr Rust the chief person in the Sanitary Commission here lately stated
by advertizement in the newspapers that all necessitous persons would
find work at the hospital of La Charité,[5] where extensive buildings are
in progress.

The number of applications however was so great that many of the
poor were disappointed in their expectation of obtaining employment;
and above a hundred of them proceeded in a body yesterday to the
Palace at Charlottenburg and asked to see the King.

His Majesty sent an Aide de Camp to them to whom they stated
their case in a quiet and respectful manner.

The King gave orders in consequence, which it was expected would
have procured them bread or work. They were not however all satisfied,

[5] Hospital in Berlin, founded 1710.

and this morning there was a disposition shewn to assemble again – but after a short time the people dispersed.

I mention this incident to your Lordship, as it is not unlikely that it may be exaggerated and misrepresented. So little sensation however did it create in the Town, that I knew nothing of it till this afternoon.

The King some time before the Cholera broke out here gave 40,000 thalers from his privy purse, to be spent in employing the Poor.

His Majesty comes to Berlin every morning, and appears every night at the play.

The indirect consequences of the prevalence of the Cholera upon the lower classes are such as cannot fail to produce discontent.

Many persons are entirely deprived of employment as whilst the pestilence lasts, there is a general disinclination to admit (unless in cases of absolute necessity) workmen of any sort into private houses. The effect upon the industrious poor in a populous Town is greater than at first sight it would appear to be. Amongst the sufferers are all those persons, who are interested in the sale of fish, fruit, vegetables – articles of food which are thought unwholesome. Poultry has also been added to this list, a mortality having lately shewn itself amongst the ducks, geese, and fowls.

The trade of shopkeepers is also generally very much diminished during the prevalence of the Cholera, as the fear of buying infected goods prevents all purchases which are not absolutely necessary.

If the determination of the Government to insulate all those houses in which the Cholera has shewn itself had not been relinquished, the consequences would probably have been disastrous: but I have not heard of any instance in which any attempt has been made to carry into effect, this, or many other of the measures of precaution, which had been however repeatedly and officially announced as being to be adopted.

The irregular manner in which the Cholera makes its advances, is the cause of much complication in the quarantine measures.

It was stated here some time ago that when the Cholera should reach Berlin all quarantine to the North, and North-East of the Capital would be raised. This determination however has been modified in favour of the inhabitants of still healthy districts, but the term of detention has been reduced to 5 days.

There are now in a Lazarette on the frontier towards Poland, English and French Doctors, who have been stopped there in their way from Warsaw to Berlin; and who are there detained, although they are only passing from one infected Town to another; because intermediate districts through which they must travel are still free from the disease – and I am told by the French Minister,[6] that if these Doctors go from

[6] Hector Philippe, comte d'Agoult.

Berlin to France they will be compelled to perform a second quarantine on the Elbe, and a third on entering the French Dominions.

These multiple quarantines have however one good consequence – They discourage unnecessary change of place and keep all those at home, who are not absolutely obliged to travel.

FO 64/174: George William Chad to Viscount Palmerston, No 424, Berlin, 13 October 1831

Information on the means employed to prevent the spread of the cholera in Berlin; question of contagion; reasons for slow spread of the disease; population's behaviour; disease not confined to the poor

In obedience to the Instructions contained in your Lordship's Dispatch N° 49 of the 27th ultimo, I have endeavoured to collect authentick information as to the means employed to prevent the extension of the Cholera at Berlin, and I have obtained the best opinions as to the causes which have contributed to the languid progress of the disease here.

The question of contagion[7] is the cause of such violent contention that almost all those who have attended to the subject of the Cholera are partizans, and their view of facts is influenced by their opinions as to this question. I have however addressed myself to Dr Becker, one of the Physicians of my district, who is attached to the board of Health, and who is unremitting in his attendance upon Cholera patients both in the Hospitals and in private dwellings.

He is, I think, the most dispassionate of those of his Profession with whom I have conversed on this subject, and although he is a believer in the doctrine of contagion, I think his opinions deserve attention; and I am sure that his statement of facts is worthy of confidence. [...]

The slowness with which the disease has spread at Berlin may, I think, in some degree be ascribed to the non-adoption of any violent preventional measures which by exciting the angry passions of the Populace, and by diminishing the comforts of the Poor render them liable to attacks of the malady. No entire dwellings have been blockaded notwithstanding the repeated orders which have been issued on this subject, the apartments in which Cholera patients have died have been shut up in some instances for 5 days but even this modified measure has not, I am certain, been carried into effect in half the houses where the disease has appeared. The measures of precaution adopted in

---

[7] Those who believed in contagion thought that cholera could only be spread by direct infection from person to person, and that environmental and climatic factors played only a secondary role in spreading the disease. Their main proposal for containing cholera was quarantine.

respect to the soldiers who form the garrison of Berlin, have consisted in a watchful attention to their diet, an addition to their food of a mess of meat-broth at supper, the distribution amongst them of warm clothing, and the strict enforcement of cleanliness, temperance and early hours.

The Garrison has been remarkably preserved from the attacks of the disease.

The People are generally orderly and well behaved, and drunkenness and rioting do not at least appear in the streets; – but on the other hand the situation of Berlin is very unhealthy; extensive inundations keep a great part of the neighbouring country up to the very walls under water for a great portion of the year, and during the whole of last February, and March and during half the month of April water stood in nearly every house in the town, and in one of the largest Squares (the Platz von la belle Alliance) it was for several days so deep as not to be passed in a carriage without danger; and at this moment there are many acres of green stagnant water within a hundred yards of the best part of the town. The gutters in the streets are all open and full of stagnant water; a Doctor who had been very conversant with Cholera in India observed last Spring when he passed through this place that he considered it as peculiarly liable by these circumstances to Cholera. [...]

As far as I have been able to judge from hearsay the disease has not been confined to persons who are insufficiently fed and clothed and whose dwellings are unwholesome; it seems to have taken a pretty wide range amongst shop-keepers and tradespeople who are quite as well clad and fed, as far as health is concerned, as the highest classes, but who are certainly not so spaciously lodged and who are in much more frequent contact with the lowest part of the population. [...]

It has been frequently and generally stated that those who feel a terror of the disease are most likely to be attacked by it, I have seen no confirmation of this assertion here.

An English surgeon[8] at this place has a patient in whom this fear brought on a fit of illness but it did not produce Cholera. Another Doctor of my acquaintance lost a Patient whose death he ascribes to the fear of the Cholera but the patient acquired no symptoms of the disease, and I have seen many persons who were in great dread of the malady but not one of them has contracted it, this statement may probably have been made by persons who having escaped the disease wish to adduce indirectly their good fortune as a proof of their strength of mind.[9]

[8] Not traceable.
[9] Enclosures: 1. Dr Becker's Memorandum of the progress of Cholera at Berlin; 2.

FO 64/175: George William Chad to Viscount Palmerston, No 465, Berlin, 16 November 1831

Eleventh week of cholera; number of persons attacked by the disease remains stable; prominent deaths not attributed to cholera

The eleventh week of the Cholera ended yesterday, and exactly the same number of Persons have been attacked in it as in the first week.

Persons of celebrity however, and members of the higher classes who die of Cholera are not reported in the lists which are given to the Publick.

Thus, Field Marshal Gneisenau died of Asiatick Cholera, and I was informed by his son (who was at his death-bed) and by a Doctor who read the medical Report addressed to the King on the occasion that there was no doubt entertained as to the character of his disease – yet he was officially declared in the Gazette to have died of apoplexy.

Again, Mr Hegel, one of the most celebrated Professors of Germany, died here in the course of this week after an illness of a few hours. One of the Physicians who attended him to the last moment has assured me that his disease was Asiatick Cholera,[10] and that he signed the usual certificate in concert with his colleague who attended the Professor to that effect – yet in the State Gazette of which I have the honour to enclose an extract, the Professor is officially announced as having died of apoplexy.[11] [...]

FO 64/175: George William Chad to Viscount Palmerston, Private, Berlin, 28 November 1831

Violation of Treaty of Einbeck; Prussia's interest in a united commercial system; main features of that system; Prussia expects greater political influence in Germany; the 'War-Party'

[...] The establishment & extension of the Commercial System [...], has been for some years a favorite object with the Prussian Gov^t. The Union[12] formed in opposition to it under the Auspices, of Hanover Saxony & Electoral Hesse, has just been broken up, by the Secession

Plan of Berlin to shew the houses where the Cholera has broken out to the 30th September; 3. Map shewing the monthly advances of the Cholera in Prussia.

[10] Asiatic cholera, as opposed to endemic cholera nostra, became an epidemic and was fatal for the majority of those who caught it.

[11] Enclosures: 1. Extract from the Prussian State Gazette, 16 November 1831; 2. Report on state of Cholera (30 August to 16 November 1831); 3. Extract from the 'Cholera Paper'.

[12] *Mitteldeutscher Handelsverein* founded 1828, cf. Volume I, pp. 45ff.

of the Elector who has signed a Treaty of Commerce[13] with Prussia, & by that of the King of Saxony, who is about to do so likewise although in direct violation of the Treaty of Einbeck[14] concluded only in March 1830. [...]

I shall only observe that the object of Prussia is to unite those German Powers whose States are contiguous, in the uniform Commercial System now established in Prussia, Hesse-Darmstadt, Coethen, & which is about to be introduced into Saxony & Electoral Hesse, & the principle of which is adopted in Bavaria & Wurtemberg, & on the point of being brought into action in the Grand-Duchy of Baden.

The main feature of this System is to abolish all Transit & all other Duties between the Countries leagued together, & to shut out from such united Countries, by heavy Duties, the produce of foreign Soils & of foreign Industry. Thus excluding from the States engaged in this Commercial league the productions of the rest of Europe, as Buonaparte endeavoured to shut out from the Continent the Production of Great Britain & of her Colonies.[15]

Prince Metternich speaking to me in the Summer of 1830 of this System called it 'Le Systeme Continental au petit pied' & added 'ne voyez vous pas que La Prusse cherche a Jacobiniser[16] toute L'Allemagne contre le Commerce de L'Angleterre?'

Prussia has made pecuniary sacrifices in order to advance this System, from which she expects not only advantageous future financial returns, but also an augmentation of political Influence in Germany; & her geographical Position although disadvantageous in many respects enables her, by making her the frontier of many different States to act upon their direct Interests & thus to acquire Influence over them.

This Commercial System would not in its present immature State survive it is thought, a war in Germany a Consideration powerfully in support of Pacific Counsels.

There is however it is true a War-Party here, composed of the Young Princes[17] of a few Ultra-monarchical Men, & of the Officers of the Army, wearied by the slow advancement here in time of Peace: & if the Contest in Poland[18] had been much prolonged, & if the Russians

[13] Treaty between Prussia and Electoral Hesse of 25 August 1831.

[14] Cf. pp. 4–5 in Frankfurt section.

[15] On 21 November 1806 Napoleon Bonaparte ordered a blockade against Britain. The conditions of this so-called continental barrier were intensified on 17 December 1808 by the Decree of Milan.

[16] This expression refers to the political grouping during the French Revolution named after their meeting place in the Dominican monastery of St Jacob. The expression passed into common usage as a negative description of supporters of the ideas of the French Revolution, radical democrats and other radicals.

[17] The sons of Friedrich Wilhelm III, Wilhelm, Karl, and Albrecht.

[18] In Poland there was an uprising against Russian rule from November 1830 until it

had proved quite unable to bring it to a successful termination, I am not sure that this party might not have prevailed in persuading the King to rush in at all hazards & put an end to it, but that Crisis being over I do not think that prospective reasons or any thing short of pressing necessity, would during the Life of the present King induce Prussia to make war. This Government stand very much in awe of Public Opinion, although it has no legal Organ here, & Public Opinion would I think be decidedly against a war of Principles, or in short against any war but one absolutely necessitated by foreign aggression.

FO 64/181: George William Chad to Viscount Palmerston, No 41, Berlin, 19 February 1832

Number of people who have contracted and died of cholera

The enclosed Report of the number of persons who have been taken ill and who have died of Cholera in all those parts of the Kingdom of Prussia in which the disease has penetrated since its first appearance, has been published in the State Gazette of this morning. Of 52,773 attacked, 30,927 have died.[19]

FO 64/182: George William Chad to Viscount Palmerston, No 82, Confidential, Berlin, 23 April 1832

Negotiations about Saxony becoming a member of the Prussian Commercial Union; Saxony's real intentions; two commercial systems similar in principle, but not in detail; commercial system could be endangered by war; Baden's position; Prussian system not 'liberal'

The Saxon Minister of Finance Mr Zeschau has been at Berlin in order to superintend the negociations respecting the proposed accession of Saxony to the Prussian Commercial system.

Before he returned to Dresden he came to me to inform me as he said frankly but in the strictest confidence of the real intentions of his Government respecting this matter. It is necessary to premise that Prussia the Coethens and the 2 Hesses on one side and Bavaria, Wirtemberg and the Principalities of Hohenzollern on the other form 2 masses who have adopted commercial systems similar in principle

was put down in September 1831. At the beginning of October 1831 most of the Polish army fled to Prussia, where it was disarmed.

[19] Enclosure: Copy from the Prussian State Gazette of 19 February 1832.

but differing in details.[20] The principle is to do away with duties and custom houses between the states uniting, and to protect by a Tarif the Produce and Manufactures of the countries within the pale, from the competition of those who are not included in it.

Commercial plenipotentiaries are now assembled at Berlin endeavouring to unite these 2 Masses and make of them one whole, and Saxony is treating with Prussia respecting her immediate accession to the Prussian Mass but her real intentions are to wait until this commission be effected and if it should take place then and not till then to treat in earnest respecting the accession of Saxony to this whole.

Mr de Zeschau is not however a Partizan of this commercial system, he thinks it likely to be deranged or broken up by war in Germany and he considers it dangerous inasmuch as if one of he states within the pale keep a bad frontier guard against contraband trade the whole Union will be supplied by smuggled goods to the detriment of the common revenue.

So little does he expect that the system can be established permanently, that he assured me that if Saxony became a member of the Union he should not sell or pull down the Saxon custom houses, because he foresees the probability of their soon becoming again necessary by a breaking up of this Union: However if the Fair of Leipzig were protected in the enjoyment of the diminution of duties of goods sold there, called 'Messrabatt', Saxony would be a gainer by becoming a Member of the Union, for most of her manufactures are better and cheaper than many of those of the associated Countries and therefore would be preferred within the Pale.

He will not however in any event take upon himself the responsibility of acceding to the Union without consulting the States of Saxony.

Mr Zeschau thinks that Bavaria is already a loser by her participation in this system because her manufactures are few & inferior to those of some of the states already included or likely to be included in the Union.

The Grand Duchy of Baden has I find been prevented for the present from joining the Association of Bavaria and Wirtemberg by the refusal of the States of the Grand Duchy to agree to the Cession of a small portion of territory which was to have been given to Bavaria as a satisfaction for Sponheim, and as the arrangement of this Sponheim question[21] was the bait by which Baden had been tempted into a

---

[20] Köthen and Hesse-Darmstadt joined the Prussian customs system in 1828, Electoral Hesse in 1831. Bavaria, Württemberg, Hohenzollern-Hechingen, and Hohenzollern-Sigmaringen formed the South German *Zollverein* in 1828 as a counterweight to Prussian expansionism.

[21] The preliminary agreement between Bavaria and Baden of 1829 merely provided for a small alteration of the border, not the cession of the whole of the Baden Palatinate as

promise to accede to a commercial system in opposition to her interests it is not likely that the promise should now be fulfilled: the States of Baden have however expressed themselves vaguely and generally as not unwilling to enter into negociations on the subject.

I find from my Hanoverian Colleague[22] that notwithstanding the defection of Electoral Hesse from the Treaty of Einbeck,[23] Hanover & Brunswick are endeavouring to carry the principle of it into effect & to make a common stock of their indirect Taxes dividing the produce of them at the end of the year in proportion to the population of the States.

It is an opinion generally entertained that Prussia has more in view Political Influence than financial advantage in advocating her commercial system. I am told however that in a late instance she was disappointed in its operation in this respect and that the Government of Hesse Darmstadt was prevented by the popular party from voting with Prussia on a late occasion in the Diet.

The Prussian System has been very incorrectly called a liberal system − it is liberal no doubt to the states who adopt it, inasmuch as the duties between countries within the Pale are removed; but it is the reverse of liberal in respect to the rest of Germany and the rest of the world & a comparison of the Tariffs of the associated countries of those without the Pale will prove the truth of this assertion.

FO 64/184: To Earl of Minto, Foreign Office, No 3, London, 7 September 1832 (Draft)[24]

Palmerston's reaction to the recent resolutions of the Federal Diet in Frankfurt (Six Articles)

The late resolutions of the Diet of Frankfort[25] have excited so great and so extensive a sensation throughout Europe, that they could not fail to attract the serious attention of His Majesty's Government. Great Britain was a contracting party to the Treaty of Vienna,[26] of which the settlement of Germany was an essential feature; and the British

originally demanded by Bavaria. Nonetheless this territorial compensation, which had arisen from former Bavarian rights in Sponheim, was rejected by the Baden *Landtag*. Thus the Sponheim question remained unresolved. Cf. also vol. I, pp. 297f.

[22] Börries Wilhelm von Münchhausen.

[23] Cf. pp. 4–5 in Frankfurt section.

[24] The same dispatch was sent to the British envoy in Vienna; cf. pp. 494–502 in Austria section; original in FO 244/31.

[25] Six Articles of 28 June 1832; cf. pp. 35–39 in Frankfurt section.

[26] Congress Act of the Congress of Vienna, 9 June 1815. The Federal Act of 8 June 1815 signed by the members of the German Confederation was part of the Congress Act; cf. nn. 136, 137 in Frankfurt section.

Government is connected by relations of friendship with the German States; whatever then may tend, either to disturb that settlement & thereby to endanger the general peace, or else materially to affect the welfare of those states, must be an object of deep interest to His Majesty's Government.

His Majesty's Gov[t] therefore, in instructing your Lordship to make to the Cabinet of Berlin the communication directed by this Despatch, conceives itself to be performing an important public duty; and is also convinced that a frank explanation of its opinions at this period, will be received by the Prussian Government as an unequivocal proof of friendly disposition. In those acts of the Congress of Vienna which relate to the settlement of Germany, two prominent principles appear to be established.

The one, that the several States of which Germany was to be composed, should enjoy an independence inviolable from without: the other that their internal welfare should be secured by representative Assemblies.[27] It further appears that whereas many of these States are small and incapable of defending themselves against a powerful enemy, and are yet so placed geographically, as to be exposed to sudden invasion, whenever the Great Powers of Europe should be engaged in war, it was judged expedient to unite the whole of Germany in a general Confederation for mutual defence. In this manner the weaker States were assured of the protection of the strong, and the strong found their defensive means encreased, by the pledged alliance of their less powerful neighbours.

It is clear that this league was intended to secure the separate Independence of its component members; for the maintenance of that Independence was set forth as one of the principal objects of the Union, and to it, therefore, the federal obligations & engagements must be considered as subordinate & conducive. The Sovereigns of the States composing this Confederation, were to be represented by Plenipotentiaries in a general Diet; which Diet was to be invested with Powers to establish rules, upon certain matters connected with the general objects of the Confederation, and these rules were to be binding upon all the members of the league; but a limit to the Powers of the Diet must be found in the principles of the Treaty by which Germany was settled, and in the inherent Independence of the component States.

The Plenipotentiaries who compose the Diet represent only the Sovereigns, who, in States where the right of representation has been established, cannot by their sole authority give validity to Acts which require by their nature the consent of all the branches of the legislature;

[27] Article 2 and Article 13 of the Federal Act of 8 June 1815. For Article 13 cf. n. 83 in Frankfurt section.

and the assent of these Sovereigns to regulations subversive of their political Independence, would be inconsistent with the engagements which they have contracted by the Treaty before referred to.

His Majesty's Gov^t however, in thus stating their general view of the principles on which the Germanick Confederation is founded, do not intend at present to exercise the right which they conceive to belong to all the Powers who were parties to the Treaty of Vienna, of discussing whether the late measures of the Diet are or are not such, in their tendency & effect, as to trench upon the independence of the separate States, or to infringe upon the constitutions which have been granted them.

But, whatever explanations may be given upon those questions, it may certainly be feared that if the authority which has been constituted within the Diet by these resolutions, were to exercise to its full extent, the power with which it has been invested, the constitutional rights of the smaller States and their political Independence might be most seriously affected. It is however to the danger which may possibly result from those measures, that His Majesty's Government wishes, on the present occasion, to direct the attention of the Court of Berlin. His Majesty's Gov^t have observed for some time past with much concern the attempts which have been made to excite discontent among the people, in several of the German States bordering upon the Rhine, & they have seen with regret the success with which, to a considerable degree, these attempts have been attended.[28] But much as H.M.'s Govt lament this disposition to disturbance, yet, believing it to proceed from temporary causes, & not to be founded upon any deeply seated political grievances in the Countries in which it exists, they have viewed it with less uneasiness than they would otherwise have felt, & they are inclined to think that a firm but temperate exercise of the Powers possessed by the Govt^s of those States, would have been sufficient to uphold the Authority of the law, & to preserve domestic peace; and in the exercise of these powers those Governments would certainly have been entitled to have applied for, & to have obtained if necessary the support of the Diet.

Considering then the late Resolutions of the Diet simply with reference to their policy, & setting aside for the present, any other question, H.M.'s Gov^t are apprehensive that those measures may go to a greater extent than was necessary for warding off the evils against which they were directed; & may produce dangers of another kind, more general & more complicated.

---

[28] Apart from the events and the behaviour of the political opposition in Hesse-Nassau, in the Grand Duchy of Hesse and in Baden, Palmerston is mainly referring to the so-called Hambach Festival in the Bavarian Palatinate on 27–30 May 1832; cf. pp. 23–26 in Frankfurt section.

Although the proceedings of the Diet have been unanimously sub-scribed to by the Representatives of the several States of the Con-federation, yet they appear to have been by no means equally assented to by the Legislatures and by the Population of many of those States.

It appears, on the contrary, that a strong & general opinion prevails throughout almost all the Constitutional States, that the resolutions of the Diet are an infringement upon their rights, and an attack upon their national Independence. Nor is this opinion confined to noisy agitators, declaiming at publick meetings, or acting by means of a licentious press; but in the contrary, as His Majesty's Government has reason to believe, it is striking a deep root, & is creating serious apprehension & extensive discontent in the minds of all classes, including the most wealthy & the most intelligent.

Should this feeling break forth, at the next meeting of the Legislative Assemblies in the Constitutional States, which it probably will, even if nothing should occur to call it sooner into action, the consequence of these measures will be a breach between the Sovereigns of those States and the great Mass of their Subjects, upon questions of the deepest national importance, and which excite the strongest passions of mankind.

Such a state of things could not exist without serious inconvenience in any country, even though that country were cut off from all external contact; but His Majesty's Government leave it to the Cabinet of Prussia to consider, how much the danger must be encreased, in countries whose geographical position is such, that if the affections & confidence of the nation should be withdrawn from the Sovereign, the people might turn their eyes to other quarters, & might be taught to look abroad for that protection and support, which they believed their natural Governors had ceased to afford them.

It is obvious that in such a posture of affairs a powerful foreign influence might grow up in the bosom of the State, – an influence too, not of a foreign Gov^t but of a foreign Faction, ready to fasten upon discontent wherever it should be found, and to make the grievances of all nations equally subservient to its own bad purposes.[29] Such are the dangers which H.M.'s Government apprehend from what has already taken place; but if the resolutions of the Diet should be pushed to their full application, and measures should be carried into execution which the people of the German States might consider either inconsistent with rights & privileges formally conferred upon them, or else delib-erately planned for the destruction of those privileges and Rights, – much more serious & extensive evils might be expected to ensue.

---

[29] This remark was prompted by the close connection between the liberal movement in Germany and in France; cf. Metternich's view on p. 501 in Austria section.

The nations of Germany are known to be firmly attached to the Constitutions under which they live; and are not likely to surrender those Constitutions without a struggle.

There has grown up too, in these States a spirit of national Independence, which can neither be safely contemned, nor easily subdued; and this spirit is the more entitled to be respected by the Governments, because it was first called into life by an appeal from the Sovereigns to their people, when the united efforts of the latter were required by the necessities of the former, to free them from the thraldom of the greatest military Power which, in modern times, has broken down the Independence of Princes, or controlled the liberties of Mankind.[30] The experience of all times, and of none more than the last three years,[31] teaches that overstrained exertions of Power, though springing from the National Government of a State, produce resistance, and may end in revolution; but how much more likely are those consequences to follow, when arbitrary measures emanate from an external authority, & are to be supported by a foreign Force. In such a case, the question of resistance, or submission, can be decided by nothing but a calculation of success; and in moments of national excitement that calculation will be made by men, upon whose judgment & discretion the peace of nations ought never to depend.

When the bulk of a people are contented, partial insurrections, of which all countries furnish occasional examples, are easily put down; but instances are not wanting to show, that where discontent is general & deeply seated, a casual conflict, or the rash act of a few desperate Individuals, may involve a whole Nation in a bloody civil war.

Should the measures of the Diet unfortunately provoke resistance, & should force, but more especially foreign force, be employed to quell it, (and the troops of Austria & Prussia would, in such a case, be looked upon by the people of the other German States as a foreign force) a war of political opinions would begin, of which it is more easy to foretell the calamities than to foresee the conclusion. But looking to the temper of men's minds in a large portion of Europe, and to the susceptible state of public feeling upon political questions, even in countries which have hitherto been least the scene of actual agitation, it is impossible not to perceive that such a war, breaking out upon the Rhine, in consequence of what would be represented and felt, as the

[30] Palmerston is referring here to France's dominance or political influence in Germany. Until the collapse of the Napoleonic system in 1813–1815, Germany had undergone fundamental changes in the secularization of church property, the abolition of the religious principalities and the territories of the imperial knights, and in the integration of most of the imperial cities into the enlarged German states.

[31] Palmerston is referring here to the revolutionary events that took place all over Europe in the wake of the French revolution of July 1830.

aggression of Power upon legal rights, might produce a general convulsion in Europe, from which the soundest Institutions and the most firmly established Thrones, might not escape unharmed.

His Majesty's Govt, therefore, actuated by conservative principles in the strictest sense of the expression, & animated by sentiments of the sincerest friendship, entreats the [Prussian] Govt, well to consider all the dangers which may attend the course, which in consequence of the Resolutions of the 28ᵗʰ June, it is apprehended the Diet may be preparing to pursue. The influence of [Prussia] in the Diet is known to be such, as the greatness of her Power entitles her to exert; the first aim of her policy is believed to be the maintenance of Peace, and the chief object of her apprehension, violent convulsions in Europe. His Majesty's Government, then, most earnestly request the [Prussian] Government to employ its influence in restraining the inconsiderate zeal of the Diet; and in preventing the adoption of Measures, of which convulsion & war would be the too probable consequence. His Majesty's Government think that in stating to the Cabinet of Berlin, thus frankly & explicitly, their sentiments upon a subject of such deep & general interest, they are no less discharging the offices of Friendship and Alliance towards [Prussia], than fulfilling the duties which they owe to their own country: and they are the more solicitous to avail themselves, for this purpose, of the present time, because, in the existing state of things, those offices and those duties are happily reconcilable, and consistent with each other.

FO 64/189: Earl of Minto to Viscount Palmerston, No 25, Berlin, 3 April 1833

Commercial treaty signed between Prussia, Bavaria, Hesse-Darmstadt, Hesse-Kassel, and Württemberg; desire to enter into commercial treaties with foreign states; treaty viewed with extreme dissatisfaction by Austria

The commercial negotiations in which this Government has for some time been engaged have terminated in a treaty which was signed two days ago by the Plenipotentiaries of Prussia, Bavaria, the two Hesses,³² and Wirtemburgh.

The determination here to encourage the Fair of Frankfort on the Oder by advantages from which Leipzig was excluded produced some hesitation on the part of Saxony, but this has now been overcome, and Saxony consenting to leave to the Commerce of Frankfort a Drawback of 15 Per Cent on foreign cotton and woollen manufactures has within

³² Grand Duchy of Hesse (Hesse-Darmstadt) and Electoral Hesse (Hesse-Cassel).

these few days notified her accession to the treaty.[33] It is also understood that the accession of the smaller Principalities[34] within these limits has been secured. The object of this association, which will comprise a population of about 22,500,000 people, is an absolute freedom of commerce, and the abolition of all interior customhouses within its limits. The Import and Transit duties will in every case be levied upon the frontier of the association, and will be shared amongst the parties I believe in the ratio of their respective population.

The substitution of duties for prohibition as existing here at present has been recognized, and the Prussian tariff has, in general, been provisionally adopted, subject, to revision [.]

In some cases indeed where the interests of the parties required a change it has been slightly modified, the cotton twist of England, for example, being necessary for the manufactures of Bavaria the duty upon the importation of that article has been reduced to a mere trifle.

A transit duty of Twelve Groschen and a half (about 15^d sterling) per quintal will be levied once and for all at the common frontier upon goods not destined for sale or consumption within the limits of the association which will be subject to no further interruption during their progress.

A right is reserved to each of the parties of contracting separate treaties with other states, provided they be first communicated to the association in order that it may be seen that they contain nothing inconsistent with the associate obligations. In most cases, however it would be found that this amounts to little more than a privilege of inviting the association collectively to contract such treaties so far as commercial interests are concerned, since almost every question which could become the subject of separate treaty is already determined by the united authority.

The arrangements and regulations by which this treaty may be brought into operation are reserved for further discussion, which it is supposed may still occupy a couple of months.

A great desire is professed here, with what sincerity I cannot yet judge, of entering into commercial treaties with foreign states upon the most liberal principles. I do not doubt however that any facilities we might be disposed to offer to the importation of the Timber, grain, wool or other productions of Germany would be eagerly invited by corresponding advantages to our industry.

This imperfect outline is all that I am at present able to give your

---

[33] Saxony joined the *Zollverein* on 30 March 1833.

[34] On 10 May 1833 all the Thuringian states (including Saxe-Weimar, Saxe-Meiningen, Saxe-Coburg-Gotha) joined together to form the Thuringian customs and trade union. On the following day it joined the *Zollverein*.

Lordship, but I shall endeavour to inform myself more fully of the details of a measure which unites nearly the whole of Germany in one system, and the political consequences of which may not be less important than those which are professedly contemplated.

This Treaty is naturally viewed with extreme dissatisfaction by Austria, who feels the influence thus acquired in Germany by her rival; and even amongst some of the parties to the treaty well founded apprehensions are entertained that their domestick prosperity may have been consulted in some measure at the expence of their political independence. [...]

FO 64/189: Earl of Minto to Viscount Palmerston, No 44, Berlin, 5 June 1833

Baron Binder's suspicious mission

Baron Binder's presence here as an unaccredited Agent, begins to give a good deal of offence at this Court. This Government has long been familiarised to Prince Metternich's system of an ostensible and a secret Diplomacy, but upon the present occasion too little pains have been taken to put a decent disguise upon it, and Monsr Binder appears almost avowedly as superseding Count Trautmansdorff in his functions. This degradation of the Minister, who is still allowed to occupy his Post is not thought very respectful to the Court at which he is accredited, but the real ground of dissatisfaction lies in the tendency of these secret Missions to inspire jealousy and uneasiness, which an appearance of concert between the two great Powers, never fails to produce amongst the smaller States of Germany. Count Clam's continued residence at Berlin after the close of the military commission,[35] and the influence he was known to have acquired with Monsr Ancillon had been notified with some alarm by the neighbouring States, and there were Members of the Prussian Government who then insinuated that Prince Metternich sought to encourage such suspicions with the view of creating a distrust of Prussia. Hence perhaps the haste of Monsieur Ancillon and others to proclaim their dislike of Monsieur Binder's Mission and the cold reception which the King has given him. But though this Mission certainly gave some displeasure, it is very possible that Monsr Binder may succeed in making an impression favorable to the views of his Government.

[35] The military commission of the German Confederation convened from September 1831 to December 1832 in Berlin. The main point of the negotiations was the reorganization of the confederation's army and discussion of military and tactical measures should France invade across the Rhine.

We cannot ascertain that he is charged with any special negotiations. But he is evidently provided with ample instructions and information on all the leading questions of the day, and is supposed generally to be thoroughly in the confidence of Prince Metternich.

If there be any single object of his Mission, I should imagine it must be that of keeping Prussia fast to the great Conservative Confederacy, as he terms it.

My language to him and others with reference to such a Confederacy as we have lately seen, if it be contemplated as a permanent system, is, that they must not imagine that other Governments could see three Great States[36] assume this imposing attitude with indifference. That if they constitute themselves a Power apart from the mass of European society, they must be prepared to see another League opposed to them. That this must be the inevitable result of their system if it be now prolonged beyond the circumstances which may in some measure have justified it, and that they should weigh the consequences of marshaling Europe in opposing camps upon such ground as each might occupy.

FO 64/190: Ralph Abercromby to John Backhouse, No 4, Berlin, 11 September 1833

Poor relief in Prussia

In reply to your Circular dispatch of the 12th August, I have now the honour to transmit the following information relative to the administration of the relief for the Poor in Prussia.

Throughout the whole Kingdom of Prussia the funds for the maintenance and support of The Poor are raised from private Charity. No law exists enabling either The Government of The Country, or the subordinate Provincial Regencies to raise Funds explicitly appropriated for the provision of The Poor, and it is only when private charity does not suffice for the exigencies of the moment, that The Government, or The Regency advance money for that purpose. But to enable them to do so, the amount must be taken from those funds which had been destined for other purposes, such as, for improvements in paving, lighting, or for the publick Buildings of a Town, or for the construction of roads, or other publick work.

In Prussia, each Town, and each Commune is obliged to take charge of the Poor that may happen to reside within them; and consequently there is no passing from one Parish to another, or refusal to maintain an Individual because he belongs to another Parish.

[36] Austria, Prussia, and Russia.

In each Town there is a Deputation, called 'Armendirection' or Society for the Poor, who undertake the collection and distribution of funds raised by Charity. In small Towns under 3,500 Inhabitants, exclusive of Military, this Society is composed of the Burgomaster, together with the Town Deputies, (forming the Town Senate) and Burghers chosen from the various quarters of The Town.

In large and middle sized Towns, including from 3,500 to 10,000 Inhabitants exclusive of Military, to the afore mentioned Individuals is always added The Syndic, (or Town accomptant) and if necessary another Magistrate. Clergymen and Doctors are likewise included in The society, and where the Police of the place has a separate jurisdiction from The Magistrate, the President of The Police has always a Seat as a Member of The Society.

Under this Armendirection the care of the poor is confided to different subcommittees formed of the Burghers, and for this purpose The Town is divided into Poor districts. (or Armenbezirke). In small and middle sized Towns these districts are again divided into subdistricts containing not above 1,000, or less than 400 Souls. In large Towns the subdistricts are to comprise not above 1,500, or less than 1,000 souls, and in these last Towns several subdistricts may, if requisite, be united into one Poor district or Armenbezirke. [...]

As regards the manner of obtaining the necessary funds, everything is done by donations and private charity. Each house proprietor, each inhabitant of a floor, or appartment is, in his turn visited by some of The Members of The Subcommittee of The Armenbezirke who, in return for the donation, delivers a receipt for the amount.

These donations from residents are generally monthly, and vary in amount according to the number of Individuals in the Family, or to the feelings of generosity of the donor. No rate, or calculated fixed Table exists, regulating the sum to be given by each Individual, or head of a Family.

Each Town being governed by its own particular Laws and Customs with regard to the management of its Poor, and each, from accidental circumstances differing from its neighbours, it is impossible to particularize any other general principle that is followed, than the establishments of The Armendirection, and of The Subcommittees, which detailed information, I have extracted as above from The Städte Ordnung, or Town Laws, as revised in 1831.[37]

With regard to the claims of The Poor, every person has a right to

---

[37] The aim of the town laws of 17 March 1831 was to create a uniform municipal constitution for the whole of the Prussian state. The town laws of 19 November 1808 only applied to the four old Prussian provinces – Prussia, Silesia, Brandenburg and Pommerania – but not to the provinces which joined the Prussian state in 1815 – Posen, Saxony, Westfalia and Rhineland.

claim relief from The Town or Commune in which he lives. If he is not a citizen of the place where he seeks relief, he cannot be admitted into The Hospitals or establishment set apart for those specific cases, he however obtains assistance from other funds, but his situation is not quite as comfortable as those who are admitted into The Hospitals.

Physical incapacity is the only excuse received for not working for the benefit of the charity during the period that an Individual is receiving assistance from The Armendirection.

Such are the general principles which are at present applied to the relief of The Poor throughout the Kingdom of Prussia. [...]

As regards the provision for illegitimate children, the laws of Prussia are most severe. The oath of the Mother that an Individual is the Father of her Child is sufficient to enforce the provisions of the law, which require, that a stated sum shall be paid for what is denominated the pains of labour, and which is calculated to defray the expenses entailed by the delivery, and that besides a fixed sum shall be paid monthly until the Child has arrived at a sufficient age to be able to procure its own living.

No person can be forced to marry a woman in consequence of pregnancy unless a document is produced containing a promise of marriage in distinct terms, or that such a promise has been given before witnesses; but the system above alluded of adjudging sums for the pains of labour and maintenance of the Child, is applicable to all classes, and fixed scales are established which can be enforced from the Nobles inclusive down to persons of light and disrespectful character.

FO 64/195: Earl of Minto to Viscount Palmerston, No 61, Berlin, 1 June 1834

M. Ancillon's opinion on the question of French or British interference in affairs of the German confederation; Earl of Minto's reply

I am not without hope that the representations of the British and French Governments and the opposition of some States of the Confederation may have the effect of arresting the measures to which the Diet was about to recur in Frankfort.[38]

M. Ancillon in conversing with me today upon this subject betrayed a good deal of irritation, and this, I have frequently observed, is apt to indicate a defeat.

[38] For the events in Frankfurt and the reaction of France and England cf. pp. 41–52, 66–71 in Frankfurt section.

He complained of our interference as being calculated to produce ill humour in the Diet at a moment when we required its cooperation in concluding an arrangement for Luxemburg.[39] He denied our right of intervention, and he said that the Diet certainly would not entertain any representations directed against its own acts in regard to the interests, and within the limits of the Confederation alone. This he said was the answer which Messieurs Cartwright and Alleye must be prepared to receive to any remonstrances they might have been instructed to offer; and he dwelt upon, what is a favorite topick with him in such questions, the inconsistency of our language on different occasions. At one time, he said, we exaggerated the influence of the Two Great Powers[40] over their Confederates, imploring them to employ it in the Diet, and almost holding them responsible for all the measures of that Body. At another, we represented them as aiming at the subjugation of the rest of Germany, and we appealed to the jealousy of the smaller States, whom we endeavoured to alarm into resistance. This, he said, was more especially the policy of the French Government, which sought to produce divisions favorable to its own influence in Germany – a policy, he said, which it had betrayed too plainly, and which being detected had only produced the effect of fortifying their Union.

M. Ancillon then proceeded to argue that as Parties of the Treaty of Vienna[41] we had not acquired the right to intrude upon the internal Government of other Powers. That undoubtedly we might have resisted any attempt to alter the Constitution of the Germanick Confederation. But that having established the Diet as the supreme Authority in Germany, it must be left to the free exercise of the high Powers which it possessed: That no foreign Court could be permitted to take cognizance of the proceedings of the Diet in regard of its Constituent States, unless indeed that State had alledged a grievance, and appealed for the protection to which it might be entitled. This, he said, was not the case with Frankfort, where our intervention was purely officious.

I told him, I was sure he could not seriously expect me to acquiesce in the pretensions he had put forward for the Diet. That in our eyes even the Smallest Member of the Confederation was an Independent State, that as such, we had an interest in its Independence, and a right to maintain it, which we should invariably assert and exercise, when we found it expedient to do so.

I need not trouble Your Lordship with a recapitulation of my argument on this subject of the Germanick Constitution, which is

[39] For the Luxemburg question cf. n. 42 in Frankfurt section.
[40] Austria and Prussia.
[41] Congress Act of the Congress of Vienna, 9 June 1815.

familiar to you; and in the course of which M. Ancillon was of necessity brought to modify many of the assertions with which he had started, and to plead a specialty in the case of Frankfort, as the seat of the Diet, which subjected it to peculiar obligations. He did not attempt to deny that the occupation of the Town, and the recent demands of the Diet were in strictness illegal, but he justified them by the necessity of the case, and the notorious inability of the Town to give the protection which it was bound to afford the Members of the Diet; and failing of which that Assembly was entitled to take such measures as were necessary for its safety. I observed that this really was not the true state of the case. That the town of Frankfort was both able and willing to afford the Diet all the protection that was necessary; but that having once obtained the admission of a Federal Force, they now rose in their demands, and insisted upon having the police and the troops of the Town placed under their authority.

With regard to the inconsistency with which he is fond of charging us; I said it was undoubtedly true that where we had a common object in view we not infrequently urged this Government to employ its great and acknowledged influence in the Diet; But, that this influence was a thing which existed independently of our will; and that it by no means followed, because we sought at any time to give it an useful direction, that we were friendly to its abuse, any more than it could be concluded, that in appealing to the interest of the inferior States in the maintenance of their independence, we must necessarily be prompted by sentiments of hostility towards Austria and Prussia. [...]

FO 64/196: Ralph Abercromby to Viscount Palmerston., No 1, Berlin, 2 July 1834

Conversation between M. Ancillon and M. Bresson about the questions discussed, and agreed on at the recent conferences at Vienna (surveillance of universities; Federal Court of Arbitration et. al.); doubts as to the effectiveness of the new regulations

I have the honor to transmit herewith a Memorandum of a Conversation between M. Ancillon and M. Bresson on the subject of the late proceedings of the Conferences at Vienna.[42] [...]

The regulations adopted with regard to the discipline of the

---

[42] Between January and June 1834, at Metternich's instigation, ministerial meetings took place in Vienna between the leading powers in the German Confederation. They ended on 12 June with the secret resolution of the 'Sixty Articles'.

Universities is the first point which attracts notice.[43] They no longer afford easy means of Instruction to the Youth of every Class, and of all descriptions of opinion; for the preliminary examination as to character will have the effect of permitting only one species of Student to enter these establishments. Supposing even, that the greatest latitude be given in favour of the admission of Students, it is clear, that if this regulation is to be acted up to as a measure of prevention, it must for some time to come shut the Universities to a large portion of the Young Men of Germany.

I beg also to call Your Lordship's attention to the penalty which is attached to the conviction of any Student found guilty of belonging to an Association, which precludes him for ever from obtaining any publick employment, and which, by destroying his hopes of future distinction, condemns him to lead a life of insignificance – and may deprive his Country of Talents, which under other circumstance might have been usefully employed.

The exact Provisions of the Reciprocal Convention are still wrapt up in considerable mystery, and there is an evident unwillingness on the part both of Prince Metternich and M. Ancillon to enter into any detail upon this point. The vague explanation that it contained regulations for the better Government of the various States of the Confederation, is so unsatisfactory, and the secrecy which is preserved as to the object and amount of mutual engagement is so little calculated to inspire confidence or security – that it cannot but be a matter of considerable suspicion, until the execution of its provision shall have proved its danger or its harmlessness. This much is however avowed, as your Lordship will see in the enclosed Memorandum, that this Convention forms the basis and source of the Compromissions-Gericht.[44] But a Tribunal possessing such extraordinary powers as this does, and which is in fact superiour to the Constitutions, cannot excite any very flattering opinion of a Convention, from which it is declared to derive its origin.

One great object of the Diet of Frankfort has been to establish, that the duties of the several Members of the Confederation, as parts of a Federal System, are superiour to their duties as Individuals in their respective Countries, and to deny to the Chambers in States where a Constitution exists, the right of refusing to the Sovereign all supplies, and consequently rendering him unable to fulfil his engagements as a Member of the Confederation.

---

[43] Articles 38–56 of the Sixty Articles of 12 June 1834 dealt with supervision of the universities; most of their provisions were taken over into the Federal University Law by the Federal resolution of 13 November 1834.

[44] For the Federal Court of Arbitration (Articles 3–13 of the Sixty Articles of 12 June

The establishment of the Compromissions-Gericht is calculated to carry this principle into execution and if its composition is examined, it is not difficult to foresee the power which the Sovereigns of Germany obtain by it over their Chambers. The Members are named by the Sovereigns. The Tribunal is final, and without appeal, and in case of non-compliance with the Sentence, the Diet, that is, the other Sovereigns of Germany, are called upon to execute the Judgment of the Court. But this is not the whole extent of the powers of this Tribunal – which is one superiour even to the Diet itself – for disputes arising between Princes themselves of a political tendency, and which are superiour to Common Law are to come within the Jurisdiction of this Court. This Tribunal bears a striking analogy to 'the <u>Supreme</u> <u>Court</u> of the United States of North America', which possesses nearly the same attributes, as does the Compromissions-Gericht; and it is curious that a Court, which has just been organized in the Cabinets of Prince Metternich, or of M. Ancillon (for both appear to lay claim to the merit of the invention) should bear so close a resemblance the one to the other. M. Ancillon, however, in M. Bresson's remarking to His Excellency this similarity seemed much surprized, and was evidently in ignorance of the existence of such a Court, or of its Powers. It is clear indeed that such a Tribunal can only exist in a Federative System, but, if my memory does not betray me, I think Prince Metternich observed to M. de St Aulaire, when explaining to him the merits of this Court, that he regretted it was impossible to establish similar ones in other Countries.

So many decrees and regulations have already been issued by the Diet, for the internal regulation of Germany, and for its preservation against the Contamination of Revolutionary Principles, – all of which nearly have proved ineffectual from the impossibility of fully executing them, – that it is by no means improbable that a similar fate may attend the results of the late deliberations of Vienna. Should this be found to be the case, whenever an occasion may occur requiring their application, they will become a dead letter, and be allowed to remain in abeyance, until perhaps other times and other circumstances may render their execution more easy. The fear of the extension of Revolutionary Principles. The fear also that those Principles would be attended with troubles, which might affect the present position and influence of the Members of the Confederation, has for the moment united all in one Common Cause – but as time passes on, and Tranquillity becomes more firmly established in other Countries, these

1834), officially established by the Federal law of 30 October 1834, cf. pp. 73–74 in Frankfurt section.

fears will naturally diminish, and it will then be seen how far the execution of these regulations is compatible with the Independence and Interests of the various States of the Confederation.[45]

FO 64/200: Ralph Abercromby to the Duke of Wellington, No 16, Berlin, 11 March 1835

Death of the Austrian Emperor

The melancholy intelligence of the death of His late Imperial Majesty The Emperor of Austria, has not failed to produce here a feeling of deep and sincere regret at the loss of a Sovereign distinguished by so many amiable and estimable qualities. His Prussian Majesty in particular has been deeply affected by the loss of a Contemporary with whom, during the various vicissitudes of a long political career, he had been in the habits of the closest alliance and affection and the touching proof of the confidence, and esteem which His late Imperial Majesty shewed during the last moments of His Illness, in the personal character of His Prussian Majesty, has naturally made this loss more deeply felt.

I am given to understand that the late Emperor strongly impressed upon His Successor[46] the expediency of maintaining the same line of policy which had hitherto been followed by His Government, and added that in the case of any difficulty he would be sure to derive the wisest and best counsels from His Prussian Majesty in the soundness and justness of whose opinions he had from long experience placed the greatest confidence.

His Present Imperial Majesty has since addressed a letter to His Prussian Majesty, couched in the most agreeable and satisfactory terms, and in which His Imperial Majesty, after recapitulating the advice which He had received from the late Emperor on His deathbed, states His earnest desire to continue the line traced out by His Imperial Father, and to maintain that intimate alliance with Prussia, which so closely united the two Countries.

His Prussian Majesty has transmitted an answer to this letter by His Son Prince William of Prussia who, it was expected, would reach Vienna yesterday.

The same publick testimonies of regret and respect for the death of Emperor Francis have been shewn as were testified at the decease of The Emperor Alexander. The Royal Theatres have been closed for

---

[45] Enclosure: Memorandum of Conversation between M. Ancillon and M. Bresson relative to the questions discussed, and agreed to at the late Conferences at Vienna.
[46] Ferdinand.

three nights, and a Court Mourning which has been extended by a Cabinet Order to the whole Prussian Army has been ordered for four weeks.

A rumour having prevailed at Vienna immediately after the decease of the Emperor Francis, that an intrigue was on foot to set aside the present Emperor a decided and strong expression of feeling was shewn on the part of the Publick to oppose such a measure, and it is clear that the Emperor Ferdinand enjoys to a large extent both the affections and good will of his Subjects.

FO 64/201: Ralph Abercromby to Viscount Palmerston, No 37, Berlin, 4 August 1835

Incidents triggered by birthday celebration of Prussian King; assessment of their meaning

The Celebration of His Prussian Majesty's Birthday[47] has not, I regret to say, gone off with quite as much tranquillity as had marked preceding anniversaries.

Several accidents having occurred last year in consequence of the permission which was usually granted allowing the discharge of fire arms and squibs by the populace in open space outside of the Brandenburgh Gate, the Police had determined to prevent the recurrence of similar accidents and had prohibited this year the hitherto usual discharge of fire arms. Towards the evening, however, some boys and students notwithstanding the opposition of the Police succeeded in firing off squibs and pistols and the Police whilst endeavouring to arrest some of these Individuals rode over some of the Bystanders.

This encreased the already growing disposition to disturbance and it was found necessary to call out some Squadrons of Lancers and Light Dragoons.

The Military after ineffectually attempting to disperse the mob by quiet means, and that some of the men and officers had received contusions from stones which had been thrown at them, charged upon the mass that had assembled and I regret to say that some lives have been lost and several persons wounded.

The exercising ground outside the Brandenburgh Gate having been thus cleared, the people were driven into the town, and in their progress down the Linden, the Gas Lamps and Benches were destroyed, and some of the windows of the Princess de Liegnitz and of the Commandant of the town were broken.

The Troops continued to patrol the Streets during the night, but it

---

[47] Friedrich Wilhelm III was born on 3 August 1770.

was not till towards three o'clock this morning that tranquillity was perfectly restored.

Prince Charles Solms, Son of her Royal Highness the Duchess of Cumberland, received a contusion on the forehead and in the side from a stone, but I am happy to say that the Prince whom I saw this morning, does not experience any severe effects from this accident.

I have gone into these details to counteract the exaggerated reports which no doubt will be circulated of this affair which bears not the smallest political character, but which arose entirely from the prohibition already mentioned, and from a dislike to the Police who perhaps acted somewhat hastily at the commencement.

Measures will be taken to prevent any assembly of persons this evening, and although there certainly is considerable excitement in the town; I trust that no repetition of the scenes of last night will again occur.

FO 64/204: To Lord William Russell, Foreign Office, No 9, London, 15 April 1836[48]

H.M.'s Government's formal protest against proceedings at Cracow

You are instructed to state to M. Ancillon that the British Government has witnessed with much pain and regret the events which have lately taken place within the Territory of the Free State of Cracow: and it would be an abandonment of those Principles by which the Conduct of Great Britain is guided, if His Majesty's Government were not to record its formal Protest against Proceedings which appear to be inconsistent both with the general Rules of International Law, and with the specifick Stipulations of particular Treaties.

His Majesty's Government has moreover a just right to complain that no previous communication should have been made to the British Cabinet of measures which were to be founded upon a construction of important Treaties, to which Great Britain was a Contracting Party;[49] and that Three Parties[50] to a general Treaty should have proceeded to carry into execution by force of arms their own interpretation of that

[48] The draft was also sent as No. 32 to Lord Durham in St Petersburg and as No. 9 to Edward Fox in Vienna.

[49] In Articles 6 to 10 of the Congress Act of the Congress of Vienna (9 June 1815) the Free Republic of Cracow was recognized under international law and declared to be independent and neutral.

[50] Austria, Prussia and Russia. In the Congress Act of the Congress of Vienna (9 June 1815) these three states were appointed as Cracow's protective powers.

Treaty, without previously making their intention, and the grounds of it, known to the other Contracting Parties.

His Majesty's Government heard for the first time in the month of February, that rumours were afloat of some hostile intentions on the part of the Governments of Austria, Prussia, and Russia, towards the Free State of Cracow; and Instructions were immediately sent to His Majesty's Diplomatick Agents at certain Courts in Europe to obtain information thereupon. His Majesty's Government learnt soon afterwards that a military occupation of Cracow had been resolved upon: but up to the present time no formal explanation has been given to the British Government by the Three occupying Powers, as to the causes which have led to the Proceeding, nor as to the grounds upon which it was conceived to be justifiable. His Majesty's Government, therefore, while it is impelled by a sense of duty no longer to delay expressing an opinion upon this Transaction, founds that opinion upon facts of general notoriety, and upon Documents which have been published to the World.

It appears that the Three Protecting Powers rest their Right to act as they have done on this occasion, upon the Stipulations of the Treaty of Vienna of 1815: but His Majesty's Government is of opinion that the Proceeding which has taken place, is not borne out by the Stipulations of that Treaty.

The three Residents, who represent at Cracow the Three Protecting Powers,[51] presented to the Senate of the Free State on the 9th of February last a note requiring the expulsion of a considerable number of Persons, not natives of the State, who were then living within its Territory,[52] and that expulsion not having been carried into effect by the Authorities of Cracow within the period of eight days prescribed for its execution, the Troops of the Three Powers entered the Territory and City of Cracow, in order themselves to execute the measure by force.

The demand for the expulsion of the Persons in question was grounded upon the Ninth Article of the Treaty of Vienna,[53] and the occupation was justified as a necessary means of obtaining redress for a breach of the Engagement, which that Article imposes upon the State

---

[51] Austria, Prussia and Russia were represented in Cracow by so-called residents, who represented the Republic of Cracow in foreign affairs. In 1836 these were Resident Liehmann for Austria, Otto Emil von Hartmann for Prussia, and Wilhelm Rembert Freiherr von Ungern-Sternberg for Russia.

[52] After the failure of the Polish uprising in 1831 Cracow became a place of refuge for supporters of the Polish independence movement. They had strong links with the Polish exile organisations in the rest of Europe. In 1835 they founded an 'Association of the Polish People' in Cracow.

[53] Article 9 of the Congress Act of the Congress of Vienna (9 June 1815) dealt with Cracow's right to neutrality.

of Cracow. But the Ninth Article of the Treaty of Vienna does not bear out the demand, and expressly prohibits the occupation.

The governing Stipulation of the Ninth Article of the Treaty interdicts the entrance of Foreign Troops into the State of Cracow upon any pretext whatever; and the primary object of that article was to secure the inviolability of the Free State. The second part of the article imposes reciprocal Duties upon Cracow: but it is to be remarked that the absolute plenitude of the first prohibition, is not declared, by the subsequent part of the article, to be limited to the period, during which Cracow shall fulfil the reciprocal Duties imposed upon her.

If it had been intended that Foreign Troops should be at liberty to enter for the purpose of enforcing the fulfilment of the Duties imposed upon Cracow, whenever the Three Powers might think that those Duties were not fulfilled with sufficient promptitude, or to an adequate extent, it would have been incumbent on the Parties who framed the Treaty, to have expressed in distinct words so important a modification of the positive and unqualified interdict contained in the outset of the Article. So material a restriction upon the independence and freedom of the State of Cracow, cannot be admitted as an unexpressed inference, drawn from a mere comparison of two separate Stipulations of the Treaty.

But it will be said, Cracow cannot pretend to be entitled to break her Engagement with impunity; and what then is the Penalty to which a Breach of Duty is to render her liable?

The Penalty to which such Breach of her engagement must subject her, is that which every State is liable to incur, when it violates its Treaty Engagements, the Penalty, namely, of War. If Cracow should refuse to fulfil towards any of its neighbours the Duties imposed upon it by Treaty, the neighbour so injured would have a right of war; a right to be exercised according to the usages of modern nations, and after all other means of obtaining redress had been exhausted; and as War supersedes all Treaties, the leading Stipulation of the Ninth Article of the Treaty of Vienna, would in such a case necessarily cease to have effect between Cracow and the Party aggrieved.

But had the Three Powers a right of war against Cracow, arising out of a Breach of the obligations imposed upon Cracow by the Treaty of Vienna? Undoubtedly not; for the demand made by the Three Powers was not a demand in conformity with the latter part of the Ninth Article of that Treaty. The Treaty entitles the Three Powers to demand that Runaways, Deserters, and Persons under legal prosecution shall be delivered up to the State whose Subject they are. The demand made was, that certain turbulent Foreigners, resident in Cracow, should be expelled from the State.

The obvious motive for the Stipulation of the Treaty was to prevent the Laws of Austria, Prussia, and Russia, from being evaded by their respective Subjects. The motive put forward by the Three Residents in their Notes was, that the Laws of the State of Cracow might be better enforced. The Residents allege that a murder had been committed, and the assassin had not been discovered.[54] That the windows of a House had been broken, and the offenders had not been detected or punished: that the Executive and judicial authorities of Cracow were, therefore, unable to perform their respective Duties to their own State: and that, consequently, the interference of the Protecting Powers had become necessary. The British Government must observe upon this, not only that the demand made, was not the demand of the Treaty, and that, consequently, a refusal to comply with it, was no violation of the Treaty; but, moreover, that the reasons alleged as the ground for that demand, strike at the very root of the Principles upon which rests the independence of Nations. Because, if it were admitted that the Troops of one Power are entitled, in time of Peace, forcibly to enter the Territory of another State, in order to execute more promptly the Criminal Law, or to carry more vigorously into effect the Police Regulations of that State, it is manifest that no State would be entitled to be called really independent, whose military means were not sufficiently great to protect its Territory from violation by its neighbours.

It is demonstrable then that the State of Cracow has not been called upon to execute the obligations imposed upon it by the Ninth Article of the Treaty of Vienna; and that the measures of violence which the Three Powers have had recourse to, cannot be justified by a reference to that Treaty.

But His Majesty's Government must be allowed to say that even if the demand authorized by the Treaty had been made, and had been refused, the Three Powers would have shewn more respect for the other Parties to that Treaty, for their own engagements, and for international usages, if, before resorting to force of arms in order to obtain redress, they had exhausted those means of remonstrance and persuasion, which are commonly employed to settle disputes without a recourse to War, when differences arise between Parties whose relative strength is less unequal.

But if the Ninth Article of the Treaty of Vienna, which has been formally appealed to by the Three Powers, is insufficient to justify their Proceeding, is there any other ground upon which that Proceeding can be maintained?

It has been asserted by various organs of the Three Protecting Powers, that the true cause of their Proceedings against Cracow was,

---

[54] The pretext for the occupation of Cracow was provided by the murder of a Russian agent by members of the radical Polish independence movement.

that a number of Refugees from the Kingdom of Poland had established themselves within the Territory of the Free State, in order to carry on from thence secret communications with the Kingdom of Poland, and with the Polish Provinces of the Three Powers, for the purpose of exciting disturbances and insurrections in those Quarters.

If such be the fact, the question naturally arises, why that fact was not distinctly alleged in the formal communications made by the Three Residents to the Senate of Cracow?

But His Majesty's Government will, for the sake of argument, assume the assertion to be well founded, and state their opinion upon that assumption.

The Right of giving refuge to Persons flying from their own Country for political Reasons, the Right, in short, of Hospitality, is undoubtedly, an inherent attribute of national Independence. But that Right, like many other Rights, should be exercised with a due regard to the duties of neighbourhood, and to the safety of friendly States: And between States, which are neighbours and Friends, or which are connected together by intimate Ties, it would afford just cause of complaint, if the shelter, which is granted by the one, as a Refuge to misfortune and exile, should be converted into a vantage ground for planning with impunity attacks against the safety of the other.

A State, whose Territory is large, may often, by a judicious arrange-ment as to the Residence of its guests, prevent such complaints, without withholding its hospitality. A small State may sometimes be unable to reconcile the continuance of its hospitality, with the fulfilment of its Duties as a neighbour; and, in such a case, the latter consideration ought undoubtedly to outweigh the former.

This may have been the case with Cracow. The British Government is not possessed of information sufficient to enable it either to affirm or to deny that proposition. But, if such was the case, and if, among the Refugees at Cracow, there were men who availed themselves of its sanctuary in order to organize from thence projected disturbances in adjoining Countries, it appears to His Majesty's Government that the demand for expulsion ought to have been limited to such Persons only; and should have been accompanied by a distinct statement of the real reasons for which the expulsion was required. Ample time should have been given to the Senate to have complied with the demand; and the course of proceeding need not have been so sweeping, so precipitate, and so violent. His Majesty's Government have also been informed that the Senate of Cracow had, during the last year, applied to the Austrian Government for Passports for a certain number of Persons, whose presence had become embarrassing to the State; but that such Passports were not granted. If that information is correct, it does not seem very consistent with justice to urge as a Plea for violating the

Territory of Cracow, the Presence within that Territory of Persons, whom the Parties by whom that Plea is put forward, had themselves prevented from previously quitting the State.

You are further instructed to say that His Majesty's Government looks forward with confidence to the early evacuation of the City and Territory of the Free State of Cracow, in conformity with the assurances which have been given to Your Lordship, and to His Majesty's Ambassador at St Petersburgh:[55] and You will also remark that the independence of Cracow rests upon the same Treaties of Vienna, by virtue of which many of the Powers of Europe hold parts of the Territories which they possess.

Your Lordship is instructed to read this Despatch to M. Ancillon, and to give him a copy of it.

FO 64/205: William Russell to Viscount Palmerston, No 70, Berlin, [no date] June 1836

On two published papers relating to the present state and future policy of Prussia; antipathy of Prussian population to a closer Prussian–Russian alliance; question of how Prussia could become Germany's leading power; expectations of the Crown Prince

Two Papers have been published in the Portfolio relating to the present State and future Policy of Prussia. One of them is an official State Paper written by the late Count Bernstorff [56] by the King's desire – the other is a semi-official Paper written ten years ago by one of the Members of the Prussian Mission at Frankfort.[57] The first treats on the means of securing tranquillity to Germany in the event of foreign War. The second on the means of extending the influence of Prussia over Germany.

As some time has elapsed since these Papers were written, it may be of importance to His Majesty's Government to know how far the opinions put forward have been acted upon, and what has been the result; for it is now as necessary to watch the feelings and will of the People as the prejudices and predilections of Courts and Governments: the former acting as a check upon the latter in all cases which affect the general state and well-being of the Nation. This I can illustrate by affirming that the Prussian People have so great an antipathy to a

---

[55] John George Lambton, Earl of Durham.

[56] Christian Günther Graf von Bernstorff.

[57] Bernstorff's memorandum is dated 29 January 1831. It looks at how, in the case of a European war, Germany could maintain its internal peace, and at what measures Prussia should take to prevent internal unrest in neighbouring states from spreading. The author of the second paper could not be ascertained.

closer Russian Alliance, that in the event of War, it would not be in
the power of the Prussian Government to carry the Nation to act
aggressively in concert with Russia – consequently, any threats on the
part of the Prussian Government to unite their forces to those of Russia
may be regarded as phrases devoid of sense.

Count Bernstorff commences his Memoir by acknowledging the
danger of the encreasing discontent of the German People, and shews
the necessity of combating this evil, which he states is to be done by
pursuing a system conformable to the general good, so as to conciliate
the enlightened and possessing, and give them an interest to rally round
their Sovereign in time of domestick danger or foreign War. He advises
that the German Princes should not show any mistrust of their own
Subjects – that they should endeavour to encrease and rely on their
moral power, which should be strengthened by the application of legal
means, that the Press should be brought to contribute to the maintenance of right and order, by placing it under the direction of writers
of talents and good opinions, that an uniform system of commerce
should be adopted, and that a general fusion of institutions should take
place throughout Germany.

The second Memoir not being an acknowledged State paper, I will
only allude to it to point out that it discusses at length that which
Count Bernstorff only hints at, which is the means of extending the
Power of Prussia over Germany, in fact of obtaining the ascendancy
formerly in the hands of Austria, which has been declining since the
Treaty of Vienna,[58] and now depends solely upon the influence of
Tradition.

Prussia in order to make herself the directing Power of Germany
must guide and govern publick opinions, and manage the machinery
of the Commercial Union; by attention to these two objects she may
in time become the Arbiter of the Confederation, dispose of the force
of Germany in War, and model her institutions in Peace. But at this
moment Prussia is far from exercising such an ascendancy. The
formation of the Commercial League has certainly added, though not
in a great degree, to her Political Power; her real power is to be gained
by adopting, exercising, and extending the means suggested by Count
Bernstorff; and these I should say the Prussian Government had
essentially neglected. The consequence is, that the small Constitutional
States so far from looking to Prussia as an Example and Support,
endeavour to take the lead in their progress towards improvement, and
regard the close Alliance of Prussia with Russia, as putting her in the
light of an enemy they should be on their guard against, rather than a
friend on whom they could rely in the hour of need. Besides, the

[58] Congress Act of the Congress of Vienna (9 June 1815).

Prussian Government after having given such development to the energies of the people appears to be frightened at its own work, and to wish to restrain those energies from acting upon the Political State of the Country; instead of following the line chalked out by Count Bernstorff, and leading publick opinion by the Press, and other legitimate means. The Prussian Press is only allowed to be a Register of facts, and the most enlightened Nation in Europe is not permitted to read the English Morning Chronicle. This erroneous system, however, whilst it prevents Prussia from having that moral and political ascendancy in Germany to which her Geographical position, as well as her Military strength, and free institutions entitle her to aspire, does not prevent her from being a tranquil, contented and powerful Nation. Tranquil and contented from the perfect justice that directs the actions of the King and Government – powerful, from the admirable organization of her immense Army. No Nation is in a better state to repel aggression than Prussia, and none, I should say at the same time, was less disposed or less fit to act aggressively.

The Prussians do not appear to me to wish to possess a political Constitution. They see the difficulty of finding proper men to represent the Towns and Provinces. The impossibility of uniting Pomerania and the Rhine in one common interest,[59] and they prefer the present system of local Government; but many wish for change in the details, or that greater encouragement should be given to one class than another. This is a source of uneasiness to those who have now got possession of place and power – this class, called by the French, – Bureaucratie –, that is, the Subalterns of public Offices are so numerous and well-organized, that their influence is felt in every department of the State, and it is believed that the Crown Prince,[60] when on the Throne, intends to destroy the power of this Class, and bring forward in their place the large-landed Proprietors.

If this is done slowly and discreetly, the progress will be safe, and the ultimate effects beneficial to the Country; but should an attempt be made to wrest the power from this Class hastily and violently, the effort might be followed by National Convulsion.

I have not however any distrust of the wisdom of the Crown Prince – from what I have seen and heard of His Royal Highness, I should think that his Character had been much misrepresented in Europe, and that certain violent or petulant speeches had given rise to the belief that his opinions were exaggerated, and his temper difficult of self-

[59] The province of Pommerania in the east of the kingdom was characterized by agriculture and feudal structures, the Rhine province by trade and an aspiring economic bourgeoisie.

[60] Friedrich Wilhelm IV.

controul. I should say that the Crown Prince was totally free from prejudice that he took a calm and enlightened view of the interests of his Country, and that when he succeeds to the Throne of Prussia, Europe will remain as secure from war, and Prussia as tranquil and contented as under the just and benignant sway of his present Majesty.

The immediate relations between England and Prussia are on a more satisfactory footing than they were. There remains still on the part of the Court and of some of the Ministers, especially Mr. Ancillon, a strong prejudice against the political opinions and conduct of Your Lordship, and Your Colleagues, which appears to me to be more founded in the erroneous view they take of that conduct, than in any sound opinions of their own.[61]

This prejudice however is by no means shared by the mass of the Nation, who look with admiration on the calm yet decided efforts of His Majesty's Government to reform and eradicate the abuses that threatened and undermined the power of the British Empire.

FO 64/206: William Russell to Viscount Palmerston, No 80, Berlin, 26 October 1836

Ordinance prohibiting Jews from adopting Christian names

Considerable sensation having been occasioned amongst the Jews in Prussia by a late Ordinance prohibiting them from adopting Christian Names, and directing that in all official Reports they should be designated only by the appellation of 'Jews', a Jewish Merchant[62] of Berlin addressed a Petition to The King of Prussia praying His Majesty to remove by some gracious expressions on His Majesty's Part the stigma which appeared to have been attached to the Members of the Jewish Persuasion.

His Prussian Majesty returned to this request the answer of which I have the honor to enclose a translation from which Your Lordship will perceive that His Majesty denies having had any intention of putting a slight upon the Jews and declares his determination to uphold the legal rights which they at present enjoy.

The Jews of Berlin have requested to be furnished with a list of the names which they are prohibited to assume, but the Government

[61] Cf. Palmerston's intervention in the occupation of Cracow by Prussia, Austria and Russia, pp. 140–145 in this section.
[62] Joel Wolff Meyer.

experiences some embarrassment in specifying them. [...][63]

FO 64/204: To William Russell, Foreign Office, No 47, London, 15 November 1836 (Draft)[64]

Occupation of Cracow; British and Prussian cabinets pursuing different political lines

I have received Your Lordship's despatch N° 81, giving and account of a conversation which you lately had with M. Ancillon, and requesting to be instructed as to what Your Lordship should say to M. Ancillon in reply, if His Excellency should again revert to the subject[65] of which he then spoke. Your Lordship states that in the course of the conversation in question, M. Ancillon said that he regretted that there was so little of confidential intercourse between the Governments of Great Britain and Prussia: that our respective Sovereigns entertain for each other the warmest affection and the firmest esteem: that there exists between the two Nations reciprocal sympathy and respect: but that the two Governments appear as much estranged from each other, as if they were severally engaged in the pursuit of opposite interests: that Baron Bülow has not been treated with confidence in England: and that His Majesty's Government has never communicated to the Cabinet of Berlin the principles of policy which have guided the conduct of Great Britain with regard to Affairs either in the West or in the East of Europe.

With reference to these remarks, I have to instruct Your Lordship to take an early opportunity of stating to M. Ancillon that you have reported to His Majesty's Government the observations thus made to you by him; and that you are requested to say in reply that the circumstances adverted to by M. Ancillon have occasioned as much regret to the Cabinet of London, as they can have done to that of Berlin.

It is undoubtedly true, and well known to all Europe, that no Two Sovereigns ever felt more real regard and deeply-rooted esteem for each other, than do The King, our Master, and His Majesty The King of Prussia.

It is also certain that the British and Prussian people have many social and political sentiments in common; and that on many of the

[63] Enclosure: Translation of a Cabinet Order addressed by His Prussian Majesty to Joel Wolff Meyer, merchant of Berlin (of the Jewish Persuasion) in answer to his petition of 22 September 1836.

[64] Original in FO 244/50.

[65] In his conversation with Russell at the end of October 1836 Ancillon discussed the foreign political situation in Europe in the light of the occupation of Cracow.

great questions of European Policy of the present day, the real interests of the two Countries are one and the same. On the other hand, it is, unfortunately, undeniable that of late there has existed much estrangement between the Governments of the two Countries; the principal cause of which unquestionably has been, that the two Governments have been severally engaged in the pursuit of objects lying in opposite directions. It has, in fact, so happened that upon some leading principles of policy, and upon many practical questions, the opinions and feelings of the Prussian Government have been entirely different from those of the Government of Great Britain.[66] [...]

Under such circumstances what inducement could the British Government feel, to make confidential communications to that of Prussia, upon matters on which the two Governments were known to each other to have taken such opposite lines? To what useful result could such communicating have led? On the one hand, His Majesty's Government could entertain no hope of altering the views of Prussia, who appears, for reasons which no doubt She deems valid, to have determined for the present to conform her policy to that of her immediate neighbours: and, on the other hand, the British Government has so fully considered the grounds of its own system, that there could not be the remotest chance that its opinions could be shaken by any communications which it could receive from Prussia.

The only effect there of attempting to communicate, would have been to give occasion to irritating disputation: and that such would have been the consequence, experience seems sufficiently to prove; for it must be confessed that the tone adopted of late by the Prussian Government in its communications upon other subjects, on which it has been addressed by the British Cabinet, has been far from calculated to inspire confidence, or to create good-will.

If then there has been of late a temporary estrangement between the two Governments, the causes of such estrangement are to be found in the nature of things, and in the conduct of the Prussian Government itself.

But M. Ancillon is mistaken, if he supposes that Baron Bülow has not been treated in this Country, with all possible respect and confidence, both in his individual capacity, and as Prussian Minister.

Baron Bülow has constantly been honoured with the most marked proofs of favour and esteem by The King, our Master; and has deservedly enjoyed the confidence and respect of all His Majesty's

---

[66] Points of difference were *inter alia* the question of the Spanish succession, in which Prussia, along with Austria and Russia, had taken sides with Don Carlos. Given the conflicts between Britain and Russia over policy in the Orient, Britain regarded Prussia's close link to Russia in foreign policy with great mistrust.

Ministers. But for some time past the same reasons which I have adverted to, as accounting for the suspension of confidential intercourse between the two Cabinets, have also by necessity limited the communications between His Majesty's Government and the Prussian Minister at this Court. It was naturally to be presumed for some time past, that Baron Bülow had no instructions from his Government to communicate with me, because he came but very rarely to the Foreign Office; and inferring from thence that the Prussian Government wished to keep aloof from that of Great Britain, I, of course, abstained from pressing upon its Minister here communications which were not sought.

There is indeed, as Your Lordship justly remarks, one great object of general policy, which both Great Britain and Prussia constantly keep in view, with equal solicitude, and with a similar determination to employ all their influence and to use all their exertions to attain it: and that is the maintenance of the Peace of the World. His Majesty's Government entertains a firm conviction that whatever particular differences may exist between the two Governments, Prussia will always be found staunch and ready to co-operate with Great Britain for this most important purpose: and that conviction very much diminishes the pain which His Majesty's Government would otherwise feel at finding itself for the present so much separated from a former Ally.

Your Lordship is, however, instructed to assure M. Ancillon that the ancient feelings of friendship towards Prussia, which have for so many years existed on the part of the British Government, are neither extinct nor weakened: and that His Majesty's Government will hail with the sincerest satisfaction the arrival of the day, when the policy of Prussia shall again be such as to lead to confidence and concert between the Cabinets of Berlin and of London.

FO 64/206: William Russell to Viscount Palmerston, No 109, Berlin, 28 December 1836

Short sketch of policy which Russell thinks should govern how Great Britain and Prussia should behave towards one another; cooperation needed to preserve peace in Europe

With reference to Your Lordship's Despatch No. 47 and to the conversations I have had with Monsieur Ancillon relative to the divergence of political lines pursued by the Cabinets of Great Britain and Prussia, I now submit to the consideration of His Majesty's Government my ideas of the system that Great Britain should require[67] Prussia to act upon in order to prevent a total separation of interests and an

---

[67] In margin in pencil 'strong'.

extinguishment of all sympathy between the two Nations.

British Statesmen appear at all times to have courted an Alliance with Prussia – from the moment the House of Brandenbourg[68] began to take part in the political affairs of Europe to the present time a friendship scarcely ever interrupted has united Prussia to Great Britain – their warriors and their Diplomatists have acted in concert in foreign fields and General Congresses. Maria Theresa exclaimed against the manifest partiality of England towards Prussia when she was required to cede Silesia,[69] and the King of Saxony felt the influence of the same partiality when half of his Dominions were exacted from Him[70] – in short the course of History for one Hundred and Fifty years marks the intimate relations existing between Great Britain and Prussia.

In spite however of the antecedents of history, of present interests and of future contingencies – Prussia has abandoned the line of policy chalked out by Her Greatest Monarch and Her ablest Statesmen. Her distrust of the British Cabinet has been made ostensible – her official language has been rude, almost insulting, her State Press has been filled with Articles offensive to His Majesty's Government and efforts are made to keep the Prussian Public in ignorance of the real state of England by forbidding the circulation of The Morning Chronicle and other liberal Papers. This hostile or at least distrustful attitude demands I think on the part of Great Britain an explanation with a view to return to a friendly and confidential intercourse based upon common interests and common objects – the basis appears to be this. The policy pursued by Great Britain with regard to the Continent is manifest. It consists simply and purely in maintaining the Balance of Power, with a view to the conservation of Peace – this principle requires that the integrity and the Power of Prussia should be upheld – Her Position is one of peril. She undertook to guard the Rhine. She has lost the iron barrier of Belgium.[71] She undertook to guard the Vistula. The Troops of Russia are in possession of, and are congregating in Warsaw – Poland has been effaced from the Map of Europe.[72] The volatile spirit

[68] The House of Brandenburg's rise to become a European power occurred under the reign of Prince Elector Friedrich Wilhelm. Friedrich II took Prussia into the realm of the European great powers.

[69] The Peace of Dresden of 1745, which confirmed Prussia's possession of Silesia, conquered in 1740–1745, was guaranteed by England.

[70] It was only under pressure from England, France and Austria that the Saxon King Friedrich August I agreed to the division of Saxony at the Congress of Vienna in 1815. Prussia allocated the territories thus acquired to the newly created province of Saxony.

[71] In 1830 the Belgian revolution led to Belgium's independence from Holland; cf. n. 21 in Frankfurt section.

[72] At the Congress of Vienna in 1815 the Duchy of Warsaw, reduced in size by the removal of Posen (subsequently Prussian province) and the Free Republic of Cracow, was unified with Russia in a personal union as the Kingdom of Poland. The river Vistula

of the French and the insatiable ambition of Russia make these dangers imminent – the crises arriving, where is Prussia to look for help? not to Austria. She can scarcely keep her own acquisitions in Italy[73] – not to the States of Germany – this jealousy of Prussia is too great to make their cooperation cordial – possibly she relies on her means of playing off France against Russia and acting with one or the other as her interests may require – but should Russia and France unite (the case is not impossible) Prussia is lost should she not be prepared for this contingency by living in harmony with Great Britain – besides this, her interest finds an immediate object of gratification in the English Markets, – where the natural productions of Prussia are sold whilst they are excluded from the markets of her surrounding neighbours. Great Britain and Prussia are cooperating to preserve the Peace of Europe – they have this great object in common – they have many interests in common they have none that clash. Yet distrust and suspicion are leading us to act on diverging lines would it not then be right on the part of the British Government to come to a frank and friendly explanation with the Prussian Cabinet before this system leads to the brink of a rupture?

No apparent cause exists that ought to subject His Majesty's Government to the cold and unfriendly tone of Prussia – for it would be unworthy of the Prussian Cabinet to object to the internal Reforms carried on in England when she herself with a boldness that never before was adopted and has never since been imitated by any other Nation set the example of reforming her whole social organization, and is now reaping the fruits of her Courage and her Wisdom in the happiness – contentment and prosperity of the Prussian People.

The Monarch whose Ancestors placed themselves at the head of religious reform, and who has placed himself at the head of political Reform cannot feel prejudice against Reformers, nor would it become the Prussian Cabinet to give the preference to a political party in England which neither enjoys the confidence of His Majesty or His Subjects to that which is in full possession of the confidence of both.

This coldness towards us on the part of Prussia is against nature, against her interest, and can only be attributed to causes unworthy to regulate the policy of Great Nations, and must take its rise from some misunderstanding. Is it not therefore advisable before the crisis that threatens Europe arrives to let the Prussian Cabinet know the views that guide the conduct of His Majesty's Government and to call for friendly and explicit language when we are denied unity of action?

thus fell under Russian control. After the failure of the Polish uprising in Warsaw in the autumn of 1831 Russia intensified its anti-Polish policy.

[73] Cf. n. 43 in Frankfurt section.

Prussia's Alliance with Russia need not call for this cold bearing towards Great Britain. She can disclaim the smallest feeling of jealousy at the demonstrations of intimacy displayed between the Royal and Imperial Courts. She demands the same candour for herself when she displays her intimacy with France.

Great Britain knows that Frederick the 2nd the founder of the Power and Policy of Prussia – called Russia who had not then passed the Duna and the Dnieper, 'the most dangerous neigbour of Prussia because she was near and it was impossible to render her evil for evil' – Great Britain knows that the hostile policy of Catherine the 2nd is still remembered at Berlin, and that the opinion of Frederick the 2nd and the conduct of Catherine must still be the great landmarks to guide the march of Prussian Statesmen.[74] Being so assured She understands and appreciates the policy of the Court of Berlin tending to neutralize by an alliance a neighbour formidable from geographical position and principles of Government and to moderate by her salutary influence the ambition of the Czar. Nor does England require that Prussia should separate herself from the Imperial Courts or make any ostensible demonstrations of a closer intimacy with herself, but she does require that confidence not demonstrative but sincere and cordial should be resumed, and that communications imparted by His Majesty's accredited minister at the Court of Berlin should be received with the Courtesy the respect and consideration that is due to the opinion of the Council of a friendly Nation. [...]

This is a short, yet general sketch of the Policy which I think ought to guide the bearing of Great Britain and Prussia with regard to each other. Should Your Lordship approve of the view I have taken, I will place it before M. Ancillon, and seriously call his attention to the conduct of Prussia towards England during the last six years – telling him at the same time that our patience is exhausted[75] – that none of the acts of His Majesty's Government entitle them to the suspicion, malevolence and irritating language of the Prussian Cabinet[76] – that we hold out once more the hand of Peace and propose oblivion of the past – that we point out fairly and frankly to Prussia the grounds on which our friendship is to be secured – that we ask no sacrifice on her part – no breaking directly or indirectly with present Allies – no organic change of policy – but simply that the basis of her system should be that which was laid down for her by the founder of her greatness[77] –

---

[74] Despite Russia's withdrawal from the anti-Prussian alliance in the Seven Years' War (1756–1763), when Catherine II came to the throne in 1762 she opposed further expansion by Prussia and the long-term occupation of Saxony by Prussia.

[75] In margin: 'strong'.

[76] In margin: 'unfriendly, too strong'.

[77] Friedrich II.

and was acted upon by Herzberg one of the wisest of her Ministers, which secured to her formerly the friendship of England and upon the presumed existence of which England still founds her Alliance. But if Prussia continues to thwart the views of England in the East and in the West of Europe, to proclaim loudly her disapprobation of our proceedings, to stigmatize His Majesty's Government as impracticable and revolutionary, to use in its official communications offensive language – then it will become His Majesty's Government to use the same coldness towards the Prussian Cabinet, to participate nothing, and to wrap itself up in the reserve and dignity that is imposed upon it by the unfriendly feeling of Prussia. The responsibility must fall exclusively upon Prussia.

FO 64/210: William Russell to Viscount Palmerston, No 19, Berlin, 31 January 1837

Opening of Prussian provincial Diets; their principles and general character

The Prussian Provincial States of Brandenburg, Pommerania, Posen, Saxony and Silesia were opened on the 29th instant, and those of Prussia and Westphalia are convoked for the 19th of February. The Provincial Rhenish States will meet in the month of May according to their wish previously expressed to The King. Various projects of Laws chiefly affecting the local interests of the Provinces were to be submitted to the States already opened – those which appear most remarkable and are proposed to be extended to the greater part of the Monarchy, are Laws for the abolition and Commutation of compelled services and feudal rights, as well as general Road Regulations. His Prussian Majesty who has the right of naming the Presidents of the Provincial Assemblies has in most instances appointed the Governors of the respective Provinces to that Office.

The Provincial States were instituted, as Your Lordship is aware, in the year 1823.[78] Property is the principle of the Representation which they establish. The States are composed in the Provinces of Brandenburgh, Prussia, Pommerania and Posen of 3 Estates, namely 1st Estate – The Chapters, Nobles and Orders of Knighthood. 2nd Estate – The Deputies of the Towns – 3rd Estate – The remaining Proprietors, Freeholders and Peasants. In Silesia, Saxony and Westphalia and the Rhenish Provinces the States are divided into 4 Estates, but the difference only arises from the classification of the Nobles into two Estates. In the several Provinces the qualifications of the Deputies with

[78] Law of 5 June 1823; cf. vol. I, p. 200.

regard to the amount of property required, as well as their numbers which vary between 48 and 95, have been respectively fixed by the Government. The Deputies are chosen for 6 years in such manner that half are renewed every three Years. Property is likewise the basis of the elective franchise in the Towns and in the Country.

The duties of the States are to examine and report upon the projects of Laws severally submitted to them – they are likewise empowered to draw up Petitions and complaints relating to the separate interests of their Provinces. The result of the deliberations of each of the States is conveyed through the Royal Commissioners to the Government which is at liberty to reject or adopt its proposals.

The convocation of the Provincial States takes place every two Years.

FO 64/210: William Russell to Viscount Palmerston, No 20, Berlin, 31 January 1837

Some information on the internal administration of justice in Prussia

The secrecy that covers all Proceedings relating to the internal Administration of Justice in Prussia makes it scarcely possible to learn what number of Criminals are brought before the Courts, of what offences they are accused, or to what punishments they are condemned. Not only the Prussians are unwilling to speak on this subject, but my own Colleagues profess to be in complete ignorance of the Proceedings in the Courts of Criminal Judicature. It is however a fact that twenty two Persons out of 140 confined in the Prisons of Berlin for political offences have been lately condemned to death on the charge of High Treason.

The King has confirmed the sentence but changed it into imprisonment for life. The remainder have been condemned to shorter intervals of confinement and to exclusion from public employment for ever. – Some of the persons condemned to death, as well as of those still remaining in confinement, were, I am given to understand, implicated in the Frankfort disturbances and were delivered up to the Prussian Government.

If the common belief is true that the filling of the State Prisons is the precursor of a political crisis, it ill becomes the Prussian Government to proclaim Great Britain on the brink of a Revolution[79] in whose Prisons not a single person is confined for crimes against the State, whilst those of Prussia are so full.

[79] This assessment is based on the intensifying social crisis in England that was accompanied by mass protests against living and working conditions, falling wages and the Poor Law of 1834.

I am told that the Prince Royal has expressed his disapprobation of the severity of the sentence, most of the Prisoners being very young, but fear appears to have blinded the Counsellors of The King whose duty it was to have advised His Majesty to confirm or mitigate the judgement of the Court.

The enclosed Extract from the State Gazette is the only notice given to the Prussian Public of the number of Persons committed to Prison – the offences are not classed.[80]

FO 64/210: William Russell to Viscount Palmerston, No 36, Berlin, 15 March 1837

Public opinion in Prussia; difficult to assess

Whilst our duty confines us to have relations solely with constituted Governments, it behoves us at the same time to observe the tendency of publick opinion, so as to learn whether the Acts of Government satisfy the Nation, and what may be expected should a divergency take place; indeed to omit altogether to observe the workings of publick opinion (the lever that now moves the States of Europe) would be to run the risk of falling into difficulties and error. At the same time it is not easy for a Foreigner and a Diplomatist to arrive at any certain knowledge of publick opinion in a Country like Prussia, where the Press is shackled and perverted,[81] and where he himself is condemned to live in an artificial society, and excluded from mixing with those who express their thoughts cautiously, yet with sincerity and openness.

I have had however a Conversation with one of the liberal Party,[82] the heads of which I will place before Your Lordship.

I told him that I was struck by the indifference, I might say, apathy of the Prussians at a moment when the Great States of Western Europe were full of commotion, threatening a change that must be felt even in Prussia. That I was surprized the Prussian Government, instead of remaining apparently indifferent to, or ignorant of, what was passing on her very frontier, had not sought to place herself at the head of publick opinion, so as to govern and controul it, and by that means to direct the whole energies of Germany to ward off or crush the impending danger, but to which, from want of foresight and preparation they might be forced to succumb.

---

[80] Enclosure: Translation from the Prussian State Gazette, Berlin, January 28, 1837.
[81] For censorship of the press, cf. pp. 199–200 in this section.
[82] Not traceable.

He replied, do not allow yourself to be deceived by the apparent Tranquillity of this Country. It is true our Government sleeps, but there burns an underground fire, which will one day burst forth, and carry with it the spirit that roused Germany from its lethargy and shame in 1813.[83]

We are prepared, he said, for events, but at the same time we shall not provoke them. When they come, and come they must, we shall endeavour to master them, and to force our Government to take that lead in German affairs, which either from fear or ignorance they have abandoned, and left at the disposal of any Minor Sovereign who may wish to play the part, that ambition or patriotism may point out. He know, he said, our own Power – we made use of it in 1813 – it has lain dormant ever since: but its force is not diminished, we should use it however with moderation, and I hope with disinterestedness. We desire no great changes – we should not even ask for a Constitution, thinking the elements of its formation too discordant to lead to freedom or happiness. But we should ask for certain concessions necessary to develop, cement, and preserve the Institutions we possess.

I asked him if they were connected with the Liberals of France, or if the French Government sought to make use of them through the means of their Minister at this Court. He said – no. We have no confidence in the French Liberals, nor in their Government; perhaps M. Bresson might have exercised an influence over us had he opened his house to us, and collected us around him, but he has avoided us, and united himself entirely to the Court. We rejoice at it, because we prefer remaining purely German. England, he continued, need not take umbrage at our views. We are enemies of the Ambition of Russia,[84] of the Immorality of France, and naturally attached to England, to whose Alliance we are drawn by our sympathies, as well as by our interest. The elements of disorder he said, do not exist in our Party. We love our reigning Dynasty, our Institutions, and our Laws; but we wish to give our Sovereign that legitimate, moral, and political preponderance over Germany to which he is entitled, and we wish to give our Laws and Institutions the vigour and virtue that belong to them, whilst at the same time we wish to see our Government emancipated from its subserviency to Russia and Austria, and our Country take the station, and play the part amongst Free States to

[83] In 1813/1814 the so-called war of liberation against Napoleon's occupation of Germany led to a national movement and the political mobilization of the public.

[84] After the collapse of the Ottoman Empire, Russia sought to exploit its powerful position in the East. The aim of Russian policy in the Orient was, *inter alia*, unimpeded passage for its trading ships through the Turkish Straits to the Black Sea. From the 1830s onwards Russia had an additional interest in the religious sites in Palestine.

which it is called by its Geographical position, its Military means, and the intelligence of its Inhabitants.

FO 64/210: William Russell to Viscount Palmerston, Separate, Berlin, 12 April 1837

Outline of the course of study required for admission into the Prussian diplomatic service

I. Three years study at a Prussian University, or at a German University recognized as such by Prussia – During this period attendance at the following Lectures is required

    a) General Philosophy – Logic –
    b) Juridical Roman Law in particular, History of Law – Institutions – Pandects – Proceedings in Civil Law – Criminal Law – Prussian Provincial Law – Canonical-Law – History of the same
    c) Municipal Financial Administration, National Economy, Statisticks

After these three years follows the first Examination – namely

II. Juridical – but only verbal – Roman and Church Law in particular – together with Prussian Provincial Law, and Police.

After this Examination one year's practice at the Administration of Justice either in Berlin or elsewhere, where the Student is employed as a Referendacy – From this he passes to the Regency, and then follows the second examination, in writing and verbally.

    a) in writing, Generally three Themes
    1st a juridical exposition, 2nd a Financial composition – and a purely administrative statement.
    b) verbally – Law of State & Subjects – Financial Administration – National Economy – Practical Legislation very minute – History and Geography – especially Statisticks.

At the Regency the Student remains at least one year, and is employed as a Referendacy in the various Departments of the same, in order to give him thorough knowledge of Prussian Administration.

IV. At last comes the third – & final Examination – the Diplomatick in writing, & verbal

    a) in writing – 4 Themes a) on the Law of Nations – as for example on the position of the German Standes-Herren in reference to the States of the Confederation – b) political – f.ex: on the origin of Royal Succession – c) on political & financial Science – f.e. the original forms of the Principle of possession stating its advantages or disadvantages in reference to the wealth of Nations − or on the admissibility and possibility of reducing the interest of the National Debt − d) Historical in French − f.e. exposition of the principal causes of the political greatness of the Low Countries during the XVIIth century.

b) verbally− History of State & Jurisprudence very much in detail − the most remarkable Treaties of Peace − also history & Genealogy of the Reigning Families − Canonical Law; & relations of States with the Holy See − Law of Subjects − Law of the German Confederation − Statisticks − Financial Gov^t, & National Economy − Part of the verbal Examination is in French.

FO 64/210: William Russell to Viscount Palmerston, No 58, Berlin, 3 May 1837

On the Prussian 'Camarilla' ministry

Since the retirement of General Witzleben (who had great influence with the King of Prussia), and the death of Monsr Ancillon the power of the Prussian Cabinet has fallen into the hands of what may be called a Camarilla, the heads of which are Prince Wittgenstein and Count Lottum. The violent, or what may be designated by being called the Ultra Tory Party, at the head of which is Duke Charles of Mecklenburgh, have failed in all their efforts to bring their friends into power. This party was so hostile to the Reigning Dynasty in France that their defeat is most grateful to the French Minister.[85] General Witzleben represented the last of the Hardenberg School[86] − feebly however and not without having incurred the censure of his Country for having contributed to the subjugation of Poland without requiring any conditions from Russia.

It is difficult to give any political color to the Camarilla Ministry − they consist of old men who have seen the dangers and vicissitudes of war, and know the uncertainty of political controversy, consequently wish to satisfy all parties by conciliation and thus preserve the Peace of Europe: by this system they obtain a strong hold on the confidence of the King who delights in being regarded as representing the Pivot

[85] Charles Joseph, comte de Bresson

[86] Karl August Freiherr von Hardenberg (Minister-President 1810–1822) represented the social and political reforms in Prussia between 1810 and 1820. However, his plans for a constitution ultimately presented in November 1820 failed due to resistance from ultra-conservative and restorative circles.

on which turns the object of all his thoughts, <u>Peace</u>, and as the Moderator of the clashing interests, and bad passions that threaten to disturb the Continent. It is in this spirit that His Prussian Majesty supported so powerfully the marriage of the Duke of Orleans,[87] and which has obtained for him from Count Molé the appellation of '<u>La Sagesse couronnée</u>'.

Whether or not the present Ministry will succeed in their conciliatory views is more than I am able to decide. Party prejudice is violent, and it is said that the aid given by the King of Prussia to bring about the marriage of the Duke of Orleans has Caused a coolness between Him and the Emperor of Russia – of this however I know nothing – in the mean time it appears to me that the part becoming the British Minister is to remain quiet, and let events work their own way the mass of the Prussian Nation leans strongly towards a British Alliance, and should circumstances arise which required Great Britain to demand the aid of Prussia, the weight of the mass would prevail, and Court and Ministry yield to the expression of public opinion.

No Minister of Foreign Affairs is yet named.

FO 64/211: George B. Hamilton to Viscount Palmerston, No 5, Berlin, 23 August 1837

Differences between Prussian government and Archbishop of Cologne on the right of jurisdiction over Catholic professors

Monsignore Cappacini, the Papal Under Secretary of State for Foreign Affairs, has arrived lately at Berlin. He came from Vienna at the express invitation of the King of Prussia, – His Majesty being desirous to avail himself of the good sense and moderate opinions of this Functionary, in order to heal the very serious differences which have lately arisen between the Prussian Government and the Archbishop of Cologne[88] on the subject of the Archbishop's right of jurisdiction over the Catholic Professors in Prussia.

Of the 7,000 Catholic Professors and Clergy existing in Prussia, 5,000 have been educated at the University of Bonn, and have attended the lectures, and been brought up in the Religious principles of a celebrated Professor of that University, named Hermes; the orthodoxy of the Doctrines of the Professor having fallen under the suspicion of the Court of Rome, he was called upon to explain them, and they were

---

[87] In 1837 Ferdinande Louis Phillippe, Duke of Orleans, married Princess Helene of Mecklenburg-Schwerin.

[88] Clemens August Freiherr von Droste zu Vischering.

condemned as schismatical, and he was admonished as to his future conduct. But the Archbishop of Cologne not content with the censure passed upon the Professor by the Pope,[89] has threatened to issue mandates to suspend the functions of all the Professors brought up in the Dogmas of Professor Hermes, and to deprive them of their Chairs.

The Archbishop is a well-meaning Fanatic, and entirely led away by a false zeal for what he supposes his duty as Head of the Catholic Church in the Prussian Provinces. But the King of Prussia will not allow the proposed measures of the Archbishop to be put into execution and asserts that as the Professors are all appointed by a Royal Patent, they cannot be deprived of their situations otherwise than by a Royal Mandate. The Archbishop on the other hand asserts his right to remove them, and there the matter stands at the present moment.

The King of Prussia would therefore have found himself obliged either to yield to the Archbishop, or to remove that Prelate from his situation, and I understand that this latter project was in contemplation, but as His Majesty is averse, on this, as on all other occasions, to have recourse to so strong a measure, He has requested the presence of Monsignore Cappacini, in order to mediate between himself and the ArchBishop, and I believe that hopes are now entertained that the present differences will be adjusted.

Monsignore Cappacini will proceed from hence forthwith to Cologne and Bonn – he will then go to Brussels and from thence to Paris. [...]

FO 64/211: William Russell to Viscount Palmerston, No 115, Berlin, 27 December 1837

Uneasiness at the dismissal of seven professors at Göttingen by the Hanoverian King

The proceedings of the King of Hanover begin to create alarm and uneasiness at this Court. The Members of all the Universities and learned bodies of Germany appear disposed in their individual capacity to take part with the seven Professors,[90] and to indemnify them for the loss of their Chairs by insuring to them by subscription an annual pension equivalent to their lost salary. The leading professors of the

[89] In September 1835, four years after Hermes' death, his doctrine was banned by the decree:'Damnatio et prohibitio operi Georgii Hermes'.

[90] Wilhelm Eduard Albrecht, Friedrich Christoph Dahlmann, Georg Gottfried Gervinus, Jacob Grimm, Wilhelm Grimm, Heinrich Ewald und Wilhelm Weber. In a letter of protest of 19 November 1837 the seven professors had objected to the repeal of the Hanoverian constitution by the patent of 1 November. On 14 December Ernst August reacted by dismissing the seven professors from the university of Göttingen. On the constitutional struggle cf. pp. 263–264 in Hanover section.

University of Berlin have given their money and this daring act is looked upon by many as the commencement of a great struggle between Kings and their subjects. The University of Gottingen is said to be broken up and for ever destroyed by the arbitrary Acts of King Ernest. His Majesty, however fearless of the consequences, is now about to change the organization of the Army, and to double the number of Cavalry Regiments by dividing each into half. This must of course greatly encrease the expense. It is supposed that he intends to change the colour of the Uniforms from red to blue, and to assimilate it as nearly as possible to the Prussian Uniform. This will displease the Hanoverian Army. In East Friseland a turbulent spirit has shewn itself, connected with a desire to be again united to Prussia. A Deputation from the Nobility of Westphalia is arrived at Berlin to intercede in favor of the Archbishop of Cologne,[91] but the King has refused to receive them.

FO 64/215: William Russell to Viscount Palmerston, No 8, Berlin, 24 January 1838

Reactions of different classes to the conflict between the Prussian government and the Archbishop of Cologne and political repercussions

[...] The state of Prussia at this moment is curious and perhaps critical. The Government has of late years (trusting too much to peaceable times and the apathy of the governed) endeavoured to create, and give consistency in the state to an Aristocracy, and in doing this has departed from the wiser policy of former Years of tempering by moderation and liberality the arbitrary principle, and giving development and strength to the democratic Institutions which form the power and beauty of the Kingdom — this error is now felt — the new created Aristocracy of Westphalia[92] having on the first emergency abandoned the Government to side with the Archbishop of Cologne,[93] whilst the middling classes who ought and would have been the firmest supporters of the Executive offended at a want of Confidence and wounded by the attempt to form an exclusive class in the social Order, stand aloof as indifferent Spectators of the Contest. Religious toleration for which Prussia was

[91] Clemens August Freiherr von Droste zu Vischering. For his arrest cf. pp. 88–91 in Frankfurt section.
[92] After 1815 the nobility in Westfalia, and indeed the Rhineland, regained many of the privileges given up during Napoleon's rule. These regained privileges included political rights in the provincial Diets, entailed estates and the reintroduction of titles and coats of arms.
[93] Clemens August Freiherr von Droste zu Vischering.

so distinguished, and which gave such harmony, with the consequent strength that arises from it, to her different Churches, is now no longer the Characteristic of Government. Last year the Jews, a rich and industrious portion of Prussian Subjects were interfered with[94] – this year the Roman Catholics have their grievances. Whilst these internal evils are agitating the Country, the Prussian Government by its timid and vacillating policy is detaching its Foreign Allies and is threatened with being left isolated amongst the Continental Nations. Austria has severely censured the Proceedings towards the Archbishop of Cologne, Bavaria still more so – all the Catholick States have done the same – National Antipathies have separated Russia and Prussia – the relations between Belgium and Prussia are not cordial, nor do I believe that those with Holland are on a much better footing – the alliance with France does not go deeper than the exchange of phrases and acts of courtesy between the Sovereigns, it has no sympathy with the Court or Nation. In the meantime Prussia is losing that hold she was beginning to assume over Germany by her apparent approval of the acts of the King of Hanover[95] which are repugnant to the Constitutional States, to the learned Bodies and to the Industrious Classes of Germany.

Such, My Lord, appears to me to be the present state of the Prussian Government surrounded by difficulties brought on by a departure from that liberal, tolerant and enlightened line of conduct for which they were so distinguished, and to which they appear to want the courage or good will to return. The crisis however may be of short duration for the Nation is full of resources with able men to direct them, who may now see the dangerous course they are pursuing, and by their energy and wisdom, place Prussia where She ought to be; at the Head of the Confederated States of Germany.

FO 64/215: William Russell to Viscount Palmerston, No 18, Berlin, 7 February 1838

Reactions to the vigorous act of arresting the Archbishop of Cologne; Metternich's comment; on the 'Bureaucratie' class in Prussia; its intentions and workings; on the importance of that class to the Prussian state

In the copies of Despatches transmitted to me by Your Lordship, I see that the vigorous act of arresting the Archbishop of Cologne[96] has surprized and annoyed Prince Metternich and excited the displeasure

---

[94] Cf. pp. 148–149 in this section.

[95] Cf. pp. 263–264 in Hanover section.

[96] For Clemens August Freiherr von Droste zu Vischering's arrest cf. pp. 88–91 in Frankfurt section.

and alarm of the Southern States of Germany. Every one indeed was astonished to see a Government so lethargic and so tolerant as that of Prussia suddenly execute a measure of boldness and of apparent intolerance, the known effect of which must have been to place the Prussian Cabinet at variance with the Courts of Rome, Austria and Bavaria and others of less note. This mode of proceeding is so different from that which has hitherto guided the Government of Prussia whose maxim has been tranquillity on any terms, a maxim put in practise by her subserviency to Russian views when Poland[97] was agitated, and her present complaisance to France in order to ensure quiet on the Rhine.

Prince Metternich goes so far as to say that the Arrest of the Archbishop of Cologne may lead to the dismemberment of the Prussian Monarchy; an opinion thus gravely given by the most experienced and clear-sighted Statesman in Europe is highly important, and makes it incumbent upon me to endeavour to explain a Proceeding that appears involved in mystery and diverges so much from the course of policy hitherto pursued by Prussia.

That Policy may generally be designated as cautious – a desire to wait upon events, rather that to bring them on, and a readiness to profit by the incautious acts of their neighbours, consequently the decision to arrest the Archbishop of Cologne, and the mode of executing the Arrest surprized the whole Diplomatic Body resident at Berlin: the explanation I am about to give is hypothetical, originates in my own mind, and is not partaken by my Colleagues, still I am disposed to think it founded in truth. Coming events will shew.

In a Despatch I addressed to your Lordship last year,[98] I pointed out the existence and power of a class of men called a 'Bureaucratie' – this class was created by Frederick the 2nd who possessed the master hand to govern and direct them – that controuling hand removed, they have felt and have occasionally exercised their own power independent of the wishes of the Executive Government, not openly and avowedly, but secretly and by unseen means. Selecting their Instruments and working on them by language and acts they alone know how and when to make use of. Such was the case in 1813. General York was their instrument and the declaration of war against France their object[99] – the Executive Government during the operations became paralysed and passive. The result accomplished, the Prussian Eagle planted on the Gates of Paris,

---

[97] Cf. n. 18 in this section.

[98] Not included in this volume.

[99] The neutrality agreement concluded with Russia without authority by Hans David Ludwig Yorck von Wartenburg in December 1812 was the start of the Prussian uprising against French rule. These wars of liberation, conducted largely by Prussian patriots and including the 'bureaucracy' mentioned in this despatch, culminated in March 1814 when the powers allied against France marched into Paris.

the influence of this class of men was withdrawn, and the Ministers and the King were allowed to fix without their controul the limits and position of Prussia. The negotiations however at the Congress of Vienna excited the high displeasure of those who had directed the war by giving their consent to the existence of so many Monarchies, as well as for having submitted Germany to the rule of the Diet, which in the words of Frederick the Great (whose opinions form the Code of this Party) is compared to 'des chiens de basse courquin aboyent à la Lune'. The intention of the Bureaucratie was (notwithstanding their occasional disapproval of the acts of their Government) to remain quiet and to avoid to trouble the latter days of a Sovereign they respected and the vicissitudes of whose Life had been so severe. The encreasing and alarming weakness of the Prussian Cabinet induced them to bring their power to act like a lever on the Government at an earlier period than they intended, at least if I am right in supposing that it is their hand which has placed Prussia in what may be called a state of transition, and they determined to give an impetus and direction to the Executive, before things became worse, and the accession of the Prince Royal[100] to the throne, acting upon principles at variance with their own, should make it dangerous to return to a line of policy considered by them the most conducive to the strength and well-being of Prussia. In this view they urged on the Government to act against the Archbishop of Cologne, selecting a religious, instead of a political victim, because in the one care they knew they would carry with them the King, – in the other they apprehended a failure at the outset – not loathe at the same time (though their object is political, and their opinions as tolerant and as philosophical as those of their Idol of the Great Frederick) to check the growing influence of the Roman Catholick Church on the Rhine, and even in Berlin itself, where an attempt was made, and almost a successful attempt to convert the Prince Royal himself to Romanism. Colonel Radowitz, the Chief Actor was sent to Frankfort. The calculations then of the Bureaucratie are these. Internally that they shall be able to give a deathblow to the Prince Royals Policy – to the Privileges of his new-created Aristocracy[101] in Westphalia and the Rhenish Provinces and check his high Prerogative Notions before he comes to the Throne – secondly that they will give vigor and character to the Government. Externally they wish to bring about a complete rupture with the See of Rome – that is –to put an end to the Popes

[100] Friedrich Wilhelm IV.

[101] The Catholic nobility in Westfalia and the Rhineland were very reserved towards Protestant-dominated Prussia and its bureaucracy. It was not until the 1830s that the nobility were gradually integrated into the Prussian state, with the help of visits by Crown Prince Friedrich Wilhelm to Westfalia in 1833 and 1836. For the privileges regained under Prussian rule cf. n. 92 in this section.

interference with the civil Law of the Land.[102] Besides this they wish to place their Sovereign at the head of the Protestant Party in Germany, not from any feeling of Religious intolerance, but because they consider this Party to be more enlightened and energetic than the Catholics – more fit to be opposed to the influence of Austria in Germany, and consequently the readiest and surest way to govern the Diet. From Russia they say they have nothing to fear and nothing to hope, indifference towards that Power, in as far as a neighbouring State can be indifferent, is their rule of conduct – they respect the family Relations of the Courts. The excessive courtesy of their Sovereign towards The King of the French,[103] they think misplaced and uncalled for, but it has entered into their calculations that their views could not be furthered at a more opportune moment, than when the Friendship of Louis Philippe for the King of Prussia gave a guarantee for the absence of French interference on the Rhine, during the effervescence created amongst the Catholic Population by the arrest of the Archbishop of Cologne. This effervescence, they think may last six month, perhaps a Year, and will then subside and be forgotten, but had Prussia been on bad terms with France, they never would have ventured to have thrown the Rhenish Provinces into such agitation. This I believe to be the true history of the causes that have agitated all Germany and alarmed and displeased many of the German Courts. I may be wrong. It is difficult to give an account of an 'Imperium in Imperio', the springs of whose conduct are not visible, of the views of a Party that has no ostensible head and with which no one can have any palpable connexion. The year 1813 gave evidence of the existence of this Party and of its Power, yet no one could put his hand upon it – it appeared nowhere – yet it existed every where – it had no Chief – yet it moved and directed the Masses of German Population, and Sovereigns bent before its Will. It is not held together by Secret Societies – they have been rooted up and destroyed. It must then be that mysterious force, public opinion, driven from its natural vents – the Press and Public Assemblies, but condensed in the hands of a class of men who manage the Machinery of Government and by them brought to bear upon the Executive by means known only to themselves. This mode of action was at all times suited to the German character, and has in the middle and modern Ages had great influence on German Governments. It is said that the Prince Royal has often declared his dislike to this class of men, and his intention to destroy their power by creating an Aristocracy that should

---

[102] For the intervention of the Pope in the question of mixed marriages cf. pp. 169–170 in this section.

[103] These friendly relations reached their zenith in 1837 when Friedrich Wilhelm II helped the son of the French King to win a daughter of the Prince of Mecklenburg as his bride, cf. n. 87 in this section.

take upon itself much of the local Administration and by that means enable him to diminish their number. This may account for their present precipitate conduct and their endeavours to accomplish Reforms before the Princes accession to the Throne enabled him to strike the first blow.

Having given this opinion as to what I believe to be the secret agency that has operated on the Prussian Cabinet, I will complete it by adding that I think the Party directing the movement will have full success, that they will emancipate Prussia from the interference of the Pope in the Civil Law of the Country, that the effervescence created by the act will subside – that Prussia will take the lead from Austria in German Politics – that Prussia will gain strength and confidence in herself by this successful act of vigor and that instead of being a Power without a Will, or at least without courage to act up to a will, She will become a really independent State.

In Foreign Alliances the class of men whose existence and power I suppose, lean decidedly towards England: former alliances, with which are connected the Grandeur and Glory of Prussia lay the foundation of this predeliction which is completed by a belief that the prosperity of Prussia depends on its Commercial Relations with England as well as on the conviction, that, should emergencies arise, it is to England alone that Prussia can look far support. Some go so far as to say that their existence as a Nation will then be in the hands of the British Government. [...]

The Prussian Cabinet is probably acting without knowing from whence it takes its impulse. It is the fate of every Government that would be absolute to be under some secret influence, some power that propels or checks it, occasionally such a Man as Frederick the Great will make his own will predominate, but such Men are rare. Even in Russia when great catastrophes threaten the Nation, the ancient Nobility of the Land come from their Retreat and dictate to the Sovereign, so it was in 1812 when they forbid Alexander to make Peace with Napoleon. In Prussia there is no Aristocracy but there is a 'Bureaucratie', a numerous class of men, enlightened, laborious, patriotic, managing the whole machinery of Administration and consequently well acquainted with the motives and acts of the Executive Government. This class of men are indispensibly necessary to the State, they could not be got rid of without destroying the working of the System of internal Government – there are no men to take their places – they must therefore know their own power, and knowing it will of course occasionally make use of it. I believe that at this moment they are making use of it – that their intention is to place their Sovereign at the head of the Protestant Party in Germany, not as a Religious but as a political Party, and through these means to take the lead in the Diet. I believe that this end will be accomplished without danger, and with the certainty of adding to the Power and Stability of the Prussian Kingdom. Austria is a vast Monarchy on the decline without resolution to commence Reformation, and Prince Metternich is unwilling to see the unhealthy state of the Country he governs. Prussia has accomplished her great Reform, is full of health and vigor, and to be kept so only requires that the spirit of her Reforms should be observed – the Executive having failed to do so, a subaltern class of men are endeavouring to force the Government into its true line of Policy. That object quietly and imperceptibly accomplished, the directing hand will be withdrawn and the Cabinet will resume its ordinary course, astonished at its own energy and determined not to risk again the tranquillity of the State.

FO 64/215: William Russell to Viscount Palmerston, No 20, Berlin, 14 February 1838[104]

Dispute between Prussian government and See of Rome regarding the question of 'mixed marriages'

The question between the Prussian Government and the See of Rome remains stationary. Each Party appears to have assumed a position from which it is unwilling to be dislodged by its adversary. In the meantime the Public Mind is actively engaged in discussing the various bearings and probable solution of the difficulty. The Ultra Protestant Party in Prussia maintains that the Policy of England should be taken as a Model and all ties with the Pope cut asunder for ever. Others would place the Relations of Prussia with the Pope on the same footing as those of Holland, taking as a Basis the declaration of Benedict 14th in 1741 by which the Catholic Clergy of the United Provinces are directed to give the Nuptial Benediction to 'Marriages mixtes' without stipulations as to the Religion of the Children. A state of things that has secured Religious Repose to Holland for a Century, without any probability of its being disturbed.

The whole dispute between the Prussian Government and the See of Rome is included in the granting or withholding the Nuptial Benediction. Pius the 8th, by his letter[105] to the Archbishop of Cologne,[106]

---

[104] Cf. pp. 88–91 in Frankfurt section.
[105] *Mischehen-Breve* (Letter on mixed marriages) of 25 March 1830.
[106] Ferdinand August Graf Spiegel zum Desenberg.

the Bishops of Treves,[107] Münster[108] and Paderborn,[109] directed the Catholic Clergy to withhold the Nuptial Benediction unless the stipulations enacted by the Council of Trent[110] were complied with. Monsieur de Bunsen succeeded in making a Convention[111] with the late Archbishop of Cologne, the Count Spiegel, by which the orders of Pius the 8th were mitigated and the wish of the Prussian Government was satisfied, which is that when Persons of the Protestant and Catholic Religion are united in marriage, the Catholic Priest should grant the Nuptial Benediction and leave the Parents to bring up the children in the Religion that should appear to them to be the best. The present Archbishop of Cologne[112] having refused to conform to the Convention signed by his Predecessor and Monsieur Bunsen was after long and fruitless negotiation arrested and carried out of his Diocese. This is, I believe, an exact and complete history of the dispute that now agitates all Germany – a dispute in which the Prussian Government can neither be accused of intolerance or injustice, though the violent act of arresting and imprisoning a Man of the Archbishop's Rank and Character admits, perhaps, of cavil or censure.

A cold observer would suppose that the difficulties standing in the way of an amicable adjustment are so trifling as to give promise of obtaining soon so desirable an end, but the moment the Roman Catholic Church enters into dispute, the line drawn between Spiritual and Temporal matters is made to disappear by the subtlety of the disputants and all is vague and open to never-ending argument. The Roman Catholic Church maintains that the Nuptial Benediction is a question purely of its own internal discipline and asserts its right to direct that discipline as well as the danger of admitting the temporal interference of another Church. The Prussian Government maintains that it is a question of State, if the civil Law of the Land, of the Liberty of the Subject who has a right to its protection: from such seeds, fresh disputes will spring with all their evil consequences unless The King of Prussia decides to cut, and not to unravel the Gordian Knot.

---

[107] Joseph von Hommer.
[108] Kaspar Maximilian Freiherr von Droste zu Vischering.
[109] Friedrich Clemens Freiherr von Ledebur.
[110] The Council of Trent (1545–1563; *Tridentium*) determined that such a marriage was a sacrament and laid down the conditions for it.
[111] Berlin Convention of 19 June 1834.
[112] Clemens August Freiherr von Droste zu Vischering.

FO 64/215: George B. Hamilton to Viscount Palmerston, No 16, Berlin, 18 April 1838

State of Prussian army; changes and promotions

I had the honor of informing Your Lordship in my Despatch N° 7, that the changes and promotions in the Prussian Army which took place on the 30 Ultimo had been more numerous than during several preceding years. But these changes have been of so marked and peculiar a nature, that I think it my duty to make some further observations upon them more particularly as they involve considerations of some political importance.

The Prussian Army consists of eight 'Corps D'Armee', and a Corps of the Guards and Three of these 'Corps D'Armee' were commanded by the three eldest Sons of the King. The Prince Royal[113] and Prince William Son of His Majesty have been removed from their respective commands, and the whole Army having been now divided into Four Sections, the Prince Royal, Prince William and Prince Frederick of Prussia have been nominated to the Inspectorship of Three of them.

Prince Charles of Prussia alone still continues to retain his 'Corps D'Armee' but as no one has yet been nominated to the Inspectorship of the 3^d Section, it its supposed that it has been left vacant for His Royal Highness, who has only held his present command during two years.

It appears that much dissatisfaction and discontent had prevailed among the old and distinguished Officers of the Army at seeing too many of the chief situations monopolized by the members of the Royal Family, who are young men without experience and to whom the Army could not look up with the confidence in the event of any contingency – and in order to conciliate the Army, the King has been determined to make the important changes I have described; but at the same time He has sought to propitiate the feelings of His Sons who have felt aggrieved at being deprived of their commands, by confering upon them the Title of Inspectors of the Four Sections, into which the Army is divided. These situations cannot however be otherwise considered than as entirely honorary, no emolument is attached to them and they are only confered for a year.

H.R.H. Prince William alone profits by these arrangements, as he received the general command of the Corps of Guards, vacant by the Death of the Duke Charles of Mecklenburgh Strelitz in addition to the Inspectorship of the 4th Section.

The nominations also which have been made by the King to the

---

[113] Friedrich Wilhelm.

Commands thus vacated are further calculated to please the army. The officers that have been selected, being distinguished more for their talents and services, than their Birth or high Political Feelings.

A change perhaps still more remarkable has been operated among the Officers immediately surrounding the Princes. Many of these were men possessing violent Ultra Political and Ultra Religious Sentiments, the latter are here designated by the term of Pietists[114] – who were continually working upon the minds of their Royal Superiors, and impelling them to acts and opinions which rendered them unpopular with the Army and the Nation. Of the Prince Royal's Establishment every Officer has been removed and many of that of Prince William's – among the latter was one who was the chief contributor to the weekly Journal of Berlin,[115] the most distinguished of all the Prussian Newspapers for its Arbitrary and Aristocratical principles. All these Officers have received destinations removed from Berlin, some with advancement, others retaining their former grade.

A strong conviction of the necessity of making these remarkable changes must have existed in the King's mind, to have determined His Majesty to have taken the steps above mentioned –and in the removal of the Officers composing the Military Households of His Sons, as well as in confering the vacant Commands in the Army on Officers who in a manner have risen from the Ranks. The King has shewn that He has thought it expedient to defer to the opinions of the Army and Nation generally, and to give a timely check to those Ultra Religious and Arbitrary impulses by which the Royal Family, and more particularly the Prince Royal, are generally supposed to be governed.

FO 64/216: William Russell to Viscount Palmerston, No 49, Berlin, 10 July 1838

Reasons for rising wool prices; expansion of home market and export; Austria's umbrage at the interference of Prussia as head of Customs Union in internal affairs of Baden, Württemberg, and Bavaria

At the great annual Wool Fair of Berlin the wool sold at so very high a price, that I was induced to ask the cause. I am informed that at former Fairs the price was regulated by Buyers for English consumption: but that the German Manufacturers are now the great purchasers, and that the English have almost disappeared from the Market. This is attributed to the immense progress lately made in Germany in the

---

[114] Cf. n. 225 in this section.
[115] Carl Gustav Schulz, editor in chief of the *Politisches Wochenblatt* founded in 1831.

Manufactures of Woollen Goods – a progress that owes its source to the confidence given by the duration of Peace, and the encrease of Capital, rather than to the creation and fiscal regulation of the Prussian Commercial Union. The German Manufacturers of Woollen Goods are not only getting possession of their own Markets, but they are exporting to America and the Levant. The States forming the Commercial Union have sent Agents to meet at Dresden to present and compare data, and take information as to the grounds on which the Union is to be renewed and regulated. Prussia continues to be a loser in the receipts of Custom, whilst other States gain considerably.

I have been told that the Question has been mooted in the Prussian Cabinet of leaving out the Southern States of Baden, Wurtemberg and Bavaria at the expiration of the first Three years of Union.[116] The Grounds for this are political and not commercial; Prussia having found that Austria takes great umbrage at the interference that Prussia as head of the Commercial League is obliged to exercise in the internal Affairs of those Countries.

Mr Wheaton, the American Minister, is gone to Dresden to learn the proceedings of the Commercial Meeting, and at his return I may be able to give Your Lordship some accurate information.

FO 64/221: William Russell to Viscount Palmerston, Separate, Berlin, 10 January 1839

On prison discipline in Prussia; reform of criminals; involvement of private charities

With reference to Your Lordship's Circular Despatch of the 20th ultimo, I have been informed by the Minster of the Interior that there do not exist any Printed Official Documents on Prison Discipline in Prussia, but His Excellency has promised to cause a Report on the subject to be drawn up, which I shall not fail to transmit to Your Lordship as soon as I receive it.

In the meantime I have the honor to forward herewith all the Papers hitherto published by the Society at Berlin for the amelioration of Delinquents, instituted some Years ago and authorized by Government.[117]

---

[116] Baden joined the *Zollverein* in 1835; Bavaria and Würtemberg had already done so in 1833.

[117] The *Verein für die Besserung der Strafgefangenen* (Association for the Amelioration of Delinquents) was founded by members of the Prussian administration in Berlin at the end of 1826. The association was supposed to 'improve' delinquents and turn them into 'pious and useful citizens'. On 10 September 1828 its statutes were approved by the Prussian Ministry of the Interior and Ministry of Justice. The papers mentioned by Russell were transferred to the Home Office and are not extant in FO 64/221.

This society, of which there are Branch committees in all the Eastern Provinces of Prussia, has the double object in view, of endeavouring to reform Criminals undergoing their Sentences, and of guarding against a relapse on their release from confinement. The means employed in both cases are, Religious Instruction and occupation afforded to those who are willing to improve their condition by their own exertions.

It would appear from these Papers that the crowded state of the Prisons, and more especially of those of the Capital, prove a considerable impediment to the laudable efforts of the society, nor does the encrease of Crime, alluded to in its Reports, present a very favourable idea of the Results of the system of Discipline pursued in the Prussian Prisons.

FO 64/221: William Russell to Viscount Palmerston, No 7, Confidential, Berlin, 23 January 1839

King of Prussia's personal style of ruling the Kingdom; effect on Prussia; Metternich's alleged influence on the Prussian King; on Metternich's 'love of order'; mutual prejudices in relations between Austria and Prussia

[...] Since the death of General Witzleben, no Minister of State has had either the confidence or a direct influence over The King. His Majesty governs His Kingdom by His own Opinions and Will, more than at any period of his former life. He admits of no interference, and shews great jealousy of the Prince Royal.[118] The system of The King is rather to adjourn and mitigate difficulties than to meet and overcome them: consequently they accumulate until the day of reckoning falls on the shoulders of the Successor to the Throne. Prince Wittgenstein, a shrewd and subtle man, but too refined a Courtier to hold language to his Master that could displease, is the link between The King and His Ministers. The result of this state of things is, that the Acts of The King partake of the tardiness and hesitation common to Persons of His Majesty's Age, especially to Persons who have experienced the vicissitudes that beset The King of Prussia during the early part of his Reign. This determination of the King to act without consulting the Heir Apparent or Minister has not only paralyzed the energy of Prussian Policy and given rise to a belief that Prussia is in a state of decrepitude, a belief on which the Pope and the Belgians have largely drawn,[119] but it has been productive of another evil, which is this. The King having no confidence in any one of His Ministers, nor yet any

[118] Friedrich Wilhelm IV.

[119] Russell is referring here to Prussia's long delay in recognizing Belgium as an independent state and to the dispute with the Pope over mixed marriages.

decided confidence in his own judgment, seeks advice in difficult cases out of his Kingdom. Prince Metternich is the Person to whose opinion and judgment he defers. In the first place this causes great delay, and secondly it gives umbrage to the Prince Royal and generally to The Kings Subjects, and produces an irritable and hostile feeling towards Austria. Prince Metternich is accused of taking advantage of his influence over The King to promote the interests of Austria at the expense of Prussia – especially on the question agitated by the Arrest of the Archbishop of Cologne.[120] He is openly and loudly accused of having fermented[121] the Religious Quarrel, and of having withheld the Power he possesses over the Pope to bring about an arrangement. As I look upon a good understanding between Austria and Prussia to be very essential to the maintenance of the Peace of Europe, I have met this language, by saying, that I could not give credence to an accusation against Prince Metternich so much at variance with every act of his Public Life. Prince Metternich, I say, has been the Apostle of Order. He has been accused of carrying his love of order even to fanaticism – it would be unjust now at his advanced time of life to accuse him of encouraging Disorder. Prince Metternich is naturally desirous of holding this influence over Prussia – his personal Vanity is flattered by it, and in all probability he makes use of it in a manner to maintain Austrian Ascendancy in Germany, and to prevent The King from placing Himself at the Head of the Protestants, to which His Majesty's Religious Feelings give a tendency. The Protestants are as a mass more enlightened than the Catholicks, and more desirous of obtaining guarantees for their Political Freedom, consequently it would ill suit the Policy pursued by Prince Metternich to allow them so powerful a Chief as The King of Prussia. In the meantime there is much National Acrimony and Jealousy between Austria and Prussia, and they are fond of depreciating each others political stability and system. Prussia represents Austria as an Empire that will fall to pieces when the Reins of Government fall out of the able hands of Prince Metternich, and the Austrians represent Prussia as a Kingdom partaking the Age and feebleness of its Monarch. Much of this may be ascribed to the jealousy of two powerful States, each anxious to direct the ponderous Machinery of the Confederation and to govern the small States that form the Diet.

[120] Clemens August Freiherr von Droste zu Vischering, cf. pp. 88–91 in Frankfurt section.
[121] Corrected in pencil, 'fomented'.

FO 64/221: William Russell to Viscount Palmerston, No 55, Berlin, 7 May 1839

Baron Werther's assessment of the political state of France; different assessments of French crisis; unstable conditions in Germany; threat of polemical discussion that may separate Protestants and Catholics; outburst from France would meet with sympathy and support on the part of the German people

In the last conversation I had with Baron Werther, I asked him if the state of France[122] caused him any uneasiness. He said, none whatever; that the last accounts from France were favorable, that King Louis Philippe was calm and in good spirits, that He was ready to accept any Ministry that had a Majority in the Chambers, that His Majesty had been everywhere well received on the 1st of May, and that he (Baron Werther) looked upon the struggle going on in France as one that only affected the internal state of the Country, and not as one which could give apprehension to Foreign Nations.

The accounts however which reach us from private sources do not accord with Baron Werther's opinion. The Mercantile Classes are very uneasy at the prolongation of the French Crisis. It is certainly much to be desired that the opinion formed by Baron Werther may be correct, for I think Germany is in a less fit state to repulse difficulties and danger accruing to Constituted Authority than it was in 1830.[123] Discontent reigns amongst various classes, and the Governments of Germany have shewn little wisdom in meeting and soothing the causes of discontent as they arose. The Prussian Government has allowed the dispute with the Court of Rome[124] to assume an alarming tendency, and Germany is threatened with a polemick discussion that may separate the Protestants and Catholicks. This is made to assist the purposes of political discontent, and an angry fermentation exists in Eastern and Western Prussia, in Poland and on the Rhine.

The King of Hanover has thrown His States into an irritable mood, and the Diet of the Confederation has very much lost the public Confidence by declining to arbitrate between The King and His People.[125] The accounts that we receive from Vienna represent that Country as unprepared to contend with difficulties. The Finances are in a deteriorated state, and the last loan is looked upon almost as a

[122] When the Chambers were re-elected in 1839 the government lost its majority. The incumbent minister-president, Louis-Mathieu, comte de Molé, resigned on 8 March.

[123] For the repercussions of the French revolution of July 1830 in Germany, cf. n. 194 in Frankfurt section.

[124] For the dispute over mixed marriages and the arrest of the Archbishop of Cologne cf. pp. 88–91 in Frankfurt section.

[125] For the dispute over the Hanoverian constitution cf. despatches in Hanover section between 1838 and 1840.

fraud – added to this the Government is said to be in the greatest confusion – small coteries and individuals contending for the Mastery, and no hand firm enough to direct an even and intelligible line of Policy.

These evils might be overcome, or made to pass off unperceived, through the patient and submissive Character of the Germans, should France remain tranquil, but an outburst from France would meet with sympathy and support on the part of the German People, whilst the energy on the part of the aged Statesmen who govern this Country would be too feeble to repel the attacks that would be made on constituted Authority.

FO 64/222: George B. Hamilton to Viscount Palmerston, No 13, Berlin, 7 August 1839

State of British trade at Koblenz; necessity of appointing a British consular agent there or somewhere else; question of which location most preferable; Prussian government's objection to appointment of consuls in inland towns

In reply to Your Despatch No. 113 of the 22nd ultimo,[126] requesting information as to the state of British Trade at Coblentz, and as to the expediency or necessity of appointing a British Consular Agent there, or at any other City in that part of the Prussian Dominions, I have to inform Your Lordship that from the enquiries I have been enabled to make from Persons whom I have considered to be best qualified to give an unprejudiced opinion, and who have been lately travelling in the Rhenish Provinces for the purpose of making Official Reports to their respective Governments on the state of Trade with England and other Countries, I do not consider that the present state of the British Trade at Coblentz is of sufficient extent to render it expedient that an English Consul should be established there.

I understand, moreover, that if it was the intention of Her Majesty's Government to propose to that of Prussia the establishment of a Consulate, that Mayence or Cologne ought to be preferred to Coblentz, both as respects their local position and the extent of Trade carried on with Great Britain. Of these Towns, I should venture to suggest Cologne as the most preferable, as, if a Consul was stationed there, he might be most useful to Her Majesty's Government in making Reports as to the state of the Prussian Trade in that most populous and enterprizing District, and in keeping a watchful eye over the improvements which

---

[126] FO 64/220: Draft to Lord William Russell, No. 113, Foreign Office, London, 22 July 1839, not included in this volume.

the Germans are daily making in their Manufactures and Industry. The selection of Cologne in the immediate neighbourhood of the great Mining Districts of Prussia, of Aix-La Chapelle, where are the chief woollen Manufactories, and of Elberfeldt and Düsseldorf would be most propitious for this purpose, but it will hardly be necessary for one in this case to point out to Your Lordship, that should it seem expedient to Her Majesty's Government to appoint a Consul at Cologne, with a view to obtaining useful information, as well as for the advantage of Trade, that such a Person should be an Englishman, or at any rate not connected with German Commerce.

The Gentleman[127] recommended to Your Lordship for the appointment of Consul at Coblentz, is, I understand, a very respectable Person, but he would not combine the advantages that might be derived from a more Independent Agent.

Social position is what is sought for generally by the Natives of a Country in desiring to be made Consuls, and I believe I may venture to assert, that, in places where there is but little Trade, more harm is frequently done by the jealousy created by conferring such a distinction on an Individual Merchant, than if a Consul did not exist at all.

It has been hitherto a principle with the Prussian Government to object to the appointment of Consuls in Inland Towns, and with regard to Mayence they refused to allow a French Consul to reside there, on account of its being a Fortress of the Confederation – and Mons[r] Engelhardt, the Gentleman who has lately been sent on the part of the French Government to confer with the Congress of the German Union, now assembled at Berlin, has resided at Mayence for sixteen years as French Commissary under the Convention for the Navigation of the Rhine[128] – a Consul in reality, though not in name. The reports of this Gentleman are supposed to have been very useful to France, and for some years past he has been enabled to keep his Government well informed as to all the Proceedings of German Trade.

I should perhaps apologize to Your Lordship for entering so much at length on this subject, but it appears to me to be one that merits the consideration of Her Majesty's Government, and I cannot but be of opinion that if such a Person as Monsieur Engelhardt was appointed to reside at one of the influential Cities of the Rhine as Consul, or in any other capacity, much advantage might be derived from such a nomination.

[127] Mr Jordan.
[128] The Rhine Navigation Commission met in Mainz between 1815 and 1831. Negotiations culminated in the Rhine Navigation Act of 1831 in which the states bordering the Rhine agreed to liberalize trade and to reduce shipping tariffs.

FO 64/222: William Russell to Viscount Palmerston, No 98, Berlin, 18 September 1839

State of things within the Zollverein; question whether a commercial treaty between Zollverein and Great Britain would be advantageous for the latter; Prussia's manufacturing and industrial development; reasons why Prussia has abstained from exercising a preponderant influence over Germany

The Members of the Commercial Union have left Berlin.[129] D[r] Bowring having been sent here by Your Lordship to observe and not to act will return to England to report the result of his observations and to obtain Instructions to act, should Her Majesty's Government think that grounds exist for forming a Commercial Treaty with the Zollverein. The state of things past and present may be stated in a few words. The conclusion of the War[130] left the Germans an Agricultural and not a Manufacturing People. Prussia proposed to England to take Her manufactured Goods on condition that England would take the natural productions of Germany. England declined. Prussia then said, we will manufacture for Ourselves and by the Union of several States do away with the Custom Houses that now form hindrances to commercial Intercourse. This Union has succeeded beyond the hopes of those who formed it. Manufactures nursed by the duration of Peace, by the encrease of wealth and the progressive wants of the People have sprung up all over Germany. Capital to an immense amount has been invested in these Manufactures. Englishmen have been brought over to direct them, and their productions not only suffice to supply the Home Markets, but they are sent to contend against English Manufactures in the Market of America and the Levant. England might still have kept in her hands, exclusively, the supply of Machinery necessary for the construction of German Manufactories, but the exportation being forbidden by Law,[131] the Machinery was at first smuggled out of the Country, and is now made by the Germans themselves − England has thus thrown away many advantages which were within her grasp and which can never be entirely recovered. It is however well that Her Majesty's Government should be prepared to profit by a disposition on the part of the British Parliament to alter the Laws that have forced Germany to manufacture for Herself, and for this purpose the intelligence and activity of D[r] Bowring will place in the power of Her Majesty's Cabinet every information. The language of the Prussian Government on Commercial

---

[129] Since July 1839 the *Zollverein* Congress in Berlin had been preparing a revision of customs tariffs and the organization of the *Zollverein*.

[130] The end of the Napoleonic Wars in 1814.

[131] An export ban was imposed for machines and blueprints from 1781 to 1786. In 1825 these conditions were modified by a license system; they were lifted altogether in 1843.

Subjects is as liberal as can be expected. They say, 'We see all the advantages of a Commercial Treaty with Great Britain – we desire no prohibitive or enormous duties – We wish our Manufactures to establish themselves without artificial protection, we will use our influence with the other States of the Union to moderate the demands they are now making for protecting duties. We will undertake to propose and carry through the Stipulations of the Treaty. But we cannot give something for nothing. Hitherto we have proposed and you have refused. We have changed (forced by You) our system. – We are content with the present state of things. It is for you to propose and we will not refuse.' This is the language of the Prussian Government. Doctor Bowring will probably confirm this Report, whilst at the same time he will be enabled to give your Lordship information in the greatest detail, and if after that, Your Lordship sees grounds on which a Commercial Treaty can be proposed, the negotiation can at any moment take place at Berlin – the presence of Members of the Commercial Union being rather an embarrassment than an advantage.

This is purely the commercial view of the Question – it has besides its political bearings which are of vast importance. It is in the power of Prussia to exercise a preponderating influence over Germany. This She has hitherto abstained from doing, partly to avoid giving umbrage to Austria, partly from a desire to remain within that timid and passive system which marks Her political course, but the day is fast approaching when Prussia must take the lead at the Diet, or abdicate in favour of a smaller Power the part that is assigned to Her by Her Geographical position, Her resources and the enlightenment of the Prussian People. To abdicate, would be to wound the pride of the Prussians and consequently to endanger the tranquillity of the State, Prussia must therefore move on with the spirit of the Age, and a Commercial Treaty with England would lead to intercourse and Union between the two Nations which could not fail to have beneficial effects on the progress of Prussia. The late refusal of Prussia to protect the Hanoverians[132] has caused great discontent and greatly weakened Her influence over the Constitutional States of the Commercial Union.

---

[132] For the dispute over the Hanoverian constitution, in which Prussia supported King Ernst August, cf. dispatches in Hanover section between 1838 and 1840.

FO 64/228: William Russell to Viscount Palmerston, No 2, Berlin, 1 April 1840

Baron Werther shows no uneasiness about the situation in France; comment on Eastern Question

I have had a general conversation with Baron Werther since I arrived here, from which I infer that the Policy of Prussia remains unchanged – that is, that the same desire prevails to act as much as possible in concert with Austria and Russia, the results of which should be the continuance of Peace. Were a difference to arise between the Countries named, it is towards Austria that Prussia would incline. At the same time there is a very friendly feeling in this Cabinet towards England and France, and Baron Werther told me that Monsieur Thiers's accession to Power[133] gave him no uneasiness. He thought his policy towards other Nations would be that of conciliation and Peace. Baron Werther has given such instructions on the Eastern Question[134] to Baron Bülow, as he thinks will be satisfactory to Your Lordship, but he fears that a speedy settlement of that Question is not to be expected: At the same time the "Status Quo" gives him no apprehension of War. He rejoiced at Baron Bülows appointment to London, as he thought him more able than any one; to explain questions, that gave umbrage to the British Government. His long service in the Foreign Office of St Petersburgh making him master of every subject, and his views being conciliatory and favourable to English Policy. [...]

FO 64/228: William Russell to Viscount Palmerston, No 9, Berlin, 22 April 1840

Quaker deputation seeks to induce King of Prussia to allow his subjects to follow the creed of their respective churches without molestation; plans to create a National Church

Mrs Fry, Mr Allen and Mr Gurney, forming a Deputation from the society of Quakers[135] lately arrived here with a Twofold object, the one to inspect the Prisons, the other (the real object of their mission) to induce the King of Prussia to allow His Protestant Subjects to follow

[133] In March 1840 Adolphe Thiers became the new Minister-President of France.
[134] Since April 1839 the European powers' policy in the Near East had been dominated by the conflicts over Syria between the Ottoman Empire and Mehmet Ali, the Ottoman governor in Egypt.
[135] As in this case, members of the Christian Quaker movement, the Society of Friends, based in Britain, worked to realize their philanthropic aims in the USA and all over Europe.

the creed of their respective churches without molestation. I informed
Your Lordship soon after my first arrival here that the King was
endeavouring to blend the Lutheran and Calvinist Churches into one,
and thus create a National Church. The Lutheran Church having
become lax in its discipline and faith, this fusion was in general brought
about without difficulty, but in Silesia a strong resistance was made by
the Lutheran Clergy: this induced the King to use force,[136] which ended
by the emigration of the Clergy carrying with them their Flocks, and
it appears from the reports of the Quakers that 1040 Prussians passed
through Newcastle last year on their way to Australia. The Quakers
look upon this persecution as a scandal brought upon the Protestant
Church, and to remonstrate with the King on behalf of Protestantism;
have made the journey to Berlin. They have been received by the
Prince Royal,[137] and by all the Princes and Princesses with great
cordiality all lamenting the effects of the King's attempt to create a
National Church but no one undertaking to speak to His Majesty on
the subject.

The King on the plea of bad health has declined to see them. They
consequently drew up a petition or remonstrance in the form of a
Letter which they requested Baron Humboldt to present to the King:
but the Baron represented to them that the persecution had ceased,
that the King was old, and made irritable by sickness, that their Letter
might rather have the effect of injuring, than of serving the Protestant
Cause; and that after the King's Kindness in throwing open the Prisons
to their inspection, and allowing them to give lectures, and hold publick
worship in an Inn, an indulgence never shewn before, and contrary to
Prussian Custom, it would ill become them to write a letter which
might offend and wound the feelings of the King. They yielded to these
Arguments, and have determined to carry their Letter to England and
send it through Baron Bülow to the King signed by the whole Body of
Quakers.

In this case I was only able to assist them with my advice, which
accorded with that given to them by Baron Humboldt.

M.rs Fry in a publick Lecture pointed out to the Prussians the defects
in their Prison Regulations which has been well received by them.

---

[136] 1834 saw the climax of the disputes between the orthodox Lutherans in Silesia, who
opposed uniting with the Calvinists to form a unified Protestant Church, and the Prussian
state. In one case it was only possible to replace an old-Lutheran clergyman with a new
pastor by means of forceful military intervention.

[137] Friedrich Wilhelm IV.

FO 64/228: William Russell to Viscount Palmerston, No 13, Berlin, 20 May 1840

Difficulty of obtaining a true account of Prussian King's state of health; arrangements resulting from his illness

[...] So much mystery is observed with regard to the state of the King of Prussia's health, that it is difficult to send Your Lordship a true account, but I am inclined to think the danger imminent.

Prince Wittgenstein told me that the King had not eaten solid food for several days, and that a Cup of broth taken at long intervals was the only nourishment he received – a rapid decline must be the consequence unless a medicine is found to restore the power of the stomach.

No one has ventured to tell the Prince Royal[138] of the danger attending the Kings illness – the younger Princes speak of it as a temporary derangement of health, and the Courtiers around the King's Person will scarcely allow that He is ill at all. The Prince Royal is consequently exposed to be called upon at any moment to take the reins of Government without any previous preparation or any knowledge of the actual state of affairs, so jealous has the King been of his Son's interference in public business.

The Government is for the moment in that state to which all absolute Governments are exposed when the Sovereign is not able to direct affairs, and has no Minister who has sufficiently his confidence to take the direction upon himself – that is, paralysed – however as no question of moment presents itself, the machinery of Government goes on and the Public do not perceive that the Head to direct is wanting. The great annual Parade of the Berlin and Potsdam Garrisons is to be tomorrow in front of the Palace instead of being as formerly in the field, when the King will look at it from his window. The arrival of the Empress of Russia[139] is announced for the 2nd of June, consequently everything is done to prevent the Public from taking alarm, but my own belief is that the King is in great danger.

---

[138] Friedrich Wilhelm IV.
[139] Alexandra Feodrovna.

FO 64/229: William Russell to Viscount Palmerston, No 20, Berlin, 18 June 1840

Late King's will; reasons why King is not regretted by the Prussian nation; many questions on internal policy still unsettled; external policy of the late King had also its defects; expectations of the new King

Since the King of Prussia's Death every thing has proceeded in the usual way. The late King left a will (drawn up in 1827) in the hands of Prince Wittgenstein. The two Codicils relating to the Funeral are alone made known to the Publick. In these Codicils the King gives directions in minute details for the disposal of His Body – the clothes in which It is to be dressed – the time It is to be exposed to publick view – the number of men from each Regiment that are to escort the Body to the Grave, and the place and space they will occupy. It is an imitation of the Will of Frederick 1st. The Body is to be buried at Charlottenburgh, and placed by the side of that of the Queen[140] which reposes in a small Grecian Temple in the Palace Garden containing the beautiful Marble Statue of the Queen by Rauch.

The King has left the money He had accumulated to His successor, liable to Legacies to the Princess Liegnitz and His Sons. It amounts to eighteen Millions of Dollar formed from the savings the King made from the Civil List of an annual Revenue of two and a half Millions of Dollars, which He assigned to Himself, and which does not appear as an Item in the Budget presented to the Nation. The King's simple habits consumed a very small portion of this Revenue, but He occasionally made grants out of it for the support of the Theatres and liberally assisted the Actors and Actresses.

The King is not regretted by the Nation. They say that He was a just and good man, but wanted the energy and enlightenment to put in play the resources and wants of the Country. He held firmly in His hand the authority of an Absolute Sovereign without attempting to give a direction to the internal or external Policy of the Country He governed; He allowed Events to arise, and attempted to avoid rather than to overcome the difficulties they presented. Tranquillity at Home and Peace abroad were the ends. He aimed at, and which He obtained by Sacrifices that will throw many difficulties in the way of His Son and Successor. The late King's famous and solemn promise to give a constitution to His Subjects contained in a Decree[141] issued from Vienna in 1815, and signed by Himself and His Minister Hardenberg, is still

[140] Luise.
[141] Decree of 22 May 1815. It contained, in legally binding form, the promise of a written constitution with representative institutions.

an unredeemed pledge. The People may or may not ask the Son to fulfill the promise of the Father; it is a question which no one can answer: but the desire to possess a Constitution by an Assembly of Representatives is not strong in Prussia: The present state of publick feeling in the East and Western Extremities of the Kingdom would make such an assembly very dangerous, and the geographical position of Prussia would make it inconvenient. It is possible that the Provincial Assemblies may ask for greater power and a controul over the publick expenditure. Besides this there are many questions of internal Policy still unsettled. The Catholick and Lutheran Churches have their griev-ances. Two Archbishops[142] of the former being still in prison, and the Pastors of the latter are still endeavouring to carry off their Flocks to Australia. The Arts and Sciences of which the Prussians are passionately fond received no support from the late King. The Universities, the members of which form a powerful Body, will not bear the same neglect from His present Majesty. These are the difficulties that present or may present themselves to Frederick William the Fourth. The External Policy of the late King had also its defects, and defects so glaring and so obnoxious to the Prussians, that a more wholesome system must be pursued. During the intimate Alliance that existed between Russia, Prussia and Austria, the King to conciliate His Allies, allowed them to exercise a rigid Policy in His Country, under the plea of keeping down revolutionary principles. Prussian Citizens who by their language or love of liberal Institutions had made themselves obnoxious to Russia or Austria, were persecuted, imprisoned or put away from employments that they exercised with patriotism and integrity. These men, including some of the ablest of the Country have their grievance and may demand redress, or legal guarantees against future persecution. Russia has ceased to interfere in the internal Affairs of this Country. Austria must do the same. Action of a vicious nature produces re-action, consequently the system is impolitick as well as unjust. All Prussians desire an intimate Alliance with Austria, but they desire it between Equal and Equal. The support given by the late King to the King of Hanover was disapproved of by His own Subjects, whilst He lost by it the confidence of all the constitutional States of Germany and His influence at the Diet.[143]

Such is the aspect of Prussia on the King's accession to the Throne. I look forward however to His meeting or overcoming all the difficulties:

---

[142] Clemens August Freiherr von Droste zu Vischering, Archbishop of Cologne and Martin von Dunin, Archbishop of Posnan. Like Droste, Dunin was also arrested for refusing to follow the Prussian laws on mixed marriages.

[143] For the dispute over the constitution in Hanover cf. dispatches in Hanover section between 1838 and 1840.

His Majesty is enlightened and just, passionately fond of the Arts, a protector of Science, and respected by His People. In His younger days He was supposed to carry to excess his love of legitimate Monarchy, to have wished, to have made War on France for the sake of Charles the Tenth, and to have marched into Belgium in aid of the King of Holland.[144] The Chivalrous notions of a young Prince will now yield to the matured opinions of a Sovereign with the responsibility of the Welfare of His people on His head, and I am convinced that He will be as firm a Guarantee for the maintenance of Peace as was the late King.

FO 64/229: William Russell to Viscount Palmerston, No 23, Berlin, 24 June 1840

New King seeks alliance with Austria; in German affairs jealousy between Austria and Prussia will continue to exist; late King never saw his ministers; new King shows new kind of leadership

[...] The opinions of the present King will I think lead Him to seek an intimate Alliance with Austria in preference to any other Power: I mean, that He will take no great step without consulting and acting in accordance with Austria. In German Affairs some jealousy will continue to exist, yet Prussia must shew Herself at the Diet the Protector of the German People as well as of their Sovereigns, or, she must submit to see the lead taken out of Her hands by some of the Constitutional States. The part taken by Prussia on the Hanoverian Question has thrown Her for the present quite into the shade.[145]

The late King never saw His Ministers: a written Report was made to Him of the proceedings of the Cabinet by Count Lottum, and the King made His observations in the margin. The present King has appointed a Day in the week to transact business personally with each Minister. He has not yet been able to appoint any one to the Ministry of Education, considered now to be the most difficult and important post, especially as the King's desire is to settle the Catholick Question and release the ArchBishops.[146] His Majesty has been occupied in receiving the Officers of the Garrisons of Berlin and Potsdam as well

[144] For the 1830 revolutions in France and Belgium referred to here cf. nn. 21, 28 in Frankfurt section.

[145] For the dispute over the constitution in Hanover cf. dispatches in Hanover section between 1838 and 1840.

[146] Clemens August Freiherr von Droste zu Vischering, Archbishop of Cologne and Martin von Dunin, Archbishop of Posen.

as Deputations from the Universities, Academies of Sciences etc. It was thought that these learned Bodies would seize the opportunity to elicit from the King some expression of His Political views, but their addresses were adulatory and feeble, and the cause of disappointment to the progressive party.

The appearance of things indicates a continuance of the Policy of the late King.[147]

FO 64/226: To William Russell, Foreign Office, No 30, London, 17 July 1840 (Draft)[148]

Explanation of why no special mission sent by Queen Victoria on the accession of the Prussian King to the throne rendered necessary

Her Majesty's Government have been informed that some of the Courts of Europe have sent or about to send special Missions to Berlin, for the purpose of congratulating His Prussian Majesty on his Accession to the throne; and in order that no misinterpretation may be put upon the circumstance that no such Mission has been sent by the Queen, I have received Her Majesty's Commands to instruct Your Lordship to explain to the Prussian Government that it has not been the practice of this Court to send Special Missions on the accession of Foreign Sovereigns, except in some special cases; and in those cases it has generally happened that the Mission had some political object connected with the events of the day, and was not merely complimentary.

But as happily there is nothing in the existing political relations between Great Britain and Prussia, which could render a Special Mission necessary, The Queen has not thought it expedient to deviate on the present occasion from the general practice of Her Court; and Her Majesty feels fully persuaded that the Court of Prussia will at once perceive that nothing can be further from the intention or wish of Her Majesty, than to show the slightest want of attention and respect to a Sovereign with whom, both on account of the ancient connection between the Royal Families of Great Britain and Prussia, and in consequence of the friendship and intercourse subsisting between the respective Countries, it is Her Majesty's earnest wish to maintain the most internal relations. [...]

---

[147] Enclosures: Copy and Translation of 'My Last Will'; Translation of Cabinet order, addressed to the Ministry of State by His Majesty Frederick William the Fourth.
[148] Original in FO 244/63.

FO 64/229: William Russell to Viscount Palmerston, No 31, Berlin, 5 August 1840

On the Treaty of London

I do not remember any Event to have occurred since I have been at Berlin which has given so much satisfaction as the signature of the Convention by England, Austria, Russia and Prussia:[149] No doubt the satisfaction would have been greater had the Government of France thought fit not to have separated their Policy from that of the Four Powers; but the obstinacy of the French Government to adhere to a line chalked out for themselves made every one see, that concession to their dictation would submit the Continent, not to the will of the King of the French, nor to the will of the French Government, but to the will, the capricious will, of the French Press, for in this case the Press of France has made both King and Government bow to its decision. Such a state of things would not long have been bearable, and great is the gratitude to Your Lordship for having come to the rescue of the Northern Nations. The general fall of the Funds, and the warlike language of France certainly creates uneasiness amongst the mass, but every one capable of forming a political opinion sees, that the success of the views of the Four Powers will secure to Europe many years of Peace, whilst submission to the views of France would place it on a foundation of sand. Yesterday the Telegraph[150] announced the intention of the French Government to call out 150,000 men and to arm and man several Ships of War. I saw Baron Werther after he received the news – he told me that he regarded the measure as wise, from its tendency to calm the French, who would probably be as well satisfied with Parade and the display of force as with action, but that it caused no apprehension to the Prussian Government. I think the King must have infused this Courage into His Government, for I am not accustomed to see them so calm on an occasion so trying. I afterwards saw Count Maltzahn who left Berlin yesterday to reside near Prince Metternich: he told me that the Prince having ratified the Convention would not flinch from going through with it.

Count Bresson has held to me moderate and reasonable language, but my Colleagues tell me that the violence of his language to them

[149] On 15 July 1840 the four powers concluded the Treaty of London to protect the integrity of Turkey and to block attempts at expansion by the Ottoman governor in Egypt, Mehmet Ali. Ali's plan to occupy the whole of Syria was supported by France.

[150] *Telegraph für Deutschland*, political literary periodical edited by Karl Gutzkow. Founded in Frankfurt in 1836, from September 1837 onwards the *Telegraph* was published by *Hoffmann and Campe* in Hamburg. In December 1841 it was banned, along with all other *Hoffmann and Campe* publications in Prussia.

surpasses all that can be imagined: his object is probably to frighten the Prussian Government as well as the minor German States: he has failed in both. The Prussian Government is firm, and the ministers of the minor States are unanimous in their approbation of the Convention. Count Bresson strove hard to prevent the Convention receiving its Ratification, but failed. It will be sent to England today.

FO 64/229: William Russell to Viscount Palmerston, No 33, Berlin, 12 August 1840

Innoculation and vaccination for smallpox regulated by law in Prussia

In reply to Your Lordships Despatch of the 31 Ultimo desiring to be informed whether measures have been taken in Prussia for abolishing by Law the practice of Inoculation for the Small Pox, I have to state that Inoculation for the Small Pox is forbidden by Law under very severe Penalties and an Institution has been formed for substituting and extending the practice of Vaccination.[151] From this Institution the Vaccine matter is sent on application gratis, to all Parts of Prussia: the result gives perfect satisfaction. I will endeavour to procure the printed Documents for transmission to Your Lordship's Office.

FO 64/229: William Russell to Viscount Palmerston, No 42, Berlin, 16 September 1840

Provincial diets' petition Prussian King for extension of constitutional rights; King against any change in the present system

Considerable sensation has been caused at Berlin by the Intelligence that the Provincial States of Prussia lately assembled at Königsberg had in their address petitioned His Prussian Majesty by a very large Majority for an extension of Constitutional Rights, and by the Reply of His Majesty, of which I have the honor to enclose a Translated Extract, and from which Your Lordship will perceive that the King has expressed Himself in very decided terms against any change of the present

---

[151] Inoculation is the injection of smallpox pathogens from the lymph of a person with the disease. In the vaccination method, the cowpox lymph is used for immunization, which entails relatively little danger to the person injected.

Institution of Provincial States existing in Prussia,[152] and against a Union of those Provincial Assemblies into one Representative Body for the whole Kingdom.

The exact terms of the Address of the States are not known, the King's Reply alone having been published, but it is understood that great unanimity prevailed amongst the Members, and some blame has been attributed to the President of the Province and Royal Commissary, Monsieur de Schön, a Statesman of known liberal opinions, for not having exercised his influence over the Diet to prevent an expression of opinion so unusually bold for a Prussian Assembly, but it does not appear that he has incurred His Majesty's displeasure, having received on the occasion of the States doing homage to His Majesty, the high distinction of the Order of the Black Eagle[153] and the Title of Minister of State. His Majesty however is reported to have expressed much dissatisfaction on first learning the demand of the States which is attributed to the preponderance in the Diet of the middle classes who have obtained by purchase possession of the greater part of the landed Property in the ancient Province of East Prussia and have thus contributed to the spread of constitutional opinions. [...][154]

FO 64/229: William Russell to Viscount Palmerston, No 49, Berlin, 7 October 1840

Fluctuating views by various parties on Treaty of London; Baron Bülow of greatest service to Quadruple Alliance; King in need of advice and support from an able cabinet

It would be to waste Your Lordship's time to give you an account of the fluctuation of the views of the Prussian Cabinet with respect to the Convention of July[155] – Parties, and fractions of Parties get the ascendancy by turns over some influential member of the Ministry, and the tone of thinking is changed accordingly. Baron Werther acts occasionally without the knowledge of his Colleagues, and I believe that the instructions he sent to Baron Bülow to sign no Treaty unless France was a party to it, were given without being communicated to the King,

[152] Since 1823 each of the eight Prussian provinces had had provincial diets. They were responsible for laws affecting ownership rights or taxes and for decrees and measures of the provincial administration. However, they only had decision-making rights in matters regarding the self-administration of the provinces.
[153] Order of the Black Eagle, the highest Prussian order, inaugurated by King Friedrich I on the occasion of his coronation on 18 January 1701.
[154] Enclosure: Extract from the King of Prussia's Reply to the address of the Provincial States of Prussia assembled at Königsberg under date of 9th September 1840, Section 3.
[155] Treaty of London of 15 July 1840, cf. n. 149 in this section.

and doubt whether His Majesty has ever seen the reserved Protocol in which the word 'Neutrality' is introduced. In the midst of this confusion Baron Bülow has been of the greatest service to the interest of the Quadruple Alliance. He explained to the King's satisfaction the causes that induced the Parties to the Treaty to withhold the communication from the French Ambassador[156] untill the signatures had been affixed.

The weakness I have alluded to in the Berlin Cabinet must lead to its dissolution and reconstruction on principles of homogenity and unity of action. I thought at one time that the King would be able to govern His Ministers, and that all action would emanate from His Will; that He would take up again the Reins which have been in feeble hands since the death of Frederick the Second, and guide the State with the firmness and foresight of His great Predecessor; but it appears that the King stands in need of the advice and support of an able cabinet. The late King allowed Him to grow up in ignorance of the Affairs of Government, and He consequently wants that confidence in Himself which His natural and acquired talents entitle Him to. Here is an instance. The Sovereigns of the South of Germany stated that they were threatened with the loss of their best horses, and requested the King of Prussia to forbid the exportation to France. The Cabinet advised it and the order was presented to the King for signature. On that day an Article appeared in the Courier Français, saying, that an interdiction put upon an exportation of horses was tantamount to a declaration of War. The alarmists acted on the King and to this day the order remains unsigned. This timid Policy naturally encourages the French to arm and to threaten.

The King has noble feelings and upright intentions, and will not abandon His Allies with levity or from ungrounded fears. The conduct of Austria, will however have great weight here. The influence of Russia is null at Berlin, yet since the signature of the Treaty, She has acted with a firmness, consistency and moderation that might be imitated by the Cabinets of Austria and Prussia. [...]

FO 64/229: William Russell to Viscount Palmerston, No 52, Berlin, 21 October 1840

Act of Homage to Prussian King by several provinces; critical reception of King's speech by Liberal Party; granting of numerous titles of nobility

The Ceremony of the Act of Homage to the King of Prussia on the part of the States of the Provinces of Brandenburg, Pomerania, Saxony,

---

[156] Charles Joseph, comte de Bresson.

Westphalia, and of the Rhine, took place on the 15th instant with great pomp and Solemnity, first, in the apartments of the Palace, and then generally in the Square fronting it where the great Body of the Citizens of Berlin, according to their several Guilds, and of the Deputies of the States, were drawn up to the amount of between 50 and 60,000 Persons, as stated in the official Accounts.

His Majesty, whose appearance was the Signal for loud and general acclamations, pronounced two Speeches, of which I have the honor to enclose a translation and which are remarkable for His repeated declaration of His Anxiety to preserve the Peace of Europe in concert with His Allies, and of His determination at the same time to maintain the present position and Institutions of Prussia.

That portion of His Majesty's Speech alluding to the absolute tenure by which He holds the Crown of Prussia and in which he appears to discourage the idea of any political changes in the Institutions of the Country, has found less favour in the minds of the liberal Party, who, without distrusting His Majesty's sincerity and good intentions, consider that a greater degree of political liberty would lend to develope the energies and enlightenment of the Prussian Nation. Numerous titles of Nobility have likewise been granted on this occasion, and the condition restricting them to the first degree of Relationship[157] and enacting that they should descend in the second degree to the actual Possessors only of the Properties conferring the title, has been generally approved of as obviating the evil of an encrease of the poorer class of Nobility. [...][158]

FO 64/229: William Russell to Viscount Palmerston, No 59, Berlin, 25 November 1840

Present state of Prussian army; Prussia's and Austria's jealousy regarding the defence of Southern Germany in case of war with France

The report of the present state of the French Army sent to Your Lordship by Her Majesty's Ambassador at Paris[159] corresponds nearly with the Report sent to the Prussian Government. there is a difference of a few thousand Men, but as the Recruits are daily joining their Standards, the difference of dates would make the difference of Men.

Lord Granville supposes that the French Army would take the field

---

[157] Direct male and female offspring of a marriage of appropriate social standing.

[158] Enclosure: The King of Prussia's Speech to the Nobility and Deputies of the order of Knighthood of the Provinces of Brandenburgh, Pomerania, Saxony, Silesia, Westphalia, and the Rhine.

[159] Earl Granville.

with about 200,000 Men, it is thought here that by leaving the Garrisons to the care of Veterans, Recruits and National Guards, 200,000 Men might be placed on the German Frontier and 100,000 on the Frontier of Italy. The German Confederation would be able in the space of four or six Months to put into motion 500,000 Men, and better Troops are not to be seen. [...]

In the Military schemes discussed and adopted, some jealousy has arisen between Austria and Prussia. In former days the defence of Southern Germany was confided to Austria. This Power has, either willingly or from negligence (I know not which) allowed her influence amongst the Southern States to diminish, and they have made known to Prussia, that they cannot trust their safety to the supineness and slow military movements of Austria – that in case of French Invasion they hope to be aided by Prussia. The King flattered by this appeal to his power, promised to send the 4th Corps d'Armée (30,000 men) towards the upper Rhine. The old Prussian Officers no sooner got knowledge of this promise than they remonstrated against it, as being contrary to the old Prussian System, and offensive to Austria. General Grollmann will probably rectify this misunderstanding at Vienna.

The King of Prussia has expressed a wish, that should war be declared, the command of the Army of the Confederation should be offered to the Duke of Wellington. This is a compliment to the old warrior as well as to England.

FO 64/229: William Russell to Viscount Palmerston, No 64, Berlin, 23 December 1840

Unintended renewal of German Confederation by France's threat of war; Austria's weak financial situation; people's demand for more liberal institutions; service England could render to Germany in case of war with France

[...] Monsieur Thiers has involuntarily rendered great service to Germany by renewing the Union of the Confederated States which has been on the wane since 1820.[160]

As far as the Sovereigns and Governments are concerned, it is now perfect. Two sources however of weakness exist, one is the deplorable state of the Finances of Austria – the other arises, or rather might arise from an encreasing desire on the part of the People to obtain Institutions more liberal, which would make them reluctant to contribute to the Expenses of a War, unless they saw that the result would bring some

---

[160] For the French foreign policy under minister-president Adolphe Thiers who propagated re-conquering the Rhine border in 1840, cf. n. 210 in Frankfurt section.

benefit to themselves. Prussia for instance contains an enlightened and industrious Population without a particle of Civil Liberty, without control over the Finances, without even having the free use of their own Judicial Tribunals. It is then scarsely to be expected that they would bear the burthen of War, without making their compact with the King.

Should war arise from the present state of things, the principal service that England could render to Germany would be, 1st To secure by Her influence the Neutrality of Belgium and Switzerland,

2nd To control the succours sent by Russia and prevent Her Troops from powering into Germany, which would weary and disgust the Germans, about 70,000 Russians would engage the Emperor in the contest, without being a burthen to Germany.

3^{d} To prevent (if possible) the War from becoming a War of political principles, and 4th To control and regulate the language of the Germans towards France, and prevent them from assuming pretention to dismember the French Territory, or by hasty invasion to play their whole Military game upon a Card – from which defeat might ensue, followed by the dissolution of Constituted Governments, consequent Anarchy, and prostration of Germany to the Arms of France.

FO 64/233: William Russell to Viscount Palmerston, No 10, Confidential, Berlin, 24 February 1841

Death of Count Lottum; Metternich's policy, style, and influence on the Prussian King; public demands; results of proceedings of provincial diets important to Europe

Count Lottum Minister of State and of the Treasury died here last week. Count Lottum and Prince Wittgenstein were the two men through whom Prince Metternich exercised such influence in the affairs of Prussia – an influence so fatally directed that Prussia is now beginning to feel its evil consequences. The policy of Prince Metternich was to check by severity all political discussion and to avert reforms – at the same time to carry Prussia with him in his Foreign Policy. Count Lottum being dead, and Prince Wittgenstein having, since the death of the late King, ceased to have any weight in the Council, the lever made use of by Prince Metternich has become useless. Prince Metternich however still hopes to exercise a direct influence over the mind of the King, with whom he is probably in Correspondence. The difficulty of the King's position is this, The enlightened part of the Prussian People say – The late King promised us a Constitution and signed the promise with His Royal Hand[161] – for reasons unknown to us He deferred the execution. We respected His Will and abided our time, but now We ask from Your Majesty, if not a Constitution, at least some concession, some Control over our Finances, some guarantee for our personal Liberty. Prince Metternich on the other hand tells the King that the smallest concession is fatal to the Conservative System, that Italy, Hungary and perhaps Austria Herself would immediately make the same pretension, that concessions once admitted, the end to them is not to be foreseen, that all Germany might be inflamed, and the Throne of every Sovereign endangered. The King of Prussia must decide to meet the wishes of His Subjects, or to follow the Counsel of Prince Metternich, a middle course is impossible, for the smallest concession is as objectionable to Prince Metternich and probably to Russia as the grant of a Constitution.

The struggle is about to begin – the Provincial States are called together in March. In East Prussia there is much agitation and the President of the Province, Mons[r] de Schoen,[162] on whom the King lately bestowed the Order of the Black Eagle,[163] has put himself at the head of the movement, and it appears that the King is afraid to dispossess him of his Charge. In Polish Prussia there is no wish to obtain a Constitution – they may demand some Provincial privileges. In Westphalia there is much Agitation. The Meeting of the Rhenish States is postponed. The King intends to visit them in Person in May.

The result of these Proceedings is important to Europe – the German Liberals are active and full of hope, and the French Liberals watch the movement with anxiety, as one, that, by disturbing the Union of Germany may facilitate their warlike Projects.

The King of Prussia might put aside, or at least postpone the critical moment that threatens Him, were He to call to His Councils Men more capable to give Him advice than His present Ministers, and with more courage to meet the difficulties that present themselves, but unfortunately they do not enjoy the confidence of the Public, and the King, although enlightened, instructed, of quick conception, just, liberal and adorned with every private virtue does not appear to have that clear sight into the consequences of a political act, nor the decision that might enable Him to govern without a Ministry – a point at which He aims – his concession to the Pope have displeased the Protestants.[164]

---

[161] Cf. n. 141 in this section.
[162] Heinrich Theodor von Schön.
[163] Cf. n. 153 in this section.
[164] When he took office Friedrich Wilhelm IV was prepared to compromise on numerous issues hitherto in dispute, for example the role of the state in electing bishops or the question of mixed marriages. This was in an attempt to appease the Catholic church and to pacify the Catholic movement in Prussia. He did not, however, reinstate

His hesitation to acknowledge the Queen of Spain[165] displeases His Subjects.

FO 64/233: William Russell to Viscount Palmerston, No 29, Berlin, 20 May 1841

Results of proceedings of provincial diets; Liberal Party gains strength; situation in different Prussian provinces

The Provincial States assembled on the 28th of February last have closed their Sessions without producing any remarkable results.

In East Prussia the Constitutional Spirit showed itself the strongest by an Address to the Crown in favour of Freedom of the Press, and by the general tenor of the Debates in the Diet, although the influence of the President of the Province, Monsieur de Schön, who had previous to the opening of the States encouraged the demands for a Constitution, was employed to allay the impatience of the liberal Party, with the view of giving the King time to mature his plans for the development of the Institutions of the Country, and on this ground the Petitions from several Towns for Constitutional Rights were laid aside by the Diet. It is to be expected however that unless His Majesty should make some further concessions during the interval of Two Years that will elapse before the re-assembly of the States, the liberal Party will gain strength at the next Elections and will show more perseverance in their demands.

In the Diet of Posen, the feeling of Polish Nationality predominated and served to check the natural leaning of the Poles towards the liberal form of Government which a Constitution for the whole Kingdom would establish, but through which they would lose their separate position.[166]

Should they however not obtain the Natural Privileges[167] they desire, it is probable that at their next meeting, they will pronounce themselves more strongly in favour of general liberal Institutions.

In the Westphalian States a powerful Catholic Party exists – the

Clemens August Freiherr von Droste zu Vischering, who had been dismissed as Archbishop of Cologne.

[165] Isabella II.

[166] In the provincial diet of Posen the majority of deputies were appointed by Poland, so that specific Polish interests could be represented. In a national representative body, on the other hand, there was a risk of becoming politically marginalized.

[167] The most important demands were that the Polish language be retained and taught in schools, and greater participation by Poles in the administration. In the Grand Duchy of Posen Poles constituted 60 per cent of the population.

Government however succeeded in carrying a Majority against a motion for an Address to the King for the unconditional Return of the Archbishop of Cologne[168] to his Diocese.

The Diet of Silesia adopted a Representation on the injury done to the Commercial Interests of the Province by the system of Prussian Prohibitory Duties and the manner in which it is enforced on the Polish Frontier, and petitioned the Government to exert its influence to put an end to a state of things inconsistent with the amicable Relations existing between the Courts of Russia and Prussia.

The States of Brandenburg and Pomerania distinguished themselves by their acquiescence in the views of Government.

The only motion of interest in the Diet of Saxony was in favour of the Manufacture of Beet Root Sugar.[169]

The States of the Rhenish Province are convoked for the 23rd of this month and it is expected that the question of the Return of the Archbishop of Cologne will be mooted by the Nobility who on the other hand will support Government against a Constitution. [...]

FO 64/233: William Russell to Earl of Aberdeen, No 4, Berlin, 10 November 1841

Germany's increased manufacturing endangers Great Britain's manufacturing interests; protective system and heavy duties on British goods under consideration; negative effects of Corn Laws

I have frequently called the attention of Lord Palmerston and I now call the attention of Your Lordship to the danger that menaces the Manufacturing Interest of Great Britain from the rapidly encreasing manufactured productions of Germany. These manufactures owe their creation, rise, and progress to the principle too long acted upon in England of selling, without buying. A few years ago British Manufactured Goods were in great demand in Germany, and now they are completely excluded from the Markets. At the great Fairs of Frankfort and Leipzic the English Merchants have ceased to appear, and whilst the activity of our Looms is declining, those of Germany are augmenting; cheered on by the hope of gaining possession of the great markets of the World. German manufactured Cottons and Woollens are exported to the Levant – to America, and are sold in London after paying the Duty. The loss of markets is not the sole evil that threatens us. We are

---

[168] Clemens August Freiherr von Droste zu Vischering.

[169] In the interests of the sugar beet industry protective tariffs on imported raw sugar (colonial sugar) were demanded. In 1841 public pressure led to the cancellation of the trade treaty concluded between the *Zollverein* and the Netherlands in 1839.

losing at the same time, the talent and enterprize, that brought our Manufactured Goods to such perfection, and with it, such wealth to the Nation. The Manufacturers are leaving England, carrying with them their gold, their industry, and their knowledge – to be bestowed upon Foreigners. In this Town the largest Cloth-Manufactory has been set up by British Capital, and is directed by Englishmen, who complain of the Laws which drove them from their native soil; Laws, which have the practical effect of the Edict of Nantes,[170] by which the industry and Gold of France was brought to England, as it is now driven out of England, by the operation of the Corn Laws.[171]

This subject requires the most serious consideration of Her Majesty's Government.

There is another bearing of this Question, which has not yet assumed a dangerous, or even a consistent form; still it should not be lost sight of a vast plan has been imagined by the execution of which our Manufactures may be destroyed. This plan has transpired by the published writings of some obscure men; It has however caught the attention of men by no means obscure. The writers propose by a system of protection to Continental Manufactured Goods, and heavy duties on British Goods, to gain such an ascendancy in all Markets, that they will soon be able to undersell British Manufactures in our own Colonies, and perhaps in our home markets. They state that the encreasing Power of England is dangerous to the Peace of the World; that She is already too powerful to be met in open War; but that a War may be carried on against the source of Her Wealth – viz – Her Manufactures; and a blow may thus be struck which She cannot parry, and which will bring Her to a level with other Nations.

It is in fact another mode of acting upon the principle of the Continental System promulgated by Napoleon in his Berlin and Milan Decrees.[172] What he attempted to do by force, they would do by commercial Treaties. This plan may appear too wild and difficult to be acted upon, but if the present Corn Laws are maintained, it will become practical and easy. I am glad to have had another opportunity of calling the attention of Her Majesty's Government to this important Question before I leave Berlin.

---

[170] Russell is referring here to the repeal of the Edict of Nantes in 1685 (Edict of Fontainebleau), which led to the emigration of the Hugenots to England and elsewhere.
[171] The Corn Laws of 1815 and 1828 imposed tariffs on the import of corn if it were to be offered below a certain price. The aim of these protective tariffs was to support British corn prices. They were repealed in 1846.
[172] Cf. n. 15 in this section.

FO 64/238: George B. Hamilton to Earl of Aberdeen, No 10, Berlin, 15 January 1842

Order of Prussian King granting greater freedom to the press; hopes raised by this order

One of the measures most loudly called for by publick opinion and the high state of Education in Prussia has just been adopted by the King. His Majesty has issued order[173] that a greater degree of Freedom should be granted to the Press. The Censorship is not in future to place unnecessary restrictions on the liberty of discussion, but to confine itself to suppressing that which is contrary to Morality and Religion, to prevent the mixing up of fanatical Religious opinions with Politicks; and to watch over the Dignity and Security of Prussia, and of the States of the Confederation.

A Free discussion of the internal Affairs of Prussia both as to the Acts of the Government and the suggestion of improvements is to be allowed, provided the articles are not drawn up in an invidious form – and the Censors in judging of the propriety of their admission are chiefly to be guided by the Tone and tendency that may pervade them, and consequently considerable latitude is left to the discernment of the Persons exercising that Office.

All offensive personal observations, and Party names are to be excluded. It is hoped, as the orders in question further state, that the more expanded field thus given to publicity will have the effect of encreasing the interest taken in National concerns of raising the National Character, and of preventing the periodical Press from endeavouring to satisfy the curiosity of its Readers by borrowing the malevolent or ill-founded correspondence of Foreign Newspapers.

Great Care is to be taken in respect to the authorization of new Periodicals or new Editors who are to be men of irreproachable character and loyalty. The same caution is to be observed in the choice of the Censors.

Such, My Lord, is the substance of the Circular addressed by His Prussian Majesty's Orders on the 24th of December last to the Presidents of the Provinces, and of which the most important feature is the liberty formerly withheld, and now granted, of discussing the internal Affairs of Prussia.

Hitherto the Prussian Newspapers contained no information on the state of Prussia, and the restraint placed upon the Press was severely felt by the numerous class of Prussian Writers and the Publick, who either remained in ignorance of Events passing in their own Country, or learnt them through the doubtful medium of Foreign Journals; and

---

[173] Circular instruction of 24 December 1841 to the *Oberpräsidenten* of the provinces.

it may be confidently hoped that much good will result from this measure, if the spirit of the King's intentions is fairly acted up to by the subordinate Authorities on the one hand, and by the Persons connected with the Press on the other – and the hidden talent of which there is so much, existing in Prussia will thus be brought to light.

His Prussian Majesty, on His side, has given a new proof of His conscientious intention of fulfilling the promise He has frequently made of gradually introducing the necessary improvements in the administration of His Kingdom, provided He should not be too hard pressed as to the period of their introduction.

FO 64/238: George B. Hamilton to Earl of Aberdeen, No 70, Berlin, 15 June 1842

'Pour le Mérite' for sciences and arts

Among the Orders of Prussian Knighthood is the Order 'Pour le Mérite'[174] instituted by Frederick the Great and only given as a Military Reward the King of Prussia has lately created a new branch of this order for Civil Merit to be bestowed on Individuals preeminent for Science and Literature. It is to consist of 60 Members, whereof 30 are to be Germans and 30 Foreigners. On the Decease of any of the German Members, each surviving Knight is to send in a Notification to the King of the Person he thinks most worthy to succeed him, and the King may or may not let His Choice fall on the Person who has the most votes. The Foreign nominations rest entirely with the King.

Sir John Herschel, Mr Thomas Moore and Mr Faraday are amongst the Englishmen on whom the King has conferred the Order of Merit.

FO 64/238: George B. Hamilton to Earl of Aberdeen, No 73, Berlin, 18 June 1842

Changes in proceedings of the different provincial diets of Prussia; project of one assembly uniting the committees of the several provincial diets; question of what function it should have

In the Month of February 1841 His Prussian Majesty opened the first Sitting after His accession to the Throne, of the different States of the Provinces of Prussia by a Royal Rescript, of which the most interesting political points were, the promised Publication of the Proceedings of

---

[174] Order founded by Friedrich II in 1740. The *Pour le Mérite* for sciences and arts was founded by Friedrich Wilhelm IV on 31 May 1842.

the States formerly withheld by the Government, the proposal that the States should meet every two instead of every three Years, and that a permanent Committee of the Members of the States should be named to assist the Government with its advice on matters of Provincial Administration during the Intervals between the Sessions.

It was also intimated that should the state of public affairs seem to require it, the King would call together the Committees of the States in one Assembly at Berlin, and consult them upon different matters that would be submitted to them – thus realizing a promise that had been made by his late Majesty Frederick William the 3rd.[175]

For some weeks past the question has been agitated in the Council of State as to the expediency of calling together the Committees of the Provincial Diets during this year. I understand that His Majesty's wishes were expressed strongly in favour of their convocation, urging as a reason, that having expressed his intention of doing so, He was desirous of showing his Subjects that His promises would be fulfilled. Several Members of the Council of State were opposed to His Majesty's Views, and the Prince of Prussia[176] expressed his opinion that the state of public affairs did not require that the Committees of the States should be called together, and considered such a measure as inopportune. I believe however that is has been decided that the convocation should take place at Berlin towards the end of October.[177] Much discussion has also arisen as to the subjects that should be submitted to this assemblage for their deliberation, and the manner in which they should be submitted. It is probable that the Government will merely acquaint the States with their intentions as to Financial measures, the new Law for the Press[178] and other subjects connected with the internal Government of the Country and that their Functions will be purely consultative. [...]

The first assembly of this Body at Berlin is doubtless a great innovation in the State and cannot be regarded without great interest although (as I have already informed Your Lordship) the Assemblage in question have only a consultative Voice – they will have little or no power and cannot reject any measure submitted by the Government for their consideration.

[175] Cf. n. 141 in this section.
[176] Prince Wilhelm, brother of Friedrich Wilhelm IV.
[177] Cf. pp. 203–204 in this section.
[178] Cf. pp. 199–200 in this section.

FO 64/239: Henry Howard to Viscount Canning [unnumbered], Berlin,
4 September 1842

*Royal Ordinance relative to the formation of the United Committee of the States; composition
of that committee; its principal occupation; disappointment of its limited function*

With reference to my Despatch of the 31st Ultimo, I have the honor to
transmit herewith a Copy and Translation of the Royal Ordinance
relative to the formation of a Committee of the States of the Kingdom
of Prussia, by which the Province of that name is meant.

Similar Ordinances, in some cases more detailed, have been issued
for the organization of the Committees of the remaining seven Provinces
composing the Prussian Dominions, and will be also be found in
Enclosure N° 1.

I likewise enclose the Copy and translation of His Majesty the King
of Prussia's Cabinet Order, published since the date of my above
mentioned Despatch, convoking a general Meeting of the several
Committees, thus formed, to commence their deliberations on the
18th of October next on the questions to be submitted to them by
Government.

Each Committee is to be composed of twelve Members of whom six
are to be chosen from the Nobility and Proprietors of Estates, two from
the Country Parishes, and four from the Towns, thus giving a Majority
to the Landed Interest and most probably to the views of Government.
These Members will be elected by each State separately during the
Assembly of the Provincial Diets (which meet every two years) and will
hold their Commission during the interval of their Sessions.

Prussia containing eight Provinces, viz: the Kingdom of Prussia,
Pomerania, Silesia, Brandenburg, Saxony, Posen, Westphalia, and the
Rhine, the General Assembly of the Committees will consist of ninety
six Deputies who will meet for the first time together on the 18th of
October next.

Your Lordship will observe that although one of the declared objects
of the Institution of these united Committees is that they may assist the
Government with their advice on important matters of State not usually
laid before the Provincial Diets,[179] whenever His Majesty may think
proper to convoke them for that purpose, yet their principal occupation
will be to reconcile and digest the various propositions and opinions of
the several Provincial Assemblies, and thus form a centre of union, of
which the want was much felt on account of the geographical position
and diversity of interests, of the Provinces. An illustration of the necessity
of this centralization is to be found in the intention of the Government

[179] For the duties of the provincial diets cf. n. 152 in this section.

to submit on the present occasion, to the Committees the question that was presented to the Provincial Diets of last Year, as to the Manner in which the annual remission, from the first of January 1843, of Taxes to the amount of Million of Dollars, should be effected. The Diets gave so many different opinions that no decision was taken by the Government.

The second proposition for the consideration of the Committees, is that of the Establishment of RailRoad communications between the Provinces with the assistance of Public Funds. This is explained by a Promise of the late King not to make a new Loan or raise the Taxes without assembling States General.[180] The third is only of local interest.

Although better informed Persons were aware that it was the intention of the Government to limit, as much as possible, the subjects to be brought before the Committees, so as not to give too much importance to their Proceedings, yet a belief prevailed amongst the Public that various Projects of Laws of general and even political interest would be presented to them. Some disappointment may therefore exist at the non-fulfilment of this expectation, but on the other hand, the many improvements His Prussian Majesty has introduced into the Admin-istration, the settlement of many intricate questions pending at the time of his accession and the choice of His Ministers have tended to inspire the greatest confidence in the Sincerity of His Majesty's Intentions, and of his wishes for the well-being of His People. [181]

FO 64/239: Earl of Westmorland to Earl of Aberdeen, No 30, Cologne, 5 September 1842

King of Prussia's arrival in Cologne; his speech at the ceremony of laying the first stone of the intended completion of the cathedral; Metternich's attendance

I have the honor of reporting to Your Lordship that His Majesty the King of Prussia arrived on the 3rd Instant, and was received with Every demonstration of attachment by the Inhabitants.

On Sunday the 4th the Ceremony of laying the first Stone of the intended completion of the Cathedral took place in presence of an

---

[180] According to the National Debt Law of 17 January 1820 new debts could only be incurred with the agreement of a Prussian diet. This condition reinforced the royal promise of a constitution of 1815 which provided for a parliament for the whole state.

[181] Enclosures: 1. *Gesetz-Sammlung für die Königlichen Preußischen Staaten*, No. 20, 30 August 1842, S. 215–242; 2. Translation: Ordinance respecting the formation of a Committee of the States of the Kingdom of Prussia; 3. King of Prussia's Cabinet orders Convoking Committees of Provincial States to a General Meeting at Berlin; 4. Translation of No. 3.

immense concourse of people, in the course of which His Majesty delivered a speech which created the greatest Enthusiasm, and which, as referring to the Union of Germany, is calculated to make a lasting and beneficial impression.

I have the Honor to Enclose a Copy of this Speech with a Translation.[182]

Prince Metternich arrived here the day previous to this ceremony, and together with the vast assembly of Princes and distinguished Persons from all Parts of Germany, was present upon the occasion, and participated in the general feeling of admiration which was Excited by His Majesty's language and demeanour. [...]

FO 64/239: Earl of Westmorland to Earl of Aberdeen, No 68, Berlin, 28 December 1842

Georg Herwegh's conversation with the King of Prussia; his published letter; press still censored

The Prussian Government has lately been considerably embarrassed by the tendency of the Press since the Order which emanated from the His Majesty the King of Prussia dated in October, and which conceded a greater freedom of publication than had hitherto been enjoyed in this Country.

Nearly at the same time with the issue of this order, His Majesty desired to become acquainted with a violent Republican writer and a Poet of considerable talent, Monsieur Herwegh, and in a conversation of some length with him, His Majesty is understood to have said 'We will be honorable Enemies'. The return this gentleman has made for the very gracious reception he received from The King has been to publish in the Leipzig Gazette[183] a letter which he first sent to His Majesty, and a translation of which I have now the honor of enclosing for Your Lordship's perusal.[184]

The animosity displayed in this publication, as well as the hostile tendency of other articles which have appeared in the Leipzig Gazette have determined the Prussian Government to forbid its introduction into the King's dominions, and as a great proportion of the subscribers to that Paper are Prussians it is thought that this measure will render

---

[182] Enclosures: 1. The King of Prussia's Speech at Cologne on laying the Foundation Stone of Cathedral; 2. Translation of the King of Prussia's Speech at Cologne, September 5, 1842.

[183] Cf. pp. 99–100 in Frankfurt section.

[184] Enclosure: Translated Extract from Leipzig Gazette 'George Herwegh's Letter to King of Prussia'.

the Publishers more cautious of the language they adopt.

The periodical Press in this Country is still under the control of Censors appointed by the Government, several of whom have admitted articles into the Newspapers which the Government complains of, the excuse given by many of them has been that they were not aware of the extent to which their vigilance was expected; to these more stringent Instructions have been issued, while others whose views were more suspected have been removed.

There certainly is a great attempt making by a Party of this country to push its Constitutional views in opposition to the established form of Government, and the King's kind and liberal feeling induces him at times to adopt measures and use expressions which are eagerly seized upon by this Party to infer concessions which were not intended.

FO 64/243: Earl of Westmorland to Earl of Aberdeen, No 13, Berlin, 1 March 1843

New censorship introduced

I have the honor of enclosing a Precis of an Ordinance issued by the Prussian Cabinet respecting the Censorship of Newspapers and Pamphlets as well as all other Publications, together with the Regulations under which a new Court of Censorship has been established, and generally embodying the system under which the Press of this Country will henceforward be controuled.[185]

Your Lordship will be aware that this question has of late excited much attention in Prussia as well as in the neighbouring States. I stated to Your Lordship in my Despatch N° 68 of last Year 'that there was a great attempt' making by a Party in this Country to push 'its Constitutional views in opposition to the established form of Government', and certainly this party mainly looked for success in the extended freedom of the Press, which it at that time had prognosticated from the liberal expressions which at times had been used by His Majesty the King of Prussia, as well as from the supposed tendency of the order of Cabinet issued in October last.[186]

The Council of Ministers have however since that period taken the whole of this subject into very serious consideration and have discussed it amongst themselves and with His Majesty, and the ordinance I now

[185] Enclosure: Précis, King of Prussia's Cabinet Order of 4 February 1843 published 25 February respecting the Censorship of Newspapers and Pamphlets.

[186] In the Order of Cabinet of 4 October 1842 censorship was abolished for all books published in Prussia with more than 320 octavo pages (20 printed sheets).

enclose has been the result of these deliberations. I believe that this measure will satisfy those Persons who have looked with apprehension at the too liberal tendency of the King's supposed policy. The Press will remain nearly in the state it has hitherto been, with the exception of Regulations which being more precise will render their observance easier. The composition of the Board of Censorship is also such as to secure an independent and impartial application of the duties entrusted to it. These changes will not affect the positive control of the Press the Government will retain in its own hands, and by which it will be enabled to maintain its engagements upon this subject with the Federal States of Germany. [...]

FO 64/244: Earl of Westmorland to Earl of Aberdeen, No 129, Berlin, 25 October 1843

Interview with Baron Bülow on Customs Union and the proposed duty on iron; different interests of Germany and Great Britain

I have the honor of acknowledging Your Lordship's Despatch N° 52. Shortly after the receipt of it I had an interview with Baron Bülow.

I have already reported to Your Lordship that I entertained some hopes that the present meeting of the Deputies of the ZollVerein might terminate without the establishment of the proposed duty upon Iron, I was therefore desirous before I mentioned the subject of Your Lordship's Despatch[187] above referred to, to ascertain from Baron Bülow whether this was the case, he told me he could say nothing upon the subject, that positively nothing was decided. I told him I lamented his answer, as I had increased evidence of Your Lordship's anxiety on the subject in a Despatch I had just received, and which I was in hopes I need not have made use of. He replied that it could be of no use as the Prussian Government would do nothing in hostility to British Interests, but only what was forced upon it by the necessities of its own and the German Iron Masters and those connected with them; that the liberal concessions I mentioned as having made by England by the new arrangement of the Tariff[188] were not exclusively to Prussia or Germany but to all the World, that we ought therefore to call upon Russia and Austria to reduce their Tariff to the level of that of the ZollVerein,

[187] In his dispatch of 17 October 1842 to the Earl of Westmorland, the Earl of Aberdeen opposed the *Zollverein*'s policy of protective tariffs. This was prompted by the discussion between the states of the *Zollverein* about raising tariffs on iron.

[188] The tariff reform of April 1842 was part of a major financial reform initiated by Robert Peel. Apart from reducing important import duties (including the import duties on wheat) this also included the abolition of export duties on wool.

before we complained of a small advance upon one article of Commerce by that Body meant only to protect its suffering interests; I answered that We had made our reduction in the Tariff knowing of the state of Tariffs he referred to, but what we complained of was that the ZollVerein was now proposing to inflict a new and encreased duty upon one of our suffering interests, and therefore and upon that ground I had received a direction from Your Lordship again to remonstrate against it. Baron Bülow said: 'No. You have no just cause to remonstrate, because you must know that we do nothing in any feeling as against You, but driven to it by our own position, and by the jealous exigencies of the States we are bound up with, and who suspect Us of a desire to sacrifice their interests.'

I stated that still we must feel our position and consequently the Despatch I held in my hand ordered me to make that clear to him. I then read Your Lordship's Despatch, beginning with Your Instruction to me to remonstrate, to the end, and pointing out particularly that the British Government would consider itself justified, in case an encrease of the protecting Duties on English Goods and Manufactures was adopted in Prussia, to recall what has been done by the British Tariff in her favour.

Baron Bülow replied that England would never do what was not just, and that he felt it would not be so to act in that manner, and that it would be most injurious if he was to make use of such an argument in the discussions he was engaged in, that if he mentioned the interest of Great Britain or any Foreign State, it would only encrease the anxiety in other Governments to establish the duty; that what he had to do was to defend what he thought right for Prussian and German Interests. How far this might lead to there being no change for the present he again declared he could not at present give me any assurance. He was not surprised Your Lordship should make the declaration I had read to him, with a view of straining every exertion in favor of the British Iron Masters, who were suffering as well as those of Germany, but that You must know that the alterations in the British Tariff had been very little advantageous to Prussia, that with respect to the alteration in the Corn Laws,[189] he had rather have had them as they were, and as to timber the only Provinces that profited by the relaxation with regard to it were those upon the Rivers falling into Baltic and those advantages were looked upon with jealousy by the Southern States of Germany as tending to withdraw Prussia as disinterested attention to their Interests.

I replied to Baron Bülow that if all these interests came to be discussed, they might be found to assume a different importance, but

[189] Cf. n. 171 in this section.

he now was again made aware how deeply Your Lordship felt upon the subject and my sincere hope was, that in pursuance of Prussian and German Interests, which never could be unconnected with their Commercial Relations with England he would be led to abstain from the alterations proposed, and that the disturbance which otherwise must necessarily follow to the Trade of the two Countries might thus be avoided.

FO 64/250: Earl of Westmorland to Earl of Aberdeen, No 62, Berlin, 17 April 1844

Formation of Prussian Board of Trade; composition of the council, its objects and tasks

[...] The formation of a Board of Trade by this Government which I have at different times reported to Your Lordship as being in agitation, has, – after many difficulties been decided upon, although it has not yet been announced to the Publick.[190] The Board or Council will consist of the various Ministers whose departments are connected with the Commerce, the Industry, the Revenue, and the Foreign Affairs of the Country, and His Majesty declares himself President of this Council, to which is to be added a Department[191] specially charged with Trade and Manufactures, and which is to be placed under Monsieur de Rönne, who is to be one of the Council, but without the rank of a Minister, and who is to report on all matters placed under his Controul.

The object of His Majesty by this arrangement is to obtain a more precise knowledge of the state of the Trade and Manufacturing Interests of the Country, and their wants and exigencies, and to bring it under the consideration of those Ministers whose Departments will afterwards be charged with the measures either internal or with Foreign Powers which may be decided upon by the General Council.

This Measure is not generally looked upon with much favor; it deranges the system which has hitherto existed as to the subjects to which it relates; it removes the controul from those Departments where it has been placed, and it is not supposed that the interests can be more efficiently attended to by a Department which is not to be entrusted with the Execution of the remedial measures which may be required.

This project has partly originated in a desire to counteract the

---

[190] The Board of Trade (*Handelsrat*) was officially established on 7 June 1844, along with the Office of Trade (*Handelsamt*).

[191] The Office of Trade (*Handelsamt*), hitherto part of the Prussian Finance Ministry, now became an independent department. However, it still had no executive authority.

projected independent Union of the Manufacturers of Germany which was to meet during the present month at Leipzic, and which was looked upon with much apprehension by the Prussian Government. It is hoped that the Board now constituted will be satisfactory to the Manufactures of Prussia, and that it will be able to resist the principles of high protection which certainly would be advocated by the Independent Union I have referred to.

FO 64/250: Earl of Westmorland to Earl of Aberdeen, No 81, Berlin, 8 May 1844

Willingness to negotiate a treaty of commercial reciprocity between Prussia and Great Britain

[...] Baron Bülow was very much satisfied with the acceptation on the part of Her Majesty's Government of the suggestion which he had made that the present would be a good opportunity for the negociation of a treaty of Commercial reciprocity between Prussia and Great Britain.

He told me he should immediately bring the subject under the consideration of the Minister of Finance Monsieur de Bodelschwingh in order that he might take the initiative in this business before he quitted that department.

Baron Bülow remarked that it might be difficult to find the points upon which it would be convenient to the two Governments to negociate, but where there was a sincere desire to meet each others views, as he was convinced was the case in the present instance, they would always be discovered.

He spoke with a great regret of the feeling of commercial jealousy against England which had been raised by the Press of the South of Germany, and which he had hoped would have removed by reasoning, but that as yet it had been unsuccessful; even the removal of the duty on the importation of foreign wool into Great Britain, which had just taken place without any reciprocity, had been found fault with by the manufacturers who were desirous of keeping in Germany what it produced of that article and had formerly obliged the Governments of the Zollverein to impose a duty upon its exportation.

Baron Bülow admitted that this was an evident proof that in measures of this nature it was impossible to satisfy every interest, that the wool growers would be greatly benefitted by it, and the interests connected with them, and by a general balance of advantages to the whole country alone could such measures be judged of or appreciated. [...]

FO 64/251: George B. Hamilton to Earl of Aberdeen, No 5, Berlin, 27 July 1844

Attempted assassination of the King and Queen of Prussia; sensation caused by the incident

It is with great regret that I have to inform Your Lordship that an attempt was made yesterday morning to assassinate their Majesties the King and the Queen[192] of Prussia which providentially has failed.

The King and the Queen were about to leave the Palace of Berlin at eight o' clock in the morning on their journey to Erdimansdorff and Ischl,[193] on descending the steps of the Palace The King received a petition from a Woman, and had some conversation with her; The Queen had got into the carriage, and on the King's following Her, and whilst the Servants were shutting the door of the carriage, a Man stepped forward from the crowd, and fired a double barrelled pistol into the carriage, and so close to it, the pannel of the carriage was burned by the flash from it.

One of the balls passed through the King's cloak, and the other so near to the back of the neck of the Queen, that had not Her Majesty been in the act of stooping forward to take leave of some the Attendants of the Court, She must have infallibly been killed, This ball lodged in the lining of the carriage close to the Queen, the other ball was found at the bottom of the carriage .

The Assassin was instantly seized by some of the Gentlemen of the Court; and so great was the exasperation of the People that it was with the greatest difficulty that the Officers and Soldiers of the Guard could prevent his being torn in pieces on the spot. The Prisoner immediately gave his name as Tschech, formerly Bürgermaster of the Town of Storckow in the Mark of Brandenburg; he had been dismissed from his situation in 1841, in consequence of his faulty administration, and had since petitioned the King to be employed in the service of the State, but without effect, and it is supposed that he was led to the commission of his atrocious crime by a desire to revenge himself on the King.

Their Majesties immediately proceeded on their journey, but the Populace stopped the Royal carriage in the Square before the Palace, to assure themselves that the King was unhurt, His Majesty threw back his Mantle, and thanked the people for their solicitude, The Queen was weeping bitterly and seemed greatly overcome.

The sensation produced in this Metropolis, by the commission of a

[192] Elisabeth Ludovika.
[193] Erdmannsdorf, Friedrich Wilhelm IV's Silesian summer residence; Bad Ischl, Spa in Salzkammergut/Upper Austria.

Crime hitherto unknown in Prussian History, is greater than I can describe, and the utmost loyalty and attachment to their Sovereigns has been shewn by the Prussian People on this occasion, and yesterday Evening the whole of the City was spontaneously illuminated.

I am happy to be enabled to inform Your Lordship that a Letter was received yesterday Evening from the Queen, giving the best account of the King's health and spirits, but acknowledging that Her Majesty Herself had received a severe shock from the trying scene.

FO 64/251: George B. Hamilton to Earl of Aberdeen, No 15, Berlin, 14 August 1844

Prussian King's intention of forming a States General on the foundation afforded by the permanent committees of the Prussian provincial diets; close friends of the King in favour of the idea

Your Lordship will probably recollect that one of the principal changes made by the present King of Prussia on his accession to the Throne, was with reference to the States of the eight Prussian Provinces – an assurance was given that the publication of the proceedings of the State would be permitted by the Government, the States were to meet every two instead of every three years, and a permanent Committee was to be named from each State to assist the Government with its advice on matters of Provincial Administration, during the intervals of the Session. [...]

I had the honor of communicating the details connected with this subject in my Despatch N° 73 of 1842 to Your Lordship,[194] and I now advert to it because I have remarked since my return to Berlin, that there is an idea pretty generally prevalent, that the King has some vague intention of forming a States General on the foundation afforded by the permanent Committees of the States of the Prussian Provinces. I do not pretend to say that the King has any matured plan for so great an innovation, or that such a measure is at all imminent; but judging from what I have heard in different quarters, & from a certain degree of uneasiness expressed by Members of the Government who are adverse to any change, when the possibility of such an event has been called in question, I cannot but think that there is some foundation for the opinion that has gone abroad. Although it may be argued, that after the declarations the King has at different times made, so adverse to any fundamental change in the institutions of the country of such importance as this, it is not likely that He should adopt such a measure,

[194] Cf. pp. 200–201 in this section.

yet as it is believed that in these opinions His Majesty finds abettors such men as General Canitz & Mr Radowitz, the Prussian Ministers at Vienna and Carlsruhe and the Chevalier Bunsen, all intimate friends of the King and consulted by him on most occasions, it is not impossible that at some future period the King may think it advisable to make such a change.

The Gentlemen whose names I have mentioned are all strongly distinguished for their monarchical feeling, but they may be of opinion that the safety of the Prussian Monarchy may probably require ere long some changes of a Constitutional tendency, although there can be no doubt that at least half the nation would oppose such a change, most, if not all the Members of the Government, and foremost of all the Prince of Prussia.

What I have had the honor of stating may appear visionary to Your Lordship, and perhaps I ought to apologize for taking up Your Lordship's time on an question which may never occur, or be very far distant, nevertheless I think I see sufficient grounds for bringing the subject under Your Lordship's notice, although I repeat that I believe the idea has only crossed the Royal Mind.

What appears really extraordinary, is the supposition that something like a representative system can be formed which should have no power over the finances of the Country, that department of the State to remain entirely under the controul of the King, thus depriving it of the power apparently most essential to constitutional Government – nevertheless such is part of the plan said to be in agitation.

FO 64/251: George B. Hamilton to Earl of Aberdeen, No 35, Berlin, 23 October 1844

Exhibition of German industrial products; demand for protection of native industry

The Exhibition, for the produce of German Industry, at Berlin being about to close, it may be proper that I should state to Your Lordship that the conclusions that I have been enabled to draw from the opinions I have heard expressed in various quarters from the Manufacturing and Commercial men assembled here, are, that a general tendency exists on the part of these Gentlemen to recommend protection (additional protection I may say) to the Governments of the States composing the Zoll Verein, as the only means of fastening and encouraging the improvement in Manufactures and the Arts, which the present Exhibition has shewn to have been making such rapid strides in the German States.

I understand that the 'protection to native Industry' has been the constant cry of the immense Assemblage of the 'Industriels', as they are denominated here, ever since the opening of this Exhibition, and they refer with pride to the present state of German Manufactures, which have so rapidly grown up and flourished under the System of protection, as a corroboration of their views on this Subject.

I cannot doubt that these representations will have some effect on the Governments composing the German Union, and I think Her Majesty's Government may be prepared for additional protective measures on the part of the Union, whenever any changes may be made in the present Tariff.

FO 64/251: Earl of Westmorland to Earl of Aberdeen, No 130, Confidential, Berlin, 25 December 1844

Prussian cabinet employed in planning a constitutional assembly; question of who should have a say in financial matters; growing political influence of provincial diets not well received by members of the Prussian cabinet

The Prussian Cabinet is employed in the very important consideration of the plan of a constitutional Assembly of the States General of the Kingdom. The King feels himself called upon to adopt some measure of this sort in consequence of the Laws promulgated by His Majesty the Late King in the Years 1815, 21.& 23. by the last of which it is enacted that no loans shall henceforth be negotiated or made a charge upon the Country unless they shall have been submitted to States General of the Kingdom.[195]

His Majesty and his Advisors consider that this Law would prove of great embarrassment if Prussia should be engaged in hostilities or difficulties of any sort requiring the aid of public credit, and should be obliged to convoke the States of the Kingdom without having taken such precautions as should remove any danger which might arise from the sudden calling together a number of Deputies, the limitation of whose powers might not have been sufficiently defined.

It is considered more advisable to prepare in time for the exigency of such circumstances, by establishing a well regulated plan for the Assembly of these States General of the Kingdom, by which the present Provincial States will be superseded and it is expected a safe development will thus be given to the wish for a Constitutional

---

[195] Westmorland is referring here to the promise of a constitution in 1815, and its confirmation in 1821 and 1823. The Order of Cabinet of 11 June 1821 and the *Gesetz wegen Anordnung der Provinzialstände* of 1823 followed the vague statement in the National Debt Law of 1820, in which the convocation of a national diet was dependent upon a further decision by the King; cf. nn. 141, 180 in this section.

Government, upon the basis of German Institutions which is prevalent throughout the Kingdom.

The object of getting rid of the Provincial States is considered of importance, as, contrary to the original intention of their establishment, they have of late entered into the discussion of the measures of the general Government of the Country, while the Ministers responsible for the Acts made the subject of discussion being absent, were unable to defend their measures, and very great inconvenience has arisen from this practise.

Baron Bülow in speaking to me upon this subject assured me that His Majesty was, as much as himself, impressed with its importance, and fully determined to use the utmost caution in all the proceedings to be taken with regard to it, bearing not only in mind the difficulties which, from any erroneous proceeding in so delicate a matter, might arise to His own Country, but to His Neighbours of Russia and Austria, and the rest of Germany.

FO 64/256: Earl of Westmorland to Earl of Aberdeen, No 52, Berlin, 26 March 1845

Governmental measures in response to alleged communist conspiracy

I have the honour to inform Your Lordship that the Prussian Government, having been for some time past aware of a Communist Conspiracy[196] which was existing at the Town of Hirschberg in Sielsia, have caused ten Individuals to be arrested, who, although with the exception of one person who is a Master Manufacturer,[197] are of no note of importance but who had nevertheless entertained very audacious designs; as among other projects, they had intended to get possession of the Fortress of Schweidnitz, seize the Arsenal, and distribute the arms it contained, among their supporters whom they hoped would be numerous.

Baron Bülow informs me that the arrest of these Ringleaders having been effected, the Government are under no apprehension of any further disturbance.

[196] The supposed communist conspiracy gave the Prussian government a pretext for proceeding against journalists and publicists who had taken up the weavers' cause (social problems, working conditions etc.) The background to this were the events in Peterswaldau and Langenbielau in Silesia on 4–6 June 1844, the so-called Weavers' Uprising (*Weberaufstand*), whose instigators were being sought by the Prussian government.
[197] Friedrich Wilhelm Schlöffel. The other people arrested were members of the Hirschberg singing club, which had been penetrated by a police spy.

FO 64/257: Earl of Westmorland to Earl of Aberdeen, No 71, Confidential, Berlin, 27 April 1845

Prince of Prussia's opinion on the subject of a new constitution intended by his father

The Prince of Prussia,[198] having called at my house to take leave of Lady Westmorland on her departure for England, took that opportunity (which otherwise, in consequence of the limited intercourse between the Princes and the Foreign Ministers, he could not easily have found) of speaking to me of his feelings and opinions upon the changes in the constitution of the Government of this Country which the King is occupied with, and which are expected by the Country.

He assured me that they caused him the greatest anxiety, that he had deeply meditated upon this subject, & that although he had convinced himself that some change had become necessary, yet he could not persuade himself of the propriety of proceeding to the length which was contemplated by the King. While he said this, he must premise that His Majesty had never yet distinctly stated, either in any document or otherwise, what was the ultimate decision to which he had come upon the subject; that he had never produced his plans, but that his views were to be collected from his correspondence with Prince Metternich, and from his conversation with some of his Ministers.

That according to the present Constitution of the Country, any fundamental change in the Government of the nature contemplated, must be submitted to the Council of State, where it would undergo a calm and deliberate discussion. He thought that if the King really made up his mind to propose this new Constitution, he would probably submit it to the Council in the months of July or August, as at that time it would be necessary to return answers to the various petitions which had been forwarded by the different Provincial States, & if it was not intended that they should again assemble in the year 1847 according to the existing regulations, it would be necessary to tell them so. It would also be requisite to give some answer to those States which had petitioned for this change in the Constitution; since, if it was intended to concede it, they could not be found fault with for having asked for it; and if it was not intended, their overzeal must be remarked upon, & repressed. The Prince of Prussia is of opinion, that, in consequence of the Decree which emanated from His Father[199] on the 17th January 1820, no Loan could now be raised by His present Majesty or his successors, without the Sanction of the States General of the

[198] Wilhelm I.
[199] Friedrich Wilhelm III.

Kingdom:[200] upon this ground therefore he is persuaded of the propriety of making such a change in the present Constitution, as would provide for the assembly of these States, but he would confine their action to the object for which he sees the necessity of assembling them; and for any further purpose for which the deliberation of the general interests of the Monarchy should be necessary, he would avail himself of the Committee of Deputies from the Provincial States, which was established by His present Majesty in the year 1842, & which, in the Autumn of that year, was assembled at Berlin.[201]

The principal reasons which induce His Royal Highness to view with alarm any more considerable change in the constitution of this extended Monarchy at the present moment, are, the extreme difficulty of forming a system of representative Government where none has ever yet existed; the little probability there would be of giving satisfaction to the numerous classes of inhabitants whose ambition would be roused by the prospects of a rise to power with which they have never yet been entrusted; the numerous changes which a popular assembly must necessarily be expected to require in the Civil and Criminal Jurisdiction of the country, which, being at present entirely secret, the Government is unprepared to alter; the danger of the interference of such a body with the Army, the expenses of which absorb one half the Revenue of the State, and yet upon which the whole power and influence of the Country depends; and, amongst other reasons, the total want of a Minister capable, either from his abilities, of the confidence of his colleagues, of carrying through so vast a project. The views of the King as they appear from his conversation, are infinitely more extended; but the Prince is in hopes that they are put forward, more with the intention of eliciting opinions & of producing discussion, than of permanently adhering to them.

Amongst the present Ministers of State, the Prince conceives that Baron Bülow would be totally incapable of taking the lead upon a question of this nature; his not being a native of Prussia, but of Mecklenburg, would of itself be a difficulty; he looks upon Count Arnim the Minister of the Interior to be more capable, but neither his power of speaking in public, nor his general habits of business would fit him for a Leader in a public assembly; in as far as these qualities are concerned Monsieur de Bodelschwingh would be more adapted for such a post, but he has neither the weight nor the consideration which would enable him to fill it.

The Prince of Prussia conceives that the example of every State in Germany in which a popular Constitution has been established should

[200] Cf. n. 180 in this section.
[201] For the United Committee of the States cf. pp. 202–203 in this section.

serve as a lesson to Prussia; not one of them have been without great and serious difficulties, yet their Governments have had the power of Austria and Prussia to support them in the arduous contests they have had to maintain; if such (by the miscalculation of the power entrusted to a popular assembly, or of the character of the representatives returned to it) should come upon Prussia, there would be no power to give her aid or protection and she would be unable to afford it to any other State. His Royal Highness stated that when he was in England[202] the Chevalier Bunsen had spoken to him of a plan which he had drawn up for a Constitution for Prussia, and that it had met with his approbation, if a necessity for such a measure was established; that he considered it of a conservative character, and unlikely to produce those evils which he foresaw from the other projects which had been pointed out to him. He stated that, with regard to his own opinion, the decree of 1820 rendered an assembly of the State General of the Kingdom necessary to sanction any fresh Loan which should be contacted contracted by the State. He was opposed by the same Minister, Monsieur de Rother President of the Direction of the State Debt, who had drawn up that decree, and who argued, that, as it referred to the assembly of the States General which had been mentioned in the decree of the late King of the 22nd of May 1815,[203] and which had never been assembled (and for which the Provincial States had been substituted) that he considered the reference to such States General of no effect, and therefore in no way either binding upon His present Majesty or his successors.

This opinion is entertained by many other Prussian Statesmen, and amongst them, it has been stated to me by Baron Werther the former Minister of Foreign Affairs.

I believe I have now stated to Your Lordship all the principal points of the Prince of Prussia's conversation with me, and I have done so with an anxious desire to put you in possession of his sentiments upon this very important question, more particularly as he expressed a wish that Your Lordship should be informed of them.

[202] In August 1844 Prince Wilhelm, accompanied by Christian Karl Freiherr von Bunsen, embarked upon a tour of England.
[203] Decree of 22 May 1815, cf. n. 141 in this section.

FO 64/257: Earl of Westmorland to Earl of Aberdeen, No 93, Berlin, 28 May 1845

Expulsion of two members of the Baden legislative chambers from Prussian territory (M. Itzstein and M. Hecker); unpopularity of this measure

A circumstance which has occurred in Berlin with respect to two Members of the Baden Legislative Chambers has excited some interest in this part of Germany.

It appears that these Gentlemen Mess.rs Itzstein and Hecker, are opposition, and highly liberal, Members of the Baden Chambers, and are supposed to be connected with the liberal or revolutionary party throughout Germany; it seems that they meditated upon coming into Saxony and Prussia to consult, first at Leipsic, and afterwards at Berlin, Stettin, and Konigsberg with the leaders of that party and to give what effect they were able to any measures which might be adopted, particularly during the King of Prussia's residence in Konigsberg, towards the advancement of their objects, and with this view they met here the reputed chief democrat of Silesia, Count Reichenbach.

It appears that all this information had been transmitted to the Police of this Capital, and that these Gentlemen having no passports were waited upon at 6 o'clock on the morning of the day after they have arrived here, by the officers of that Establishment, who ordered them immediately to depart from Berlin for Leipsic by the Railroad train which was to leave at ½ past 7.

These Gentlemen went to their Minister[204] resident here to seek for protection but as he was still at that early hour in bed, the Porter refused to disturb him and they were obliged to leave according to the orders they have received.

Upon their arrival at Leipsic they were greeted by the Students and persons of liberal principles, and were treated as martyrs to the good cause, and they have forwarded a protest to their Minister here who has presented a note upon the subject to this Government.

No answer has yet been returned.

The fact of these Gentlemen being without any passports, is a justification of the Police, in taking some measure with respect to them, but it is thought it would have been better (as they are Deputies in the Chambers of one of the States of Germany) that their Minister should first have been made acquainted with the order about to be given or that they should have been allowed more time to prepare for their departure.

[204] Karl von Franckenberg-Ludwigsdorf.

FO 64/258: Earl of Westmorland to Earl of Aberdeen, No 124, Berlin,
2 July 1845

Reply of Prussian government to Baden Minister regarding expulsion of M. Itzstein and M.
Hecker; reasoning on Count Arnim's resignation

The answer has been given by this Government to the representations
made by the Baden Minister against the conduct pursued by the Police
of Berlin towards Messieurs Itzstein and Hecker.[205] This reply is couched
in courteous language, but states that it was a measure taken under the
circumstances of the moment, that no explanation of those circumstances can be given to a Foreign Government, but that the
measure was not intended to place any stigma upon the characters of
the Gentlemen against whom it was taken.

The right of any Government to send Foreigners out of the country
is stated to be undisputed, and the example set by Baden herself,
who some years ago, removed a Prussian Functionary in an very
unceremonious manner from its State, without consenting to explain
her reasons for it, is cited in confirmation of this doctrine.

Baron Bülow has signed this note, but he has very openly declared
his disapproval of the measure taken against these Deputies and of the
mode in which it has been done, and his feeling upon the subject has
become known to the public.

Count Arnim is to leave the Ministry of the Interior and to retire
from the Government. The natural inference from this circumstance,
which takes place so immediately after the measure that Minister had
taken towards Messieurs Itzstein & Hecker is, that it is in consequence
of it, and indeed the expression of Baron Bülow upon this subject
would lead me to adopt that opinion, but Count Arnim himself declares
that it is not so, but that he has tendered his resignation to the King
before this event took place, and that it was occasioned by his
determination not to be a party to the answers which the King proposes
should be given to the Petitions of the Provincial States and in which
some announcement of the future Constitution for the Country is to
be set forth.

It would appear from the language of Count Arnim that these
answers will be given in the Autumn of the present year, but as they
take some time to prepare he retires now before the task of drawing
them up is undertaken.

Your Lordship will conceive that the retirement of Count Arnim at
such a juncture gives rise to much discussion, those persons who are
known to profess a sincere attachment to the established institutions of

---

[205] Cf. pp. 218 in this section.

this country greatly lament that a Minister who took a measure, although harshly carried into effect, to prevent the King from meeting with persons in his journey through his States, whose object is ascertained to have been, to raise a revolutionary clamour against Him amongst the democratical portion of His subjects in the Province of Prussia, should not have been upheld by his Sovereign; while others, who have presented addresses couched in the most violent languages against their own Government rejoice that a victim has been sacrificed to them, and an evidence afforded of the King's disregard of the character of his Minister.

Both these reasonings are exaggerated, there is no doubt the mode of sending the Baden Deputies out of the country was harsh, but it is equally certain that these Gentlemen came into Prussia with no good intentions towards the King's Government, and I believe that Count Arnim had the most certain knowledge of this fact. The part which the King has taken in the transaction, according to the statement of Count Arnim as to the cause of his resignation, is very different from what, as I have above stated, it is represented, and it is therefore lamented that the time chosen for Count Arnim's retirement should give a colour to such erroneous impressions.

I believe the King was displeased with the conduct of Count Arnim in this Affair, and with the consequent unpopularity it has brought upon His Government but I am assured that it is without reference to this subject that he has consented to accept his resignation.

Monsieur de Bodelschwingh who was formerly Minister of Finance will it is understood take the duties of Minister of the Interior until a permanent appointment takes place.

FO 64/258: Earl of Westmorland to Earl of Aberdeen, No 192, Berlin, 31 December 1845

Opinions on the resignation of Sir Robert Peel

I feel it my duty to report to Your Lordship the intense anxiety which was excited in this capital by the resignation of Sir Robert Peel's Cabinet, and which has now been allayed by its return to power.[206]

I should be unwilling to state the distress and alarm created by this event, as I might be suspected of a bias of party, if the fact was not so general and notorious, as to make it impossible to doubt or deny it.

---

[206] The governmental crisis was caused by differences of opinion over the Corn Laws, which Peel and others wanted to repeal because of the famine in Ireland. For the Corn Laws cf. n. 171 in this section.

From the first moment that the intelligence of the retirement of Sir Robert Peel arrived here, I received from His Majesty and the Royal Family the strongest assurances of their deep regret, and I can assure Your Lordship that the same feeling was deeply participated in and expressed by the Kings Ministers the Corps Diplomatique, and by the public.

The money market in this Capital was very seriously affected by it, and general apprehension was spread amongst the persons most connected with the trade and commercial interests of the country.

The return of Sir Robert Peel to Her Majesty's Government has allowed all these feelings to subside, and as a mark of the great satisfaction felt personally by the King at this event His Majesty sent for me in the Theatre to His private room to express this feeling and to beg me to convey it to Your Lordship, to Sir Robert Peel, and to the Duke of Wellington. [...]

FO 64/263: Earl of Westmorland to Earl of Aberdeen, No 33, Berlin, 19 February 1846

Arrest of a conspirator; precautionary measures

Baron Canitz has informed me that one of the chief conspirators[207] in the insurrectionary plot lately discovered in Posen, has been arrested.

This person, a Pole by birth, is an emissary of the Paris and Brussels Propaganda, and had been exceedingly active; a large sum of money was found upon him, and it is expected that some important information will be obtained from him. The number of persons arrested is not yet known but the whole proceeding was carried into effect without creating any disturbance.[208]

The Bazaar and the principal Inns were occupied by the military and numerous patrols marched through every part of the Town, some pieces of Cannon were placed in the two principal Squares, as well as a Battalion of Infantry and a Squadron of Hussars.

The Gates of the Town as well as the Bridges which had been closed during the day were opened towards the Evening.

The whole of these measures were merely taken out of precaution lest any injury should happen to the peaceful inhabitants of the Town.

---

[207] Ludwik Mierowslawski. The aim of the uprising planned in Posen and Cracow was the liberation of Poland from Russian rule, cf. pp. 528–529 in Austria section.

[208] Altogether about seventy people were arrested.

FO 64/264: Henry Howard to Earl of Aberdeen, No 14, Berlin, 17 June 1846

Considerations of the general Evangelical Synod of Prussia

The general Evangelical Synod[209] of the Kingdom of Prussia, the assembly of which has already been reported to Your Lordship,[210] has formed itself into 8 Committees for the consideration of the following subjects from the materials prepared by the Provincial Synods which met in 1844.

1. Questions of Doctrine and Faith including that of the obligation of ordination for the Clergy.
2. Constitution of the Church and Church Ritual.
3. Examination of the proposals concerning the preparatory education for the Ecclesiastical State.
4. Examination concerning extension of sphere of action of parochial Clergy.
5. All questions concerning the public celebration of Divine Service and private worship.
6. Discussion of the relations of the Churches with the Schools.
7. Preparatory deliberations concerning the Relations referred to in the Protocols, with other Churches and Religious Societies.
8. Connexion of the Church with the civil legislation more particularly with regard to matrimonial Statutes and the tendering of oaths.

The labours of the first Commission, embracing as they do matters of doctrine and faith will, present the greatest difficulties on account of the great diversity of opinion concerning them prevailing amongst the Members and Clergy of the Evangelical Church and the Rationalist tendency which has of late years developed itself in Germany, where a feeling in favour of a freer individual interpretation of the Scriptures than is authorized by the Confession of Augsburg[211] has gained considerable strength, and where the uneasiness of the public mind on political matters has communicated itself also to Church Questions.

It is not perhaps to be wondered at that differences of opinion should

[209] The General Synod was the first general representation of the Protestant church in Prussia. Like the synods at local and provincial level established under Friedrich Wilhelm III in 1816, the General Synod, consisting of thirty-seven clergy and thirty-eight laymen, only had an advisory function.

[210] FO 64/264: Earl of Westmorland to Earl of Aberdeen, No. 199, Berlin, 13 May 1846, not included in this volume.

[211] *Confessio Augustana*, a confession written by Melanchton in 1530 for the *Reichstag* in Augsburg, which became the most important doctrine of the reformist church.

exist in the Evangelical Church of Prussia, when it is considered that the Union of the two Confessions, the Lutheran and the Calvinist, into one common Church called the Evangelical, was effected by the late King after the Peace with considerable effort, and in some cases even, as for example in Silesia, not without the employment of force.[212]

His Majesty, the present King of Prussia, has it much at heart to bring about a lasting union in spirit as well as in form, between the two amalgamated Churches and to this object much of his attention is directed. His views extend further and he is desirous of establishing a uniformity of belief and practice throughout the whole Protestant Church in Germany and with this intention he assembled the Ecclesiastical Congress of the German States, which separated however without any positive result. [...]

FO 64/265: Earl of Westmorland to Viscount Palmerston, No 14, Berlin, 28 July 1846

Principal features and regulations of the new 'Preußische Bank'

Since the date of my despatch N° 10 to Your Lordship, a Cabinet Order dated the 18ᵗʰ instant, has been published by which His Prussian Majesty approves of the new organization of the Bank proposed by the Head of that Institution[213] and Minister of State Monsieur Rother in the annexed draft of Bank Regulations.

Of both of these documents I have the honour of enclosing copies together with a Précis of their more important contents.

The principal features of the contemplated measure are the following.

The King sanctions the raising, by private subscription, of 10 Millions of Prussian Dollars in shares of 1,000 dollars each, and the issue by the Bank of Notes to the amount of 15 Millions of dollars to which will be added a further issue of 6 millions of Notes upon the repayment to the Royal Treasury of the Bills (Paper Currency) formerly advanced by it to the Bank.

This total sum of 21 Millions of dollars cannot be exceeded without the Kings special permission.

The Capital of the State, to which the 10 millions of private

---

[212] On the occasion of the 300th anniversary of the Reformation in 1817 Friedrich Wilhelm proclaimed the union of the Calvinists (reformed) with the Lutherans in a unified Evangelical church. There was opposition to this church policy from the Rhenish-Bergish Calvinists and sections of the Silesian orthodox Lutherans (old Lutherans). Between 1830 and 1834 in particular the state reacted to this opposition by dismissing clergy, imprisoning them, and banning meetings.

[213] *Preußische Bank* founded in 1765 as the *Königliche Bank*.

subscription are to be associated, will be formed by the balance at the end of the year 1846 of the Assets over the Liabilities of the Bank. The funds of the Bank will consist of the 10 millions of dollars in question and of the Deposits which Courts of Guardians of Minors, of Justice and the Administrators of the Property of Churches, Schools and charitable Institutions, are by Law forced to make in the Bank of the Funds at their disposal under the special guarantee of the State, and upon which a very low rate of interest is given. One of the stipulations of the new regulations is that the interest upon any such deposits cannot be raised without the consent of the Shareholders. [...]

It is proposed to retain the whole administrative and executive authority of the new Bank which, if the subscriptions for the 10 millions of Dollars are filled up, will be established on the 1st of January 1847 under the title of the 'Prussian Bank', in the hands of the Head of the Bank who acts as Royal commissioner and is responsible to the King alone, and of the Bank Directory which is subordinate to that Functionary. The Shareholders will however be represented by an Assembly of 200 of those amongst them who possess the largest number of Shares. This assembly will meet once a year to receive a report upon the state and operations of the Bank. It will elect for 3 years a Central Committee formed of 15 persons for the purpose of Controling the operations of the Bank and which will in its turn elect 3 Deputies who will be in constant communication with the Bank Directors and will offer their advice on all matters connected with the transactions of the Institution. At the Branch Banks and Country Houses to be established in the Province the Shareholders will likewise be represented by a certain number of Delegates, but with one or two exceptions, the Representatives of the Shareholders will only have a consulting voice and the powers vested in the Head of Bank as Representative of the King will be unlimited, however much they may be virtually controled by the moral influence of the Shareholders whose Capital will so far exceed that of the State as Your Lordship will perceive from the balance Sheet of the Assets and Liabilities of the Bank on the 13th of May last annexed to the enclosed Precis; the surplus in favour of the Bank which is to form the Capital advanced by the State being at that period only 990,344 dollars, from which ought to be deducted the difference between the nominal and the real value of the Stocks in hand, whilst the forced Deposits of the Property of Minors &c have served as the principal Basis of the operations of the Bank.

Upon the Constitution of the new Bank the general Guarantee of it given by the State will cease, the special guarantee for the property of Minors &c being alone retained. The Capital of the Bank above described will be answerable for its liabilities. [...]

Monsieur Rother in virtue of the Kings authority has published the terms of the proposed subscriptions; they are substantially the same as are contained in the Draft of Bank Regulations with the additional clause that every Subscriber will on subscribing have to furnish a security of 10 per cent; the subscriptions to be opened on the 1st of August and to close at the end of the Month.

The complicated measure, the details of which I have thus laid before Your Lordship, has given rise as might naturally be expected to a great deal of discussion, so that it is impossible at the present moment to form any correct judgment as to the value of the different opinions which are set forth with regard to it.

The great power and control which is placed in the hands of the Royal Commissioner is looked upon by some persons as calculated to deter the publick from placing their Capital in this newly created Bank, while others are satisfied that the well known integrity of Monsieur Rother and his acknowledged ability in financial affairs will afford the best chance of its successful management and in confirmation of this view it is understood that several Capitalists have already notified their intention of becoming Shareholders.

An increase of the circulating medium is much wanted in the Country and if this measure is formed to ensure this object upon a safe and intelligible principle it will meet with the publick approbation.[214]

FO 64/265: Earl of Westmorland to Viscount Palmerston, No 16, Berlin, 29 July 1846

New law issued concerning the judicial proceedings in criminal cases (introduction of oral proceedings, publicity etc.)

I have the honour to enclose herewith to Your Lordship copies in original of a new Law just issued by His Prussian Majesty introducing some important changes in the manner of conducting the Juridical Proceedings in Criminal Cases before the Court of the 'Kammergericht' and the Criminal Court at Berlin.

His Majesty states that since His accession to the Throne his intention has been to ensure a more expeditious administration of Justice in the Tribunals in the Provinces of His Kingdom subject to the common Law, by the establishment of a system of oral Proceedings, and that for the present he has resolved to introduce it in the two above mentioned

---

[214] Enclosures: 1. *Allerhöchste Kabinets-Ordre die Betheiligung von Privatpersonen bei der Bank betreffend* (Supreme Cabinet Order concerning the participation of private individuals in the bank) 18 July 1846; 2. Précis of King of Prussia's Cabinet Order dated Sans Souci 18 July 1846 concerning the participation of private Individuals in the Bank addressed to the Minister of State Rother.

Courts at Berlin where its application can be effected without difficulty.

The Law then provides that from the 1st of October next, the Proceedings of those Courts shall be carried on orally and not by written procedure as heretofore.

A crown Advocate, named by the King and dependant on the Minister of Justice, will be appointed to conduct the Prosecutions, the initiative of which is transferred to him from the Courts themselves and the Police Authorities in which they are now vested. The examination of the Prisoner and of the Witnesses, the Charge of the Crown Advocate and the Pleading of Counsel in defence will be by word of mouth.

The number of Judges to try a cause will vary, according to its more or less serious nature from 3, 6, & 8 to 10. A majority of their votes decides upon the condemnation or acquital of the accused.

When the votes are equal the more lenient opinion prevails.

The specifick interpretation at present imposed by Law of particular grounds of proof is done away with and full Latitude is left to the Judges to pronounce their opinion according to their views of the merits of the case and of the evidence brought forward.

The general forms of proceeding are in other respects greatly simplified and expedited.

A certain degree of publicity will take place, in as much as all Lawyers and persons connected with the Law will be admitted to attend the Courts in question.

The Provisions of this Law will take effect with respect to all cases not decided in the first Instance at the period of its coming into operation on the 1st of October, and it is supposed that its first application will be the case of the Poles charged with being implicated in the late conspiracy[215] and who will be transferred from the Grand Duchy of Posen to Berlin for trial before the Court of the 'Kammergericht' which takes cognizance of all offences against the State.

As far as I have yet been able to learn, the contemplated changes are likely to be viewed with great satisfaction as establishing very important reforms in the Administration of Justice in this part of His Prussian Majesty's Dominions.[216]

---

[215] Cf. p. 221 in this section, and pp. 528–529 in Austria section.
[216] Enclosure: *Gesetz-Sammlung für die Königlichen Preußischen Staaten*, No. 21, 25 July 1846.

FO 64/266: Henry Howard to Viscount Palmerston, No 12, Berlin, 7 October 1846

Agricultural information; second year of bad harvest; potato disease; necessity to import grain

I have the honour to enclose the copy of a report from Mr Vice Consul Peterson relative to the corn Trade at Stettin.[217]

From the general information which I have received, I understand that the results of the harvest in Prussia, excepting in the Provinces of Saxony and Silesia, are by no means satisfactory. The Wheat crops have varied of course according to the locality and nature of the soil, but they may, I believe, be said to be below the average. The greatest falling-off has been in the Rye crops, so that in many places, Rye which is so essential an ingredient for the brown bread almost exclusively eaten and preferred by the poorer and agricultural classes in Prussia is selling nearly as high as Wheat.

This is especially the case in the Province of Westphalia where the Crop is stated not to amount to more than one third of the usual Produce. Other Kinds of Grain are considerably risen in price. Of all, the Barley crop is said to have been the most productive.

The great heat and long drought which, excepting in some wet soils, have exercised either in the quality or in the quantity such an unfavorable influence on grain, have been in a higher degree injurious to all kinds of vegetables.

The Potatoes do not appear in general to have been hitherto attacked by precisely the same disease as last year; but the stalks have withered and rotted and there is a very great deficiency in the quantity and quality of the roots, the bulbs being remarkably small and affording but little nourishment. Other species of vegetables, such as Cabbage &c, of which as well as Peas and Beans a greater use is made amongst the poorer classes in Germany than in England have likewise suffered considerably from the same causes and their failure will add to the anticipated distress.

Upon the whole therefore it may, I think be said that with respect to grain the harvest in Prussia has been very indifferent and that taken by itself and without reference to the stocks in hand or importations from Poland, the production would hardly, if at all, be more than what is required for home consumption.

Monsieur de Rönne, the President of the Board of Trade who has just returned from a six weeks tour in Westphalia and on the Rhine, tells me that the deficiency has been so great there that corn is being imported from the Bonding Warehouses in Great Britain and that

---

[217] Enclosure: Copy, Peterson to Westmorland, Stettin, 2 October 1846.

considerable orders have been sent to North America for grain and Indian Corn.

FO 64/266: Henry Howard to Viscount Palmerston, No 23, Berlin, 17 October 1846

On several religious movements in Prussia

The religious movement in Prussia forms one of the most interesting features in the affairs of Germany at the present day. Many causes have assisted it and amongst them the tendency of Modern German Philosophy, the intolerance of Religious Parties and the fermentation of the publick mind which, checked on political matters by the restrictions laid on the Press, found a vent on Church questions left more open to discussion.

To indicate the origin of this movement it would be necessary to go back to the forced Union of the Lutheran and Reformed Churches by the late King of Prussia in 1817, to the persecution of the Lutherans in 1834[218] and to the Religious dissensions which arose in consequence of the removal of the Archbishop of Cologne from his Diocese in 1837.[219] Taking it up however from the Commencement of the present Reign when the King of Prussia showed a most anxious wish to calm all religious excitement the following more immediate causes may be assigned to it.

First of all came the Gustavus Adolf Association,[220] the object of which was to contribute to the support of indigent Protestant Communities and to establish a closer connexion amongst the different Protestant Confessions in Germany and in other Countries. The very name given to the Association with its historical recollections, the circumstance of the Protestant cause having long been allied with the liberal cause in Germany, although the distinction has now in great measure disappeared, the wide extension of the Association and the freedom of discussion that prevailed at its meetings, all proved that it might become an instrument in the hands of political Agitators. The King of Prussia therefore hastened to put Himself at its Head within His own Dominions and has thus been enabled to exercise a certain control over it.

Then followed the Pilgrimage to Treves[221] which, although it went

[218] Cf. n. 136 in this section.
[219] Cf. pp. 88–91 in Frankfurt section.
[220] The Gustav Adolf Association was founded in 1832 in Leipzig to mark the 200th anniversary of the death of King Gustav II of Sweden. In 1843 it amalgamated into the Protestant Association of the Gustav Adolf Foundation.
[221] Cf. n. 223 in Frankfurt section.

off in a very orderly manner, was pretty generally considered as an untimely and illjudged demonstration on the part of the Catholicks.

It gave occasion to the celebrated letter of Ronge and furnished the pretext for the formation of the Sect of the German Catholicks[222] which found numerous adherents in those parts of Prussia where the discipline of the Catholick Church was most relaxed or where its religious wants were least provided for, and which likewise recruited itself from a large class of freethinkers who, though in reality not practising any Religion, nominally belonged to the Evangelical Confession.

It was impossible that a Sect so composed without any fixed religious tenets should not very soon assume a democratic character.

Such was in fact the case, and so inflammatory was the language and so great the disorder that attended the meetings held all over Germany by the itinerant Apostles of the new creed, that the Prussian Government which did not at first appear to attach much importance to the proceedings in question took measures to put a stop to the agitation by directing the Preachers to confine themselves to the Districts for which they might be chosen and by withholding their recognition of the Sect.

Since that period the Catholick Dissenters have separated into two different Parties, the one under Ronge, called the 'German Catholick', which admits of every latitude of belief, the other called the 'Christian Catholick' of which Czerski is the head, and which is disposed to retain more of the doctrines and forms of the Christian Religion.

The split that has thus taken place, the want of talent and character of the leaders and of pecuniary Funds on the part of the Communities, as well as the Government measures to which I have alluded, have all tended to impede the progress of the Sect which may be said to have lost all consideration and to have sunk comparatively into the shade.

In the mean time the spark had communicated itself to the Protestant Church, the 'Friends of Light'[223] shewed themselves and threatened its Unity. They professed extreme Rationalist opinions and like the German Catholicks put forward democratic principles. But here the Prussian Government, alive to the danger, lost no time in interfering, prohibited their meetings, proceeded against and finally removed from their Parishes two Clergymen of the Evangelical Church Mr Wislicenus of Halle and Dr Rupp of Königsberg who, with different shades of opinion,

---

[222] For the German Catholics cf. pp. 102–104 in Frankfurt section.

[223] The Friends of Light, a free-religious movement that had existed since 1841, held the view that the Bible was not the only valid norm of Christianity. Religious self-determination should take the place of the orthodox belief in the Revelation. As precursors of liberalism within the church, and indeed as proponents of liberal and democratic ideas in the political sphere, they attracted quite a following. Their meetings were banned by the Prussian government in 1845.

lent their support to the Doctrines in question and have since formed two separate Protestant Communities, which, labouring under all the disadvantages of unacknowledged Sects, and of pecuniary difficulties, are neither numerous nor prosperous.

Indeed the object of the Protestant Rationalists seems hitherto rather to have been to procure the triumph of their opinions within the Evangelical Church, than to separate from it whereby they would entail upon themselves the maintenance of any religious worship they might think necessary to set up. All these circumstances however contributed to embitter the feelings and the controversy between two Parties in the Evangelical Church in Prussia long in opposition to each other.

One of these Parties professes opinions closely allied to those of the 'Friends of Light' considering the confession of Augsburgh[224] as antiquated, consequently rejecting the Symbols and all restraint upon free and scientific interpretation of the Scriptures.

This Party numbers its chief followers in the Province of Saxony where the Philosophical opinions of the Theologians of the University at Halle have had considerable influence over the Clergy.

The other Party on the contrary, which goes under the name of the 'Pietist',[225] is for strictly adhering to the Doctrines of the Reformation and to the observance of all the practices and external forms of Religion and is favourable to an Augmentation of the power of the Clergy. It is accused by its adversaries endeavouring, under the cloak of religion, to advance its worldly interests, and the fact of several of its most prominent Members occupying high Government Offices and Posts about the Person of the King has gone some way towards accrediting the accusation amongst the Publick.

There is however a third Party which had a decided majority in the late Synod[226] assembled by the King, and which I believe to be the most numerous in the Country, both amongst the Clergy and Laity. It is in favour of retaining the generality of the doctrines of the Protestant Faith as laid down at the Reformation whilst it considers that the spirit in which the Reformation was based requires that great liberty should be left to individual interpretation, and that the Evangelical Church ought to develop itself in a manner conformable to the spirit of the Age. It is termed the Party of Progress.

I believe the Prussian Government to be sincerely desirous of reconciling these differences of opinion, at the same time that they are determined to uphold the Established Church in Prussia. It was for this

---

[224] Cf. n. 211 in this section.

[225] As a theological revival movement, in which the religious awakening of the believer was the main issue, the pietists described here opposed liberal and rationalist tendencies within the church. The traditional pietists' precept of tolerance played no role here.

[226] Cf. pp. 222–223 in this section.

purpose, and in order to obtain some rules for their guidance in their contemplated changes in the Government of the Church that they convoked the General Synod which met last June.

But as I reported in my Despatch N° 14 to the Earl of Aberdeen, this measure did not completely attain its object, for the composition of the Synod was in the first place objected to and afterwards it took itself a freer line than suited the Government.

Again I hear that latterly a certain reaction in an orthodox sense has taken place and that a considerable number of Clergymen have protested against the looseness of the Formula of Faith proposed by the Synod for Clergymen taking orders whereas by another Party it is held to be too stringent.

Notwithstanding this state of things, the religious agitation appeared to have abated when the exclusion of Dr Rupp, the Head at the Free Church at Königsberg[227] from the annual meeting of the Gustavus Adolphus Association held at Berlin in the beginning of last Month, furnished fresh matter for strife and angry polemical discussion throughout Germany. Dr Rupp was sent as a Deputy from the Königsberg Association, but the General Assembly at Berlin decided by small majority not to admit him, as he had seceded from Evangelical Church. The other Party contended that all the General Assembly had to look to was whether Dr Rupps full Powers were in order and that it would be contrary to the principles and spirit of the Association to reject a Member who though not an 'Evangelical'[228] was nevertheless a Protestant.

Thus new subjects of dissension are constantly occurring and it is to be feared that we have not yet arrived at their end, but hopes may be entertained that the cause of Order and Religion will ultimately prevail, with so enlightened a People as the Germans are, over tendencies of an opposite nature produced in part by the excitement of the times.

FO 64/272: Earl of Westmorland to Viscount Palmerston, No 18, Berlin, 28 January 1847

Statement of force and composition of Prussian army

In conformity with the directions contained in Your Lordship's Despatch N° 47 Confidential of last Year, I have the honor of laying before you

---

[227] The Königsberg Free Church, under the leadership of Julius Rupp, was formed by secession from the Protestant regional church on 19 January 1846.

[228] Collective attribute for the Lutheran and reformed Calvinist churches in Prussia which had joined to form the Evangelical Union, cf. n. 212 in this section.

a Statement of the Force and Composition of the Prussian Army which I have taken every pain to make as correct and comprehensive as the nature of the subject will allow.

The Military Force of Prussia consists

of 1st the Standing Army
2nd the Landwehr of the 1st Levy
3rd the Landwehr of the 2nd Levy
and 4th the Landsturm.

The standing Army and the Landwehr of the 1st Levy compose appointed to take the field.

The Landwehr of the 2nd Levy is destined for the Garrisons of Fortresses &c; and the Landsturm includes all men between the Age of 17 and 50 who have not been enrolled either in the Line or in the Landwehr; this Force however is never called together except at express command of the King in case of hostile Invasion for the purpose of defending the Interior of the Country.

The conscription by which the Recruits are raised for this Army is based upon the principle that every Prussian is bound to serve in the Army, consequently every Year in the Provincial Circles the number of Men which according to the Exigencies of the Year are required are chosen by Ballot from the Young Men who have attained their 20th Year.

In addition to this Mode of raising Men for the Army, Volunteers are received after they have attained the Age of 17 and these are allowed to choose the Regiment they will serve in. All the Men raised in either of the above Modes are required to serve 3 Years with the Regiments of the Guards to which they may have been attached and two Years with the other regiments both of Cavalry and Infantry. They then pass into the Reserve for two or three Years according as they belong to the Guards or the Line, in order to make up the period of five Years during which they belong to their respective Regiments, and are liable to be called into active Service at any moment, and it is from this body of Men that in time of War the Regiments are at once increased to the War Establishment.

After this period of the Soldier's service he passes into the first Levy of the Landwehr and into the Regiment of Landwehr corresponding with the one to which he has originally belonged, with the exception of such Men as have served in Regiment of the Guards and who have been brought from distant Provinces, and who are placed in the Landwehr Regiments in the Districts to which they belong. All these Men are required to serve in The First Levy of the Landwehr for seven Years, at the expiration of which they have attained their 32nd year; during the period of this service they are assembled in Battalions,

Squadrons, or Brigades of Artillery once a year for a fortnight; and in those Years in which the Corps d'Armée to which they belong are brought before together for field Maneuvres, and which takes place once in four years, they are called out for the space of one Month in Regiments.

After the Men have completed their service in the first Levy of the Landwehr, they are placed in the Landwehr of the 2nd Levy in which they are enrolled for seven Years more till they have attained the age of 39 during which period they are not in time of Peace called upon for any Service, but in time of War are subject to be called upon to join the Regiments to which they have already belonged either in Active Service, or in Garrisons or Reserves.

The nature and duty of the Landsturm has been described above.

The conscription is furnished by eight districts or Provincial Circles, each Corps taking its recruits from the Circle assigned to it.

The number of Recruits required each year from the conscription to fill up the vacancies occasioned by the men who pass to the Reserves depends upon the exigencies of the Corps which is to be completed to its establishment and varies, first according to the deaths or casualties which may have arisen, next, according to the number of Soldiers who having served their two Years are desirous of remaining upon capitulation, and thirdly, according to the number of Volunteers who come to enrol themselves either for one or for three Years, which Class is more numerous in the Northern districts than in the Rhenish Provinces.

The average number of Recruits required yearly by the eight Corps d'Armée is 34 000, and out of those taken by the Line the Number of Recruits required for the Guards is selected by Officers of the Guards who chose them from all the different Corps. [...]

In concluding this report, I think it my duty to remark that I consider the Prussian Army at present in a state of discipline which renders it a most effective Army.

It is certainly to be borne in mind that a Recruit who joins his Regiment for only two Years, or, as in the case of the Guards, for three Years, cannot be regarded by Officers who know what is required in active Service as formed Soldiers. In the short period however of two years under the direction of well instructed and zealous Officers & non-commissioned Officers, these Recruits are so well drilled as to go through all the movements of field exercise and general maneuvres with the most perfect order and precision, and a foundation is laid, so that when they are called upon to join the Regiments on the War Establishment from the Reserves, or in the 1st Levy of the Landwehr they soon become efficient and well disciplined Soldiers.

In the Cavalry, the time of the Recruit's first Service whether of two or three years is certainly too short for the perfect training which he requires, and as when he passes into the Landwehr he has no horse to ride except for the fortnight or month in the year during which he is called into active service and then upon horses which generally have had no previous training, it is impossible that he can be considered as a perfectly formed Cavalry Soldier; notwithstanding however these disadvantages, the degree of regularity which these Men attain and the good management of their Horses is quite extraordinary, although it is certainly would not be till some time had elapsed after this Landwehr Cavalry had been called out upon the War Establishment that it could be considered as in a fit state to meet an enemy in the field.

The Artillery is in a very efficient State and both Officers and Men are very highly instructed, and although the Recruits remain but so short a time at their first joining still they have the opportunity under active and able instructors to make very great progress in the knowledge of the Service which at a future time may be required of them.

With respect to the Officers of the Prussian Army I believe there is nowhere to be found a more zealous or a better educated body of Men, they are almost exclusively taken from the noble families of the Kingdom, they are admitted as Officers after a very severe examination as to their attainments in the different Sciences and Languages as well as in Military Tactics which it is thought necessary for them to be acquainted with. Before they have passed this examination (from which many are turned back as was lately the case with the Son of one of the King's Ministers)[229] these young men serve as Soldiers or as Corporals in the Regiments and there learn their duties from the earliest Stages.

These Officers are constant in their attention to their duty and are present at all the Stages of the Instruction of their Men.

The Promotion in the Army is slow, many Officers remaining 17 to 20 Years as Lieutenants before obtaining their companies and then the advancement is not much accelerated, but it is conducted with great justice and impartiality.

The General Officers are consequently, under the present system, and during peace, a long while in obtaining their rank, many who are now active General Officers owe their early advancement to the casualties which brought them forward in the last War, and some distinguished Men have since been favorably promoted so that in case of War there are many General Officers of great merit who would take their place in command, while the necessary promotion would bring forward a Body of Active well informed and zealous General Officers who would command the confidence of the Army and of the Government and Country. The Military Spirit in Prussia is certainly very

---

[229] Not traceable.

great, and the recollection of their former renown would lead the people to make the greatest sacrifices in case of necessity. The character of the Soldier is that of temperance good order and activity, he was distinguished during the War for bravery, and I feel that he may be relied upon as a most formidable opponent to any enemy which he may be called upon to stand up against, and it may truly be remarked that throughout the Prussian Army there is a feeling of entire devotion to His Majesty and of anxious zeal in defence of the institutions and independence of the country.

FO 64/273: Earl of Westmorland to Viscount Palmerston, No 74, Berlin, 11 April 1847

Opening of the United Diet (Vereinigter Landtag); King's speech

I have the honor of reporting Your Lordship that His Majesty the King of Prussia opened the States General of the Kingdom this day, by a speech from the Throne, a copy of which I will endeavour to transmit to you with this despatch.[230]

His Majesty proceeded this morning, according to the Programme which I have forwarded to Your Lordship in my despatch N° 73, to the Cathedral where, in company with all the Protestant Deputies of the States, he attended Divine Service, while the Deputies of the Roman Catholick Religion attended their Service in the Church of St. Hedwig.

His Majesty on his return on foot from the Church to the Palace was constantly cheered by the people; and after the Deputies, the Princesses and the Younger branches of the Royal Family, and the Heads of the Diplomatick Missions had taken their Seats in the Weisse Saal, the Hall destined for their meeting, The King made his entry in State, and was received with the strongest expression of loyalty and respect by the whole Assembly.

After the Speech which His Majesty delivered, he invested the Marshals of the Upper as well as the Lower Chambers with the Insignia of Office, and then directed the Minister of the Interior Monsieur de Bodelschwingh to declare the opening of the Session; after which Prince Solms, as Marshal of the Upper Chamber, replied to the King's Speech by expressing in a few words the hope that His Majesty would find in the conduct of the States all that he expected from them and concluded by a cheer for the King which was responded to by all the Deputies.

[230] Enclosure: Speech published in the Prussian Universal Gazette, 12 April 1847.

His Majesty then retired in the order of procession according to which he had entered.

The Kings Speech, which I hope will accompany this despatch, although it is not yet published and the hour of Post is nearly arrived, is characterized by a strong desire in every way to consult the best interests of his country, a desire which was ever uppermost in the mind of His Father, whose wishes he has now carried out by calling this Meeting of the States; but at the same time by a declaration that he will abide by what he has now effected, and that he will steadfastly maintain inviolate the system he has established.

He enters at some length into the reasons which have induced him not to grant a Constitution according to the modern acceptation of the word which would be entirely unfitted to the State of Prussia and which he never will agree to. He assures the States that if he finds in the result of their proceedings that their meeting has been useful to the best interests of the Kingdom, he will frequently call them together and after describing the prosperous state of the country at the present time and pointing out to them the subjects upon which they will be called upon to deliberate, He terminated His Speech by saying to them with the warmest feeling of his heart 'Welcome'. [...]

FO 64/273: Earl of Westmorland to Viscount Palmerston, No 75, Berlin, 11 April 1847

Difficult question of determining the legal position of various sects of Protestant and Catholic dissenters in Prussia

The formation of various Sects of Protestant and Catholick Dissenters of late Years having produced numerous complications and embarrassments,[231] the attention of His Prussian Majesty and his Government has for some time past been directed towards the question of determining the legal position of such religious Communities, and of extending the limits of Religious liberty already established by Law.

With this view His Majesty issues on the 9th instant the Patent and Ordinance, of which I have the honor of transmitting a Copy in Duplicate, together with a Translation and Precis respectively, – containing general Regulations concerning the Formation of new Religious Societies applicable to all those Parts of the Kingdom where the Common Law is in force – that is to say, with the exception of the Rhenish Province, where the Code Napoleon[232] is in operation.

---

[231] Cf. pp. 228–231 in this section.
[232] Cf. n. 192 in Frankfurt section.

His Majesty after having declared in His Patent his determination to maintain the two Established Churches in his Dominions, viz the Evangelical and Roman Catholick Churches, in the full enjoyment of their Rights and priviledges, states that he is equally resolved to uphold the Religious Freedom of his subjects.

Everybody is at liberty to separate from his Church and join a new Religious Society sanctioned by the State without incurring the loss of his Civil Rights. The Conditions of that sanction are as fixed by the Common Law, that no doctrines are taught in such a society in compatible with Respect towards God, with the Laws and publick morality.

A distinction is made between those Religious Societies who do not essentially differ in point of Doctrine and Belief from the Religious Parties acknowledged in Germany at the Peace of Westphalia,[233] and other Religious Communities not answering to that description.

To the Clergymen of the former, the right of performing Civil Acts with full legal force will be granted. The Lutherans have since the Accession of the Present King been placed on that footing. The Persons celebrating the Religious Rites of the Societies mentioned under the Second head will not enjoy the same privilege. As prescribed by the Royal Ordinance issued together with the Patent, those tolerated Societies will be subject to the Control of the Local Magistrates by whom all births, marriages or deaths will have to be registered,

A marriage is not legal until so registered, previous to which various formalities are to be observed, amongst them the publication of the Bans by means of a Notice posted at the Court of Justice or Town Hall or Parish building.

The provisions of the Ordinance are likewise applicable to cases of Births, Marriages and Deaths in the Families of Persons who have separated from their own Church and have not yet joined any other Religious Community. For the legality of their Marriages the publication of the Bans and the personal declaration of the Parties before the Magistrate that they consider themselves as Man and Wife, are the principal Conditions.

Your Lordship will perceive from the above statement that considerable latitude is given for the establishment of new Religious Societies; it is hoped however that by the removal of many of the restraints which virtually impeded their formation, that spirit of opposition which in some instances gave rise to them will to a certain extent die away, and that the effect of this measure may not be, as might otherwise be apprehended, to add materially to their numbers.

---

[233] In the Peace of Westphalia of 1648, Calvinism, Lutheranism (Augsburg Confession), and Catholicism were all recognized.

Before I conclude this despatch I will remark that neither the Protestant Dissenters forming the Free Church,[234] nor the German Catholicks[235] have been recognized by the Prussian Government. In the Case of the former all Civil Acts, to be valid, have to be performed by the Clergymen of the Evangelical Church, as members of which, in the eyes of the Law, they are still counted. The Baptisms of the German Catholicks are performed by their own Clergymen but registered in the Evangelical Church and their marriages have to be solemnized by a Clergyman of that Church. It is to put an end to a similar state of things that the present measures have been enacted.[236]

FO 64/273: Earl of Westmorland to Viscount Palmerston, No 77, Berlin, 12 April 1847

Disappointment at the limited power of the United Diet; but no conflict envisaged

[...] Your Lordship will be aware that at the first meeting of the General States of this Kingdom which are composed of so many Members[237] there are those who represent every shade of opinion, and therefore that both before and after the opening Speech of His Majesty[238] there were many persons who expressed disappointment at the limited nature of the Constitutional concessions granted, and at the manner in which the King had declared that he would not enlarge them, these persons had expressed very generally their intention of stating these sentiments, and of calling upon the King in the address to concede a regular yearly Assembly of the States, and to grant many other privileges, but it appears that these feelings in the meeting of this day had passed away, and that a general desire of responding to the King in a manner which may be agreeable to him was manifested. [...]

---

[234] Cf. pp. 229–231 in this section.
[235] For the German Catholics cf. pp. 102–104 in Frankfurt section.
[236] Enclosures: 1 *Gesetz-Sammlung für die Königlichen Preußischen Staaten*, No. 12, 9 April 1847; 2. Translation: Patent concerning the formation of new religious Societies.
[237] In the United Diet all 613 members of the provincial diets were represented.
[238] Cf. pp. 235–236 in this section.

FO 64/273: Earl of Westmorland to Viscount Palmerston, No 84, Berlin, 15 April 1847

United Diet's discussion about its address in reply to the disappointing speech by the King of Prussia; wish to secure the rights of the assembly

The Committee appointed to draw up the Address in answer to the King's Speech have completed their task and have this day submitted the result of their deliberations to the United Diet where it is now being discussed.

I have not yet been able to see this document which has been distributed only for the use of the Members, but I understand that while it expresses devotion and Loyalty to the King, yet it recalls the rights which have already been conceded to the Nation by the Ordin- ances of the late King and also makes some allusion to the pain which had been occasioned by some of His Majesty's expressions.

I apprehend that a considerable discussion in the General Assembly will take place upon these paragraphs, which will be supported by those members who have hitherto been distinguished for their opposition to the Government in the Provincial Chambers, and by those also, who, although not having hitherto belonged to any systematic opposition, yet are desirous of securing as their right the periodical Assembly of the General States, which from the expressions in the Kings speech, as well as from the proposed establishment of the Committee of the States which is to represent them when they are not assembled, they fear it might only be his intention to carry into effect at his own pleasure and at distant periods.

The reasoning of these persons is that by the late King's ordinance of January 1820,[239] the periodical assembly of the General States of the Kingdom was established as the Law of the Country, and therefore that it ought no longer to be at the option of the King to decide when these meetings should take place, and more particularly that it should not be made to depend, as stated in his speech, upon the good behaviour of the present Assembly.

These feelings are believed to be entertained by a majority of the present Diet, so much so, that although they probably will not be embodied in the Address, yet they will be shewn by the refusal of that body to nominate the committee which is to replace the General Assembly so that the duties which by the Kings letters Patent of the 3rd

---

[239] National Debt Law of 17 January 1820 (*Staatsschuldengesetz*), cf. n. 180 in this section.

of February[240] are to be executed by that committee must remain unperformed unless the General Assembly is called together.

It is expected that some compromise may take place upon this point to which allusion is already made in most respectful terms in the amendment to the proposed Address which has been moved by Count Arnim and which seems to have met with the approbation of the Assembly, and it will be most fortunate if such should be the case and if it is effected by a concession from the King.

The general spirit of the Members composing the United Diet may be traced to that of which for may years past they have given evidence in their Provincial Diets; the most ardent in the pursuit of free and liberal institutions are the Representatives of East Prussia and they were so much disappointed with the speech of His Majesty on the opening of the Diet that a majority were inclined to leave Berlin with a declaration that their attributes being reduced to a mere shadow their presence could no longer be of any service, they were however restrained from this proceeding by the persuasions of the Deputies from the Rhine Provinces who, being next in rank to them in the freedom and constitutional liberality of their principles, yet not feeling so unfavourably as to the sentiments expressed by the King, succeeded in persuading them to relinquish their intention.

The Deputies from the Polish Provinces are not inclined to be supporters of the Government and the King in the short speech he made to them after the dinner which he gave on Monday last to all Members of the Diet, expressed the hope that by their future conduct they might efface the recollection of the tears of sorrow which had been shed throughout their Country.[241]

The Deputies from Silesia and Pomerania are generally supporters of the Government while those of Brandenburg, Saxony and Westphalia are almost entirely so.

The report which is given of the sitting of this day is that the general feeling of the Assembly is favourable to the Amendment of the Address proposed by Count Arnim and which goes to leave out those expressions as to the rights already granted to the Country, and as to the unfavorable impression made by some expressions in the Kings speech, and sub-

[240] *Patent die ständischen Einrichtungen betreffend vom 3. Februar 1847.* The duties of the *Vereinigte ständische Ausschuss* (United Committee of the States), which was to be elected by the United Diet, were to advise on laws proposed by the government, and to petition the king. Only the United Diet had the right to make decisions on taxes and state finances

[241] The Polish deputies, overwhelmingly from the Province of Posen, feared further erosion of the rights of the Polish population and maintenance of the anti-Polish measures (i.a. increased press censorship), adopted by the Prussian government in reaction to the Polish Uprising of 1846. For the Polish Uprising, cf. p. 221 in Prussia section, and pp. 528–529 in Austria section.

stituting the loyal expression of the hope that His Majesty will still
further extend his concessions to the Country but assuring Him that it
is with perfect confidence they rely upon his decisions. [...]

FO 64/273: Earl of Westmorland to Viscount Palmerston, No 91,
Berlin, 22 April 1847

'Bread Riots' in Berlin

[...] I regret to have to announce to Your Lordship that in consequence
of the high price of Provisions, riots of a somewhat serious character
took place in this capital during the course of yesterday and of the
night, and have been partially continued this morning.

The Mob assembled yesterday at the market Place and proceeded
to seize the stores of Potatoes belonging to a Dealer of the Town which
were selling at a very high rate, and in the evening broke the windows
of several baker's and Confectioner's Shops and attempted to pillage
their contents, and these excesses were carried to such an extent that
is was found necessary to call out the Military who remained under
arms and patrolled the Streets during the night.

This morning a notice has been issued by the Police Authorities and
placarded in the Town forbidding all assemblages of Persons in the
Streets and calling upon all Tradesmen to keep their Journeymen at
home.

Notwithstanding this, some further disturbances took place at one of
the Market Places; measures have, however, been taken to prevent
their recurrence and no political object is attributed to them.

FO 64/274: Earl of Westmorland to Viscount Palmerston, No 152,
Berlin, 17 June 1847

Discussion of laws regulating the position of Jews in Prussia

[...] This Chamber[242] has [...] been occupied with the discussion of the
Law proposed by the Government to regulate the position of the Jews
throughout the Kingdom.

The regulation affecting the affairs of religion and education, and
the rights and government of these persons are very different in the

---

[242] Lower chamber; in matters not relating to state finances the representatives of the
chamber of peers and the other members of the United Diet, comprising representatives
of the knights, the towns, and the rural districts, met in separate chambers.

respective Provinces of Prussia, and the object of the Government is to bring them under one uniform system.

The Jews are not favorable to these changes, and most of them will probably be rejected by one or other of the two Chambers.

The Lower Chamber has already decided upon one part of the Government proposal by which the Jews were to be formed into distinct Communities, which were to elect their own Committees, to whom were entrusted the management of their civil as well as religious rights.

It has been felt by a majority of the Deputies that this regulation, which would tend to keep the Jewish population separated from the Christian, was neither conformable to their wishes nor advantageous to the State; the Chamber has therefore rejected the part of the Law which entrusted these communities with the management of civil rights, but has retained that portion of it which refers to the Affairs of religion. [...]

Since I commenced this despatch the Lower Chamber has decided upon the most important paragraph of the Law relating to the civil and religious rights of the Jews, and has adopted an amendment by a majority of five which has entirely changed the dispositions proposed by the Government, and has placed the persons professing this religion nearly on the same footing with all the other subjects of the Kingdom, admitting them to Offices of the Government, to most of the Professorships in the Universities, and to the Municipal Councils.

The Upper Chamber has also been engaged in the discussion of this Law, but in the Votes that have as yet been agreed to, the same concessions have not been sanctioned which have been adopted by the Lower Chamber, and it is presumed that there will be so great a discrepancy in the decisions come to by the two Chambers, that the Law will altogether be abandoned by the Government. [...]

FO 64/274: Earl of Westmorland to Viscount Palmerston, No 161, Berlin, 25 June 1847

Question of which proceedings should govern the election of committees (after closing the first session of the United Diet) of the eight Prussian Provinces; competence of these committees; results of the first working session of both chambers of the United Diet

Since I had the honor of addressing You in my despatch N° 160[243] of yesterday's date, I have received a copy of His Majesty's reply to the

---

[243] Not included in this volume.

petition[244] of the Diet together with his declaration as to the bearing of the Patent of the 3rd of February[245] and his announcement to the Diet that their sittings will be closed tomorrow by the Royal Commissioner.

I enclose the printed copies of theses documents together with their translations.

The Diet is to assemble this day in order to proceed by Provinces to the Election of the Members of the Committees, which is to take place by Orders in each of the eight Provinces, six deputies for the equestrian Order, four for the Towns and two for the rural districts to which are added eight deputies from the Chamber of Peers.

The most important question agitated since the commencement of the Sittings of the Diet has been whether the Deputies would name these Committees; it is now brought to an issue and the general impression appears to be that they will conform to His Majesty's wishes.

If such should be the case, the termination of this first Session of the States of the Kingdom of Prussia will have taken place without any collision with the Crown, but without the adoption of any of those measures of public utility which this assembly was expected to carry into effect and with the great mass of petitions which had been laid before it undecided upon. [...]

The declaration of His Majesty as to His intention of consulting the Diet upon all Loans and Guarantees by the state have been most explicit, and his desire to see the Committees appointed with the view of submitting to them and taking their opinion upon the Criminal Code proposed to be adopted has pointed out the nature of the duties with which those Committees are immediately to be charged. The other points referred to in the petition of the Chambers and which related to the Deputation of eight Members for the control of the State Debt and for the assistance of the Government if called upon to contract a loan in time of War have been so clearly defined and the attributes of this Body so restricted, that there can hardly remain any doubt as to the probability of their appointment.

The answer of the King upon the prayer of the petition for the periodical assembly of the States, as upon the other question brought forward in that document is nearly conformable to the terms I had reported to Your Lordship in my despatch N° 148 as likely to be adopted, but as this document will be before You I need make no further remarks upon it.[246]

[244] The sitting of the United Diet on 23 June 1847 concluded with a petition to the King for the periodical assembly of the diet. This would make the election of the committee to take over its responsibilities when it was not sitting, superfluous; cf. n. 252 in this section.

[245] Cf. n. 240 in this section.

[246] In his message to the Diet of 24 June, Friedrich Wilhelm IV merely stated that he

I am in hopes that it will be well received by the country, it holds out the prospect of the firm establishment of Constitutional liberty, while it maintains unimpaired the free action of the Crown in the concessions it may deem it expedient to make.

As the proceedings of the present Diet are now nearly brought to a close, it may in justice be remarked that they have been distinguished for order and regularity, and that the Members of both Chambers have shewn throughout the discussions which have taken place a feeling of Loyalty to the King and attachment to the State, which has redounded to their honor and secured to them the consideration of the country.

Many of the Deputies have given proof of talents of the highest order, and have secured themselves a distinguished position in the future development of the Constitutional liberties of this Country.

With regard to the development of those liberties there can now remain no doubt whatsoever, it is manifestly the King's intention, and the country has taken so decided an interest in the proceedings of the Diet, and in its endeavors to secure the firm establishment of the Constitutional rights conceded to it, that it would be impossible, without creating general dissatisfaction to delay for any length of time its re-assembly.

It is to the honor of the Government of this country, that when for the first time the representatives from every part of the Kingdom have been brought together, there should have been so few subjects of complaint against any part of the administration, and that no reforms of any national importance have been asked for or appear to be required.

The few propositions of the Government which were laid before the Chambers were considered as ameliorations which it would be useful to adopt, but which were not necessarily required, so that, as from causes apart from their intrinsic merit, these measures have been rejected, neither the country nor the administration will suffer from it.[247]

The King within the last week has received all the Deputies of the two Chambers at two fêtes given at Potzdam, and has thus taken leave of them, he proceeds tomorrow to Breslau to be present at the inauguration of the statue of Marshal Blücher and He instructs to

would take the question of the periodical assembly of the United Diet and the requested extension of its sphere of responsibility 'into careful consideration'.

[247] Apart from the government's two main proposals, the law on the *Landesrentenbanken* and the law on the eastern railway which was to finance a railway link from Berlin to Königsberg, the United Diet was also asked to consider laws for reforming the tax system and a new law on Jews.

Monsieur de Bodelschwingh the duty of announcing to the Diet the close of their Session. [...][248]

FO 64/275: Henry Howard to Viscount Palmerston, No 6, Berlin, 14 July 1847

Festive receptions for returning deputies of United Diet; hope for concessions by Prussian King; next session will have more liberal deputies; assessment of the first session

Accounts from all parts of the Kingdom relate the festive receptions which have either been given to, or are in course of preparation for the Deputies on their return to their homes, and particularly for those who have been the foremost in asserting what they consider to be the Rights of the Diet accruing from the Laws anterior to the Royal Patent of the 3rd of February last.[249]

I have the satisfaction to report that hitherto all these demonstrations, which have been very generally participated in, have been conducted in the most orderly manner and that great loyalty has been shown toward the Person of the King.

This feeling would no doubt, notwithstanding the painful impression produced by His Majesty's Speech on opening the Session, have been turned into enthusiasm, had His Majesty thought it consistent with the dignity of His Crown to hold out any distinct prospect of those concessions which he will probably sooner or later see the expediency of making in answer to the Petitions of the Diet,[250] and without which it is to be feared that the harmony which it is so desirable should exist between the Executive and the Chambers will not be established.

The longer they are delayed the greater will be the political agitation in the Country and although this agitation in Prussia is of a very passive nature yet it is not without inconvenience for the Government.

Moreover, it might perhaps have been advisable to have taken advantage of the composition of the present Chamber of Deputies, which was elected in great measure at a time when less interest was taken in politics than will hereafter, in all probability, be the case, and

[248] Enclosures: 1. King of Prussia's Message to the United Diet concerning the interpretation of Paragraphs of Ordinances of 3rd of February 1847 respecting loans, Berlin 24 June 1847; 2. King of Prussia's Message to the United Diet relative to Petitions for changes in the Patent & Ordinances of the 3rd of February 1847, Berlin 24 June 1847; 3. King of Prussia's Message to the United Diet concerning its close on the 26th instant, Berlin 24 June 1847; 4. Translation of No. 1; 5. Translation of No. 2; 6. Translation of No. 3.

[249] Cf. n. 240 in this section.

[250] Cf. n. 244 in this section.

which showed its moderation in rejecting demands not founded on former Laws to which such frequent reference was made and which were issued upwards of 30 years ago.[251] Within the next four years a considerable part of the Chamber will be renewed and from the feelings prevalent in the country it may be inferred that the Elections will fall on the more liberal candidates. It would therefore have been an object to have brought, if possible, all questions of Rights to a satisfactory settlement during the first Session, so that the next may be more exclusively occupied with the discussion of the material Interests of the Country.

It was with the view of bringing about this desirable end and of evincing a spirit of conciliation that the Second Chamber waived its original resolutions in respect to the laws of February last and adopted such of the amendments of the first Chamber as it considered compatible with the principles of its existence.[252]

Hence arose the disappointment, when by the Royal Messages at the close of the Diet, some of the Prayers of the joint Petition of both Houses were rejected and the answers to others were either postponed or left vague and uncertain.

However, notwithstanding the unfortunate differences between the Crown and the States on some important points, the first Assembly of the Diet has not been unproductive of good, for it has brought strongly to light the Patriotism which animates the representations of the Nation and has formed a bond of Union between the distant Provinces of the Kingdom.

The further development of the Constitutional Institutions of Prussia appears only to be a question of time, and when His Majesty by granting the Periodical Meeting of the Diet, shall have added real value to the boon he has conferred upon His People, and when mutual confidence shall have been restored, the Government will find a strong moral support in the advice and countenance of an Assembly which notwithstanding the defects in its composition, represents so considerable a Mass of Property and so many influential Classes in the Country.

---

[251] Howard is referring here to the two constitutional promises of 1815 (Decree of 22 May 1815) and 1820 (National Debt Law of 17 January), cf. nn. 141, 180 in this section.

[252] The first chamber (chamber of peers) agreed to the periodical assembly of the diet, with the proviso that the king himself must decide how long the periods between sessions should be. The first chamber also agreed to reduce the authority of the United Committee of the States, which was supposed to continue the work of the diet once its sitting was over. Moreover, the election of the United Committee was to be postponed. However, the proposal by the second chamber that the United Committee be abolished altogether did not gain a majority.

FO 64/276: Henry Howard to Viscount Palmerston, No 25, Berlin, 5 August 1847

Collection of Prussian laws regulating the position of Jews and the exclusion of persons of tainted reputations from assemblies of the States

The enclosed number of the Collection of Prussian Laws, published this day, contains the new Laws regulating the position of the Jews and the exclusion of Persons of tainted reputations from the Assemblies of the States, as well as His Majesty's Cabinet Order of the 23rd Ultimo[253] authorizing the publicity of the proceedings of Town Councils.

The Law concerning the Jews answers to the anticipation I conveyed in the Memorandum[254] enclosed in my Despatch Nº 14. It declares Jews to enjoy the same Civil Rights as the Kings Christian Subjects, but excludes them from all Government or Communal Offices with which judicial, police, or executive authority is connected, from the management or superintendence of all Affairs concerning the Worship or Education of Christians, and from the exercise of all Rights appertaining to the elective franchise of to eligibility as members of the States.

On the other hand the Civil corporations proposed to be instituted in the former Project of Law submitted to the Diet[255] have been abandoned and the Jews are to be admitted (which they have hitherto not been) to certain specified Professorships at the Universities the Statutes of which do not prevent their employment,[256] and to places as Teachers in Schools of Arts, Trade, Commerce and Navigation.

The Law for the exclusion of Persons of tained reputation from the assemblies of the States shows that the recommendations of the Diet have in great measure been attended to, as compared with the original Project. It provides that penalty for all persons who shall have incurred have the sentence of a criminal Court of Justice, who shall have been pronounced by an Assembly of States as unfit to sit as a Member, or be excluded from a Municipal Corporation, for <u>dishonorable conduct</u>.

[253] Law on the situation of the Jews of 23 July 1847.
[254] Henry Howard wrote a 'Memorandum relative to the Prussian Legislation concerning the Jews, to the project of Law submitted to the Diet, and the discussions which took place concerning it'; FO 64/275: Henry Howard to Viscount Palmerston, No. 14, Berlin, 22 July 1847, not included in this volume.
[255] The government proposal of 30 March 1847 foresaw the creation of political corporations for the Jewish population. This was supposed to do away with individual political rights.
[256] According to the new law, Jews were allowed to work as professors of medicine, mathematics, natural sciences, geography, and philology, as long as this accorded with the statutes of the university in question. In Prussia, however, this only applied to the University of Berlin.

The same rule has been applied to the sentences of Military Courts of Honor but the number of cases entailing a loss of representative Rights in consequence of a judgement of those Courts has been restricted.[257]

---

[257] Enclosure: *Gesetz-Sammlung für die Königlichen Preußischen Staaten*, No. 30, 5 August 1847.

HANOVER

HANOVER

FO 34/27: John Duncan Bligh to Viscount Palmerston, No 6, Hanover, 14 June 1838

Situation in Hanover; difficulty of getting real information; reasons for the delays in the proceedings of the Hanoverian Landtag; problems caused by the King's management; no results in the lower chamber

I am apprehensive that I shall be able, but very inadequately, to satisfy the desire which Your Lordship will naturally feel to learn something, from my personal observation, of the state of things in this Country at this interesting period[1] of its history; if however I fail, in giving you much information, I trust that the shortness of my Residence here, and the expediency of my keeping somewhat in the background, until the return of the King enabled me to present my Credentials, will be a sufficent excuse.

Indeed, if circumstances had allowed me more means of observation, it would not, I perceive, be very easy to ascertain the real state of things; for that which must at the present moment be the most interesting, namely, the proceedings of the states of this Kingdom, does not transpire in any authentic manner, as the sittings are secret, and the Press is entirely under the influence of Government; whilst Individuals who are privy to what is going on, give it that colouring which suits their own predilections and hopes.

The common channels of information will have made known to Your Lordship that for some time after the States were convoked by the King according to the forms of the Constitution of 1819, they were not in sufficient number to deliberate, in consequence of the refusal of most of the Towns to elect Deputies; by degrees, however, many of them gave way; and that impediment to the march of business was removed, though still several of the principal Towns, such as Luneburgh,

---

[1] The death of William IV in June 1837 saw the end of the personal union between Britain and Hanover that had existed since 1714. William's brother, Ernst August, became King of Hanover. On 1 November 1837 Ernst August repealed the basic state law of 1833, which he had already protested against as heir to the throne. This, and the subsequent reintroduction of the 1819 constitution, led to conflict that reached well beyond Hanover.

Osnabruck, Stade &tc &tc still remain unrepresented.[2]

In the First Chamber the opposition to the consideration of the Royal project of a Constitution was overcome, and they have proceeded with it; but in the Second Chamber it was, upon one pretext or another, put off during the absence of The King at Berlin; and it was thought by many, and desired by some, that His Majesty would on His return take some decisive step with the States in consequence of their delaying to deliberate upon affairs of such paramount importance. No proofs however of the Royal dissatisfaction have transpired further than those reported in my former Dispatch upon the Presentation of the Birthday Address[3] and if, as it is thought, The King has made up His mind not to dissolve the States, they probably, will, if they do not soon come to some decision, melt away gradually, and ere long find that they are not in sufficient number for business. In that case it is supposed the King will (as a Budget has been voted for a year) carry on the Government for the present, in the hopes of finding the Representatives of the People more tractable when He shall have to require their assistance, which hope, History and experience tell us is not unlikely to prove vain.

Some people think that The King's determination not to give up the abrogation of the Constitution of 1833 is so great, that He would in that case attempt to continue to levy the taxes now voted for a definite period; I will not venture to speculate how far the desire for things remaining unchanged may lead His Majesty to give such proofs of His thinking Germany nowadays as manageable as when He was here in His youth, but I have seen enough here to think that such an experiment upon the phlegm of the Hanoverians, and even upon their voted devotion to their Rulers, would not be safe; especially as the changes made during the present Reign in the dress of the Army, and other particulars for the purpose of assimilating it to that of Prussia have caused great and universal dissatisfaction.

It was rather expected the day before yesterday that the Lower Chamber would decide something, but I understand that no result was arrived at after a somewhat stormy sitting, in which the question of their competency was attempted to be moved, and was met by a declaration on the part of the President that it could not be entertained.

---

[2] Also not represented were the towns of Hanover, Hildesheim, Emden, Münden, Buxtehude, Fürstenau, Leer, and Norden. The 1819 constitution, according to which the *Landtag* had been called together, laid down that at least thirty-seven of the seventy-three deputies must be present for the second chamber to be able to pass resolutions.

[3] On 10 June 1838 Ernst August had refused to accept the birthday address of the city of Hanover. His condition was that Hanover's protest in the *Landtag* against the repeal of the 1833 constitution should be withdrawn. This was not accepted by the citizens of Hanover.

FO 34/27: John Duncan Bligh to Viscount Palmerston, No 13, Hanover,
12 July 1838

The Hanoverian chambers' intention to petition the Federal Diet of the Confederation against the royal abrogation of the constitution of 1833; Hanoverian King's misperception of people's real political feelings; belief that extending the franchise would secure government's majority

[...] It has been reported (though I cannot ascertain that any step of such a nature has positively been taken) that the opposition in the States purpose following the example of some of the principal Towns such as Osnabrück, Hildesheim, Buxterhüde, and Münden by petitioning The Diet of the Germanic Confederation against the Royal Abrogation of the Constitution or fundamental Law of 1833; the Government however, does not seem to apprehend that Petitions of that nature will be favourably received at Frankfort, but of course your Lordship will have much better means of judging upon that head than I have.[4]

In the mean time The King does not disguise His satisfaction with the turn which things have taken, and the conviction that He has established so firmly His popularity by His late Tour,[5] that He has no grounds for apprehending any serious or permanent opposition to His proposed Constitution, or even to His governing, as He would probably prefer, without the restraint of the States.

His Majesty details with particular pleasure what passed at the Audience which He granted to some of the Citizens of Osnabrück, for the purpose of receiving from them a Petition in favor of the maintenance of the fundamental Law of 1833 which he compelled those who presented it to acknowledge they had never read. His Majesty and those who are most in His confidence, I have reason to think, argue from this and similar incidents that the Inhabitants of the Towns are either indifferent, or are favorable to His measures, and that they are made the tools of needy Lawyers who gain by political agitation, or of the Corporations, in whom in fact is vested the election of the Members of the States, and who fear that their local importance might be diminished by any change.[6] On that account some would, I believe, go so far as to advise The King to enlarge the Rights of voting by giving it to all Householders of a certain value which they think would ensure

[4] For the *Bundestag*'s reaction to the petitions cf. pp. 94–96 in Frankfurt section.

[5] In June 1838 Ernst August embarked upon a journey of about two weeks through the provinces of the Kingdom of Hanover.

[6] The electoral law of the towns provided for so-called electoral colleges consisting, in equal proportions, of members of the city council, the so-called *Bürgervorsteher* (generally representatives elected by the citizens), and other representatives elected by all the citizens. Thus the majority of the citizens had no right to vote directly.

at the present moment an increase to the adherents of Government in
the Chambers, while the measure would be popular as bearing the
semblance of a liberal Policy; but it is not likely that The King's
repugnance to every thing in the shape of Reform would be overcome
so far as to induce Him to try the experiment.

FO 34/29: George Edgcumbe to Viscount Palmerston, No 12, Hanover,
20 February 1839

*Second chamber unable to transact business; on King's motives in annulling constitution of
1833*

I have the honor to inform Your Lordship that the States of this
Kingdom assembled on the 15th Inst.

The Second Chamber which is composed of Seventy three Members,
and requires thirty seven to be present in order to form a House, is
unable to transact business from the fact of only Twenty Nine Members
having arrived, the others have absented themselves, fearing that their
presence might be construed into a recognition of the Constitution of
1819.[7]

His Majesty has published a Proclamation and address explaining
His motives for annulling the Constitution of 1833, and restoring that
of 1819.

As these documents fill fourteen columns of the Hanover Gazette, I
have thought it advisable to give Your Lordship merely the most
important points.

'Not to leave His faithful subjects' as it is said 'in doubt or uncertainty
as to the motives which have actuated His Majesty in this affair, every
point in which the late Constitution differs from that of 1819 in any
way infringing in the privileges of the Crown is brought forward to
justify the present measures.'

It would be very difficult to notice all these judicial arguments, but
they appear to rest chiefly on the facts before adduced, that many
clauses in the late Charter were inserted without the consent of the
States, that they were at variance with the fundamental laws of the
Country, and that although the Chambers eventually thanked His late
Majesty William the fourth for granting that Constitution, still as His
present Majesty had never acquiesced in the changes then made, it

---

[7] This was the danger envisaged by the absent members of the second chamber since
the Hanoverian *Landtag* was elected and constituted according to the principles of the
1819 constitution that had been reintroduced.

was His fixed determination to adhere to that of 1819.[8] In His Majesty's letter to the General Assembly of the States which accompanies this Proclamation the subject is pursued in still greater detail, in the course of which His Majesty states that as His desire to come to some understanding with the Chambers on the project of a new Constitution submitted to them last Session had not been met by a corresponding desire on their part, His Majesty now withdraws the proposal alltogether, and commands the Presidents[9] of both Chambers not to allow any discussion on the subject, on the present occasion, adding that 'his steps have been well considered on all sides and that His will is unalterably fixed' to be guided solely by the Charter of 1819; [...]

FO 34/29: John Duncan Bligh to Viscount Palmerston, No 3, Hanover, 18 April 1839

Growing opposition to the government; Hanover question will be decided by the Federal Diet; Prince Royal averse to government's policy

From all I can hear there is little Prospect of the States meeting in sufficient numbers for the transaction of business, whenever the King shall convoke them, and it is very certain that the Country is daily becoming more and more united in opposition to the policy of The Government.

That part of the population of The Towns which has the elective franchise,[10] have from the first been opposed to the change in the Constitution which the King attempted to effect at His accession; amongst them the determination to resist has gained strength, and is now pretty generally extending itself even in the rural districts, so that not only do the electoral Bodies refuse to proceed to new Elections, or, if they do, retain the same Representatives, who have been sent back to the Constituencies by the assumption on the part of The Government that they had vacated their seats; but an opinion seems to be gaining ground, that a still more effectual resistance will be offered to the Government by a refusal to pay the Taxes after the term for which they had been voted, viz July next.

[8] In the opinion of Ernst August the repeal of the 1819 constitution in 1833 contravened Article 56 of the Vienna Final Act of 1820, in which protection of the constitutions was laid down. In support of this argument it was pointed out that a series subsequent changes to the government's draft in 1833 were not approved by the *Landtag*. In contrast to the prevailing legal view, Ernst August did not regard the silent sanctioning of these changes by the *Landtag* as binding.

[9] The president of the first chamber was Karl Graf von Platen-Hallermund, of the second chamber Friedrich Karl Jacobi.

[10] Cf. n. 6 in this section.

As encouragements to the People of this Country to pursue such a course, publications have appeared, which deny, on various grounds, the idea, that the Resolution of The Diet which empowers the Governments of the representative States of the Germanic Confederation, to levy such an amount of Taxes as has been once voted, is applicable to the present circumstances of Hanover.[11] There seems then to be little doubt that the matter will have to be decided by the Diet, and it is thought that the visit to Berlin of Prince Bernhard of Solms, who was a few months ago appointed President of the Council, may have reference to this matter; and that he has been instructed to sound the Prussian Cabinet, as to the course it would be likely to pursue at Francfort, and as to the support which The Government of the Country might expect from their powerful Neighbour, in case their Proceedings should provoke any more serious matter of dissatisfaction than those which the patient Hanoverians have hitherto shewn. It is supposed that The Prince Royal[12] of Prussia is very averse to the policy pursued by the Government of this Country, and The Prince of Solms will not receive much encouragement in his Mission. [...]

FO 34/29: John Duncan Bligh to Viscount Palmerston, No 9, Hanover, 6 June 1839

Reasons why Hanoverian chambers still unable to proceed; even with requisite number government cannot be sure of a majority

The Proceedings, or rather the attempts to proceed, of the Hanoverian Chambers would be altogether ridiculous, but for the serious consequences, which are but too likely to result from the state of things, which impedes the march of Government in this Country.

Since my last Report to Your Lordship, the number of 37 necessary to constitute the lower Chamber would have been complete but for the unexpected resignation of one[13] of the Members, upon the absurd plea that a residence in the Capital did not suit his health. What made this retreat the more remarkable was, that The King had actually condescended, as it were, to canvas him, and to exact from him a Promise to attend, when His Majesty a few days since visited a village about ten miles distant from here, where this Member was the principal

---

[11] This restriction on the budgetary rights of the *Landtag* was imposed according to articles 20 and 21 of the federal resolution of 12 June 1834 (cf. pp. 135–138 in Prussian section). If not adhered to the *Landtag* in question could be dissolved, if necessary by military intervention on the part of the German Confederation.

[12] Friedrich Wilhelm IV.

[13] Deputy Willers resigned on 3 June 1839.

Magistrate, of which visit a long account was published in the News-paper. The fact is that upon his arrival here he was so much pressed by his Friends to continue his opposition to the Government, that he had not courage to keep his promise.

Upon another occasion a Member,[14] whose attendance would have completed the requisite number, applied Leeches to his person as a excuse for his absence. Another attempt has been made by the Partizans of Government to effect an Election in the Capital during the last few days, which totally failed; in short everything proves, that the opposition to the Government is daily acquiring strength and consistency, which is encouraged by the late pressing demands made by the Diet at Francfort, for explanations from this Government respecting the changes which they have been attempting to make in the fundamental law of the Country.[15]

Thirty seven members of the Lower Chamber attended yesterday to present their respects to The King upon the return of His Birthday, which they could do without committing themselves, as in consequence of the holiday there could be no regular Sitting. This circumstance makes the King and Baron Schele sanguine as to their meeting in sufficient numbers today, which if they do, I will report to Your Lordship by the present opportunity.

Should this however be the case the difficulties of The Government will not be at an end, for the competency of each Member will have to be tested by both Chambers, and in neither can the Government be sure of a majority who will approve of the Mode in which some of the Elections have been made; as in many cases they have, in the opinion of many, been irregular, a few of the Members having been returned by one two or three votes, the other Electors having refused to attend.

Then again supposing the Chambers meet in sufficient numbers, and that the Government succeed in passing the Budget the indisposition which I have reason to believe exists in the Country to the payment of Taxes, imposed by a power which was even, last Year, considered by so many to be illegal, is not likely to be diminished should the same Imposts be enforced by an authority which is still more questionable.

It is evident that the present unfortunate state of things creates a great uneasiness in all classes of society which I am sure is participated in by the Government in spite of the air of confidence which they assume.

Thirty eight Members of the Lower Chamber having assembled today they will be competent for the transaction of business if they can

[14] Deputy Strohmeyer.
[15] At the Federal Diet's session on 26 April the envoys from Bavaria and Baden once again requested that the Diet should deal with the question of the Hanoverian constitution. To this end a commission was set up, proposed by Baden. At the *Bundestag* session of 27 June Hanover responded with a draft of numerous legal grounds for the procedure.

but be kept together. The Upper Chamber have been occupied during the day in the discussion of an Address to the King.

FO 34/29: John Duncan Bligh to Viscount Palmerston, No 14, Hanover, 26 June 1839

King proud of 'never giving in'; Bligh's reply

[...] My fears that the partial success[16] obtained in the late Session would encourage the King, in the consistent opposition to anything like concession upon which he plumes himself, were confirmed the other evening at a Party at the Palace, given to The Prince of Prussia,[17] when The King who seldom speaks to me upon the Affairs of this Country, said, after congratulating himself upon having got rid of The States, 'I have never given way upon a single point to these Gentlemen, have I not been right?' When I replied 'Yes because Your Majesty will thus be enabled to give up with a good grace, those points, where concessions may eventually be found to be expedient', when The King who does not like, and for some time has been unused to, opposition to his views, changed the conversation.

FO 34/29: John Duncan Bligh to Viscount Palmerston, No 15, Hanover, 11 July 1839

Change of law regarding tithe payer; government cannot rely on compliance by both chambers

[...] One of the Laws presented by The Government to The first Chamber, for its adoption during the late short Session, went to make a most important alteration, in a Law passed, soon after The Constitution of 1833 came into force. That Law empowered the Tithe Payer to capitilize his Tithe, and obliged the owner to receive The Capital, whenever it might be offered to him. This was certainly a one sided arrangement, and The Government wished to alter The Law, so as to give to The Tithe Owner a reciprocal right to demand, whenever convenient to him, the Capital from The Payer.[18]

Although The first Chamber is composed entirely of landed Pro-

---

[16] Before its session on 20 June 1839 the *Landtag* approved large sections of the budget – including use of the budget surplus.

[17] Wilhelm (I).

[18] *Grundherrschaft* was abolished by the decree of dissolution of 23 September 1833. From then on peasants could claim unrestricted ownership of their land by paying twenty-five times their annual dues.

prietors they reflected this in a more summary way, than any of the other Laws presented for their adoption; not permitting it even to appear upon the Minutes of their proceedings; as they knew how unpopular such a measure would be in the Country at any time, much more whilst The Legislature must, from circumstances, be possessed of so little of the public confidence.

I mention this fact to shew how little the Government can rely in either Chamber upon compliance with their wishes, should they endeavour, either to set aside, without a compromise the fundamental Law of 1833, or even make any new Laws, until something shall have been definitely settled respecting the Constitution.

FO 34/29: John Duncan Bligh to Viscount Palmerston, No 19, Hanover, 7 August 1839

Governmental measures against magistrates of Hanover; restoration of peace by civil and military measures; evidence of continuing sympathy for the opposition; Osnabrück's protest; critical sentiments of several towns of the kingdom; attempt to bribe M. Rumann

My anticipation, as communicated to Your Lordship in my last despatch, that in consequence of the proceedings of this Government against the Magistrates of Hanover,[19] the public peace would not for the present, at least, be again troubled, and that the other Corporations in the Kingdom would make common cause with the Capital have been fully verified. The prompt and vigorous measures taken by the civil and military Authorities to restrain and overawe the few who were inclined to resort to violent modes of shewing their dissatisfaction with the measures taken against the Magistrates of Hanover, have had the result which was to be expected, and not even the slightest disturbances, such as I have before expected, have been renewed. On the other hand ample evidence has been afforded of the full sympathy which is felt by the other Citizens of the Kingdom for their Brethren in the Capital. Addresses have arrived from all sides testifying such to be the case, and also their readiness to give them, and especially M. Rumann every support in their power.

Osnabruck as might be expected (from having been throughout the reign of the present King conspicuous in opposition to his measures) has not been backward upon the present occasion; A numerous Deputation was sent thence with an Address to the King begging the

[19] On 15 June 1839 the magistrates of the city of Hanover sent a petition to the Federal Diet to protest against the repeal of the basic state law of 1833, cf. pp. 94–96 in Frankfurt section. King Ernst August reacted by dismissing the city governor, Rumann, who was then accused of high treason.

reinstatement of M. Rumann, and the Chief Magistrate of that Town[.] M. Stuve[20] who is the cleverest and most influential of the opponents of the Government, has undertaken the defence of M. Rumann before the Tribunal to whom his case will be referred.

It will be needless to specify the other Towns from which similar proofs of their feelings as to this particular matter have been received; but I will mention a few circumstances which prove what is the animus of the inhabitants, especially of the Corporations, as regards the Government in General.

At Hildesheim a Pamphlet was lately published and circulated with great diligence, which blamed the Petition of the Corporation of Hanover to the Diet, and was at the same time highly laudatory of the measures taken by the Government in consequence.

This was seized by the Magistrates and suppressed, and several of those who had been employed in its distribution were imprisoned.

Several of the principal Inhabitants of Hameln, a short time since, presented a Memorial to their Magistrates in which they stated that they only consented to pay the Taxes which they consider to have been voted by a Chamber illegally constituted, once more, because they hope that the Diet will interfere to put things upon a legal footing before they shall be called upon again for similar payments; and the Memorial was not only received, but the Magistrates signified their approbation of it, in consequence of which, I understand, that the Government have it in contemplation to take legal measures against those Authorities.

These circumstances are sufficiently indicative of the difficulties which the Government are preparing for themselves in all parts of the Country, and I will only mention one more which has occurred at Osnabruck, which, though as it were a feather, shews that the popular breath is not unlikely to turn even against the Sovereign in whose favour it has, in this Country, been so much and so long accustomed to be. A number of persons having been sued for various Rates for which they were in default, publickly sold Portraits of the King, which they had hung up their houses, for the purpose of paying them.

Apprehensions were entertained at one time, that disturbances would have taken place at Osnabruck, Troops were in consequence moved to that Town from East Friesland, and General Halkett in whose Military district it is, was ordered to proceed there. That Officer is so much beloved and respected that his presence tended materially to calm any unruly disposition which might have excited, and he was enabled to dispence with the presence of the additional Troops.

It is said to have been intimated to M. Rumann, from Authority,

[20] Johann Carl Bertram Stüve.

that if he would resign quietly his Office all legal measures against him and his Brother Magistrates would be stopped, and that a Pension equal to his endowments as Director of the City would be secured to him, which he peremptorily declined; this would not tally with the confidence which is possessed to be felt by the friends of the Government as to the result of the said legal measures, but would rather justify the very positive language in which (in their Petition to the King praying for Rumann's restoration to his Office) the Citizens of Hanover deny the legality of the measures which have deprived them for a time of their Chief Magistrate.

The King refused their Petition so that the Law must take its course. In the mean time this once quiet Country is daily becoming more and more agitated, and knowing what the elements of its Government are it is difficult to foresee how its tranquillity is to be restored.

FO 34/29: John Duncan Bligh to Viscount Palmerston, No 21, Hanover, 5 September 1839

Federal Diet's decision in favour of Hanover government; King's satisfaction; opposition not over unless conciliation is made by the Hanoverian King; Federal Diet has suffered in the public esteem by its decision

The Decision[21] of the Diet in favor of the King of Hanover's abrogation of the Constitution of 1833 (the particulars of which your Lordship will doubtless have heard directly from Francfort), has, of course, caused great satisfaction to this Government; and although the Protocol, and official Notification of this Decision has not, even yet, reached Hanover, the King could not conceal the joy he felt upon receiving this news, ten days ago, from His Plenipotentiary[22] at Francfort; when His Majesty was pleased to tell me, that He considered it as 'the triumph of the Monarchical Principle, and the severest blow the Radicals had received since 1830'.[23] In short His Majesty seems to think that all His difficulties are now removed. But I have before seen instances of His prematurely flattering Himself in a similar way; and although, doubtless, the spirit

---

[21] At the *Bundestag* session of 22 August Austria, in agreement with the Hanoverian government, put forward the view that since the constitution of 1833 had been repealed, the constitution of 1819 was valid. Prussia also supported this view and on 5 September 1839 the *Bundestag* decided that the German Confederation had no reason to interfere in the question of the Hanoverian constitution. Petitions in favour of this were rejected; cf. pp. 94–96 in Frankfurt section.

[22] Karl Friedrich Freiherr von Stralenheim.

[23] For the events following the French revolution of July 1830 cf. n. 194 in Frankfurt section.

of opposition to His measures will be somewhat impaired by the failure of all hope of foreign support; I still feel convinced that, unless the King should submit to the States, when again convoked, as the result of the labours of the Commission,[24] now acting under His orders, a Project of Constitution which shall shew Him to be guided by a spirit of conciliation, and a wish to consult, in some measure, the popular, as well as His own Sovereign will, that He will not find He has to deal with as tractable a People as He is sanguine enough to expect.

The Decision of the Diet is said to be accompanied by an earnest recommendation that early steps should be taken for endeavouring to meet the wishes of the Nation in settling its future Government, but I apprehend, now that the King is pleased to imagine that He will have every thing His own way, that He will have a deaf ear to such counsels, and be less than ever disposed to concede.

What will be the moral effect throughout Germany of a Decision so lightly setting aside a Constitution granted by a Sovereign, and acted upon for several years, it may be idle to speculate about; but I cannot think this Act of the Diet will raise that Body in public estimation either here or elsewhere. [...]

FO 34/31: John Duncan Bligh to Viscount Palmerston, No 7, Hanover, 20 February 1840

Baron Schele's confidence that lower chambers will have sufficient members to proceed; opposition well organised; King of Hanover in a more favourable position; brief recapitulation of the circumstances; project of a new constitution

I am still unable to pronounce with any certainty as to the effect of the Royal Proclamation[25] for convoking the States, or to give any opinion founded upon positive data as to the probability whether the Lower Chamber will meet in sufficient numbers or not.

Baron Schele, who however is perhaps wont to be over sanguine, professes to entertain little doubt on the subject, and whilst he affirms that the Proclamation has generally produced a favorable impression, expresses a confident expectation, that although three out of the Members, who were barely in sufficient numbers to form the Lower Chamber during last Session, have resigned,[26] more than enough new Elections will take place, or other Members will be induced to attend,

[24] The constitutional commission, in which deputies from the second chamber also took part after initial opposition, was convened in August 1839.

[25] The *Landtag* was convened for 19 March 1840 by the Royal Proclamation of 10 February 1840. Its task was to deal once more with the draft constitution.

[26] Deputies Merkel, Schaf, and Lang resigned.

as will obviate the danger of the Royal Summons proving a fruitless measure. At the same time he does not seem prepared to support this opinion by any facts indicative of a change in the tactics of those who are opposed to the Government, of whose proceedings and intentions he seems surprisingly ignorant, though all their late measures prove them to have been at length acting upon a well organized system. He anticipates good effects from that Paragraph of the Proclamation which assures the Electors that in the exercise of their Rights, as such they are not expected to pronounce any opinion as to the fundamental Law or Constitution, by which they are called upon to exercise those Rights, and that consequently they will no longer be apprehensive of committing themselves to anything positive by electing their Representatives, and will therefore not be backward to do so.

It cannot be denied, whatever opinions may be entertained as to the justice and sound policy of the taking away by one Sovereign of Rights and a fundamental Law given to a People by his Predecessor,[27] that in the present cases circumstances have placed the King of Hanover in a much more favourable position than He might have found Himself in if his Subjects had known how to defend those Rights in the possession of which they were upon His Accession; if in fact they had not played His game instead of their own.

A brief recapitulation of the circumstances will I think make this sufficiently evident. In the first place as to the right of King Ernest to abrogate the Constitution given to the Hanoverians by King William in 1833. It is indisputable that the former when Heir Presumptive to the Throne constantly refused his adhesion to the change then effected, which refusal might be some sort of justification for his attempting to alter at least those parts of the new fundamental Law of which He did not approve, and there is little doubt that He would have been able to have accomplished his wishes by submitting to the States, as then constituted, measures calculated for the purpose.

Upon the plea however that such a course would commit Him to a tacit approval of the fundamental Law which, before He was the Sovereign, He had rejected, He chose by a <u>Coup d'Etat</u> to abrogate it altogether, and to convoke a new Chamber according to the Patent or Fundamental Law of 1819. Against this no remonstrance was in the first instance made, nor was any opposition, either active or passive offered; The Electors exercised their Rights as set forth in the revived fundamental Law; Those elected according to its forms obeyed the Royal Summons, took the oaths prescribed, constituted themselves as a Chamber, voted the Budget and passed some insignificant Laws, and it was not until parts of the fundamental Law itself came under

---

[27] William IV.

discussion that the Opposition appeared to be aware of the false steps they had taken, and declined to acknowledge their competency to consider such matters, thereby stultifying all their anterior proceedings.

That Chamber was consequently dissolved and another being convoked the Electors in many places, and the majority of them in many more, abstained from voting, and many of the Members who were elected were backward in taking their seats.

This System had it been acted upon from the first, would have seriously embarrassed the King, but it was now adopted too late for any practical purpose, for by some means or other (many of them perhaps of questionable regularity) a sufficient number of Deputies were collected to vote the Budget &c and another Prorogation took place upon their declining to enter, whilst so uncomplete, upon the question of amendments in the Constitution.

In the mean while the Diet of the Germanic Confederation after rejecting all the Petitions[28] which had been presented to them, from different Bodies of Hanoverians declared their incompetency to interfere in the internal disputes of this Country, and recommended an early settlement of them, between the Government and the then existing States. Cavils have been raised, and much has been written as to the precise meaning of the expression under lined above, but as far as I can learn the German expression dermalig cannot fairly be otherwise interpreted, and nobody can deny that there are States existing, for in two different Sessions Budgets have been voted, and other business has been transacted. [29]

The King declares in His last Proclamation that He has the Project of a New Constitution ready to lay before the same States which having already met have consequently recognized their own legitimacy and competency to discuss it; as then no further hopes of Foreign support can be entertained; as the Opposition themselves must see how seriously they have compromised their means of resistance by their foolish proceedings in the first instance; as there must, and does exist a desire in the People generally to have the Constitution settled upon an undisputed Basis, so that the material and pressing wants of the Country may be attended to; and as those who are acquainted with its provisions represent the Project as being concocted upon fair and acceptable terms, it is not unreasonable to expect that the States will not only meet at the time for which they are summoned, but will seriously occupy themselves with the consideration of the King's Proposals.

[28] Cf. pp. 94–96 in Frankfurt section.
[29] For an interpretation of the formulation 'then existing' cf. n. 39 in this section.

FO 34/31: John Duncan Bligh to Viscount Palmerston, No 13, Hanover, 2 April 1840

Most remarkable points of the projected new constitution

As the Project of a Constitution has been taken into consideration by the Chambers of the Hanoverian States, and as it will probably be much discussed both here and elsewhere, I have had it translated and have the honour of enclosing a Copy herewith.

As however it will probably be too long for Your Lordship's perusal I have compressed into as small a Compass as possible in this Despatch the most remarkable points of the Project, as follows.

§2 declares that all Decrees of the Germanic Diet are to be valid as soon as promulgated by The King.

§9 gives to The King the power of stopping proceedings in criminal Processes.

§33 qualifies in some measure the hitherto existing exemptions from billeting Troops &c &c which had been granted in 1822.

§35–36 states that the exemptions hitherto enjoyed by Persons <u>and Things</u> (which are enumerated)[30] from the jurisdiction of certain Courts of Law will be qualified by a Law to be made.

§38 confirms a most important Law passed by the States elected in virtue of the Constitution of 1833, and which has been acted upon to so large an amount throughout the Country as would have rendered it impossible for the King to dispense with it altogether, though endeavours were made last Session to induce the States to alter it so far that it should not be imperative upon the Possessors of the Rights in Question to sell, when required to do so. The Royal Domains have sold them to a very large amount, some say 8 000 000 Dollars.

From §42 to 58 inclusive are detailed the privileges of communities and Corporations and §55 also defines the Principles upon which New Charters which are promised to be given by The King are to be framed, against the Justice, and propriety of which it appears to me that nothing can be advanced.

From §59 to 76 inclusive the Rights, and Privileges appertaining to the Clergy and to establishments for Religion, Charity, and Education are defined, and there is nothing particular to remark, except that the

---

[30] Persons: 'the higher Royal Authorities, the Proprietors of equestrian estates eligible to sit in the Assembly of the States, the Noble freeholders, the higher Royal Servants, the higher Clergy, the present holders of Office as Magistrates & Towns and the Officers'. Things: 'The Royal Palaces, Castles, Gardens and Buildings as also Estates belonging to the Crown, Foundations, Monasteries, those Possessions of Knights entitled to sit in the Chamber of the General States, and the Grounds belonging to these as well as to all the beforementioned estates.'

influence, and Controul of the King, the non-interference of the Pope in all matters not entirely religious, and the inalienability of the Property are guarded, and laid down with great precision.

§77–78–79 establish the continuance of Provincial States in the districts which are named,[31] and the maintenance of the Rights which they at present possess, except where they merge into those of the General States. §80 declares that the General States are to consist of two Chambers.

From §81 to 84 inclusive the Constitution of the first Chamber is given.

From 85 to 88 inclusive that of the second Chamber. From 89 to 97 inclusive the attributes common to both Chambers are detailed.

§89 renders it imperative upon all Voters to proceed to elect when called upon, by which the difficulty which at present prevents so many Elections from taking place (upon the plea of Elections by a Minority of Electors being invalid) will be got over.

§95 Forbids Members to fetter themselves with Instructions from their Constituents; a provision which obviously cannot be enforced.

§96 Gives cases in which the Right of voting by Proxy or Substitute is allowed in the first Chamber.

§97 Gives to the King the Right of sending Commissioners to either Chamber to assist at their deliberations without voting, a provision likely to produce, an improper Controul over the Proceedings.

From 98 to 116 inclusive are defined the Powers of The States General which it might be worth while to peruse in extenso, and it will be sufficient for me to state generally the Regulations which are made as follows.

The duration of each Parliament or <u>Landtag</u> is to be 6 years, and is to be convoked every 3 years, and the Session is generally not to exceed 3 months. To the States is accorded the Right of sanctioning the remission, the repeal, the alteration of, and of giving an authentic interpretation to [a] all Laws relative to the Taxes [b] which immediately effect private Property, [c] which impose new Burthens upon the People in General, or upon Separate Classes, or which increase those already in existence. The States will only be required to give their opinion and advice, upon all other Laws without having the power of making any addition to them.

---

[31] 'There shall be Provincial States 1, for the Principalities of Calenberg, Göttingen and Grubenhagen together with the former Hessian Bailiwicks in the Principality of Göttingen and for Eichsfeld on this side, 2, for the Principality of Lüneburg including the Dukedom of Sachsen-Lauenburg on this side, 3, for the Counties of Hoya and Diepholtz with the former Hessian Bailiwicks in those Provinces, 4, for the Duchies of Bremen and Verden, 5, for the Principality of Osnabrück, 6, for the Principality for Hildesheim together with the Town of Goslar, 7, for the Principality of Ostfriesland and the Harlingerland.'

The King retains the Right of passing them according to the Principles laid down by the Constitution and afterwards promulgating them.

Petitions, and Proposals from the States to The King can only emanate from both Chambers conjointly. In case of necessity The King can issue Laws to be afterwards submitted to the States for their opinion. Courts of Justice are to administer Laws published by The King without examining whether they have been agreed to by the States, the Proceedings of the States are not to be published by the Members.

From §118 to 154 comprise the Chapter upon Finances, to which as it forms the Portion of the Project most likely to offer difficulties for an arrangement between the Sovereign and His States, I would most invite Your Lordship's Attention in the enclosed Translation, and I shall only mention the most important points in this Despatch.

The King reserves to Himself the Management, and expenditure of the Crown Domains and Royalties, and the States are to have no right to interfere in the matter unless the King, under particular circumstances, should require it; but upon the opening of each Landtag, or Parliament, a statement of the income, and expenditure of the Royal Treasury will be communicated to them. The nett Revenues from these sources will be applied to the Payment of the Interest upon the debts due by the Domains, and to the gradual Reimbursement of the Capital; to the expenses of the Royal Family, and to other expenses of the Government. They will no longer be paid into the same Treasury as the Taxes, but the separation of the Royal, and State Treasuries is to be reestablished in the same way as it existed up to the 1ˢᵗ July 1834. An arrangement is to be made between the King, and the States respecting the Partition of certain classes of expenditure between the Royal and State Treasuries, which can only be altered, or annulled by mutual consent.

A Budget of the expenses to be borne by the State Treasury is to be laid at each ordinary Session (id est every three years) before the General Assembly of States, who will have the right to examine it, and agree to it, and at the same time an estimate of the amount of Taxes which will be required is to be submitted to them; and their consent to the levying of the Taxes will be requisite, and will be valid for the succeeding financial period of three Years. The King gives up to the State Treasuries the Land Tolls, and Navigation dues (Royalties, which have annually produced to the Royal Treasury 230,000 Dollars) upon the understanding that an equal sum be made good to the Royal Treasury. The Stade Duties contribute the principal share of these 230,000 Dollars. If the States do not assemble in sufficient numbers, without having voted the Taxes proposed to them by The King, He is to have the right of continuing to levy for the ensuing Year the Taxes, which had been voted for the previous financial Period.

The direct, and Indirect Taxes are to be paid into the State Treasury, the management of which will appertain, under the superintendence of the Minister of Finance to the Schatz Collegium, which will be established, under Royal authorization, partly by the nomination of the King partly by election in the States.

From §155 to 166 inclusive the appointment, and functions of the Ministers, and Council of State, of the Judges, and other public Servants are detailed, as well as the circumstances under which they can be dismissed from office.

§167 States that no Change can be made in the Constitution unless voted in two successive Landtags by at least 2/3rd of the Members present.

§169 In case of any unconstitutional infringement of the Constitutional Charter the Schatz Collegium is empowered and bound to petition The King to support the Constitution, and to appeal for that purpose to the General Assembly of States, and should that means fail, to invite the Germanic Confederation to defend the Constitution.[32]

FO 34/32: John Duncan Bligh to Visount Palmerston, No 22, Hanover, 28 May 1840

Birthday celebration for Crown Prince; feared blindness of the Crown Prince; difficulties resulting from his illness

[...] A Dinner was given at Court yesterday in celebration of the Crown Prince's[33] Birthday, at which the Grand Duke of Oldenburgh,[34] who arrived unexpectedly, and the Queen's daughter the Duchess of Dessau,[35] who came by invitation, assisted; the Court afterwards proceeded to the Theatre where the Crown Prince was received with considerable applause. D'r Graeffe is expected to arrive from Berlin in the course of next month for the purpose of operating, if practicable upon the Crown Prince's eye and His Royal Highness is anxious that no further delay should occur in ascertaining whether He is partially to recover his sight, or to be condemned to perpetual blindness; I regret deeply to have to state that it is pretty generally feared that the latter alternative will be the sad lot of His Royal Highness.

[32] Enclosure: project of a Constitution for the King of Hanover.
[33] Georg.
[34] August.
[35] Luise Wilhelmine.

This melancholy state of things as regards the heir to the Crown; the age of the King; and His Majesty's late serious illness, have caused a general, and deeply felt anxiety that some provision should be made for the case of a blind Successor to the Throne.

In the project of a Constitution now under consideration by the States, the contingency of mental incapacity in the Sovereign is specially provided against, but bodily ailments which prevent the due exercise of the Royal Functions do not appear to have been contemplated, and it is feared that the King has not hitherto made any arrangement, in a less public way, for obviating the disadvantages which both his Successor and his Subjects would labour under if the former should become King without the power of knowing what he may have to sign, and without anyone being officially designated to testify the sign manual.

FO 34/32: John Duncan Bligh to Visount Palmerston, No 23, Hanover, 28 May 1840

No results from chambers' daily deliberations; both chambers' struggle for more legislative power; many deputies employed by government therefore subservient; chambers not really supportive of people's liberties

The States continue their daily deliberations upon various matters of local interest, as well as upon the more important affair of the Project of Constitution without however anything resulting worth Your Lordship's notice except that the Second Chamber have read a second time, without any amendment, that portion of the Project by which the King withholds from the States the power of refusing to pass Laws except of such a nature as are therein specified.[36]

The first Chamber will not easily, as far as I can ascertain, give way upon this point and some Members of it have expressed to me a hope that upon the third reading, the Second Chamber will see the expediency of following their example, or at any rate that in a Conference between the two, some middle term will be found by which they will agree to contend for the possession of a little more of the real attributes of a legislative Body than the King seems disposed to concede to them.

This want of union between the two Chambers upon so important a point will of course fortify the King's resolution not to give way, and will induce His Majesty to hold to his threat (should the present project be altered by the States in any important particular) of governing the

---

[36] Cf. summary of the government draft in FO 34/31: No. 13, 3 April 1840: 'To the States is accorded the Right of [...] the proceedings of the States are not to be published by the Members.'

Country according to the Constitution of 1819 which is in some particulars less favorable to his Subjects than that which He at present offers them.[37]

It is painful to see that portion of the States which is entirely elective and which ought to be the most watchful over the liberties of the people so subservient to the wishes of the Government, but when it is known that a large proportion of its members are in the employment of the Government and that many have been sent to the States by a small Minority of the Electors, the circumstance however disreputable ceases to be surprising.

It is impossible that such a decision of a Body so constituted can be satisfactory to the Country if there really exists among the People a desire to have a Constitutional Form of Government, – I really believe however that as long as the material interests of the Country are flourishing, as at present, German Phlegm and apathy will prevent their making much of a struggle for political rights. [...]

FO 34/32: John Duncan Bligh to Viscount Palmerston, No 34, Hanover, 6 August 1840

Constitutional project; gains and losses; not clear whether substituted constitution will satisfy the country; dissatisfaction of towns, Hanover in particular

The Constitutional Project as amended by the States and sanctioned by the King not having yet been published and officially promulgated, I shall not at present attempt to make an analysis of what the Monarch and the People have gained or lost in the late struggle.

It does not appear however that after the alterations which have been made in the original Royal Project,[38] the King will be found to have gained much beyond what the fundamental Law of 1833 gave to the Sovereign, except the separation of the Royal and the State Treasury, and everybody seems to think that this point, and any other which could have been reasonably desired, might have been obtained by the Government from the States which the King found assembled upon his accession without such a waste of time, and without the ill

---

[37] The 1840 constitution was a compromise between the constitution of 1819 and the Basic State Law of 1833. On the one hand the new constitution limited the rights of the *Landtag*, underlined the monarchic principle and emphasized ministerial responsibility. On the other hand it also retained certain key features of the constitutional state. Apart from a constitutional guarantee of basic individual rights, this meant, above all, involvement of the *Landtag* in legislation. The composition of the *Landtag* was only very slightly different from the constitution of 1833.

[38] For a detailed inventory of the constitutional project cf. pp. 265–268 in this section.

blood and excitement which has been occasioned by the overthrow of a Constitution by the Successor of the Sovereign who had granted it to the Country.

Whether the Constitution now substituted for that of 1833 will satisfy the Country remains to be seen. The Towns will doubtless protest against the competency of the States, elected as the last were, to have a voice in such a matter, but the Diet will in all probability refuse to listen to their Protestations, as in fact the King has, according to the recommendation of that Body, settled his differences with His <u>then existing States</u>.[39]

If then the Diet gives their Guarantee to the Constitution lately agreed upon, the Hanoverians who, with few exceptions, like tranquillity and wish for a settled state of things, will probably submit quietly.

The Magistrates of Hanover as well as the Citizens sent an Address to the King the day before the question of the Constitution was settled, praying His Majesty not to sanction it.

Everybody is surprised that the King who, up to the last moment, expressed a determination not to yield upon the point of a deliberative voice for the Chamber in all Laws, should have so suddenly given way. I believe his Ministers and Counsellors unanimously expressed their conviction that the First Chamber would adhere to their opinion and that His Majesty therefore yielded rather than allow the whole thing to fall to the ground in the face of the urgent recommendation supposed to have been given to His Majesty by the King of Prussia to bring his disputes with his people to an end. [...][40]

FO 34/32: John Duncan Bligh to Viscount Palmerston, No 35, Hanover, 20 August 1840

Austria and Prussia approve the new constitution; no hurry to obtain approval of smaller member states of the Federal Diet

[...] In consequence of the strenuous opposition to the measures of the Hanoverian Government which was shewn last year by the minority in the Diet,[41] it has been judged more prudent not to press that Body

[39] Bligh was hinting here at the disputed interpretation of this formulation by the *Bundestag*. Since the *Landtag* had been legally dissolved before the edict of 1 November, the formulation 'then existing state' refers to the chambers convened in 1838 according to the constitution of 1819.

[40] Enclosures: 1. Translation, Address of the States to the King; 2. Translation, The King's Answer to the Address.

[41] Bavaria, Baden, Württemberg, the Saxon dukedoms, and the free cities opposed the procedure proposed by Hanover and favoured intervention in the constitutional conflict by the German Confederation.

at the present moment to give their guarantee to the new Hanoverian
Constitution, but as this Government are assured of the entire satisfaction felt by those of Austria and Prussia that an end should have
been put to the disputes between the King and His States, they are in
no particular hurry to obtain the formal approbation of the other
Members of the Confederation. [...]

FO 34/32: John Duncan Bligh to Viscount Palmerston, No 42, Hanover,
15 October 1840

*Ban on export of horses to hinder French war preparation; Prussia not preparing for war;
doubts whether a concerted line of action could be achieved in case of war against France*

[...] A Royal Ordinance which was published a few days since forbidding
the exportation of Horses was in consequence as I am informed by
Baron Schele of an agreement amongst the Powers of the Germanic
Confederation to adopt such a measure; which, if generally carried into
effect, will materially impede the French Government in one branch
of their preparations for the War which they appear, so unaccountably
and so unjustifiably, to be provoking.[42] Should Hostilities unfortunately
result from the excitement in France and should Germany be an object
of attack, the Disturbers of the Peace of the World would, as far as I
can ascertain, meet from the People of these Parts with very little
sympathy, and with much animosity, both on account of their past and
present proceedings; whether the somewhat discordant Interests of the
different parts of Germany would allow the Governments to adopt
cordially any common line of action I am not competent to give a
decided opinion; but I am inclined to fear the contrary. The total
abstinence from ostensible preparation for war upon the part of Prussia
already excites suspicion here; but Hanoverians are ever ready to cairl
with their powerful Neighbour, – it is to be hoped in this case
unreasonably, and that the admirable organization of Prussia both for
<u>Peace</u> and <u>War</u> may render it less necessary for Her, than for others,
to make extraordinary preparations for the latter state of things, even
when there may be threatening appearances of its approach, and when
She would be one of those most likely to bear the first brunt of an
attack. [...]

---

[42] For France's behaviour during the so-called Rhine Crisis cf. n. 210 in Frankfurt
section, and pp. 192–193 in Prussia section.

FO 34/37: John Duncan Bligh to Earl of Aberdeen, No 13, Confidential, Hanover, 7 July 1842

King's intention to govern without the chambers; plans to realize his intention; open tensions between King and Estates result in a 'party spirit' difficult to overcome

Having heard from a source on which I can generally rely, that the King, disgusted by the opposition which he is continually meeting with in the States, entertained, not only the wish, but seriously the intention, of governing without the intervention of those inconvenient Bodies, I could hardly believe it, as, independent of the difficulties which might be met with at home, quiet and submissive as the Hanoverians have ever been, I imagined that His Majesty must be aware of the obligations imposed upon him, by the Act which regulates the Germanic Confederation, to maintain such Bodies,[43] I was farther told however that His Majesty threatened to get over any difficulty of that sort by separating Himself from Confederation forgetting that He has not the power of doing so.

I took an opportunity of asking the Austrian Minister[44] if he had ever heard a report of this nature; when after expressing his surprise at my knowing anything about it, as that was a proof that the idea had been more seriously entertained than he had supposed, he confessed that the King had upon one occasion after urging him to endeavour to obtain for Him the support of Austria at Frankfort, threatened, if unsupported there, to separate Himself from the Confederation.

I have been informed also that one of the objects of the King's last visit to Berlin was to sound the Prussian Cabinet as to his separation from the Confederation as a preliminary to doing away with the States, and that of course His Majesty met with no encouragement there.

It really cannot be wondered at that the States should not feel well disposed to the Government, as not only is nothing done to conciliate them, as might be done at very little cost and trouble; not only are they summoned from their homes in the depth of winter sit for two months in perfect idleness in the Capital, but the King omits no opportunity of expressing most openly his contempt for them in language which it would not be decorous for me to use in my official correspondence. The immediate consequences are that the Government is now opposed in almost every measure by at least as strong a majority, as they had in their favour at the commencement of the Session, the ultimate consequences will assuredly be to excite a Party spirit in the

[43] Article 13 of the Federal Act of 1815, cf. n. 83 in Frankfurt section.
[44] Baron Friedrich Kress von Kressenstein.

Country, which a short time since was not thought of, but which it will be very difficult to overcome.

FO 34/39: John Duncan Bligh to Earl of Aberdeen, No 4, Hanover, 19 January 1843

No Prussian support for Hanoverian King; King's irritation at the appointment of M. Dahlmann to a professorship at Bonn; censorship in Prussia

The King was so much irritated by some late proceedings in Prussia, and of the inattention to his feelings and wishes on the part of the Cabinet of Berlin which they appeared to betray, that it is probable that he had no intention when He left this of extending his journey to Berlin, but His Prussian Majesty having so much pressed Him to do so when so near as Dessau, His Majesty could not resist the temptation of revisiting a Place for which He has such strong predilections,[45] whilst at the same time His doing so would give Him a good opportunity of prolonging, in an agreeable manner, his absence from His own Capital where, as His occupations are not of a pleasing, and his recollections are of a sorrowful, nature, He appears not to wish to be, longer than His duties require.

By personal communication with His Prussian Majesty He would also have an opportunity of receiving explanations respecting the circumstances to which I have alluded to above; and I have every reason to believe that He has not only received them, but has found them to be satisfactory, inasmuch as Baron Schele tells me that the appointment to a Professorship at Bonn by M. Dahlmann, (which was one of the grievances) took place without the King of Prussia having been made aware that, being one of the Professors who had been expelled from Göttingen,[46] his appointment would naturally be disagreeable to the Hanoverian Government; He has received the strictest injunctions to abstain in his Lectures, or in any way from giving umbrage to this Country; but I am told that he still retains so strong a feeling of irritation for his treatment at Göttingen as to find it very difficult to refrain from giving expression to them in public.

As a remedy for the causes of complaint which have been found here against several of the Prussian Newspapers, in which, offensive Articles have appeared, of late questioning the right of the Crown

---

[45] By marriage to Princess Friederike of Mecklenburg-Strelitz, the sister of Queen Luise of Prussia, Ernst August was a brother-in-law of King Friedrich Wilhelm III. Ernst August's close connection with Prussia was also illustrated by his long visits to Berlin and his close links with ultra-conservative Prussian politicians.

[46] For the dismissed professors cf. pp. 162–163 in Prussia section.

Prince[47] to succeed to the Throne, other Censors have been appointed who it is hoped will not be remiss in the performance of the Duties of good neighbourhood. The strong measures which have been taken by the Prussian Government against the Press by the exclusion of the Leipzic Newspaper[48] will also tend to reconcile the King to the offence which had been committed against Him by those of Prussia. [...]

FO 34/39: John Duncan Bligh to Earl of Aberdeen, No 11, Hanover, 30 March 1843

Present position of Hanover regarding the Commercial Union

The following appears, as far as I can ascertain, to be the present position of Hanover with reference to the great Commercial Union of Germany.

In consequence of a pressing invitation to that effect this Government, some time since, communicated to the Cabinet of Berlin an outline of the terms upon which Hanover might be disposed to join the Union; but they were found to be so inadmissible as to have led to the inference that they were propounded more with the view of not acting ungraciously towards the Prussian Government, than with any serious expectation of their being accepted. [...]

I do not imagine that the opinions of the King have undergone any material change upon this subject; He declared not long ago, that He would not join the Zollverein without communication first with Her Majesty's Government, and He has assured my Austrian Colleague[49] that He would not join it unless Austria did. The public feeling is, I am sure, as strong against it as ever, as it cannot but be evident that Hanover would lose by being absorbed in the great League, so that, if even the Government were to be gained over and alter their policy in this matter, I do not think they would, at present, at least, be able to prevail upon the States to sanction the change.

The Prussian Government has doubtless made considerable efforts to prevail upon this Government to unite with them commercially; my Prussian Colleague Count Senckendorff has been very ardent in the cause, and not long since was even sanguine of success; he now however, has changed his tone and seems to think that the time is not yet come. It is indeed the fashion to say, 'the Union must take place sooner or

---

[47] Crown Prince Georg went blind in 1833. His right to the succession was secured by the constitution of 1840, since according to the new constitution only minors or the mentally ill could be precluded from succeeding to the throne.

[48] *Leipziger Allgemeine Zeitung* cf. n. 215 in Frankfurt section.

[49] Baron Friedrich Kress von Kressenstein.

later', but situated as this Country is, I see no absolute reason for it. At any rate I tell all with whom I speak on the subject that the game is in their own hands, as they have nothing to gain by abandoning their independent position, and that if ever they were to yield, it should be at the price of most favourable conditions.

Oldenbourg being, as I believe she undoubtedly is, favourable to a Commercial Union with the rest of Germany, does not alter the position of this Country, as from the Geographical situation of the former, she must, almost inevitably, follow, in this particular, the lead of Hanover. [...]

FO 34/39: John Duncan Bligh to Earl of Aberdeen, No 23, Hanover, 15 May 1843

M. Rumann's sentence; sentence confirmed by Superior Court of Appeal

About four years ago, as a reference to the correspondence from this mission would shew, he the City Director Rumann and his Brother Magistrates were by order of the Government removed from their Posts and cited before the Chancery of Justice to answer for their conduct in appealing directly to the Diet at Francfort against the Government in the affair of the Constitution then under discussion.[50]

After mature deliberation the Chancery of Justice, in August 1841, condemned the Magistrates to various terms of imprisonment or to proportionate fines, which, in the case of Rumann was eight weeks confinement or the payment of four hundred Dollars; upon which he choose the alternative of the fine, expressing at the same time his readiness to resign, which would have settled the matter, and as it has turned out would have relieved the Government from considerable embarrassment.

The King however thinking the punishment inadequate, and encouraged by the Minister of Justice, contrary, as it is said, to the opinions of his other Counsellors, determined that a Reference of the case should be made to the Superior Court of Appeal at Celle, which has within these few days unexpectedly pronounced a decision, confirming that of the inferior Tribunal; by which the Government and a Subject are placed, unfortunately, in the false positions of the latter gaining a sort of victory over the former.

It is hoped that Rumann may again be induced to resign his situation, and retire upon a Pension; and that the King will not endeavour to exercise the prerogative, secured to Him by the Constitution, of

---

[50] For Rumann's dismissal cf. pp. 259–261 in this section.

dismissing such Functionaries from their Posts by the advice and with consent of the Council of State, as that Body might fairly hesitate to sanction a proceeding, in opposition to the Decision of the two principal Courts of Justice in the Country.[51]

FO 34/43: John Duncan Bligh to Earl of Aberdeen, No 9, Hanover, 14 March 1844

King of Hanover does not want to join the Zollverein

[...] I have been lately surprised by hearing, in an indirect manner, that the King imagines Her Majesty's Government to have been under the impression that He had been disposed to join the Zollverein; should such have been the case I can confidently assert that it cannot have been derived from my Correspondence, as I have invariably maintained the existence of a strong Bias on the part of His Majesty against such an Union. Indeed I have always asserted my belief that the true interests of the Country were too well understood both by the King and His People to make it at all probable.

It is true that external circumstances may at one moment have induced His Majesty to be especially anxious for a complete Union of Germany, and to entertain the Question whether a juncture with the Zollverein could be made compatible with the interests of His People.

Prussia by availing herself of the favorable junction might have entangled this Government in negotiations which might possibly have resulted in the total disruption of the Steuer Verein,[52] if, instead of at once rejecting the conditions upon which Hanover proposed to treat, she had suggested some middle term for an accommodation.

I think however that, the menacing aspect of things on the other side of the Rhine having in the mean time calmed, Hanover was not sorry to find that her overtures at Berlin had been rejected, and was not at all disposed to renew them.

A few days ago the King told the Prussian Minister[53] in presence of

---

[51] At the end of May the Rumann affair was settled. Once the city of Hanover had paid 3,000 Talers from its own coffers for Rumann's pension, King Ernst August declared that he was prepared to take over payment. At the same time Rumann and his condemned colleagues were released from having to pay the fine.

[52] In 1834 Hanover, Brunswick, Oldenburg, and Schaumburg-Lippe joined together in a fiscal union, as a North German counterweight to the customs union. Like the *Zollverein* the *Steuerverein* had a unified, though much lower, external tariff. The founding of the *Steuerverein* prevented the *Zollverein* from expanding to the North Sea coast. In 1841, following disputes with Hanover over customs policy, Brunswick joined the *Zollverein*.

[53] Graf Theodor von Senckendorff-Gutend.

our Austrian Colleague,[54] that it was contrary to His Policy, as regards England, to join the Zollverein; which declaration, however satisfactory the feeling which gave rise to it may be to us, I was sorry for, as such expressions may tend to increase the bitterness of the attacks against this Country for its unpatriotic feeling, with which the German Press abounds; and they are unnecessary, because the internal interests of this Country indicate much more clearly what its course should be, than any foreign influence and sympathies however powerful or innate. [...]

FO 34/43: John Duncan Bligh to Earl of Aberdeen, No 39, Hanover, 14 August 1844

Product of national industry displayed at exhibition every four years

Although this Country may be considered amongst the lowest in the scale of manufacturing progress, and hitherto its Capital has for the most part been employed in improving its means of communication, its agriculture and extensive waste Lands, rather than in struggling to produce what is to be procured far better and cheaper from other Countries, there has nevertheless for some time past[55] been an exhibition every four years of the product of National Industry, one of which has lately been opened here, and it may not be wholly uninteresting to Your Lordship to be made acquainted with what I have observed and heard respecting it.

It seems to be considered that improvement has on the whole taken place during the last four years, and although complaints are made that some manufactures, who formerly were amongst the principal contributors, have sent nothing upon this occasion the collection of objects is more numerous than heretofore; and although there are many things exhibited of a very common description, there are a few which merit attention.

The common Linens of the Provinces of Göttingen and Osnabruck appear to be good and reasonable in price, and the coarser sorts of Cloth are cheap; there are some very good specimens of Cabinet work and inlaid Furniture; the Fire Arms of Hertzberg in the Hartz are highly finished and made after English Models; evidence is given of the great encouragement which has of late years been bestowed by the Court upon the works in Bronze in this Capital by some good specimens

---

[54] Baron Friedrich Kress von Kressenstein.

[55] In 1835 a trade exhibition was held in Hanover for the first time. It was organized by the Trade Association of the Kingdom of Hanover, founded in 1834.

of Lustres made after French patterns, and considerable improvement
has been made in this particular branch; there are Articles of Leather
of a very good description; every thing of Cotton seems to be very
ordinary; and, altogether, however the Hanoverians themselves may be
pleased, as they appear to be, by the progress which they assert that
native Industry is making, Foreigners have little reason, from what it
can at present produce, to fear anything from its competition. [...]

FO 34/45: John Duncan Bligh to Earl of Aberdeen, No 12, Hanover,
6 February 1845

Reasons why balls at court should not be held on Sunday; England as an example

[...] The Crown Prince[56] continues in complete seclusion, on account
of the delicate state of His Eyes; the Crown Princess[57] always remaining
with His Royal Highness, except when ordered by the King to attend
the Balls, which, as was the case also last year, His Majesty gives every
Sunday. Repeated but ineffectual attempts were made by those who
are supposed to have influence over the King to induce His Majesty
to be pleased to select another day for his Entertainments; upon the
plea that as the whole Society in this small Place is put in motion by
a Fête at Court, the Domestics and many Persons in inferior Stations
are deprived of their customary Holiday.

As the King expects to see the Corps Diplomatique upon these
occasions, I attend, and as soon as I have made my Bow, I retire: but
I cannot help wishing that Her Majesty's Servants abroad might be
allowed (and that their having that option might be made known to all
Courts) to follow their own inclinations as to the observance of the
Sabbath; and then, no offence could possibly be taken by their acting
up to the practice of the English Court and Nation in this particular;
especially when called upon, not occasionally only, but, systematicaly
to deviate from it. It might be, also, that the example of England, and
of those who represent Her (which can never be altogether unheeded
in matters however trifling) might eventually have a beneficial effect
upon others, as well as upon Her own Subjects resident in foreign
Countries.

---

[56] Georg.
[57] Marie Alexandrine.

FO 34/45: John Duncan Bligh to Earl of Aberdeen, No 27, Hanover,
22 May 1845

Indifference or reluctance towards subject of railroads in Hanover

I cannot help regretting to observe here an indifference on the subject
of Railroads which may prove as prejudicial to this Country as the
contrary extreme threatens to be in some other parts of the world.
They appear to be looked upon in the light of evils, necessary perhaps,
but to be staved off as long as possible.

Thus about nine years ago the Country between this place and
Harburg was surveyed by an eminent English Engineer,[58] plans and
estimates were prepared, English Capital was forthcoming for the
scheme, which, had it been carried out, would have given to this
country the first work of the sort in Germany, but being opposed by
the Government it of course fell to the ground. Having however at
length seen the necessity of not being altogether left behind in the race
of improvement the Government has decided upon carrying out almost
the same plan as had been previously proposed to them, and as the
only work of the sort which they are actually proceeding with is in that
direction it is probable that their intention of completing in the course
of next year the new Port at Harburg and the communication by
Railroad with it will be carried into effect; I find however that that
part of it as far as Celle which was to have been ready this month will
not be opened until the Autumn. [...]

A Treaty with Bremen for connecting it with this place by Railroad
has been ratified, but though it will be the same line for a certain
distance as that proposed to Minden and Cologne there seems to be
no hurry to act upon it.

FO 34/45: John Duncan Bligh to Earl of Aberdeen, No 43, Hanover,
11 September 1845

Potato blight

I am sorry to say that the extraordinary disease which has affected the
Potato crop of this year in so many parts has also made its appearance
in this Country, to such a degree, as to cause considerable alarm.[59] To

---

[58] Not traceable.

[59] Potato blight is caused by the false mildew mushroom (*Phytophtora*). In the 1840s
potato blight was imported from France. In 1846/1847 it caused a food crisis in many
states of the German Confederation.

tranquillize the public mind and to guard against any dearth of this Produce, which has become almost indispensable advice and directions respecting the treatment and preservation of the Crop have been published by the Government coupled with assurances that measures will be taken to make up as far as possible for any deficiency in this particular.

I understand that all the rice at Hamburgh has already been bought up for Holland and Belgium.

The grain Harvest in this Country is nearly completed and has generally been very productive.

FO 34/47: John Duncan Bligh to Earl of Aberdeen, No 11, Hanover, 12 March 1846

Statistics and analysis of Hanoverian population

According to a statement which has lately been published the Population of this Kingdom on the 1ˢᵗ July 1845 amounted to 1,773,711; the increase since the year 1836 having been 85,426.

My attention being drawn to the fact of the average annual increase up to 1842 having been about 11000, whilst from that period to 1845 it had decreased to about 6000, I was desirous of ascertaining whether this, as was probable, was attributable to an increased drain by Emigration, and the result of my enquiries shews, that the taste of explanation which has long prevailed in the Southern parts of Germany is at length gaining ground in this Country, and entirely accounts for the smaller average annual increase in the Population which is now observable. Thus in the Province of Osnabrück, the principal Seat of the Linen Manufacture which of late years has not prospered, from whence alone Emigration to any amount formerly took place, the number of Emigrants has doubled since 1836, viz from 2253 to 4537, whilst in the Province of Hanover during last year it was 1967, and in that of Hildesheim it was 1437. I have no returns of the Emigration from the other Provinces, but I know it to be inconsiderable.

From Bremen, the principal point of departure for German Emigrants, the number of those who embarked last year was 31849 of which 28224 went to the United States, 2134 to Texas, and 491 to Australia. I understand the whole Number who emigrated from Germany last year was about 56000, of which about 19000 by way of Antwerp.

FO 34/47: John Duncan Bligh to Earl of Aberdeen, No 17, Hanover,
9 April 1846

Open disregard of so-called Sabbath Ordnung (Regulations for the Sabbath)

It cannot be said that any extraordinary regard is shewn here to the
outward observances of Religion, nevertheless people have been of late
scandalized by an unprecedented neglect of them in influential Quarters
in despite of the Law for defining them which is called the Sabbath
Ordnung (Regulations for the Sabbath.)

Last year the Theatre, which had hitherto invariably been closed
from the Eve of Palm Sunday until Wednesday in Easter week, was
open to the Public on Palm Sunday and the two following days in
Passion Week, a precedent which has been followed this year, besides
which the usual weekly Ball was given at the Palace on that Sunday, a
thing hitherto unheard of here.

As all festivities and public Entertainments are still strictly forbidden
under pain of heavy fines at this Season in all Places except those
under the immediate control of the Court, it is easy to imagine the bad
effect which must be produced by this open disregard of the Laws
which is shewn by those to whom the execution of them is entrusted,
especially when it is notoriously in the teeth of remonstrances which
have been addressed to them by the Consistory, to whom is assigned
the superintendence of such matters.

Unfortunately the Clergy, being generally men neither of high birth
nor acquirements, do not possess much influence or consideration, nor
are they likely to obtain more from the fact of their being exposed to
severe reprimands if they should, from their Pulpits, touch upon matters
distasteful to the Authorities, of which several recent instances might
be given.

I have thought it beyond my province thus slightly to touch upon
matters which, though not strictly of political interest, cannot fail
indirectly to influence the social condition of the People of this Country.

FO 34/47: John Duncan Bligh to Earl of Aberdeen, No 22, Hanover,
7 May 1846

Regulations for duelling in the army changed

A few Months ago some Regulations were issued to this Army respecting
Duelling, the principal one being, that no dispute should be settled in
such a manner until a Court of Honor composed of Officers had

investigated the particulars of each case, and pronounced the necessity of having recourse to that extreme measure.

I did not think it worth while to trouble Your Lordship by mentioning a measure having only reference to the internal arrangements of the Military Service; but the first application of it has been altered with circumstances which have been much canvassed here, and I venture to trespass on Your Lordship with this matter, which, although trifling in itself may be considered of some interest as shewing how much interference of the highest Authority makes itself felt in every particular.

About two years ago instructions had been given to Count Platen,[60] an Officer of the Guards, to regulate the measure of the Music at Balls here. Having heard that at one patronised by the Garde de Corps about three Months since the music had been too quick, that Officer threatened to punish the Master of the Band[61] which led to a dispute between him and the Director of the Ball[62] in question. It was hushed up at the time but having been subsequently revived in consequence of some gossiping reports, the King as Colonel in Chief of the Guards ordered the matter to be submitted to a Court of Honor which decided that Count Platen must fight with Count Kielmansegge an Officer of the Garde du Corps. The Duel, (as well as another between Count Platen and one[63] of the Royal Chamberlains which originated in the same cause), which ensued was, fortunately, bloodless; had they been otherwise, amongst other effects which would have been to be deplored, the disagreeable impression would have been increased which has been occasioned by the direct interference of the Sovereign in a private quarrel, and by allowing it to be pushed to extremity with his perfect cognizance.

FO 34/50: John Duncan Bligh to Viscount Palmerston, No 17, Hanover, 30 July 1847

King's former predilection for everything Prussian and its effects; increasing influence of Austria and reasons for the diminishing influence of Prussia in Hanover

A notable change has taken place in the Policy of this Government, as regards the leading Powers of Germany, since it first became my duty to observe it, which I think it may be well to point out, and to try to explain to Your Lordship.

---

[60] Gustav Graf von Platen-Hallermund.
[61] Not traceable.
[62] Not traceable.
[63] Not traceable.

In 1838 the struggle was at its height between The King (who, never having adhered to the Constitution granted by His Predecessor,[64] was determined to alter what He conceived to be prejudicial to His rights and interests) and his people, who, were naturally striving to preserve the guarantees for their Liberties and influence in the Government which they had once been allowed to possess.

From his long residence at Berlin,[65] The King came to the Throne with strong predilictions in favor of every thing Prussian, and this was immediately shewn in a variety of ways and acts, which it is needless here to particularize. One of the most remarkable of them was the adoption of the Prussian Uniform for the Army which sorrowfully remonstrated, but in vain, against the loss of a Color under which so much Glory had been acquired.[66] At the same time the most intimate relations were kept up between the Governments here and at Berlin; and all this much to the dissatisfaction of the Hanoverians who eschewed all close connexion with their powerful Neighbour of whom they entertained a naturally inherent jealousy. The unpopularity which this course of Policy added to the discontent occasioned by the attempt to overthrow the Constitution of 1833 was disregarded; Prussia was still courted and imitated; amongst other reasons, doubtless, because it was convenient to be sure of having at hand the material as well as moral support of a Power, able and willing to assist if necessary in keeping that discontent within bounds.

At length the perseverance of the Government aided by the support at Frankfort of the principal Powers of Germany prevailed, and in 1841 a new Constitution was established.[67] Up to that time the Prussian Cabinet was almost without a Rival with this Government, although the influence of Austria had already begun to make itself felt.

At Vienna, the importance was perceived of securing in the North of Germany some counterpoise to the increasing influence which the establishment of the Zoll verein was acquiring for Prussia. Baron Kress had been sent here as Austrian Minister, and the more active support of his Government had been afforded to this Government in the Constitutional struggle which was in progress. That Minister whose previous Career had been in the Chancery of Prince Metternich, and at Hamburgh, had never resided at a Foreign Court, and flattered as may be supposed by finding Himself in immediate contact with a Sovereign, fully carried out in his own person the Policy of his

[64] William IV.

[65] From 1818 to 1837 Ernst August and his family lived mainly in Berlin.

[66] The Hanoverian army's greatest achievement was fighting alongside England and Prussia during the Seven Years' War (1756–1763). At this time it consisted of about 50,000 men.

[67] The new constitution came into force on 6 August 1840 and not in 1841.

Government by complying with the somewhat exaggerated pretensions of this Court, more completely than many might think necessary for one in the independent position of a Foreign Minister. The interchange of Orders soon took place. The King and Crown Prince receiving that of St Stephen,[68] Prince Metternich the newly created one of St George[69] and Baron Kress the Guelph,[70] and in the meanwhile the Constitutional question had, as before stated been settled.

The support of Prussia had now become less necessary, and her influence was gradually diminishing from various causes. Considerable dissatisfaction had been felt here by the employment in Prussian Universities of some of the Professors who had been dismissed from that of Göttingen[71] soon after The King's accession to the Throne. Although General Canitz, who at that time was still Prussian Minister here, had in reality done the Hanoverian Government much service during the constitutional struggle, he was personally distasteful to the King who then took little pains to disguise those feelings which are still bearing their fruits in the rejection of that Minister's Son-in-Law Count Westpahl.

Then came the separation of Brunswic from the Steuer Verein and its junction with the Zoll Verein,[72] a proceeding so manifestly contrary to the interests of that Country that it was attributed, in part at least, to extraneous influence and Prussia naturally had to bear the blame. She, at any rate as the directing Power of the Zoll Verein had to take a prominent part in the Negotiations consequent upon that proceeding, which at one time were carried on with much acrimony, and Count Seckendorff who had succeeded General Canitz here was personally made the Victim of the ill humor felt at this Court on the subject, to such an extreme, that he was on the point two years ago being withdrawn from his Post.

The convocation of the States General at Berlin,[73] a measure so peculiarly repugnant to the Conservative principles of The King of Hanover was the bathos of disfavor into which the Prussian Government had been gradually falling in the estimation of this Cabinet; and this was soon after followed by the nomination of Count Westpahl as

---

[68] Order of St Stephen, Austro-Hungarian order, created by Empress Maria Theresia in 1764.

[69] Order of St George of Hanover, created by Ernst August in 1839 as an order of 'Court Honour and Merit'.

[70] Order of the Guelph, created by King George IV in memory of the war against France and dedicated to the ancestors of the Hanoverian royal family.

[71] Friedrich Christian Dahlmann was offered a chair in Bonn in 1842; Jacob and Wilhelm Grimm at the Berlin Academy of Sciences in 1841. For the dismissal of the so-called *Göttinger Sieben* cf. pp. 162–163 in Prussia section.

[72] Brunswick joined the *Zollverein* in 1841 cf. n. 52 in this section.

[73] Cf. pp. 235–236 in Prussia section.

Minister to this Court, and his public and peremptory rejection upon the Plea of his being a Roman Catholic.

The King still keeps a private Correspondence with the Sovereign and Princes of Prussia, but it will not be easy to restore cordiality between the two Governments.

In the meanwhile the Austrian Government has gone on profiting by its opportunity of increasing its favor here, which appears to have reached its Climax from the following somewhat insignificant cause. The Emperor ascertaining the great prediliction of the King for Hussars, appointed His Majesty Chief of one of his most distinguished Regiments of that Arm, at which I am told His Majesty could not disguise his satisfaction. A general Officer was immediately sent with His thanks to the Emperor; a fresh interchange of Orders took place; a Tailor[74] was summoned from Vienna to make His Majesty's new Uniform, and somewhat to the scandal of those who think that such distinctions should be reserved for Persons of a Higher Grade, and for more eminent services, he returned home with a Snuff Box ornamented with the King's Cypher as a Present from His Majesty. I hope I shall be excused for mentioning such a trivial circumstance, but trifles sometimes become of importance even in serious affairs; at any rate Austria has played a not unwise game most successfully, and her influence is now paramount in this portion of Germany; nor do I consider it likely that in the natural course of things, future circumstances will operate for its diminution; as the Crown Prince not only adopted the intimacy with Austria earlier, but is to all appearance more firmly attached to it even than The King.

FO 34/50: John Duncan Bligh to Viscount Palmerston, No 40, Hanover, 4 November 1847

Crown property and its management

It was always unquestionable that The Crown of Hanover had a large and direct pecuniary interest in the overthrow of those arrangements by which the late King had given up all direct controul over the Regal Domains; and that this was the principal cause of the change in the Constitution which the present King effected after a protracted struggle, thereby restoring to The Sovereign the management of the property of the Crown, a management which is nominally but very imperfectly

[74] Not traceable.

superintended and controlled by the Schatz Collegium.[75]

It may not however be altogether uninteresting to Your Lordship to be shewn in figures the result of some observations I have made on the subject.

The whole surface of the Kingdom is calculated at 9,041,406 Morgens (a measure somewhat less than an English acre) of which the Domains and suppressed Convents (both being under the immediate direction of The King) possess 1,521,299 Morgens, or 17 per Cent of the whole.

This statement, however, will give a very imperfect idea of the extent of the Crown Property, if unaccompanied by that which follows.

Up to the year 1833 the whole soil, not altogether owned either by the Crown, the suppressed Convents or by the Nobility, was in the hands of the Yeomanry or Peasants (as they are here called) or of the Gemeinde or Parishes. It was however charged with various burthens payable either in money, in kind or in labour to the Lord in fee; of which rights the Crown and the Convents were the principal Proprietors. A Law was then passed for the redemption by money of those rights, according to a certain recognised scale, of which the Peasants have to a very great extent availed themselves; so that The Crown has already received upwards of 11,000,000 of Dollars, and is daily receiving, in addition, a part of about an equal sum which it is calculated will eventually be derivable from this source, whilst the whole public Income for this year is not more than 4,121,619 Dollars. Of this sum about 2,000,000 have already been laid out in Land, but the high price it bears, both from the number of Purchasers and from the very great disinclination of the Peasantry to part with it, renders this sort of Investment very difficult and the greater part has necessarily been lent on good Security of other kinds.

This difficulty of increasing the landed possessions of the Crown is consolatory to those who already view with jealousy their immense extent, and who deprecate the diminution in the number and influence of the Independent Yeomanry.

I will not trouble Your Lordship with further details having stated enough to shew how important to this Crown was the struggle which was successfully carried through for securing the predominating influence which its immense possessions must ensure for the Sovereign.

[75] The Treasury College was first introduced by the constitution of 1819. It was supposed to control state expenditure and the income from the royal domains. When it was abolished by the basic state law of 1833 the royal domains were taken into state ownership, a civil list set up for the royal court and the *Landtage* given more of a controlling function in state expenditure. Following the introduction of the new constitution in August 1840 the Treasury College was re-established by the patent of 24 December 1840; the separation of royal expenses and state expenses that had prevailed until 1833/34 was thus re-established.

SAXONY
(DRESDEN)

DRESDEN

FO 68/33: Edward Michael Ward to Earl of Aberdeen, No 16, Dresden, 29 June 1830

300-year Commemoration of the 'Confessio Augustana'; tensions resulting from a Catholic royal family and a mainly Protestant population

Three days of the last week have been devoted here to the Third Centenary Commemoration of the Publication at the Diet of Augsburg of the Articles of the Protestant Faith as adopted by Luther and his Followers.[1]

On this occasion whatever of Party Zeal the existence of a Catholic Family on the Throne keeps alive here, was called into action.

A Drunken Riot originating in some insult offered to a Bust of Luther which took place on the first night, occasioned much alarm to the Authorities of this, at other times, very peaceable Town, and the Military were called out to disperse the crowds assembled.

Patrols of Horse and Foot paraded the Streets during the following nights. No rioting took place, but the people were not to be prevented from testifying their Zeal for the cause in shouts in Honor of Luther and Melanchton, of that of their popular Preachers who had officiated during the day, and also of all Protestant Princes – the King of Prussia by name. Cheers were likewise given for Prince Frederic the Heir to this Throne, it being the popular belief that His Royal Highness is less strongly attached to the Romish Tenets than the other Members of the Royal Family.

There have been also some tumultuous proceedings on the part of the Students at Leipzig, who were guilty of some acts of insubordination in consequence of being prohibited from displaying their Zeal for the Memory of Luther by a public Procession.

It does not however appear that any apprehension of further disturbance of the public Peace need not be apprehended.

---

[1] *Confessio Augustana* cf. n. 211 in Prussia section.

FO 68/33: Edward Michael Ward to Earl of Aberdeen, No 25, Dresden, 6 September 1830

Student insubordination; workmen's riots

On Thursday last some of the Leipsig Police having given offence to a party of Students who were, on the occasion of a Festival which took place on that day, amusing themselves somewhat riotously in the Streets, these latter assembled tumultuously and attacked the house of the President[2] of the University which they nearly destroyed.

The President is very Unpopular amongst the Young men.

This Act of insubordination on the part of the Students is, however, unconnected with Riots amongst the Workmen which took place on Saturday night, when several houses belonging to members of the Senate of the Town were attacked.

The extent of damage done I have not heard.

The alleged motive of discontent was an Order for Iron bedsteads for the Hospital having been given to the manufacturers of some other Town. There being no Garrison in Leipsig, some Troops were sent from hence in Carriages Yesterday immediately on the receipt of the above intelligence.

The Students were aiding the magistrates in their endeavours to restore Order.

It does not appear that any Political feeling has been manifested in these disturbances.

FO 68/33: Edward Michael Ward to Earl of Aberdeen, No 28, Dresden, 10 September 1830

Serious riot in Dresden; Prince Frederick proclaims an armed citizen guard ('Bürgerwehr')

[...] In this City a serious Riot took place last night in which the Town Hall was attacked by the populace and the furniture and Archives taken out and burnt in the Street.

The Police House was also completely destroyed and the Prisoners detained there set at liberty.

The windows of the Minister Count Einsiedel were also broken.

The Military who were called out were unable to oppose effectual resistance to the Mob without firing on them, and that it was thought advisable not to do. A few blank shots were only discharged.

I have heard that some of the Officers have been wounded by stones thrown and it is reported that some lives have been lost.

---

[2] Karl Heinrich Konstantin von Ende.

Today Prince Frederick (who has lately been appointed Commander in Chief of the Army) has issued a Proclamation[3] calling upon the Citizens to turn out in defence of the Public tranquillity and Arms are now in the Act of being distributed to them.

In defect of a sufficient quantity of these they are desired to arm themselves and in lieu of Uniform to wear a white handkerchief on the left Arm.

The Town is at present perfectly quiet but if the Spirit of the Riot continues to prevail, its security must depend upon the Exertions of the Burgher Guard and other armed Citizens, the number of regular Troops being from the drafts made to Leipsig and other temporary circumstances at this moment quite insufficient for the purpose.

General Minckwitz[4] with whom I have spoken considers that no Political feeling whatever manifested itself on this occasion, and seems inclined to attribute the Violences of the Mob to the innate love of Disorder always to be found amongst the lowest Classes and now excited to action by the accounts of tumults received from so many other Quarters.

There is however no doubt that considerable dissatisfaction respecting the amount of certain Municipal Taxes which affect the necessaries of life, has for some time prevailed.

FO 68/33: Edward Michael Ward to Earl of Aberdeen, No 29, Dresden, 12 September 1830

Grievances and demands of lower classes and bourgeoisie; organisation of a 'Bürgerwehr'; limited number of military troops in Dresden

No Disturbance whatever has taken place since the first night of the Riots.

The operatives in those Excesses were certainly of the lowest Class, but from many things which have come to my knowledge, I suspect that they were abetted by some of a better Class, with a view of intimidating and drawing the attention of those in Power to the Grievances of which they, the Bourgeoisie, complain.

These Grievances refer mainly, I believe, to municipal Exactions or Police Regulations.[5]

In this they have succeeded, as the King has named a Commission at the head of which is Prince Frederick, which is to sit tomorrow for the purpose of hearing the representations of the Citizens.

---

[3] Proclamation by the Commission for Upholding the Peace, 10 September 1830.
[4] Johannes von Minckwitz.
[5] For the demands cf. p. 295 in this section.

The Citizens on their part met to day and chose six persons to act in their name. In a day or two we shall see what is the extent of their Demands, such, I hope, as may be complied with, for in the first six or eight hours of Alarm, the Government in order to procure a sufficient Force to keep down the rabble during the night, which was coming on, gave out from the Arsenal, two thousand five hundred stand of Arms and five hundred Sabres to any person whatsoever who chose to present himself and demand them, authorising at the same time others, who could not get these, to arm themselves, and The whole of these Volunteers, designating themselves by a white handkerchief on the left Arm to unite by fifties and chose their own Officers.

Many more Arms than the above number have since been given out, but with more circumspection. The first imprudent precipitation having been with reason much blamed.

These Volunteers in plain clothes, added to an already formed Burgher Guard in Uniform, but all of the same Class, amount probably to above four thousand men and they have possession of all the posts in the Town.

When I wrote my last Dispatch I was not aware of the circumstance of this Burgher Guard, which turned out some time after the breaking out of the Riot, having forced the King's Troops, who were endeavouring, however ineffectually from the smallness of their number, to resist the Mob, to retire to their Barracks.

The number of the Troops now here does not exceed a Portion of a Regiment of Riflemen (the Remainder having been sent off to Leipsig,) seven hundred Artillery, two hundred Guards and five hundred Cavalry, the latter arrived yesterday, but are not allowed to come into the Town being quartered in the neighbouring Villages.

Thus the National Guard is in possession of Dresden and are tomorrow to become as many thousand armed Petitioners.

A numerous Meeting of the Citizens took place to day, when six Persons[6] were named to draw up a Statement of their Grievances. Both in Leipzig [!] and here, the immediate exciting cause of discontent among the lower class of Citizens was doubtless the heavy, unequal and oppressive dues levied by the Municipalities, of the amount or Employment of which they render no account.

If their demands should now confine themselves to these points, matters would perhaps be arranged in tranquillity, as the Municipality has declared its readiness to give way. There is however reason to believe that the Petitioners may take a wider Range now that they

---

[6] Seven people in all were involved – amongst them the popular community judge Friedrich August Rätzsch – who were commissioned to prepare an address by the citizens of the old town of Dresden. It was delivered on 16 December 1830.

perceive the impression which they have produced on the Government.

Accounts of Excesses being committed at Chemnitz, a considerable Manufacturing Town, have arrived and a Battalion of Light Infantry has been marched from hence thither, this draft diminishes still farther the small number of disposable Troops in this Garrison.

FO 68/33: Edward Michael Ward to Earl of Aberdeen, No 32, Dresden, 14 September 1830

Demands of citizens

The Demands which the Citizens mean to make have not yet been definitively agreed upon by them but the following heads have been being handed about as being proposed to be brought forward.

Demands of the Citizens

N° 1. that the Police shall not be reorganised in its old form.

2. a new form of City Constitution and participation of the Citizens in its Administration.

3. reduction of the Taxes on Bread, Meat, and Flour, to 1/3 of the present rate.

4. the Monopoly of the Mills (which belongs to the Crown) to be done away with.

5. abolition of high Pensions and Salaries enjoyed by idle and undeserving People.

6. abolition of secret Expences of the Court for objects which are unknown to the Country.

(NB. this alludes to Relics, Indulgences &c. &c. procured at Rome.)

7. higher Duties on foreign Goods.

8. the Court is requested to buy in Saxony all those Articles which can be furnished by the Natives.

9. removal of those Servants of the State who have countenanced the old abuses.

10. that the Town of Dresden should send two Deputies chosen from the Citizens, to the Meeting of the States.

The Municipality has already promised to admit the Citizens to examine the accounts of its receipts and Expenditure. This Concession has been made known by a public Advertisement[7] signed by Prince Frederick as Chief of the Commission for the preservation of the public Peace.

Your Lordship will however see that this falls very short of the notions which now seem afloat amongst the Petitioners, inspired by the

[7] Cf. n. 3 in this section.

consciousness of their own strength and the utter weakness of the Government.

Government has in fact no means to control them or resist any demand which they may now chuse to insist upon if they continue united among themselves.

FO 68/33: Edward Michael Ward to Earl of Aberdeen, No 30, Dresden, 14 September 1830

King's proclamation announcing Prince Frederick as Co-Regent; removal of Count Einsiedel

The King being thrown into great alarm by the Information that a general popular Manifestation in favor of His Nephew Prince Frederick's being called to the Throne was in agitation, came yesterday to the sudden resolution of issuing a Proclamation[8] announcing that he had determined to name Him Co-Regnant with Himself and that the Prince's Father Prince Maximilian spontaneously resigned in his favor all reversionary Right to the Crown.

Translation of this Proclamation I have the Honor to inclose.

The removal of Count Einsiedel from the Ministry was also resolved upon and made known.

These Changes which were announced late in the Evening appear to have given satisfaction the Town having been generally illuminated in consequence.

Prince Frederick's Popularity depends upon the belief that he is less strongly attached to the Tenets of Roman Catholicism than the other Members of his Family.

M. de Lindenau lately Saxon Minister at the Diet at Frankfort has been named in Count Einsiedel's room.[9]

FO 68/34: Edward Michael Ward to Viscount Palmerston, No 7, Dresden, 2 March 1831

Proposed new system for composition of Saxon chambers; mode of election

I have herewith the Honor to inclose a Translation of that Part of the Project of the New Saxon System submitted to the States, which relates to the Composition of the future Chambers.

[8] Proclamation of 13 September 1830.
[9] Enclosures: Original and Translation of the Proclamation of King Anton and Duke Maximilian, dated 13 September 1830.

The Upper Chamber is partly hereditary, partly depending on the holding Office and Ecclesiastical Dignities, and partly elective for Life.

It is to be observed that this hereditary Right to sit in this Chamber is in no instance separated from the entailed Inheritance which gives the Qualification. It is therefore landed Property and not Birth which qualifies.

The lower Chamber is composed of Representatives of landed Property, Representatives of Towns, and Representatives of the Yeomanry. The two latter being together to the first as ten to three. A Proportion of this Chamber is renewable every three years.

The mode of Election for the Town and Yeomanry Deputies is not direct. The Electors themselves being first to be chosen.

It being only since yesterday that the States have been in possession of the Project and it not being yet in public Circulation, I am unable to say with what favor it may be received. I can however imagine that that party which looks to France as its model, will not find the composition of the Chambers sufficiently free from the Clogs of fixed and tangible Qualifications, which its Framers have thought requisite in order, in this little inland state whose Boundaries are neither traced by nature or consecrated by time, and which is not even distinguished in language from its surrounding Neighbours, to identify the interests of the Members with that of the Country itself. On the other hand the little regard with which it treats Nobility of Birth may perhaps find little favor in the eyes of those who at present enjoy exclusive Privileges in virtue of this qualification.[10]

FO 68/34: Edward Michael Ward to Viscount Palmerston, No 10, Dresden, 7 March 1831

Summary of proposed changes regarding the new Saxon chamber

I have herewith the Honor to transmit a Translation of the Decree read by the President[11] of the Conference to the Deputation of the Sates of the Kingdom, in presence of the King and Prince CoRegnant,[12] when H.M. delivered to them the Project of the new System for the Government and Legislation of the Country.

I have already submitted to Your Lordship a resumé of the proposed changes in the Legislative Body and I now briefly notice some other changes alluded to in this Decree.

---

[10] Enclosure: Translation. Project of the new Saxon System submitted to the States relative to the Composition of the future Chambers (§§ 58–65).

[11] Gottlob Adolf Ernst von Nostiz und Jänckendorf.

[12] Friedrich August.

Summary of proposed Changes

The States now sitting in one Chamber to sit henceforward in two.

1) The Number of Members to be reduced from the present Number (nearly four Hundred) to sixty five in the lower Chamber and to between thirty and fourty in the Upper Chamber, making together about one Hundred, more or less;

2) The Revenues of all Crown Property and the Produce of all those Taxes which, not depending on the States, have hitherto never been accounted for by the Crown, are now to be paid into the Treasury. The Crown to receive fixed Income from the Treasury for the maintenance of its dignity under the Denomination of the Civil List. The Jewels of the Crown, the Royal Library, Armory, Picture Gallery, Porcelain Museum &c. &c. declared Heir Looms of the King and His Heirs for ever.

3) A Tribunal to be appointed for Trials of Impeachments of Ministers and Members of the State

I likewise annex a Statement of the Heads of the Estimates of Receipt and Expenditure for the current Year, now for the first time communicated to the Public. I have reduced the Sums into Pounds Sterling at the rate of Three Shillings to the Saxon Dollar.

With respect to the feelings with which this great change is received, I will only observe in corroboration of what I, in my Dispatch N° 7, had the honor of stating, that it is probable it will give satisfaction to no Party or Persons excepting its immediate Framers and Friends.

First, the Pounds, Shillings and Pence calculators remark that above one fifth and a quarter part (one Hundred and Thirty Five thousand Pounds) of the Revenue of the Country, is demanded for the Civil List. This comprises the whole of the King's Expences, the allowances to Three married Princes and two Princesses, the Theatre and Royal Catholic Chapel, together with Extras (amounting to 18,000 a year) of which no detail is given. It is however to be remarked that the Revenues of the Crown Lands £113,000 and the Hereditary Revenue, such as Post Office, Mines, Tolls &c. £149,000, now given up, amount together to £262 000.

Next, the Members of the States, in number near four hundred, of whom the greater portion are under the new System disenfranchised, can hardly be expected to be contented with it.

The Deliberation on the whole plan which is now going on daily, Article by Article, is not however sufficiently advanced for me to be able to learn what may be their result.

There does not prevail an entire unanimity in the view taken of the Project within the States and it is to be remarked that whatever may be surmised to be the private feelings of many of its Members on the subject, it does not follow that they will all venture openly to oppose the Minister, so much more or less is the majority under the influence of the Crown.

The deliberations are carried on with closed doors.[13]

FO 68/34: Charles Townshend Barnard to Viscount Palmerston, No 7, Dresden, 18 April 1831

On the so-called 'Bürgerverein'; government's prohibiting measures

An Association has been lately formed here under the name of 'Bürger Verein'[14] at which many Citizens were in the habit of assembling at a Coffee House. It was known that the greater part of its Members were discontented persons who had belonged to the late National Guard,[15] and that the language held at their Meetings was of a very revolutionary nature.

The Government issued an Order, forbidding these Meetings, this order however not being attended to, two[16] of the most violent Members were arrested on the Evening of the 16th Inst and confined at the Town Hall. Yesterday afternoon about forty persons belonging to this Association came armed to the Town Hall, where a small number of the Communal Guard were on Duty, and succeeded in rescuing their companions, whom they escorted to their respective houses.

The Governor[17] of the Town and his Aid de Camp[18] arrived on horseback but were obliged to retire. Several large Stones were thrown at the Governor while passing through the Streets. The Military and the Communal Guard assembled very soon and quiet was again restored. The Populace took very little part in the disturbance. Several of the Rioters have been arrested and removed immediately to the Fortress of Königstein. Both the Citizens who were rescued from the Town Hall have been again arrested and are now in confinement.

[13] Enclosure: Translation. Decree addressed to the States relative to the new constitution of Saxony, 1 March 1831.

[14] The *Dresdener Bürgerverein* was founded in December 1830. Under the leadership of the lawyer Bernhard Moßdorf it became increasingly influential and supported democratic ideas.

[15] The National Guard was disbanded on 4 December 1830 because its members had participated in the disturbances in Dresden.

[16] The two merchants Karl Friedrich Wilhelm Schramm and Heinrich Moritz Müller.

[17] Heinrich Adolf Freiherr von Gablenz.

[18] Carl Friedrich Anger.

FO 68/34: Charles Townshend Barnard to Viscount Palmerston, No
9, Dresden, 22 April 1831

*Tranquillity restored; arrests of some ringleaders; alleged dangerous tendency of 'Bürgerverein';
lenient punishment for rioters*

Since I had the Honor of addressing Your Lordship, this Town has
been perfectly quiet. The Military remains on Duty in the Streets, day
and night. Several Citizens have been arrested in consequence of
denunciations made by those who were taken as Ringleaders in the
riot of the 17th Ins[t].[19] However insignificant in point of number and
means, yet it appears that the association ('Bürger Verein[']) had a very
dangerous tendency. Among other papers found in the Houses of some
of the Members of this Society, is a printed Sketch of a Constitution[20]
of which a great many Copies were to have been distributed by
Emissaries in the Country. The Expulsion of the present Dynasty, and
the massacre of several ministers and other persons in Office was, it is
said, also in contemplation. All papers found are of a revolutionary
and republican nature. Many of the persons concerned in this Conspiracy belong to the Communal Guard, which has now proved itself
to be a very disaffected Body and not to be relied on in cases of
emergency. The principal Actors in the plot are low tradesmen and
Attorneys, but the whole plan was so absurdly arranged and the number
so small that it never could have been carried into execution. As
long as the Military remain in the Town, no further disturbance is
apprehended, but if the Government does not act with more energy
and firmness and make some severe examples of the persons now in
prison, it will be difficult to prevent future Riots. Not a single person
who has been arrested in the different disturbances since September
last, has been punished beyond a few days imprisonment. There is no
regularly organized Police in the Town and the people entertain neither
fear or respect for any of the Authorities.

[19] Cf. p. 299 in this section.
[20] This was the 'Constitution, which the Saxon people want' (*Constitution, wie sie das
sächsische Volk wünscht*), drawn up by Bernhard Moßdorf.

FO 68/35: Charles Townshend Barnard to Viscount Palmerston, No 15, Dresden, 20 May 1832

Austria, Russia, and Prussia wish to have all Polish refugees removed from Saxony

The Ministers of Austria,[21] Russia[22] and Prussia[23] have according to Instructions received from their respective Courts, addressed a Notes to the Saxon Government demanding the immediate removal of all Polish Refugées[24] from this Kingdom. The necessity of this measure is grounded on the apprehension that the discontented Poles, if permitted to establish themselves in Dresden, which is so central a point, will eventually become too numerous here and that the Saxon Government may then be embarrassed by the Intrigues which will be carried by them and their Countrymen at Paris, Dresden having already been pointed out by General Bem as a Town well situated for the seat of a Polish Committee.

The answer to these Notes merely states that the Saxon Government is anxious to meet the wishes of the Three Powers, that many Poles have been already sent away – that none, against whom any cause of complaint can be made, will be ever permitted to remain here, and that the difficulties made in general by the Police to their residing here, will it is hopes in time prevent their resorting to this Country.

FO 18/35: Charles Townshend Barnard to Viscount Palmerston, No 28, Dresden, 29 July 1832

Sensation created by the Six Articles; protest initiated by members of the Old Saxon States

The Sensation created hereby the Protocol and Six Articles of the Diet of Francfort[25] has greatly subsided, although the general impression is that the Measure is an Infringement on the Rights, Privileges and Liberty guaranteed by the Constitution. These opinions and feelings although no longer expressed, can only be considered as dormant for a time, as whatever may be thought, yet nothing can be done till the Meeting of the States; the old Parliament having been dissolved last year, the Elections will not take place before September and the States will probably not assemble before November.

[21] Franz Graf von Colloredo-Wallsee.
[22] Andrej Andrejewitsch Schreder.
[23] Johann Ludwig von Jordan.
[24] After the failed Warsaw Uprising of 1831 many Poles temporarily settled in Saxony; cf. n. 18 in Prussia section.
[25] For the Six Articles of 28 June 1832 cf. pp. 35–39 in Frankfurt section.

A few Persons,[26] Members of the Old States, have drawn up a Protest against the Protocol of the 28th Ult° and laid it before M. de Lindenau, with a view of obtaining his sanction to its publication here. This however, it was assured, could not take place, as nothing of the kind would be permitted to appear in the public Papers. The Protest, signed by a very small number, has been since forwarded to Augsburg in the hope of its being inserted in the Allgemeine Zeitung[27] as well as to Altenburg to the Editor of the Bürger-Zeitung[28] and also to Paris where it will doubtless appear in the Constitutionel.[29] I am assured that M. de Manteufel had not unlimited Instructions to sign the Protocol of Frankfort and that he has been severely reprimanded by this Government for the unconditional way in which he has rendered Saxony a Party to this Measure.

FO 68/36: Francis Reginald Forbes to Viscount Palmerston, No 35, Dresden, 10 September 1833

Public opposed to commercial treaty between Saxony and Prussia; Austria unreliable partner; Prussia's interest in Saxony

The Report of the Committee upon the late Commercial Treaty[30] between this Country and Prussia was laid before the Second Chamber yesterday, but the Publick were excluded, nor will they be admitted whenever the Subject is to be discussed in the Diet, which will probably take place in he course of this week. The Feeling of the People here is decidedly opposed to this Measure, as drawing them into a still closer connection with Prussia, at the same time that it was impossible to avoid acceding to this commercial System, unless Austria had made some Concessions. The Minister of Finance, M. de Zeschau said to me openly that Saxony had been completely sacrificed by the former Power and that he was still so firmly convinced that this Union could not last, that in all his Financial Arrangements, he had provided for the Changes, which he looked forward to as inevitable. In a few days I shall be able to transmit to Your Lordship a more detailed Statement of this Measure, which has been rendered still more unpopular by the Language which

[26] Otto Friedrich von Watzdorf and Peter Wilhelm Graf von Hohenthal.

[27] For the *Allgemeine Zeitung* cf. n. 33 in Bavaria section.

[28] *Allgemeine deutsche Bürgerzeitung für Alle, die an der Entwicklung des constitutionellen Lebens im Vaterlande Theil nehmen*, founded and edited by Ferdinand Philippi in 1832; from 1833 onwards published as the *Constitutionelle Staatsbürgerzeitung*.

[29] *Le Constitutionnel*, founded in Paris in 1815, important organ for liberal and anti-restoration policy in France.

[30] Saxony joined the *Zollverein* on 30 March 1833.

many of the Prussians hold in respect of this Kingdom. The Prussian Minister[31] at this Court has not scrupled to say more than once that Prussia is arrived at that degree of prosperity, that she must extend her Territory to maintain it, and that this Country is almost necessary to her. All this has given rise to a number of Reports, such as that Saxony was to be exchanged for the Prussian Provinces on the Rhine, or that the Kingdom of Poland was to be given to His Saxon Majesty instead of His present Dominions, and these however groundless, have created so much Excitement that the Ministers have probably thought it better that the Publick should not be admitted to the Debates upon the commercial Treaty.

FO 68/36: Francis Reginald Forbes to Viscount Palmerston, No 38, Dresden, 23 September 1833

Plans to send Polish refugees to America; question of supporting those wishing to go to England; regrettable behaviour of Saxon ministry in this matter

The Austrian Government proposed some short time back to that of Saxony, that the latter should make an Arrangement with them for sending off to America, those few Polish Refugees[32] who were still remaining in Dresden; but with an apparent understanding, that a semblance of Freedom was to be left to these unfortunate Persons in their option of going or remaining.

An Agent of Police[33] was sent off from this [Capital] to Prague, to make the necessary Preparations, and returned about the 20th – and I was told today by the Minister for Foreign Affairs,[34] that an Estafette had arrived here late in the Afternoon of the 21st with Intelligence that all those Poles who had chosen to go to America, must set out immediately for Brünn to join the Party who were to leave it for Trieste – Late in the Evening of the 21st and early on the following day (which was Sunday) Police Officers were sent round to all the Polish Emigrants to announce to them that before midday of the 22nd, they must chuse between being sent off to America, or the being given up to the Russian Authorities, and that they must sign a Declaration, that they went there voluntarily, whilst all who refused to submit to these Conditions were to be arrested, until they could be sent back to Poland. I need scarcely say to Your Lordship that not one of the few who

---

[31] Johann Ludwig von Jordan.
[32] Cf. n. 24 in this section.
[33] Not traceable.
[34] Johannes von Minckwitz.

remain here, would submit to such ridiculous and degrading Conditions, and they were in consequence of their refusal, immediately arrested and carried off to Prison. There does not remain here above Ten or Eleven Poles in all, out of whom only Seven were unprovided with Passports, and out of these Seven, I had already refused to countersign for Three, as well as from the Fear of their not having sufficient Means for living in England, as from the Idea that it was better for them to remain here, where their Remittances could reach them with more Facility.

I was apprized of all this on Sunday Morning by a Polish Lady[35] of Rank and Respectability, who came to me to beg for God's Sake that I would exert myself to assist them in their miserable situation, that there were only <u>Seven</u> remaining but that if they could obtain Passports for England, not only the Saxon Government would be delighted to send them off there, but that I could perhaps procure them a short Interval of delay to make the few Arrangements which their means could command previous to leaving Dresden. I explained to her frankly, what Your Lordship's Instructions[36] were, but said that provided they could only make out enough money to live in England for a certain time, that I felt convinced that in such an Extremity, I could trust to Your Lordship's Humanity for forgiving my not acting so strictly up to them; still that no Consideration should make me grant a Passport to a Man of bad Character, and that I put it to her Honour as to whether any on the List could be considered as such; on which she instantly erased one of the Names. I immediately took measures for ascertaining how the remaining Six, had conducted themselves here and on what Funds they have been existing. The Answer from the Police was, that they were all Individuals of very respectable Character, and who paid every thing on their Receiving Remittances from Poland, so that at this moment they could set out from Dresden without leaving a Debt behind them. On my attempting to persuade them that they could live more comfortably and with more freedom of action in America, they all said that their Means of Existence were so irregular, that the distance would put them to the greatest Inconvenience by the delay in the transmission of Money from their Relations, and besides most of them have families, from whom they cannot bear the idea of being separated by the Ocean. Under all these circumstances I hope that Your Lordship

[35] Not traceable.

[36] According to Palmerston's instructions of 28 May 1833 passports could be issued to those Polish refugees, 'who have the means of supporting themselves, the number of course of those who could avail themselves of this permission not being such as would create any inconvenience here. Passports should not be given to those Poles who, having no means of maintaining themselves here, would soon after they arrive find themselves in distress; nor to any whose character and conduct have not been entirely unobjectionable'.

will not disapprove of my having granted Passports to Six of these unhappy Individuals, one of whom, however, will probably be able to return to Austrian Poland, where he was born, although his Property was in Russia.

The manner of executing an Order already so severe in itself could not but create a general outcry in all Dresden, and I immediately wrote in an inofficial Form to the Ministers of the Interior[37] and of Foreign Affairs,[38] putting to them in very plain terms how cruel it was to force these unfortunate Gentlemen to leave Dresden in Twenty Four Hours, the notice to do so having been given on a Sunday, when all Banks and Shops are closed, and that they must also take into Consideration the disagreeable Light in which this Measure must place the Saxon Ministry in all those Countries where it could be freely discussed. I am happy to say, that I succeeded in procuring a delay of a day at least. This Act of unnecessary Severity coincides with the arrival of Count Nesselrode, who reached Dresden on his Return from Münchengrätz[39] on the Morning of the 21st Ult° and leaves it again tonight for Russia. The Emperor Nicholas having decided on returning through Poland it was probably thought advisable to bring forward this Proposal of their going to America, as a Means of securing all the Polish Refugees here, and under the supposition, that there was no possibility of their saving themselves from so arbitrary a Proceeding: and I must freely admit to Your Lordship, that at a moment when the whole Policy of the Eastern Part of Europe seems directed against the constitutional Governments and their Views, I was not sorry to have an opportunity of proving that a British Minister was ready to come forward for the purpose of saving some very respectable Individuals from a most unmerited Persecution. The greater part of these Poles have no wish to remain in England, where whatever money they carry with them could only suffice for a very short time: They intend proceeding to Belgium, Portugal or any part of the Continent, as soon as they can arrange it; they are also sure of receiving assistance from those of their exiled Countrymen, who still possess some Fortune.

I am sorry to say that the Conduct of the Saxon Ministry in this business and their evident Obsequiousness to Foreign Influence cannot but increase the already great Unpopularity of the Government, and as I think very highly of many of the Individuals who compose it, I must the more regret they should have allowed themselves to be in a manner driven to a Proceeding which though now rendered less odious,

[37] Bernhard August von Lindenau.

[38] Johannes von Minckwitz.

[39] In Münchengrätz, negotiations took place in autumn 1833 regarding measures to be taken against the Polish independence movement. They concluded with the Alliance of Münchengrätz between Austria, Prussia, and Russia of 15 October 1833.

cannot but create a bad Impression against them in all the independant part of the Population.

FO 68/37: Francis Reginald Forbes to Viscount Palmerston, No 9, Dresden, 25 March 1834

Jews petition for participation in all civil rights

[...] A Petition from the Jews born in Saxony praying for a participation in all civil Rights on condition of fulfilling all the Duties of Citizens and which had been received by the First Chamber in the course of last year, was lately presented to the Lower Chamber, and has been referred to the Ministry, although a strong opposition was shown to even receiving it, and Counter Petitions were sent up from a great number of Towns. Their Prayer will probably be granted but under certain restrictions, such as, that they will not be allowed to buy Houses or Land, unless with an obligation of not selling them again before the lapse of Ten Years. Their Number in Saxony is said not to exceed Eight Hundred, but they still labour under many severe restraints in different parts of the Kingdom. For instance no Jew can enter or even pass through the Town of Freyberg, without being accompanied by a Police Officer, wherever he goes during his stay there. The Committee for Petitions proposed to the Government that this ridiculous Regulation should be immediately done away with.

FO 68/37: Francis Reginald Forbes to Viscount Palmerston, No 15, Dresden, 9 May 1834

Precautionary measures due to rumours of an alleged conspiracy

An Estafette arrived here from Munich before Daybreak on the 4th Ultimo with Despatches for the Saxon Government apprizing them that Intelligence had reached the Bavarian Ministers of a Conspiracy having been formed for a general Insurrection throughout Germany, which was to break out on the 4th, with the professed Object of assassinating all the reigning Sovereigns on the same day.[40] However extravagant and impossible the Idea of such a Plot must appear to every one, the Government still thought it necessary to take some

---

[40] News of the supposed conspiracy originated in a letter of Metternich's to Karl Philipp von Wrede of 21 April 1834. According to Metternich, Germany should also be part of a pan-European revolution on 4 May led primarily by Polish emigrants.

Precautions: the Guards at the Palace were doubled and His Majesty was accompanied by a greater Number of Officers in going to and returning from Church. A Messenger was also sent off to the Prince CoRegent,[41] who was then at Leipzig, transmitting to His Royal Highness the Despatches received from Munich, with a Detail of the Measures taken in consequence of them, but accompanied with the strongest assurances of utter disbelief of such absurd Intelligence. I need scarcely add that the day passed over without the slightest disturbance, although the circumstance of an increased Guard at the Palace, could not but give rise to some anxiety, as soon as it was known. [...]

FO 68/37: Charles Townshend Barnard to Viscount Palmerston, No 2, Dresden, 12 August 1834

Arrests of politically engaged artisans belonging to a Union for upholding the Rights of Man

Within these few last days eight Persons have been arrested here, who with the exception of one Lawyer,[42] are all artisans of this Town. They are now in prison and are accused of being Members of the Union for upholding the Rights of Man,[43] and are all sworn to exert themselves in accomplishing the subversion of Thrones, the Suppression of Nobility, a complete Liberty of the Press, a diminution of Taxes and an equal division of Property. The Government has long been in possession of the names of many people here, connected with the Association, but was unwilling to take any decided Step until some sufficient proof could be brought forward against them. Those now arrested have been denounced by a Citizen[44] of this town, who is in prison as one of seven accomplices in a murder committed here a few months ago, and who declares that it was the Lawyer by whom the Oath was administered to him on his initiation into the Union.

The dwellings of twelve other persons have been searched in the hope of finding papers relative to this Affair, but nothing further has transpired. It was intended that the object of this association should have been put into execution on the 4th of May last, when the German Sovereigns were to have been assassinated, but the Bavarian Government, having received information of the subject, apprized

[41] Friedrich August.
[42] Not traceable.
[43] *Gesellschaft für Menschenrechte* (Society for Human Rights), successor to the *Dresdener Bürgerverein*, cf. n. 14 in this section. Whether there was a connection with the organization of the same name founded by Georg Büchner in 1834 is unclear.
[44] Not traceable.

several of the neighbouring States.[45] There can be no doubt that,
however extravagant the object may appear, yet the association has
not only very extensive ramifications in Germany, but has also its
Agents and connexions in France and other Countries, as proved by
Documents which are in the hands of this and of other Governments.

FO 68/38: Francis Reginald Forbes to the Duke of Wellington, No 3,
Dresden, 17 January 1835

Saxony's advantages from joining the Prussian Commercial Union

[...] A year has now elapsed since the Accession of Saxony to the
Prussian Commercial Union, and M de Zeschau informs me that this
Country has gained considerable advantages from it. Great apprehensions were entertained a first that the Trade of Leipzick would
suffer from the competition of other Towns, but Four Fairs have now
been held there and the Improvement is evident. In the Revenue there
is a large Diminution, but this is more than made up to the Country
by the Merchants having no longer to pay the Transit Duties to Prussia,
which amounted to between Two and Three Hundred Thousand
Dollars. The Exports from Saxony to Bavaria are very great and consist
principally of manufactured Goods, while the latter Kingdom has
nothing to give in return but Beer.

FO 68/40: Francis Reginald Forbes to Viscount Palmerston, No 13,
Confidential, Dresden, 10 April 1836

Changing attitude towards Prussia; foreign affairs; England seen as only reliable supporter

[...] The Position of Saxony between two such powerful Neighbours as
Austria and Prussia, along with the open manner in which the Prussians
always speak of the great advantage it would be to them to gain
Possession of the remaining Part of this Kingdom, could not but create
a strong Feeling of Enmity towards that Power, which had made the
Country sink into comparative Insignificance, and this naturally inclined
them to look up to Austria, who can have no views of aggrandizement
on this side. The Chain of Mountains between Saxony and Bohemia
form such a naturally strong Frontier, that the incorporation of this
Country into the Austrian Dominions would be rather a Disadvantage
than otherwise: In addition to this the Fact of the Saxon Royal Family,

---

[45] Cf. pp. 306–307 in this section.

DRESDEN 309

being Catholicks favoured this Feeling which was also kept up by the frequent Intermarriages of the Two Royal Families.

I must now say, that even since I have been here, a great Change is perceptible in what regards Prussia. The Commercial Union[46] has brought the Two Countries into much closer Contact, the Saxons are now accustomed to seeing Prussian Agents in their Country, and the Manufacturers have gained so largely by the doing away of the Customs Houses, that the Expressions of Dislike to their Northern Neighbours are no longer heard as often as formerly. In proportion as this Feeling gains Ground, they become more alive to their Sovereign and His family being of a different Religion from the generality of the Inhabitants; and I did not expect the strong Burst of attachment which showed itself on the Celebration of His Majesty's last Birthday,[47] and which was fully due to His Virtues and Kindness. Of these I can not speak in Terms of sufficient Praise: His Majesty's greatest Pleasure is doing good without Distinction of Religion, and His Death will be severely felt whenever the Country has the misfortune to lose Him. If the Prince Co-Regent[48] had had Children, it is thought he would have had them educated in the Reformed religion, but his Brother Prince John is a devoted Catholic, who would never hear of such a Step. A great Point however and which surprized every one, was gained by his having appointed as Tutor to the young Princes, a M. de Langen,[49] one of the best informed and most enlightened Men here, and a Protestant. Of the Feelings here towards the other parts of Germany, I can hardly presume to speak: at the present moment there exists a certain Jealously of the House of Saxe Coburg, which is easily understood, but until lately the Influence exercized in Saxony by Russia was surprizing.[50] I think that this is now lessening, and can only attribute it to the Confidence inspired by the strength of His Majesty's present Government.

With the example of the misfortunes into which Poland had been drawn by the assurances of the Republican Party in France,[51] who had not the Power, (if they even had the Will) to assist them, it was but natural that the Saxon Ministry who were surrounded by Persons constantly preaching that the Reforms which had become inevitable in

---

[46] Saxony joined the *Zollverein* on 30 March 1833.

[47] On the occasion of King Anton's 81st birthday on 27 November 1835 numerous celebrations were held in Dresden, including a great procession.

[48] Friedrich August.

[49] Friedrich Albert von Langenn.

[50] The house of Saxe-Coburg-Gotha owed its prominent position to its dynastic connections with Belgium and Portugal. Russia's influence resulted from its role in maintaining the kingdom of Saxony in 1815.

[51] Forbes is referring here to the support given to the Polish independence movement by Republican circles in France.

England,[52] were an overthrow of all Monarchical Principles, should be more than cautious about doing any thing which could give Umbrage to Russia, and consequently to Prussia. I repeated over and over that they ought to feel their own strength, and that no one could dare to attack them openly as long as their Affairs were so well conducted, but then in all and every Emergency (even in respect to the Poles) the Representative of France[53] hesitated to come too much forward, and was seldom provided with Instructions. Now the case is different: His Majesty's Government gains strength every day, both at home and abroad, and M. de Zeschau, who is at the head of the Saxon Ministry said to me himself, long before there was any Idea of his becoming Minister for Foreign Affairs, 'I do not deny that Reform is disagreeable for the higher Classes, but come it must; our neighbours will be forced to submit to it, and we must take care to leave nothing reasonable undone – we need not then fear any danger from what must happen in Prussia, but may be the Gainers.'

These Opinions must incline him to look to England, and I lose no opportunity of raising them in their own opinion, for nothing could be more advantageous to England than the Existence, in the very Centre of Germany of a Constitutional State, and none of those in the South can be compared to Saxony in the management of her Affairs under the new Institutions.

It may appear too great Presumption on my Part to offer to Your Lordship's attention the great Influence, which any Distinction conferred by His Majesty would have, as well on the King of Saxony, as on the whole Country, for now that they are beginning to feel themselves a Constitutional State, they would be alive to every thing of this sort, and would be flattered by an undeniable Proof of the Interest which great Britain feels for them. I know that His Saxon Majesty's greatest wish is to have the Garter,[54] (on His last Birthday He received the Black Eagle[55] from the King of Prussia.) He is the Head of the House of Saxony, to which the British Royal Family are doubly allied,[56] and as an Individual it could not be conferred a more respectable nor excellent Sovereign. It would also have its weight with the future Sovereign[57] who (as well as his Consort[58]) are fully sensible of the Value of such an Order, and who have certainly no Reason to like Russia.

[52] Cf. n. 79 in Prussia section.
[53] Jules Edmond Louis Baron Renouard de Bussière.
[54] Senior English order of knighthood established in the fourteenth century.
[55] Cf. pp. XX in Prussia section.
[56] Adelaide von Saxe–Meiningen was the wife of William IV; Marie Luise Viktoria of Saxe–Coburg-Gotha was the mother of Queen Victoria.
[57] Friedrich August.
[58] Maria Leopoldine.

I hope that Your Lordship will forgive me for venturing to say this much: I am aware that it is great Presumption on my Part, but I see even in the Prince Co Regent, who is generally cold, a very visible alteration of manner, which has become less restrained and more confidential towards myself; they must see that England is the only Country on whom a steady Reliance can be placed, and the Encouragement of this Feeling, must be the proudest, as well as greatest object of every Englishmen.

FO 68/40: Francis Reginald Forbes to Viscount Palmerston, No 24, Dresden, 7 June 1836

Death of King of Saxony

It is with Feelings of the most real and sincere Regret, that I have to announce to Your Lordship the Decease of His Majesty Anthony King of Saxony, who expired yesterday at Pillnitz at Half past Eleven in the Forenoon. In the last two Days, His Majesty's sufferings were painful to witness, but He supported them with the greatest Courage and Resignation. The Evening before His death He called all the Royal Family round Him and took a most affecting Leave of Them. He was beloved as He deserved by all who had the Honour of approaching Him, and to me personally, whom He had always been pleased to distinguish in such a gracious manner His Loss will be very great. [...]

His Majesty Frederick Augustus came into Dresden immediately after the Demise of the late King and presided the Council of Ministers: He is deeply affected and attended upon His late Majesty during this last Illness the utmost Tenderness.[...][59]

FO 68/40: Francis Reginald Forbes to Viscount Palmerston, No 30, Dresden, 21 November 1836

Opening of Saxon diet; agenda (i.e. national debts; proposed criminal code et al.)

The Report read by M. de Lindenau at the Opening of the Saxon Diet is much too long for me to transmit the whole of it, and a greater Part can be of no Interest excepting in Saxony; The Points, which appear to me most worthy of Your Lordship's Notice are the following.

The Abolition of the Evangelical Consistories in Dresden and Leipzig,

[59] Enclosures: 1. Translation of a Note from M. de Zeschau; 2. Translation of a Proclamation of King Frederick Augustus of Saxony on ascending the Throne.

as well as partially that of the Catholick Consistories in Dresden and Bautzen, enacted in the pregoing Diet, has been effected:[60] their juridical Functions have been transferred to the inferior Tribunals and those of Appeal, while the Administrative Part has been given to the Directions of the Circles and to the general Evangelical Consistory of the Kingdom. A more suitable Demarcation of the Boundaries of Parishes has been begun. The Treasury has issued Supplies to the higher Schools in Towns in aid of their better Establishment and much has been done to promote Education amongst the lower Classes, according to the Law[61] passed for that Purpose.

Separate Reports will be laid before the Diet respecting.

The Division of the Parochial Charges,

The Foundation of a Fund for the Widows and Orphans of those employed in Schools and Churches.

New Academical Laws for governing the Students.

The Connection between the Department 'des Cultes' and of the Interior, now charged with the Management of Part of the Evangelical Affairs.

and, the Exercize by the State of its general Rights in all Matters of Religion, over the Catholick Church.

The Administration of Justice has been so simplified by the Laws passed in the late Diet[62] and since brought into Effect, that not one Appeal has come before the Privy Council and scarcely any Arrear of business remains since the Formation of one Supreme, and of Four Provincial Courts. The apparent Increase of Crime is only to be attributed to the Activity of the minor Tribunals and Police, by which many Misdeeds have been brought to Light and punished, which had before escaped Discovery. A Code of Civil Laws for the Tribunals is drawing up and the Project for a Criminal Code has been prepared and laid before the Commission named by the last Diet for its Examination who will present a Report upon it to the present Chambers. A Law has been prepared for simplifying the Trial of small civil cases, and obviating Delay, as well as for proceeding in those which are sent to the Supreme Tribunal (Staatsgerichtshof).

The national Industry has increased in the most extraordinary

---

[60] Based on a resolution of the Saxon *Landtag* of 10 April 1835 a decree was issued concerning a change in the organization of the church authorities.

[61] Education Law of 6 June 1835.

[62] The main points in the laws concerning the organization of the courts and the administration of justice, which came into force on 1 May 1835, were the separation of justice and administration, the establishment of new supreme courts, the introduction of administrative jurisdiction, and the three-stage appeal procedure.

Degree, since the Introduction of the new System of Customs[63] – the Receipts in most Branches of the Revenue far exceed the estimated Sums: there are scarcely any, where a Diminution has occurred and many Manufactories now give a clear Profit which were formerly worked at a Loss.

Every Means have been employed to regulate the National Debt, which after a careful Discussion of its Nature and Origin has been partly paid off, and partly brought into a Course of progressive Extinction.

Communications will be made by the Government upon, Several Points to regulate the Laws concerning the indirect Taxes, Arrears and Disputes as to the Taxes on Persons and Trades, the alienated Crown Land, the national Debt and the adding to it that of Upper Lusatia, the preliminary Steps for a new Land Tax, a further Improvement of the Commercial Union, and State Lotteries. New Conventions have been entered into with the Upper Lusatia and the Family of Schönburg, by Means of which (with few Exceptions) a Similarity of laws has been effected for the whole Country.[64]

Notwithstanding the many Alterations, which have been made since the last Diet in the interior Administration of the Country, the following still remain to be brought forward: The Abolition of Excommunication, the Prohibition of Participation in Foreign Lotteries, a Punishment for gambling at Lotto, the Organization of Banks, Regulations for all Undertakings by Shares, and (if practicable) the laying down on general Parochial System for the Management of their Business.

The Supplies granted by the last Diet for the Army have enabled it to be put on the best Footing and to be completely supplied with Arms: the Law[65] respecting Substitutes has succeeded perfectly well, and separate Projects of other Laws will be brought forward respecting,

The Second Part of the revised Military Code,[66] with the Punishments for Offences.

The Military Pensions, and

The Compensations to be made to the Treasury for having taken upon itself to furnish several Supplies to the Military, which were before derived from other Sources.

---

[63] When Saxony joined the *Zollverein* on 30 March 1833 this meant not only a new and uniform customs tariff, but also reform of the entire fiscal system.

[64] The Oberlausitz region and the territories of the princes of Schönberg were not completely integrated into the kingdom. Their special rights were further diminished by agreements reached in 1835.

[65] Law regarding compulsory military service of 26 October 1834.

[66] In the revised military code of 14 February 1835 punishments for soldiers were made less severe and brutal methods of punishment abolished.

FO 68/41: Francis Reginald Forbes to Viscount Palmerston, No 13, Dresden, 5 May 1837

Motion for the abolition of first chamber of Saxon diet; discussion about emancipating the Jews

A few Days ago, a Motion was made in the Second Chamber of the Saxon Diet by a Deputy of the Name of Dieskau for the Abolition of the First: this is much to be regretted, for it is the first Time that any Thing of a Democratic Spirit has shewn itself, and although the Motion not having been seconded, was not even put to the Vote, the Occurrence will be made the most of by the Enemies of the Constitution. In Discussion of a Law for partially emancipating the Jews was carried on in the first Chamber with very great Illiberality; it is calculated that their Number in Saxony, of both Sexes, does not exceed Eight Hundred, and that scarcely a Fourth of these is engaged in either a Trade or Profession; notwithstanding which they are not allowed to settle in any other Towns than Dresden or Leipzig and are excluded from a great Number of Trades[.] Amongst others, they cannot in Saxony become Booksellers, although at least one Fourth of these in other Parts of Germany are either Jews or Persons of this Nation who have been baptized. Prince John exerted himself very much against many of the severest Restrictions, but His Royal Highness' Amendments were in great Part rejected and the Law was passed with a great Majority.[67]
[...]

FO 68/44: Francis Reginald Forbes to Viscount Palmerston, No 3, Dresden, 4 January 1838

Public interest in affairs of Hanover; special family compact to save the Crown of Saxony and to secure independence

The Russian Minister at this Court, M. de Schröder, left this Capital a few days back for Hanover, where he is equally accredited. He professes to have done this without any special orders from his Court, and that he merely proceeds there for the purpose of communicating to the Russian Government, 'the extraordinary and interesting Events of which Hanover is now the scene'.

The Interest felt here by the Publick on the Affairs of that Country encreases instead of diminishing, and Subscriptions have been made in

---

[67] The law of 18 May 1837 allowed Jews in Dresden and Leipzig – the only two cities in which Jews had the right of abode – to form religious communities and to build synagogues.

almost every Town in Saxony, for the Professors who have been forced to leave Göttingen.[68] The Austrian Minister[69] was directed by his Government to remonstrate strongly against the Articles which appeared in the Leipziger Allgemeine Zeitung,[70] and which were evidently drawn up by some very clever Man;[71] of late they are much shorter, but quite as bitter, and have brought this Journal into very general notice. Should an appeal be made to the Germanic Diet against the Overthrow of that Constitution, there is no doubt that the Saxon Government must support it, although it will not be assisted by the Influence of the Duchies of Saxony, whose Rights are put aside by the Constitution of this Kingdom.[72]

A Family Compact had existed for Centuries, by which on the Failure of the Male Line, the Crown of Saxony would have gone to the Branch of Weimar, whilst by the Constitution, Females may inherit, when all the Male Branches are extinct.

This is the Circumstance which has hitherto prevented Saxony from seeking to obtain the Sanction of the Germanic Diet for her new Form of Government, any Step of the sort would be immediately met by a Protest from the other Branches. If the Affairs of Hanover be brought before the Diet, it is expected here that that Body will declare that it can take no Cognizance of the Overthrow of a Constitution which had never been submitted to it for the Purpose of its Approval. [...]

FO 68/44: Francis Reginald Forbes to Viscount Palmerston, No 16, Dresden, 29 May 1838

Meeting of a monetary commission to establish uniform value between the coins of North and South Germany

I have the Honour to acknowledge the Receipt of Your Lordship's Despatches N° 4 and 5 the latter of which reached me yesterday. I shall carefully attend to the Instructions conveyed to me in it, and watch the Proceedings of the Commissioners from the States of the Prussian Commercial Union, so as to report any alterations made in the Import Duties on British manufactured Goods.

At the present moment a Commission of Persons appointed by all the States of Germany (excepting Austria, Hanover, and Brunswick) has met here, whose object is to establish one uniform Rate of Value

---

[68] Cf. n. 90 in Prussia section.
[69] Franz Freiherr von Binder-Kriegelstein.
[70] On the *Leipziger Allgemeine Zeitung* cf. n. 215 in Frankfurt section.
[71] Wilhelm Adolf Lindau.
[72] Constitution of 4 September 1831.

between the Coins of the North and the South of Germany.[73] It is more than probable that Saxony will end by adopting the Prussian monetary System, for notwithstanding the Denominations are the same, and accounts are generally kept in Prussian Currency, there are still some Payments which must be made in Saxon Money, and tend to create a good deal of Confusion.

This Commission has held but two Meetings, and has not yet come to any determination, but Monsieur de Zeschau informs me that the principal object is to draw up a Convention for the Signature of all parties, so as to preclude any such arbitrary Measure respecting the Currency as occurred not long ago in the Duchy of Coburg.[74] [...]

FO 68/44: Francis Reginald Forbes to Viscount Palmerston, No 27, Dresden, 17 November 1838

Catholic clergy's intolerance of mixed marriages; extensive schism expected; population under influence of clergyman called Stephan; emigration increases

The Catholick Clergy in this Kingdom, who hitherto had remained passive Spectators or the late Events in Prussia,[75] have at last begun to shew the same spirit of Intolerance respecting Marriages between Persons of different Persuasions, and one of those established in this Capital, has refused to perform the Ceremony, unless with a previous Engagement, that the Children should be educated in the Catholick Religion. The more enlightened Persons of that Faith are sorry that the Question should have been raised here, where the subject had been fully discussed in the last Diet, and decided in a spirit of Conciliation towards them, although the Mass of the Inhabitants of Saxony are too much opposed to the Doctrines of the Church of Rome to admit of their bearing with patience any attempt at Encroachment on the part of its Followers.

If this is pushed too far it may lead to scenes of Violence, in which the Military who are almost all Protestants would probably not assist their opponents.

It is much to be regretted that an extensive Schism should have arisen in this part of Germany in the Reformed Religion, at a moment

---

[73] For the division into a north German and a south German currency area cf. n. 169 in Frankfurt section.

[74] In a decree of 4 December 1837 Duke Ernst of Saxe-Coburg-Gotha ordered coins of reduced value to be minted for regional trade. The new Coburg coin ran counter to attempts at uniformity, but also suppressed 'more valuable' currencies in neighbouring duchies.

[75] Cf. pp. 88–91 in Frankfurt section.

when it would be for their Interest to remain as much united as possible, but this is unfortunately the Case. A Clergyman, named Stephan, a Bohemian by Birth, has for some years past brought himself into very great notice by his preaching, his Sermons which are remarkably eloquent being directed against the abuses which he states to have crept into the pure Lutheran church. Prior to the Revolution in Eighteen Hundred and Thirty, he was very much protected by Count Einsiedel, then Prime Minister, who was supposed to have adopted his Doctrines, and was in the habit of consulting him respecting the nomination of Clergymen to different Parishes. Stephan of course recommended his friends, whose opinions coincided with his own, and through them, his Tenets have been widely propagated, not only in Saxony, but in Prussia.

His Talents which are of the highest order, are unluckily coupled with great Immorality, and the Police was forced to interfere and to put a stop to nocturnal Meetings, which were said to be similar to those which occurred not very long ago at Königsberg.[76] Stephan has been arrested more than once, but such is his Influence over his Followers, that it was very difficult to obtain Proofs against him, although the Facts were notorious; but finding that the Government were determined not to allow these disgraceful proceedings, he declared that he and his Proselytes were persecuted on account of their Doctrines, that they ought not to remain in a Country where they were so illtreated, and proposed their emigrating to North America. The idea was eagerly caught at and his Followers proceeded to sell their Property and have acted with a degree of Fanaticism, which appears strange in the Nineteenth Century. On the other hand, the Government who were well aware of the risk, if they punished him of transforming a clever Profligate into a Martyr and foreseeing that from the immense increase of the Population, an Emigration at their Expence, must sooner or later take place, have done every thing to facilitate their Departure, which was consistent with the security and maintenance of those Individuals of Families who did not chuse to desert their County. They have already left Saxony in the number of between Eight and Nine Hundred persons, and are supposed to have collected about one Hundred Thousand Dollars (say Fifteen Thousand Pounds) with which they have bought Lands near St. Louis, on the Mississippi, where they intend to establish. The Emigration from Prussia is still more numerous.

[76] Stephan organized night-time 'edification and relaxation' sessions.

FO 68/46: Francis Reginald Forbes to Viscount Palmerston, No 20, Dresden, 9 July 1839

300-years anniversary of the Reformation

The secular Anniversary of the solemn Establishment of the Reformation in Dresden, was celebrated on Saturday last the 6th Ultimo, with a degree of Splendour, which I did not expect to have witnessed. On that day Three Hundred Years ago, the first divine Service according to the Rites of the Reformed Religion, was celebrated in the Church of the Cross, under the sanction of the Duke Henry, and at a Moment when there are such Dissensions in Prussia between Protestants and Catholicks,[77] it was determined to spare no Expense in honouring this Festival. There was an Idea of postponing it to the following day, Sunday, but on an application made to the King Himself, His Majesty was pleased to order that it should take place on the very Day. There was a Procession of all the Trades with their Banners, was well as of the several Schools, who attended divine Service in the Church, after which they proceeded to the great Square, where accompanied by thousands of Spectators, they sang a Hymn[78] composed by D[r] Luther, one of whose direct Descendants[79] was present.

In the Evening the whole City was brilliantly illuminated. The Church of Our Lady was one of the most splendid spectacles I have ever seen. The Dome which is immensely high, was illuminated to the Top of the Cross, and the Name of the Duke Henry, as well as the Date of 1539 were marked on it with lamps in letters of such immense size, that they were distinctly legible at a distance of many Miles. None of the Royal Palaces were lighted up, nor did any Member of the Royal Family appear in Dresden, but all Sects, with very few exceptions had illuminated their Houses. His Majesty is said to have given Two Thousand Dollars from the Privy Purse towards the general Expences.

I am happy to say, that although the Crowd was immense and that many thousands had poured in from Leipzig and the whole of the Kingdom, the Evening passed off without the slightest accident or disturbance.

---

[77] For the dispute over mixed marriages in Cologne cf., *inter alia*, pp. 88–91 in Frankfurt section, and pp. 169–170 in Prussia section.

[78] *Eine feste Burg ist unser Gott*; the hymn is based on the 46th psalm.

[79] Not traceable; it was one of Luther's descendants from Prussia.

FO 68/48: Francis Reginald Forbes to Viscount Palmerston, No 3, Dresden, 23 February 1840

M. Thielau's motion concerning affairs in Hanover; report of a special committee

In my N° 33 of last year[80] I had the Honour of informing Your Lordship that on the 11th November, one of the cleverest Deputies[81] in the Second Saxon Chamber had moved that the Two [Chambers] should address a point request to the Government, begging for a detailed and satisfactory Communication of the Transactions which have taken place in the Germanic Diet, respecting the Affairs of the Hanoverian Constitution,[82] as well as of the Part which this Government had acted in them, and of the result of the same.

This motion was referred to a Committee of Seven Members for the purpose of their drawing up a report on it, which last was laid before the Chamber about a week ago. It begins by examining the late occurrences in Hanover according to all Principles of Constitutional Law, whether ancient or modern and after stating that the ground taken by the Government towards the Germanic Diet has fully justified the Confidence reposed in it by that of Saxony, proceeds to state on strong but moderate language, that in consequence of the Failure of all the Efforts made to adjust the Differences between His Hanoverian Majesty and His People by peaceful and legal Means, and of the Diet declaring itself incompetent, there no longer existed a Tribunal to which an Appeal could be made in the Event of the Constitution of a Country being overturned, and its States dissolved as the most convenient way of getting rid of those who protested against such violent Measures. The Arguments for and against the Validity of the Hanoverian Constitution of 1833, as well as the Explanations in the Hanoverian Proclamation of the 10th of last September[83] (which published the Decision of the Germanic Diet) are then severally criticised, with the remark that neither of these Documents can be consonant with the Views of this Government.

The report then points out the consequences of the Course followed with respect to the Affairs of Hanover, that the Foundation of every Constitution in Germany is shaken and the monarchical Principles

[80] FO 68/46: Francis Reginald Forbes to Viscount Palmerston, No. 33, Dresden, 16 November 1839; not included in this volume.

[81] Friedrich Erdmann August von Thielau.

[82] Cf. pp. 263–264 in Hanover section.

[83] In its proclamation of 10 September the Hanoverian government interpreted the federal resolution of 5 September as official recognition of the repeal of the 1833 constitution, even though it only established that there was currently no reason to intervene.

endangered, and that the Institution of some Tribunal of final Appeal for the security of constitutional Rights, which must be fixed, independent and immoveable can only answer the objects intended in forming the Germanic Diet.

The Committee therefore unanimously proposed the following Motion, founded upon the foregoing Arguments and Principles.

That the Chambers should jointly solicit the Government to exert every Means in its Power with the Germanic Diet for the Reestablishment of the public Rights in Hanover, which have been annihilated by the forcible overthrow of the Constitution of 1833, and further that they should in the first place require from the Germanic Diet a clear explanation of the Term used in their Decree (as published by His Hanoverian Majesty) 'the then existing States'.[84] Secondly that the Proceedings of the Diet shall be printed and published as ordered by itself on the 14th November 1816,[85] and thirdly, the Institution of a Tribunal to replace the ancient Tribunal of the German Empire, where not only the Complaints of the several States or Diets, but of Corporations and even of Individuals respecting the overthrow of Constitutions, as well as the Refusal of Justice might be heard and decided upon according to the Principles of National Law.

The Committee ends their Report by advising that the Petitions for placing the Saxon Constitution under the Guarantee of the Germanic Diet, should not be received, as the well known Faith, Honour and Conscientioness of His Majesty afforded a sufficient one for the Country.

On the 20th Ultimo, this Report of which I have given the principal Points, was discussed in the Second Chamber and gave Rise to some very violent Speeches, so much so that M. de Zeschau called one Speaker three times to order, – on the last occasion where he had quoted a Line from Schiller 'that the Sword was the last Ressource of the People'.[86] His Excellency stigmatised his speech as revolutionary and threatened to move that the Galleries should be cleared, which were filled to the utmost with Spectators of the higher and better Classes.

The Thanks of the Chamber to the Committee were voted by Acclamation, an attempt was then made to obtain a Declaration by vote, that the Chamber disapproved of the above mentioned Speech, but it was lost by an immense Majority.

The Propositions of the Committee were finally passed unanimously, as was the whole Report, the Deputies being called over by Name.

---

[84] Cf. n. 39 in Hanover section.

[85] On 14 November 1816 the provisional rules of procedure for the Diet of the German Confederation were passed.

[86] Quotation from *Wilhelm Tell. Ein Schauspiel*, Act II, Scene II.

FO 68/50: Francis Reginald Forbes to Earl of Aberdeen, No 24, Dresden, 20 November 1841

On Saxony's agriculture

Since the Receipt of the Despatch marked Circular of the 20th of last October, which was addressed to me by Your Lordship's Orders, I have taken the greatest Pains, in Consequence of the Instructions conveyed in it, to seek to ascertain and make out a Return of the Quantity of the several Qualities of Grain raised in this Kingdom, but I am sorry to say that applying to Three of the Ministers of State here, they have all answered, that it was totally out of their Power to furnish me with any satisfactory Documents on this Subject. The Quantity of Corn of Different sorts raised here in Saxony is so inadequate to the Consumption of the Country, that from Six to Eight Hundred Thousand Scheffels are annually imported, partly from Bohemia partly from Prussian Saxony.[87] The Climate is so severe in the Chain of the Mountains, the Erzgebirge, which form the Frontier between this Kingdom and Bohemia, and constitute a great Part of Saxony, that very little Corn can be grown there: even the Crop of Potatoes, which are the principal Sustenance of the Inhabitants is very uncertain. This arises from the Formation of these Mountains, which run nearly from East to West, and although their Height is not very great, they are very abrupt on the Side of Bohemia, whilst towards Saxony the Inclination is very gradual and the Land is consequently exposed to the Cold of the North.

Very little beet root is now cultivated for making Sugar, the Speculation having completely failed: a few Years back there were Eight Manufactories, but this Summer there were only Three remaining one of which has since stopped.

The Cultivation of Tobacco is still more inconsiderable, for the Tax on it produces to the Government only One Thousand Dollars yearly, (about £150) and there is scarcely any Hemp grown in this Country. Wool being their principal Export a large Portion of the Land is devoted to Pasture for Sheep and as great a Part of the Remainder as can be spared from the Cultivation of Potatoes and Corn, is employed in raising Flax, but I have not been able to procure any certain Return of the exact Quantity grown in Saxony.

Millet and Buckwheat are also cultivated to a certain Extent: the latter is much used by the lower Classes, in Soup.

---

[87] The Province of Saxony, formerly the northern part of the Kingdom of Saxony, which fell to Prussia after the division of Saxony in February 1815.

FO 68/51: Francis Reginald Forbes to Earl of Aberdeen, No 4, Dresden,
1 March 1842

Work regulations in Saxony (food, wages, employment of children et al.)

The hope that some general Regulations would at last be established
in the Saxon Factories, had induced me to postpone answering a
circular Despatch, which I received last Autumn from the Foreign
Office, requiring, Information respecting them, the Food consumed
therein, and the Wages; but as I see no Prospect of any thing being
published, I think it more advisable to inform Your Lordship (for the
purpose of being laid before the House of Commons) that up to this
time there exist no general Regulations for the treatment of workmen
in the Saxon Factories. The want of them has been often felt as well
by the Proprietors as the Workmen; the Association for promoting
National Industry[88] has indeed put forward a Project for this purpose
and the Authorities have made some local Regulations with the same
view, but no definitive Measures have yet been framed.

Some special Orders have however been issued to particular Trades,
as for instance the Lace Weavers and those who make it with Bobbins.
The Masters in this Trade are positively forbidden to pay their
Workmen or working Children in Kind; this has been latterly so often
transgressed (and with serious Loss of the Workmen) that new and
more severe Regulations are under Discussion.

The Director[89] of the Circle of Zwickau (where the most of the
Manufactories are situated) has published a set of Regulations to define
the position of the Apprentices. So in the Factories for printing Calicos,
but these contain little of importance, they refer principally to the
conditions under which Apprentices or Workmen can be hired, such
as their having passed their Examination at certain Schools, their being
forced to attend Sunday Schools, and the Punishment for an Apprentice
leaving his Master before the Expiration of the Five Years and a half
for which they are hired (having already passed six months on Trial)
or for a Master seducing away the Apprentices of others.

Nothing whatever is mentioned in their Regulations as to Wages,
which are a Matter of private Agreement with the Proprietor, nor as
to the Food; this last however consists principally in fictitious Coffee
(made generally of burnt Endive) Bread and Butter and some Soup.

According to the Criminal Code, Workmen who combine to strike
work and will not conform to the Orders of their Masters, are liable
to Imprisonment for any Term between Eight Days and six months,

---

[88] *Sächsischer Industrieverein*, founded in 1830.
[89] Karl Konstantin Freiherr von Künßberg.

those who betray the Secrets of their Masters belonging to their Trade, as well as the Persons who induce them to commit this Breach of Confidence, are liable to an Imprisonment not exceeding Four Months or to a proportionate Fine. It is moreover enacted that any Master who takes advantage of his Situation to force his workmen to receive in payment any sort of Coin other than they have agreed for, or an unreasonable Proportion of small Money, is liable to a Fine, not exceeding Twenty Dollars.

A Law made the 6th of June 1835,[90] enacts that all children employed in Factories who have completed their sixth Year, must regularly attend the Schools until the Expiration of their Fourteenth Year or of such farther time until they have attained a competent knowledge of reading, writing and Arithmetick and particularly a clear Insight into the Principles and Truth of Religion, as well as of the Contents of the Holy Bible. These Schools can only be established with the Sanction of the Authorities and after a strict examination of the Teachers.

The same Law forbids the afternoon Schools for Children, and orders that the Lessons shall be given in the morning or Forenoon, unless an imperious necessity can be brought forward for holding them in the afternoon. The Manufacturer can establish no general Regulations with his Workmen, unless submitted to and sanctioned by the Government.

The Wages paid are optional, but generally speaking, are so low, that no Englishmen could live for even very much more, than what contents the frugal habits of the Saxons. If I can obtain any further Information I will not fail to transmit it to Your Lordship.

FO 68/51: Francis Reginald Forbes to Earl of Aberdeen, No 22, Dresden, 5 September 1842

Some disturbances during the anniversary celebration of the constitution

Some Disturbance occurred here in the Course of last Night, which although of little Importance in itself, is sure to be exaggerated in the Foreign Newspapers and besides afford an other dangerous Instance of the Weakness of this Government.

The Fourth of September, being the Anniversary of the Proclaiming the present Constitution,[91] is always celebrated by an Illumination of some of the publick Buildings, where Bands of Musicians are stationed. Between Twelve at Night and One O'clock this Morning, an Number

---

[90] Education Law of 6 June 1835.
[91] The Saxon constitution came into force on 4 September 1831.

of persons collected in one of the Squares, and proceeded to the Principal Police Office, to which, on seeing them approach, the armed Police had retired and had shut themselves in, without attempting to disperse them. The Mob, after crying out, 'Down with the Police', 'Down with the Magistrates and the Town Council', proceeded to break the Windows of this as well as of the Town House and pushing themselves uninterrupted, marched through different Parts of the Town, and passed before the Main Guard, who remained passive Spectators, crying out, 'Down with the Constitution', 'Long live the King, let Him reign <u>alone</u>', 'Bread, Bread, before it goes as far as in England'.

In the mean time Intelligence of this paltry Riot had reached the Commandant of the Town, who immediately ordered out the greater Part of the Garrison, with their Musquets loaded, a Part of whom were marked over to the Old Town, to which these Disturbances were confined.

In a short Time, the whole affair was at an End, and might have been put down at once by the Civil Power alone, without the Aid of the Military; but the Garrison passed the whole Night under Arms.

The Town Council and Magistrates have rendered themselves very unpopular by their Partiality, and the lower Classes attribute to them the present Increase in the Prices of different Articles of daily Consumption, whilst it is owing to the Want of Rain, which is now become very alarming. [...]

FO 68/52: Francis Reginald Forbes to Earl of Aberdeen, No 2, Dresden, 28 January 1843

Debate in Saxon chambers on amendments in the criminal procedures weakens government

A Debate in the Saxon Chambers on a Law presented to them by the Government for the purpose of introducing certain Amendments in the Criminal Procedures of this Kingdom has terminated in a manner which can scarcely fail to weaken the salutary influence of the Crown: in most former Diets the Proposals of the Ministers have been so favorably received by the Chambers, as to prove that they possessed the Confidence of the Country, and the flourishing State of the Finances is such (the Surplus of Revenue above the Expenditure amounting in round numbers to nearly two Millions and a half of Dollars) as scarcely any other Country can boast of: it is therefore deeply to be regretted that any of Their Measures should be rejected by the great Mass of the People, and still more so, that it should be persisted in.

As soon as this Law was laid before the Diet, it was referred to a Committee in each Chamber: in the First, an Amendment proposing the confrontation of Witnesses with the accused as well as the Admission of the Publick to the Trials was only lost by a Majority of Five Votes, three of whom have since declared that they voted with the Government from having misunderstood the Motion and imagined that Trial by Jury was a necessary consequence of the Amendment, for which the Country is certainly not fitted. In the second Chamber, the defeat of the Government was complete, for Their Proposition was thrown out by <u>Seventy one</u> Votes against <u>Four</u>, whilst two other Motions – the one 'that the Government should be requested by this Chamber to submit to the next Diet, if not sooner, a more comprehensive Law for Criminal procedures grounded on the Principles of Publicity, Confrontation of Witnesses, and Prosecution on the Part of the Crown' – and the other, for abolishing all private Jurisdiction in Criminal Matters – were carried against Ministers, the first by Sixty seven votes to Four, the second by Sixty to Fifteen.

Yesterday a Royal Message was communicated by the Government to the First Chamber to the effect that His Majesty had been induced by the existing Circumstances to withdraw the above mentioned Project of Law which He had ordered to be laid before them and that He reserved for His farther Consideration whether in particular cases the Accused might be confronted with the Witnesses before the competent Tribunals, without infringement of the Principles hitherto acted upon, for that He still had serious objections to a Criminal Jurisprudence combined with Publicity and Confrontation.

It remains now to be seen what the Chamber will do, for I cannot think that they will submit without a Struggle to the Government acting so directly in Opposition to the Wishes of the Mass if the Population. The small Majority in the First Chamber was only owing to a Mistake, and the leading Members of it are said to declare openly that, if the Question be again brought forward, they will vote against Ministers, and not oppose the almost unanimous opinion of their Country.

This is the second time during this Diet that Ministers have been left in a Minority and Their refusal to alter the Proceedings in criminal Cases is openly attributed to Foreign Influences.

FO 68/55: Francis Reginald Forbes to Earl of Aberdeen, No 6, Dresden, 6 February 1844

Dresden population census

The Census of the Population of this Capital, which is taken every three years, is now concluded; and Dresden contained up to the 1st of December 1843 Eighty Six Thousand, Six hundred and one Inhabitants, including a Garrison of Seven Thousand, Six hundred and Thirteen Men.

Of the different Religious Denominations there are Seventy Three Thousand and Thirty Seven Lutherans, Four Thousand Six hundred and Thirty Five Roman Catholicks, Six Hundred and Nineteen of the Reformed Religion, Seventy one Greeks, and Six Hundred and twenty Six Jews.

In the whole Population there were but Ten Persons above Ninety years of Age, and one Hundred and Seventy Seven between Eighty and Ninety. The Foreigners of all Classes are Three Thousand Two Hundred and Forty Three, but during the Summer Months an additional Increase of between Five and Six thousand is calculated upon.

The Increase of the Population since the last Census in 1840 is Five Thousand, Five Hundred and Twenty three, but when I recollect that on my Arrival here Eleven years ago, Dresden was not supposed to contain above Sixty Thousand Inhabitants, the present Population appears enormous.

FO 68/55: Francis Reginald Forbes to Earl of Aberdeen, No 10, Dresden, 16 February 1844

Double residence of Court of Saxe Coburg constant source of complaint; effects on diplomatic corps

I had the honour of receiving on the 1st of this Month (transmitted by Your Lordship's Order) Copies of a Letter from Mr Barnard to Viscount Canning, requesting Authority to charge in the Extraordinary Account of this Mission[92] the Expenses of his official Journies to Gotha, as well as of the Reply to it. I now enclose a Letter which I have received this morning from Mr Barnard on the above-mentioned Subject, and in consequence of the Request expressed by Viscount Canning, I take the Liberty of adding a few Observations.

The double Residence as well as the frequent Journies of the Court of Saxe Coburg Gotha from one to the other are a constant Source of Complaint to all those whom it affects. Even Monsieur de Lepel, when I alluded once the Chance of the Branch of Saxe Meiningen becoming extinct, answered; 'For God's sake don't let us think about of the Possibility of a third Residence: two cost us too much money already.' I cannot therefore refrain from stating frankly to Your Lordship that the Application of Mr Barnard seems to me to be perfectly natural and

---

[92] From July 1841 the British envoy in Dresden was also accredited to the court of Saxe-Coburg-Gotha.

worthy of being taken into consideration: Coburg is, generally speaking, more expensive than Dresden: almost every Article for the Table comes from a Distance, (even Vegetables from Bamberg) for the Fortunes are so small, that few will risk providing more than what is sufficient for daily Consumption, and the little above this is taken by the Court. I am convinced that the additional Salary granted to Mr Barnard does not cover the Increase of Expenditure to which his Position subjects him, and that he is forced to spend more than he did formerly in Dresden.

The Inhabitants of these small Residences live on a different Footing from what is either possible or, I may say, decent for Her Majesty's Chargé d'Affaires, and no English Person can submit to, may enforce the minor Economies they practise. At the Time when it was first arranged that I should pass six Months of each Year at the Ducal Court of Coburg, I took some Trouble to ascertain Prices etc. (+ Ambersand) so that my opinion is not formed solely on Mr Barnard's Representations.

I hope that Your Lordship will not be offended at my taking the Liberty of mentioning here, that I know it to be the greatest Wish of Two of the other Sovereigns of the House of Saxony, that I should be accredited to Their Courts; I allude to the Grand Duke of Saxe Weimar,[93] and the Duke of Saxe Meiningen,[94] who have personally spoken to me on the Subject, and said that it was most unpleasant for them that the English Minister should only pass through or near Their Residences; The Grand Duke is in Blood the Head of the whole House of Saxony, and in proceeding to Gotha I must always travel through Weimar. I have not the Honour of being personally known to the Duke of Saxe Altenburg, but I must equally pass His Residence on my way to Coburg: Meiningen is merely six or eight German Miles from either Coburg or Gotha, so that the Increase of Expense could not be very great, were I accredited to all the Court of Saxony, as the greatest Part of my colleagues are, which has perhaps given rise to the Wish I mention above, independent of the near Connection with the Count of Meiningen and now with that of Altenburg.

[93] Karl Friedrich.
[94] Bernhard.

FO 68/57: Francis Reginald Forbes to Earl of Aberdeen, No 5, Dresden, 9 March 1845

Progress of German Catholics; their proceedings

My temporary absence at the Court of Gotha (from which I returned on the Evening of the 1ˢᵗ) has prevented me from sooner informing Your Lordship of the Progress which the Seceders from the Roman Catholick Church[95] have been making in this Kingdom; and, though the Saxon Government has now begun, very unwisely, to throw impediments in their way, their increase, as well as in numbers as in the respectability of the individuals themselves, is but more sure from being slower, and their tenets are spreading in the Class of rich citizens, which possesses much real influence in this Country. The Nobility are, with few exceptions, poor, whilst the Merchants and Tradespeople are rich, and their habits so economical, as to add daily to their Fortunes.

On the 7ᵗʰ of last month a considerable number of Catholicks met at one of the hotels in this Capital, for the purpose of concerting measures for the Establishment of a Catholick Church independent of Rome, but no Committee was definitely chosen, because the individuals who composed the meeting were, generally speaking, unacquainted with each other, (a fact which speaks for itself); however on the proposition of a Professor Wigard, above fifty Catholicks signed a declaration that they would attend the next general meeting, for the purpose of a more minute discussion of the Matter. On the preceding day, a similar meeting of Catholicks had been held in Leipzig, where a number of persons of the very lowest Class had sought by every means to interrupt the Speakers, (it is of course said, that they had been bribed by the Catholick Clergy) – and at last proceeded to acts of violence against the promoters of the Assembly, so that the Police was called in, the ringleaders arrested, and the remainder turned out without ceremony. A second meeting was held in Leipzig on the 12ᵗʰ of February, at which the German Catholick Congregation was formally established and the confession of Faith of Breslau[96] (which must already have reached Your Lordship) unanimously adopted and signed: a Protestant also attended on behalf of his Catholick wife, and presented a chalice and a subscription of 1700 Thalers in aid of the new congregation, which had been collected amongst his immediate friends.

---

[95] For the German Catholics cf. pp. 102–104 in Frankfurt section, and pp. 228–229 in Prussia section.

[96] The Breslau branch of German Catholics led by Johannes Ronge represented an extreme theological rationalism. In contrast to the Schneidemühl branch, it recognized only two sacraments, baptism and communion.

The subscriptions in Leipzig now exceed the sum of six thousand Thalers.

The second meeting of German Catholicks in Dresden was held on the 15th of February, and Professor Wigard was unanimously chosen President. He began with the Lord's Prayer, and after stating in a very impressive manner the object for which they had met, put the questions; first, as to whether the meeting were ready to constitute itself into a free German Catholick and Apostolick Congregation; secondly, as a necessary consequence of the first, whether they were ready to throw off all subjection to Rome and to the Pope.

Both questions were unanimously carried, a Committee of seven persons was chosen to correspond with Leipzig and Breslau, and the meeting broke up in the most peaceable manner.

At another meeting on the 22nd of February the articles of Faith were submitted to and signed by the Members present; they are nearly identical with those which had been adopted at Leipzig and Breslau, and differ but slightly from those of our Church.

The fourth meeting, on the 1st of March, was marked by an incident which has left a most painful impression. Professor Wigard, on taking the Chair, after an account of the increase if the subscriptions had been given, informed the members present, one hundred and seventeen in number, that he had an important communication to make to them: that he had been sent for that morning by the Ministers of the Interior and of Publick Instruction,[97] who had declared to him, that though the Government did not intend to throw any Obstacles in the way of their Meetings, the Galleries must in the future be closed to the Publick, and that a publick notice of them, which had hitherto appeared in one of the newspapers, would no longer be allowed. That the motives assigned for these prohibitions were, that a publick notice of meetings had the appearance of seeking to gain proselytes (altho' it was only addressed to 'the Members of the Congregation'), and that the Roman Catholick Clergy had petitioned the Government to protect the rights of their Church, which could not be refused: – that the Minister of Publick Instruction had added, that they were not, in fact, a Congregation, for the Government had never acknowledged them as such. The President now proposed to the Meeting, to take legal steps against this prohibition; first with the Government, and if this were not attended to, to petition the Diet. He added, that he had already apprized the two Ministers of his intention to make this proposition to the Meeting. He further proposed to enter upon their Protocol, that until they were formally recognised as a Congregation, they should in future style themselves a

[97] Johann Paul Freiherr von Falkenstein and Carl August Wilhelm Eduard von Wietersheim.

'Society', against which there was no existing law. All the speakers followed in the same sense; it was agreed to call themselves 'the Society of German Catholicks' or 'Society of Catholicks in Dresden for the Discussion of religious Affairs', and to leave the Choice of the name to the proper Authorities. Several of the members proposed to arrange the calling of an extraordinary meeting at their private expense, but it was agreed that they should assemble on every Monday until further notice.

The draughts of the three addresses voted in the last meeting, were then submitted to the Members; viz, to the Department of Publick Instruction – to the Town Council of Dresden – and to the Congregations of Leipzig, Breslau, and Schneidemühle.

In the first, the Meeting declare that they have not the slightest intention of founding a new Sect – that they are Catholicks, and remain Members of the Christian Catholick Church, and have no other object that to purify it, and correct the errors and abuses which do not properly belong to it – that they therefore petition for the free exercise if their religion, as well as the preservation of all their rights and privileges as citizens, both of which are guaranteed to them by certain Paragraphs in the Constitution: and they end by requesting that a certain share of the Funds allotted by the Diet for the maintenance of the Roman Catholick Church should be granted to them for the support of their Clergy and Church, and that henceforward the members of this Congregation should no longer be called upon to contribute to the support of the Roman Catholick Clergy or their Schools.

In the address to the Town Council, they first express their grateful thanks to the Burgomaster[98] and Magistrates for the use of their Hall for their Meetings, and request that they would grant them a Church for the celebration of Divine Service, for which they will offer a remuneration as soon as their funds enable them to do so – and that if the Government do not assign them a Place of Worship, they hope hereafter to be able to buy ground to erect one for themselves.

The three other addresses were drawn up in a Christian and brotherly sense, stating the necessity of Union, and pointing out that a Synod should be held as soon as possible to put an End to divergence of opinions – that the Laity should alone be called to it, although the Clergy might be present to assist the deliberations without voting.

These Addresses were all voted, and the meeting separated after adopting some regulations as to the admission of new Members.

There have been several other meetings in Leipzig, where the number of the new Catholicks, as well as the funds for their Support,

---

[98] Carl Balthasar Hübler.

are rapidly increasing: according to the last accounts, one hundred and fifty heads of families had already signed the declaration.

I need hardly remark to Your Lordship, that the obstacles thrown in the way of the New Church are uniformly ascribed to the influence more of the Royal Family than of his Saxon Majesty, whose good sense and moderation are universally recognised and esteemed as they deserve. But Prince John is much more violent, and this places the Government, and particularly M. de Zeschau in a very delicate position, which makes His Excellency rather averse to speaking much on the subject. My Colleagues of Austria[99] and Bavaria[100] (and particularly the former) are indefatigable in their Efforts to support the Roman Catholics. In a conversation with M. de Zeschau, I pointed out to his Excellency that the nomination of the Clergy must eventually fall into the hands of the Government, as soon as the separation from Rome was fully established, and that this would add to its influence. I recalled to him also what he had said to me concerning a sect, called 'Stephanists',[101] which sprung up here a few years ago, 'that the most foolish proceeding was to make Martyrs of them; that if the thing were good they could not overthrow it, but if bad, it would fall of itself', which last was the case with the above mentioned sect. He admitted the justice of my remark, but dropped the Conversation, for he is too well informed not to know the Unpopularity which momentarily presses upon some Members of the Royal Family, as well as the utter impossibility of stopping the impulse now given. It is a remarkable fact, that the 'Allgemeine Zeitung',[102] printed in Bavaria, which had hitherto taken little or no notice of the German Catholick Church, has in N° 64 of the 5th of March given a plain and fair statement of all the proceedings as well as the names of the principal towns which have declared for it, and without any violent comment.

FO 68/57: Francis Reginald Forbes to Earl of Aberdeen, No 28, Confidential, Dresden, 11 September 1845

Saxony's future prospects; real causes of difficulties in the country; tensions due to religious questions; imprudence of Catholic clergy; internal peace superficial

Although I returned to this Capital on the Evening of the 4th, I have purposely delayed writing to Your Lordship that I might be better able

---

[99] Franz Graf von Kuefstein.
[100] Klemens August Graf von Waldkirch.
[101] Cf. pp. 316–317 in Saxony section.
[102] *Allgemeine Zeitung*, cf. n. 33 in Bavaria section.

to form some opinion, as well concerning the present state of Saxony as its future prospects; I am sorry to say that the result of my observations is favorable to neither.

At this moment all is again quiet, but this apparent tranquillity is only superficial, and can never be permanent under circumstances, which, at least for the present, afford but little hope for the change for the better.

The real causes of the Evil are; first the difference of the religion of the Royal Family from that of the Country,[103] and secondly (I am sorry to add) the personal character of Prince John, the presumptive heir to the Crown,— who with every moral virtue, and with a degree of scientifick information rarely to be found, has not that tact, that friendliness of disposition, which alone contribute to win personal attachment, however his other virtues must command respect.

I need hardly recall to Your Lordship, that the religion of the reigning Family was invidiously put forward by their Enemies in the years 1812 & 1813, and again later in the years 1830 & and 1831:[104] but unfortunately, at the moment of the Revolution, when the King gave up voluntarily much more than was either asked or expected, the most important condition of all was not insisted upon by the then dominant party – that of the future heirs of the Crown being educated in the Protestant Religion. Had this point been then firmly pressed, it would certainly have been conceded, and Prince John's Eldest son, Prince Albert, was then only three years old. There is but one way of accounting for the omission; that M. de Lindenau, to whom the present Constitution is attributed, got frightened at the Extent of Concession, and wished to reserve to himself one Merit with the Royal Family.

It is a great Misfortune for this Country that the King should have no Children – for His Majesty is so tolerant in Matters of Religion, although sincerely devoted to his own, that he would in all probability submit to necessity, and see that, sooner or later, a change must occur if the reigning Family wish to preserve the Crown. Even at this moment, frequent allusions are made to the elder branch of the Saxon Family,[105] who lost the title of Elector from their attachment to the Protestant religion, and as long as the King lives we may probably have no serious disturbances, but were His Majesty now called away from this world, I much doubt whether Prince John would be allowed to succeed.

[103] In 1697 Prince Elector August converted to Catholicism in order to become King of Poland. The population of Saxony, on the other hand, was overwhelming Protestant.

[104] During the Napoleonic Wars of 1812/1813, when Saxony was France's ally, and also during the revolutionary events following the French revolution of July 1830, the Saxon royal house felt itself to be on the defensive as regards its subjects, on confessional grounds.

[105] Ernestine line of the House of Wettin; in 1547 it lost the title of Elector.

Prince John on the contrary is well known to be a devoted Catholick in the strictest sense of the term, and to be completely under the influence of that Clergy, so that no hope can be entertained of his sanctioning, much less promoting, any change of Religion. In the first Diets,[106] he was always at the head of all the Finance Committees in the Chambers, and was the first to propose (at least his name was always at the head) reductions in the Salaries of all those employed in the publick Offices &c: and when Your Lordship is informed, that many of these have to support themselves and their families on £45 to £60 a year, you will understand how unpopular this must make a Prince, whose own habits are very economical, and who certainly never would propose any reductions which could affect himself. He has no inclination to military studies or pursuits, and has therefore no friends in the Army, whilst his constant interference in the Diet, where he is always speaking on every Question, indisposes a class against him, who, on their return to their provinces, speak without reserve of these minor shades, whilst his really good and excellent qualities are forgotten.

At the moment of my departure for Coburg, the Ministers had issued a decree,[107] signed by them all, in which they declared that they will abide their oaths to support the Lutheran Religion as established by Law, and forbid all those Meetings among the Protestants which had no other view than to take the nomination of the Clergy to Parishes out of the hands of the Government, and to make in purely elective; a measure replete with danger. The Ministers also declared that they would sanction neither encroachment nor alteration in these affairs, unless with the consent of the Diet. This decree made a great Sensation, and a few days after its publication, Mr Ronge paid a visit to Leipzig which only served to add to the already great excitement. This was the moment which Prince John chose for proceeding there to review the <u>Communal</u> Guard, as it is called, without mentioning his intention to any of the Ministers. The Governor of the Circle, M. de Broitzem, was unluckily absent, and the few remaining authorities seem not to have known what they were about. The unhappy result[108] is already known to Your Lordship, but the share which His Royal Highness appears to have had in it, has left an impression which can never be forgotten. Two addresses to the King and Prince John were lately proposed in the Town Council there, deprecating the late tumults, and giving the usual assurances of loyalty &c; they were voted by 36 votes to 16, after an animated and violent discussion.

[106] The first Diet constituted after the new constitution of 4 September 1831 convened on 22 January 1833.
[107] Ministerial Decrees respecting the Protestant Church, issued on 17 and 19 of July 1845.
[108] On 12 August eight citizens of Leipzig were killed and many injured during a demonstration against Prince Johann and the anti-liberal system he represented.

The Number of Catholicks in the whole Kingdom somewhat exceeds thirty thousand in a population of more than one Million, seven hundred and fifty thousand; but their Clergy are imprudent to an incredible degree – and it was but last Sunday, that one of them, who was preaching in the presence of their Majesties and the Royal Family, said 'that no thing now remained for the faithful, but to take up arms, and defend their religion by exterminating the heretics'. Two Catholick Gentlemen[109] who dined with me mentioned this with astonishment.

The attitude of the Ministers, and particularly of M. de Zeschau is all that can be wished: they are calm but firm, and determined to resist all the attacks of the democratical Party, whether openly made or under the cloak of Religion: but it is a strange contradiction in human nature, that the inhabitants of this part of Germany, who are inclined to believe in every thing that is mysterious, should seek to explain away Religion and to reduce to the level of human understanding that into which we are forbidden to pry: and it is impossible to deny the fact, that Deism and Materialism are making rapid strides, and that the prospects of this Country are not very cheering, although the Administration be perfect, the taxes light, and the industry daily increasing.

With such blessings it is doubly painful to think, that the internal peace may be interrupted at any moment, and that the only means of preventing this are at best only problematical – whilst foreign Agents are not wanting who take advantage of this state of things, for objects which can never be a matter of indifference to any Saxon.

FO 68/57: Francis Reginald Forbes to Earl of Aberdeen, No 32 [B], Dresden, 24 October 1845

Bitter disagreements when second chamber debates on the answer to King's address

[...] A most animated debate has taken place in the Second Chamber respecting the address to the King, in answer to His Majesty's Speech from the Throne,[110] which lasted several days. It began on the 17th, when the Committee brought up their report, and after some discussion the general draught of the Address was passed unanimously – but the debate on its separate paragraphs adjourned to the following day.

A great part of this is unimportant, but the Second Chamber pronounced generally its opinion against the system of prohibitive duties which the Southern States of the Customs Union had sought to

---

[109] Not traceable.

[110] The second chamber in Saxony was opened on 14 September 1845 with an address by Friedrich August.

introduce at the Carlsruhe Meeting[111]. In reference to the late Treaty for the Navigation of the Elbe[112], M. de Zeschau agreed that the transit duties were too high, and expressed a hope that at the next revision of the act, it might be possible to procure a diminution of them.

The principal debate was on the paragraph referring to the melancholy events which occurred at Leipzig in August last,[113] And this gave rise to such bitter animadversions on the line of conduct followed by the Government, that M. de Zeschau called upon the President[114] not to allow such revolutionary doctrines to be uttered in that Chamber. The President, who had already called the Speaker to order, rose again and said, that however sorry he must be to differ from the Minister for Foreign Affairs,[115] he must state that the Speech, though out of order, could not be designated as revolutionary.

The Minister of War,[116] in answer to an interpellation from a Deputy, respecting an order of the day praising the Military for the part they had taken in that tumult, answered boldly, that no order of the day had been issued in which allusion had been made to their having fired, – but one, in which their discipline, their alacrity in returning instantly from furlough, and their cheerful submission to the many privations they had to endure whilst forced to remain in their barracks, had been deservedly praised. He added later, (in answer to another Attack) that he must soon visit Leipzig, and would repeat personally to the Garrison the same Sentiments as those contained in the order of the day.

The Minister of the Interior[117] said that the Government were fully prepared to defend their Measures, when the Report in the Leipzig tumults was brought up, but that all those who blamed them, had only spoken of the melancholy results, and had passed over in silence the events which had led to them. [...]

[111] Cf. p. 395 in Württemberg section.
[112] Convention between Austria, Prussia, Saxony, Hanover, Denmark, Mecklenburg-Schwerin, Anhalt-Coethen, Anhalt-Dessau, Anhalt-Bernburg, Lübeck, and Hamburg relative to the regulation of the Brunshausen and Stade Toll. Signed at Dresden, April 13, 1844.
[113] Cf. n. 108 in this section.
[114] Karl Braun.
[115] Heinrich Anton von Zeschau.
[116] Gustav von Nostitz-Wallwitz.
[117] Johann Paul Freiherr von Falkenstein.

FO 68/60: Francis Reginald Forbes to Earl of Aberdeen, No 2, Dresden, 6 January 1846

Severe sentences for rioters create universal feeling of dissatisfaction

The unusual Severity of the sentences passed upon some of the individuals concerned, last August, in the Leipzig riots,[118] and which were lately made publick, has created, not only there but in the whole Kingdom, an universal feeling of dissatisfaction, nay disgust. Eight persons have been convicted, and, as far as one can judge, not on the very clearest testimony: the two[119] most implicated are condemned, one to Eight years', the second to four years' detention in a House of Correction of the first Class, which is what is called in French 'une peine infamante', and is severer even in its consequences than its infliction.

One appeal still remains open to them, and has been made; but should this last resource fail, it is to be hoped that this Government will see the necessity, as well for their own sakes as for that of the Presumptive Heir of the Crown, of extending Mercy to these very young men, and remitting part of their punishment. The name of His Royal Highness Prince John cannot but be associated with these sentences, which are all, more or less, severe.

FO 68/60: Francis Reginald Forbes to Earl of Aberdeen, No 4, Dresden, 7 January 1846

Proceedings in the Estates of Saxe-Coburg-Gotha lead to their dissolution; growing democratic spirit

The accounts which I have received from Her Majesty's Chargé d'Affaires at Coburg,[120] are far from satisfactory, and His Royal Highness the Duke of Saxe Coburg-Gotha[121] has been forced to dissolve the States. A violent and democratical spirit has shewn itself in all their proceedings, for the Deputies are completely under the influence of an Attorney of the name of Brieglep,[122] who openly professes principles of the most radical tendency. The Government had already conceded the Admission of the Publick to the Sittings, but the States rejected as utterly useless a Law proposed by them respecting the

---

[118] Cf. n. 108 in this section.
[119] Not traceable.
[120] Charles Townshend Barnard.
[121] Herzog Ernst II.
[122] Moriz Briegleb.

Responsibility of the Minister, and declared that they preferred having none at all.

On one occasion they went as far as to vote a declaration of their want of Confidence in the Government, on which His Royal Highness sent them a Ministerial Message desiring them not to meddle with questions where they had no right of interference. The same motion was announced for the 19th of last month, and M. de Lepel made his appearance then for the first time. On His Excellency enquiring why this Motion was not brought forward, the President[123] got up and said, that in consequence of the illness of the said Monsieur Brieglep which prevented his Attendance (and which was but a pretext) it must stand over to another day. M. de Lepel then rose, and said that although the Government had nothing to fear from it, but that the Assembly persisted in a line which did not belong to them, he had received the Sovereign's orders to dissolve the States, and read an order to that Effect which he had just received.

There is this advantage resulting from the measure, that His Royal Highness will retain the valuable services of M. de Lepel for (at least) some time longer, but I fear that he is getting very tired of the senseless opposition, and will not finally consent to remain.

A few days after the dissolution, a publick dinner was given in honor of this M. Brieglep, to which about fifty persons subscribed. The Duke's health was drunk with apparent Enthusiasm, but it is much to be feared that the Elections for the States, which must take place the End of February or the beginning of March, will be as unfavorable to the Government as the last.

The Court left Coburg for Gotha on the 5th of this month.

FO 68/60: Francis Reginald Forbes to Earl of Aberdeen, No 5, Dresden, 10 January 1846

Petitions against the suppression of 'Sächsische Vaterlandsblätter'; violent debate in second chamber; growing 'radicalism'; ministry has no party in the chamber

On the 7th of this month several petitions, which had been addressed to the second Chamber of the Saxon Diet, were presented and read by the Members who had received them, and amongst others, three or four from Dresden and other towns, respecting a remarkably clever paper, called 'the Saxon Vaterland's Blätter',[124] which the Government had lately suppressed. After reading the petitions, some very severe and

---

[123] Haubold von Speßhardt.
[124] Cf. n. 221 in Frankfurt section.

cutting censures were made upon Ministers, and the debate became extremely violent. One of the Deputies[125] is said to have declared that Saxony must blush at being governed by Men, who were completely under the influence of other Powers, and who were afraid of allowing the truth to be spoken about themselves. There was violent applause from the Galleries, and a Member got up and proposed the instantaneous adjournment of the Sitting. In this he was overruled by the President,[126] who threatened to have the Galleries cleared, but did not put his threat into Execution.

The debate continued, but grew so animated, that a motion was made and carried by a considerable Majority, 'that the Subject had been sufficiently discussed'.

On the following day, a still more violent scene occurred, which originated in one of the radical members[127] getting up, and requesting permission to correct an error which, according to his statement, had fallen from one of the speakers in the course of the preceding debate, and was in fact 'an Untruth'.[128] The confusion became then past description, the spectators loudly applauding the first speaker, and as soon as order was partially restored, the Member assailed, a M. de Thielau (a Gentlemen of birth, fortune, and of moderate liberal principles) rose and said, that in these two sittings, he had been three several times accused of having uttered an Untruth – that if this was the case, as he must conclude from the Chamber submitting to it, he at least would not bear it, but considering himself unfit to sit there, he begged leave to resign his seat into the hands of the President – and prepared to leave the Chambers.

His friends however interposed, and after a great deal of discussion, the President put the Question, 'Does this Camber believe, that the honorable Member[129] in his quotation of yesterday, did not purposely assert an Untruth'; this was voted unanimously, and they passed to the order of the day.

I need not say to Your Lordship what a bad impression these two sittings have left behind, nor how much they tend to lower the Government in the Eyes of the Publick. It was but a week ago, that the whole Edition of a work,[130] containing some severe censures upon

[125] Carl Gottlob Todt.
[126] Karl Braun.
[127] Wilhelm Michael Schaffrath.
[128] Wilhelm Michael Schaffrath was refering to deputy Thielau's false interpretation of a memorandum by Carl Biedermann. According to Thielau, in this memorandum to the Berlin church conference Biedermann had described Jesus and his Apostles as noisy seducers of the people.
[129] Friedrich Erdmann August von Thielau.
[130] Not traceable.

them, was seized by the Authorities at Leipzig, and a few days later a Ministerial order appeared, to say that the work was again allowed, as the attack on the Government was so base and so unworthy, that nobody could attach importance to it.

The Ministers have literally no party in the Chambers on in whom they can depend with certainty, and not one law, nor even motion, is allowed to pass in the form in which they have presented it. It is not easy to say whence their hesitation proceeds, but their whole proceedings are so vacillating, and shew so little firmness, that they must feel a want of confidence in themselves, or in some other source to which they ought to look for the firmest support.

FO 68/60: Francis Reginald Forbes to Viscount Palmerston, No 26, Dresden, 21 August 1846

Secret association with republican principles discovered; members arrested; alleged connection with 'Junges Deutschland' (Young Germany)

[...] A secret association has been discovered in the principal School[131] of this Capital, which is frequented not only by the sons of Citizens but even by those of the Nobility. A great number of individuals are involved in it, and fifteen or sixteen have been already arrested and brought up several times for Examination. It appears that their Principles and views are quite Republican, and that they are connected with similar societies in almost every Capital or City in this part of Germany. The Police are actively employed in tracing the ramifications of this so called 'Young Germany',[132] which is the more serious from the accused being principally sons of rich Merchants and Shopkeepers, by far the most influential Class in these Countries. The young men are generally of the age of from sixteen to seventeen, and this being a preparatory School for College, there is every reason to fear, that their principles are widely diffused in the several Universities, and particularly at Leipzig where there is already so strong a democratic tendency.

---

[131] *Kreuzschule* (Holy Cross School), founded in the thirteenth century.

[132] On the secret organization *Junges Deutschland* as well as the literary movement *Junges Deutschland* which have nothing to do with the case here; cf. nn. 151, 158 in Frankfurt section.

FO 68/60: Francis Reginald Forbes to Viscount Palmerston, No 39, Dresden, 19 December 1846

Special session of Saxon diet to discuss railway project; question of fundraising

A proclamation has been issued, calling the Saxon Diet together for a Special Session, but which is not to last longer than four weeks; the day appointed for the Meeting is the 18ᵗʰ of January next. The object is to provide funds for the completion of the Railway from Leipzig to the Bavarian frontier, the Expense of which already so far exceeds the Estimates, that the Company having completely failed in their Efforts to raise even a part of the requisite funds, have been too happy to hand it over to the Government. The Saxons are beginning to cure of the Railway Mania, and the inhabitants of Dresden and Leipzig have discovered that foreigners depart with as much facility as they arrive, and that they will prefer a milder Climate for the Winter. The Bavarian Railroad, as far as it is finished, is admirably constructed for without any perceptible ascent it terminates now on the top if a Mountain with an immense Valley in front (over which it is to be carried), and the town of Reichenbach considerably below it. [...]

FO 68/64: Francis Reginald Forbes to Viscount Palmerston, No 6, Dresden, 16 February 1847

Meeting at Leipzig initiated by Robert Blum; petition to protest against Saxon diet's measures; German Catholic's petition to the Saxon diet

The Publick are almost excluded from the Sittings of the present Diet, which are entirely occupied, in the second Chamber, with discussing measures for finding the funds required for completing the several Railroads. I am told that the Government is excessively embarrassed, as to whence they are to be provided, and is calling in several large Mortgages.

A very important Meeting was held at Leipzig the day before yesterday, which was called by three[133] of the Town Council of that city. The first of the three, Robert Blum, is at the head of the German Catholicks, and the Government managed to annul his Election to the second Chamber, under the pretence that the duties of the two were incompatible with each other. He, as well as another person[134] similarly situated, formally protested against this decision.

---

[133] Robert Blum, Carl Biedermann, and Wilhelm Michael Schaffrath.
[134] Not traceable.

At the above mentioned Meeting, to which none but Electors and eligible persons were called, it was proposed, to enter and transmit to the second Chamber, a solemn protest against all and any measures carried in the present Diet, the composition of which was a violation of the Constitution; and to petition said Chamber to declare itself incompetent, and to demand the convocation of a Constitutional Diet.

After a very short discussion <u>Seven hundred and ninety</u> persons, out of one Thousand present, signed the petition, which was immediately sent off to Dresden.

A strong petition has been presented to the Diet, from the German Catholicks, protesting against their being forced to pay the regular dues to the Roman Catholick Church, and claiming that freedom which the Constitution in Saxony guarantees to all Christian Religions.

FO 68/64: Francis Reginald Forbes to Viscount Palmerston, No 11, Dresden, 4 April 1847

Reflections on anti-English articles in German press, 'Allgemeine Zeitung' in particular; questions of commercial policy

I had the honor of receiving on the 28th of last month Your Lordship's despatch marked N° 3 of the 20th of March, inclosing to me several copies of a letter addressed to the Foreign Office for the purpose of refuting the unjust attacks on the Commercial policy of Great Britain, which have lately appeared in some of the German Newspapers, and principally in the 'Universal Augsburgh Gazette'.[135]

I had long noticed the illiberal tendency of the above-mentioned Journal towards England, which is not confined to publick Affairs but is even directed against individuals and not many weeks back there was an Article, dated Rome, purporting to give a description of the last days of the Carneval, but which teemed with scurrilous abuse not only of the English in general, but even of some by name. This Journal has fallen considerably in publick's estimation since the death of M. de Cotta, its original Editor, whose known talents and respectability had increased the numbers of subscribers to an immense extent – but of late years it has attacked almost every country, excepting Austria, the Government of which have declared that they will prohibit its entrance into the Austrian dominions the moment that it contains anything offensive to them: it is even said that a separate Edition is printed for that Empire alone. By a curious coincidence the very day on which I

---

[135] For the *Allgemeine Zeitung* cf. n. 33 in Bavaria section.

received Your Lordship's despatch, the Leipzig Universal Gazette[136] published translations of two letters from Your Lordship and from Sir Robert Peel addressed, and in answer to the late Mr List (the originator of all this Abuse, as well as Editor of the Zollvereins Blatt),[137] and accompanied them with very sensible as well as liberal Comments.[138] This however has been taken up by the Augsburgh Gazette of the 31st, and has given rise to a very virulent Article, which may chiefly to be attributed to the fact that the Leipzig paper, edited and published in a town where the advantages of free trade are fully understood and acknowledged, is becoming daily more popular, whilst its Rival is losing ground in the North of Germany.

Saxony has the advantage that the wages of labour of all sorts are almost incredibly low, and the Manufacturers are contented with a less profit compared to what is looked for in other Countries – but the great cause of the partial outcry in Germany in favor of prohibitive duties is, that on account of the smallness of the Capitals in the possession of individuals, most of the Manufactories are founded by subscription, and each person is anxious to get the highest possible interest for the share which he has rested in the concern. [...]

FO 68/64: Francis Reginald Forbes to Viscount Palmerston, No 13, Gotha, 11 April 1847

Petition in favour of a constitution for Gotha

[...] A Petition requesting His Royal Highness[139] to grant this Duchy a Constitution, or in their Words, to do away with all those ancient Institutions with which the Nobility and respectable Inhabitants are perfectly satisfied, had been got up by some meddling Lawyers as well as secondrate Burgesses and Shopkeepers, and lay for Signature in one of the publick Rooms. As it always occurs, many of the better Classes, who in the Beginning had loudly disapproved of the Measure allowed

---

[136] For the *Leipziger Allgemeine Zeitung* cf. n. 215 in Frankfurt section.

[137] The *Zollvereinsblatt* was published from 1 January 1843 until 1846. It was the organ of supporters of the economic unification of Germany and of a German policy of protective tariffs.

[138] The published letters contained the reactions of Sir Robert Peel (22 August 1846) and Lord Palmerston (8 September 1846) to the memorandum *On the Advantages and Conditions of an Intimate Alliance between Greatbritain [!] and Germany*. In this Pamphlet (the so-called Alliance Memorandum), List stressed the significance of Anglo-German trade relations and called for England's support in further extending the German *Zollverein* and for the English government to tolerate the German policy of protective tariffs. Both Peel and Palmerston rejected List's suggestions.

[139] Ernst II.

themselves to the be persuaded into signing their Names and a
Deputation was chosen to present it to the Duke. Monsieur de Stein
informs me, that His Royal Highness answered, that the existing
Institutions had been sanctioned by the Lapse of Centuries, independent
of which, there were others (the Princes of Hohenlohe)[140] whose Rights
must not be overlooked, and that He would take it into consideration.
I trust however that His Royal Highness will use the greatest Caution
in attending to any Part of this Petition, and that He never will consent
to allow any Interference in the Ducal Domains. [...]

FO 68/64: Francis Reginald Forbes to Viscount Palmerston, No 15,
Dresden, 24 April 1847

*Prussian King's inconsistencies and contradictions create feeling of bitterness in the very highest
Saxon circles*

[...] I should deceive Your Lordship were I not to say that the King of
Prussia's speech on opening his Diet, has produced the worst Effect
here on all Classes.[141] In more than one instance His Saxon Majesty
and his Government have been placed in the most embarrassing
positions by His Prussian Majesty's inconsistencies. During one of his
visits here, the King of Saxony spoke to him unreservedly on the
subject of the German Catholicks, and said that he himself, being a
Roman Catholick Sovereign over a Protestant Country, was most
anxious to know what line would be pursued in Prussia, that he might
follow the same. His Prussian Majesty gave the strongest as well as
repeated assurances that he would avoid as long as possible acknowledging them as a Sect, and above all would not allow them a publick
celebration of their service. In a few weeks afterwards, he granted them
the use of a Church at Dantzic.

During his last visit here, this Sovereign equally sought to ascertain
what were His Prussian Majesty's intentions as to alterations as well in
the administration of Justice as in the admission of the Publick to
trials – and received in answer the declaration that he would change
as little as possible – that only a very limited number of persons should
be admitted to criminal trials, and none to civil ones. He has now
published an Edict admitting every one indiscriminately to all trials
whatsoever.

The above mentioned circumstances, however they may create a

---

[140] The Hohenlohes belonged to the *Standesherren*, not the ruling houses. In the dukedom
of Gotha their feudal rights were secured by the old Saxon *Ständeverordnung* of 1653–1666.
[141] Cf. pp. 235–236 in Prussia section.

feeling of bitterness in the very highest Saxon circles, were still but partially known – but his Speech is so full of contradictions and inconsistencies, that it is universally ridiculed. It must end by lowering in the general opinion a Sovereign who is full of talent and virtues, and the Publick looks forward to what may occur in Prussia with painful attention, and but little confidence.

FO 68/64: Francis Reginald Forbes to Viscount Palmerston, No 29, Dresden, 17 August 1847

Food riots; potato blight reappears

[...] There have been some riots in several provincial towns, principally against the bakers, but of no importance. There has been a partial reappearance of the Potatoe blight in Lusatia, but it is confined to a very small spot. The peasants here strew the plants with lime, for the purpose of killing the Animalcula from which it is supposed to originate, and which are said to eat their way down the stem into the root. This remedy is said to have succeeded in most instances.

The heat is unexampled, and the Corn harvest has been all carried home.

WÜRTTEMBERG
(STUTTGART)

STUTTGART

FO 82/24: Edward Cromwell Disbrowe to Earl of Aberdeen, Stuttgart, No 12, 30 March 1830, Copy

Death of Grand Duke of Baden revives the still unsolved Sponheim question

An Officer[1] is just arrived with an official account of the death of the Grand Duke of Baden which took place this morning at a quarter past three o'clock. The Officer will return direct to Carlsruhe.

I have not the slightest doubt that as soon as ever the King of Bavaria receives this intelligence, that he will give orders to take such steps as he deems necessary for laying claims to the succession of Sponheim.[2]

I enter on this question at once, as your Lordship will probably recollect that in my despatch N° 43 of last year, I stated that it has been a subject of discussion at Frederickshaven during the visit of the King of Bavaria.

On that occasion the King of Bavaria promised the King of Wirtemberg that he would not take any measures in this business likely to disturb the publick Peace and repose of Germany, but that he certainly would put in his claims and enter his protest at the diet if he did not receive satisfaction.

I must however add that so violent is the temper of the King of Bavaria whenever this question is agitated, and so bent is he on obtaining a portion, however small, of the Palatinate which he thinks he may obtain to compromise these claims. The King of Würtemberg who knows his character so well, is, I am confidentially informed, inclined to fear that he will not be as moderate as he professes. The Prince of Fürstenberg, brother in law of the Grand Duke, who was at Stuttgart when the news arrived, has been authorized by the King of Wurtemberg to assure the Grand Duke that he holds the promise of the King of Bavaria that he will not resort to hostility to enforce his claims.

Two years since when the Grand Duke was supposed to be dying, orders were given to some regiments to be ready to march and enter

---

[1] Not traceable.
[2] For the Sponheim question cf. n. 21 in Prussia section.

the Palatinate, but on the present occasion I do not believe anything of that sort will take place, even though the probability of His Royal Highness death was foreseen by the King of Bavaria before he set out for Italy.

His absence in Italy at this moment by giving time for his ardour to cool is rather a fortunate circumstance with regard to the declarations by the Courts of London, Vienna and Paris, that signed by your Lordship is deemed the most satisfactory to the Court of Carlsruhe and it certainly will be brought forward as soon as the question is mooted. [...]

FO 82/24: Edward Cromwell Disbrowe to Viscount Palmerston, No 74, Stuttgart, 30 December 1830

Critique of election proceedings in Baden

[...] The election of the Deputies in the Grand Duchy of Baden is concluded.

For the first time since a constitution has been established in the Grand Duchy,[3] the Government has not interfered with Elections.

The Grand Duke having forbidden all persons connected with Government from interfering under pain of his displeasure, as he wished to know the real sentiments of his people.

Honourable as such a feeling is, I regret to say that some doubts exist of the effects likely to be produced, not so much, because such an attempt is in itself detrimental to the interest of the Country but because the Electors having been in the habit of being taught beforehand whom they were to elect (and in fact they almost universally abided by the expressed wishes of the Magistrates,) they were by no means prepared for the sudden change by any intermediate Steps, the Elections have therefore in many instances fallen, not on persons who are acquainted with the local wants of the Circles, but on persons totally and entirely unconnected with, and unknown to them, and who have obtained their situations by intrigues and other means. [...]

---

[3] The constitution of Baden was introduced on 29 August 1818.

FO 82/25: Edward Cromwell Disbrowe to Viscount Palmerston, No 13, Stuttgart, 24 March 1831

Reports that Baden and Württemberg will support France in case of war between Austria and France

During the last three or four Weeks Reports have been in Circulation that in Case of War between France and Austria[4] the King of Wurtemberg and the Grand Duke of Baden had entered into a secret Agreement with the French Government, not only to declare themselves in all Cases neutral, but even to admit the French Troops to pass through this Country to attack Austria; and to defend this measure on the Ground of their Incompetence single handed to resist the Aggression of France, and because the German Confederation is not prepared to protect the Independence of Germany, and it has also been argued that such is the only safe line for a constitutional Sovereign to pursue in a Contest between Constitutional France and despotic Austria. [...]

If I had believed such a Step was really about to be taken, it would have been so serious in its Consequences and so complete a death blow to the Germanic Confederation as to have rendered it my duty not delay a single hour in conveying the Intelligence to Your Lordship. [...]

As regards the Grand Duchy of Baden I can only argue from Probabilities.

I have already had the honor of stating to Your Lordship my opinion of the Weakness of that Government and of the Situation of the Country, and my Attention has been drawn to several minor Circumstances as indicating a vacillating if not a treacherous Policy.

Among other circumstances the proposition for throwing three Bridges over the Rhine.

I must confess on this particular head, though I believe the fact, I am not inclined to attach much importance to it, because supposing a secret understanding to exist between the French Government and the Grand Duke (and if this idea is abandoned the case is not worth arguing) the Pontoons at Strasbourg would, (in the present advanced State of the science of War) afford such an ample means of crossing the River without opposition, as to render this as regards to the Bridges, to say the least, useless for the object in view and would only serve to awaken suspicion in Germany.

I therefore must say I believe that the three Bridges to have a

---

[4] The tension between France and Austria grew out of their rivalry in Italy; the immediate cause was a revolutionary rising in Rome, Modena and Parma, which had been going on since February 1831.

Commercial and not a Military destination, although indubitably they might also serve the latter purpose.

It should be remarked also that in His Speech at the Opening of the Chambers, the Grand Duke expressly calls on the Estates to enable him to fulfil all his Engagements towards the Confederation.

As far therefore as I am able to judge I should conceive no Stipulations with France contrary to the Engagements of His Royal Highness with the Confederation exist, but should war unfortunately take place and a large French Army attempt to cross the Rhine, I do not think the Grand Ducal Government has that Energy in itself or that Confidence in and Reliance on the Spirit of its People as would induce it to offer all the Resistance in its Power in Conformity with its Engagements until the Confederation could come to its Assistance.

The Effect of such submission would undoubtedly bring the French in three marches to Stutgard and the King being deprived of two thirds of the Army destined for the defence of this Part of Germany would be entirely disarmed.

Both the Governments in question cannot but recollect the sufferings they have formerly brought on themselves and their people by a to hasty submission to the French Government and too much confidence in French promises.

They have it is true been respectively raised to the Rank of King and Grand Duke[5] but this was the Effect of the after policy of Bonaparte not of their submission to the early revolutionary Armies of France professing to fight for the independence of Mankind.

They cannot either forget how difficult it is to get the French Armies out of it, when they have once entered into Germany, nor the Contributions with which they will be obliged to supply them the payment for which may be stipulated for, but can be scarcely be relied on.

Nor if it comes to this point, can the people be entirely blinded to these Considerations or induced cordially to fraternize with the French, whatever temporary force this eventful Period may lend to such a feeling.

Bearing therefore all these Considerations in Mind I cannot I confess, bring myself to believe any stipulations with France to exist, because I cannot conceive these Governments, however they may have contemplated the Possibility of being compelled to submit to force, can be blind enough to adopt, a priori, those measures of all others the most likely to bring such Misfortunes on their own head, but I must add that such appears to be at this moment the Weakness of the Bond of

[5] In return for accepting French hegemony, Friedrich I had been raised to the rank of king in the Peace of Pressburg (26 December 1805).

Union which unites the Confederation, that unless some of the more powerful Members puts itself at its head in Case of War it will most likely fall to pieces.

If the point of Union is more firmly combined these dangers will naturally cease.

Austria for reasons I have stated in my former Correspondence continues unpopular and is looked on with some degree of Suspicion – if therefore the King of Prussia should put himself forward and take the lead in the Counsels of the Diet (I speak as regards the feeling of this part of Germany) it would be popular as Prussia is considered to be purely a German Power and as a more completely & entirely bound up in German Interests than Austria, and the Want of a head to whom to look, for latterly Austria has carried not one Measure in the Diet, is fully admitted whether the Policy of the Times should require a neutrality or render it necessary for these Powers to precipitate themselves into a War, and I must add that in Case of a War for, or in, Italy, Neutrality, if it can be maintained is the Policy these Countries would wish to adopt. [...]

FO 82/25: Edward Cromwell Disbrowe to Viscount Palmerston, No 15, Stuttgart, 28 March 1831

Public opinion in Baden of the proceedings of the Landtag; replies of both chambers to the opening speech by the Grand Duke of Baden

In a period of such general Agitation as the present, it cannot I presume be uninteresting to Your Lordship to be informed from time to time, of the march of public opinion in the Grand Duchy of Baden, when the States are assembled at the commencement of a new Reign, (if not of a new dynasty), and when its members have been chosen, as I have already had the honor to point out, on new principles entirely free from the Control of Government.

I have already had the honor of drawing your Lordships attention to the only remarkable passage in the opening Speech of the Grand Duke.[6]

It will be now my endeavour to point out such portions of the Replies of the two Chambers, as I may think worthy of your Lordship's notice.

[6] In his speech of 17 March 1831, Grand Duke Leopold called on the chambers and asked them 'to enable Him to fulfil all his Engagements towards the Confederation given the tense situation abroad'. This referred to Württemberg's financial and manpower commitments to the common army of the German Confederation.

I avail myself of a Newspaper translation of them, and I have taken the liberty to mark such passages as are more particularly worthy of notice.

The Corvées, which were one of the real grievances felt in the Grand Duchy, will probably be abolished, those who profited by the abuse seem disposed to relinquish them voluntarily.

The Second Chamber acknowledges those Duties the fulfilment of which, the Confederation has a right to demand, and does not shew any disposition to resist them, but it expresses the hopes that the Voice of Baden will be raised in the Diet against 'the Laws of Exception'.[7]

The Laws of Exception here alluded to, are the regulations placing restraints on the liberty of the Press, in certain cases throughout the Confederation, the same Laws, which were lately attacked in Bavaria, and I must say, I believe the connection between the opposition in the two Countries might without much difficulty be traced. [...]

The only remaining Passage, in the reply of the Chambers of Deputies worth noticing is 'Nous reconnaissons que, malgré les obstacles qu'éprouvent le commerce et l'industrie à l'extérieur, ils sont parvenus dans notre Patrie à un degré satisfaisant de perfection, et nous nourrisons l'espoir de voir bientôt s'accomplir le vœu just et universel de la Nation Allemande, de voir disparaître toutes les difficultés et les entraves de la liberté du commerce dans l'intérieur de l'Allemagne'.

The sentiments here expressed do not I conceive, indicate any approximation to the Commercial Union with Würtemberg and Bavaria but the contrary.

Before the Badois could be brought to agree to such a measure, the Pact itself must undergo great modification.

On the spirit which animated the debates themselves and the violent language of some of the Deputies, I shall take the liberty of making a few remarks, on a future occasion.

A deputy a professor[8] from Fribourg made a most violent speech against any restraints on the liberty of the Press, calling for the entire abolition of all Censorship, and in praising the 'les trois glorieuses Journées' of the French Revolution,[9] added if the wishes of the people were not complied with they must or would be tried in the Grand Duchy.

In the House and the galleries the speech was received with applause, but I believe the good sense of the people out of doors, was not led

---

[7] On 20 September 1819 the German Federal Diet passed four exceptive laws on the basis of the Carlsbad Decrees. These including the Federal Press Law referred to here, which made censorship of the press obligatory.

[8] Karl Theodor Welcker.

[9] Cf. n. 28 in Frankfurt section.

away by, or inclined to applaud such an outrageous and indecent declaration.

The Prince Augustus Nephew of the King has accepted a Commission of Captain in the Guards of the King of Prussia, His Highness will set off in a few days for Berlin.[10]

FO 82/25: Edward Cromwell Disbrowe to Viscount Palmerston, No 47, Stuttgart, 12 December 1831

Württemberg's accession to commercial treaties with Prussia; Württemberg's expectations; Grand Duke of Baden anxious to accede to the Commercial Union

Your Lordship will without doubt have been informed of the note presented at Berlin by the Minister of Hesse Cassel[11] on the Subject of the accession of that Country to the Commercial Treaties and of the difficulties relative to the Country of Hanau.[12]

I have now the honor to inform your Lordship, that the Commissioners who are to be joined to the Ministers of Wurtemberg and Bavaria[13] at the Court of Berlin for negotiating a Treaty of Commercial Union with Prussia on the same footing as these two Countries are united, will set out almost immediately for their destination.

By the treaty of 1828[14] the Tariff on the Entrance of Colonial goods was to be raised in Wurtemberg and Bavaria to the Tariff of Prussia, which would be an encrease of about eight Kreutzers per centner.

The Government of Wurtemberg is extremely anxious that on the contrary in this new Treaty of Union the Prussian Tariff should be lowered to the standard of Wurtemberg and Bavaria, indeed it was made a sine quâ non in the instructions, but as hopes are now entertained that the Prussian Government may be induced to include the Rhenish Provinces, and as by the accession of Hesse Cassel and Darmstadt[15] a continuity of the Custom Houses down to the frontiers of Germany will thus be obtained. I understand a Latitude will be left in the negotiators in this Article.

Possibly the facility which will be afforded to the Circulation of

[10] Enclosure: *Journal de Francfort*, No. 85, 26 March 1831.

[11] Karl Friedrich Freiherr Wilkens von Hohenau.

[12] Electoral Hesse joined the Prussian Customs Union on 25 August 1831. The province of Hanau in the south saw this as threatening its trade with the neighbouring states of Frankfurt and Bavaria.

[13] Friedrich Wilhelm Graf von Bismark and Friedrich Graf von Luxburg.

[14] Bavaria and Württemberg established the South German Customs Union on 18 January 1828.

[15] Hesse-Darmstadt (Grand Duchy of Hesse) joined the Prussian Customs Union on 14 February 1828.

Merchandise may lead to encrease the consumption of Colonial Produce, but if the Tariff is lowered to correspond in any measure with the entrance Duties in the Grand Duchy of Baden, I conceive it will indubitably have that effect.

The Grand Duke is anxious to accede to the Commercial Union and intends sending his Plenipotentiary to Berlin with a view to that object.

The Report of the commission of the Chambers of Baden, (which I have the honor to enclose) will, if acted on entirely shut out the Grand Duchy. The Government pretends that the Chamber has no right to tie up its hands, which may be true, but they indubitably must be consulted hereafter when the present entrance duties are to be altered by Law.

I therefore entertain but little hopes of the arrangement as concerning Baden taking place at least for the present; but the fact of having entered into negotiation at all must facilitate the point, all these Governments have in View that of doing away with the Lines of Custom Houses in the Interior of Germany.

As matters now stand Colonial Produce comes up the Rhine with transit duties, pays the low entrance duties into Baden, and is to a very great extent smuggled across the Wurtemberg frontier and circulated without difficulty throughout Wurtemberg and Bavaria.[16]

FO 82/26: Edward Cromwell Disbrowe to Viscount Palmerston, No 1, Stuttgart, 8 January 1832

Elections to Württemberg's Landtag completed; 'mixed' composition

[...] The Elections for the Kingdom of Wurtemberg are now completed, the Choice is of a very mixed Character. Three of the Proprietors of the Hoch Wächter,[17] an ultra liberal Paper, have been chosen as well as one or two more of the same Class of unprincipled Agitators. It is possible the Election of the three Individuals above alluded to may be annulled in Consequence of a Judgement pronounced and punishment awarded them some Years ago, great part of which was remitted by the King.

M. de Wangenheim, formerly Minister of the Interior is likewise to

[16] Enclosure: *Journal de Francfort*, No. 329, 26 November 1831.
[17] Gottlob Tafel and Fredrich Rödinger were the proprietors and editors of the newspaper, *Der Hochwächter, Volksblatt für Stuttgart und Württemberg* (cf. n. 46 in Frankfurt section). In 1831–1832 they were refused permission to take their seats as deputies in the *Landtag* because of past convictions.

become a distinguished Member of the Opposition, but He is in general considered as a wild Visionary.

The political Events of the day, at the period of the Meeting of the Chambers will probably decide the strength of the respective parties which it would be vain to analize at this moment, in the mean time the Government flatters itself that it has a Majority sufficiently considerable to enable it to manage Matters with a little discretion. [...]

FO 82/26: Edward Cromwell Disbrowe to Viscount Palmerston, No 8, Stuttgart, 15 February 1832

On the character of newly elected deputies; ministry no longer in majority; discussion on Württemberg's treaty for the Commercial Union with Prussia; Disbrowe's own assessment; Austria regains influence on German governments

Having just learnt that Lord Erskine will pass through this City in an hour or two without stopping I am desirous of availing myself a few Moments to write to Your Lordship a few Lines which I should not be willing to commit to the public Post.

The more the character of the deputies who have been elected to the Chambers of the Kingdom of Wurtemberg is considered, the worse it appears.

Pettifogging Attorneys, Editors of radical Newspapers and smaller Employés of Gov^t, who having served a given number of Years are entitled to certain Provisions independent of the Will of the Crown, and who having failed in the advancement they expected, find a Trafic in Agitation and Ultra Liberal Doctrines more profitable, particularly when coupled with their pay as Deputies, have been elected in very considerable numbers as Members. In fact I do not believe the Ministry any longer flatter themselves they will be in a Majority.

M. Pfizer Author of a pamphlet[18] I mentioned in a former despatch in which He puts forward the Doctrine of a German National Union, which would do away with the independant Sovereignities of which it is composed has been elected in consequence of advocating that doctrine.

A doctrine which in different States has been more or less covertly advocated by the Members of Opposition in Baden, Messrs Welcker and Dutlinger & by M Hoffmann in Darmstadt.

Their plan impracticable in the present State of Germany or in any probable State to which that Country could be brought except through means of Blood would most likely if successful reduce it to an infinite

---

[18] *Briefwechsel zweier Deutscher* (1831) (Correspondence between two Germans).

number of federated Republics with or without Royal heads but of which the factious demagogues of the day would become the real Arbitrators.

Proofs sufficient are in Existence, and in my former despatches I have pointed out some of them when treating of the Grand Duchy of Baden, to elucidate the complete Connexion which exists among the Radical Party in Germany.

The Scene of Contest will shortly be transferred from Carlsruhe and Munic to Stutgard and I am sorry to say that the Administration destined to meet the Storm appears nearly as disorganized as that of Baden.

The new Minister of the Interior[19] is considered as a complete failure by his Colleagues and I believe by the King.

Gen¹ Hugel[20] Minister at War a vain flippant but well meaning man deep in every money speculation is totally unfit for times of difficulty.

Count Beroldingen totally incapable of public speaking.

M de Varnbuhler[21] Minister of Finance, once an Ultra Liberal, feels himself in such difficulties from the publication of some of his former Speeches & opinions that He pleads ill health and will I think resign before the meeting of the Chambers.

In the mean time the Treaty for the Commercial Union with Prussia at present negotiating at Berlin has given rise to an angry and able discussion in the public prints too important to be passed over in Silence.

Under pretence of arguing a mere commercial Point, (whether it is more advantageous for Southern Germany composed of States enjoying representative Constitutions to unite themselves, politically with France 'the Key Stone of the Liberties of continental Europe or with Prussia whose Sovereign has never fulfilled his Promise of granting liberal institutions to his Subjects') the political Question is in fact the one which is discussed.

The papers in the German Language are very long and if I was to forward the Translations the Attempt to wade through them would be a useless Occupation of your valuable time.

It is sufficient for the purpose to state the Substance of them and I am anxious to do so because I do not think the French Government or at least the French Mission entirely strangers to the publication.

In some points they coincide too remarkably with a Speech of M. Casimir Periers in the Chamber of Deputies some Months ago in which that Minister in reply to an Observation stated 'that it is not worth

---

[19] Sixt Eberhard von Kapff.
[20] Ernst Eugen Freiherr von Hügel.
[21] Karl Eberhard Friedrich Freiherr von Varnbüler.

while for France to enter into a Commercial Union with so small a State as the Grand Duchy of Baden but that if a Union of Constitutional Southern Germany took place it would be worth Consideration in every point of view'.

I noted it at the time and I regret exceedingly at this Moment I cannot lay my hand on the Debate.

I believe it will be better to throw the precis of the paper into an Inclosure and I take the Liberty of drawing Your Lordship's Attention to these Remarks, not because I conceive for one moment that it is of importance to England whether this or that Ministry is in a Majority in Wurtemberg or Baden but I dwell on the Subject because I see in it a wide spreading and well directed plan for encreasing the democratic power in Germany because I see a fair chance of success to a considerable Extent, and because in that Success a tremendous Encrease of French Influence if not a complete Control both commercial and political of that Country over Southern Germany and which I cannot suppose Your Lordship will think unimportant. [...]

I consider the Question of the Treaty of Commerce now negotiating at Berlin as in a great Measure a Question between Prussian and French political Influence in Germany.

Whether that Treaty will be beneficial or the contrary to British Manufactories I here keep quite distinct.

When the former treaty with Prussia[22] was signed the influence of Austria in Germany was very low. The Wheel has now turned. Political Events of the last 18 Months have restored her to her antient Influence in the Cabinets but not in public opinion.

If any Jealousy of Prussia induces Austria to thwart the present Treaty of Commerce I fear the Consequence under actual Circumstances will be an Encrease of French Influence not of Austrian Ascendancy.

The Scene of Combat will shortly be concentrated in the Chamber of Deputies of Wurtemberg and in the Treaty negotiating at Berlin. If Prussia takes for her basis her present high scale of duties I think it will fail.

Would it were equally easy to point out the Remedy.

The Mass of the people are good and still but slightly tainted they have some theoretical and a few practical Evils to complain of All of which the Governments are anxious themselves to remove at least the latter Class.

If the Master Spirit fit to meet the difficulties of the times with firmness and Moderation arises all will soon be right and Germany preserved from sinking under French Influence.

[22] The trade treaty of 27 May 1829 between Prussia and South Germany laid the foundations for a common customs area. The freedom of trade agreed here, however, applied only to domestic products.

But I think he is not yet found. It appears to me that to do good He must arise in one or other of the Representative States of Germany, not in Monarchical Prussia or in despotic Austria.

It must be hoped also that He will be found soon for mischief is in the mean while taking root rapidly.[23]

FO 82/26: Edward Cromwell Disbrowe to Viscount Palmerston, No 23, Stuttgart, 22 May 1832

Partial change of administration in Baden; resistance to Federal Diet's influence on internal affairs; predicted victory of liberty of the press; mass of people allegedly unaffected; Hambach Festival announced

I have the honor to inform Your Lordship that a partial change of Administration important to this part of Germany is about to take place in the Grand Duchy of Baden.

At a Meeting which took place at Manheim last week a certain M[r] Itstein[24] made a speech on the Subject of the Liberty of the Press, in which after passing Encomiums on the Grand Duke and his Government for having proposed the Law[25] on the Liberty of the Press to the last Chamber of Deputies, moved a declaration to the Effect that they were all ready to lay down Lives & fortunes in defence of the Grand Duke & his Authority.

The real Object was to deter the Diet at Frankfort by the Means from making any attempt to induce or compel the Grand Duke to modify the late Law. The Receipt of the Address consequent in the declaration embarrassed the Grand Duke excessively. As on the one hand the Maintenance of the present Law threatens to bring him into Collision with the Confederation, on the other there is very little chance in the temper of the present times, (particularly after the failure of the Government Prosecution of the Freisinigen),[26] that His Royal Highness will be able to induce the Chamber to take the Repeal into their Consideration.

Under these Circumstances the Grand Duke has had Recourse to

[23] Enclosure: Precis; On the Commercial Association between Prussia, Wurtemberg and Bavaria.

[24] Adam von Itzstein.

[25] The press law which lifted censorship in Baden came into effect on 28 December 1831. However, articles dealing with the concerns of the German Confederation and other German states were still excluded from the freedom generally granted to the press.

[26] *Der Freisinnige* was published in Freiburg from March 1832 until it was banned in July 1832. The editors of this organ of the Baden opposition were Karl Rodecker von Rotteck, Friedrich Gottlieb Welcker, and Johann Georg Duttlinger.

the Advice of Monsieur de Reitenstein[27] a Gentleman of an advanced Age formerly in Office and one of the Persons consulted in drawing up the Constitution and He will be shortly become the Grand Dukes Prime Minister.

M de Reitenstein was formerly suspected of a leaning towards France and French Politics.

I dwell on this Nomination because I conceive that in it in some Measure is involved the Question of the Liberty of Press in Germany.

It is expected that Reitenstein will show more firmness than the present Ministers have done, that (had he been in office) He would not have consented to the Law on the Press which was proposed by his Eleve M. de Winter but that that Law being passed He will not consent to a Coup d' Etat.

If therefore the Diet comes to a Conclusion and insists on the modification of that Law in the Grand Duchy in order 'once more to bring its Institutions into harmony with those of the Confederation' He will refer the Case fairly to the Chambers and if a Modification is refused, which I am pretty certain it will be, the Question appears to me decided; the Contest may be carried on some time longer but the Liberty of the Press must within a short period be established in the South of Germany.

I hardly know as yet with what Eye the Communication will be received at this Court, but I do not think it will be well received as if my information is correct it will add to those difficulties which already embarrass the Government in chaining up the Law on the liberty of the Press[28] which shall at once be in harmony with the Times and not militate against the Authority and the Conclusions of the Diet.

Not many Years ago the Centre of the Resistance to the Diet was to be found in this Court whilst that Body relied for support on Baden & Bavaria.

Now its main Support in the South of Germany is to be found here.

In my Correspondence during the last 18 months I have had the honor to point out step by step the changes and Causes of these changes it is therefore unnecessary I should repeat them here.

Your Lordship may also possibly recollect that I have stated that the strong desire for Innovation which is abroad is confined to the Class of Newspapers writers and Professors and that the Mass of the People was still unaffected by it.

The first great Attempt to bring all Classes together is to be made

---

[27] Sigismund Freiherr von Reitenstein.

[28] In Württemberg the freedom of the press was introduced by the press law of 1817, and confirmed by Article 28 of the 1819 constitution. None the less, the Württemberg government excerised censorship.

on Sunday next the 27 May at an old Castle near Neustadt in Rhenish Bavaria.[29]

Persons from Wurtemberg Bavaria and Baden are flocking to it.

The Governor[30] of the Rhenish Bavarian Provinces had prohibited the Meeting but he subsequently allowed it on the Guarantee of a Number of wealthy Individuals of those Provinces that no disturbance and nothing offensive to the Government should take place. I do not think they can fulfil the second part but I do not apprehend a disturbance.

Trees of Liberty as in 1792[31] have been planted in most of the Villages of Rhenish Bavaria but nothing indicative of an Approximation of feeling towards the French has manifested itself.

FO 82/26: Edward Cromwell Disbrowe to Viscount Palmerston, No 32, Stuttgart, 17 July 1832

Public reaction to the 'Six Articles'

I think it my duty to lose no time in referring to the Spirit in which the first news of the Resolutions[32] of the Diet of Frankfort of the 22nd Seance have been received by the public in this part of Germany. [...]

Having already had the honor in my former Despatches to trace out the progress of Public Opinion in the Towns among the Possessors and Editors of Newspapers, and on the other hand among the People of the Country there will remain but a few words to add.

The Liberal Party have received the Intelligence with Consternation. It has been to them a blow which they were not prepared to parry.

They have not however been altogether silent. I can state that in some of the large Towns (as Stutgard Geppingen & Ludwigsburg) they maintain in Conversation that it is equivalent to annulling all the Constitutions of Germany.

I have not however as yet heard of any attempt at assembling to petition or otherwise.

It they do so in Wurtemberg it will be in direct Violation of the Proclamation[33] of the King published previous to the Conclusum, a Proclamation which M. de Weishaar the Minister of the Interior, (a

---

[29] Hambach Festival, cf. pp. 23–26 in Frankfurt section.

[30] Ferdinand Freiherr von Andrian-Werburg.

[31] Trees of liberty, which had been erected in 1792 in the areas on the left bank of the Rhine under French occupation, were a symbol of the French Revolution.

[32] Cf. pp. 35–39 in Frankfurt section.

[33] Political gatherings were forbidden by the ordinance of 12 June 1832. A ban on political associations had been in force since 21 February 1832.

Man much inclined to Liberal Doctrines himself and of the firmness of the Constitution) drew up and countersigned. He must therefore consider it legal; but many of the principal Lawyers have in a public Meeting declared it to be contrary to the Wurtemberg Constitution and such a one as no Court of Law can take cognizance of:

In the Grand Duchy of Baden the Freisinningen[34] has published several very violent Articles on the Subject. [...]

The Paper calls it a death blow to German Liberty one to which they must silently submit or resist but that it will require time to reflect & choose between the two alternatives, that the German Princes are willing Slaves of Austria & Prussia, that the Constitutions are as good as abrogated. It touches on the Right of granting public money. Says that the G^d Duke of Baden was popular because He was believed to be sincere but that He has played a double Part &^{c}; that Baden had set a most glorious Example which is eclipsed by her Sovereign acceding to the Resolutions [,] that from this Side there is no more hope there is but one only one last Remedy, the Power of the People which has legality on its Side, that the People must do nothing contrary to Law that they are despised because they do not know the Use of Arms &^{c}.

A Wurtemberg Newspaper has written quite as violent an Article calling it Tyranny an unconstitutional Proceeding and repeatedly reminding the Sovereigns that Charles X signed his famous Ordinances from the Thuleries[35] & that now he dates from Holyrood.[36]

I mention the latter Article because it was suppressed and can for reasons with difficulty appear in the same Shape in another Paper & what is perhaps more remarkable is that the same weighty Reasons it might have been expected that the particular would have been more moderate in its oppositions to the measure.

I hardly dare take the Liberty of making any remarks on the Redaction of this Conclusum. Some step was become necessary as to the Liberty of the Press & to ensure some Uniformity still I cannot help thinking that if the Declaration had brought more into the front of the Argument the great detriment which the present Excitement, kept up entirely by designing Men, was causing to the Wealth Happiness & prosperity of Germany, instead of relying so much on the Acte finale du Congres de Vienne[37] it would have obtained the support of a

[34] Cf. n. 26 in this section.

[35] The Tuileries, the chief residence of Charles X in Paris.

[36] The ordinances of Charles X (restrictions on press freedom; dissolution of the chamber of deputies; reduction in the number of deputies in parliament; curtailment of the suffrage) triggered the revolution of July 1830 in Paris. After his abdication, Charles found a temporary residence at the Palace of Holyrood House, Edinburgh.

[37] Vienna Final Act of 1820.

valuable Class of Men in the South of Germany who will now at best be neutral.

It certainly appears to Me, as Matters now stand, that it will be impossible to allow the Freisinnigen and other Liberal Papers in the Grand Duchy of Baden to be published without shortly raising a violent Storm.

I have reason to believe that the Cabinet of this Country flatters itself that it has been instrumental in softening down many of the Expressions in these Resolutions but it has not by such Conduct disarmed a single Enemy.

The new Law on the Liberty of the Press in Wurtemberg will of course be framed in Conformity with the Resolutions of the Diet & will I have little doubt be rejected by the Chambers.

A Dissolution therefore and a new Election will probably take place at the beginning of next year.

FO 82/26: Edward Cromwell Disbrowe to Viscount Palmerston, No 35, Stuttgart, 5 August 1832

Württemberg's minister of the interior ignorant of Federal Diet's resolutions; astonishment about Federal Diet's right to interfere

[...] In my former Despatch I mentioned that it was very generally believed that M. De Weishaar holding the important Office of Minister of the Interior was ignorant of the Resolutions of the Diet[38] until they made their appearance and that He disapproved of and refused to countersign them.

Singular as it may appear that M. de Weishaar filling the confidential & high situation of Minster of the Interior should be kept in ignorance of so very important a Measure (to which He must be ultimately made a party) I can assure Your Lordship it is not incompatible with the usual Manner of proceeding in this Country.

The nomination of a Minister by the King of Wurtemberg bears no analogy to a similar Proceeding in Great Britain. Each Minister named separately is only answerable for his own Department and there is not necessarily any Unity in the Administration.

It is true therefore that M. de Weishaar was not made acquainted with the Progress of the negotiation nor with the Resolutions till they appeared. He disapproved of their Policy. He hesitated to sign them. He wished to refer the Matter to the King but He at once admitted

---

[38] Six Articles of 28 June 1832, cf. pp. 35–39 in Frankfurt section.

their Legality and the Obligation this Government was under to submit to the decisions of the Diet.

The same Observations generally will hold good with respect to M. de Reitzenstein & de Winther they likewise admitted the Legality but demurred to the Policy of the Act.

(In the Grand Duchy of Baden there exists a United Responsibility on all the Ministers) [...].

Many persons even those engaged in political Life were ignorant of all the obligations of the States towards the Diet with which they had never previously found themselves so directly in competition, they are astonished at the Right of interference and Extent of protection claimed by Austria and Prussia through the Diet. And although these Resolutions will receive the Sanction and force of Law in each seperate State, I am much mistaken if a quiet but systematic Reaction does not commence almost immediately with the Object in view of curbing the Influence of those two Powers, and if an Opportunity offers many would go even as far as forming a Confederation from which those two Powers would be excluded and such a Measure would even receive the Sanction of several Statesmen who under the present Circumstances have supported the Resolutions of the Diet. [...]

FO 82/26: Edward Cromwell Disbrowe to Viscount Palmerston, No 49, Stuttgart, 30 September 1832

Reaction to Palmerston's note in Württemberg; 'evil' in Germany caused by false system of education; on 'Landsmannschaften' and 'Burschenschaften'

According to Your Lordship's instructions I have communicated to Count Beroldingen, the Minister of Foreign Affairs Your Lordship's despatch to Sir Frederic Lamb dated the 7th September No. 83, and requested His Excellency to put The King of Wurtemberg in full possession of the views of His Majesty's Government on the important question to which it relates.[39]

A few days ago Count Beroldingen in reply informed me that His Majesty had received the communication as a mark of confidence and as such it had given him pleasure.

That the King was far from wishing to dispute the right of Great Britain to interest itself on this question. His Majesty admitted our right to take an interest in it on the specific ground of our being a party to the treaty of Vienna,[40] and on the general grounds that any steps by

[39] Cf. pp. 123–128 in Prussia section.
[40] Act of the Vienna Congress of 9 June 1815.

which the Independence of any of the States of Europe were threatened would affect the general tranquillity.

But His Majesty conceived that the measures taken by the Diet would contribute to restore tranquillity without attacking or injuring any of the separate rights of the States forming the Confederation;

That the Wurtemberg Government had done much to modify the redaction of the six articles,[41] in order that nothing illegal or unconstitutional should be contained in them;

That the union which existed among the discontented rendered it necessary to take some measures; that if these measures were not taken in common some of the Governments might have gone too far, others not far enough, and others again have taken measures not compatible with the existing state of things, and not analogous to the present state of public opinion, and thus have rendered matters worse, and would have ultimately called for even stronger measures in self defence.

Since the above conversation I have had the honor to see His Majesty, when The King in allusion to the despatch said, that as a matter of friendly advice, as it was represented by me to he from one Court to another it was all very well, but he did not exactly see how it was called for. His Majesty trusted that there would be no mistake in supposing that the discontented who had assembled in London,[42] for the purpose of making individual reputation for themselves, were speaking the voice of the German Nations, that if they were not listened to, he did not know who it was that had complained, or on what ground of complaint it was that this advice was now given.

I assured His Majesty that I did not believe that it was grounded on any complaints but was merely meant as the advice of one friendly court to another in a matter of great public interest, and that the communication was directed by a friendly feeling towards the minor Courts of Germany. [...]

The explanation given in the King's name by his Ministers and the Royal declaration from Leghorn of the 3rd of August, have I believe given umbrage at Berlin and Vienna and have been interpreted as a proof of Something like tergiversation on the King of Wurtemberg's part. I am most confident the interpretation is erroneous, that His Majesty never had the slightest intention of ceding one iota of his own Constitutional power, or allowing the Diet to touch in the slightest degree on that of his subjects.

The Committee of the Chambers have declared the 6 articles not to contain any thing unconstitutional.

---

[41] The Six Articles of 28 June 1832 cf. pp. 35–39 in Frankfurt section.

[42] In the summer and autumn of 1832, German emigrants and internationally orientated British liberals met at the Crown and Anchor Tavern in London in order to draft a note

I must add things are much quieter in Wurtemberg than they were, and that many of the liberals and parliamentary Opposition have declared themselves satisfied with the Royal assurances, but add they must watch to see the Diet does not go any further.

The Diet seems resolved to follow up the blow it has struck against the public press by suppressing every periodical publication which in any way displeases it.

The public prints have already furnished the list of these decrees.[43]

It is remarkable that among them is to be found the Allgemeine Europäische Annalen,[44] first published in 1795 and never prosecuted even under Bonaparte.

I am not aware of the exact article which called for this measure of the Diet, but as since the suppression of the Freisinnigen,[45] this periodical has to a certain degree supplied its place, I conceive it to be on account of its general tendency. [...]

Shortly previous to the Hambach feast[46] the Freisinnigen counted 2000 odd hundred subscribers, but on the division which took place among the liberals about that period, they fell off to 1500, so that in fact these newspapers were gradually losing their influence, although I believe unless suppressed, they would not have died out, but they might have been controlled by the Individual States, and have become comparatively innoxious.

I venture to say they would not have died out because there is a Party in Germany, which is not the creation of the newspapers, but who wants a newspaper at its command, nor are they creatures of the French Revolution.

I fear the cause of the evil in Germany lies much deeper and is more difficult to cure. It lies in the false system of education, which for the last 17 years has prevailed in Germany. It takes its rise in the absurd and dangerous constitution of the Universities.

When the excitement among the youth in Germany in 1814 and 1815 had lost its food by the liberation of their Country, and the retreat

---

protesting against the Six Articles. Their aim was to persuade the British government to intervene with the German Confederation.

[43] After the censorship regulations were tightened by the Ten Articles, promulgated on 5 July 1832 (Measures for the Re-establishment of Legal Order and Tranquillity in Germany), the Federal Diet banned a number of publications between July and September 1832.

[44] The journal meant here was the successor publication to the Europäischen Annalen (1795–1820). Also published by the Cotta Verlag, it was edited from 1830 by Karl Rodecker von Rotteck under the title Allgemeine politische Annalen. It was banned by a resolution of the Federal Diet of 16 August.

[45] Der Freisinnige, which was also edited by Karl Rodecker von Rotteck, cf. n. 26 in this section.

[46] Cf. pp. 23–26 in Frankfurt section.

of the French, it looked to some fresh aliment and a point of union, it took refuge in their Universities.

The Landmanschaft and the Bursenschaft[47] took their use, and established their own code of laws not only in spite of the professors, tutors and magistrates, but as a sign of their direct defiance of them, and the proof they gave that the 'Bursen ist frei' (their watchword of freedom) was that they opposed all University regulations merely because they were made and the student, as a free Bursen, would submit to no law not made by his own society and class.

If his own Bursen or society had established law based on common sense, or on any thing like a principle of liberty, such institution might, with all its faults, have sown in the youthful mind some idea of true liberty, which hereafter would have borne its fruit, when matured by age, and have contributed to the happiness of the Country, but the contrary is the case. It is quite notorious that among themselves they enjoyed nothing of freedom but the name. Thus in their meetings to attend which they dare not refuse for fear of losing Cast, they were absolute slaves. They were at liberty to insult a professor provided he had offended their leaders or thrash a citizen, and to do it with impunity, but beyond that circle they were free to do nothing. In short they were in the enjoyment of exactly that species and measure of liberty which the factious demagogue usually allows his favoured followers.

In my earlier acquaintance with Germany I have often heard it argued that such facts though true were of no consequence in a political point of view, as they were absorbed in the general mass, and forgotten on quitting the University. I have long thought the contrary, and I fear this succession of youths educated in their false and nefarious principle of despising all law, merely because it is law, is now beginning to shew its effects, and that we must look deeper than radical newspapers, or French revolutionary doctrines for the cause of the present agitation in Germany.

What I have ventured to state is but an opinion, and perhaps it would be but becoming in me to apologise for venturing to offer it. I may be mistaken, but at least the period at which this agitation had made its appearance coincides with that period of life in which the Individuals who first began this system of education are around at the age of 35 to 40, consequently at that time of life when they are most likely to influence the Government of their Country.

I do not mean that they will endeavour to introduce the absurdities

---

[47] *Landsmannschaften* and *Burschenschaften* were student associations at the German universities. They had been officially banned since 1819, but many continued to exist clandestinely.

of Bursenschaft law into actual life, but I mean to say the early education of these men was founded on a principle of false liberty, and that the symptoms of the present day partake too much of that feeling. It is much more prevalent also in the towns, where these University companions were apt more to meet and discourse over their old fetes than in the Country, where in fact comparatively few if any underwent that system of education, which I have taken the liberty to point out.

But although, I venture to state an opinion that such a system of education has unfortunately established a great latitude of feeling subversive of all law, and is ready to furnish fit tools for the factious demagogues of the day, I beg to guard myself by saying that I do believe that in a majority it is so much softened down by reflection as to leave hopes that that majority are not swayed by their absurd and mischievous theories. Still I cannot help thinking that whilst the German States are attacking the press as the cause they are overlooking the real aliment which keeps alive the flame of discontent. At the same time it must be admitted that a free system of commerce would most considerably contribute to the peace and tranquillity of Germany.

FO 82/27: Edward Cromwell Disbrowe to Viscount Palmerston, No 21, Stuttgart, 14 April 1833

Rumours of Poles arriving from France to assist radical party in Germany

Since I closed my Despatch of yesterday's date an estafette has arrived bringing the intelligence that three or four hundred Poles left the depot at Dijon & Besançon on the 7th and 45 officers of the same nation from other depôts.

Where they are gone to is not yet known – The circumstance of some fires having been seen on the hills in the neighbourhood of Frankfort induces the supposition that they are marching in that direction and that this movement in connected with the late coup de main in that town,[48] though it is not possible they could have reached that neighbourhood on the 12th and they may direct their march on Manheim.

There exists unfortunately much bad blood in the universities of Germany, much excited feeling and but a small portion of judgement to direct it to useful and practical ameliorations; but whatever tumults may be brought about by such means, aided by the hatred which the late measures emanating from the diet have created in a certain class the arrival of any band of foreigners to the assistance of these parties

[48] Cf. pp. 41–45 in Frankfurt section.

is more likely to prove prejudicial, as I am inclined to believe, than useful to their cause.

The facility with which the majority of the conspirators made their escape from Frankfurt carrying some of their wounded, and that with which they have since concealed themselves, the slight attempt at a disturbance at Manheim, and other circumstances indicate a state of feeling which calls for the greatest vigilance on the part of the Governments, but for open resistance or civil war the Country is not prepared. [...]

FO 82/28: Henry Wellesley to Viscount Palmerston, No 32, Stuttgart, 22 May 1834

Württemberg's position on the forcible occupation of the city of Frankfurt in answer to Palmerston's intervention; King not inclined to listen to British advice; conflicting interests between individual states and German Confederation

In obedience to the instructions contained in Your Lordship's despatch No. 7 of the 15th Inst. I yesterday communicated to Monsieur de Maucler, the President of the Wurtemberg Council, who, in Count Beroldingen's continued absence consented to my addressing myself to him, the contents of Your Lordship's despatch No 24 of the same date to Mr Cartwright.[49] After pointing out His Excellency the light in which the forcible occupation of the City of Frankfort by the federal Troops was received by the British Government, I requested that the Wurtemberg Representative[50] at the Diet might be instructed to use his influence for the amicable arrangement of the questions at issue between the City and the Confederation.

As it was only through courtesy that Monsieur de Maucler received my communication, I did not expect him to enter at all into the subject with me. He merely remarked that he did not think that this would become a matter of serious difference between Great Britain and the Diet, but that Frankfort had latterly become the very foyer of revolution, and that it had been absolutely necessary to provide for the personal safety of the representative members of the Confederation. He promised to submit my communication to The King, and to let me know His Majesty's answer as soon as possible.

From private information I fear that His Majesty will not separate Himself from the policy pursued by Austria and Prussia on this occasion.

---

[49] The dispatches mentioned (not included in this volume) referred to the occupation of the Free City of Frankfurt by confederal troops. For the British standpoint cf. pp. 66–68 in Frankfurt section.

[50] August Heinrich Freiherr von Trott zu Solz.

If my informant be correct ere this the decision will have been taken at Vienna to enforce the resolution of the Diet relative to a continued occupation of Frankfort by federal troops, and placing the City under the command of a General to be named by that body, and I have now but little doubt that the Courier[51] mentioned in my despatch No. 31 of the 20th Instant as having been sent from here to Vienna was the bearer of the King of Wurtemberg's adherence to that decision. What with the state of things in Switzerland, and the facility given to revolutionary adventurers to take up their abode there and at Frankfort, and what with the fear inspired by the French propaganda, His Majesty thinks that there is no safety to Germany but in a firm and cordial union of all her States. On this grounds I am afraid that His Majesty, whatever His private opinions may be, will not listen to the advice of the British Government on the present occasion, unless His more powerful Allies take the lead.

It is argued that the interests of an individual State, member of the Confederation must always be subservient to the interest of the Confederation as a body; that if therefore any State becomes the rendezvous of persons promulgating doctrines subversive of the institutions, and dangerous to the welfare and public tranquillity of the other States, and that its Government is either unable or unwilling to get rid of such persons, the Confederation has a right to employ whatever means it may deem advisable for putting an end to the evil. That the Diet of Frankfort must be considered in the same light as the Diet of Switzerland, or the Representative Assembly in the United States of America; that if the latter have the power of enforcing laws in Cantons or States, however much those Cantons and States may dislike them, so has the Germanic Diet the right of enforcing its resolutions, however adverse they may be to the wishes and views of an individual member. That from the moment that a State refuses to acknowledge this principle, it ceases to be a member of the Diet, or the federal Union is at an end. These and such like arguments I have heard from a person much in the King's confidence. Whether he speaks The King's sentiments or not I cannot pretend to say. I report them to Your Lordship, as you may like to know how far arguments can be pushed in support of a measure which the British Government discountenances and condemns.

[51] Not traceable.

FO 82/28: Henry Wellesley to Viscount Palmerston, No 58, Stuttgart, 3 September 1834 (Cypher)

French criticism of smaller courts' obedience to Austria and Prussia

The French Minister[52] represents the French Government to look with much anxiety at the evident tendency that exists among the smaller Courts of Germany to obey without hesitation the dictates of Austria & Prussia, in all measures, whether of internal administration, or as regarding their relations with Foreign Countries, that it may seem good to those two Courts to propose.

FO 82/29: Lord William Russell to Duke of Wellington, No 1, Stuttgart, 4 January 1835

English language newspaper published in Stuttgart; censorship forces Germans to seek information from liberal foreign press

A newspaper[53] published in the English language made its appearance in this town on the 1st Instant. The object of the publisher[54] is to circulate through Germany a paper conducted on the model of Galignani's Messenger,[55] the price of which is too high to enable many persons to read it. The success of this new publication will indicate an encreased cultivation of the English language amongst the German People.

The publisher has probably been tempted to engage the speculation by the immense sale of French newspapers in Germany, which is to be attributed to the excessive severity of the censorship of the German Press, a severity carried to lengths not only absurd, but offensive to the German people, by shewing a distrust of their prudence, which they consider unjust, and a desire to withhold the truth from them, which they consider a useless precaution. This, like all state policy partial to extremes, has operated in a sense diametrically opposed to the intention of the legislators who schackled the press, that is, it has forced the Germans to seek for that information from a free foreign press, which they ought to obtain from their own, the consequence of which is, an enormous sale of French papers to the detriment of the German, French publicists receiving the profits of the Germans, French opinions

---

[52] Anne Louis Gabriel, vicomte de Fontenay.

[53] *Stuttgart Evening Post*; it contained the latest news from English, French and North-American Journals.

[54] Paul Neff.

[55] *Galignani's Messenger*, an English-language newspaper which had been published in Paris since 1814.

and tastes propagated, and above all a general conviction of public feeling by French agitators finding ground unoccupied on which they can sow their vitiating seed, productive only of agitation and discontent, indeed the only produce they desire. The Tribune,[56] French paper, was lately prohibited by the Diet from circulating in public reading rooms, which has only encreased its sale by adding to its individual subscribers, a strong proof of the ardour of the Germans to read all that is published, and of the inefficiency of the federative laws to prevent them. Had the German Diet sought to encourage its own Press by granting it more freedom, whilst it restrained its licentiousness, it would have been a support to all existing Governments, and the soreness and irritability that now prevails would have been removed. As it is the position taken by the Diet is full of difficulty and danger – to add to the restrictions on the press will add to the discontent. – to take them off will be to expose themselves to a torrent not easily controlled. Yet I consider the latter of the least dangerous course of the two, for the liberty of the press is the great object of the German People, and they will never rest satisfied until they have obtained it.

The paper of which I send Your Grace an example, does not appear to have any political views.[57]

FO 82/29: Lord William Russell to Duke of Wellington, No 8, Stuttgart, 12 March 1835

Death of Emperor of Austria; speculations on future political course of his son; question of Austria's future influence in German affairs

The death of the Emperor of Austria has made a deep sensation in Southern Germany. All classes had the greatest respect for the character of that excellent Monarch; but besides sincere sorrow, His death has given rise to vague conjectures as to what will be the policy pursued by the Reigning Emperor, and what influence that policy will have on the general system of Germany. All are agreed in regarding the death of the Emperor Francis as a link broken in the chain that held together the different States, and made them act as one body. The Emperor's character, His efforts during the revolutionary war, and the circumstance of His having been crowned Emperor of Germany, whereby He had a fast hold in traditionary recollections still cherished by Germans, had

[56] *La Tribune des Départements*, a republican newspaper of the radical opposition, established in 1829.

[57] Enclosures: 1. *Evening Post*, No. 1, Stuttgart, 1 January 1835; 2. *Albion: A Weekly Chronicle of Literature, Science and the Fine Arts*, No. 1, Stuttgart, 4 January 1835.

together placed a Power in His hands, and given Him an authority over the Councils of the Confederation, which will not be inherited by His Son[58] with the Imperial Crown. Prussia will probably attempt to exercise this Power. The Commercial Union gives her an excuse for sending her Agents into every State – Her efforts will be supported by Russia with the hope that her own influence will be extended, and by the liberal party with the hope that Prussia will become constitutional, and give a protecting hand to Constitutional States. Unless Austria can counterpoise by some external support this fearful union of separate interests, she must sink from the high station she has held amongst the Nations of Europe. [...]

FO 82/29: Lord William Russell to Viscount Palmerston, No 18, Stuttgart, 3 June 1835

King's opinion on the state of things in Germany; his attitude towards the Federal Diet

[...] I had a long Conversation with His Majesty on the State of Germany. I told him it was Your Lordship's opinion that the stability of the German Constitutional Governments, and the peace of Europe depended, very much on the smaller Powers not allowing themselves to be coerced by the Diet into the Commission of acts that might be considered by people to militate against their Constitutional rights. His Majesty said that the interests and privileges of His subjects always had been and always should be His first consideration, but that at the same time it was necessary to promote and ensure such prefect harmony in the Diet as would enable all Germany to act like one Nation against foreign aggression and He thought that much good would arise from the Commercial Union, which would gradually lead to an identity of laws, money, &[59] that would tend to consolidate and strengthen the German Empire, which, constituted as it is, was an object to be desired, whilst the plan now agitated of creating one vast Empire or Republic was pernicious and chimerical. His Majesty thought the German People too much attached to their respective Governments, and too much guided by the antecedents of History ever to consider favorably a change so complete and experimental. The notion is however actively propagated by many able writers. [...]

---

[58] Ferdinand.
[59] Space left in original.

FO 82/29: Lord William Russell to Viscount Palmerston, No 19, Stuttgart, 16 June 1835

Public opinion in Southern Germany

The Policy of the King of Wurtemberg is so dove-tailed into that of the Germanic Diet, that no event of importance can occur here which would not either arise immediately from, or bear eventually upon the general interests of all the States united by the Confederation.

I will therefore endeavour to make Your Lordship acquainted with public opinion in Southern Germany. Such at least as appears to me after six months residence.

Two Opinions are in conflict, and approaching daily nearer to collision, the one is conservative or for maintaining things as they are; the other progressive or for reforming abuses, the first is supported by the Courts and Aristocracy, the second by the Mass of the People engaged in Literature Commerce and Agriculture. Men of Letters demand the liberty of the Press, commercial men the free navigation of rivers, and the Agricultural interest will not rest satisfied until Tithes are abolished whilst all Classes are united in their condemnation of the interference of the Diet in the internal affairs of the smaller States, which paralyses all their efforts to do themselves justice. So this interference is in some degree to be attributed the slow progress that this Party has made in obtaining its ends, but it may be still more attributed to their own variety of opinions as to the mode of action to be followed. Some were for relying entirely upon France, and coercing their own Government through her means, but now loudly accuse the King of the French of having abandoned them. Others prefer to rely upon their own resources, and propose to constitute Germany into the vast Empire, whose Power can protect them from the arbitrary opinions of Russia on one hand, and the vascillating opinions of France on the other, This idea is pleasing to Yeomen in acumination and is gaining ground aided by many able writers. Lately the liberal Party has looked towards England, where events[60] are watched with intense anxiety, not in the belief that any political assistance will be afforded to them, but from the conviction that the Yeomans will be encouraged by the example of the English to demand reforms more stoutly that they have hitherto done. This feeling caused the return to office of the present British Ministry to be viewed by the Court Party with vexation and regret, by the popular party with joy and hope.

The conservative Party defends the system pursued by pointing out the general well-being and contentment of the Yeoman People, and

---

[60] Cf. n. 79 in Prussia section.

the necessity of preserving Union in the Diet, but a most material fact is lost sight of. Which is that the Confederation instead of having consolidated the Power and Strength of Germany, has diffused her Power, and paralysed her Strength. Germany is dependant upon events in France, and subject to their immediate influence, consequently her tranquillity is never secure, but she lies still more at the mercy of the smallest of her Native Sovereigns, should any one of them from ambition, from pique or from conscientious motives, declare his independance the clumsy machinery that upholds the Diet would fall to pieces, and his will would be irresistable. This is a temptation never averted from their eyes, & is the cause of much suspicion, and a system of watching and reporting, to which none are more subject than the King of Wurtemberg, owing to his former liberal opinions.

A Remedy to this unsatisfactory state of things might be found in concessions to public opinion, a remedy however that will not be resorted to so long as a chance remains of maintaining the present system. That chance tho diminished is not hopeless, for it is not probable that convulsions will arise in Germany whilst France remains tranquil, and the war of words and pens may continue for years without producing any result, but it can scarcely be doubted that an outbreak in France against the established Authority, would be followed by the same consequences in the South of Germany extending rapidly to the North and East. The important fact to be deduced from the actual state of things is this. That the confederation is weak and that its means of defending Germany against foreign aggression would probably fail in the hour of need, not from any deficiency of the composition of its troops but from the general wish of the German People to rid themselves of the arbitrary Government of the Diet.

FO 82/30: George Shee to Viscount Palmerston, No 12, Stuttgart, 6 March 1836

Debate on the law for the redemption of seigniorial rights; proposals

The question which I reported to Your Lordship in my despatch No. 4 dated January 23rd [61] as likely to occupy the Chambers during the present Session, namely, the law for the redemption of the Seignorial rights enjoyed by the Nobles, has at length, and after much acrimonious discussion been disposed of in the second Chamber.

They have acceded to the proposed arrangement upon the following terms.

---

[61] Not included in this volume.

The seignorial rights are to be surrendered by the present possessors at twenty years purchase, upon an estimated value; ten years of the purchase money to be paid by the Individual, over whom those rights are exercised for personal services: and sixteen years for services derived from occupation of land; the remainder of the purchase money in both cases to be paid by the Government, who, moreover, in every instance in which two thirds of a Commune signify within the space of three years their willingness to purchase, undertake to advance the whole purchase money for each individual in that commune, receiving back the amount from them afterwards by periodical instalments. In those Communes in which such consent shall not have been signified within three years, the individuals are to be left to their own means of liquidation. The value of the services to be redeemed is to be estimated upon a moderate reduction from its marketable price, and the reduction is to be made upon the principle that compulsory and reluctant service must necessarily be less efficient than that for which remuneration is received. The question was carried in the second Chamber by a majority of 72 to 14 – Of the latter number eight were of the rank of Nobles (ordre equestric) who objected to any sale at all of the seignorial rights, and six were of the extreme opposition, who, for a very different reason, equally disapproved of any purchase. The members of the Equestrian order who voted for the proposed arrangement were four in number. Three of those yielded their assent in the avowed hope that the measure would undergo important modifications in the Upper Chamber, and one only professed a patriotic motive for his vote.

The bill has now been carried into the Upper Chamber, and the prevailing opinion seems to be that it will there be forthwith rejected.

FO 82/35: George Shee to Viscount Palmerston, No 58, Stuttgart, 12 November 1839

Federal Diet's interference in discussions between Hanover and Württemberg

Having heard it stated that the Diet at Frankfort had interfered authoritatively in certain discussions which had arisen between the Courts of Hanover and Wurtemberg, and in which the Hanoverian Government had applied to the Diet for assistance I took the opportunity this morning of asking Count Beroldingen whether there was any truth in the report.

From Count Beroldingens reply it would appear that the following is the state of the Case.

The Corporations of Hanover having some time ago referred to certain Foreign Universities of which that of Tubingen was one, for their opinion upon the great Constitutional question[62] then at issue, between their Sovereign and themselves. The University of Tubingen expressed on their part an opinion favorable to the Claims of the Corporations and hostile to he pretensions of the King.

This reply of the University of Tubingen together with the answers of the other Universities having been afterwards printed and published as a collective Document at Weimar, the Government of Hanover addressed a complaint at the Würtemberg Government against the Professors of Tubingen for the opinions which they appeared in that Document to have expressed upon the subject, and in consequence of that opinion demanded their dismissal. In reply the Government of Wurtemberg, explained first that the Professors of Tubingen had themselves not consented to the publication in question. Secondly That the publication took place in Weimar not in Würtemberg and thirdly, that even had the Document been published in Würtemberg, its pages exceeded the Number to which the Law of Censorship in Germany extends.[63] Under these Circumstances the Government of Würtemberg declined adopting any measures of severity against the Professors of Tubingen, beyond a reprimand which from the intemperate language of one passage they appeared to have justly incurred.

Count Beroldingen then admitted it to be true that the Hanoverian Government not satisfied with the above answer from the Government of Würtemberg had appealed to the Diet upon the subject, and that the decision of the Diet[64] carried by a very small Majority was hostile to the Professors of Tubingen, Count Beroldingen however stated that the decision merely suggested that the Wurtemberg Government should inflict some severer punishment upon the Professors but did not in any way attempt to prescribe to the Government of Würtemberg any mode of proceeding in the Case. As far as I could collect from Count Beroldingen the Government of Wurtemberg would on no account have submitted to dictation upon the subject and in point of fact the whole question seems now to be considered as virtually at an end.

[62] Cf. pp. 263–264 in Hanover section and pp. 85–88 in Frankfurt section.

[63] Under the terms of the Federal Press Law of 20 September 1819, publications longer than 320 pages were exempted from pre-censorship.

[64] On 30 September 1839 the further dissemination of the document produced by the law faculty of the University of Tübingen on 26 January 1839 was banned by the Federal Diet. At the same time the government of Württemberg was instructed, under the terms of the Federal Press Law of 1819, to prosecute the Tübingen professors for their personal misdemeanours.

FO 82/36: Henry Wellesley to Viscount Palmerston, No 7, Stuttgart, 19 July 1840

Conversation with M. von Blittersdorf about the construction of new federal fortresses

Since I had the honor of addressing Your Lordship on the 10th Inst, respecting the Military Commission[65] which has been sitting at Carlsruhe, I have had an opportunity of conversing with Monsr de Blittersdorff who presided over it. Monsr de Blittersdorff entered at great length into the circumstances which had given rise to the formation of this Commission.

He said that ever since the idea of constructing a new federal Fortress had been seriously entertained, so many different opinions as to the most eligible place had been broached, that it seemed almost impossible to reconcile them all. Austria proposes Ulm, as the strongest Town from its natural situation, thinking that Rastadt was too near France, and liable to fall into the hands of the French at the first attack. She also made it a condition of her agreeing to the fortification even of Ulm, that it should be garrisoned solely by Austrian Troops. The King of Wurtemberg demanded that the approaches to the Black Forrest should be secured, without which His Whole Kingdom was open to invasion, and was therefore in favor of Rastadt, though He had no objection to Ulm being fortified also, and Baden for similar reasons supported Wurtemberg; while Bavaria would have neither Rastadt nor Ulm, but insisted on Germersheim. Lastly, Prussia, though less interested in the question, supported Austria from an unwillingness to give her Umbrage.

Such being the State of the question the four smaller Powers, Bavaria, Wurtemberg, Baden, and Hesse Darmstadt, agreed to meet in Conference at Carlsruhe and to endeavour to come to some decision upon a common line of policy to be pursued before the Diet and their Plenipotentiaries have at length drawn up a convention containing the following propositions to be submitted to that body.

1 That Ulm and Ratsadt should both be fortified, and a Tête du pont erected at Germersheim at the expence of the Confederation.
2 That for the execution of the latter part of the plan, a small exchange of territory should be made between Bavaria and Baden.
3 That these Fortresses should not be garrisoned by federal Troops in time of peace, but by the Troops of the respective Countries in which they are situated.

[65] The *Bundesmilitärkommission* was set up in 1819 by the resolution of the Federal Diet in order to organize and supervise the military concerns of the German Confederation. It met in a number of different places by turns.

4 That as the Twenty Millions already existing[66] would not suffice for the execution of this plan, the remainder should be paid by the Confederation.

Mons[r] de Blittersdorff anticipates great opposition to these proposals on the part of Austria, and thinks that she will agree to nothing, which does not place the defence of Ulm, entirely and unreservedly in her hands, but there were, he said, so many inconveniences attending the system of placing foreign Garrisons in the federal Fortresses, that the countries interested would do all in their power to oppose it on the present occasion. It wounded the national feelings of the inhabitants, and the Army to see one of their Towns surrendered to Foreign Troops, as if their own were not competent to defend it, and there were besides continual jealousies and disagreements with the persons placed in command. They were perfectly willing to agree that the plans of fortification should be submitted for the approval of the other States, members of the Confederation, who should also have the right of inspecting the fortresses at any Moment, and even a Voice in the appointment of the Officers to command them, but Mons[r] de Blittersdorff is afraid that this will not satisfy Austria, and that the whole question will eventually be deferred on account of her opposition although he assured me that Prussia had latterly promised to support the proposals when brought before the Diet.

Mons[r] de Blittersdorff observed in continuation that this was a question, which was not only of importance to the Countries more immediately concerned but to all Europe likewise, and he proceeded to explain to me, the advantages which he thought were to be derived from the plan proposed.

At this moment, he said, neither Baden, Wurtemberg, nor Bavaria could oppose a sudden invasion from France, they must be overpowered, their Countries overrun, and their Governments in all probability forced to adopt a policy they repudiated. But in the event of these Fortresses being constructed, there would be a line of Fortifications on the Rhine, garrisoned by 100,000 Men, who at all events could keep an enemy sufficiently in check, to give time for the assembling of larger forces in their rear. He thought that Germany might then be considered as in no danger from foreign invasion. He observed likewise that in the event of any thing like a revolutionary spirit manifesting itself in Germany these Fortresses would go far to repress it, and to maintain internal tranquillity, on which the strength of a Country depended as much as on her other resources. He concluded by saying that it was for the Members of the Diet to consider these advantages and if they

[66] Cf. n. 208 in Frankfurt section.

rejected the proposals about to be made to it, they would be responsible for the consequences which would inevitably ensue on the breaking out of any future War.

I asked Monsr de Blittersdorff whether in the event of any Town being fixed on by the Diet, it was in the power of the Sovereign of the Country, in which it was situated, to refuse to allow of its being fortified, and he told me that it certainly was.

Such, My Lord, is the substance of the Statement made to me by Monsr de Blittersdorff, but I have since been informed, that although Prussia was at one moment inclined to act as he describes, she has since changed her tone. It seems that when the Arch Duke Albert went to Berlin to congratulate The King on His accession to the Throne, he was instructed to press strongly on His Majesty, the Views of Austria with respect to Ulm and that The King has since declared that in this as in all other Matters his policy will be directed by His fathers last will, and that he holds himself bound to act in concert with Austria.

The King of Wurtemberg has likewise insisted on the whole of the existing twenty Millions being expended on the fortification of Rastadt alone, and that the expence of the others, if carried into effect, shall be borne by the Confederation at large, but it remains to be seen whether the Northern States will not demur at being called upon to contribute towards the erection of Fortresses from which they can derive no immediate advantage. [67]

FO 82/36: George Shee to Viscount Palmerston, No 29, Stuttgart, 9 October 1840

King of Württemberg on European state of affairs, France's aggression in particular; Metternich's vanishing influence

During the Audience which I had the honor of having yesterday of The King of Wurtemberg, His Majesty entered at great length into the present state of affairs in Europe. [68]

He commenced by asking me how I thought this crisis was likely to terminate, I answered that threatening as appearances might be as far as I was informed, I had every hope that the peace of Europe would not be disturbed, and such I believed also to be Your Lordship's opinion, and that I could at all events assure Him that no endeavours would be wanting on the part of Her Majesty's Government to preserve

---

[67] Enclosure: *Grossherzoglich Badisches Staats- und Regierungsblatt*, Carlsruhe, 9 February 1843.
[68] Cf. n. 210 in Frankfurt section.

it. In short I conceived that nothing but the most wanton aggression or a declaration of war, on the part of France could disturb that tranquillity which had now so long existed and that considering that a War let it be successful or not for France would probably lead to the fall of the Orleans dynasty the danger of breaking the peace would not be lightly risked by the King of the French.

His Majesty said that he was inclined also to think that there was no immediate danger still He could not contemplate without anxiety the continued Armaments of France. Her Government might really intend them only for defence, but any one who knew the internal State of France must be aware that it was a dangerous thing to have 500,000 Men on foot, and that the caprice of a Minister or the slightest shew of popular feeling might convert what was meant only for defence into an engine of Attack. He thought also that Monsieur Thiers would find it very difficult to make an honorable retreat from the position which he had taken up, and He hoped that his fall would be the consequence.

His Majesty went on to say that though this Country was small they were equally interested in great European questions, that its frontier was within four days march of the french frontier and open to the first attack. 'Thanks' He said, 'to Mons.r de Metternich who has so long prevented a fortress being built to defend us. But his influence among us is gone. His policy has always been to forward the interests of Austria at the expence of those of the rest of Germany, and he may depend upon it, that let the events turn out as they may, our eyes are open to the mischief he has done, and it will not be his councils that will direct us.'

He was not satisfied in general with the organisation of the Austrian Army and was afraid that in the event of a war its insufficiency would be severely felt.

His Majesty continued that He had been much gratified by the behavior of the troops at the late Manoeuvres, and that the French Officers who were present had confessed they were surprised at the excellence of them. [...]

FO 82/38: George Shee to Viscount Palmerston, No 24, Stuttgart, 29 May 1841

Dissatisfaction about Commercial Treaty between Great Britain and states of the Commercial Union; hostile feelings also in Württemberg

Your Lordship has I presume learned from other sources that the

Commercial Treaty[69] lately concluded between Great Britain and the States composing the Germanic Commercial Union has excited great dissatisfaction in several of those States.

That dissatisfaction so far as Bavaria, Hesse Darmstadt, and Baden are concerned had it appears been loudly expressed through the medium of the Public Journals, but until within the last few days I had no reason to believe that it had extended to this Country.

Now however it appears that in Wurtemberg also a feeling hostile to the Provisions of that Treaty has arisen, and it has manifested itself, first in Articles written with some bitterness upon the subject – inserted in the Augsburg Gazette.[70] Secondly – In meetings of various Merchants and Manufacturers of Wurtemberg for the discussion of the Treaty which they consider to be a grievous infliction upon them. Thirdly – In the preparation and presentation of an Address to The King by those Individuals praying His Majesty to exercise the right reserved to Him by the Treaty of cancelling it at the expiration of the present Year.

Upon learning the above facts I took no time in calling upon Count Beroldingen to enquire from him the particulars of the Case, and above all to ascertain if possible the course which it was the intention of the Wurtemberg Government to pursue respecting it.

In reply the Count informed me, that beyond all question a strong feeling had been excited in Wurtemberg against the Treaty in question. And that it was also true that the Address to which I alluded had been presented to The King. But he assured me that neither The King himself nor His Majesty's Government had any intention whatever of yielding to the panic which prevailed.

The objections made to the Treaty by the complaining parties appear from Count Beroldingen's report to have been in substance as follows.

First – They state that England from the right which the Treaty gives her of entrance into the Elbe and Weser and other Rivers named therein would through the great extent of her general Commerce be enabled to penetrate into the heart of Germany, with goods of which the sale would interfere with Manufactories already existing there, while those States including Wurtemberg which would suffer from such Sales, would from the small extent of their Commercial transactions derive no counterbalancing advantage from the right which the Treaty gives them of admission into the Ports of Great Britain.

Secondly – That the Article which grants to Great Britain the

[69] Convention of Commerce and Navigation between Great Britain, on the one part, and Prussia, Bavaria, Saxony, Wurtemberg, Baden, the Electorate of Hesse, the Grand Duchy of Hesse, the States forming the Customs and Commercial Union of Thuringia, Nassau, and Frankfurt, on the other part; signed at London, 2 March 1841.

[70] *Allgemeine Zeitung*, cf. n. 33 in Bavaria section.

privilege of introducing Rice and Sugar into the States of the Germanic Union upon the footing of the most favored Nations might eventually be productive of serious inconvenience to the Kingdom of Wurtemberg. The complainants pretend for instance that it might hereafter be of great advantage to Wurtemberg to enter into Commercial Treaties with France or perhaps with Belgium, and that great advantages might perhaps be obtained by Wurtemberg from either of those States if the power existed of granting to them a preference over England in the importation of the Articles above mentioned. That such preference perhaps might form the only effective equivalent which they could offer for the advantages which they would be desirous of obtaining, and that the Treaty therefore in question might eventually be closing a most important avenue to the Commercial prosperity of the Country.

Thirdly – The Complainants state that it has always been deemed an essential object with the States of the Germanic Union to obtain the accession thereto of Hanover and the Hanseatic Towns. But that that object would now be in all probability frustrated for that at the present moment those States are under no obligation to admit the Rice and Sugar of England upon the footing of the most favored Nations.[71] Whereas by the provisions of the Treaty in question every State becoming a Member of the Germanic Union must at the same time become a party to that Treaty. Such a necessity therefore – they say – must of course materially increase the reluctance which the above mentioned States have hitherto manifested to the junction, and without that junction the complainants insist that the Confederation can never as to its essential objects be considered complete.

The above objections my Lord on the part of the Wurtemberg Complainants, might as Your Lordship will perceive be easily disposed of, but in my interview with Count Beroldingen I found it quite unnecessary to discuss them. Count Beroldingen on the contrary assured me that The King had received the Address presented to Him by the Wurtemberg Traders with much displeasure, that He had distinctly informed them that they utterly misunderstood the Question upon which they had taken upon themselves to express their Sentiments to Him and finally that He has had dismissed them without giving them the smallest encouragement to expect any change on His part in the course which he had thought proper to pursue.

---

[71] Britain concluded trade treaties to this effect with Hanover on 12 June 1824, and with the Hanse Towns of Lübeck, Bremen, and Hamburg on 19 September 1825.

FO 82/38: George Shee to Viscount Palmerston, No 4, Carlsruhe, 27
July 1841

Animated discussion in Baden's second chamber about the so-called 'Urlaubsstreit'

Since the assembling of the Chambers[72] in this Capital the Second
Chamber has been engaged in various discussions – some of them
extremely animated – upon a subject in itself of no great moment, but
important from a Constitutional principle which it involved.

Two Individuals[73] holding subordinate Offices under Government
being at the same time Members of the Second Chamber. The Grand
Duke was advised to forbid their quitting their Official duties for the
discharge of their Legislative functions. It does not appear that these
Individuals were of any consideration personal or official, but the cause
of the proceedings was as follows.

According to the Constitution of Baden the Officers of Government
are not removable, except for flagrant disobedience of Orders or by
modes of proceeding of which the practical difficulties are considered
insurmountable. But many of these Individuals having become Members
of the Second Chamber have been engaged for some time past in
organizing a formidable opposition to the Government. Their strength
is now very considerable, their principles appear to be democratic, and
Government in apprehension of the mischief to which the combination
might ultimately lead, have at length adopted the above expedient as
affording the only means by which their scheme could be defeated.

The opposition on the other hand perceiving at once the drift and
tendency of the course which the Government were pursuing determined to resist it at the outset. They instantly therefore protested
against the prohibition which the Government had issued declared that
their Assembly was incomplete so long as the secluded Members were
prevented from attending, and passed a very strong resolution denying
peremptorily the right of the Government to exercise the Authority
which it had assumed.

This resolution was to have been presented to the Grand Duke in
the form of an Address. But by the Baden Constitution no Address can
be presented to the Grand Duke by a single Chamber, the Concurrence
of both being required and in this Address the Upper Chamber
unanimously refused their acquiescence.

Foiled in this object the opposition then caused Addresses to be
prepared in some of the principal Towns of Baden for presentation to
the Second Chamber, approving of the Conduct of the opposition

---

[72] The *Landtag* assembled on 17 April 1841.
[73] Joseph Peter und Gerhard Adolf Aschbach.

party and censuring the Government to which they were opposed. These Addresses after some resistance upon the part of the Government were received. But as no ulterior proceeding could by the Constitution of the Baden Legislature be founded upon them, Monsieur de Itzstein the Leader of the Opposition, a man of dangerous principles but considerable ability, brought forward a new resolution declaring the incompetency of the Second Chamber to pursue their deliberations during the compulsory absence of the Individuals who had been forbidden to attend.

This resolution the Government were fortunate enough to defeat by a Majority of 14 Votes, and the consequence of the Victory has been that the whole struggle has for the present terminated. The opposition retaining their original protest upon their records, and the Government on the other hand declaring that they will persevere in the Course of proceeding which they have adopted.

At some future time the Contest will probably be revived.

In the mean time I am happy to inform Your Lordship that no attempt has been made by the opposition party to interrupt the ordinary march of Government. The Supplies have been voted, the renewal of the Germanic Commercial Union has been agreed to, and all the other measures have been passed which the Government had brought forward for the general benefit of the Country.

FO 82/40: George Shee to Earl of Aberdeen, No 27, Confidential, Stuttgart, 30 May 1842

Course which Baden government means to pursue in present crisis; opposition gains strength; government determined not to make concessions; tensions between government and chambers continue; ministerial plan of operation to strengthen governmental party; appeal to Federal Diet hopefully avoidable

With reference to my Despatch N° 25 dated the 27th Inst.[74] in which I apprized Your Lordship of the reopening of the Baden Chambers, and of the communication addressed to them upon that occasion by Monsieur de Rüdt[75] – the Minster of Interior – I have now to acquaint Your Lordship that since the transmission of my Despatch, the Chargé d'Affaires of Baden[76] at this Court has shown to me confidentially a

[74] Not included in this volume.
[75] Franz Freiherr Rüdt von Collenberg-Eberstadt. On 20 May, on the re-opening of the *Landtag*, Rüdt announced 'that the only subjects with which they would have to occupy themselves during the remainder of the session, would be the completion of the Budget for the Years 1842 and 1843'.
[76] Ludwig Freiherr Rüdt von Collenberg-Bödigheim.

Circular, upon the subject which has been recently been addressed by Monsieur de Blittersdorf to the Diplomatic Ministers of Baden at Foreign Courts, and of which the object is to explain to those Ministers the course which the Baden Government mean to pursue in the present crisis of Affairs.

The general impression appears to be, although the fact is not absolutely ascertained, that the party opposed to the Government again possesses a Majority in the Second Chamber, and further that in the prosecution of the hostility which they have been long carrying on against the Government they mean again to take every possible advantage of their strength.

On the other hand however it is evident from Monsieur de Blittersdorf's circular that the Grand Ducal Government are quite determined to make no concession whatever to that party but that they have resolved to resist to the utmost any proceedings on their part that might either endanger the Authority or be inconsistent with the dignity of The Grand Duke.

Your Lordship will in the fist place have remarked in my last Despatch that when the Chambers reassembled not only was no speech delivered to them by the Grand Duke himself, but that His Minister of the Interior in his address to them consented himself with simply prescribing to them the subjects for their future deliberations. In addition to this however Monsieur de Blittersdorf states that The Grand Duke purposely abstained even from showing to the Individual Members of the lower Chambers upon their reassembling any of those personal courtesies which are usual upon such occasion. He added that this system will be continued during the progress of the present Session and that the personal attentions of The Grand Duke to Individual Members will in future be strictly regulated by the conduct which each Member may pursue.

In the next place Monsieur de Blittersdorf states that the utmost efforts are immediately to be used for the formation of a Government party in the lower Chambers, a party which has not as yet existed there, but which however weak at first, will it is expected increase gradually in strength and it is hoped, should the Session last, that what in England is called a working Majority may ultimately be obtained.

Thirdly – It has been determined that the Ministers who although possessing no Votes in the lower Chambers have a right to appear there and to speak as they habitually do upon subjects under discussion shall during the present Session not avail themselves of their privilege unless when absolutely necessary, and further that they shall refuse to answer any questions that may be put to them by Members of the opposite party, except after formal Notice and upon days previously fixed upon for their replies.

Fourthly – It has been determined that if the opposition party in confidence of their strength, shall again evince their intention to adopt any course of proceeding by which the March of the Government may be impeded and that they shall appear likely to succeed in their designs, such intentions shall be at once met and counteracted by another dissolution and

Lastly – It has been resolved that should the extreme case occur that the opposition availing themselves of their power, shall adopt at once measures by which not only the course of the Government might be obstructed but the principles of the Constitution be infringed, then that the Baden Government in discharge of that duty which binds them to the preservation of the Constitution shall at once tender to the Grand Duke their advice that His Royal Highness at the same time that He dissolves the Chambers shall make his appeal upon the subject to the Germanic Confederation, praying that the Constitution of His Country which is under the protection of that Body,[77] and which in its working has at length proved itself unequal to fulfill the proposes for which it was framed, may be carefully revised by them and undergo such modifications at their hands as may enable The Grand Duke to exercise those powers to which he is legally entitled, and which he has no desire to employ but for the real welfare of His People.

From the Ministerial Plan of operations which I have above described Your Lordship will perceive that the State of Public Affairs at Baden is at the present moment somewhat critical; and from all that I can learn of the relative strength and the mutual feelings of the contending parties I fear that the struggle must terminate in a fresh dissolution of the Chambers.

The appeal to the Diet however I trust will be avoided, and it seems most desirable that it should, for however small the Theatre of Action, the conflict must be between the Monarchical and the Democratic principles, and but little benefit can result either to Germany itself or to Europe at large from having those principles brought any where at the present moment into direct and open collision.

---

[77] Article 56 of the Vienna Final Act of 1820 enshrined the protection of the constitutions in the states of the German Confederation.

FO 82/40: George Shee to Earl of Aberdeen, No 85, Stuttgart, 18 November 1842

Railroad projects

The Committee of the Chamber of Deputies who have been employed for some time past in considering the Question of Rail Roads to be established in The Kingdom of Wurtemberg, have at length decided upon recommending three lines for the adoption of the Chambers when they reassemble.

One is to be in a Western direction towards the Frontiers of Baden.

A second to the East and South will be carried to Ulm and then descend to Friedrichs Hafen. And a third – a species of Cross Road is to be carried from Plochingen by Reutlingen and Tubingen to Rothenburg.

This last Road however will it is thought be left as an object of private speculation, the State guaranteeing $3\frac{1}{2}$ p C^t Interest upon the Capital to be subscribed for it.

I am further informed upon good Authority that of all the above Rail Roads, that which will lead to Friedrichs Hafen on the lake of Constance, is the Road which the Government intend to press primarily and most urgently upon the attention of the Chambers.

FO 82/42: Henry Wellesley to Earl of Aberdeen, No 3, Stuttgart, 5 January 1843

Georg Herwegh's interview with the King of Prussia; King of Württemberg's embarrassment

I should hardly venture to call Your Lordship's attention to an interview with which the King of Prussia lately favored a person of the name of Herwegh (an account of which the latter caused to be published in a Leipzig newspaper)[78] were it not that it has given great umbrage to the King of Wurtemberg.

This Herwegh was a soldier in the Wurtemberg Army, but made himself so obnoxious, by the Republican doctrines which he disseminated, and the insubordination, which he showed, that he was dismissed the Army, or rather he was given an unlimited leave of absence, in order to get rid of him. He has since published some works in which the same republican principles are advocated.

He however managed to get himself presented to the King of Prussia by Dr Schönlein His Majesty's Physician, and according to the account

[78] Cf. pp. 204–205 in Prussia section.

he sent to the newspapers of what passed at the interviews he was treated by His Majesty with much condescension, and his opinions were made rather the subject of joke than serious animadversion.

This has given great offence to the King of Wurtemberg the more so, as His Majesty has taken every opportunity of shewing his respect and partiality for the King of Prussia. It is to be hoped that the measures taken by the latter Monarch, of prohibiting the Leipzig gazette throughout his dominions and sending Herwegh under a police escort, out of the Kingdom, may allay the irritation at the present felt.

FO 82/42: Henry Wellesley to Earl of Aberdeen, No 3, Carlsruhe, 13 January 1843

On the present state of the Grand Duchy of Baden

Your Lordship is no doubt aware that the Grand Duchy of Baden, from its proximity to France, and the more than liberal tendency of its Chambers has been an object of distrust and anxiety to the other States of Germany, and that its proceedings have consequently been carefully watched by them. I trust therefore that I shall not be considered as intruding unnecessarily on Your Lordship's time if I proceed to address a few lines to You on the present state of the Country.

Sir George Shee's despatches will have informed Your Lordship that when The Grand Duke prorogued his Chambers in September last, it was not done in cordial terms. The opposition, although they passed the Budget, were in a decided majority, and were supported by public opinion and the Ministers were many of them personally disliked, especially Monsieur de Blittersdorf, the Minister for Foreign Affairs.

The Chambers will not meet again before next Winter, and I have endeavoured to find out whether in the mean time the Government has done or is inclined to do any thing to conciliate public opinion, or strengthen themselves.

From all I can collect the contrary is the case. The Government has endeavoured to revenge itself on Towns, where Elections have gone against them, and on Individuals who are hostile to them, but even here their conduct has not been consistent for it has constantly happened that an Individual displaced one week, has been decorated and given another place the week after. In short nothing can be more inconsistent and, pusillanimous than all their proceedings, nor is the Government united. Monsieur de Blittersdorf complains that he is not supported by his Colleagues who are in their turn afraid of him.

Were the personal character of the Grand Duke more esteemed, some amelioration might be hoped for, but He is unfortunately as weak and inconsistent as His Ministers. To give Your Lordship an instance of it. A short time ago Monsieur de Radowitz the Prussian Minister, took occasion to tell The Grand Duke publicly at a dinner to which he had been invited by His Royal Highness, that The King of Prussia was much displeased at the State of Affairs in the Grand Duchy of Baden. The Grand Duke after answering with great warmth that he did not care for the opinion of the King of Prussia but should pursue that line of conduct which appeared to Him most conducive to the happiness of his own Subjects, left the room and sent Monsieur de Blittersdorf to complain of this insult the following day to the Austrian Minister. Yet in six weeks afterwards, He sent Monsieur de Radowitz His principal decoration, and has constantly invited him since privately to the Palace to the exclusion of the other Members of the Diplomatic Body.

His Royal Highness' declaration therefore that he will stand by His Ministers does not carry much weight with it.

Throughout the Country there is a spirit of discontent and this is fomented by a set of intriguing Lawyers, who have nothing else to do, and I am sorry to add, by the Clergy, especially the Roman Catholic part of it.

Nothing can be at lower ebb than the Royal influence so much so that a project for selling some of the Crown Lands to meet the expences of the Rail Roads now constructing instead of contracting a debt as mentioned in my Despatch N° 2 of yesterday's date,[79] was abandoned at the entreaties of the Austrian and Prussian Ministers who feared that if the Crown Lands were passed with the Royal influence would be entirely gone.

But the State of this Country has become comparatively less interesting to Germany from the rapid strides that are making towards more liberal institutions in Prussia. The hopes of all German liberals (of whatever shade their opinions may be, or to whatever State they may belong) formerly centered in this small Duchy, are now turned towards that Country, and its proceedings viewed with corresponding anxiety, I may even add, distrust, by the different Sovereigns.

[79] Not included in this volume.

FO 82/42: Henry Wellesley to Earl of Aberdeen, No 7, Stuttgart, 23 January 1843

Friedrich List and his commercial considerations; anti-English tendencies of his publications

I observe that the public press in England has taken notice of a new weekly publication which has appeared at Augsburg under the name of 'Das Zollvereins Blatt' (The Customs Union Paper) edited by a D[r] List.[80]

The tendency of this Paper is so much against British Commercial Interests, that since its appearance I have been at some pains to trace its parentage, with a view to writing to Your Lordship on the subject.

I find it is a mere continuance of a series of Articles that have from time to time appeared in the Augsburg Gazette[81] in the same sense and by the same Author. The Author D[r] List, a Wurtemberger by birth. He was formerly a Professor at the University of Tubingen, which he left from incapacity. He was then chosen as a Deputy to the States, but expelled on a Criminal prosecution and confined in the Fortress of Asperg. After suffering the half of his punishment, the other half was remitted upon condition of his leaving the Country. He went to America, and succeeded in getting named American Consul at Leipzig. He there established a Paper called the Rail Road Journal,[82] and was a Member of the Committee of the Leipzig and Dresden Rail Road where however he made himself so disagreeable by his meddling that they gave him money to get rid of him. He has since written for various Newspapers, particularly for the Augsburg Gazette. He is much protected by Monsieur de Cotta the proprietor of that Journal and a report, of which Monsieur de Cotta was the drawer up, was presented to the lower Chamber during their last Session, embodying exactly the same views as those advocated by D[r] List.

Those views may be shortly stated to be excluding England from the German market to the advantage of America.

I took an opportunity of speaking to Monsieur de Herdegen the Minister of Finance on the subject to see if he was an Advocate of the same doctrine, and I was glad to find that he considered the writings of Dr List as wild an visionary, and not for a moment to be entertained by any sensible person either here or in any other part of Germany.

---

[80] Cf. n. 137 in Saxony section.

[81] *Allgemeine Zeitung*, cf. n. 33 in Bavaria section.

[82] The *Eisenbahn-Journal und National-Magazin für neue Erfindungen, Entdeckungen und Fortschritte im Handel und Gewerbe, in der Land- und Hauswirtschaft, in öffentlichen Unternehmungen und Anstalten, sowie für Statistik, Nationalökonomie und Finanzwesen* was published from April 1835 to July 1837.

I beg to enclose copies of the papers which have as yet appeared [.][83]

FO 82/42: George Shee to Earl of Aberdeen, No 46, Stuttgart, 4 November 1843

Opposition majority secured in Baden chambers; hostilities towards M. von Blittersdorf; tensions between government and chambers expected

The new Baden Chambers are expected to assemble towards the end of the present month, and I am sorry to acquaint Your Lordship that the result of the late Elections is highly unfavorable according to general belief to the Government of that Country.

The opposition have it is thought secured a decided Majority in the Chambers and it is moreover expected that they will avail themselves of their strength for the promotion of the most factious objects.

In the first instance it is supposed that their hostility will be directed against the Minister for Foreign Affairs Baron Blittersdorff who is at the same time the leading Member of the Government. Baron Blittersdorff is a Gentleman of considerable Abilities, of sound Political principles, and of unquestionable loyalty to his Sovereign.

He is also a distinguished Speaker in the Chambers. But these qualities are unfortunately counterbalanced by an impetuosity of temper and a rigid unbending spirit which prevent his exercising that tact in the management of Individuals which is so necessary in a Country when the Government is constitutional, where Parties are nearly balanced, and where a Democratic Spirit is actively at work.

It is much to be regretted that the complications which are likely to arise during the approaching Session of the Baden Chambers from Baron Blittersdorff's personal unpopularity were not obviated at the commencement of the late Elections by the voluntary retirement of that Minister. His retreat at that period would have been subject to no legitimate criticism whatever, whereas after the assembling of the Chambers it may possibility become a compulsory measure and then The Grand Duke by acquiescing in it may find both His character injured and His Authority impaired. The Act would bear the double disfigurement of surrender to a hostile faction and abandonment of a meritorious public Servant.

It is further to be remarked that had this point of collision between the Government of Baden and its opponents been removed prior to the assembling of the Chambers a different tone might perhaps have

[83] Enclosures: *Das Zollvereinsblatt*, No. 1, 1 January 1843; No. 2, 8 January; No. 3, 15 January; No. 4, 22 January.

been given to their future proceedings. The acrimony of even their most hostile adversaries might have been to a certain degree allayed, and it is moreover well known that there exists in the opposition a moderate Party who if their personal dislike of Baron Blittersdorff were gratified by the removal of that Minister would show themselves decidedly indisposed to carry out to their full length the ulterior objects of their friends.

In the foregoing Statement however my Lord I am far from wishing to convey to You that the Government or the Constitution of Baden are exposed to any imminent peril from the party to which I have alluded. Your Lordship is aware that both are sufficiently protected by the laws of the Germanic Confederation.[84] But the result of their exertions if successful would in this way be injurious that they would impeded the march of the Government in the administration of Public Affairs for the general improvement of the Country, and what is of still greater importance would tend very much to increase the dissemination of those democratic principles which are already too widely diffused in Germany and which are alike adverse to local improvement and to the promotion of social order.

FO 82/42: George Shee to Earl of Aberdeen, No 47, Stuttgart, 6 November 1843

M. von Blittersdorf's resignation

With reference to my Despatch N° 46 dated November the 4th relative to the approaching Session of the Baden Chambers, I have the honor to acquaint Your Lordship that Count Beroldingen received yesterday morning a Letter from Carlsruhe reporting to him the resignation of Baron Blittersdorf.

It is stated that Baron Blittersdorf is to resume the charge of the Carlsruhe Mission to the Diet at Frankfort a post which he formerly held, and that its present occupant Monsieur de Dusch will succeed him as Minister for Foreign Affairs.

This timely retreat of Baron Blittersdorf will I expect – and Count Beroldingen concurs with me in the opinion – be productive of very great advantage to The Grand Duke of Baden and to His Government. The Chambers not having yet met it will be received by the party hostile to Government as a boon, and wearing all the appearance of a gratuitous concession it will probably be attended with those conciliatory

---

[84] The relevant provisions are in the Federal Act of 1815 and the Vienna Final Act of 1820.

results which as I stated to Your Lordship in my last Despatch might reasonably be expected from such a measure.

I beg to add that the 21st of this Month is the time fixed for the Assembling of the Chambers.

FO 82/47: Alexander Malet to Earl of Aberdeen, No 6, Stuttgart, 4 February 1845

Building railroads between Baden and Württemberg; problems arising from the project

As the final execution of the Rail Road intended to traverse the Kingdom of Würtemberg and to connect the great lines of Baden and Bavaria is a question of general interest, Your Lordship will perhaps allow me to call Your attention to a part of the Speech of The King of Würtemberg on opening the Session of the States of this Kingdom alluding to this matter, which I had not time to do at the Moment of transmitting my preceding Despatch enclosing that Document.

His Majesty speaks of the arrangements to be made with the neighbouring States of Bavaria and Baden with reference to the points of the communication by Rail Road already commenced in His own territories, as if He entertained the expectation that the plan as traced by the Engineers of this Country would be acceded to by these two Governments for the several points of junction.

It is however notorious that this very important question meets with serious difficulties; and that Bavaria especially, has hitherto shewn very little disposition to accept the proposals of Würtemberg.

Less difficulty may be expected in a final arrangement with Baden. But while the works in Würtemberg are being carried on in the direction of Heilbron and along the Valley of the Neckar, requiring a branch from the Baden Rail Road from the neighbourhood of Heidelbergh, it is known that the Baden Government presses for a totally different line, and that the branch of communication should proceed either from Bruchsal, or from Carlsruhe itself by way of Pforzheim.

On the side of Bavaria the Würtemberg Rail road is traced to cross the Danube near Günzburg. The Bavarian plan would take their terminus to Ulm, a point which is said to present insurmountable difficulties to the engineer on the Wurtemberg bank of the Danube.

There exists as Your Lordship is aware a great want of cordiality between this Government, and that of Bavaria, and this feeling seems likely in the present instance in which the advantage is decidedly on the side of that Country, to produce serious inconvenience and embarrassment to Wurtemberg in the prosecution of plans undertaken without due consideration.

The Royal Speech says nothing of the Loan of Forty Millions of florins contemplated for the completion of the projected Rail-Roads – but as it announces that the ordinary revenues of the Country will cover the expenditure without any recurrence to augmented taxation – it is evident that the surplus of Two Millions on the last Budget is calculated on for paying the interest on this Loan till the Rail Road becomes productive. [...]

FO 82/47: Alexander Malet to Earl of Aberdeen, No 28, Stuttgart, 31 May 1845

Sensation caused in Baden by the expulsion of M. Itzstein and M. Hecker from Prussian territory

A very considerable sensation has been created in the Grand Duchy by the Expulsion from Berlin and the Prussian Territory of Messieurs Itstein[85] and Hecker, Members of the Lower Chamber of this State, and leaders of the Opposition.

These Gentlemen ostensibly traveling for their amusement, had been received at Leipsic and other places on their Route with marked attention, and having quitted Leipsic for Berlin with the intention of returning to the former Town in a few days to partake of a publick Dinner offered to them, they received on the morning of the 23rd, the day after their arrival in Berlin, peremptory orders thro' the Medium of the Police, to quit Berlin and the Prussian Territory without a Moments delay.

Having complied with this order, Messieurs Itstein and Hecker reached Mannheim their ordinary residence on the 27th and have lost no time in addressing themselves to their own Government to demand redress, not only for what the represent as a personal indignity, but an insult offered to the Legislative Body of an independent State; alledging that no cause was assigned for their Expulsion, and no time allowed them to obtain the protection of the Baden Minister at Berlin.

I learn that the Motive likely to be assigned by the Prussian Government for this proceeding, will probably be a charge of irregularity in the Passports of these Gentlemen, while it is surmized that the real cause is to be found in their visits to the various Towns in which the New Sect of seceding Roman Catholicks[86] are established, and with which the Prussian Government either suspect or know, that these

---

[85] Adam von Itzstein.

[86] This refers to the German Catholics (*Deutschkatholiken*) who were led by Karl Ronge.

Members of the Baden Chamber, generally regarded as leaders by the German Ultra-Liberals, have some intention of connecting themselves with political views.

It will be a matter of no difficulty for the Prussian Government to give satisfaction to the official remonstrances which may be addressed to it by that of Baden in this affair, but it is likely to excite much clamour amongst the liberal portion of the German Publick, and may create serious Embarrassments to the Grand Ducal Ministry, should the Affair be taken up, as may naturally be expected, by the Appraition in the Chamber of which Monsieur Itstein is the popular Leader.

FO 82/47: Alexander Malet to Earl of Aberdeen, No 31, Stuttgart, 12 June 1845

Württemberg manufacturers demand increased duties; different views regarding duties within Customs Union

The annexed Paper is a Statement and translation of the alterations in the Tariff which the Wurtemberg Manufacturers wish their Government to propose at the approaching Congress of the Zoll-Verein at Carlsruhe.

It is doubtful whether increased duties to the extent proposed will be supported by this Government, at any rate it is known here that so great an augmentation will be opposed by Prussia.

Notwithstanding the demands for protection made upon the Government by the Manufacturing interest of this Country there are not wanting persons of intelligence and even Manufacturers themselves who see its impolicy, especially in the tendency of such measures to render the Mill Owners careless and retarding progress.

A vast majority however are in favor of increased duties and this feeling has even led to the expression of a wish in the Chambers, that if at the ensuing Congress Prussia should be opposed to them, steps might be taken for separating from Prussia, and forming a New Commercial Union elsewhere, with an evident allusion to Austria.

The indication of the existence of this feeling is too important to escape Your Lordship's notice; the realization of such a project would doubtless be advantageous to Southern Germany, and Your Lordship may rely on my watching the development of any such tendencies with the attention they deserve.

I need scarcely add that it would be of great advantage to me in view of this plan assuming a tangible shape to be put in possession of the opinions held upon it by Her Majesty's Government as a guide to my language and conduct in such Contingency.[87]

FO 82/47: Alexander Malet to Earl of Aberdeen, No 54, Stuttgart, 7 October 1845

Jealousy of British influence among delegates to the Commercial Congress at Carlsruhe; invitation of British envoy not accepted

I found a jealousy of British influence to exist among the delegates to the Commercial Union Congress at Carlsruhe and those Gentlemen kept themselves so much aloof from general Society, that it became impossible, as well a inexpedient expedient for me to associate with or offer them any attention during the progress of their deliberations.

When I had obtained the certitude that their labours as far as regarded British interests were brought to a close, by the signature of the Tariff I thought the time was arrived when without exciting their susceptibilities I might venture to invite them to a dinner together with the Baden Minister of Foreign Affairs[88] and my Colleagues of the Diplomatic body, having first taken the precaution of consulting one of the Delegates Monsr Vahinger[89] the Wurtemberg Commissioner as to which of two days Saturday the 4th or Monday the 6th of October would be most convenient for himself and his Colleagues to do me this honor, and that Gentlemen having fixed on Monday I invited all the Commissioners on that day.

On the 2^d Inst., two days after my invitations had been sent, I received an intimation that none of the Commissioners would accept them excusing themselves on the plea of a Conference; and on my offering to alter the day I was informed that my invitation could in no case be accepted, and I was confidentially told that the actual ground of non acceptance was the apprehension which the Commissioners one and all entertained of what might be said upon such an occasion by the Press.

I should hardly thought it worth while to report this Circumstance to Your Lordship as the refusal of these Gentlemen to accept so trivial a civility from me was accompanied by all the forms of politeness which I could expect or require, did I not apprehend that the fact which can hardly escape publicity might probably be conveyed to Your Lordship in some other than its true light.

[87] Enclosures: Statement of the demand of Wurtemberg Manufacturers for augmented duties, Original and translation.
[88] Alexander Dusch.
[89] Vayhinger.

FO 82/49: Alexander Malet to Earl of Aberdeen, No 10, Confidential,
Stuttgart, 22 February 1846

Approval of Sir Robert Peel's reform policy

It may not be without interest for Her Majesty's Government at this
moment to gather the opinions entertained on the course which Sir
Robert Peel has entered upon, by Persons whose position may exercise
a congenial or counteracting influence on the policy of Foreign States.

I think it my duty therefore to acquaint Your Lordship that the King
of Würtemberg took occasion to speak to me yesterday in very warm
terms of approbation of Sir Robert Peel's measures.[90]

It was impossible, His Majesty said, that a policy based on such
principles should not be followed by other States.

The elements of calculation were too clear, and the conclusions
drawn from them too rigorous, not to compel assent to the arguments
laid down by the British Minister.

The mischievous influence of the Corn Law League is destroyed,
and a failure of success in carrying the measure (which, however His
Majesty observed there seemed no reason to apprehend,) would be a
general misfortune.

His Majesty was pleased to express His great personal admiration of
Sir Robert Peel and said with great energy 'combien j'admire votre Sir
Rovert Peel! c'est un homme qui aime véritablement son pays, et qui
sait écarter tout ce que est personel'.

I ventured to express the great satisfaction with which I listened to
the expression of His Majesty's sentiments on these questions, and my
hope that His approval of the system of removing restrictions on
Commerce of which England was giving an example would not be
without effect on other States which had hitherto followed a contrary
policy .

His Majesty received my observations most graciously, and with a
degree of cordial assent which leads me to auger favorably for the
nature of the instructions with which the Wurtemberg Commissioner[91]
to the ensuing Congress at Berlin will be supplied, and at all events
the high value attaching to His Wurtemberg Majesty's talents and
opinions throughout Germany is not likely to be without results.

---

[90] Malet is referring to the attempt by the British prime minister, Sir Robert Peel, to
repeal the Corn Laws in the winter of 1845–1846 (cf. n. 171 in Prussia section).
[91] Loechner.

FO 82/49: Alexander Malet to Earl of Aberdeen, No 16, Stuttgart, 24 April 1846

Opening of Baden chambers fixed; results of recent election cause Grand Duke's anxiety

I have the honor to inform Your Lordship that the opening of the Legislative Chambers of the Grand Duchy of Baden is fixed for the 1ˢᵗ of May.

Mʳ Craven writes me from Carlsruhe that the result of the recent Elections, and the general aspect of affairs in the Grand Duchy cause much anxiety to His Royal Highness The Grand Duke, to a degree affecting His Royal Highness' health.

The Baden Government have in Mʳ Craven's opinion, committed an error in seeking to balance the Radical and Ultramontane Parties, and in their dread of the ascendancy of the latter, which would he conceives, if skilfully employed, have supported conservative principles, have mismanaged their influence so as to allow of the former securing an increased Majority in the reelected Chambers.

FO 82/49: Alexander Malet to Viscount Palmerston, no number, Confidential, Stuttgart, 16 October 1846

King of Württemberg on political issues

I think it my duty to acquaint your Lordship confidentially with the nature of the views and opinions which I have recently had means of ascertaining to be entertained by the King of Wirtembergh on several points of political importance and general interest upon some of which the recent connexion formed by His Majesty with Russia,[92] and the deference shewn to Him by that Court, must give His advice and counsels a weight and influence which they have not hitherto possessed. [...]

With more immediate reference to Germany His Majesty expresses more dislike than fear of Prussia. He is of opinion that Her Rhenish Provinces are insecure, that they are a slip of Territory too much Geographically disconnected, and too favorably affected to France, not to be easily laid hold of by that Power at the first European convulsion. For their greater security, they should, The King thinks, be given with some additions to a Prince of the House of Saxony, that Family being Roman Catholick.

---

[92] Malet refers here to the marriage between Crown Prince Karl of Württemberg and Grand Duchess Olga Nikolajevna of Russia in August 1846.

While much too prudent to encourage disaffection, His Majesty is one of those who regard the duration of the present state of things in Germany, as impossible, divided as it is, according to His Majesty's expression, 'en 38 morceaux'.

It is not improbable that some of the apprehension His Majesty would naturally feel at the prospect of any serious European convulsion, such as would lead to new territorial divisions, is lessened by the persuasion generally entertained that such an event would, in consideration of His Majesty's present character be favourable to Himself. His position however as a Constitutional Sovereign is very different at present from what it was at the commencement of His reign, and it is not likely that the ultra liberal Party which then looked up to Him as a Leader would be now willing to regard Him in the same light. [...]

FO 82/52: Alexander Malet to Viscount Palmerston, No 8, Confidential, Stuttgart, 18 February 1847

Sensation caused by promulgation of Prussian constitution; public opinion; censorship cannot prevent spread of radical opinions

The promulgation of the Prussian Constitution[93] has naturally caused a considerable sensation in this Capital as well as in the rest of Germany, and I think it my duty to report what I conceive to be the general tone of public feeling in its appreciation of an event of so much importance and which has been for so long a time looked forward to with anxious expectation.

Those who may be regarded as Opponents of the Constitutional System, and those who desire its extension, are equally agreed in opinion that the concessions granted by the Royal prerogative are of as limited a nature as it was possible to make them. – The first class, who I must observe are here by no means numerous, while they think it would have been wiser to abstain from any change in the lately existing order of things, express their hopes that with due precautions, The King of Prussia will be enabled successfully to resist further concessions; Moderate advocates of a more liberal policy say that what is done is a good beginning, but cannot suffice either to satisfy the governed or to secure tranquillity to the ruling Power; while those, and they are numerous, whose views go farther, speak of the whole arrangement as illusory and defective, and declare that the so called Constitution will only have the effect of exciting into dangerous activity, the discontented spirits hitherto kept quiet by the prospect of substantial

[93] Cf. pp. 235–236, 238–241 in Prussia section.

reforms, and now cheated in their expectations by a cruel mockery.

There exists however a general persuasion that whatever small portion of real concession is to be found in the Prussian Ordonnances emanates from the Sovereign, while those who analyze them most severely, observe that each consecutive clause contains some phrase or provision attenuating or abrogating any thing that might be virtually liberal in the one that preceded it, and this tendency is attributed to the counsels and influence of the Prince Heir[94] apparent to the Throne.

There is one point of view, as respects her foreign policy, in which this foreshadowing, (as it is generally felt to be,) of a constitutional Government in Prussia, is generally favorably regarded in this part of Germany, viz: that it will detach her from Russia, and that each step made in the career, now felt to be only entered on, must widen the breach.

Much will depend on the attitude assumed by the newly constituted Prussian States in their ensuing Convocation, as well as on the temper of the Nation generally. Should any serious degree of fermentation occur in any portion of that Kingdom it would I have reason to think find sympathy and support in the greater part of Southern Germany in any attempts that mighty be made to wrest larger concessions from the Crown.

The existing laws in all these States against the expression of public opinion and the operation of the Censorship are ineffectual in preventing the spread of opinions amongst the Masses hostile to arbitrary Government, and which are the more dangerous that they circulate by secret and forbidden channels. I do not mean to express a belief of the existence of any imminent peril, but looking to the spirit of the times and the means taken in this conjuncture by the Government of Prussia to conciliate that spirit by concessions generally felt to be inadequate to the emergency, I only make myself the Echo of the prevailing opinions of the Country in which I reside when I report to Your Lordship that the promulgation of this Constitution instead of promoting Security, has had the opposite effect of creating much disquietude and serious apprehension for the future amongst the friends of order, while it has revived the hopes and the activity of the Partisans of anarchy and confusion.

[94] Wilhelm.

FO 82/52: Lord Augustus Loftus to Viscount Palmerston, No 3, Stuttgart, 21 April 1847

New law for the regulation of the press in Germany; three different periods when the legislation of the press has occupied German Sovereigns

Prior to my leaving Carlsruhe I was privately shewn the Project of a New Law for the regulation of the Press in Germany, which had been submitted by the Prussian Cabinet to the Government of Baden, and I believe equally to all the German Sates, previously to its being brought under the consideration of the Germanic Diet.

The change proposed by this New Law is of an extensive and important nature: and the object sought to be attained, and which is generally admitted throughout all Germany to be of essential necessity, is a unity of principle and legislation as regards the Press throughout all the German States.

I may here remark to Your Lordship, that there have been 3 different periods at which the Legislation of the Press has occupied the attention of the German Sovereigns, and when it has undergone certain changes 1. At the Treaty of Vienna. 2dly at the Congress of Aix la Chapelle. and 3dly soon after the French Revolution in 1830.[95] At these periods it was generally decided that the Germanic Diet was to occupy itself with the framing and organising a general and united system of Legislation for the Press in Germany. This has hitherto never been carried out, and the 32 States forming the Germanic Confederation – although acting on the same principle of Censorship, have till now admitted separate and distinct regulations as to the administration of that Censorship in each state. This has been found in its general application to Germany to be both vague in execution and fruitless in the result desired; for many instances have occurred where the Censor of one State imposed prohibition, while the neighbouring State granted permission, of publication: and thus have arisen constant subjects of litigation and jealousy among the different States, as well as frequent subjects of discontent in the publick mind.

The plan now submitted by Prussia, and to be shortly laid before the Germanic Diet consists of the abolition of the Censorship and the

[95] Loftus refers to the following stages of press legislation in Germany: Article 18 of the Act of the German Confederation of 8 June 1815 held out the prospect of a uniform press law for the whole of the German Confederation. The Federal Press Law of 20 September 1819 went back to resolutions of the Aachen Congress (September/October 1818) and the Carlsbad Conferences (August 1819). After the French revolution of July 1830, a number of states began liberalizing their laws; but measures taken by the German Confederation in 1831 and 1832 (*Maßregeln-Gesetz* of 5 July), and 1832 and 1834 (Articles 28–36 of the Sixty Articles of 12 June 1834) resulted in a considerable tightening up of press legislation again.

repression of the Press by its subjection to the Judicial Laws: and in case of their infraction, the infliction of Fines and in extreme cases, the penalty of imprisonment. Every Editor is to be made responsible for his publication, and no work is to be printed without having the Editors and Printers name. A right of appeal is to be likewise given to the Diet in cases where doubts may exist as to the propriety of sentence pronounced by the Judicial Court.

The acceptance of this new Law if sanctioned by the Diet, is to be voluntary on all the German States, and in case of their non-acceptance, they will be bound to abide by the existing Law of Censorship.

I have thus endeavored cursorily to convey to Your Lordship what I have learnt to be the principle of the New Law submitted by Prussia; and I may state that it is the intention of the Grand Ducal Government to support this proposal at the Diet, with some unimportant modifications.

With respect to Wurtemberg, I have to inform Your Lordship that at the Extraordinary Session of the Chambers held in February last – as reported in Sir Alexander Malets Despatch to Your Lordship No. 5[96] the Majority decided that the Petition which had been presented against the Censorship, should not then be taken into consideration, but referred to the ordinary Session: the Government then stating that when that period arrived, the States would be informed of what had been effected relative to that subject.

I have now learnt that His Wurtemberg Majesty deeply imbued with the necessity of a united Legislation for the Press throughout Germany, and feeling convinced that the existing Law of Censorship can no longer be maintained without disseminating an overpowering spirit of discontent in the publick Mind, has given His adhesion to the general views entertained by Prussia, and will support the new Project of Law relative to the Press, when laid before the Diet.

I have also privately learnt that His Wurtemberg Majesty has been in correspondence with Prince Metternich on this subject and that His Majesty has strongly urged on the Prince, the urgent necessity of a solution of this important subject.

I have been further informed that in the Event of the above mentioned Project of Law being rejected by the Diet (which is not probable) Prussia will propose that each State of the Confederation shall be at liberty to legislate for the Press, as each may respectively deem advisable for its own Welfare.

---

[96] FO 82/52: Alexander Malet to Viscount Palmerston, No. 5, Stuttgart, 5 February 1847, not included in this volume. The united diet of February 1847 was convened in order to provide 'funds for the system of railroads undertaken by the Government'.

FO 82/52: Lord Augustus Loftus to Viscount Palmerston, No 6, Stuttgart, 5 May 1847

Food riots in Ulm and Stuttgart

I have to inform Your Lordship that on the Evening of the 3^{d} Instant a disturbance took place in this Capital, a Mob having assembled for the purpose of attacking the Houses of different Bakers and Corn Merchants: His Majesty The King of Wurtemberg, (Who had been apprized of this intended attack, and who had accordingly postponed His departure for Baden) – attended by His Royal Highness the Crown Prince[97] and His Staff immediately repaired to the scene of disorder, hoping by His Presence to restore tranquillity. I regret to say however that His Majesty was disrespectfully received, and His Person assailed by stones as well as by opprobrious epithets. His Majesty fortunately escaped any contusion.

The Military were obliged to fire twice before the Populace would disperse or desist from their acts of violence.

Two lives among the Populace were lost, and a great number wounded by the Cavalry. Several of the Military suffered severe contusions from Stones, the only Weapon which the Mob could command.

A Riot had occurred a few days previously at Ulm: where similar excesses were committed: but it was quelled without the loss of Life.

Though the scarcity of grain, and the consequent high price of provisions may be accounted as the ostensible cause of this disturbance, it is surmised that political Emissaries have been at work in disaffecting the public mind and in diffusing the principles of communism: and I regret to say, that the presence of that Sovereign who had always been regarded with adoration by His People, in this occasion elicited Expressions of anger and discontent, as well as outward marks of insult.

Every military precaution has been taken by His Majesty Against any further outbreak, and I am happy to report to Your Lordship, that, tho' much Excitement exists, the public Peace has not since been disturbed.

[97] Karl.

FO 82/52: Lord Augustus Loftus to Viscount Palmerston, No 7, Stuttgart, 7 May 1847

Restoration of peace; arrests of workmen and artisans; causes for unrest; King's decree against Communist societies

[...] I am happy to be able to report to Your Lordship that the peace of this Capital has not been again disturbed, and that perfect tranquillity reigns.[98] The resolute and determined measures adopted by His Majesty, have succeeded in overawing the discontented, and in giving confidence to the well disposed.

A great number of persons, composed of Workmen and artisans have been arrested, and amongst them but one individual of a higher condition, who having refused to state his name and address, is supposed to have been a principal instigator in the late disturbance. It is worthy of remark that the class of workmen who were engaged in this revolt, on the plea of starvation, is the one which is in the receipt of daily work and pay, and who cannot therefore have been driven to these Excesses by want or distress, It is generally thought that this moment of scarcity has been seized by Political Agitators in order to feel the pulse of the German Publick and to serve as a Barometer in ascertaining the temperature of Publick opinion. The Republican writings of Heinsen[99] who is now in Switzerland have been secretly circulated through this Country, as well as the Grand Duchy of Baden, and it is supposed that their circulation is effected by Private agents, who at the same time infuse into the minds of the Lower Classes the deadly poison of hatred to all Sovereigns and Governments, while they hold out the illusory advantages of Communism, as an incentive to revolt.

His Majesty the King of Wurtemberg only a few days previous to the late Riot, had published an ordonnance against Communist Societies, which I have the Honor to enclose herewith to Your Lordship in original and in Translation.

I must likewise report to Your Lordship a gratifying Circumstance which offers Evidence of the Loyal spirit of the rising generation. At Tübingen where a similar attempt at Riot was manifested for the sake of plunder, the Students of the University in that Town volunteered to the Municipal Authority to preserve peace and order, and accordingly by their means the first attempt at disturbance two days ago was quickly arrested.[100]

[98] For the food riots cf. p. 403 in this section.
[99] Karl Heinzen.
[100] Enclosures: 1. Königliche Verordnung, betreffend das Verbot von Vereinen mit kommunistischer Tendenz, 21 April 1847; 2. Translation

BAVARIA

(MUNICH)

MUNICH

FO 9/60: Lord Erskine to Earl of Aberdeen, No 44, Munich, 14 August 1830

Reaction of the Bavarian government to the French revolution of July 1830

The great events which have recently taken place in France[1] have excited the interest of this Government and Court, as much as they appear to have done all parts of Europe.

There was in the beginning a great display of popular feeling in the towns of Munich and Augsburg in favour of the insurrection of the people of France against the late overstrained exercise of the Royal Prerogative in that Country, so much so that His Bavarian Majesty's attention was drawn by some of his Courtiers near his person to this sudden ebulition of political sentiment, with a view to induce him to take measures for its suppression.

The King, however, declined interfering, alleging that as a Constitutional Sovereign he could not help being of opinion that Charles the tenth of France had abused his authority and forfeited any claim to the support or sympathy of other Sovereigns of Europe.

This information I received from good authority, and I believe [it] to be in substance at least, well founded.

FO 9/60: Lord Erskine to Earl of Aberdeen, No 54, Munich, 27 September 1830

Disturbances caused by tax imposed on beer and meat; 'beer-riots'; governmental measures

As it is not improbable that Your Lordship may have heard some reports that disturbances have taken place amongst the populace of this Residence, I have thought it right to mention to you, that, in consequence of the high price of the two chief articles of the subsistence of the common people, beer and meat, various complaints were preferred to the Government, who directed enquiries to be instituted upon the subject, and finding that the price of those articles had been much augmented by a tax lately imposed by the competent authorities

[1] Cf. n. 28 in Frankfurt section.

of the town and with the permission of the King, ordered the above mentioned tax to be discontinued in future and the price of beer to be changed from six Kreutzers (about two pence in English money) the Maass[2] (between a pint and a quart) to three Kreutzers and a half, which material alteration completely satisfied the working class of the Community.

Measures have been also taken to lower the price of meat.

The soldiers of the Cuirassier Regiment had also complained upon the same topics, but repectfully and not in a body to their Colonel Prince Charles[3] (the King's brother) who promised his interference to endeavour to remove the grounds of their complaints.

I feel strongly persuaded that no tumultuous proceedings are likely to take place, as the people of this Country in general are well satisfied with their Government and have no well founded grievances.

If any disturbances should be made by illdisposed individuals, they will be easily suppressed by the Police and Guard, whose numbers have been recently increased. [...]

FO 9/60: Lord Erskine to Earl of Aberdeen, No 63, Munich, 31 October 1830

On the disposition of the labouring classes in Bavaria

[...] I consider, however, that the great cause of the quiet and peaceable disposition of the labouring classes of the people of this country may be attributed to their easy and independent state. The inhabitants of the country towns and villages at least generally possess a house or a cottage, or some land more or less, the care of which occupies their time and creates an interest in the establishment and continuance of order and obedience to the laws which are equal for all and are usually impartially administered, and it is curious to remark how very small an interest in such property produces that useful effect. The knowledge of this I have derived from actual observations of my own, having during my stay for the summer months, in this country and in Wurtemberg for six years past, had opportunities of perceiving the strong attachment evinced by the common people and peasants for the enjoyment of this independence.

---

[2] 1 *Maß* = 1 litre.
[3] Karl Theodor.

FO 9/61: Lord Erskine to Viscount Palmerston, No 7, Munich, 10 February 1831

Considerable opposition in the chambers anticipated; King's veto on the election of leaders of the opposition

I have the honor to inform you that the two Legislative Chambers are summoned to meet on the 20th instant at this Residence and will be opened by The King in person.

Although His Bavarian Majesty's Government expect to find the majority of the Chambers moderate and reasonable in their views, yet it should seem as if considerable opposition is anticipated since the King of Bavaria has thought it proper and advisable to exercise a power vested in him by the Constitution,[4] to put His Veto upon the Election of the five following principal Leaders of the Opposition, Messrs Behr, Hornthal, Bestelmeyer, Tauffkirchen and Closen, who by chance happen to hold some small Post or Pension from the State. One[5] of them indeed is only a Magistrate of a Provincial Town.

The policy of this measure is much questioned and it is confidently said, and I believe with truth, that most of His Bavarian Majesty's Ministers were against it.

Already, indeed, it is said to have caused considerable commotion in several large Provincial Towns, for which some of the before mentioned Deputies were elected, and it will without doubt occasion warm discussions in the Chambers, when they meet.

FO 9/62: Lord Erskine to Viscount Palmerston, Separate, Munich, 23 December 1831

Question of what to wear when meeting the Bavarian King and Queen

I feel considerable reluctance in troubling Your Lordship upon a matter that would have been too insignificant, and perhaps even unworthy of being communicated to Your Lordship, had it not been for the importance attributed to it by His Bavarian Majesty's Government.

The Secretary of State for Foreign Affairs, Count Armansperg conveyed to me the request that I would change the uniform in which I have been accustomed, (as well as all others of His Majesty's Servants), to appear before My Royal Master, and Her Majesty, The Queen, and

---

[4] According to §44 of the Edict on the Assembly of the Estates of 1818 (Appendix X to the Constitutional Document of 1818) civil servants needed the permission of the King before they could take up a position as a deputy.

[5] Johann Georg Bestelmeyer.

to substitute for the trowsers, (I am almost ashamed to mention so trifling a subject) short breeches and silk stockings.

This communication was made to me after I had been in the habit, the greater part of a year, of appearing at His Bavarian Majesty's Court, upon all occasions, in the uniform of Our Royal Masters Servants, without any observation having been made, further than the remark by the Grand Master of the Ceremonies[6] that he supposed it was my uniform and that of course I was right in wearing it.

The occasion upon which this request for a change in my costume was founded, (I have full reason to believe), upon the circumstance of the French Legation appearing in trowsers also, which, I understand is the dress of the French Court; because on that same night the Grand Master of the Ceremonies observed to me that there could not be any objection taken to my costume as it was the usual uniform of my Court; but that he doubted that being the case with respect to the costume of the French Legation.

I ought not to omit to observe to Your Lordship that uniforms of all kinds from different parts of the world, with or without trowsers, are to be continually seen at the Bavarian Court, and that half of the Officers wear boots. This I remarked to Count Armansperg, at the time he mentioned the subject to me; and I reminded him that I had presented many of my Countrymen with various costumes, and amongst others a Scotchman[7] without any pantaloons or breeches at all and that the dress had been[8] generally much admired, and even by His Bavarian Majesty Himself who joked with me repeatedly about it. This Scotch gentleman was not in the Army.

I may also add that Greek, Slavonian, Georgian, Circassian and numberless other costumes, at different times appear at this Court, and I asked Count Armansperg, whether at any time there was any objection raised to the persons, wearing them, being received at Court. He replied in the negative, when the uniforms were those of their Country. My answer was obvious, viz: that my costume was the Diplomatic uniform of Our Royal Masters Servants.

I do not, My Lord, presume to ask you to lay this letter before Our Royal Master, or to ask of His Majesty the slightest attention, to so ridiculous a topic, and I would much rather submit to all the consequences or injury, which could arise to me personally from the displeasure of His Bavarian Majesty for my nonattendance at His Court; but if Your Lordship should be pleased to send me orders to acquiesce in this demand of His Bavarian Majesty, I shall of course obey.

[6] Cajetan Peter Graf von und zu Sandizell.
[7] Not traceable.
[8] Pencilled in margin: 'by the ladies?'.

In the mean time I have not given any refusal to Count Armansperg to comply with that demand, but shall excuse myself at Court, until I should be acquainted with Your wishes upon the subject.

FO 9/61: To Lord Erskine, Foreign Office, London, 16 January 1832 (Draft)[9]

Palmerston's reply on the dress regulation question

I have received and laid before the King Your Lordship's separate despatch of the 23^d December relative to certain new regulations respecting Dress which have recently been made by the Court of Munich and asking for instructions for your guidance thereupon; and I am commanded by His Majesty to inform you that if it be established as the <u>general</u> rule of the Court of Munich that all who present themselves there, as well Foreigners of all nations, as natives of Bavaria, shall appear in short Breeches and stockings and if it be the invariable rule that Pantaloons or Trowsers, and Boots shall not be worn, in that case it is the King's pleasure that the Individuals composing His Majesty's mission shall conform to such Rule. But if the Rule be not general, and if it be not established & declared regulation of the Court applicable to <u>all</u> who attend the Court, then and in such case His Majesty does not see any Reason why such a partial Regulation should be applied to His representative and he cannot admit it to be so applied.

I am further commanded by the king to say that if notwithstanding this decision of His Majesty which you are authorized to communicate to the proper quarter, any insurmountable difficulty should still be experienced by you with respect to the Question about Breeches & Trowsers, Your Lordship is at liberty to appear at Court in your Militia uniform, if by so doing you would put an end to a difference of etiquette upon a subject in itself so extremely trivial.

FO 9/64: Lord Erskine to Viscount Palmerston, No 7, Munich, 19 January 1832

King's anger towards those entertaining liberal opinions

As I have an opportunity of sending this Despatch beyond the frontier of this Country, I will take the liberty of writing more freely respecting some circumstances which have lately occurred at this Court.

---

[9] Original in FO 149/24.

His Bavarian Majesty has appeared, since a year past, to have been extremely irritated against what He conceives to be the progress of dangerous principles of democracy, and has evinced, more especially within a short time past, a violence of feelings, very unusual I believe, and certainly very extraordinary.

He takes every occasion, in private, of expressing the bitterest anger against those who, as He thinks, entertain liberal opinions and has declared that He feels quite happy, now, that He has got rid of a Jacobinical Ministry,[10] and finds Himself in a right political career. – He would, undoubtedly, earnestly wish to join Himself to the other Great Powers of the Continent in any war against France, from His hatred of the principles by which that Country has been directed since her last Revolution;[11] but I do not believe that His Bavarian Majesty would meet with any support from His People unless an attack should be made by France upon Germany without any just provocation. This conviction I derive from an attentive consideration of the sentiments of the Representatives of the People in the Chamber of Deputies and also in the Country at large. [...]

FO 9/64: Lord Erskine to Viscount Palmerston, No 8, Munich, 19 January 1832

Composition of the new ministry

The present Ministry may be now said to be fully in action, although most of them have been only provisionally appointed.

The Secretary of State for Foreign Affairs, Baron de Gise, and who still holds the appointment of Minister to the Court of St Petersburgh, is generally considered as a person of good abilities and quick in business. With respect to his political opinions I believe that they are not very violent or exaggerated and that he is extremely desirous that the peace of the Continent should be preserved; but all the information which I have received seems to concur that he would not be likely to interpose his own political sentiments, whatever they might be, to those of His Royal Master, which I have explained in my preceding Despatch, N° 7, sent herewith.

The Minister of the Interior Prince Oettingen Wallerstein of a Mediatised family, is supposed not to be deficient in ordinary abilities and acquirements and is plausible in his manners, but his talents are not equal to his pretensions. He was formerly a great liberal, but

---

[10] The new government was formed on 31 December 1831; cf. pp. 412–413 in Bavaria section.

[11] Cf. n. 28 in Frankfurt section.

changed considerably in the complexion of his political opinions. – He himself, however, in conversing with me, the other day, upon the present serious position of the Affairs of the Continent, declared that his own sentiments were as firm as ever they had been, in favour of free institutions and rational liberty; and that he had so explained them to His Bavarian Majesty when it was proposed to him to accept the post of Minister of the Interior; and he added that he would not give his assistance in carrying on the Government on any other principles. It is true that most people would be inclined to doubt this assertion of his, in as much as having once essentially changed his system, his firmness might be questionable.

The Minister of Justice, Baron Zu-Rhein is a very clever man and very active in business, but has hitherto been but little acquainted with the branch of Administration over which he is now called upon to preside. He has been formerly employed by His Bavarian Majesty on topics regarding Commerce, and has been found to have well executed his charge, and is thought also to have been a good Commissary-General. His manners are lively and conciliatory. His political opinions are supposed to be moderate, and according as he represents them, pacific.

Of M. de Mieg, the Minister of Finance, and was Commissary General at Ansbach, the common opinion seems to be that he is a man of considerable talents and dexterity in business, but has never given his attention particularly to Financial matters. His political views are now said to be moderate, although formerly he was reputed to be an alarmist as to the approach of dangerously free political sentiments.

The several Ministers, here before mentioned, were hardly before acquainted with each other, and it is a curious fact that His Bavarian Majesty has lately expressed Himself, as but little satisfied with the composition of His own Ministry.

I will only add that the Minister of War, Monsr de Weinrich, retains his post although universally considered to be unfit for it in all respects.

M. Grandaur, whose office of Cabinet Secretary had been abolished by the Chambers, has been named by His Bavarian Majesty, a Counsellor of State, provisionally.

FO 9/64: Lord Erskine to Viscount Palmerston, No 11, Munich, 24 January 1832

Some observations on political topics; England's attitude towards constitutional states in Germany; hopes of preserving their constitutional form of government rest on England

I hope Your Lordship will pardon me if I should seem to exceed the usual limits of the Diplomatic Correspondence of this Mission in presuming to make a few observations upon some political topics, which, though general in their nature, have also a particular application to this Country.

The opinions which have been lately promulgated through public Journals that England would not interest or exert Herself, for the protection of the Constitutional Liberties of the smaller States of Germany, on account of the probable danger of involving Herself in a war with the Great Continental Powers, has produced the greatest effect in emboldening the party adverse to sentiments of Liberty and Free Institutions, and in discouraging the firmest advocates of those principles; and to such an extent, indeed, as to threaten the gradual, and perhaps even, total, destruction of Constitutional Govts.

I am well aware, My Lord, that His Majesty's Government does not attempt to interfere with the public Journals or to controul the Liberty of the Press, but if it was possible, in any way, to cause to be known the general views of Government upon these important points, it would greatly tend to promote the good will of those States of Germany towards England and to further the cause of Freedom well defined and guarded by wholesome Laws, against the encroachments of arbitrary power, which, I am sorry to observe to Your Lordship is making most daring and rapid approaches.

This is not merely an idea on my part, My Lord, but I could give Your Lordship numberless and strong proofs of the truth of this remark, which, I am persuaded, You must have had confirmed from other parts of the Continent.

Every hope of preserving Constitutional forms of Government rests solely on England. France could have done a great deal towards their support, but unfortunately the opinion of her instability and fickleness of purpose has greatly diminished the confidence in her assistance.

FO 9/64: Henry Howard to Viscount Palmerston, No 2, Munich, 20 February 1832

Government's arbitrary and contradictory manner in treating the Bavarian press; need for definite laws; publication of a state gazette; sentiments of the inhabitants of Bavarian territories on the Rhine

[...] I have indeed observed that the majority of the smaller Journals surpass even in violence those of almost any other State. The rejection of the Bill upon the Press,[12] proposed during the last Session of the Chambers (by which Trial by Jury would have been established) and the continuance of the Censorship upon Foreign Affairs, which only tends to promote a more immoderate use of the freedom which exists as regards Domestic Affairs, have contributed much, in my opinion, to keep up in this Country that confusion with respect to the Press which originated with the obnoxious ordinances[13] of a former Minister of the Interior M. de Schenk, issued a year ago, but which has since been withdrawn. The punishment of offences by the Press, in the absence of definite Laws, now chiefly rests with a Police which is but illcontrouled, which often acts in an arbitrary and contradictory manner and occasionally causes much embarrassment to the Government itself. Nor do I see any remedy for this state of things until some efficient measure shall have been passed by the Legislature; general satisfaction, however, I am inclined to think, will not be produced until the entire Liberty of the Press so energetically called for by the late Chamber of Deputies shall be granted.

On the first of next month a State Gazette[14] will appear here under the direction of the Govt, for the purpose of defending its general measures and the Persons of the Ministers who have been so severely attacked by the Opposition-Journals. The Editor[15] who has been selected was formerly remarkable for his writings in favour of liberal Principles; he is thought to have changed, but he himself professes the contrary.

To revert to the subject of the Bavarian Possessions on the Rhine,[16] I have reason to believe from every thing I have learnt during my stay in this Country that although the Inhabitants of that Province carry their ideas of Liberty further than their fellow subjects of ancient Bavaria, yet they do not wish again to be united to France, but might at the same time be desirous of seeing such improvements made in the Constitution as would be congenial to the Spirit of the Times. [...]

[12] The resistance of the second chamber prevented the new press law from being passed in August 1831.

[13] The Press Ordinance of 28 January 1831 had considerably tightened censorship. Political reportage had, without exception, been subjected to pre-censorship. This ordinance had been revoked on 13 June by King Ludwig I, that is, before the more moderate press bill presented to him had been debated by the *Landtag* (cf. n. 12 in this section).

[14] The *Bayerische Staatszeitung*, which was published in Munich from 1832, had only a brief existence, despite massive state subsidies.

[15] Friedrich Ludwig Lindner.

[16] The Palatinate (on the left bank of the Rhine), which had been under French rule since 1795, became part of Bavaria in 1816. The continued validity of the French administration, justice and legal systems gave it a special status.

FO 9/65: Lord Erskine to Viscount Palmerston, No 29, Munich, 12 June 1832

Measures triggered by the Hambach Festival

In transmitting the report of the occurrences at Hombach[17] furnished to me by His Bavarian Majesty's Government I have not also sent, as is customary, a translated Copy of it, as it is of too great length to admit of its being done in time, and as besides it does not contain any facts that are not already known to Your Lordship.

It is currently reported, and I believe with truth, that a considerable force of troops commanded by Prince Wrede[18] is about to set out immediately for the Circle of the Rhine to reestablish order in that Province in which other disturbances have lately taken place.

A very general sentiment prevails of the necessity of an immediate and effectual repression of these unlawful and dangerous proceedings.[19]

FO 9/65: Lord Erskine to Viscount Palmerston, No 35, Munich, 26 June 1832

Bavaria's attitude to the Six Articles; their acceptance by Bavaria crucial; effects caused by the articles; England interested in the preservation of rights and independence of constitutional states in Germany

In the course of another interview which I had yesterday with the Minister for Foreign Affairs, he explained to me that the reason why he could not furnish me with a copy of the six propositions of Vienna[20] was that it was as yet uncertain whether the President[21] of the Diet would cause them to be generally known, or not, as the acceptance of them on the part of His Bavarian Majesty was of a qualified nature and might require further consideration at the Diet; and the more so, as the consent of some of the other States was to depend upon that of Bavaria, which might therefore embarrass and delay the decisions of that Assembly.

He appeared, however, to be deeply impressed with the importance of the state of Affairs in Germany at the present moment, frequently

---

[17] Hambach Festival, 27–30 May 1832, cf. pp. 23–26 in Frankfurt section.

[18] Karl Philipp Fürst von Wrede.

[19] Enclosures: *Das Hambacher Fest aus officiellen Quellen dargestellt*; Translation: an account of the festival of Hambach from official data.

[20] For the Prussian–Austrian propositions, which were accepted by the *Bundestag* as the Six Articles cf. pp. 28–30 in Frankfurt section.

[21] Joachim Graf von Münch-Bellinghausen.

repeating that it was a 'moment bien critique'. He said that he cherished the hope that it might be possible to reconcile the rights of the Constitution of Bavaria with any future measure or course of policy directed by the Diet. He seemed anxious to discover what might be the probable chance of obtaining support in case the independence of Bavaria should be in danger of being infringed. This enquiry was not made directly of me, but I collected from the general tenor of his conversation that it was a point upon which his mind was very strongly bent.

Baron de Gise avows himself to be a firm Constitutionalist, but I can evidently perceive that he feels his position to be a very difficult one and that he is at a loss how to guide his political conduct. He is a very well meaning, sensible man and extremely desirous of preserving a moderate system of policy. Several other principal Members of the Government entertain similar sentiments.

I did not of course find myself authorized to convey to the Minister for Foreign Affairs any intimation of what might be the views of His Majesty's Government upon this very delicate and highly important subject; I considered myself, nevertheless, justified in assuring him that I was fully persuaded that His Majesty's Government would feel greatly interested in the preservation of the rights and independence of Constitutional States in Germany, as far as might be consistent with their reciprocal engagements to each other for their mutual protection.

Your Lordship will best judge whether it would be right to instruct me hereafter as to any language that I should hold, should any future attempts be made to ascertain, through me, the sentiments of His Majesty's Government. [...]

FO 9/66: Lord Erskine to Viscount Palmerston, No 1, Munich, 11 January 1833

Negotiations pending between Württemberg, Bavaria, and Prussia for a commercial treaty; Prussia's willingness to sacrifice revenues in order to obtain political power in Germany; Austria's proposal for a treaty unlikely to succeed; willingness to integrate Great Britain under certain circumstances

I find that all the Ministers and Chargés d'Affaires of the German States, (my colleagues at this Court), are of opinion that the negociations now pending between Bavaria Wurtemberg and Prussia for a commercial Treaty are likely to terminate in an arrangement favorable to their interests reciprocally, as it is expected that Prussia will give way sufficiently with respect to her Transit duties as to satisfy the other Contracting Parties.

It is frequently remarked to me that the Hanoverian Propositions[22] do not even go far enough in the principles of liberal commerce to meet the views of the German States above mentioned, but the great distinction and difference appears to me to be, that, by commercial Treaties being established between certain States separately, the general interests of Germany are not likely to be thereby so well attended to and promoted and still less the fair principles of Trade and Commerce with respect to other Nations.

There may still be a chance, however, that Prussia, may not be willing to sacrifice so much Revenue as She must do by acceding to such arrangements, but the Minister for Foreign Affairs[23] assured me yesterday that he fully expected that She would acquiesce in the propositions which are now under Her consideration, in the hope of obtaining a political influence in the Diet and in Germany generally by such a commercial alliance

Whilst these negociations are pending, it is not likely that the propositions made by Austria for a commercial Treaty with Bavaria and Wurtemberg[24] will make much, if indeed, any progress, because although there are no principles of commerce, I believe, opposite to those contained in the projected Treaty with Prussia, yet I can hardly think that Austria would be enclined to cede her restrictive system of commerce generally, unless from the hope of gaining, by that means, a political influence and support from the German States in the Diet.

The Ministers of the German States which are in treaty with each other for these commercial arrangements continually declare that they would all be willing to admit into their views and connexions any other Countries which would agree to reciprocally free principles of commerce; and when I have asked whether it was meant that Great Britain, for instance would be allowed to join such an alliance, the answer has always been that they did not doubt it, provided that She, on Her part, would change Her Corn Laws and make Her Custom House duties conformable to the rules which are to be established amongst the Contracting German States.

---

[22] In 1832 Hanover filed an application in the *Bundestag* for a unified customs system (including the free movement of goods on all roads and rivers) to be introduced in the territory of the German Confederation, in line with article 19 of the Act of the German Confederation of 1815.

[23] August Friedrich Freiherr von Gise.

[24] Since August 1830 Austria had been trying to conclude a trade and customs agreement. The negotiations, which Austria had raised to a new level of intensity in March 1832, had little priority for Bavaria and Württemberg against the background of negotiations for entry into the *Zollverein*.

FO 9/66: Lord Erskine to Viscount Palmerston, No 31, Munich, 9 July 1833

Strictness of police due to discovery of alleged political intrigues; involvement of Poles; more careful treatment of English travellers envisaged

In the course of an interview which I had lately with Prince Wallerstein, the Minister of the Interior, he explained to me the reasons of the extreme strictness of the Police at present in Bavaria which had been ordered in consequence of the many Discoveries that had been made of political intrigues and even of extensive projected revolutionary movements.

He stated to me that many Poles[25] had been engaged in exciting a disposition to disturbance amongst the Students and others and that a wide spread intercourse had been traced and a conexion even with the Propaganda Societies of France.

When I enquired him of whether proof of such conexion had been obtained, he acknowledged to me that they had not actual proofs; but that there were the strongest reasons for believing it, derived from many letters in the possession of various persons who have been arrested.

He assured me that some of the most horrible assassinations had been spoken of as necessary, and the necessity of a general conspiracy against all kings and great aristocratic personages as the only means of obtaining the emancipation of Germany.

He did not pretend to justify some of the detentions of English travellers of which I had preferred several complaints; but on the contrary informed me that he would give directions to the Police and other authorities to be more careful and discriminating in future. [...]

FO 9/66: Lord Erskine to Viscount Palmerston, No 48, Munich, 4 December 1833

Considerations on the effects of the Zollverein; question of whether it is potentially damaging to British interests

The more I consider the object and the probable effect of the German Commercial League so often alluded to in my late Despatches to Your Lordship the more I am struck with the unfriendly tendency of it towards the interests of Great Britain.

[25] For the presence of Poles in the states of the German Confederation cf. n. 63 in Frankfurt section.

I have no means of knowing and no right to suspect that the intention of it is hostile to England – but its consequences (if the Tariff should be so high as it is expected to be) might be more injurious than the unjustifiable Berlin and Milan decrees of Buonaparte[26] because they were unwillingly received and therefore imperfectly carried into effect by the different Countries of the Continent: whereas the high parties of the commercial League propose uniting their most vigorous efforts against any infringement of its regulations.

It appears to me, My Lord, that the great services rendered by Great Britain to the security and independence of the Continent of Europe have either been ungratefully remembered or most unaccountably overlooked when the great exertions and extraordinary sacrifices of England during a long protracted war for the common cause are considered.

I have frequently drawn the attention of His Bavarian Majesty's Government for several years past to this view of the effect of the commercial League; but the answer uniformly given has been, that the intention of it was entirely confined to advancing the interests of the Countries engaged in it and not against any other Power – but surely the imposing of such extravagant duties and severe restrictions on the Commerce of other Countries upon the great rivers and internal communications of so large a part of the best Countries of Europe can be viewed in no other light than as an unfriendly exclusion.

Whether it may be possible for Great Britain to elude its injurious effects will be a most important question and will no doubt meet with all the attention due to it from His Majesty's Government. [...]

FO 9/69: Lord Erskine to Viscount Palmerston, No 4, Munich, 14 February 1834

Question of whether the constitutions of several Germans states are threatened by the proposals made in Vienna (i.e. alterations in censorship; restrictions on freedom of debate in the chambers)

During an interview which I had yesterday with Baron Lerchenfeld the Minister of Finance (who is acting also at present as Minister for foreign Affairs) some observations were made by him which I consider of sufficient importance to relate to your Lordship.

Upon my mentioning to him that reports prevailed generally that propositions were about to be made to the Congress of Vienna[27] for

[26] Cf. n. 15 in Prussia section.
[27] Cf. pp. 135–138 in Prussia section, and pp. 503–505 in Austria section.

changing parts of the Constitution of some of the States of Germany he assured me that no such propositions would be made and that if any such should have been made that His Majesty the King of Bavaria would never have consented to violate a Constitution which His Father had given and which He himself had sworn to maintain.

It is possible that it may be intended to give an interpretation at the Congress of Vienna of a larger extent as to the power of the Confederation of Germany in general for purposes of mutual defence against external danger but that no attempt would be made or at least would be likely to succeed to extend the power of the German Diet to an interference with the internal affairs of any separate State.

The only important alteration likely to be effected has indeed for some time past been established namely the <u>Censure of the Press</u> to which notwithstanding many objections have been urged no attempt at open resistance has yet been made nor do I think will be likely to appear.

Some of my Colleagues believe that there will be propositions made in the Diet for endeavouring to put some restraint upon the freedom of debate in the Chambers which is considered by many as having been extended even to too great a licence; but it appears to me that it would be very difficult to accomplish such an object without mainly interfering with the rights and independence of separate States.

Your Lordship will of course be much better informed than I can be respecting what has passed or is likely to pass at the Congress of Vienna; but I have thought it my Duty to relate to your Lordship the foregoing particulars respecting this Country which has a representative there at present in the person of M. de Gise but who is expected shortly home and Mr de Mieg at present Bavarian Minister to the Diet of Frankfort will go there in his place.

FO 9/69: Lord Erskine to Viscount Palmerston, No 45, Munich, 24 June 1834

Royal projects (Library; canal between Rhine and Danube); moderate behaviour in the chambers proves that liberal constitutions may be consistent with rights of monarchy

The Chambers have just voted a hundred thousand florins to be devoted to the completion of the building for the Royal Library which was left in an unfinished state for want of funds.

This appropriation has given great pleasure to His Bavarian Majesty who had taken very great interest in this establishment which will now be soon finished and on a scale very considerable and will be a great addition to the many publick buildings which already adorn this City.

A sum of two millions of florins, which is not however to be appropriated until two thirds of the amount required for the enterprise has been raised by subscription, has been lately voted for carrying into effect the project for joining by means of a Canal the Rhine with the Danube[28] has also given great pleasure to His Majesty as he was pleased to inform me last night when His Majesty condescendingly honoured me with a visit at a chateau on the Lake of Starnberg which I have hired for the summer months where His Majesty has a palace which he occasionally frequents.

His Majesty dwelt for some time and with great earnestness on the great advantages which he anticipated would result from that important undertaking which he said had been first imagined by Charlemagne the Great and which he hoped would be of the greatest use to Bavaria & at the same time contribute highly to the commerce and interests of Germany in general.

His Bavarian Majesty appeared to be perfectly satisfied with the whole conduct of the Chambers this Session which has certainly been extremely moderate and considerate and must have a great effect towards proving that liberal Constitutions in Germany may be consistent with the rights and political advantages of a Monarchy and at this particular moment is likely to be of the greatest consequence in encouraging the hopes of the practicability and usefulness of such a System of Government.

The Chambers will separate in a few days and His Bavarian Majesty and the Court will quit this Residence for some months unless any particular circumstances should occasion the necessity of returning to it. [...]

FO 9/71: Lord Erskine to Duke of Wellington, No 7, Munich, 15 January 1835

Prussia's customs deficit due to Zollverein; disadvantage to manufacturing interests of Great Britain; willingness to enter into negotiations with any foreign power

In reference to my despatches N[os] 3, 4, 5 and 6 upon the subject of the German Commercial League, I beg leave to state to Your Grace that I find very great importance is attached to the deficit in the receipts of the Prussian Custom House from the product of it before the treaty.

Many reasons are brought forward to show that the deficit is only likely to be temporary; but it is not attempted to be denied that if so

---

[28] The canal project was to connect the Danube with the Main and not, as the dispatch suggests, the Rhine. Building works began in 1835 and were completed in 1846.

large a deficit should in future be incurred it would tend to weaken the confidence in the advantages to be derived from that commercial league.

How far it might be favourable to the general interests of Germany is as yet uncertain, but there can be no doubt that the treaty would be highly disadvantageous, if carried into full effect, to the manufacturing interests of Great Britain, as already the English goods have very much disappeared from the towns and other places in the States of the contracting parties to that league in consequence of the extravagantly high duties which have been imposed upon them beyond those of German Manufacture, although the German manufactured goods are not only greatly inferior to the British but really of a very bad quality particularly for instance the cotton, and long woolen, and flannel goods.

Those articles are hardly to be found in this town, and always of an inferior kind and very dear. Whenever the Tarif of the Commercial German League is spoken of as being high as respects articles of foreign manufacture the answer always given is that it is not half as high as the tarifs of England and France on manufactured goods imported into those countries, and especially with regard to corn and wood, the principal articles which some of the German Countries could send to England in great quantity, but which they cannot do on account of the high duties, so that, in fact, (as it is said) those countries have nothing to send.

It would perhaps be presumption in me to consider the important question of how far it might suit the Policy of Great Britain to make any further diminution in her import duties, or any change in her Corn Laws,[29] but I am persuaded that if it ever should be thought advisable or possible to do so, an arrangement might be made with the German States of the commercial league, as they are well aware of the difficulties, expense, and trouble of guarding the introduction of contraband goods.

I have considered it however to be my duty rather to endeavour to explain to Your Grace the state of things as I conceive it to exist in these States than to presume to suggest any alterations in the system which has been adopted in our own country.

I will only however venture to add that I have always been assured by my colleagues that the members of the German commercial league would be willing to enter into negotiations upon fair terms of a commercial treaty with any foreign Powers.

[29] Cf. n. 171 in Prussia section.

FO 9/71: Lord Erskine to Viscount Palmerston, No 26, Munich, 19 October 1835

Detailed account of the Munich 'Oktober Fest'

In commemoration of the twenty fifth year of the marriage of their Bavarian Majesties the anniversary October Fête has been celebrated with more than usual ceremony and display.

Although it would, perhaps, be unnecessary to trouble Your Lordship with a long, detailed account of the various exhibitions which took place that day (the 4th of October) I may perhaps be allowed to mention that the different towns and districts of Bavaria sent up to Munich a certain number of their inhabitants, representing, and dressed in the costume of, the various trades and occupations of their respective countries, arranged in waggons adorned with garlands of flowers and covered with other ornaments in a most picturesque and even elegant manner.

The whole effect of these precessions as they passed by the Tent in which their Majesties and the Court were placed, (the weather being fine,) was extremely good, as very great pains had been bestowed by the various deputations in preparing the numerous ornaments and devices in honour of the day.

It was indeed remarkable how much ingenuity, and even taste, was displayed by some of the towns and villages in these different representations, which were entirely furnished and imagined by the inhabitants themselves, though it might have been supposed that some director of a theatre had planned them.

Sometimes these processions were attended by a hundred or more horsemen, generally preceded by musick, – sometimes by considerable numbers on foot in the costumes of their respective countries and trades; and the greatest order prevailed whilst all these deputations were passing, and the strongest demonstrations of loyalty towards their Majesties were displayed.

The whole of the expence of these ceremonies was defrayed by the communes themselves respectively, and was entirely at their own suggestion as his Majesty when first applied to for his permission that such marks of the people's loyal affection should be shown, rather objected to it, on the ground that the period of their Majesties' marriage had not been long enough to justify such a display, but on its being remarked that twenty five years of marriage was called the silver, and fifty years was called the golden period, His Majesty was graciously pleased to give way to the requests of his People.

The various amusements lasted ten days, amongst others there was a company of wrestlers in ancient costume, who not only displayed a great deal of strength and agility but at the same time the contests were carried on in front of the Royal tent in a very graceful manner, and in perfect good humour.

The Wrestlers were all Bakers by trade, and when asked, by order of the King, what sort of recompense they would like to have, replied, that if His Majesty would condescend to direct that a band of musick should play at a ball they were about to have, they should be highly flattered and satisfied.

There were also horse and foot races and other amusements which took place on the occasion. I ought perhaps to apologize to Your Lordship for troubling you with these details, but all strangers agreed in saying that it was a very curious and interesting display by the people of processions, games, and amusements, such as on so large a scale they had never before seen exhibited.

FO 9/72: Lord Erskine to Viscount Palmerston, Separate, Munich, 12 September 1836

Appearance of cholera; precautionary preparations in case cholera reaches Munich

As doubts were entertained whether the disease that has made its appearance at Mittenwald in Bavaria (four Posts from Munich on the road to Italy) was the real Cholera or not, I did not trouble your Lordship with any account of its progress, but it has now been pronounced by some Physicians who have been sent there expressly by the Gov[t] to be the real Cholera of which about nine or then persons of the place (which contains about 1600 inhabitants) have died daily.

It is considered uncertain whether the complaint will extend itself, or not, and in what direction as it seems to have passed over without affecting the town of Innsbruck (the capital of the Tyrol) as well as several other towns and villages round about.

It is said that Mittenwald is situated in an unhealthy position but the large town of Mantua in the North of Italy is placed in a much more marshy and unhealthy Country and has not been attacked by the Cholera although it has raged in a violent degree in the adjoining Countries.

Every preparation has been made in Munich to treat that Disease (if it should make its appearance) in the best way possible, but from what I have heard the Physicians do not entertain great confidence in any one particular mode of cure as they say it must depend very much upon the particular state of the different persons who may become affected by it.

They all however seem to entertain strong hopes that Munich would be likely to suffer less than most other towns of the same size, from its position and local circumstances.

FO 9/72: Lord Erskine to Viscount Palmerston, No 67, Munich, 9 December 1836

State of cholera in Munich

The state of the Cholera has varied but little since my last account although it was expected that the late very high winds might have had some effect by changing & purifying the air of this neighbourhood, but the disease was rather increased than lessened.

The new cases daily are from 33 to 50 & the Deaths from 16 to 24; but the number of persons affected in different degrees by a Diarrhaea which is considered as part of the Epidemy has been very great indeed – amounting it is said to 4000, – whose cure has been effected by remedies administered in the early stage of the attack; but with respect to the violent cases of the disease more advanced, it is remarkable that the proportion of Deaths has been as in most other places something less than half of those attacked, notwithstanding there have been & still are many Physicians who declare that they are acquainted with a specific cure yet few are agreed upon the remedies to be employed, & generally differ in the use of them.

I have been requested to transmit to His Majesty's Gov^t a letter addressed to Our Royal Master enclosing a publication upon the disease by Dr. Wilhelm Physician to Her Majesty the Dowager Queen,[30] who has a good reputation & I have therefore thought it right to forward it herewith to your Lordship to be disposed of as you may deem fit & proper.

It has been universally remarked that since the prevalence of the Cholera in this town the slightest irregularity in the manner of living has a tendency to produce some symptoms of that disorder and that almost every body has felt an occasional indisposition of that character which caused at first great alarm but which has now partly subsided.

The whole number of persons who have been seriously affected by the Cholera from the middle of October up to the present time has been between 1300 & 1400 & the number of Deaths according to the official report has been between 600 & 700.[31]

[30] Karoline.
[31] Enclosure: *Praktische Bemerkungen des Professors Dr. Wilhelm in München über die Cholera, das schützende Verfahren vor und bey derselben, wie die Behandlung derselben*, 5 November 1836 (Practical comments on the cholera, on preventative measures and treatment, by Prof. Dr Wilhelm in Munich) (Publication with accompanying letter to the English King).

FO 9/74: Lord Erskine to Viscount Palmerston, No 10, Munich, 30 January 1837

Liberal attitude to public press in Bavaria; offensive articles against British government

[...] The Rules which are laid down for the Regulation of the public press[32] in this Country are different from those which prevail in Prussia, although there is a Censorship in both Countries but in the 'Allgemeine Zeitung'[33] printed in Bavaria (& which is received in all the Countries of Europe) there are to be found articles extracted from the British Press seldom violent on either side and reasonably fairly selected and the newspapers of all the different political opinions are permitted to come into the Country upon the same terms though all are liable to be suppressed and sometimes are so by the authority of the Gov^t.

A very scandalous article[34] of personal attack, it is true, has appeared in the number of yesterday extracted from the Times against the members of His Majesty's Gov^t which it appears to me ought not to be permitted in a Country where the Censorship of the Press is established; but I have hesitated to make any remonstrance upon the subject as it does not come precisely under the Principles laid down in Lord William Russell's letter to M. Ancillon.

FO 9/74: Lord Erskine to Viscount Palmerston, No 54, Munich, 5 September 1837

Apanage for King Otto

In the course of a discussion lately in the Chamber of Deputies on the subject of the budget, the Minister for Foreign Affairs, Baron de Gise, expressed himself in the following manner.

'I am enabled to declare most distinctly that His Majesty King Otho has not only not renounced all His rights as a Bavarian Prince, but, on the contrary, that, under certain conditions, He has expressly reserved His claims to the Throne of Bavaria.'

---

[32] Press Ordinance of 28 January 1818.

[33] The *Allgemeine Zeitung*, from 1810 also known as the *Augsburger Allgemeine* (after the place of publication), had been established by Johann Friedrich von Cotta in 1798, and from 1832 was continued by his son, Georg von Cotta. It was among Germany's most important newspapers in the nineteenth century.

[34] The *Allgemeine Zeitung* published the article in question, taken from *The Times* (London), in German translation on 29 January 1834, without any commentary. In it, doubt was cast on the political competence and the moral suitability of Sir Robert Peel's entire government.

The sum of 80,000 florins was accordingly voted for six years as an Apanage for King Otho.

FO 9/74: Lord Erskine to Viscount Palmerston, No 56, Munich, 5 October 1837

Change in the Bavarian ministry no proof of King's inclination towards a more liberal policy

Various reports have prevailed here for some time past that a change in the Ministry of His Bavarian Majesty is likely to take place, but I have not as yet been able to ascertain whether they are correctly founded or not, though I am inclined to think Baron de Gise will give up the Post of Minister for Foreign Affairs, as in the course of an interview which I had with him a few days ago, he intimated to me that he had resolved many years since to retire about the present period from public life to the enjoyment of that repose which his health required and his inclination induced him to seek; and this communication seemed to me to confirm the reports to which I have alluded and which have been in general circulation, that Prince Wallerstein would be appointed as Minister for Foreign Affairs and that M. de Mieg, (at present Minister to the Diet) (should his health permit it) would replace the Prince as Minister of the Interior.

Should this alteration take place it is not considered that it would be any proof of an intention on the part of His Bavarian Majesty to change the system of the Bavarian Gov^t towards a more liberal course of Policy, but that it would only be a change of persons as it is known that the King still continues to entertain the same apprehension of the march of liberal opinions, which had produced so strong an impression upon His Majesty at the period of the French Revolution of 1830[35] and has continued ever since to influence his political conduct. [...]

FO 9/74: Lord Erskine to Viscount Palmerston, No 57, Munich, 23 October 1837

Both chambers agree on budget spending; possible effects of this; Prince Wallerstein offers resignation; King's reaction

I avail myself of the opportunity of sending by a Queen's Messenger an account of the remarkable and important occurrences which have lately taken place in the two Chambers of Legislature of this Country.

[35] Cf. n. 28 in Frankfurt section.

It had been observed by the Chamber of Deputies that a full and correct account had not been rendered in the Budget which was laid before them; they therefore came to a resolution by a very considerable majority that the sum which according to their estimate remained to be disposed of, should be devoted to the improvement of the publick roads & Buildings which have been considered for a long time to be in a very bad state.

This Resolution was then sent up to the Chamber of Peers, and to the astonishment of everybody was acceded to by a majority of eighteen to three, (the vote however of the President the Maréchal Prince de Wrede[36] making a fourth) although it was known that His Bav^n Majesty was opposed to that measure and was highly desirous that it should not be carried. But the most remarkable circumstance was that the Minister of the Interior Prince Wallerstein spoke strongly in favor of that resolution, & supported it by all his influence with the Peers, which was considerable and mainly contributed to their acquiescence in the resolution alluded to, which had been passed by the Chamber of Deputies.

The course of conduct which was adopted by Prince Wallerstein on this occasion naturally offended His Bav^n Majesty and there is no doubt that Prince Wallerstein will retire from the Post of Minister of the Interior & indeed he has already offered his Resignation, but the pleasure of His Bavarian Majesty upon the subject has not yet been made known.

I should mention to your Lordship that His Bav^n Majesty, when he learnt what had been the resolution of the two Chambers, called together the Council of State[37] and consulted them upon the Constitutional Question as to whether His Majesty had a right to direct the employment of the savings of the Revenue in such manner as he might think proper, when eleven out of twelve gave their opinion that His Majesty had that right.

It is unknown at present to the persons who have given me the forgoing information (and who are in the best situation to be well informed) what steps His Bavarian Majesty may think it proper to take under the existing circumstances, but one of my Colleagues, whom I consider to be good authority on such a subject, thinks that the Gov^t will endeavour to make a compromise with the Chamber of Deputies, which, consisting as it does in great part of persons under the influence in some way or other of the Gov^t may be persuaded to accept a

[36] Karl Philipp Fürst von Wrede.

[37] *Staatsrat*, the highest authority, in an advisory capacity, in the kingdom. It was composed of Crown Prince Maximilian, Prince Karl Theodor, the ministers, six councillors of State nominated by the King, and one secretary general.

promise on the part of the King of Bavaria to pay some attention to their recommendation.

I will not fail to let your Lordship know the result (whatever it may be) of the state of things above described but I beg leave at present to draw your attention to the singular circumstance that a Minister of so distinguished a Reputation for talents (as Prince Wallerstein is) and backed by a large Majority of both Houses of the Legislature in so important a measure of Finance should be obliged to retire while all the other Ministers who were in a small Minority but supported by the King should retain their Posts – Baron de Gise is now firmer than ever in his place.

FO 9/76: Richard Camden Bingham to Viscount Palmerston, No 5, Munich, 4 January 1838

On the King's motives for a Royal decree establishing a new territorial division of his kingdom; expenses involved; measure not considered to be popular

I have the honor to enclose herewith an abstract translation of a Royal Decree, which appeared last month in the Government Gazette, establishing a new territorial division of this Kingdom.[38]

I have endeavoured with as little success to ascertain the origin of this measure, as to discover any good likely to result from it. It would seem to have emanated from the King alone, who, it is well known, did not even consult the Presidents of the different Circles respecting it, and to have no other cause than His Majesty's ardour in the revival of historical associations, and desire of blending his own name in their transmission to posterity; I am therefore unwilling to give credit to the reports prevalent with respect to His Majesty's supposed real motives: namely, that these changes are a prelude to the establishment of Provincial States, in substitution for the existing States General, reports which may owe their origin chiefly to the King's well-known sentiments upon the late Coup d'État in Hanover,[39] and to the dissatisfaction with which he lately separated from his Chambers. I think that they are, however, of sufficient importance to be brought under Your Lordship's

[38] Under the terms of the Ordinance of 29 November 1837, the eight circles of the Kingdom of Bavaria, which had so far been named after rivers, were renamed: 1. Upper Bavaria (former Circle of Isar), 2. Lower Bavaria (former Circle of Lower Danube), 3. Palatinate (former Circle of the Rhine), 4. Upper Palatinate and Ratisbonne (Circle of Regen), 5. Upper Franconia (Upper Maine), 6. Middle Franconia (Circle of Rezat), Lower Franconia and Aschaffenburg (Lower Maine), 8. Swabia and Neuburg (Upper Danube).

[39] Cf., among others, pp. 263–264 in Hanover section.

notice; the more especially as the King's Circle has been the most active in giving them currency.

The expence which this measure will occasion to the country is not the least feature belonging to it, as a million of florins, it is supposed, will scarcely defray the complicated transfers attendant upon it. The Circle of Upper Bavaria, formerly the Circle of the Isar, containing the Capital, alone receives, from the change, an augmentation of 100,000. inhabitants.

The inconvenience of every kind produced to the Provincial Authorities has not tended likewise to render the measure popular, and the Bavarians in general consider it as opposed to the system of nationality[40] which it had been the object of their chief man of State, Count de Montgelas, during many years, to accomplish.[41]

FO 9/76: Richard Camden Bingham to William Fox-Strangways, unnumbered, Munich, 5 March 1838

Publication of Görres' work 'Athanasius' on religious differences arising from the arrest of the Archbishop of Cologne

I transmit to you herewith a work[42] in duplicate which has appeared lately at Munich upon the religious differences which have arisen out of the affair at Cologne.

This publication, which has gone through many editions, has excited deep interest in this country. It has been prohibited in Prussia; the Prussian Minister[43] at this Court even made a representation to this Government, previously to its appearance, with the view of its suppression, which was so little attended to that the King permitted the Author to deliver it to Him in a private Audience and addressed to him the most flattering compliments.

The Author, Mr Görres, who is at the head of the Ultramontane Party and Professor of History at this University, was in 1793 a leading demagogue in France. He became afterwards Editor of the 'Mercure

[40] The main components of Montgelas's reform policy were the internal modernization and reordering of Bavaria, which had been enlarged and elevated into a kingdom in 1806. Montgelas is considered to be the father of the modern Bavarian state.

[41] Enclosure: Extract from No. 58 of the *Regierungs-Blatt*, 29 November 1837.

[42] *Athanasius* by Josef von Görres was published in January 1837. An indictment of Protestantism and the Prussian state, it was the first significant document of political Catholicism in Germany.

[43] August Graf von Dönhoff.

du Rhin'[44] and in 1814. & 1815. preached revolt against French dominion
in Germany.

   The work is considered in this Country as a counterpart to the
'Paroles d'un Croyant'[45] and the most remarkable composition that
has, as yet, appeared from the Congregation Party, having for object
to establish the supremacy of Church over State; its tendency is besides
revolutionary in so far as it demonstrates the impossibility of Catholick
Populations remaining subjected to Protestant Sovereigns, and on that
account I view the work as likely to offer interest to The Majesty's
Government.[46]

FO 9/78: Lord Erskine to Viscount Palmerston, No 31, Confidential,
Munich, 3 December 1839

*On the King's right to strike out names of deputies he objects to; his intention to increase his
influence in the chambers*

[...] The King of Bavaria, after having dissolved, not long ago, one
legislative Assembly, before it met, upon slight grounds, is now exercising
a right of striking out the names of all such Deputies who are obnoxious
to him, of the Legislative Chamber recently chosen.

   This right is given to him most strangely by the Constitution[47] in
cases of all those who hold employment under Government, and as by
far the greater part of those who are likely to be chosen as Deputies
are in that position, as collectors of taxes, or holders of some kind of
office in the Towns and villages, it naturally gives a most extensive
power to The King of Bavaria, of influencing the composition of the
Chamber of Deputies.

   But in order to obtain a still further power to accomplish that object,
The King of Bavaria, some years ago, decreed[48] that all advocates
should have the dignity conferred upon them (as His Majesty was
pleased to term it) of being in the Royal service, by which means they
are all brought under the controul of the right which I have above

---

[44] *Rheinischer Merkur*, founded in 1814 by Joseph von Görres in Koblenz; banned in
1816.

[45] *Paroles d'un Croyant* (1834), containing a democratic programme advocating religious
freedom and the separation of church and state, by Hugues-Félicité-Robert de Lamennais.

[46] Enclosure: Copy of Goerres Work (*Athanasius*) on religious difference existing in
Germany.

[47] Cf. n. 4 in this section.

[48] Paragraph 44 of the Edict on the Assembly of the Estates was cited in justification
of the exclusion of advocates. This practice, which was based on a decision taken by the
council of ministers (*Ministerrat*) in 1818, was not legally anchored in legislation until 23
May 1846.

described, which is given to the King, of striking out the names of those Deputies who enjoy any post under Government.

His Majesty has accordingly not only rejected all such Deputies who are obnoxious to him for any reason, but when other persons are proposed to him as substitutes for those who have been struck out, he has, in many cases, accepted those who had the fewest number of votes of the electors in their favor, which The King also, by a curious Law of the Constitution, has a right to do.

In making the foregoing observations, My Lord, or in any which may follow, I do not mean to insinuate that His Bavarian Majesty has violated the Constitution, but I feel it to be my duty to remark, that The King has invariably of late, in the exercise of his privileges, rejected from the Legislative Chambers many of the most enlightened Deputies, who had been chosen by large majorities of the electors, in their respective districts.

This strong measure His Majesty has adopted, under the impression that danger to the tranquillity and even safety of Bavaria, may be apprehended, from the diffusion through the country of Democratic principles, or even from the influence of such persons (however otherwise respectable) who entertained liberal political opinions.

These fears have been, I believe, created in His Majesty's mind, by the political events which occurred in France in the year 1830[49] and since that period, and having, in my opinion, if I may venture to express it, been more alarmed than the occasion justified, He is acting in a manner as much injurious to his own interests, as it is contrary to the advantage and best interests of his people.

FO 9/78: Stephen Sulivan to Viscount Palmerston, No 4, Munich, 24 December 1839

Baron von Gise's reply to Palmerston's critical note concerning cruelties committed in Greece

I have the Honor, herewith, to transmit to Your Lordship a copy of the reply of the Baron de Gisé to the notes which, according to Your Lordship's directions, were addressed by Lords Erskine to His Excellency on the 25th and 26th November, relative to the cruelties committed in Greece.[50]

---

[49] Cf. n. 28 in Frankfurt section.

[50] The British government's complaints about the Greek government concerned the use of torture, and the involvement of innocent people in proceedings against members of the opposition, tax evaders, and thieves. The Bavarian government reacted to British interventions against state sanctioned terror in Greece by pointing out that King Otto was independent of his father, the Bavarian King Ludwig I.

At an Interview which I had with the Baron de Gisé, yesterday, I observed to His Excellency, that I could not refrain from expressing my surprize at the note in question, the tenor of which appeared to me to be quite inconsistent with the language latterly held by His Excellency to Lord Erskine, upon the subject of Grecian affairs.

The Baron de Gisé stated in reply, that the language which he had held upon the affairs of Greece, since the year 1832, had undergone no variation. He said that the Government of Bavaria had always been of opinion, that Greece would do well to look to England, as to her best friend and her firmest support; That he had, upon many occasions assured Your Lordship that such were his sentiments; but that the Bavarian Government never had interfered, and never intended to interfere with the internal affairs of Greece. He said, that it was a mistake to suppose that The King of Bavaria exercised any influence over the councils of his son; that such an influence might have been exerted during the period of the Regency, and that if it had been so exerted, it would probably have been advantageous for Greece, but that now, His Bavarian Majesty had not the Power, even if he had the will, of influencing in any way, the proceedings of King Otho.

I observed to the Baron de Gisé that Your Lordship had certainly never desired, that the Government of Bavaria should interfere in the internal affairs of an independent Power like Greece; but that as it was natural to suppose that the Bavarian Government must feel a deep interest in the welfare of that country, and that advice tendered by a sovereign so intimately connected with His Grecian Majesty, could not fail to have great weight at Athens, Your Lordship had been desirous that the Bavarian Gov^t should recommend to King Otho the pursuance of a different system, in certain points, from that which His Grecian Majesty appeared to be at present pursuing, and which did not seem likely to be ultimately conducive to His Majesty's Interests, or to the happiness of His subjects.

I said that if the repeated assurances made by His Excellency were of any value, they must lead to some practical results, and that His Excellency's note of the 17th Instant, after the renewed assurances made to Lord Erskine a short time ago, and the belief which Lord Erskine had expressed in their sincerity, could not fail to create in Your Lordship much surprize and disappointment.

The Baron Gisé after again repeating those vague assurances which have, from time to time, been reported to Your Lordship, proceeded to remark, that there appeared to be a great discrepancy between the reports received by Her Majesty's Gov^t, of the state of affairs in Greece, and those which were received by himself. He said that, according to the statements which reached him, Greece was in a happy and prosperous condition; that the revenue was increasing; that the Government of King Otho gave universal satisfaction; and that the Greeks vied each other in sentiments of loyalty and of affection towards their Sovereign. [...][51]

FO 9/78: Stephen Sulivan to Viscount Palmerston, No 6, Munich, 26 December 1839

Alterations in the composition of the Bavarian chambers due to governmental intervention; expected subjects of debate in future proceedings; question of control of public expenditure

The number of members of the new Chamber of Deputies whose elections have been cancelled by Royal order, and the substitution, in the stead of the rejected members, of Individuals whose opinions are little known, has so entirely altered the composition of that Body, that it is difficult to form any conjecture as to the course which the Chambers may pursue. As however fifty four Protestants have been elected, one of whom, a Professor[52] of the University of Erlangen, is looked up to as the great defender of the Protestant cause, it is conceived that the grievances under which that portion of His Bavarian Majesty's subjects are laboring, will form a principal topic of discussion.

The two points upon which the Protestants chiefly ground their complaints, are 1st The Royal Decree,[53] according to which, in contradiction to the 72nd Article of the Constitution,[54] the adoration of the Host is expressly enjoined upon all Protestants serving in the Bavarian army or in the Militia (Landwehr).

2dly The constant refusal of the Minister of the Interior,[55] to permit Protestant Churches to be built, or the rites of the Protestant religion to be celebrated, in various towns in the Bavarian Dominions.

The discontent occasioned by the first of the above mentioned grievances, has been so great, that The King of Bavaria has been compelled to rescind that portion of the Decree which concerned the Militia, the Landwehr of Augsburg having, upon a recent occasion refused to obey, and having addressed to His Bavarian Majesty a Protest against the Decree in question; but the adoration of the Host still remains compulsory upon the whole of the Bavarian regular army.

---

[51] Enclosure: Note from Baron de Gise to Lord Erskine, 17 December 1839, stating in reply to his Lordship's notes, that the King can not interfere with the internal Affairs of Greece.

[52] Adolph von Harleß.

[53] Genuflexion Ordinance (*Kniebeugeorder*) of 14 August 1838.

[54] Paragraph 2 of the Preamble to the Bavarian Constitution of 1818 provided for the separation of church and state.

[55] Karl August von Abel.

Upon these questions, as well as upon question of the right which the Chambers abrogated to themselves of enquiring into and controuling the expenditure of the public money, both Prince Charles[56] the brother of the King, and the Prince Royal[57] have been strongly opposed to the system pursued by His Bavarian Majesty. The Prince Royal has endeavored, but without effect, to convince His Royal Father of the impolicy of the course which he was pursuing; and being, on the one hand, unwilling, by a surrender of his Principles, to compromise his future position, and on the other hand, feeling the impropriety of entering into open opposition to the views of the King, His Royal Highness requested that he might be allowed to be absent from Munich, at the period of the opening of the Chambers, and to take this opportunity of paying his brother the King of Greece, a visit which he has long meditated.

I have been informed that the King has as yet positively refused to consent to the departure of the Prince Royal, and that slight hopes are now entertained that His Majesty will grant his consent; although His Majesty has expressed his willingness to permit The Prince Royal to go any where excepting to Greece, upon condition that His Royal Highness will first declare his adhesion to the system pursued by his Royal Father.

Under these circumstances great efforts have been made by Prince Wallerstein and some of the leading members of the House of Peers, to induce their colleagues to consent, that the question of the right of the Chambers to controul the public expenditure, shall not be mooted during the present Session, but shall be postponed till the year 1842, when the new Budget will be brought forward by the Government.

The Prince Royal has, on his part, declared, that in obedience to His Bavarian Majesty's orders, he will be present at the opening of the Chambers, but that nothing shall prevent him, at the commencement of the discussions, from retiring to his country seat at Hohenzwangau.[58]

FO 9/80: Stephen Sulivan to Viscount Palmerston, No 20, Munich, 9 March 1840

Question of the Bavarian chamber's right to inquire into public expenditure

The Committee of Finance in the Chamber of Deputies have concluded their task of examining into the public accounts submitted by the

[56] Karl Theodor Maximilian.
[57] Maximilian.
[58] Hohenschwangau.

Government for their Inspection. The Committee having ascertained, that, at the close of the year 1838, there existed a surplus revenue of upwards of twenty millions of florins, to which no allusion had been made by the Minster of Finance,[59] and of which no account had been given, applied to the Government for further information upon the subject.

The Portfolio of the Finance Department having been entrusted, ad Interim, to Mons' Abel the Minister of the Interior, on account of the ill health of the Minister of Finance, M. Abel was summoned before the Committee, and was required to explain the purposes to which so large a surplus had been appropriated.

His Excellency stated to the Committee, in reply, that the duty of the Chambers consisted simply in voting the supplies which were required by the Government; That it was not their business to enquire into the manner in which any surplus revenue was disposed of; and that he should give no further Information upon the subject, unless he received The King's commands to do so.

The Question of the right of the Chambers to enquire into the expenditure of the public money, was submitted to the Council of State on the 7th Instant. Seven members of the Council voted in favor of the view which had been taken by His Bavarian Majesty; and four members, among whom was The Prince Royal, voted in favor of the right claimed by the Chambers.

I have been informed that a meeting of the leading men among the Deputies was held this day, at which it was decided, that if The King still adhered to the declaration[60] made by His Majesty when he dissolved the Chambers in the year 1837; and if he persisted in denying the right of that Body to enquire into the manner in which the Revenue was expended, – a solemn Protest should be drawn up by the Chambers against the view which his Majesty had taken upon this subject; and that this Protest should be entered upon the minutes of their proceedings.

As the Chambers are not called upon to vote any money for public purposes, during the present Session, no further steps can be at present taken, but if the Protest above-mentioned is actually entered upon the Journals of the House, it will be followed up, during the ensuing Session, when the Budget is brought before the Chambers, by their refusal to vote the supplies, until the right, which they arrogate to themselves, shall have been acknowledged by the Sovereign.

[59] Ludwig von Wirschinger.
[60] In closing the session of *Landtag* on 17 November 1837, King Ludwig emphasized that the Bavarian constitution did not ask for evidence of how the budget surplus was used.

FO 9/80: Lord Erskine to Viscount Palmerston, No 6, Munich, 17 April 1840

Duel between M. Abel and Prince Wallerstein

A violent altercation has occurred between M. Abel the Minister of the Interior, and Prince Wallerstein his predecessor in that post, and a hostile meeting took place between them in consequence of it.

After the duel, which had no serious result, Mr Abel recanted all the violent personal accusations[61] which he had made against Prince Wallerstein in the Chambers.

This affair has caused the greatest excitement among the members of the two Chambers and among the Court here, and it is conjectured that the influence and power of Mr Abel are likely to be much shaken by the occurrences which have taken place.

I propose to renew my observations to Your Lordship on this topick, to be forwarded by the Queen's Messenger, in the course of a few days.

FO 9/80: Lord Erskine to Viscount Palmerston, No 36, Munich, 9 December 1840

Precautionary preparations in case of war with France

I learnt today from one of my Colleagues that General Hesse[62] an Austrian General of distinction arrived here yesterday, having been sent by his Government to examine (as Colonel Radowitz has done on the part of Prussia) into the actual state of the Bavarian Army and other military Preparations in case of War.

It appears, from all the accounts that I have received, that a perfect Union of opinion exists between Austria, Prussia and the other States of Germany, as to the propriety and even necessity of placing their respective Countries on a strong footing of defensive preparation for any future emergency, even should any present apprehension of War be removed; as it is fully perceived by them that their best and only sure grounds of reliance for their safety and independence could be rested on their firm Cooperation.

As these measures are only precautionary and on a Scale of Peace Armament, no objection can be justly raised to them in France as

---

[61] In a speech to the first chamber on 9 April 1840 Abel had accused his predecessor in office, Oettingen-Wallerstein – without naming him directly – of serious misconduct and dishonourable behaviour. The duel took place on 11 April.

[62] Heinrich Freiherr von Hess.

indicating any hostile Attitude or purporting any menace towards her, and are therefore not likely to have any effect in disturbing the tranquillity of Europe; but on the contrary tend to preserve its equilibrium; and are calculated to promote the best interests of England which are deeply concerned in the strength and independence of United Germany.

FO 9/82: Lord Erskine to Viscount Palmerston, No 6, Munich, 19 February 1841

King's opinion on the idea of a French invasion of the Rhenish Provinces

I beg leave to mention to Your Lordship a circumstance which though not of itself important tends to shew the feelings of the King of Bavaria as to the Idea of the possibility of the Invasion by France of the Rhenish Provinces.[63]

His Majesty has directed a handsome Cup to be executed by the celebrated Artist Schwanthaler with the Inscription 'Der Pfalzgraf am Rhein, (one of the Titles of the King of Bavaria) dem Sänger des Rhein Lieds' and to be presented to Nicolaus Bekker[64] – Author of the Song 'Sie sollen ihn nicht haben' (they shall not have it)[65] which Song, as Your Lordship may perhaps have heard, has been very universally known, as having been composed as a National German Air, which expresses a Sentiment of a determined Antipathy to an Invasion by France of the German Territory.

FO 9/82: Lord Erskine to Viscount Palmerston, No 9, Munich, 24 March 1841

King of Prussia's measures concerning religious subjects will have beneficial effect on the Bavarian government's attitude to mixed marriages; agitation of an ultra-conservative priest in Munich

I avail myself of the Opportunity of writing confidently to your Lordship by my Son,[66] who is going to England in a few Days.

The measures[67] lately adopted by the King of Prussia, which have

[63] For the Rhine crisis cf. n. 210 in Frankfurt section.

[64] Nikolaus Becker.

[65] *Rheinlied: Sie sollen ihn nicht haben, den deutschen Rhein* (Song of the Rhine: they shall not have it, the German Rhine), first published by the newspaper, *Trierische Zeitung* on 16 September 1840.

[66] James Stuart Erskine.

[67] Cf. n. 164 in Prussia section.

shewn such a spirit of toleration and liberality on religious and political
Subjects, have produced a great Sensation in this Country and have
had a very considerable Influence in calming a religious animosity
which prevailed a short time ago in Bavaria and was not even
discouraged (as I have been well informed) by His Bavarian Majesty.

A Bavarian Catholic Priest, of the name of Eberhardt,[68] had for
some time continued to preach in a Church in Munich against
Inter marriages between Catholics and Protestants and had not only
employed the most violent expressions and denunciations of punishment
in a future world to such Catholics as should contract them, but had
also declared that such mixed marriages would be illegitimate, although
the Bavarian Laws distinctly recognise such marriages and although
Her Majesty The Queen of Bavaria[69] is a Protestant and also Her
Majesty the Dowager Queen,[70] no steps were taken by the Bavarian
Government to interdict this unjustifiable and even unlawful preaching;
and it was said to have been encouraged by the Minister of the Interior[71]
who is reputed to be a most bigotted Catholic, until a general sentiment
was raised against the scandalous conduct of M[r] Eberhardt and it was
represented to His Bavarian Majesty that to tolerate such an abuse
would have a most mischievous tendency and at a moment too when
an adjoining Protestant Monarch (the King of Prussia) was evincing so
much religious moderation. These remonstrances induced His Majesty
to prohibit M[r] Eberhardt from preaching such doctrines.

I feel also deeply persuaded that the liberal political views which have
been shewn by the King of Prussia will have a most beneficial Effect upon
the course of Government of this Country, because His Bavarian Majesty
without intending, no doubt, deliberately to violate the Laws of the Constitution has assumed to himself the right, contrary to the opinions of
seven Eights of both Chambers of the Legislature, which decided against
the right claimed by His Majesty of disposing of the surplus Revenue[72] of
the Country, amounting at present to twenty Millions of florins and it
is suspected generally that His Bavarian Majesty had relied upon the
Assistance of the Austrian and Prussian Monarchs in the Event of any
resistance occurring in Bavaria to his authority.

It is now hoped, and generally supposed that His Bavarian Majesty
will give way to the Opinions upon this Subject of his Chambers when
they next assemble and will be more disposed than formerly to be
influenced by their advice, to which he has shewn for many years past
but little disposition to pay attention.

[68] Anton Eberhard.
[69] Therese.
[70] Karoline.
[71] Karl August von Abel.
[72] Cf. pp. 429–430 and n. 60 in this section.

FO 9/82: Lord Erskine to Earl of Aberdeen, No 6, Secret, Munich, 19 December 1841

Interment of the late Dowager Queen

I venture to convey to Your Lordship the following communication by the safe opportunity afforded me by the Prussian Secretary of Legation (Baron de Canitz) who will set out for London tomorrow, having been lately appointed to the Court of Her Majesty.

The manner in which the Interment of the remains of the late Dowager Queen[73] of Bavaria had been conducted, had caused a great deal of dissatisfaction among Her late Majesty's Friends, because the Protestant Clergymen who attended the Coffin to the door of the Catholic Church, were not permitted to accompany it into the body of the Church, and also, because none of the usual solemnities such as lighting the Church, or the Priests appearing in their splendid dresses, were then observed, and as the remains of Her Majesty who was a Protestant, were obliged, in accordance with the usages of the Kingdom, to be interred in that Catholic Church; it was considered by Her Majesty's Family and Friends, and amongst them the Prince Royal[74] and Prince Charles[75] the King's Brother, as a great want of respect to Her late Majesty, and as disgraceful to those who had the management of the Ceremonies of the Church, and all moderate and reasonable Catholics were ashamed at the want of decorum and propriety of conduct on that occasion.

The Persons who had the charge of arranging the solemn Ceremonies of the Funeral, were, on the part of the Court, the Minister of the Interior (Mons\u02b3 Abel) The Minister for Foreign Affairs, (Baron de Gisé) and the Grand Master of the King, (Count de Rechberg) who being much and generally blamed, excuse themselves by saying that they consulted with the Pope's Nuncio,[76] and Archbishop of Munich[77] as to the forms and solemnities that should be observed on the occasion; and that all their deliberations and decisions had been regularly laid before His Bavarian Majesty and were signed by him in due form.

His Majesty has declared that he did not particularly examine the Papers which were laid before him for his signature, supposing them to be all in order, but when he found so much general dissatisfaction had been excited, His Majesty blamed those who had charge of the solemnities on the occasion.

[73] Karoline.
[74] Maximilian.
[75] Karl Theodor.
[76] Michele Viale-Prelà.
[77] Lothar Anselm Freiherr von Gebsattel.

But I am bound to state to Your Lordship, that a very unfavourable impression has been made upon the public mind in this Kingdom; as the King and his Prime Minister[78] are known to entertain very strong and even violent Catholic principles of religion. It is a remarkable fact that the Catholic Bishop of Augsburg[79] had caused to be performed at that place which is only at the distance of thirty miles from Munich a Funeral Service for the late Dowager Queen in full Ceremony at the same moment when in the Church of Munich similar solemnities were withheld from being performed.

His Majesty has testified his approbation by Letter of the conduct of the Bishop of Augsburg on that occasion in the highest terms.

His Majesty as I learn, has taken all necessary measures that full Solemnities and Honours should be observed in the Church when the demise of the present Queen who is also a Protestant should take place.

FO 9/83: Lord Erskine to Viscount Canning, [unnumbered], Munich, 18 February 1842

Information about factories in Bavaria; living conditions of the labouring class

In compliance with Instructions communicated to me from Viscount Palmerston through Mr Backhouse I endeavoured to procure the information required respecting the Factories in Bavaria; but as it happens not to be a manufacturing country and to have but very few and insignificant Factories in it, and these very much dispersed; I have not been able to collect much important information.

It appears however from what I can learn that the rate of Wages for a workman daily varies from one shilling up to the value of twenty-pence a day except in Brewhouses which a very numerous, and many of them very prosperous owing to the extensive use of Beer in this country and in some of these Brewhouses in the principal towns the wages often amount to two shillings a day besides board, which is not allowed in other Establishments.

It should however be stated that in consequence of the cheapness of provisions in Bavaria, a labouring man can amply supply himself with provisions for 18 Kreutzers or 6 pence a day, and as the population of the country is only half of what it is considered capable of supporting, it is seldom that a competent workman fails of obtaining employment.

I should remark that as provisions are so cheap, the price of really good beer so low (being only three halfpence for more than a quart)

---

[78] Karl August von Abel.
[79] Johann Peter von Richarz.

the difference of the work people being provided in the Factories with their daily food is not of so much importance, as in Countries where food is dearer.

All labourers in this Country when they can get employment, can do well, but constant employment is not in general easily found. There are however few people of the working classes who do not possess either a cottage or some land, or a part of each[.] Extreme poverty is therefore rare.

FO 9/83: Lord Erskine to Viscount Canning, [unnumbered], Munich, 23 February 1842

Conditions in the Munich orphan asylum

In compliance with the Instructions transmitted to me by your Lordship in your Letter of the 10th inst by the direction of the Earl of Aberdeen, I endeavoured immediately to procure the information therein required respecting the Orphan Asylum at Munich.

I learnt through the Director and principal Physician[80] of that establishment that Scrofulous Disorders are very prevalent among the Children particularly the Girls, and in both sexes mostly confined to the fair complexioned children, however the exact proportions not having been taken at the Institution cannot be given.

The origin of Scrofula amongst these children of whom two thirds had that disease, showing itself principally in glandulous tumours, and inflammation in the eyes has been attributed more to dirt and want of attention (previous to admittance into the Institution) than to hereditary causes although the latter certainly exist.

The best Diet for Scrofulous patients has been found to be Milk and Meal, and not Flesh; as to the Medical treatment, Iodine is thought to be of little efficacy; the means resorted to being regular exercise, Tisanes (as for instance Sarsaparilla continued for a length of time) and boarding in the country is now most extensively adopted.

Owing to the number of children who died before reaching ten years of age which is stated to have amounted to three fourths of the whole, the Establishment was long in bad repute, but at present the proportionate number of deaths is considerably diminished, and the Institution appears to be established in the best manner.

The whole number of children in the Establishment is three hundred of which two hundred and sixteen are boarded out which is always found to have the best effects.

[80] Felix Berr.

I herein enclose My Lord, a statement in German (with a translation),
which was furnished to me of the daily course of diet given to the
children during the week, as much importance is attached to that
regular regimen.[81]

FO 9/83: Lord Erskine to Earl of Aberdeen, No 22, Munich, 17
October 1842

*Marriage of Prince Royal of Bavaria and Princess Mary of Prussia; Princess Mary's
reception in Munich*

The marriage of The Prince Royal of Bavaria[82] with The Princess
Mary of Prussia was celebrated on the 12th Instant at 12 o'clock, in
the Royal Chapel of this Residence with great ceremony, and the
arrangements upon the occasion were conducted with much attention
to order and imposing effect, and were very successfully combined.

After the Marriage ceremony the Court repaired to the Palace,
where Their Royal Highnesses received the homages and felicitations
of all those who had been presented at court.

This ceremony was conducted with the greatest splendour in the
presence of all the Royal Family assembled in the great Hall of the
Throne, which had been lately built and was first opened on this
occasion, – and is one of the largest and most magnificent rooms in
Europe.

I may perhaps be allowed to mention to Your Lordship a peculiarity
in the forms adopted on the reception of these homages.

The Diplomatick Corps was first admitted into the Hall alone, and
advanced towards the Royal Family, who were at the end of it, at a
distance of 160 feet, – and, after having had the honour of paying their
homages, retired (backwards of course) over a variegated polished
marble floor. Then followed the foreign Ladies and Gentlemen, in the
same manner, – and then the Nobility and Gentry of this Country –
all appearing in Gala dresses.

The reception of Her Royal Highness The Princess Mary in the City
of Munich has been welcomed by all ranks of the people, with the
highest respect and strongest marks of Cordiality; the houses of the
Town were decorated on the 14th Instant, in a manner which I had
never before seen, as not only flags, wreaths, and colours were displayed,
but emblematick devices were suspended on the walls, which had an

[81] Enclosure: *Kostordnung* (Diet Sheet) (translation not extant in FO 9/83).
[82] Maximilian.

effect similar to illuminations from the manner in which they were painted and coloured.

The enthusiasm of the People in favor of the Princess has been very general, notwithstanding that, at first, the circumstance of Her being a Protestant had, amongst the middle and lower classes, caused a momentary prejudice against the Princess, which, however, the Character of Her Royal Highness, confirmed as it was by Her personal appearance, Her grace, and attractions, soon dispelled, and She is now deeply esteemed and admired.

The political importance of this connexion of the Courts of Prussia and Bavaria may be expected to be considerable, and very favorable to the several States of Germany for their mutual protection.

FO 9/84: Stephen Henry Sulivan to Earl of Aberdeen, No 12, Munich, 31 July 1843

Railroad projects in Bavaria

A long discussion has taken place in the Bavarian Chamber of Deputies, relative to the question of the rail-roads in this country, and the Chambers are at length agreed upon the Bill which they have laid before His Majesty, for his approval.

It appears that the expence of the rail-road from Hof by Bamberg to Lindau, is calculated at the sum of 51 millions and a half of Florins or £1.125000 – S6 – D8, but the Chamber of Deputies are of opinion, that that amount will not be sufficient, and they consider that it would be for the general advantage of the Country, if a larger sum was fixed. The Chamber is anxious that the Government should act in concert with the Government of Wurttemberg, as regards the projected rail-road from Augsbourg to Lindau, but the feeling of jealously which exists between the respective Sovereigns of Bavaria and of Wurtemberg has prevented the wish of the Chamber being brought to effect.

The Chamber has proposed an extended system of rail-roads which should comprise the whole line of rail-roads from west to east.

It is intended that the principal rail-roads should be constructed at the expence of the Government, whilst on the other hand the branch rail-roads will be made, at the expence of private companies, guaranteed by the Government at 4 Per Cent interest.

The Chamber has authorized the Government to effect a loan of 15 Millions of Florins, but they have blamed the Government for having entered into a rail-road Convention with Saxony without having previously consulted the Chambers.

The Chamber of Deputies is of opinion that a line from Bamberg by Coburg to Leipsic would have been preferable; but they have not insisted upon the line of rail-road abovementioned, and I have been informed that they have consented to leave the arrangement of the principal lines of rail-road, in the hands of the Government.

The rail-road from Ludwigshafen to Bexbach upon the Rhine, is also guaranteed to the share-holders, at 4 Per Cent Interest, and the Chamber has recommended that after 25 years, the Government should purchase the value of that rail-road, upon equitable terms.

The Chamber of Peers has agreed to the proposal of the Chamber of Deputies, with some slight alterations but which are too unimportant to be reported to your Lordship.

FO 9/84: Stephen Henry Sulivan to Earl of Aberdeen, No 15, Munich, 13 August 1843

Debate about the Maine-Danube canal project

A debate has taken place in the Chambers of Deputies relative to the Canal, called the Ludwigs-canal, which is intended to form a junction between the Maine and the Danube.

The immense work, one of the most favorite projects of His Bavarian Majesty was originally calculated at the sum of 8.530.000 Florins (£710833).

It has already cost the Country 13 millions and a half of Florins, and it appears probable that still larger sums will be required to bring the work to a completion. Great doubts are entertained by well-informed persons with respect to the ultimate success of the abovementioned canal, on account of the badness of the soil, and the apparent impossibility which exists of rendering it serviceable for commercial purposes, owing the shallowness of the water. A long period has already elapsed since the first commencement of this canal, but as yet, the only portion which is at present navigable is that portion between Bamberg and Nuremberg.

The Minister of the Interior has stated to the Chamber of Deputies, that His Bavarian Majesty has removed the members of the Commission charged with the completion of the work, and has appointed other and more experienced persons, and His Excellency has stated that he has no doubt, that in two or three years more, the canal might be entirely completed.

Much opposition has been made to the grant proposed by the Bavarian Government and many Deputies were of opinion, that the canal was an useless expence entailed upon the Country; but the Chambers have at length agreed to acknowledge the amount which has been required. The Chamber of Deputies has however protested against the agreement which the Government have entered into, with the House of Rothschild,[83] and which does not appear to be advantageous to the Bavarian Government.

FO 9/87: John Ralph Milbanke to Earl of Aberdeen, No 22, Munich, 16 April 1844

Royal Order regulating the attendance of the military at religious ceremonies

I have the honor to inclose the translation of the substance of a Royal Order[84] lately published in the Allgemeine Zeitung,[85] for regulating the attendance of the Military at certain religious Ceremonies, and publick worship.

In order to explain to Your Lordship the circumstances which led to the issuing of this Order, it will be necessary for me to refer back to the proceedings in the last Session of the Bavarian Chambers.

For some years past it has been a grievance with the protestant Clergy, that the Rules of the Service compelled the Soldiers of that persuasion to kneel whenever the Host was carried past them, though I do not find, whatever their feelings might have been, that the soldiers themselves made any complaint or objection on the subject. However, in the course of the last Session, a motion was made in the Lower Chamber, for a Representation to the King to exempt the Protestant Soldiery from this part of their prescribed duties, and to allow them on such occasions merely to present arms, as was the custom previously to the year 1838; but is was met by an amendment to the effect, that such a motion would be an encroachment upon the Royal Prerogative, and it was therefore proposed to omit the word 'Soldiers' and to let the motion stand: – that His Protestant subjects should not be coerced in matters of Conscience, – which being agreed to, it passed the Lower Chamber in that form.

When it reached the Upper Chamber an intimation was received on the part of the King, that if the two Chambers would desist from prosecuting the matter further, His Majesty would give a promise that something should be done to remedy the evils complained of in this part of the military service, and hereupon, a Conference took place between the two Chambers, who gave a vote of confidence in the good

---

[83] On 7 May 1835 Rothschild, the Frankfurt bank, was instructed to set up a public limited company for the construction of the *Ludwigs-Canal*.

[84] The Royal Ordinance of 26 March stated that Protestant soldiers could no longer officially be ordered to attend a Catholic service, and vice versa.

[85] For the *Allgemeine Zeitung* cf. n. 33 in this section.

intentions of His Majesty, and determined to await the fulfilment of the Royal Assurances.

The above transactions were, at the time, watched with much attention and anxiety not only by the Protestants in Bavaria, but by those in other parts of Germany, who have taken alarm at the extraordinary activity which has of late characterised the attempts of the Catholic Party throughout Europe to regain ascendency in the management of public affairs. In this country its efforts have been eminently successful. The Nuncio,[86] as its chief, is well chosen to advance the interests of the Church of Rome to the full extent which circumstances will admit, and in some instances to push even beyond what considerations of prudence might suggest, and he is zealously aided and supported in his endeavours, by the Austrian Minister, as I must presume, in pursuance of instructions from his Court. The Bishops too, particularly those of Passau[87] and Ratisbon[88] have been lately endeavouring to render religious discipline in the army more strict with respect to fasts and confession, and representations have been addressed by them to The King, complaining of the laxity which prevailed amongst the troops on these points. The Consequence has been a sort of compromise. The former of theses Dignitaries is a most uncompromising enemy to everything Protestant, and has succeeded in displacing almost all persons professing that doctrine from the public employment within the limits of his Diocese, filling up their places with Catholics, and this so gradually and imperceptibly, as not to have excited very much attention.

In the matter now before us I have reason to believe, that The King would most willingly be relieved from the embarrassment which He has become involved in by the promulgation of the Order of 1838,[89] and would gladly replace the system on its former footing, could any mode, short of actually yielding to the demands of the Protestant party, be found for setting the question at rest; but the present Decree is looked upon by the Protestants as an evasion, and so far from responding to the hopes entertained by them, has on the contrary been received with such general dissatisfaction as to leave little doubt on the minds of those acquainted with the subject that not a moment will be lost in recurring to it with renewed energy and determination in the next Session, unless some further concession be obtained before the Chambers meet again.

In the mean time, persons interested in the question have not failed

---

[86] Michele Viale-Prelà.
[87] Heinrich von Hofstätter.
[88] Valentin von Riedel.
[89] Cf. p. 435 in this section.

forcibly to impress upon The King's mind the dangerous predicament in which He might find Himself placed, were the protestant Soldiers to refuse in a body to conform to the order of 1838. The utter impossibility of making an example of so many has been made manifest to His Majesty, and these observations have been acquired additional weight from facts which have, as I am told, come to the knowledge of the Government, that in some parts of the Country, especially in Franconia, the protestant Clergy have of late been busily inculcating sentiments of opposition in the minds of the Common Soldiers, and pointing out to them the almost certainty of impunity in any combined plan of resistance to what they are teaching them to regard in the light of an arbitrary attempt to controul their freedom of conscience. In short, if what I hear of the proceedings of the so-called Ultramontane party in this Country be true, it is preparing a fertile source of future discord in the State, and I am credibly informed that ramifications of it are extended all over the Continent, as well to other parts, not excepting Ireland.[90]

FO 9/87: John Ralph Milbanke to Earl of Aberdeen, No 28, Munich, 15 May 1844

Excesses committed during the celebration of Princess Hildegard's marriage

I should not have thought it necessary to trouble Your Lordship with any allusion to the excesses committed by the populace in this Capital during the Fêtes given on the occasion of the Princess Hildegarde's marriage,[91] had I not observed in the publick papers so many exaggerated and distorted accounts of what took place.

They commenced I believe in a drunken brawl at a Beer house, amongst some Soldiers belonging to the Cuirassier Regiment stationed here, who objected to an additional ½ Kreutzer which the Brewers had obtained permission to impose upon the pint of beer. This led to the breaking of windows &c, and on the Soldiers being joined by other idlers, they proceeded to commit similar excesses at the different Breweries, and thereby came to blows with the Police Force which, being very small in numbers, was soon overpowered, and thus the employment of the Military became necessary, when one man was killed by accident, and several others wounded on both sides. It is said that the men of the Cuirassier Regiment shewed much disinclination to turn out, when it was known that they were to act against their own

---

[90] Enclosure: Translation, Extract from the *Allgemeine Zeitung*, 7 April 1844.
[91] To Archduke Albrecht of Austria.

Comrades and against their own interest; but I do not believe, as has been said, that they refused to mount.

The Authorities probably not attaching much importance to what was going on were, it cannot be denied, somewhat supine in their measures of repression, and to this want of energy is most likely to be attributed the renewal of these culpable attempts on three successive nights. However, at length it was thought proper to make a demonstration of force, which had the desired effect, and the price of the beer being lowered at the same time, the publick peace was no more disturbed.

On one of the days that the Capital was thus agitated, The King accompanied by the whole of The Royal Family and The Archdukes,[92] drove in procession through the town which was decorated for the occasion, and certainly was not saluted with any very excessive demonstrations of loyalty, which seemed to have reserved for the Crown Prince, who was loudly cheered. The truth is that His Majesty is by no means popular; – His excessive love of building and other attempts to improve and beautify His Capital compel a very considerable outlay, no small part of which falls in different indirect ways to the share of the inhabitants, who naturally murmur at the increase which the measures taken to meet these expences, occasion in the price of the necessaries of life, for an object in which they take no interest and from which they derive no benefit. There is also, I am told, much discontent amongst the Employés under Government, arising from various causes, but the principal is the mode of paying them, as it is usually contrived that they should receive only the pay of the rank next below that which they hold. The same may be said of the Officers, particularly the superior ones, in the Army, and the system is of course productive of a similar effect.

FO 9/87: Stephen Henry Sulivan to Earl of Aberdeen, No 15, Munich, 15 August 1844

Reasons for the rapid succession of disturbances in Bavaria

I have had the Honor to report to Your Lordship, from time to time, the account of various disturbances which have occurred in Bavaria. Although each isolated fact would be a matter of but little importance, yet the rapid succession of those events, in a part of the country, noted for the apathy of its inhabitants, has led me to institute an enquiry into

---

[92] Karl und Albrecht.

the present state of Bavaria, and I hasten to lay before Your Lordship the result of my investigations.

It appears that ever since the demonstration made at Hambach[93] in the Palatinate, in the year 1832, great dissatisfaction has existed, in consequence of the strong measures taken by the Bavarian Government, with a view to checking the development of liberal institutions generally.

That dissatisfaction has broken forth upon many occasions, in the Chambers as well as out of doors; partly in consequence of the spread of liberal sentiments in Baden, Wurtemberg, Saxony, and even Prussia; partly in consequence of the fact that the people of Bavaria have, for many years, perceived that their King is less inclined to listen to their reasonable wishes than some other German Sovereigns are.

If I refer to His Bavarian Majesty himself, it is because there is not a shadow of Ministerial independence, and scarcely one of responsibility in Bavaria. The animosity therefore which might, sooner or later break forth, would be directed, not against a Ministry of an individual Minister, but against the Sovereign himself. During the last Session of the States, a conflict has actually taken place between the Crown and the Chamber of Deputies, which threatened an open rupture, to avoid which The King was compelled, after a long struggle, to abandon the disingenuous interpretation of the Constitution, by means of which it was intended to secure to the Crown the uncontrolled disposal of all the surplus revenue,[94] for the increasing of which, budgets artfully prepared, had been submitted to the Chambers for a series of years, and which in the year 1843 had already amounted the sum of 38.569.286 Florins or £3.214.000 Sterling. [...]

I have been assured by persons whose experience enables them to form a correct estimate of the Bavarian people generally, that it was less the amount of the sum above mentioned, – applied, for the major part, to public works, – which created an universal discontent throughout the country, than the want of fairness and of candour which may be traced throughout the whole tenor of the King's proceedings, a line of conduct which has already alienated entire classes of the population. Moreover, the point at issue has not been satisfactorily settled, as the said speech from the throne pretends; for the doctrine started in the Chamber of Peers by Prince de Wallerstein,[95] for the sake of extricating the Crown from the dilemma in which it found itself,

[93] Cf. p. 23–26 in Frankfurt section.

[94] Cf. pp. 428–430, 436–437 in this section.

[95] The *Reichsrat* (chamber of peers, the first chamber) doctrine of 14 June 1843 resulted in a compromize in the dispute about the *Landtag's* right to approve the use of budget surpluses. In future, any budget surplus was to be considered part of the state's revenues and would thus be subject to the chambers' right to participate in making budgetary policy.

threatens to become, – in the autumn 1845, – a fresh source of attacks upon the Government, as it is to be expected that they will hold to this new interpretation, with the view to regaining for the Crown as much of the lost ground as possible. The refusal of the King to grant the amnesty solicited in the year 1843 by influential members of the Chamber of Deputies, in imitation of the Emperor of Austria and the King of Wurtemberg, has created much discontent.[96]

Great restrictions are laid upon the liberty of the press. No criticism upon any measure whatever, or upon any grievance of longer standing, is allowed to be discussed, and even the debates of the States themselves are either entirely or partly suppressed. At Munich, all the papers, without exception, are prevented from reproducing the speeches of the opposition-members, and are confined to giving the replies of the Ministerial organs. These restrictions are the more complained of, as in Wurtemberg, Saxony, Baden and even in Prussia, the press has long since been free, to a degree which creates much envy in Bavaria.

These vexatious restrictions are not confined to news-papers alone, for even scientific men, strangers to any political bias, are obliged to have their works printed in some other part of Germany, if they contain a single observation upon any particular point in the Bavarian organisation.

In addition to the grounds of complaint which I have had the Honor to mention to Your Lordship, there are others no less cogent.

The Government has been endeavouring to establish, as a right of the Crown, a system of exclusion from the elections, which, if carried through all its bearings, would deprive the country of every species of representation, as was proved in the last Session, in the Bavarian Chamber of Peers, by the Prince de Wallerstein, and which has already led to the exclusion of all lawyers from the Chamber of Deputies.[97]

The assumption of the Crown to the right of levying all the indirect taxes, without the formal consent of the Chambers, is viewed as a fresh proof of the desire of the King to encrease the Royal prerogative.

In many parts of Germany, a demand has been made for the publicity of the courts of law, and for trial by Jury; both of these important points have been lately granted by the Governments of Wurtemberg and of Baden;[98] they have both been urged upon the

[96] In Austria, Emperor Ferdinand had granted a general amnesty after his accession to the throne in 1835. In Württemberg, an amnesty for political offences was declared on 25 September on the twenty-fifth anniversary of King Wilhelm's accession.

[97] The law of exclusion that applied to civil servants also applied to lawyers (cf. pp. 432–433 in this section). This practice was enshrined in law on 23 May 1846.

[98] In Württemberg the code of criminal procedure came into effect on 22 June 1843. The code of criminal procedure discussed by the *Landtag* in Baden and approved by the government in 1843–1844 was even more progressive. However, it was not officially published until 6 March 1845.

Bavarian Government, but it is feared that they will not be alluded to in the various bills which are being prepared by a Government Commission (after twenty five years of constant solicitation on the part of the Deputies) as the King has made no mention of those subjects either in the answer from the throne, or in the ordinance appointing the said Commission.

The bills above alluded to are of the highest importance to the country as they are intended;

1st to incorporate into one single body, fifty five different and dissonant civil legislations now in force in various parts of Bavaria; to examine them; to reject many obsolete parts contained in the fifty four legislations which exist on this side of the Rhine, and to establish one uniform code for the whole country, in imitation of that of France. Several successive Commissions have been previously engaged upon this task, but the Government did not think fit to lay the result of their labors before the Chambers.

2nd To examine into the present criminal jurisprudence, and to do away with some barbarous remains of the middle ages.

3d To establish a mercantile code of which the country is as yet destitute.

4th To revise the civil and criminal proceedings at law.

Should those new codes really be brought forward in the next Session, they will furnish ample materials for recrimination, and it is feared that the Government will take that excuse to withdraw them altogether and leave the country in the same condition as heretofore.

The systematic and excessive parsimony under which every branch of the administration has, for many years been labouring, for the purpose of creating this 38 Millions Florins above alluded to, has produced general discontent. The repair of Churches, roads, and bridges, have been neglected. The hospital establishments; lunatick asylums, seminaries, workhouses, etc., the respective amounts of which had been incorporated into previous budgets; have been, from year to year unattended to. The provision for the Universities, and schools of all kind, have been grievously curtailed, as have also been, the salaries of almost every servant of the State; coupled with the practise of discharging those old servants of the State who may happen to be in the point of being entitled to a pension equal to their salary. The money voted for the maintenance of the army has been misapplied, and sacrificed to The King's taste for building, a fact which led, a few years ago, to the removal from the War Office of the Baron de Hertling, who refused to comply with the King's unconstitutional demands.

The repeated attempts to destroy the authority of the French laws, in force in the Palatinate,[99] have created, in that populous and industrious province, a great degree of distrust of the intentions of the Government, and have led the inhabitants to prefer the imperfections of their present system of legislation, to any alteration.

Mr Milbanke, in his despatch N° 22 of the 16th of April, has reported to Your Lordship, the excitement created in Bavaria, by the attempts made by the Catholick propaganda, to harass the consciences of Protestants, and by degrees to put down that faith altogether. In pretending that the adoration of the Host, – an act[100] which all the Protestant authorities of the county agree in considering as a violence done to the conscience of every Protestant soldier, – is nothing but a movement of military discipline. In declaring the offspring of marriages between Protestants and Catholicks, as bastards. In enticing Protestant children to embrace the Catholick creed, without the knowledge of their parents, a proceeding which has lately been indirectly authorized by a decision of the Government.[101] In refusing to Protestant funerals, the tolling of the church-bells, in places where the former Catholick clergy, had allowed it. In establishing a new cemetery at Munich by which the dead Protestants are to be separated from the Catholick. In impeding the formation of new Protestant communities. And, finally, in forbidding every Bavarian Protestant subject to contribute towards an association for the advancement of Protestantism, lately formed in Saxony and in Prussia;[102] or from receiving any support from that fund. I have not mentioned to Your Lordship the coarse and offensive language used by the writers of various Catholick pamphlets, who have had recourse to calumnies and to misrepresentations which have gone far to irritate the peaceful disposition of the Protestant inhabitants of Bavaria. I cannot however avoid mentioning to Your Lordship the fact, that even Catholick Priests, in the Chamber of Deputies, have reproached the Government with favouring the establishment of Convents, and of trying to bring back the Jesuits, while the secular clergy is purposely neglected, and almost put aside. Those measures of the Bavarian Government, in respect to religious matters, are certainly not the result of religious conviction; for in Austria, where the Protestants enjoy no political rights whatever, but are merely tolerated, as the Jews are in Bavaria, the Government has ever been anxious to avoid any interference in religious matters, though the Protestant population amounts only one tenth of the Catholick, while in Bavaria, the former is one half of the latter.

[99] Cf. n. 16 in this section.

[100] Genuflexion Ordinance of 14 August 1838, cf. pp. 447–449 in this section.

[101] A ministerial decree of 4 November lifted the prohibition on converting minors in exceptional cases.

[102] For the *Gustav Adolf Verein*, which was banned in Bavaria on 10 February 1844, cf. n. 220 in Prussia section.

In conclusion, I will only observe, that if the present evil system should continue in Bavaria, and if some unforeseen event should disturb the peace of Europe, it is to be feared that the attachment of the Bavarian people to their Sovereign will be found to be greatly shaken, and that they will be found to be accessible to revolutionary ideas and instigations, the results of which are scarcely, at present, to be foreseen.

FO 9/87: John Ralph Milbanke to Earl of Aberdeen, No 38, Munich, 15 October 1844

Growing aversion to the King and his ministry; numerous reasons for complaints

Since my return to this Capital all sorts of rumours of existing discontent against The King and the Government, said to pervade almost all classes, have been in circulation, and various are the causes to which it is ascribed. They are, I believe, a matter of surprize to no one, excepting perhaps to the King Himself, though of not altogether unfounded apprehension to many. In my previous Despatches to Your Lordship, I have touched upon some of the points which have been gradually leading to this unsettled state of things. Alarming, at the present moment, it can hardly be called, but it is admitted on all sides and by all parties, that the feelings of the middle and lower classes of the population, and especially in the capital, are in a state of excitement which, though probably without any definite object now, may lay the foundation of very unpleasant consequences for the future, when acted upon, as is believed to be the case, by disappointed and discontented individuals, of whom there are not a few in this country.

Hitherto the only positive manifestations of aversion to the Person of The King and His Ministers have consisted in the circulation of pasquinades publickly placarded in the streets, and of course removed immediately by the Police. It would however seem from the precautions taken by the Government, that more practical demonstrations of discontent are expected, and certainly if any encouragement were required to induce the factious to recommence their excesses, it would be found in the feeble conduct of the Authorities during the disturbances which took place here in the Spring. It will be sufficient for me to remind Your Lordship, that on that occasion the object of the rioters was fully and completely attained, and that on a subsequent occasion, during my absence, a mere demonstration on the part of the publick led to an equally successful result, viz: the lowering the price of articles of subsistence. I should be unnecessarily taking up Your Lordship's time were I to enter into a history of the rise and progress of the evil, which has rapidly increased within the last few months, in proportion as it is remarked that no effective measures are adopted to remedy it. The Government seems to exist only to give daily proofs of its' want of tact, and insensibility to the Complaints which reach it from all quarters. The men composing it are all chosen by The King from a position which renders them dependent upon His favour; they are, with perhaps one exception – that of the Minister of Interior, Monsieur Abel, devoid of talent, without energy, jealous of each other, and consequently disunited in all but one point, upon they think perhaps with reason, depends their tenure of Office, and that is excessive parsimony. To be able at the end of each year to make a merit with The King of having effected a Saving in their respective branches of administration is I may say nearly their only object. To effect it no subterfuge is considered too mean, no sacrifice of the true interests of the Country too great. Every branch of the publick service is going to decay from pure neglect and want of support from the Government. The post, Roads, Hospitals, Churches, Schools and other institutions are one and all calling for reform and assistance which they cannot obtain. One might have thought, that in the midst of so many discordant elements, attention would at least have been directed to secure the good will of the Army. This however is not the case. The soldiers are half starved, and like the Officers miserably paid; the latter, most of whom are without any private fortune, find the greatest difficulty in maintaining even that shew of respectability which their station requires. The unwise system adopted in most cases of continuing to them when they attain promotion the pay of a Step below that to which they have reached, renders, in reality, the favor of no positive advantage to them; the shifts to which the Government has recourse to cheat those who have become entitled to a hard earned pension for long service of the full amount due to them. Add to this the gradual rise which has taken place, in this neighbourhood, in the price of all necessaries of life, which weighs heavily upon the lower orders, and it must be admitted, that the Government has singularly ill chosen the moment for pursuing so fatal a system of economy, the fruits of which are unmitigated discount both in the civil and military branches of the Service. [...]

I have still to take into account the complaints and grievances of the Protestant Subjects of this Country, particularly applicable to the Soldiery in the often discussed matter of genuflexion,[103] which promises to become a fertile source of future trouble to the Government at the next meeting of the chambers. Already within the last month has this point been agitated in the Protestant Synod assembled at Baireuth, and would Probably have assumed a form very inconvenient to the Government, had not the Royal Commissioner[104] declared it to be The

---

[103] Cf. pp. 447–449 in this section.
[104] Ludwig Friedrich von Voltz.

King's pleasure, that it should not be touched upon. A protestation was immediately entered against this, as it was termed unconstitutional interference, which however appears to have been foreseen, and the question has been revived in the Synod now assembled at Ansbach, where if it meets with no better success, it has been resolved to address a Petition to the King, and should this not have the desired effect, to make it a subject of energetic remonstrance at the next meeting of the Chambers. Such is the account which has reached me of what is passing on this subject, and I have reason to believe, that even the most violent section of the Catholic party begins to regret that The King should have revived a Custom which had ceased to exist.

I am told, that The King is deeply affected at the want of loyalty displayed towards Him, and cannot understand why He, who within the last 20 years, has done so much for the Capital, should have become so unpopular; such however is undoubtedly the case, for on a recent occasion, when His Majesty appeared in public, I did not hear a single expression of loyalty, and the whole affair passed off in a sort of sulky silence.

Those persons who are attached to The King lay the entire blame upon the Ministers who, they say, are afraid to tell Him the truth. Others maintain that His Majesty is well acquainted with what is passing in the publick mind, but holds to the doctrine that a King should never be forced. I myself am inclined to adhere to the latter opinion, for I have heard, that shortly after His Majesty's return here, He sent for the two Burgomasters,[105] and to them made use of some very strong expressions of dissatisfaction at the State of Affairs in the town, telling them, that if the inhabitants thought Him weak, they were very much mistaken. Ministers, He said, might sometimes shew Signs of weakness, but He never would – and thus dismissed them.

Notwithstanding the assurances given to the last Chamber on the subject of the employment of the Savings effected in the expences of the State, it is openly stated, that a considerable portion of them has again been diverted to purposes other than those for which they ought under those promises to be employed, – and accordingly the Executive must be prepared to defend or excuse their conduct in this respect, or be exposed to the reproach of having acted with want of faith towards the country; but as it is well known, that is has been done by The King, the odium will naturally fall upon His Majesty. Unfortunately The King's inordinate love of building and decoration of His Capital has led Him into a System of extravagance for which the ordinary sources are altogether insufficient, and has finally placed Him personally in a false position; and I very much fear, that ultimately He will be

---

[105] Jacob Bauer (first burgomaster) and Kaspar von Steinsdorf (second burgomaster).

compelled, with however bad a grace, to return to more sound principles of Government. The whole question between Him and His Subjects is, at the present time, one of money; the religious part of it is, I verily believe, a mere accessory but may, and certainly will, be made a powerful use of when the other points come to be discussed.

In proportion as the popularity of The King decreases, seems to augment that of The Prince Royal,[106] and as the want of cordiality subsisting between them is a matter of notoriety, the publick do not fail to ascribe it to the endeavours of the latter to persuade His Father to pay some attention to their well founded complaints, and consequently have, in their own minds, invested Him with character of Friend of the people, and of chief of the opposition. Whether the latter is merited or not, I can hardly venture to say. His Royal Highness left this Capital a few days ago for His Country Seat, from whence He will proceed to Bamberg to pass the winter.

Much observation was called forth at neither The King nor The Prince Royal having been present at the annual national Fête given a few days ago. The absence of His Majesty was excused by indisposition, and that of The Prince was said to be in conformity to injunctions not to appear imposed upon Him by the King.

Having in the course of a conversation with Baron de Gisé adverted in a general manner to the above topics, His Excellency did not attempt to deny the existence of much discontent, but observed, that there was no legitimate foundation for a great part of it, and he made efforts to palliate and excuse the conduct of the Executive upon those points where he could not so easily refute or explain away the justice of it.

FO 9/89: John Ralph Milbanke to Earl of Aberdeen, No 12, Munich, 16 March 1845

On the South German Monetary Union; Germany divided into two monetary systems; question of tariff and protection within Zollverein

Plenipotentiaries from the States forming what is called the South German Monetary Union, consisting of Bavaria, Wurtemberg, Baden, Hesse Darmtadt, Nassau, Frankfort, Saxe-Meiningen, and one or two smaller States, are at this moment assembled at Munich for the purpose of signing a Treaty of which the provisions are already nearly agreed upon, (the only difficulty being to fix upon what is to be the reverse of the new Coin to be struck,) for operating a change in a portion of the Silver money hitherto in circulation in Germany.[...]

[106] Maximilian.

The operation will, as I am informed, be effected at a comparatively small expence, and that will partly be repaid by the Gold which the old dollars are said to contain.

The expediency has long been felt of establishing the currency of all the States composing the Zoll verein upon an uniform footing, but difficulties of an insurmountable nature have hitherto stood in the way of any satisfactory understanding in that respect, – Prussia and the Northern States being desirous of adhering to the Prussian Dollar of 3 shillings, whilst those of the South pronounce it to be impossible to introduce that denomination of coin into circulation, and thus at present Germany is divided into two monetary systems, inconvenient in some respects, but still a decided improvement upon what was the case previously.

It will perhaps not be out of place here, that I should allude to reports which are current, of the intention of the Southern States of Germany to make an attempt, at the next meeting of the Deputies of the Zoll-verein, to have the Tariff raised upon certain manufactured articles, such as Cottons, Linens, Twist &c. I have been in the habit of hearing complaints on the subject ever since I arrived here, but as the period for the meeting approaches, they appear to assume more consistency. It would seem however that the complaints on this subject are not confined to the South, or to the articles above mentioned, for a calculation appeared a day or two ago in the Allgemeine Zeitung,[107] purporting to come from the Banks of the Rhine, in favor of protection, which, after adverting in a cursory manner to Cotton Twist and Linen Goods, enters at great length into question of the support which ought to be given to the Iron manufactures of Germany. The principal point to which attention is directed in connexion with the Iron trade, is of course the formation of Rail Roads; and I shall therefore endeavour to give Your Lordship a short summary of the arguments used. The writer[108] sets the Rail Roads finished or in course of construction, within the precincts of the Zoll verein, at 340 geographical miles, and calculates that a double line of Rails will require 5,100,000 centners, costing 40 millions of florins. The time required for completing the work between 5 and 6 years, so that there will be an average annual outlay of 8 millions. The durability of the Rails differs under circumstances, but may be said to be about 15 years. Arguing upon this basis, and supposing in the course of some years the length of Railway within the territories of the Zoll verein to attain 1000 miles, 75 must be renewed every year, creating a demand for upwards of 950,000 centners of Iron

[107] *Die Eisenbahnproduction und der Eisenbedarf für die Schienenwege* (Railway production and the demand for iron for railway lines), *Allgemeine Zeitung*, no. 71, 12 March 1845.
[108] Not traceable.

in different shapes. The whole production of Rails in the Zoll Verein is about 110,000 centners, scarcely an eighth of what is requisite for future renewal, and not a ninth of the supply required for the next few years.

Last year the Zoll verein states imported above a million of centners of Rails from England and Belgium to pay for which between 7 and 8 millions of florins were carried out of Germany, and the importation in the next years to come must increase in a still more unequal proportion, unless proper measures are adopted to enable those States to produce in greater quantity than they do at present.

That there is more than ample to meet the demand cannot be denied, and it only therefore becomes a question of giving such protection as will induce speculators to invest Capital in this branch of Industry.

The article then proceeds to examine how far it would be prudent to exclude foreign competition, since such exclusion would not only occasion a great increase of expence in what is already likely to cost enough, but probably also defer the completion of the lines to a remoter period than the publick advantages to be derived from them ought to allow. Still it becomes a question whether what at first sight appears to be a useless increase of outlay, is in fact, when everything comes to be considered, really so, for the capital laid out in the purchase of Rails would have its' influence in numberless other Articles of Manufacture and thus essentially benefit the home trade.

The principal impediment in the way of competition with England and Belgium lies in the abundance and cheapness of coals in those countries. But in spite of this advantage, the writer is of opinion that the Trade may be fostered by the imposition of a moderate protective duty, and concludes by saying that this must shortly form a subject for consideration.

FO 9/89: John Ralph Milbanke to Earl of Aberdeen, No 41, Munich, 13 November 1845

Information on the agricultural situation in Bavaria; effects of bad harvests

The absence of published statistical documents, in this Country, by which it would be possible to acquire an accurate, or even approximative, knowledge of the produce of the Harvest, has hitherto prevented me from adverting to the subject; but an opportunity has lately been afforded me of obtaining from official sources information which I can communicate without fear of misleading my Government, & which may prove not altogether uninteresting at the present crisis. By it, I am warranted in stating that the Harvest throughout Bavaria has fallen far short of the usual average.

Before entering into details which will be necessary to convey to Your Lordship a clear idea upon the subject, I must premise, that in Bavaria, where Wheaten Bread is unattainable as an article of food by the middle & lower Classes, the chief Articles of Consumption are Rye & Barley – the latter being consumed in the shape of Beer which has become an object of first necessity, & the price of which, as well as the quality, is fixed by the Government. In the course of last year, I had occasion to allude to the disturbances of the publick peace, in consequence of a rise in the price; & a renewal of them is what is again apprehended, as many of the Brewers have declared their inability to continue to sell at the rate established.

I come now to a statement of the ordinary annual produce of the Harvest in Bavaria, assuming what I believe to be correct, that the Scheffel is less by 1/3 than the English Quarter.

It is as follows, of Wheat (superior quality) 1,340,000 Scheffels, (inferior quality red) 1,660,000 Scheffels, – Rye 3,260,000 Scheffels, – Barley 1,850,000 Scheffels, – Oats 3,600,000 Scheffels, – making a Total of 11,710,000 Scheffels – from this however must be deducted 2,710,000 Scheffels reserved for seed, so that the total amount for consumption does not exceed 9,000,000 of Scheffels, which is absorbed thus. Barley 1,250,000 Scheffels to the Brewers of the Country – 4,000,000 Scheffels of different descriptions Wheat, Rye, & Oats consumed in the Provinces – 400 000 Scheffels exported annually into Switzerland, and Austria &cr – and 3,350,000 Scheffels of Wheat Rye & Oats necessary for the consumption of all the Towns.

According to these returns, the produce of the Country does not, in ordinary years, exceed the quantity requisite to nourish its' own population, & fill the publick Granaries which the Government is bound to provide for, but which have latterly been entirely neglected, & the consequence is, that at the present moment, they contain only a very small quantity of Corn, & that of but indifferent quality. Such as it is, however, it is now thrown into the Market, at a low rate, in the vain hope, that it may keep down the Prices which have already reached such a height as to threaten a demonstration of popular discontent, symptoms of which have begun to manifest themselves in the Capital.

The causes are obvious. In the first place the Harvest, this year, instead of yielding to meet the wants of the people, 9,00,000 Scheffels, will not attain beyond 5 or 6,000 000 at the outside. An amount quite inadequate to the consumption of the Country itself; But as there is also a great scarcity in Switzerland, & speculations to a large amount are being made in Germany for the English, & other Markets, the

Prices of all descriptions of Corn have risen enormously, & wheat is actually selling in the principal Markets, at a higher average than the last accounts brought it from London, as Your Lordship will perceive from those which I here cite. Wheat is now quoted at 25–14 florins the Scheffel which is equivalent to 62 Shillings the Quarter – Rye 24 florins – Barley 20 florins – & Oats 8–34 florins. During the few days which have elapsed since this quotation was made, the prices, I am told have again risen, & with every prospect, that they will be yet higher.

Another circumstance which has contributed to the pressure, is a step taken by the Government to repair its remissness with respect to the publick Granaries which were meant to meet cases like the present.

The occupiers of the Crown lands are, if required, bound to pay a portion of what is here called 'Zehnten' or Tithes, though it is in fact Rent, in kind, but as the collection of this species of Return was found to be a cumbrous & expensive operation, the Government has of latter years received the value of its dues in money, at the average price of the Markets & has only taken in kind between 40 & 50,000 Scheffels instead of 5 or 600,000 to which it was entitled. This year however I hear it has announced its intention of insisting upon having delivered in 200,000 Scheffels, which is, with reason, considered to be a most harsh & unwise measure, inasmuch as the Peasants will find extreme difficulty in providing for the emergency without purchasing at ruinous prices, which cannot fail to influence the Markets in a sense directly contrary to what is hoped & intended.

The Government is in truth greatly embarrassed what course to pursue, & since I have been occupied in writing this despatch, two Royal Orders[109] have appeared: The one forbidding the sale of Agricultural produce otherwise than in a publick Market, & under particular restrictions directed more especially against foreign purchasers, by whom, however, they will be easily evaded; and the other, authorizing the Brewers to sell an inferior & cheaper sort of Beer. Both may be looked upon as temporary expedients – neither of which will answer its' purpose of correcting the evil.

In the mean time, the complaints so loud & general, that the subject must I think necessarily be treated in the Chambers which are convoked for the 1st of December.

The observations I have made above upon the Corn Harvest, will apply with equal force to the Potato Crop, which seems to have failed, in nearly the same proportion; but this article of food is likely to become still more scarce from the circumstance, that the

---

[109] Royal Ordinance concerning the Trade in Grain, 11 November 1845; Royal Ordinance concerning Brewing, 11 November 1845.

landed Proprietors, most of whom possess distilleries, finding, that the disease[110] attacks the Potatos equally after they are housed, are hastening to convert them into the Spirit in use amongst the common people of the Country. It was expected, that a Royal Order putting a stop to this practice, would have been published, but as yet it has not appeared.

The accounts which arrive from other parts of Germany, on this subject, are by no means of a cheering nature; and the Tone adopted by some of the Journals is sufficiently remarkable to attract attention. That which has established itself as the Organ of the Zoll-Verein[111] has a long Article written, it would seem, upon the bare Rumour of the possibility of the opening of the Ports of England to the importation of foreign Corn, to prove, that such a measure must bring down imme- diate & inevitable ruin upon all German industry together, both agricultural, & manufacturing, unless the Tariff be raised in proportion upon British Manufactures. I cannot say that the outcry for higher protective Duties against England has at all diminished; – and when the altered Tariff of the Conference at Carlsruhe was published a short time ago, the Bavarian Government insinuated a Threat, meant for the Northern States, that it would not sanction the existing Duties on Iron for more than one year longer, unless a corresponding increase was laid upon Linen yarns & Cotton Twist &[ca]. It may be in your Lordship's recollection, that this Country was, with difficulty, induced to accede to the imposition of an additional Duty on Iron, & only yielded out of deference to the wishes of Prussia, & other States in the North.

FO 9/92: John Ralph Milbanke to Earl of Aberdeen, No 2, Munich, 16 January 1846

Proceedings in the upper and lower chambers (i.e. so-called 'Urlaubsstreit'; publication of the constitution; act under which the chambers are summoned; difficulties resulting from Palatine's separate system of administration; law concerning the responsibility of ministers et al.)

Since the Chambers have resumed their Sittings which were interrupted for a short time at the close of the year, a number of projects for new laws or amendments of those now subsisting in the Palatinate, principally have been submitted to them on the part of the Government. Hitherto, however, the Lower Chamber has been too much occupied with questions relating to the manner in which the late Elections were

---

[110] Cf. n. 59 in Hanover section.
[111] *Zollvereinsblatt*, cf. n. 137 in Saxony section.

conducted, to admit of their taking any of these projects into consideration. One or two of them have arisen from the exercise of the power vested in the Sovereign to refuse leave absence from their Official Duties of Persons considered to be in the Publick Service. A doubt respecting the extension of this Principle to the Palatinate, for it is from thence, that the most interesting of these complaints comes, has been raised by one of the Deputies[112] chosen in that Province, to whom permission to take his Seat in the Chamber was refused by the Government, on the ground, that exercising the Profession of a sworn Advocate, he must be comprehended in the above Category. Long and angry discussions, which occupied the attention of the Lower Chamber for several days, and threatened to produce a Collision between it and the Crown, and which only terminated two days ago, ensued, not upon this one isolated case, but upon the general Principle; & the Majority of nine in favour of the Government which was at length obtained, is in reality equivalent to a reverse, since it was the result of an assurance from the Minister of the Interior,[113] that the Government intended shortly to propose a Law explanatory of the Paragraph of the Constitution,[114] of which the interpretation has caused so much Strife, and Agitation, in the Publick Mind.

I am credibly informed, that had the decision of the Chamber been in a contrary sense, the King had made up his Mind to dissolve the Assembly at once. An Act of Sovereign power which would have been in opposition to the Advice of His Majesty's Ministers, and could only be deplored by all who wish well to the Throne.

Another question also which has given rise to animated debates in the Chamber of Deputies, and has been no less turned to account by the Opposition, as offering an equally fair and practical basis of Attack against the Government, dates so far back as the year 1818 and has its origin in the circumstances connected with the publication of the Constitution itself.

By that Act,[115] under which the States were summoned, was prescribed the Mode in which the Elections were to take place, as well as that, in which the representation was to be decided. – It was as follows – $\frac{1}{8}$ was given to the Nobility enjoying certain juridical Rights, – $\frac{1}{8}$ to the Clergy, – $\frac{1}{4}$ to the Towns, – and $\frac{1}{2}$ to the Holders of Land – that is to say the Country in general, in the proportion of one Representative to every 7,000 Families, subject however to the necessary qualification of the annual payment of an insignificant sum, in the Shape of Taxes.

---

[112] Friedrich Justus Willich.

[113] Karl August von Abel.

[114] Cf. n. 4 in this section.

[115] Edict on the Assembly of the Estates, Appendix 10 to the Constitutional Document of 1818.

Now the cause of the present discussions in the Lower Chamber, is the alleged unequal partition of the Deputies in regard to the Palatinate. According to the Official Journal giving notice of, and published just previously to the Elections, the number of Families in the whole Kingdom is estimated at 985,511, and the number of Deputies fixed at 141. In the Palatinate, the number of Families is given at 123,039, and consequently that Province would be entitled to send 18 Representatives, instead of 15, which latter number was the quota settled by the Government. The disproportion appears the more striking, when it is considered, that the Palatinate contains something above ⅛ of the whole Population of the Bavarian dominions. But it may in some degree be explained by the peculiar usages and Customs of the Province itself, wherein the Nobility in the enjoyment of the prescribed Rights and Privileges does not exist at all, and thereby it is deprived of one entire Class of Electors. [...]

The result can scarcely be looked upon otherwise than as a defeat sustained by the Government, but it also conveys an indication of the feelings which prevail, for it is generally admitted in publick, that the conduct of the Government is justified by the letter of the Constitution.

Without entering further into the niceties and technicalities of the case which I have selected from amongst several others as best calculated to give Your Lordship some insight into the merits of the dispute, the Evil may I think in some respects be ascribed to the prevalence of different usages, and the existence of a separate system of administration within the same dominions. The inconvenience resulting from the operation of the French Code[116] is strongly felt both here, and in the Prussian Rhenish Provinces, particularly in legal transactions for although both Countries have been compelled to establish in their Capitals, Courts of Appeal, it not unfrequently occurs, that the Tribunals are obliged to have recourse to, and be ruled by, precedents furnished by the French law Courts. In the present instance these peculiarities led to various modifications in the original publication of the Constitution, which are now beginning to bear fruit.

I must now advert to the proceedings of the Upper Chamber in which a Proposal has been made by Prince Wrede[117] to impeach the Minister of the Interior for divers infringements of the Constitution. These he has detailed in a long list of grievances, some of which have already been negatively disposed of, and as the whole of them bear a

---

[116] Cf. n. 192 in Frankfurt section, and n. 16 in this section.
[117] Karl Theodor Fürst von Wrede.

marked character of personal enmity to the Ministers, I do not doubt that the remainder will experience a similar Fate. M. d'Abel himself treats them very lightly.

With the intention apparently of giving force to the preceding motion Prince Wrede has also called upon the Chamber of Peers to invite the Lower Chamber to join in petitioning the King to cause to be submitted to them without delay the Project of a Law touching the responsibility of Ministers, which shall clearly designate and define the penalties and punishment to which they may render themselves amenable by their own Acts.

Here also the personal feelings of the Prince led him into what is considered here rather strong and unparliamentary language. He observes that the present Minister of the Interior has not only followed the Spirit of the Constitution, but has knowingly violated many important points of it: He has rendered null as far as lay in his power the Constitutional Claims of the Protestants to the enjoyment of equal civil and political Rights; and it is not his fault that the love of so respectable a portion of the Bavarian people has not been entirely alienated from the King: He has destroyed also the Sovereign Rights of the Crown since instead of defending the Monarchical Principle against the arrogant usurpations of the Court of Rome, and the Clergy, become under his administration dependent upon it, he has entirely enslaved it to this Party whose ultramontaine tendencies he has to the best of his ability encouraged & assisted.

In conclusion the Prince asserts, that through the present Policy of the Government which is considered to be opposed to all advance or improvement, the Bavarian Nation has most materially lost in the estimation of Foreign Countries.

The Debates have in general borne a strong impression of hostility to the Government, or more properly speaking to the only one individual in it who possesses any talent, and a decided disposition has been evinced in both Chambers to force a change upon the King. In spite however of what may still be expected, I adhere to my opinion, that their endeavours will be unsuccessful. The elements of opposition undoubtedly exist, and may be said to be gaining ground, but they have not yet assumed the consistency necessary to give them much weight. At the same time the example furnished at this Moment by the States of the Grand Duchy of Baden does not seem to be thrown away; and much depends on the Conduct the Government shall pursue in the intermediate time which will elapse between the present & the next Session at which the Budget must again be brought forward, and with it in all probability a revival, with renewed acrimony of the half settled dispute about the disposal of the Publick Money. [...]

FO 9/92: John Ralph Milbanke to Earl of Aberdeen, No 27, Munich, 12 June 1846

Lower chamber enjoys more public esteem; King jealous of the prevailing independent and liberal sentiment

[...] The Upper Chamber frittered away more than six Months in confessional disputes which had their origin in personal intrigues, & enmity, & it has lost much in publick estimation in consequence. The Lower Chamber is open in part to a similar reproach but its' proceedings have on the other hand been marked with a much firmer character of independence than has ever yet been manifested. The example of other German deliberative Assemblies has evidently not been lost upon it, & any one who has watched with attention the rapid progress made in liberal principles throughout Germany, of late years, must predict a strenuous resistance to all efforts to maintain absolute Power. Upon this point the Sovereign of this Country is jealous to a degree, but I am not alone in the opinion, that he would do wisely to bestow a thought upon the future, & study to reconcile to his Person & Government the discontented Population over which he rules. So long as Europe enjoys a state of peace, & the Confederation is in a position to interpose its weight & authority no serious difficulties are to be apprehended, but elements of discord which touch the real interests of the People subsist in the Country, & by no means the least among them, is one which has just caused so much anxiety to the Austrian Monarchy in its' Northern Provinces – I mean the remnants of the Feudal System, or connection between the Peasant, & his Lord.

FO 9/92: John Ralph Milbanke to Earl of Aberdeen, No 30, Munich, 15 June 1846

Influence of M. Abel; several Cabinet members dismissed; objections to Count Bray as foreign minister; plan to remove Prince Wallerstein

The change of Ministry which I announced in a former despatch as having occurred here, may be ascribed in part to the intrigues which have been carried on in the bosom of it, with more or less of activity, ever since I have resided at Munich, but the result may perhaps have been hastened by the turn the discussions took in the Chambers towards the end of the Session, & the effect produced by them on the Mind of the King.

I have in the course of my correspondence frequently alluded to the unpopularity of M. d'Abel, the Minister of the Interior, principally arising from his avowed connection with the high Catholick or Ultra-montane Party, to the advancement of whose ends, he is accused of sacrificing the best Interests of his Country.

A strong Opposition comprehending all the Princes of the Royal Family, having at their head the Prince Royal,[118] has long been forming against him, & every effort seems to have been made to undermine his influence with the King. The Tact, however, and energy which he displayed in conjuring the stormy discussions in the Chambers, on religious, & other matters, which had rather begun to create apprehension in the mind of His Majesty, & his general aptitude for conducting the business of the Government, the burthen of which chiefly falls upon him to which perhaps may be added the jealousy of the King at anything which bears the appearance of an attempt to interfere with the Royal prerogative in the choice of his Ministers, have all combined to bring about a result far different from what was hoped by his Opponents, & have ended in a signal triumph for M. d'Abel, whose position has thereby acquired much additional strength. The consciousness of intellectual superiority over his Colleagues, which even his enemies do not deny, may probably as is said of him, have led him to exhibit in the Council a haughty & overbearing manner, towards some of them, which was exceedingly offensive, & in the course of the discussions which took place there on religious points, he frequently encountered opposition from the Minister for Foreign Affairs, Baron de Gisé, the only Protestant in the Ministry, who sought to modify some of M d'Abels confessional measures.[119] His seniority also of Service conferred upon him the Presidency; & his removal therefore became indispensable for the double reason of doing away with his opposition, & bringing M d'Abel a step nearer to the President's Chair.

Intrigues were consequently redoubled, & some Members of the Bavarian Corps Diplomatique are said to have been enlisted in them, in the hopes of being selected to fill his place. Various improbable reasons are assigned for his immediate fall, & amongst them an intercepted correspondence with the Prince Royal who has been for some time absent, at Berlin. The mode of his dismissal is generally considered by his friends to have been most ungracious, when his long Services are taken into account. It consisted of a short Note from the King which came quite unexpectedly, informing him, that he was to be placed on the Pension list, but adding, that he was not to look upon the arrangement as a Mark of disgrace. The Minister of Justice,[120] also M. d'Abel's senior in the Ministry, was disposed of in the same summary

---

[118] Maximilian.
[119] Cf. for example p. 454 in this section.
[120] Sebastian Freiherr Schrenck von Notzing.

manner, merely, however, making place for his Son[121] by whom he is succeeded, & in whom as he was entirely brought forward under his auspices, M. d'Abel probably expects to find a person who will be entirely subservient to him.

The objections which I have heard brought forward against the nomination of the Count Bray as Minister for Foreign Affairs are made principally on the ground of his want of Experience in the complicated System of German Politicks, & his consequent dependence for advice on M. d'Abel.

These transactions have created a great sensation, & much outcry, especially amongst the Protestants who see in them an earnest of what they have to expect in the way of removal of their grievances, & who now begin to entertain doubts as to the sincerity of the promises made to them on the part of the Government.

At present the King may be said to be completely in the hands of the Minister of the Interior: His Majesty observed the other day to one of my Colleagues, that upon the whole he was pretty well satisfied with the manner in which the Session of the Chambers had terminated, but he said he owed its entirely to M. d'Abel that he had got off so well.

The most curious part of these Intrigues is still to be told. Prince Wallerstein who has been a thorn in the side of the Ministry during the whole Session, & who is particularly obnoxious to M. d'Abel as a vehement opponent of the Ultramontane Party which he says is gradually sapping the foundations of all social order in Germany, has been named Bavarian Minister at Paris, solely for the purpose of removing him for a time from this Capital. As his absence was considered to be necessary to the repose of the Government, it was determined to send him as Minister to Turin, & the King accordingly sent a verbal message to him acquainting him with this decision, & adding that if he did not set out before the 1st of August his pension would be withdrawn. To this Communication the Prince prudently replied by a request to have the substance of it in writing, but for some days heard nothing more on the Subject. Subsequently however His Majesty again sent to him, not however for the purpose of enforcing his commands, but what was more characteristick, of departing from them, by offering to the Prince the Mission to Paris, which he has ended by accepting as he tells me with a proviso, that he shall be allowed to return to Munich to attend his place in the Upper Chamber during the next Session, if he shall then occupy the same Post.

I cannot describe the state of publick feeling here during all these strange proceedings which require no comment from me; & I reproduce them on paper merely to give your Lordship some insight into the

---

[121] Karl Freiherr Schrenck von Notzing.

characters of those to whom the Government of this Country is at present entrusted.

During the King's progress to Aschaffenburg, I hear he has been lecturing the Burgomasters of the different Towns he has passed through, for allowing Representatives to be chosen who were unfavorable to his Government.

FO 9/92: John Ralph Milbanke to Viscount Palmerston, No 13, Munich, 15 October 1846

Bavarian government's views on Schleswig-Holstein question

It may not be improper that I should endeavour to give Your Lordship some insight into the views of the Bavarian Government in the Schleswig-Holstein succession question, which has lately agitated the whole of Germany in such an extraordinary manner.[122]

The King of Bavaria, as is probably known to Your Lordship through the Public Press, has more especially drawn upon himself attention, by the answers which he has on one or two occasions returned to address from certain small towns and communities in Bavaria, in which His Majesty approves of the 'true German feeling' expressed by them. These sentiments have been re-echoed by the Public Press, and His Majesty has been held up as a model for all German Princes who have the Union of the German Nation at heart.

Notwithstanding that a strong feeling subsists among all classes in reference to this question, it is not unmixed with regret that the King should have pronounced himself hastily and unadvisedly on it. Indeed His Majesty seems subsequently to have had some misgivings as to the prudence of his own conduct, for I have reason to believe, that he caused a sort of explanation to be given to my Austrian Colleague,[123] to the effect that he had no intention of prejudging the question of Right, but merely wished to show that he was animated by a desire to preserve the Union of Germany. [...]

[122] The succession in the duchies of Schleswig and Holstein, hitherto united with Denmark in a personal union, was not clear because there were two different laws of succession. The vehement discussions of 1846 were sparked off by a public letter of 8 July from the Danish king, Christian VII, to his subjects, in which he upheld the principle of undivided succession in the area ruled by the Danish royal house.

[123] Friedrich Christian Ludwig Graf Senfft von Pilsach.

FO 9/92: John Ralph Milbanke to Viscount Palmerston, No 26, Munich, 16 December 1846

Public opinion on occupation of Cracow; reflections on 'German Unity'

[...] From the information which has reached me I am led to conclude that the general effect produced in Germany by the incorporation of Cracow into the Austrian Monarchy[124] is highly unfavorable towards the Imperial Government, and has greatly shaken the confidence for so many years reposed in it by the smaller Powers, who have been accustomed to consider it the best and perhaps the only guarantee for the existing order of things as established by Treaties. Here, I believe the feeling on the subject to be a divided one. The King, with His absolute notions, approves in His heart what he looks upon as an act of energy against democratick principles, but is not quite at His ease when He reflects upon the possible future consequences. He has, I am told, since the event occurred, been heard to drop expressions intimating His Conviction that in present times the closest Union amongst the German States has become absolutely necessary to the common safety. The Organs of the Ultramontane Party express their undisguised satisfaction also, and to them the ultimate effects of the measure are matters but of little moment.

On the other hand almost all moderate and reasonable men deplore it as a violation of the Compact upon which the Peace of Europe is founded, and a dangerous precedent for the future; and not many days ago one of the King's Ministers speaking to me in this sense, observed: 'it is a principle to which there are no bounds, and no one can tell how soon France may think proper to apply it to our own Provinces beyond the Rhine'.

The expectations also which have so long been held out, and which I understand to be now fast approaching their realization, of the Constitution of an Assembly at Berlin reviving the Character of the States General[125] on a very liberal basis, is viewed at Munich with much dissatisfaction, I presume from the apprehension which is felt that it may render the Bavarian Chambers less easy to manage at their next meeting.

To my mind 'German Unity', about which so much has been written and said of late years, is an impracticable Chimera. I see in none of these Countries any of the Elements of frankness or internal Concord indispensable to the carrying out of such an idea. On the Contrary

[124] An uprising in February 1846 led to the occupation of Cracow by Austria on 3 April, and the protocol of 6 November incorporated it into the Austrian Empire as part of the Kingdom of Galicia.

[125] Cf. pp. 235–236, 238–241 in Prussia section.

jealously and want of confidence in one another's designs is daily
manifested in their intercourse, and should any pressure from without
occur, I cannot but think that it would be the signal for a general
Confusion amongst them.[126]

FO 9/95: John Ralph Milbanke to Viscount Palmerston, No 8, Munich,
17 February 1847

Resignation of the whole Bavarian ministry; King's reaction to it; ultramontane party fails to
regain authority; Lola Montez's relationship with King of Bavaria; conduct of clergy

I have to acquaint Your Lordship that the whole of the Ministers
tendered their resignations to the King a few days ago,[127] but His
Majesty has only thought proper to accept of that of Monsieur d'Abel,
to whom He has accorded a Pension. To the others[128] He has given
leave of Absence for various periods, in order to allow them time for
reflection, and as it would seem in the hopes of retaining them in His
Service. In the mean time their places are filled by persons nominated
ad interim, for the purpose of carrying on the business of the different
Departments, but their appointments are not intended to be permanent.
Not one of them, except Monsieur Maurer who has undertaken the
management of the Foreign Department, as well as that of Justice, and
who was formerly in Greece, can be known to Your Lordship even by
name, and I therefore pass them over.

The immediate cause of this proceeding altogether unusual in this
Country is not easily explained. It is alleged to have been a refusal by
the Council of State, – on the Ground that the prescribed legal forms
had not been observed, – to consent to the preparation of an Instrument
conferring the Rights of Citizenship upon The King's new Mistress,[129]
who is a Foreigner, to the validity of which Document the Signature
of the Minister for Foreign Affairs was indispensable, but which he
declined to affix to it for reasons which he explained to the King in
the Council, and being thus placed in opposition to His Majesty he
thought proper to tender his resignation. Not being able to overcome

---

[126] Enclosure: Translation, Declaration made by the Minister of War of Electoral Hesse
to the Chambers respecting the interpretation by the Government of certain articles of
the Constitution.

[127] Cf. pp. 474–475 in this section.

[128] Otto Camillus Hugo Graf von Bray-Steinburg (foreign minister), Karl Freiherr
Schrenck von Notzing (minister of justice, culture, education and church affairs), Karl
Graf von Seinsheim (finance minister), Anton Freiherr von Gumppenberg (war minister).

[129] Lola Montez.

Count Bray's scruples, and anxious to keep him in his present Post, The King did not accept of his resignation, but gave him leave of absence for some months to visit Italy, intending to obtain the Signature of the Person who should have the direction of his Department during his absence. In this however His Majesty was failed, for that Person, Monsieur de Flad, also refused to sing the Document, and this rendered a further change necessary, which after many attempts on the part of The King to gain His point by negotiation, led as I have already stated, to the resignation of the whole Ministry. The general opinion seems to be that the step was wholly unjustifiable and that it was merely intended, as it has done, to embarrass The King by throwing the administration of Affairs into Confusion.

In order to give some elucidation of this attempt to force The King to yield to the Will of His Ministers in a matter in which, according to the Constitution, His Majesty has power to act as He pleases after going through the form of hearing the opinion of the Council, I must advert to the influence which the High Catholick or Ultramontane Party has been long supposed to exercise over Him, and I have little hesitation in Stating my Conviction that what has just passed is the fruits of an ill managed intrigue to regain that authority which it was in danger of losing, or rather has already lost by The King's devotion to a Mistress who rules Him with unlimited sway. She has unfortunately by her caprices urged Him into the commission of more than one Act of injustice, and thereby done Him much harm in the publick estimation. Monsieur d'Abel has been long known to be a zealous and powerful instrument in the hands of this Party, and his fall will be hailed with unbounded satisfaction throughout the Kingdom, as well by the Protestants as by the moderate Catholicks. His unpopularity has been long on the increase, and his only support was the apparent hold he had upon The King in religious matters. I have from the first doubted, or more properly speaking I have been long satisfied that the supposed religious thraldom of the King was a fallacy. His Majesty kept Monsieur d'Abel as Minister simply because he was useful to Him, and He imagined him to be thoroughly acquired to His interests through his own. Monsieur d'Abel's talents undoubtedly brought His Majesty safely through two difficult Sessions of the chambers, but he greatly miscalculated his power over The King when he made the present attempt – Having failed in it, the unceasing efforts of the Party are now directed towards preventing the formation of a new ministry, and The King, after many refusals, has only after some difficulty succeeded in carrying on the Government in the manner I have described above. His Majesty is always in hopes that a portion of the late Ministry will be induced to return, but I hear on all sides that this will not be the case. When therefore the periods of their leave of Absence shall have expired, which will be in about a month, the same scene will probably be gone through again, and we shall still find ourselves in the same predicament.

That Count Bray should have offered to resign, is I think, under the circumstances quite natural; but that the other Members of the Cabinet should have thought proper to make a matter in which not one of them was directly concerned, a Ministerial Question, seems to me somewhat inexplicable. It was no doubt hoped that The King would give in to such a publick demonstration, and dismiss His Mistress, but those who cherished such ideas could have but little knowledge of His Majesty's Character. Even now however they are not abandoned.

The conduct of the Clergy in all this business is I am told highly reprehensible. As a powerful engine of the Ultramontane Party, it has been set in motion to stir up men's minds against the Sovereign, and other means also are being resorted to for the same end. The result is great irritation in the publick mind throughout the Country, but especially in the Capital where it is rather apprehended that some popular demonstration may be made; but although great discontent and bitterness undeniably pervades all classes, I confess I do not anticipate anything very serious in that way, and I know the King is determined to act with vigour should the publick peace be disturbed. He says he will not submit to dictation from any party, and is glad to have had an opportunity of settling that of the Jesuits once for all, within His Dominions, where their reign is now over. As far as this question of naturalization is concerned His Majesty must be admitted to have the law on His side, – but on the other hand it cannot be denied that He has been acting for the last three months in open defiance of publick opinion, repeatedly and Strongly expressed as well against His violation of decorum, as against His arbitrary and self-willed proceedings. I can as yet scarcely hazard a surmise as to the formation of a new Ministry. To have the power of doing good in the Country, it ought to be composed of moderate Catholicks, and it would not surprize me to see Prince Wallerstein, now Bavarian Minister at Paris, at the head of it; but before anything permanent can be constituted, means must be found to get over the difficulty which was the pretext for the dissolution of the late Ministry.

FO 9/95: John Ralph Milbanke to Viscount Palmerston, No 10, Munich, 26 February 1847

Collective letter of the resigning ministers; King unimpressed by resolution

I stated in my Despatch N° 8 that the Ministers had sent in their resignation to the King, and I am now able to forward to Your Lordship herewith, a translation of the Collective Letter by which that resolution was made known to His Majesty.

It will be almost unnecessary for me to direct attention to the extraordinary tone of it throughout; but I am at a loss to understand how any men of Common Sense could, for a moment, have indulged in the supposition that the portrait of a weeping Bishop,[130] however pathetick, could make any impression on the King's mind in a matter in which He considers, and certainly not without some shew of reason, the interference of His Ministers as altogether misplaced and uncalled for.

The allusion to the Prince-Bishop of Breslau[131] is alone sufficient to betray the origin of the letter; but the most extraordinary part of it is that in which a sort of menace is conveyed, that in case of need the Armed Force will refuse to do its duty, and that to this menace should be attached the Signature of the Minister of War[132] himself, whose special duty is usually to maintain the Army in a State of discipline and obedience to the Sovereign. A more melancholy picture of the manner in which the Government of this Country has been conducted, or more condemnatory of their own System by the ex-Minister themselves, could hardly have been drawn. To a certain extent there is truth in it, but it is overcharged in many respects. [...][133]

FO 9/95: John Ralph Milbanke to Viscount Palmerston, No 12, Munich, 2 March 1847

Formation of the new Bavarian ministry; reasons for student disturbances

I have the honor to inform Your Lordship that the formation of the New Ministry may now be considered as completed.

It is as follows: Baron de Zu-Rhein, a member of the Upper

[130] The memorandum of 11 February reads: 'Men like the Bishop of Augsburg [Johann Peter von Richarz], whose fidelity and devotion to Your Majesty are raised above all doubt, shed bitter tears over what is passing & over results that are daily gradually developing themselves.'

[131] The memorandum reads: 'The Prince Bishop of Breslau [Melchior Freiherr von Diepenbrock] had no sooner received information of a Report circulated here, that he had pronounced an opinion in palliation of the said state of things, than he immediately sent a letter here with directions to declare in the most positive manner this statement to be untrue, wherever the subject might be mentioned, and to express his decided disapproval. His letter is no longer a secret, and will soon be known throughout the entire Country, and what will be the effect produced!'

[132] Anton Freiherr von Gumppenberg.

[133] Enclosure: Translated Letter, dated February 11 1847, from the Bavarian ministers to the King, stating the grounds of & tendering their resignation.

Chamber, is named Minister of Finance, and also has charge of that Department of the Ministry of the Interior which relates to Ecclesiastical Affairs and Publick Instruction. Monsieur Maurer is Minister of Justice, and manages the Foreign Department in the Absence of Count Bray. Monsieur Zenetti has been transferred from the Post of President of the Government of Landshut to that of Minister of the Interior, and General Baron de Hohenhausen is appointed Minister of War.

These nominations have been made, as is customary here, at first merely what is termed provisionally, but I do not doubt they will be subsequently confirmed. Generally speaking there seems to be no great objection to be made to any of them; and I conceive the new Ministry may safely lay claim to at least as much Talent as distinguished that which has just quitted Office. The Minister of Finance is decidedly the most distinguished Member of it, and on him will principally devolve the task of carrying on the Parliamentary business in the next Chambers.

I have already stated in a former Despatch that Count Bray will not again resume the direction of the Foreign Affairs, at least not for a permanency; so that the Post of Foreign Minister may still be looked upon as unfilled.

All the late Ministers, with the exception of the Minister of Finance who remains a Counsellor of State, as I believe at his own desire, without office, have received different Appointments, but only one which I need advert is that of Monsieur d'Abel, who has been named Bavarian Minister at the Court of Brussels.

Publick tranquillity was a little troubled here yesterday evening by the Students at the University, but beyond the breaking of a few Lamps and Windows no mischief was done. The immediate Cause, or rather pretext, for the disturbance was the deposition by order of The King of one of their Professors,[134] in consequence of his having proposed to make a sort of Publick demonstration on the part of the University towards Monsieur d'Abel. As this Professor is known to belong with many others to the Party now in disgrace, His Majesty interpreted the proposed step to imply a condemnation of His Conduct in what has lately passed, and had recourse to the above mode of conveying the expression of His displeasure to the University.

[134] Ernst von Lasaulx.

FO 9/95: John Ralph Milbanke to Viscount Palmerston, No 14, Munich, 15 March 1847

King's behaviour, conduct, and state of mind; his irritation with high Catholic party; Austria's influence weakening; state of public feeling; limited possibilities of new ministry; reasons for M. Abel's removal from Munich; Count Senfft's departure from Munich

I have no change worthy of notice to record since I last had the honor of addressing Your Lordship on the events, which have recently occurred in this Capital, and which have created so much sensation throughout Germany. The Cause still subsists, and The King still pursues the new System, if such it can be called, upon which He has entered. His irritation against the High Catholick Party is not in the least abated, but on the contrary, all His energies are turned towards measures which He hopes will weaken its' influence within His dominions, and He omits no opportunity of publickly expressing His hatred towards it.

My Prussian Colleague[135] read to me confidentially a Report addressed by him direct to his Sovereign, containing a relation of what passed at an Audience with which he has recently been honored by The King, and as it affords some clue to the present state of His Majesty's mind, I shall endeavour, as far as my memory will serve, shortly to recapitulate what fell from Him. His Majesty made some allusion to the resignation of the late Ministers, at which His astonishment, He said, had been great, especially as there were amongst them two[136] whom He had for many years regarded as His personal friends, and one[137] of whom, in particular, had often warned Him against the machinations of the Ultramontane Party. That these men should have been seduced to take a part in this demonstration against Him, He had seen with equal grief and surprize.

His Majesty said He had been watching the intolerant spirit which distinguished all the manoeuvres of the High Catholick Clergy ever since their indecent conduct at the Interment of the late Queen His mother,[138] and He admitted that He had to reproach Himself for not having paid more attention to the warnings which He had at that period received from the late King of Prussia, and which had been subsequently renewed by the present Sovereign, both of whom had repeatedly told Him that if He did not interfere in time, His Son[139]

[135] Albrecht Graf von Bernstoff.
[136] Karl Graf von Seinsheim, Anton Freiherr von Gumppenberg.
[137] Anton Freiherr von Gumppenberg.
[138] The funeral of the Protestant Queen Mother, Karoline, in 1841 had given rise to a public scandal because the cortège had been received by the Catholic clergy in Munich not wearing their liturgical vestments.
[139] Maximilian.

would never sit on the Throne of Bavaria. He made rather a curious confession – that he had at times sacrificed political considerations to His wish to conciliate this Party, and instanced as an example His conduct in the memorable dispute relative to the Archbishop of Cologne,[140] which He now had reason to regret deeply. He observed, that all things considered, He was not sorry the Crash had come during His lifetime, since he possessed the firmness and determination necessary to cope with these enemies, which he feared the Prince Royal did not; although he was disposed to give him full Credit for the very best intentions. He had written to him, He said, as well as to Prince Luitpold, and did not doubt that Both of them would fully approve of what He was doing. His Majesty concluded this remarkable avowal, of which I give a mere summary, by desiring Count Bernstorff to convey the substance of it to his Sovereign, and with it the assurance that the reign of the Jesuits in Bavaria was for ever terminated.

Observations in a similar sense have been made by The King to others of my Colleagues, and amongst them to the Dutch Minister,[141] to whom His Majesty said: 'the Ultramontane Party is a dangerous one to have any dealings with. It serves you well enough as long as it is allowed to have its own way; but the moment you shew a disposition to curb its influence, it becomes a double edged weapon and cuts both ways'.

With me the King has only on one occasion made allusion to the subject, but in a manner to lead to the conclusion that it was uppermost in His Mind – He accosted me in the Street, and almost without any preamble said: 'Sir, the empire of the Jesuits is over in Bavaria, over for ever' and then pursued His way.

The result of all this turmoil, politically speaking, consists, as it appears to me, in the annihilation for the moment of Austrian influence in the Councils of this Country, and the appearance of some symptoms of a leaning towards Prussia; but the nature of The King's Character is so vacillating and uncertain as to render it impossible to count upon what He may do next, and in myself for one, it would hardly excite surprize to see His passion suddenly diverted to some other object, and Himself fall back into the hands of the very Party from the trammels of which He now seems to think Himself once and for all emancipated. If therefore it were thought worth while to attempt to turn His present tendencies to account in anything relating to Commercial matters, no time ought to be lost in taking advantage of them.

It would be difficult to draw a correct picture of the state of Publick

---

[140] Clemens August Freiherr von Droste zu Vischering; cf, for example, pp. 88–91 in Frankfurt section.

[141] J.C. Gevers.

feeling in this Country at this moment. In the upper ranks of Society it is still exhibited in expressions of marked reprobation of His Majesty's conduct.[142] In general, however, I should be disposed to say that the Anger and bitterness displayed at the Commencement of this unfortunate business, have either given way before the countenance assumed by The King, or have exhausted themselves of their own accord, and in despite of the efforts of the evil disposed to keep the lower classes in a state of excitement. Still it would be an error to suppose that manifestations of popular opinion will not again recur should any new extravagance or arbitrary measure afford a decent pretext. The causes of complaint against the Head of the State are too numerous and, though sometimes exaggerated, in the main too well founded, and touch too closely the material interests of the Country to be allowed to slumber long in peace.

The new Ministry I understand hold out hopes of some ameliorations in the administration of Affairs. For my own part however, I do not imagine that they will be able to deviate very much from the line followed by their Predecessors. Any radical change of System would require far too large an expenditure ever to meet with The King's sanction, and the expectations formed in some quarters, as to the commencement of a new era, cannot fail to be disappointed. The most that the new Ministers will under present circumstances be able to effect, will not amount to much. They may introduce a little more impartiality in ecclesiastical and educational matters as regards the Protestants, and they will no doubt seek to transfer the mass of temporal patronage, which has hitherto been almost exclusively in the hands of the Higher Catholick Clergy, into a more legitimate channel. Some talk there is of granting more freedom to the Publick Press, but I confess I put but little faith in the rumour.

Apprehensions seem to be felt by some Statesmen in Germany, and I understand Prince Metternich is of the number, that The King in His anxiety to liberate Himself from the domination of the Ultramontane Party, may run into the opposite extreme, and throw Himself into the arms of the Liberals. Such fears however betray but a very superficial knowledge of His Majesty's absolute character. The truth is that the change has come so suddenly and unexpectedly, that there has been little time to reflect on its' probable consequences.

The fact that the late ministers have, with only one exception,[143] accepted subordinate places under the Sovereign whom they publickly accuse in their memorable Manifesto[144] of having brought the Country

---

[142] Cf. pp. 472–474 in this section.
[143] Karl Graf von Seinsheim.
[144] Cf. pp. 474–475 in this section.

to the verge of dissolution, must naturally appear singular to those who are unacquainted with the Power exercised by means of the patronage which most of the German Rulers have contrived to keep in their own hands, and upon which far the greater portion of official men in Bavaria are dependent for their very subsistence.

The nomination of Monsieur d'Abel to the post of Bavarian Minister at Brussels, to which that of the Hague has been added, was made no doubt for the purpose of removing him to a convenient distance from the Capital, but is viewed with some uneasiness by my Prussian and Dutch Colleagues. The former has I am told gone so far as to observe upon it to Monsieur de Maurer as calculated to afford a new focus of intrigue to the High Catholic Party in the Rhenish Provinces. The latter has not expressed any opinion upon it to the Government here, but he informed me that he entertained great doubts as to the cordiality of the reception Monsieur d'Abel was likely to meet with at the Hague, arriving there under such circumstances, and known as the particular friend of Count Senfft, the Austrian Minister, who some years ago, in conjunction with other Members of the Diplomatick Body, was known to have leagued himself somewhat too closely with the Ultramontane Party in Holland and Belgium.

On the present occasion Count Senfft has contrived to get his name so mixed up in what has passed, and The King has shewn such a marked Coolness towards him latterly, that he has felt his position here to be untenable, and accordingly left Munich for Vienna yesterday, as he says, on leave of absence for three months, but the general opinion seems to be that he will not return; and I have good reason for believing that he has been actually recalled at the request of His Majesty. At any rate he took his departure without having solicited an Audience of the King, which it is usual to do at this Court on similar occasions.

Since I commenced writing this Despatch, I have also heard that a Change is likely to be made in Monsieur d'Abel's destination, and that after all he will not go to Brussels and the Hague. I am at present unable to say whither he will be sent, but I think it will be in all probability to Turin.

FO 9/95: John Ralph Milbanke to Viscount Palmerston, No 17, Munich, 20 March 1847

Wish to strengthen common interests of Southern Germany; Austria's position unclear

The Ministers of Wurtemberg and Baden[145] at this Court have received

---

[145] Ferdinand Christoph Graf von Degenfeld-Schonburg and Ludwig Freiherr Rüdt von Collenberg-Bödigheim.

instructions to express officially the satisfaction which is felt by their Governments at the change of System which they believe to be in progress in this Country, in consequence of what has recently occurred here. They are in hopes that it will enable them to unite more closely for what they consider the common interests of Southern Germany, as they term them, to counterbalance those of the North, with which they do not altogether identify themselves. That the change was welcome there can be little doubt, – that it was unexpected is equally clear from a Conversation which took place a very few days before it occurred, between a person[146] who repeated the substance of it to me, and the King of Wurtemberg, in the course of which His Majesty lamented the subservience in the Councils of this Country to Austrian influence, and deeply regretted the little chance there was of detaching her from it, and inducing her to follow a more enlightened course of administration, and one more in accordance with the wishes of her other Neighbours.

Rumours of all sorts have been in circulation to the effect that the Austrian Government had signified to the King of Bavaria in very strong terms its disapproval of His Conduct. I mention them merely to contradict them, as the Austrian Chargé d'Affaires[147] assures me that he has not received a single word from Prince Metternich on the Subject.

The new Ministers seem to give general satisfaction, and they on their side pronounce the state of publick feeling in the Country to be all they could desire. No doubt there is some exaggeration on both sides; but I believe local demonstrations in that sense have been made.

FO 9/95: John Ralph Milbanke to Viscount Palmerston, Private, Munich, 16 May 1847

Violent disposition of population of market towns; effects of three meagre harvests in succession

[...] The German Journals are teeming with accounts of excesses committed by the Populace in all the Market Towns, & it is greatly feared that this riotous disposition is gaining ground. I hear that the Wurtemberg Gov.[t] has proofs in its hands of an affiliation between the individuals engaged in the late disturbances in that Country,[148] & the radical or Communist Party in Switzerland, more probably at Geneva; & there is no doubt that Emissaries from thence now overrun the whole of Germany. Luckily the effect of an increase of the Price of

---

[146] Not traceable.
[147] Adolf Freiherr von Brenner.
[148] Cf. pp. 403–404 in Württemberg section.

Corn, which was apprehended from the restrictive Measures of Austria,[149] has not followed. On the contrary a trifling diminution was perceptible in yesterdays Markets, but every description of Grain is still enormously dear. There has now been a succession of three indifferent Harvests, & the consequence is that the Granaries are entirely empty. At present the agricultural Reports are favourable, & it is devoutly to be hoped that they may continue so until the Harvest, for I am convinced that a fourth bad one would bring with it consequences which these Governments may well tremble to contemplate.

FO 9/95: John Ralph Milbanke to Viscount Palmerston, No 35, Munich, 5 June 1847

Changes in the administration of Justice

[...] One of the recent Acts of the new Ministry in Bavaria has been to introduce into the organisation of the Tribunals, numerous changes with a view to simplifying the present system of the administration of Justice, in both civil and criminal processes, by giving, amongst other things, a more extensive jurisdiction to the inferior Courts and thereby enabling them finally to decide cases of minor importance without reference to the higher Tribunals.

The Royal Ordonnance, on this subject, regulates the mode of conducting the proceedings as well in civil as criminal matters, through the different stages of appeal allowed by the German Law, but which I should have some difficulty in explaining to Your Lordship. It decrees, that both in civil and criminal processes, the proceedings shall be conducted verbally before the Court upon which it devolves to pronounce judgment, and that Officers shall be appointed, on the part of the State, to watch over them in its name, and especially to assist in the examination and carrying through of complaints. [...]

The Law Authorities have on different occasions in vain endeavoured to introduce, founded upon the ancient principles, a better and more expeditious system in civil Processes. Equally pressing is the necessity for a fundamental reform in the criminal code. The number of crimes, as appears from the result of the latest statistical returns, has increased in such proportion as urgently to demand the attention of the Government, in as much as the former mode of proceeding lamed the arm of Justice, and in most cases assured to the hardened criminal

---

[149] In May 1847 the Austrian government placed a ban on the export of grain from Bohemia to Saxony and Bavaria.

on almost certainty of escape from judgment, by a steady denial of his crime. [...]

FO 9/96: John Ralph Milbanke to Viscount Palmerston, No 76, Munich, 17 November 1847

Radical party gains ground

[...] Reviewing all that has passed in a political sense, it is impossible not to be struck with the victorious attitude of the Radical Party. At the Commencement of the Session its numbers in the Chambers of Deputies were small and insignificant, whilst on the other hand the Aristocratick Party was numerous in both Assemblies, and was ready to place itself under the direction of the Government, to which it would have ensured an overwhelming Majority. But the hesitation and indecision of the Ministry and its want of Tact in not availing itself of this advantage, speedily operated a fatal change. The Radical party seized the moment and gained over all the waverers, and the result has been the defeat of the Aristocratick Party in detail.

Prince Wallerstein, with whom I was talking over these matters today, observed to me that the turn affairs had taken was much to be deplored from the pernicious example it would afford to other States in Germany, and he added that it would require all the Tact and energy either of the present Ministry or that which would succeed it, to regain the lost ground before the Chambers next met to discuss the Budget. A change of Ministry is imminent, and I cannot for a moment doubt that Prince Wallerstein himself will be the Minister upon whom this task will devolve.

FO 9/96: John Ralph Milbanke to Viscount Palmerston, No 79, Munich, 30 November 1847

Public discontent grows; expected effects; King most unpopular; Prince Wallerstein's nomination as chief of ministry; King's answer to the work of the Landtag; 'Landtagsabschied' on closing the session of the Bavarian chambers

[...] It is impossible, My Lord, not to perceive that feelings of discontent are taking deep root in this Country, and I cannot but apprehend that unless a change of System calculated to allay them is speedily entered upon, very unpleasant consequences may in the end ensue. The democratick party favored by these circumstances is indubitably gaining ground, and I really do not see on what the Sovereign can lean for support. I am using a mild expression when I say that The King is most unpopular with the mass of the People; the Nobles are dissatisfied beyond measure with what is going on; and judging from their language in the Chamber and the accounts which reach the Capital from the Provinces, the Clergy, whether Catholick or Protestant, are alike making use of the Power they possess to excite the Publick mind against him. In any other Country such a state of things could not endure long without a crisis; but the patience of this People does not seem to admit of estimation by the ordinary rules.

The moment is certainly most unpropitious for the entrance into power of the new Ministry which is now fixed for tomorrow or next day. Prince Wallerstein will, as I have already stated, be the chief of it and in fact the only one I need name, for the others, although I am told they are men of business who have held subordinate offices, are wholly unknown beyond the Frontiers.[150] It is clear however that they are not very sanguine as to the stability of the Ministry they are about to compose, for it is said that every one of them, not excepting Prince Wallerstein, has made it a condition to his taking part in it, that the post he now occupies in the Administration, shall be kept open for him to retire upon in case his position as Minister should become untenable, and they have further insisted on being appointed as Ministers ad interim only. It is generally supposed that they will be unable to cope for any length of time with the difficulties of their position, and I do not hesitate to confess that looking at the circumstances under which they come in, I am strongly disposed to partake of that opinion. I shall however reserve my remarks on this subject to some future opportunity.

I had written thus far when the 'Landtagsabschied' or document by which the States are prorogued, and which contains The King's assent to the Laws passed, and His answers to the different Prayers and Petitions of the States, was placed in my hands. It sanctions the Provisions above enumerated relative to the Rail road funds, but passes over in silence nearly all the expressed wishes of the States for ameliorations in the internal administration of the Country, – such as the liberty of the Press, the discontinuance of the Lottery, with many others, and amongst them the introduction of a Law to enable the occupiers of Land to purchase their Freedom & to which however the Minister of the Interior has pledged himself in the Chambers.

The only one of these wishes to which any allusion is made, is that relating to Post regulations and the establishment of a Penny Post or

---

[150] In addition to Oettingen-Wallerstein (foreign minister, church and school affairs), the cabinet consisted of: Karl Friedrich von Heres (finance minister), Franz von Berks (minister for the interior), Hermann von Beisler (justice minister), and Leonhard Freiherr von Hohenhausen (war minister).

something similar, which His Majesty promised to take into consideration. The Conclusion is remarkable from the manner in which it is worded, for after saying that the States had been convoked for a special purpose[151] at an earlier period than is fixed by the Constitution, His Majesty continues to say that He does not the less reserve to Himself the faculty of dealing with the different wishes and proposals addressed to Him, according <u>to His own views, and on His own responsibility</u>. As I cannot find any English expression which corresponds exactly with the Phrase I have endeavoured to translate, I have the honor to inclose a copy of the 'Landtagsabschied' in the original German.[152]

[151] It was the task of the *Landtag* to discuss the regulations for financing the construction of the railways (that is, to specify the interest rate).

[152] Enclosures: 1. The *Landtagsabschied* on closing the Session of the Bavarian States, 30 November 1847; 2. Translation.

AUSTRIA
(VIENNA)

VIENNA

FO 7/222: Lord Cowley to Earl of Aberdeen, No 79, Vienna, 28 June
1830

Financial state of Austria

I have taken great pains to procure an accurate account of the Finances
of this country, a task of some difficulty as the subject is purposely (as
it is supposed) involved in obscurity by the Government. I believe
however that the accuracy of the enclosed may be relied upon, and I
shall take care from time to time to apprise Your Lordship of any new
measure, or of any variation which may occur in the system.

From the enclosed statement the following conclusions may be
drawn.

The revenue of Austria as compared with the extent of her territory,
12.000 geographical square miles, and the amount of her population,
30 millions, would appear upon the first view to be inadequate to her
expences. But the expences falling immediately upon Government in
several of the most important Departments are much less, comparatively, than those of many other states.

In most parts of the Austrian Empire the expences of the local
administration, of the judicial Courts and of public works are defrayed
by the nobility and the towns. The Clergy are paid from revenues of
their own, and the army excepting in time of war is maintained at a
very cheap rate.

Austria is not in a state to bear in case of emergency the imposition
of new direct taxes, and the only practicable way of improving revenue
is by a better distribution of those taxes already existing.

Notwithstanding the unceasing endeavours of the Emperor and
the frequent appointment of Committees of reform no considerable
diminution of expence is to be expected. This is principally owing to
the number of Employés whom it has been always found impossible to
reduce.

The amount of the debt of Austria at the end of 1829 was 839.285.169
florins (= about 83.928.516£S^g): of this rather more than 432 millions
(43.200.000£S^g) bears an interest of 5 p. C^t and is called <u>new debt</u> or
metallicks, being paid in coin, the remainder, constituting the <u>old debt</u>,
only 1 p. C^t or 2½ in paper.

The average revenue of Austria is estimated at about 122 millions of florins or 12.200.000£ - the average expenditure at 123 millions of florins, or 12.300.000£S^g - leaving a deficit of 100.000£.

This is ostensibly the annual deficit, but it can be proved that the real annual deficit of Austria up to the year 1829 had been nearly 800.000£ and that to provide for it has been the principal object of the different loans contracted under various pretences.

In the year 1829 a considerable encrease of revenue was obtained by a new arrangement of the taxes[1] and the result of the new measures of finance then adopted will leave the deficit for the next ten years, calculating the expence according to the probable estimate of 1830, at about 4 ½ millions of florins or 450.000£. But should the reduction, which the Minister of Finance[2] expects to be able to effect, of the interest of the new debt from 5 to 4 p. C^t take place, this deficit will be provided for - But even in the event of a failure of this measure, still at the expiration of ten years Austria having paid off the Lotteries will have a revenue exceeding her expenditure.

The payments of the old debt by means of the Sinking Fund will require 38 years.

Every new loan henceforth will have a Sinking Fund of 1 p. C^t created for it.

Such is the view taken in the enclosed of the financial state of Austria and of the system by a steady adherence to which it is expected that in a few years she will have a clear and flourishing revenue.

On the other hand it is to be observed, that her credit depends chiefly upon that of Her National Bank, the credit of which can scarcely be said to be founded on a solid basis, for its issue of bank-notes amounts to 120 millions of florins, while its capital in specie amounts only to 25 millions. The principal issue of notes has been made to fill up the vacuum created by the withdrawal of the Paper Currency (the Scheins)[3] - 50 millions only of the latter remaining in circulation in small notes for the daily purposes of life, these will probably be allowed to continue, since their discharge might create an embarrassing and dangerous demand upon the bank for small coin.

A continuance of peace may enable Austria to place her credit upon a solid basis. Should a general war take place she could not meet its

---

[1] The Imperial Patent of 1 November 1829 introduced a standard rate for the consumption tax levied on wine, beer, cider (*Most*), spirits, and meat. This superseded the numerous regional regulations which had previously existed.

[2] Peter Joseph Freiherr von Eichhoff.

[3] In 1816 instructions were issued for the *Wiener Währung* (Viennese currency), which had been introduced only in 1811, to be exchanged for the *Conventionswährung* (Convention currency). The aim of this measure, which coincided with the founding of the Austrian National Bank, was to get the inflation caused by the fiduciary issue of banknotes under control.

expences without a new paper currency, a measure which could hardly fail to be injurious to the credit of the bank, particularly if the expedient resorted to should be (as suggested in the enclosed paper) that of converting the bank-notes into a paper currency by stopping the payments of the Bank. But supposing such a measure to be resorted to, it must not be forgotten that during the last war after two failures, amounting almost to national bankruptcies, Austria at the conclusion of peace was by degrees enabled to bring the notes of the Bank into circulation at par and thus to restore her credit.[4]

FO 7/222: Lord Cowley to Earl of Aberdeen, No 102, Vienna, 14 August 1830

Reaction to revolution in France; line of conduct pursued by Austria and Russia

Your Lordship will not be surprised to hear that the attention of this Government is anxiously directed to the state of affairs in France.

The publication of the French Ordonnances had prepared Prince Metternich for some serious convulsion in the Capital, and as soon as the account reached him of the proceedings[5] of the 27th 28th and 29th Ult° he determined upon returning to Vienna. On his way through Carlsbad he had an interview with Count Nesselrode, and the two Ministers after agreeing upon the line of conduct which they should advise their respective Sovereigns to pursue, drew up a short paper which was shewn to me by Prince Metternich and of which the following is the substance:

'To take as a general basis of the line of conduct to be pursued by Austria and Russia, that they should abstain from all interference in the internal disputes of France, but that they should not on the other hand suffer France to do anything to the prejudice (porter atteinte) of the general interest of Europe, as established and guaranteed by treaty, or to disturb the internal tranquillity of any of the States of which Europe is composed.'

Prince Metternich upon his return from Bohemia waited upon the Emperor at Baden, who had given his full sanction the adoption of the course pointed out in the above Memorandum, and it would appear by dispatches received yesterday from Berlin, and which were communicated to me by His Highness, that the Prussian Government suggests the same course as that which it will be proper for the Great Powers to pursue with respect to France.

[4] Enclosure: *Memoire sur les Finances de l'Autriche.*
[5] French revolution of July 1830, cf. n. 28 in Frankfurt section.

The return of Prince Metternich and the language which he has held to the Diplomatick Agents at this Court has tended to correct an opinion which prevailed among some of them, that according to the Treaty of November 1815[6] the Allies were bound to maintain the King of France upon his Throne, and that an immediate war must be necessary consequence of the late proceedings at Paris.

Your Lordship will see that nothing can be more moderate than the resolutions proposed to be adopted by the three great Continental Powers,[7] and as His Majesty's Government will probably be desirous of having early information upon this subject I have charged Mr. Livesey, whom I have occasionally employed as a Messenger, with my dispatches of this day's date.

Prince Metternich will I believe send a Courier to Prince Esterhazy in the course of a day or two.

FO 7/227: Lord Cowley to Viscount Palmerston, No 1, Private and Confidential, Vienna, 7 January 1831

King of Württemberg's answer to the turmoil in Southern Germany; Metternich's conduct; Austria's policy

[...] Prince Metternich was lately much excited by the arrival at Vienna of Prince Schönburg, the Austrian Minister at Stuttgart, who appears to have been sent by the King of Wirtemberg with (as I believe) very exaggerated representations of the state of Wirtemberg, of Baden, of Hesse Darmstadt, and of Hesse Cassel, the People of which Countries are, it is stated by the Prince, rife for revolt, and the only remedy which the King of Wirtemberg has been able to discover for such a state of things is an immediate war with France.

It must be admitted that the language of Prince Metternich to his intimate Friends upon passing events, is not always as prudent as might be wished – and when it goes forth to the world before His Highness has had time to correct his first impressions, it gives rise to a belief that he is an Advocate for War. – But his measures, which are seldom taken without due deliberation, are usually wise and moderate, and the preservation of Peace is so necessary to Austria, that I feel persuaded His Highness would not embark on a War without the best possible cause [...]

---

[6] Second Paris Peace of 20 November 1815.
[7] Austria, Prussia, and Russia.

FO 7/235: Frederick Lamb to Viscount Palmerston, No 66, Vienna, 6 June 1832

Hambach Festival triggers Metternich's plan for reaction; Austria and Prussia agree to employ their contingents for suppression of revolt in Germany; on the alleged initiators of unrest; news from Paris

I was sent for this morning by Prince Metternich whom I found in a state of much agitation. – He said the proceedings at Hambach[8] had torn the veil asunder, that the Question now was whether the Sovereigns of Germany should descend from their Thrones without a struggle, or whether their Authority should be asserted by force, that hitherto their Counsellors had represented to them that concession would secure the love of their People, that now they were told in plain terms that their reign was ended and that the German Republic one and indivisible was to begin, that it was perhaps lucky for them that all illusion was over, that Mr de Münch would immediately set out for Frankfort, that the Laws of the Confederation would be affected without a dissentient voice, and that wherever resistance should shew itself force would be employed. – I had before been apprized that Austria and Prussia had agreed to employ their contingents for the suppression of revolt in Germany, a decision from which they had heretofore held back. The practical application of this principle appears to be at hand, & it is impossible not to foresee that it may be the forerunner of the most serious events. – Prince Metternich begged me to remark to Your Lordship that the events which are passing in Germany can not be safely judged by an English Standard, – That if such a meeting as that of Hambach had passed at Leeds or Birmingham, he should have thought it no more serious than they generally are in England, but that in Germany it is revolution. – What Nations can support (he added) is determined by their previous habits, if ever you should see such a meeting in Vienna or a charivari given under my windows, be assured that the Austrian Empire is at an end. – While I was with him he received a Dispatch from the Austrian Minister[9] at Stuttgart representing the King of Wurtemberg to have expressed to him the same sentiments which His Highness was stating to me. – He thinks that the Mass of the People and the higher ranks of the Bourgeoisie are still attached to Monarchical Government and Enemies to this agitation, but that the Press, the Professors, the Students and the Employés who are exorbitantly numerous are its

---

[8] Cf. pp. 23–26 in Frankfurt section.
[9] Heinrich Eduard Fürst zu Schönburg-Hartenstein.

active promoters. – Prince Metternich's opinions and consequent determination have received an active stimulus from the Meeting held at
Paris simultaneously with that at Hambach, whereof an account is
given in all the French papers of the 28th.[10] According to these it is the
Sainte Alliance des Peuples which is proclaimed as about to supersede
the Holy Alliance of Kings,[11] and the toasts given by a Patriot of each
Nation to the Health of the Revolutionists of some other Country and
to the success of their cause were read to me by the Prince as
apparent and undeniable proof of their intentions. – The Laws of the
Confederation which are about to be enforced are those of 1815 and
1820,[12] no new ones are to be asked for and the existing ones are
considered by the Prince as sufficient; but his manner as well as the
matter of his communication convinces me that he feels the Crisis to
be decisive, and I shall not be surprised if further military movements
should immediately take place.

FO 7/235: Frederick Lamb to Viscount Palmerston, No 137, Vienna,
21 September 1832

Metternich's comment on Palmerston's note; his denial of Great Britain's right to intervene

I yesterday had the honor to communicate Your Lordship's Dispatch
N° 83 to Prince Metternich.[13] Upon reading the two first paragraphs
he at once denied the right of the British Government to interfere in
the internal concerns of the Confederation, saying it was no more
entitled to do so, than the Diet would be to interfere with the measures
of the British Parliament. – This, however, was only a hasty and
inconsiderate movement, for on representing to him the difference
between the two positions, and the Rights which accrue, from the act
of the Congress of Vienna, to the Powers who signed it, he at once
abandoned the ground he had taken, and allowed that anything, which

[10] The French newspapers *Tribune* and *National* published an appeal for the establishment
of a Parisian branch of the *Preß- und Vaterlandsverein*, which had initiated the Hambach
Festival. Later renamed *Deutscher Volks-Verein*, this was the first political association founded
by German emigrants in Paris.
[11] Declaration of intent by the rulers of Russia, Austria and Prussia, 26 September
1815, which was joined later by all the crowned heads of Europe, with the exception of
the British monarch. With the aim of defending the legitimacy of the monarchies, the
Holy Alliance agreed to offer mutual support, and to work for the preservation of the
principles of the Christian religion.
[12] The Act of the German Confederation of 8 June 1815, and the Vienna Final Act of
15 May 1820.
[13] An identically worded dispatch was also sent to Prussia, cf. pp. 123–128 in Prussia
section.

should tend to infringe upon the Federal Act, or alter its nature, would be within the competence of the Powers, who were Parties to the final Act of Vienna.[14] He then went through the Dispatch with much attention, applying his comments upon it so distinctly to its individual parts, that I have thought it best to consign them to a separate Paper, to which I beg to refer Your Lordship.

With regard to Prince Metternich's doctrine as to the relative Rights and Power of the Diet and the Representative Assemblies, I need hardly remark to Your Lordship that it is open to much controversy; scarcely any two Germans are agreed upon the interpretation of the knotty points whereof it treats, and if they were to be subjected to accurate discussion, I have no doubt but it would be protracted to a length, and be found to involve difficulties, of which it would be impossible to anticipate the extent.

With regard to the practical part, Your Lordship will observe that the Prince concurs in the general scope of your reasoning.

The Questions between you are only Questions of fact.

He unequivocally denies the intention, upon the presumption of which Your Lordship's apprehensions are founded, – that of carrying the Measures of the Diet[15] to an extent inconsistent with the independence of the several German States, or subversive of their Constitutions; and he is at issue with Your Lordship upon the fact of the feeling which has been excited in Germany by the Decrees already promulgated.

Upon the first of these points, I am disposed to give full credit to Prince Metternich's assertions. – It is not in the character of his Policy to do more than is necessary for the exigency of the moment. – This is already provided for. – The licence of the Press is curbed, nor is any further extension required to the measures by which this end has been attained. – If, indeed, the States, upon their assembling, should contest the right of the Diet to do what it has done, a disagreement will arise between these Jurisdictions, but even in this case it will be in the character of the Austrian Policy to conduct the Question with great caution and prudence, and with such an exact observance of legal forms, as is apt in Germany to evaporate a grievance in protracted discussion. – The only other point, upon which collision is perhaps apprehended, is that of the obligation of the States to bear their proportion of the Federal burthens, and the question, on which this difference may come into action, is the one treated of in my No. 35[16] of April last. – the maintenance of military Contingents. – This point

---

[14] Cf. n. 131 in Frankfurt section.
[15] Six Articles of 28 June 1832, cf. n. 66 in Frankfurt section.
[16] Not included in this volume.

is vital to the very existence of the Confederation, nor can any State wish to divest itself of the burthen, without aiming at the dissolution of the Compact.

It is to be hoped that prudence on both sides may avert the catastrophe, and I am informed, that in this spirit the Commission[17] sitting at Berlin proposes to diminish the amount of the Contingent to be kept on foot in time of peace, a measure which is represented to me as indispensible for the financial relief of the smaller States.

With regard to the second point, – the effect which has been produced in Germany by the Decrees of the Diet, I am ill placed for forming an opinion. – Every thing which comes here may be expected to take a tinge from the predominant opinion of the Place, but it is only by a comparison of these opinions coming from different Quarters that Your Lordship can hope to arrive at a just estimate of the truth. – It may therefore be useful to state that all the information, I can collect, tends to confirm Prince Metternich's view of the subject. – Some of the Ministers of the Minor Courts have lately returned from travelling through the North of Germany. – They represent the whole of it, including the Prussian Rhenish Provinces to be decidedly friendly to the Measures of the Diet, and hostile to the Journalists, who have been silenced, – My information from the South of Germany is less distinct, it is derived only from Letters, and from the opinions of persons engaged in Commerce, who might be supposed to be peculiarly susceptible to apprehensions of disturbance. – These, however, as far as I have been able to learn their opinions, are uniformly impressed with the belief that the danger of serious troubles in Germany (which was extreme and imminent) is decidedly at an end. – They admit the possibility of differences of opinion, and discussions in the Chambers, and even of partial disturbances, but they are convinced that nothing serious is to be apprehended.

In stating this as the result of my enquiries, I am far from claiming, or even from giving implicit credence to it. – I am aware that nothing is more difficult than to estimate the amount of national feeling, or to prejudge the conduct of popular Assemblies. – My statement, therefore, upon the subject is only intended to add an item to the mass of data, upon the comparison of which, Your Lordship's estimate must be formed.

According to Your Lordship's Orders I left a Copy of the Dispatch with Prince Metternich, who expressed his intention of sending an answer to it.

Enclosure: appended Minute:

[17] Military Commission of the German Confederation, cf. n. 35 in Prussia section.

Extracts from Viscount Palmerston's Dispatch No. 83 to Sir Frederic Lamb[18]

Prince Metternich's Comments upon parts of Viscount Palmerston's No. 83 to Sir Frederic Lamb

1. 'In those Acts of the Congress of Vienna, which relate to the settlement of Germany, two prominent principles appear to be established: the one, that the several States of which Germany was to be composed, should enjoy an Independence inviolable from without; the other, that their internal welfare should be secured by Representative Assemblies.'

1. In the first of these principles Prince Metternich fully acquiesced; from the second he dissented.

He said that the words Etats had not been lightly inserted in the 13th Article of the Federation Act.[19] – It had been adopted after long consideration, and much discussion. – An Article demanding Representative Assemblies could never have been signed by Austria. The Etats contemplated in the Article are those which have existed from a distant period,[20] and which still subsist in all the various Provinces of which the Austrian Empire consists. – When the Emperor acquired Saltzburg, He immediately organized an Assembly of States in that Country, without which it would have been authorized to have called upon the Diet to enforce the execution of the Federative Act.[21] – The King of Prussia in like manner has complied with the Provisions of that Act by creating Etats throughout the various parts of his Monarchy. – The Federative Act therefore does not demand Representative Assemblies, but it does not preclude them, and those

---

[18] For comments on this dispatch, an identically worded version of which was also sent to Prussia, cf. pp. 123–128 in Prussia section.

[19] Cf. n. 83 in Frankfurt section.

[20] Pencil in margin: 'But Query are they not representative assemblies?'.

[21] The Duchy of Salzburg, which fell to Bavaria in 1809, was returned to Austrian rule on 1 May 1816.

Sovereigns who conferred them upon their Countries went beyond it, though not in opposition to it.

2. 'In this manner the weaker States were assured of the protection of the strong, and the strong found their defensive means encreased by the pledged alliance of their less powerful neighbours. It is clear that this league was intended to secure the separate independence of its component Members; for the maintenance of that Independence was set forth as one of the principal objects of the Union, and to it, therefore, the Federal Obligations and engagements must be considered as subordinate and conducive.'

2. In this reasoning Prince Metternich fully coincided, adding that it might have been carried further, that the Confederation was intended not only to give support to its weaker Members against external aggression, but also to protect them against the encroachments of their stronger Neighbours, but he added that the omission of the mention of this principle was well judged, and he felt grateful for it.

3. 'The Plenipotentiaries who compose the Diet represent only the Sovereigns, who, in States where the right of Representation has been established, cannot by their sole authority give validity to Acts which require by their nature the consent of all the branches of the Legislature; and the assent of these Sovereigns to Regulations subversive of their political independence, would be inconsistent with the engagements, which they have contracted by the Treaty before referred to.'

3. The Prince insisted that no Constitution could contain a Clause subversive of the Confederation. − Such a Clause would be of itself null and the Diet would be entitled to reject it. When the Sovereigns granted the Constitutions, several of them wished to place them under the guarantee of the Diet; − others, − as the King of Bavaria, abstained from this measure. − Austria objected to the Diet giving the required guarantee on the ground that it would thereby acquire the right to interfere in the purely internal concerns of these States; all that She could admit was that the Diet should accept these Constitutions as a deposit to be appealed to equally by the Sovereign or by the States, in the event of differences arising between them. − Cases have already occurred among the

minor States in which the Chambers have applied to the Diet and in all such, its interposition has been effectual; in cases such as that of Bavaria, in which the Constitution was not deposited with the Diet, it does not less possess a right to interpose, but by a longer and more complicated process.

The law of the Press promulgated in Baden was at variance with the provisions of the Constitution deposited with the Diet, it was equally at variance with the Laws of the Confederation, and the Diet was therefore entitled to demand its revocation.[22]

---

4. 'But whatever explanations may be given upon those Questions, it may certainly be feared that if the authority which has been constituted within the Diet by these Resolutions, were to exercise to its full extent, the power with which it has been invested, the Constitutional Rights of the maller States, and their political independence might be most seriously affected. – It is, however, to the danger which may possibly result from those Measures, that His Majesty's Government wishes, on the present occasion to direct the attention of the Court of Vienna.'

4. The Argument is true, but applies to a state of things which does not exist. – No Measures of the nature described have been taken, nor will any such be resorted to.

---

5. 'And they are inclined to think that a firm but tempered exercise of the powers possessed by the Governments of those States would have been sufficient to uphold the authority of the Law,

5. The Sovereigns had neglected to employ their authority till it had escaped from them, they possessed no longer the means of helping themselves, and it was their own sense of this their helplessness that

---

[22] For the debate on the press law in Baden cf. n. 51 in Frankfurt section.

and to preserve domestic peace; and in the exercise of these Powers, those Governments would certainly have been entitled to have applied for, and to have obtained, if necessary, the support of the Diet.'

induced them to apply to the Diet. – Would the King of Bavaria, who had so highly prized and upheld his independence, have resorted to such a measure, unless in the last extremity? If the measures of the Diet had been delayed but a few weeks, Germany would have fallen into a state of anarchy; the object and the effect of its Decrees were to restore to the Governments of Germany their independence and power of action, not to encroach upon them.

---

6. 'It appears, on the contrary, that a strong and general opinion prevails throughout almost all the Constitutional States, that the Resolutions of the Diet are an infringement upon their Rights, and an attack upon their national Independence.'

6. All this is a mistake. – The Magistrates have universally expressed their acknowledgements to the Sovereigns for having interposed their authority to avert the anarchy which menaced Germany. – They represent the satisfaction with the Decrees of the Diet to be general throughout all Classes, and assert that even those, who had been infected by the contagion of the times, have returned to a better way of thinking.

The President of the Diet[23] writes that if, when he left Vienna some months back, the extent of the amelioration which has taken place in the state of public feeling in Germany had been predicted to him, he should have considered the prediction as impossible to be realized.

---

7. 'Should this feeling break forth at the next meeting of the Legislative Assemblies in the Constitutional States, which it

7. This the Prince admits, but he observes that if he were to establish in argument, that in case the Chambers in Bavaria were to erect

[23] Joachim Graf von Münch-Bellinghausen.

probably will, even if nothing should occur to call it sooner into action, the consequence of these measures will be a breach between the Sovereigns of those States, and the great mass of their Subjects, upon questions of the deepest national importance, and which excite the strongest passions of mankind.'

a Republic, and connect themselves with a Party aiming at Republicanism in Germany and France, much danger should result from it, the British Government would be among the first to assent to the proposition; but what, he asks, would be gained by such a course of reasoning. – They are two extreme cases, neither of which is likely to occur; I occupy myself, he adds, with the middle course, averting the evils of either extreme, and in that course I shall remain.

8. 'It is obvious that in such a posture of affairs, a powerful foreign influence might grow up in the bosom of the State, – an influence, too, not of a Foreign Government, but of a Foreign Faction, ready to fasten upon discontent wherever it should be found, and to make the grievances of all Nations equally subservient to its own bad purposes.'

8. The state of things described here as contingent, is that which actually existed. The correspondence of Doctor Wirth and others, which has been seized, contains letters from Lafayette, Odillon Barrot, and Mauguin, which prove the proceedings in Germany to have been directed from Paris. The object of the Governments has been to withdraw Germany from the connection with a Foreign Faction, into which it had actually fallen, but which is now represented as likely to result from the very measures, which have in fact destroyed it.

9. 'Such are the dangers which His Majesty's Government apprehend from what has already taken place; but if the Resolutions of the Diet should be pushed to their full application, and measures should be carried into execution, which the People of the German States might consider, either inconsistent with rights and privileges formally conferred upon them, or else delib-

9. Upon this paragraph of the Dispatch Prince Metternich gives the assurance that no such Measures are in contemplation.

erately planned for the destruction of those privileges and rights; much more serious and extensive evils may be expected to ensue.'

10. 'The experience of all times, and of none more than the last three years, teaches that over-strained exertions of Power, though springing from the National Government of a State, produce resistance, and may end in Revolution.'

10. Prince Metternich admits the principle, but denies it's having any application to the present case.

11. 'Should the measures of the Diet unfortunately provoke resistance, and should force, but more especially Foreign force, be employed to quell it (and the troops of Austria and Prussia would, in such a case, be looked upon by the People of the other German States as a Foreign Force) a war of political opinions would begin, of which it is more easy to foretell the calamities, than to foresee the conclusion.'

11. Prince Metternich utterly denies that the Austrian Troops would in any case be looked upon as a Foreign Force. – Is the Garrison of Mayence,[24] he asks, considered as a Foreign Force? on the contrary, wherever an Austrian Regiment shews itself, it is received with open arms. – The first instruction to the President of the Diet has always been – touch no Federal Right – infringe the independence of no Sovereign; and the strict observance of this rule has secured to Austria the general confidence of all Germany.

12. 'His Majesty's Government, then, most earnestly request the Austrian Government to employ it's influence in restraining the inconsiderate zeal of the Diet, and in preventing the adoption of Measures, of which convulsion and war would be too probable consequences.'

12. The request is unnecessary as no measures of the sort are in contemplation.

[24] As one of the Confederation's five fortresses, the 'Garrison of Mayence' was under the direct control of the German Confederation. Austrian, Prussian and Hessian troops were stationed in Mainz; the Commandant was provided by Austria and Prussia alternately.

FO 7/241: Frederick Lamb to Viscount Palmerston, No 63, Vienna, 24 April 1833

Metternich deeply annoyed by the progress of commercial affairs in Germany

Lord Erskine has communicated to me his Dispatches to Your Lordship upon the Commercial Affairs of Germany, numbered 15, 16, and 17. Prince Metternich professes to believe that the Treaty concluded between Prussia and the Southern States[25] will not be ratified by the latter, but I learn from Persons on whom I can rely that he is deeply annoyed at the progress of this Affair. Your Lordship will recollect the confidence with which in the beginning he spoke of the certainty of the failure of the attempts of Prussia to extend her System over the South of Germany, and how fully he counted upon the conclusion of a Commercial Treaty between Austria and Bavaria. The fact seems to be that he has been duped in common with many others by that Power. The German Ministers with whom I speak consider the extension of the Prussian System as a serious blow to the ascendancy of Austria in the Confederation, and they reproach to Prince Metternich that he took up the Affair too late, and prosecuted it too slackly.

I understand that a project is in contemplation for a Treaty between Austria and the Commercial Confederation for permitting an exchange of certain commodities upon the Frontier, but it has not yet assumed a shape in which any thing can be said of it with certainty.

FO 7/243: Frederick Lamb to Viscount Palmerston, No 170, Vienna, 30 October 1833

Vienna conference on the affairs of Germany (i.e. on Prussia, liberty of the press, question of authorization); Metternich's intentions; difficult position of the participating ministers; limited effects of such conferences

If the decision of the King of Prussia announced in Lord Minto's N° 65 to decline entering into a Conference upon the Affairs of Germany is known here the secret is well kept, for not even any of the German Ministers are aware of the fact. Two things however are allowed to be not yet fixed, the place, and the time. Prague had been designated, but it is now admitted that the Conference, if it is to do anything, can not last less than six weeks. This time would probably be found insufficient, but even this is more than Prince Metternich could spare from his

---

[25] Bavaria and Württemberg, which had comprised the South German Customs Union since 1828, joined the Prussian Customs Union on 22 March 1833.

duties in this Residence. He is therefore labouring to procure the assembling of the Conference at Vienna. The same plea which induces him to decline himself from Vienna will probably deter M. d' Ancillon from coming to such a distance from Berlin, and thus if Prussia persists in Her objection to the Conference a plausible pretence may be found for getting rid of it. [...]

If the Conference meets I have no hesitation in pronouncing before-hand that it will do nothing effective. The points which the Prince would wish to carry are the suppression of the publicity of discussions in the Chambers, and that of the liberty of the Press. It is supposed also he would wish a Committee to be appointed to examine how far the Constitutions which have been granted are compatible with the previously existing Laws of the Confederation but in truth the whole question is comprised in the two points first stated. If these are not carried nothing is done, and he has no chance of carrying them. He has already stated to the Courts of Germany that nothing is to be overthrown, that the strict limits of legality will not be overstepped – this at once betrays his sense of his own weakness, and places a limit which is incompatible with his objects. The avowed purpose of the Conference is to give to the Diet a power of execution which it does not possess, and to trace out to the Sovereigns the cases in which to apply it, and the mode of application. The march proposed to be followed is that the Conference shall receive from the smaller Courts statements of the embarrassments which each is enduring in its Interior, and a demand for aid to remove them. At this very first step the difficulties would begin. No Court would come forwards with such a statement, unless perhaps that of Wurtemberg, and Austria and Prussia would find themselves forced to take the initiative.

But the Ministers to whom the propositions would be made, being placed in quite a different position from that of the Proposers, having to return home, and not only to face the opinion of their Countries, but to defend their measures before Chambers which it is not proposed to overturn, would either avoid going the length required of them, or on their return home would be placed between the alternatives of abandoning the measures they had consented to, or of being themselves abandoned by their Colleagues, and defeated in the Chambers. The Decrees of the Diet of 1832[26] had the effect of resisting intimidation of another sort; they took the questions then in agitation out of the hands of Mob Meetings to leave them in those of the Chambers, within which, and between which and the Diet they are properly placed. Within this limit their effect has been beneficial, but these Conferences or attempts at Conferences without the courage to go the length of

---

[26] Cf. n. 66 in Frankfurt section.

overthrowing the Constitutions, and of backing that resolution if necessary by force, can only serve to shew the liberal Party that within legal limits they have nothing to fear.

FO 7/247: Frederick Lamb to Viscount Palmerston, No 24, Vienna, 15 March 1834

Polish agitation in Germany; participation of Polish officers in a conspiracy in Baden; fear of revolution unites European governments

I learn from Prince Metternich that the Tribunal at Lemberg charged with the trail of the Poles who last summer made an incursion from Galica into the Kingdom of Poland,[27] ascertained not only that they had come from France for that object, but also that they were connected with the troubles which about the same time were on foot in Germany. In consequence of this discovery application was made for further information to the Tribunal charged with the Trail of the Military Conspirators at Louisbourg,[28] and the Answer was given by the communication from one Tribunal to the other of such of the depositions of witnesses as bore upon the subject. There was no interference either of the Governments or the Police of Austria or Wurtemberg – the depositions are judicial Documents entitled to full credit until contradicted by better evidence, nor do I suppose that Your Lordship will have any difficulty in procuring them.

Those which were read to me establish that a Body of Polish Officers amounting to between twenty and thirty were sent by the Polish Committee[29] in Paris with orders to establish themselves in the Swiss Villages nearest to the Frontier of Baden, and upon the breaking out of insurrection to throw themselves into the black Forest, and raise the country; they were told to expect that a French Column, which they were to join, would cross the Rhine, and the Countries designated as destined to be the center of the insurrection were Baden, Wurtemberg and the two Hesses. These Poles were furnished with false Passports as residents at Strasbourg by the Prefect of that Town, and they repaired

[27] An attempt by a group of partisans from Galicia to stir up a general revolt in Poland through acts of sabotage and propaganda never got off the ground. Most of the Poles involved were arrested by the Russian police; some were sentenced to death, while other were imprisoned or banished to Siberia.

[28] The planned military conspiracy in Ludwigsburg in Württemberg was part of a concerted revolutionary campaign in southern Germany, whose aim was to establish a republic in Germany.

[29] The Polish National Committee was founded in 1831 by Polish emigrés in Paris. The members of this organization, which gave rise to the Polish Democratic Society in March 1832, were involved in a large number of revolts throughout the whole of Europe.

to their destination, but hearing nothing of the promised insurrection, one[30] of them, whose name is given, advanced to Louisbourg, where he put himself in communication with the Lieutenant[31] who was the head of the military Conspiracy in that garrison. The communications which passed between these persons are detailed, and prove the extensive ramifications of these Conspiracies, and the active intercourse which is carried on between their Movers.

This communication was made to me by Prince Metternich some time back, and I take the first opportunity of stating it to Your Lordship as pointing out a channel for obtaining more exact information upon this subject than may perhaps have yet reached you.

It is one which effects the position of all Europe.

The fear of the Propaganda, resting its lever upon France, not only keeps the three Powers[32] united, but also cements all the minor States to their System. Hence it is that we see the German and Italian Governments united in one compact mass with Austria and Prussia, and the influence of France formerly so powerful among them reduced to nothing. On the other hand the fear of a Republican Propaganda excites one in an opposite sense, and rallies to its support a great portion of the most valuable class of every Community, which would otherwise range itself on the side of free Institutions. The success of the Republicans would produce universal disorder, while the mere apprehension of it is subversive both of national independence and of Constitutional liberty. [...]

FO 7/248: Frederick Lamb to Viscount Palmerston, No 50, Vienna, 12 May 1834

Question of how to enforce the measures adopted at Vienna; F. Lamb's opinion; Lamb's conversation with M. Ancillon on the subject; Russia's position; Metternich's 'real' opinion about Germany; no official information passed to French or British minister at Vienna; vanishing influence of France in Central Europe

Imperfect as the account is which is contained in my Confidential Dispatch there is yet enough to shew that no plan has been hit upon to ensure execution, and execution has always been the weak point of the Confederation. – There has long since been legislation enough – the censure of the Press has never been abrogated in Germany. – Various regulations have been adopted at different times with respect

---

[30] Not traceable.
[31] Ernst Louis Koseritz.
[32] Austria, Prussia, and Russia.

to the Universities – but the censure has been slackly exercised, and
the regulations have slept. – While the German Governments feel a
common interest in enforcing these new enactments it is possible that
they may be acted upon, but no longer, and that common interest
depends upon their fear of a common danger. – Upon this subject I
may remark that Lord Granville in his N° 130 observes, in remarking
upon a Dispatch of mine, 'that Prince Metternich wishes it to be
believed in England that it is to the abetting of the Propagandists by
the Duc de Broglie that is owing the sacrifice of the independence and
separate interests of every German and Italian State to the maintenance
of the connexion with Austria and Prussia.' – As I do not know upon
what this assertion is founded I can not controvert it, but I can safely
say that I never heard Prince Metternich volunteer an opinion of the
sort, nor do I believe that he would willingly bring the fact it goes to
establish into notice. – That such is the fact, that the fear of revolutionary
movements connected with the French Propagandists does unite Austria
and Prussia to Russia, and all the minor States to these three Powers,
that this apprehension and this union is adverse to all national independence, and to all progress in Constitutional liberty is stated in my
N° 24[33] as my opinion, and not as Prince Metternich's, and I here
advert to it because a suspicious origin will sometimes prejudice the
fair estimate of a statement and I consider this to be one of which it is
deeply important that a just estimation should be taken. – The opinion
I have stated is the fruit of my own observation, it is in itself so self-
evident as hardly to admit of contradiction, nor have I ever heard it
controverted by any one to whom I have submitted it. It so happens
that I never mentioned the subject to Prince Metternich till yesterday,
and then only in part. – He fully admitted the truth of my opinion
with regard to the minor Powers. – To M^r d'Ancillon it so happened
that I had occasion some time back to bring it forwards though in
other terms. – He was expatiating upon the moderation which had
been shewn by Austria and Prussia in the conduct of the German
Conferences,[34] those two Powers having uniformly withdrawn every
Proposition to which the slightest objection was made by any of the
Minor States. – Don't tell me, I said, of your moderation, I have known
Germany long enough to know that it's natural predominant feeling is
fear and jealousy of your influence and of that of Austria. – This has
given way to it's greater apprehension of your game Republicanism
supported by France. – This it is which unites the Minor States to you
for the moment, your game is to give them confidence, and you will

---

[33] Not included in this volume.
[34] For the Ministers' Conferences in Vienna cf. pp. 135–138 in Prussia section, pp.
503–505 in this section.

not play it so ill as to startle them by insisting upon unacceptable Propositions instead of reassuring them by deference to their wishes. – This and no other is the secret of your moderation. – He admitted the truth of the Statement; and it is with the exception of what relates to the connection of Austria and Prussia with Russia precisely the same as that which is contained in my N° 24.[35] I dwell upon this subject because it's ramifications extend everywhere, Russia alone holding a position independent of the fears which operate upon all the other European States can sell Her assistance to them at Her own price. – This price is blindness to Her system of encroachment in Asia,[36] and it is to be apprehended that this abandonment of positive interests in order to cement a league against a contingent danger will become so engrained into the European System as to survive the danger (should it ever be entirely got rid of) which it was originally designed to oppose. – Present remedy there is none, but by fairly looking at the truth we may at least aim at preventing the encrease of the evil, and this aim will best be fulfilled by shewing the other European Governments that France and England although friendly to the growth and development of Constitutional liberty are yet decidedly hostile to revolutionary attempts, and determined to cooperate in their prevention.

I have asked Prince Metternich what is his real opinion about Germany; whether he considers it to be permanently tranquil, or whether he expects agitation to revive. – M^r d'Ancillon in answer to the same question had told me that Germany had been tranquillised for the moment by the Conference at Vienna, and was no more than in a state of expectation of the result. Prince Metternich spoke more decisively, and said that it was more tranquil than it had been, and would remain so unless disorder were to revive in France. – I mention this as a strong corroboration of the statement I have often made, that he feels the maintenance of Louis Philippe's Government to be essential to the repose of Europe. – This opinion of the improved state of Germany has reached me from many quarters. – I am assured by Persons residing habitually in several of it's States that there has arisen a general disgust at the agitation which some time ago prevailed there, and that not only the Peasants but the Inhabitants of Towns who are possessed of Property, consider that Property as liable to be endangered by the preponderance of the violent liberal Party.

When the Decrees of the Diet[37] were promulgated they were represented as likely to create revolt by the disgust they would excite. – At that time I ventured to represent that their effect might possibly be

[35] Cf. p. 506 in this section.
[36] For Russia's Oriental policy cf. n. 84 in Prussia section.
[37] Six Articles of 28 June 1832, cf. n. 66 in Frankfurt section.

directly to the reverse. Whether proceeding from thence, or other causes, this expectation has been fulfilled.

The fever which had reached its height at the meeting at Hambach[38] has gradually subsided.

The licence which pervaded Germany would in all probability never have reached the height it attained without great weakness in the Governments, and a toleration of it which arose in part from a competition for popularity among several of the German Sovereigns and their Ministers. − It was only when the revolution of 1830[39] had placed them upon the brink of the abyss by the ferment it excited that they fairly united among themselves and laid aside their jealousy of Austria and Prussia. − The result has been that they are now the strongest, and although the more violent of the Ultra Royalist Party are disappointed in the results of the Conference, and express an expectation that agitation will recommence in Germany with more violence than ever when the small amount of these results is understood, I can not implicitly adopt this opinion. − There is little doubt but what an effort at agitation will be made, and perhaps a formidable one, but if, as it is to be hoped, the Governments remain the strongest, it will be essential to our own interests to cultivate their good will by every shew of sympathy in their well-being and to lead them to a greater sense of independence than they now possess, and to a more separate view of their several interests than they now dare to indulge in, by encreasing their confidence in their own security.

One remarkable fact may be stated in confirmation of this reasoning. − It is that throughout these long Conferences no one Government has been found so impressed with the importance of cultivating the friendship either of England or of France as to empower it's Ministers to make the slightest communication upon what was passing to Monsieur de Ste Aulaire or to myself. Yet we have been upon the best terms with all the Members of the Conference, and with many I have for years been in habits of confidential intercourse. − It is to the private friendship of one of them that I am indebted for what I know, but no Government has felt either a sufficient jealousy of the greater German Powers, or a sufficient wish to secure an eventual support against their encroachments, to induce it to enter into confidential intercourse with either of us. − Does not this fact sufficiently speak to their thoughts? The influence of England upon these central States has not often been great, but that of France in many of them habitually counterbalanced that of Austria. Am I not justified in saying that it is now extinct? If it is to revive, that can only be when the Governments

---

[38] Cf. pp. 23–26 in Frankfurt section.

[39] French revolution of July 1830, cf. n. 28 in Frankfurt section.

shall feel that they have more to hope than to fear from Her; and in saying this I speak not of the Government of Louis Philippe, nor of any individual Minister, but of France at large, and of the practices which, whether connived at or not by her Government, have been carried on from within Her frontier, and have thereby de facto received Her protection.

FO 7/253: William Fox-Strangways to Duke of Wellington, No 14, Vienna, 26 February 1835

Metternich's comment on newspaper article regarding the Holy Alliance

I have the honor to enclose the accompanying Article extracted from the Austrian Observer, with a Translation.

Prince Metternich told me that the above Article was intended as an answer not only to the Standard, but also to the Times and other Papers, in which ill founded representations respecting the Holy Alliance[40] frequently appeared. He said that he had seized with pleasure the opportunity of publishing his own statement in correction of such erroneous Doctrines.

He said that it was one of the most disagreeable circumstances connected with his position, that he was forced to hear principles attributed to him, and even engagement stated to have been entered into by the Austrian Government which he could not with propriety publicly contradict, although they had not the slightest foundation in fact. The so called 'Holy Alliance' as represented by Newspaper scribblers is a thing which he says, he not only does not acknowledge, but does not even understand.

He said that the Act of 1815, so often alluded to was one of the many favourite schemes of the Emperor Alexander, and that before signing it, he had strongly warned Him against the consequences of it which he even then foresaw. He told Him that in putting forth a solemn Act, which after all only professed what honest Governments might take credit to themselves for without making any profession at all, he was preparing not only for Himself, but His Successors, a continual Embarrassment. Make he said, an Article for the Journals, it will be just as well understood, but no Manifesto.

As notwithstanding these views the Emperor of Austria signed the Act of 1815, it is to be inferred that the feelings of Prince Metternich at that time were less strongly expressed than at present. The designation of an act as useless or needless, is in his mouth, a strong condemnation.

---

[40] Cf. n. 11 in this section.

He has told me on other occasions, that it is not to publicity that he objects, but to Polemics, and that the difficulty of obtaining one without engaging in the other, is the cause of the silence of this Government in a number of Cases in which it has no other reason for not uttering its sentiments.[41]

FO 7/253: William Fox-Strangways to Duke of Wellington, No 23, Vienna, 2 March 1835

Death of the Austrian Emperor; Austrian policy will not change

After placing in my hands the official Rescripts announcing the Death of the Emperor, Prince Metternich requested that I would state to Your Grace that, except in the Person of the Sovereign, it would be found that Austria had changed nothing.

He said that the same feelings, principles, and friendships would be found to animate her Alliances and guide her conduct, as during the late Reign, without change or diminution.

He wishes this to be generally understood, in order that if in some quarters expectations may have been formed that the contrary would be the case, it should be known that they would be totally frustrated. In short, he said, though it cannot be denied that it is a great Event, Austria will still be found the same, excepting only what God has taken away and man cannot replace.

The Prince spoke throughout with composure, but not without much feeling.

FO 7/253: William Fox-Strangways to Viscount Palmerston, No 58, Vienna, 21 July 1835

Metternich's opinion on the Prussian Commercial Union

Prince Metternich congratulates himself upon the fulfilment of his predictions with respect to the Prussian Commercial Union.

He says that in one year Prussia has felt a deficit in the receipts of Revenue derived from that source, of not less than three millions of dollars, which She has had to pay to the smaller States in conformity to the principle of division laid down for the produce of the duties.

Bavaria he says has been a principal gainer; and he considers the

[41] Enclosures: Original and Translation, Article from Austrian Observer, 25 February 1835.

system to be so hazardous to Prussia that She must before long propose for her own sake some modification of it.

The great fault of the system he says is the having taken a false principle for the repartition of profits. Each State shares not in proportion to its consumption but its population; and as these are in various proportions, the gains and losses will also vary respectively. Had Germany been divided into a threefold system, a Northern, Western, and Southern Union; the States composing them might have prospered under it; but their circumstances, wants, and productions are so different as to make the same system inapplicable to all, and as it appears from a short experience, unjust in its effects. But such a threefold division would not suit Prussia, the two masses of her Territory[42] would have each formed the bulk of a separate Union, dissimilar one from the other, and not favourable to that union of interests between Her Provinces which She desires, as a means of attaching them to each other.

The alarm spread in Austria by the establishment of the Prussian Union, was great, particularly in Bohemia; and the junction of Bavaria greatly increased it. Prince Metternich, however, says that the Manufacturers have suffered but little, and that the contraband exportation of Austrian goods into the countries of the Union is making up for what they had lost.

He says that accession to the system would have been ruinous to Austria, and that She is as much opposed to it as England, though on different grounds. It is however the general opinion that she will suffer by its adoption in Germany.

The Prince tells me that he is having prepared for publication an important work on the Statistics of the Austrian Empire.

FO 7/257: Henry Edward Fox to Viscount Palmerston, No 15, Vienna, 3 May 1836

Metternich's reaction to Palmerston's note relating to the occupation of Cracow; Metternich's own version of what happened at Cracow; Lamb's detailed assessment

I received on the 26th Your Lordship's Dispatch N° 9 relating to the occupation of Cracow,[43] on the 27th I waited upon Prince Metternich,

---

[42] Prussia's western provinces, the Rhineland and Westphalia, on the one hand, and the rest of Prussia's provinces in the east of the territory covered by the Customs Union on the other.

[43] An identically worded dispatch was also sent to the diplomatic missions in Prussia and Russia, cf. pp. 140–145 in Prussia section.

and after reading to His Highness the whole Dispatch, I left a Copy in his hands according to Your Lordship's Instructions.

Prince Metternich listened with great attention, holding his own Copy before him in order to follow me with greater precision while I read. When I had concluded, he observed that to a Paper of such length involving so many important Questions, and communicated so formally from Government to Government, it was impossible to expect that he should make any verbal reply – that to such a formal 'acte d'accussation' he should reserve to Himself the power of replying by a similar official channel, namely though the Austrian Chargé d'Affaires[44] in London. [...]

Prince Metternich then entered into a recital of what had occurred at Cracow. He began with narrating to me at considerable length the very unfavorable opinion the late Emperor Francis entertained from the first of such a creation as that of the Republic of Cracow.[45] He assured me that its existence as an independent State was owing to the spirit of false generosity which so often misled the Emperor Alexander – that on this subject the Emperor Francis had personally conversed with the Emperor Alexander, and had frankly avowed His total disapprobation of the policy pursued with regard to Poland. He had said 'I do not disguise from you that a real independent Poland would be a creation I should approve of – even would I make sacrifices to facilitate it, but this you do not wish to create – why then give them the name and phantom of independence without the reality? why keep up the Name of the Kingdom of Poland,[46] and still more why create an independent Town? a Temple of Liberty – where the sacred national fire of Vesta is to burn in unsullied purity. – why create for yourself and your Neighbours a place of resort where all the discontented, all the visionary can fly, and in safety adore the imaginary freedom of Poland.'

To these representations however the Emperor Alexander was deaf, so completely was he carried away by the hope of establishing a mock nationality in Poland which might render Him personally popular, and perhaps acquire for Him the reputation of magnanimity and generosity for which he so ardently panted. Cracow remained a Place of no political consequence, though always, observed His Highness, a most convenient refuge for culprits, deserters and smugglers till after the Polish Revolution in 1830–1831,[47] at the conclusion of which Cracow

[44] Paul Anton Fürst Esterházy von Galántha.

[45] The European Powers had agreed on the creation of the Free Republic of Cracow in the Act of the Vienna Congress, 9 June 1815.

[46] At the Congress of Vienna in 1815 the Duchy of Warsaw, excluding Posen and Cracow, was united with Russia in a personal union as the Kingdom of Poland (Congress Poland).

[47] Cf. n. 18 in Prussia section.

was overrun by political Refugees – indeed such was their number – such their influence, that they got complete possession of the Town – the Police (such as it was) was carried on by Polish Refugees – the Troops (such as they were) were composed of Persons of the same description, in fact the Senate, the President, and the whole Town was under their dictation.

Prince Metternich then added that though he would not reply at present to any of the points in Your Lordship's Dispatch as to the justice or injustice of the measure, he should notice one observation with respect of the execution of the occupation, namely, as to the shortness of the time given by the Protecting Powers[48] for the delivery of the Refugees – that though he granted at a distance and without a full knowledge of the particular circumstances fixing eight days might appear violent and peremptory, yet it was thus fixed in mercy to the Troops charged at that severe season of the year with the harassing duty of hemming in a Town, and guarding all the outlets night and day to prevent the escape of the Delinquents. His Highness was very anxious to remove from my mind any idea of the Russian Government having urged and pressed this measure, he assured me that the Emperor Nicholas had shewn Himself most anxious to avoid any harsh measures, and was only animated by a desire of preventing the evil-disposed Refugees in Cracow from exciting fresh turbulence in the Kingdom of Poland. [...]

From the whole tone of Prince Metternich's conversation I gathered that the existence of Cracow as an independent state has been discovered to be, as the Emperor Francis predicted, very inconvenient at least to one of the Protecting Powers, and that by the consent of all three of those Powers very violent measures have been resorted to to remedy that momentary inconvenience – perhaps the Three Protecting Powers may be satisfied with having removed the causes of immediate annoyance, but I own, from the tone of Prince Metternich's conversation and from the great stress he laid upon the absurdity of having raised Cracow into an independent Republic, it would not surprize me, if some project was in contemplation effectually to prevent the recurrence of similar inconveniences by virtually, though perhaps not nominally, crushing its independence.

---

[48] Austria, Prussia, and Russia.

FO 7/258: Frederick Lamb to Viscount Palmerston, No 23, Vienna, 9 October 1836

Probable motives for Count Kolowrat's retirement

The enclosed report from Mr Fraser conveyed to me the first intelligence of the remarkable event to which it relates. Subsequent enquiries have given me no absolute certainty as to the causes of Count Kollowrath's retirement. Those which are most currently reported are,

1st the abandonment of the System of disarming in consequence of the danger which threatens Italy from the adoption of the Constitution of 1812 in Spain,[49] in consequence of which a new Loan will be required in direct contravention of the Policy which Count Kollowrath prevailed in imposing upon the Government last year.

2dly His opposition to the reestablishment of Jesuits in Austria under the protection of the two Empresses[50] and of some of the Archdukes.

3dly The Tariff duties upon Sugar.

As the knowledge of the Truth is confined to few Individuals, each suits his own taste in the selection of a Motive. The profound thinkers lean to the first on the list, the change of measures with regard to the diminution of the Army, but upon enquiry I find that by the budget for the current year the deficit does not exceed £800.000 which are already provided for, & that the Budget for 1837 differs but little from that of the present year. Of one at least of these Budgets I hope shortly to be able to send Your Lordship a Copy, and the account I have received of them, convinces me that they offer no adequate motive for Count Kollowrath's resignation.

The second reason alleged has I doubt not contributed to determine the event, though alone it is inadequate to account for it. The Jesuits are supposed by the Public to have been established for some years in this Capital under the name of Liguorianer.[51] A fresh establishment of

---

[49] The most important points in the Constitution of Cadiz (1812–1814) were the separation of powers and the introduction of an unicameral system, the abolition of the privileges of the aristocracy, and the establishment of economic freedoms and a centralized administrative system. The Constitution of Cadiz attained symbolic value in 1820, when a revolutionary rising forced the Spanish king to reintroduce it – at least temporarily. In 1821, during unrest in the Kingdom of Piedmont–Sardinia, attempts were made to introduce the Constitution of Cadiz in Italy as well.

[50] Karoline Auguste Charlotte and Maria Anna.

[51] The *Liguorianer* were a missionary order, founded in Naples in 1732, which devoted itself mainly to missionary work among the poor. They filled the gap left by the dissolution of the Jesuit Order in 1773, but had no institutional links with the Jesuits, who had been permitted again in Austria since 1814.

them has lately been authorized at Lemberg under that of Redentori[52] &
they enjoy the protection of a great part of the Imperial Family while
they are odious to the Public. Prince Metternich as I am assured
favours them from the Notion that no successful opposition can be
made to the spread of Liberalism but by promoting a belief opposed
to that of its propogators. If this be really his view it is a short sighted
one. Instead of being a support to Monarchy in this Country Jesuitism
is a weight upon it. The Power of the Emperor is an object of
veneration, but popular as it is, it cannot wisely charge itself with so
odious a burthen as the introduction of the Jesuits.

The third reason which seems the most inadequate of the three, will
yet I believe be found to have been the immediate cause of the event
in question.

After the departure of Count Kollowrath and Prince Metternich
from the Capital, the Archduke Louis upon the representations of those
who are interested in the Manufacture of Sugar from beet-root,
suspended upon his own Authority the operation of a Law already
promulgated by which the duties upon Foreign Sugar had been lowered.
This was in itself a strong measure, but was confirmed by the Council
at Prague in opposition to Count Kollowrath who in conjunction with
the Minister of Finance[53] had been the original mover of the measure.
Upon this he determined to retire from Office, and although it is
probable that he will be induced to return to it, yet is it equally to be
foreseen that he will not long remain in it. The occurrence has shewn
how much of strength has been lost by the Death of the Late Emperor, &
is in truth but the first step towards the changes through which this
Empire is destined to pass changes which if not begun in time, if
suffered to be brought on by the pressure of circumstances instead of
being submitted to skilful guidance while they are yet capable of it,
may shake the fabric solid as it is to its foundation.

Prince Metternich and the Archduke Louis are the Representatives
of the System of immobility. Count Kollowrath on the other hand
denies the possibility of this System, and calls for an assimilation to
the progress of other Countries. Upon this slight alteration in their
Commercial Policy, and perhaps upon the two other Questions the two
Systems are brought into collision, and their first shock overthrows the
Government which was looked to to continue the System of the Late
Emperor.

From this first incident may be judged what is to follow. The triumph
remains for the moment with the stationary Party, but they dare not

profit by it, they fear to stand alone and leave no effort untried to recall Count Kollowrath to their assistance. Their motives for this are many: the chief strength of the Government left by the late Emperor consisted in the idea that it was almost a continuation of his reign. If this spell be broken by the retirement of one of its chief Members a main element of its strength will be lost. The next reason is personal to Count Kollowrath. Under the head of mere talent it might not be difficult to replace him, but there is attached to him a general confidence in his integrity and a reliance on the purity of his motives which from whatever reason is not felt in the same degree towards the rest of the Ministry.

This examination would be imperfect if I omitted to add to it the modifications resulting from the personal character of Count Kollowrath. He is little known to the Members of the Diplomatic Body, he having carefully avoided all intimacy with them, as I conclude, from the apprehension of exciting Jealousy in Prince Metternich. I can therefore only speak of him from Report, and from the evidence of his public conduct. It is the fashion among Prince Metternich's friends to represent him as a man of limited views and of narrow conceptions, I know not upon what ground.

Those who approach him say directly the reverse; His views as transmitted to me through them, have nothing of the character attributed to them, & his public measures as contrasted with those of Prince Metternich are by no means calculated to justify the imputation.

He is however of a fretful and irritable disposition which is liable to be aggravated by constitutional infirmities, and being devoid of ambition and free from interested motives, whenever any thing counteracts him, the resource to which he immediately flies is the resignation of his office. This occurred repeatedly with the late Emperor, and I am assured that at Prague[54] he maintained an attitude of discontent towards the Arch-Duke Louis which is assigned as the reason why His Imperial Highness has refused to participate in the military promotions which have been conferred upon the other Archdukes.

In this character are to be found sufficient elements of discord, and the Master hand which combined these differences has been removed. Hence it is that I consider personal as well as general considerations to oppose themselves to a long duration of the present Ministry. If Count Kollowrath retires, it is understood that M. Eichof the Minister of Finance will accompany him. Prince Metternich on the other hand is anxious to remove M. Eichhof while he retains Count Kollowrath.

If the Finance Minister retires, from whatever cause, it is probable

[54] Emperor Ferdinand I of Austria was crowned King of Bohemia in Prague on 7 September 1836.

that Prince Metternich will cause Count Münch the President of the Diet to be named for his successor. [...]

While wiring this I have received information that Count Kollowrath has consented to resume his office. Both the Empresses, the reigning and the Dowager, wrote to him to request it. He subsequently had an Interview with The Arch-Duke Francis Charles at Kladrub, and the result is what I have stated. My anticipation therefore has thus far proved correct, but I feel little confidence in the future.

There are here great Elements of stability, but the unity of purpose derivable from a single head is wanting, and without this, it is difficult to understand how either the old System of Government can be perservered in, or a new one entered upon with advantage or even with safety.[55]

FO 7/258: Frederick Lamb to Viscount Palmerston, No 35, Vienna, 20 December 1836

Details of composition and organization of Austrian government

Much negotiation took place after Count Kolowrath's return to Vienna, before his return to office was finally arranged.

The organization of this Government differs so much from that which has been adopted in other European States, that in order to understand the difficulties which have arisen, it is necessary to enter shortly into the details of its composition.

Count Kolowrath was not the immediate head of any department, but the heads of all with the exception of those of War & Foreign Affairs reported to him, and he was the sole organ of communication between them and the Emperor. This gave him the effective direction of the departments of the Interior, of Finance, and of Justice, and the Chanceries of Bohemia and Hungary, and the Governors of Lombardy and the Venetian States stood in the same relation to him.

Besides this he presided in the Council of State, whenever affairs relating to the Interior were before it. This formed a situation of immense Power and responsibility, and it was believed in the Public, that since the Death of the Emperor, Count Kolowrath standing alone, and having frequently to act without the orders of an effective Sovereign, and consequently without his support, felt the responsibility to be greater than he was willing to continue to incur.

The simple mode of discharging him of a part of it was to recur to

---

[55] Enclosures: 1. Private Letter from Mr Fraser to Sir Frederick Lamb, 28 September 1836; 2. Copy and translation of a letter from Count Kolowrath to Baron Eskales, 19 September 1836; 3. Extract of a letter from Count Kolowrath to Baron Eskales, no date.

the ancient practice of allowing the heads of Departments to report directly to the Emperor, and this is supposed to have been the plan proposed to him after his return, but not to have met his approbation. The measure which has been resorted to, is the creation of a Conference,[56] consisting of the Archdukes Louis and Francis, Prince Metternich, and Count Kolowrath, which is to decide in the last resort. It is in fact a Regency, and the subsequent report to the Emperor is a mere form. By this arrangement Count Kolowrath's position is wholly changed. Instead of being the Director of every branch of internal administration throughout the Empire, he will henceforward have to submit all questions of importance to a Conference, where in case of a difference of opinion, the majority is not likely to be of his way of thinking.

To this must be added that the heads of Departments and those who aspire to become so, are anxious to be affranchised from a Superior and to have the uncontroulled direction of their own Affairs. These reasons combining with his irritable temper and uncertain health are felt by the Public to promise no long duration to the present arrangement.

FO 7/264: Frederick Lamb to Viscount Palmerston, No 13, Vienna, 26 February 1837

Removal of Protestants from the Zillertal; general policy against differences of worship in same community

There has long been a question of removing certain Protestant Families from the Ziller Thal where their not conforming to the Catholic rite gives scandal to the great Majority of the Population, who are Catholics.

It has been finally determined to remove them at the end of three Months to a Protestant Commune securing to them the possession of their property.[57]

This is represented to me as consonant to the general Policy of this Government which has always set its face against the differences of Worship in the same Commune, but is not therefore the less a hardship upon those it affects. There is a doubt how far this measure is consistent with the Federative Act, and with the final one of 1820.[58] The Protestant

---

[56] On the decision of the Emperor, the Secret State Conference met on 12 December 1835.

[57] Protestants who refused to join the Catholic Church were compelled to emigrate by an imperial decree of 12 January 1837. The majority of the c.400 people involved subsequently went to South America.

[58] The Act of the German Confederation of 8 June 1815 specified that the religious communities of the recognized Christian denominations were to be treated equally. Therefore the granting of civil and political rights could not be made dependent on membership of a particular denomination. The Vienna Final Act of 15 May 1820 does take a position on this issue.

Ministers at this Court have represented the case to their Sovereigns and it is possible that it may become a subject of discussion between them and Austria.

FO 7/266: Frederick Lamb to Viscount Palmerston, No 88, Vienna, 20 December 1837

Metternich's confidential opinion on the arrest of the Archbishop of Cologne; Prussian minister at Vienna defends his Government's action

Prince Metternich's mind has been for some time engaged exclusively with the arrest of the Archbishop of Cologne,[59] an event which he considers to be fraught with the gravest consequences, and to tend to the dismemberment of the Prussian Monarchy. M. de Bunsen passed through this Town on his way to Rome, and communicated to the Prince by order of the King of Prussia all the acts which had led to the result in question.

The Prince after reading them, and after two long conversations with M. Bunsen, gave to me his <u>confidential</u> opinion that the Prussian Government had been wrong from the beginning to the end, and that the form in which the arrest had been made was as unjustifiable, as the proceedings which had led to it. He has not concealed this opinion from the King of Prussia, offering at the same time his good offices to smooth, if it be possible, his differences with the Court of Rome.[60] Prince Metternich says that Louis Philippe has had the address put to himself on a better footing with that Court than any other Sovereign in Europe, and he regards the differences between Prussia and her Roman Catholic Subjects as tending to throw the Rhenish Provinces into the arms of France. He does not believe that the Clergy of Belgium deserve the accusation which has been made against them by the Prussian Government of having excited these religious differences, but he makes no doubt they will now interfere to widen them.

On the other hand the Prussian Minister[61] at this Court is far from satisfied with the tone which has been taken here on this occasion. His language is that of persistance in the course which has been entered upon, and speaking <u>confidentially</u>, he has even gone the length of citing to me the example of Holland, and pointing out a schism which should separate the German Church from that of Rome as a remedy to be

---

[59] Cf. pp. 88–91 in Frankfurt section.

[60] For the differences between Prussia and the Vatican on the question of mixed marriage cf. pp. 169–170 in Prussia section.

[61] Joachim Karl Ludwig Mortimer von Maltzan.

resorted to in the last resort. Should this be attempted Prince Metternich's apprehensions may be realised. Rash as such an enterprise may appear, it is to be borne in mind that Prussia has for some time been obstinately following a course of proselytism, which had hitherto shewed itself in preferences to her Protestant Subjects, and vexations to those of the Catholic persuasion in her antient Provinces, but which has now been applied in such a shape as to place the King of Prussia on one side in a position from which Prince Metternich himself allows he can not recede; and the Pope on the other on a ground which it is impossible for him to abandon. In such a situation it is to be feared that extreme measures may finally be resorted to by the Prussian Government as a matter of necessity, not of choice, and I therefore place the case before Her Majesty's Government in all its gravity.

FO 7/291B: Frederick Lamb to Viscount Palmerston, No 170, Vienna, 11 November 1840

Frontier States of the German Confederation feel threatened by France and appeal to Austria; complaint about Austria's inaction; Prussia is taking the lead; 'spirit' of Germany; Metternich takes credit for anti-French feelings

The frontier States of the Confederation have for some time past been addressing themselves to this Court upon the threatening aspect of France.[62] Their language has been that of resistance to French aggression and of complaint at the inaction of Austria. Baden Wurtemberg and Hesse Darmstadt have represented that they can bring 60,000 Men into the field, but that they do not propose making this effort in order to retire upon the Inn, that the utmost retreat they can admit of is to the Lech, and that in order to maintain themselves there they must look to Bavaria for a corps of 40,000 Men, and to Austria for 80,000 to cover their left flank while Prussia acts upon their right. The King of Bavaria has answered that He will give 60,000, and Austria engages that the contingent required from her shall be in line, if necessary, by the first of March.

All this passed before the meeting of the Chambers in France. If the division upon the Address should promise peace, it is probable that the preparations in contemplation will be delayed, but otherwise they must be pushed forward without the loss of a moment. A comparison of dates and distances will shew Your Lordship the necessity of this. Such measures would however in all probability be preceded or accompanied by an invitation to France to explain herself. General Grollman is

---

[62] Rhine crisis, cf. n. 210 in Frankfurt section.

expected here daily from Prussia for the purpose of making the necessary military combinations with this Court.

It is Prussia which takes the lead, and to Her all Germany looks in case active measures should become necessary, but thus stimulated and supported Austria will not in case of need remain behind.

If I can trust Prince Metternich's assurances coupled with those of all the German Ministers with whom I converse the spirit of Germany has been thoroughly roused by the juggling and boasting of France; there is no feeling towards her in Germany but a disgust at her constant state of internal change and agitation, and a lively indignation at Her assertions that Germany admires and is ready to affiliate with her. Far from this, the feeling of Germany is entirely national and its object is independence and peace; but if these should be violated there is every appearance that the whole country would rise as in 1813 to vindicate them.[63] [...]

Prince Metternich takes credit to himself for all this, saying that if He had addressed himself to the States of the Confederation, they would have enquired of him what Syria and Egypt were to them, whereas by waiting, the question with France has become the prominent one, and He has only to answer to their call. Thus timidity and procrastination usurp the praise of foresight.

FO 7/305: Robert Gordon to Earl of Aberdeen, No 56, Confidential, Vienna, 12 October 1842

Metternich's visit to King of Prussia disappointing; increased ascendancy of Prussia; common interests of both countries in limiting liberties of the press; Russian-Prussian convention for extraditing offenders will not be renewed; advantages of the Commercial Union

Judging from what I could observe during my visit to Johannisberg and Coblentz, I should be inclined to doubt whether Prince Metternich's visit[64] to the King of Prussia at the latter place has proved altogether as satisfactory to His Highness as he had promised to himself.

As a demonstrative measure imposing especially upon France the conviction that all Germany was united and exulting in the display of a military force upon her frontiers which had the power & the resolution to defend them, the presence of the Austrian Minister was doubtless of importance, but the increased ascendancy of Prussia became only the more apparent from it, and the whole demeanour of the King must have shewn the Prince that His Majesty is by no means disinclined to

[63] Cf. n. 83 in Prussia section.

[64] In mid-September 1842 Prince Metternich visited Friedrich Wilhelm IV, who was at the Burg Stolzenfels near Koblenz to celebrate the building of Cologne Cathedral and for the German Confederation's military manoeuvres in the Rhineland.

assume for Himself that leading position among the German States which may be said heretofore to have appertained to the House of Austria. Upon certain questions purely German wherein Prince Metternich may have thought through his personal influence to guide the opinions of the King, neither the opportunity nor the power to do so seem to have been granted to him by His Majesty, who whilst shewing a constantly marked civility to the Prince, did not as I suspect once invite him to a private interview, but saw him only in the presence of His own Minister[65] during their five days residence at Coblentz.

In one instance Prince Metternich hopes to have succeeded with the King, that is in securing His endeavours to curb the extraordinary licentiousness of the press in Prussia, which is producing according to His Highness' belief, the most pernicious effects throughout Germany. In Konigsberg and eastern Prussia where the greatest exasperation prevails against Russia, it may not be an easy task to controul the expression of publick feeling in the journals upon that head, and I understand the King says He hopes to correct the evil rather through the just and straight forward measures of His own Government than by force or cajolery. It is not true that the Convention[66] for the extradition of offenders betwixt Russia and Prussia which is so odious in eastern Prussia, and which expires next year, has been, or is to be renewed. The King of Prussia has however privately consented to continue to act in the spirit of it, and some slight commercial favours have been promised to be granted in return for this by Russia.

In matters of trade no approximation to the Prussian System has been come to by Austria, nor is it probable that She will ever see any benefit to be derived from Her associating with the Zoll-verein.

The establishment and extension of this League has given advantages and a preponderance to Prussia which are beginning to be regretted by some of the minor states. In Baden for instance, the advantages of the League are more than problematical, and I have been credibly informed that already many of the manufactories in that Country are on the decline, and it is considered that they have been sacrificed to those of Prussia.

With regard to the religious disputes[67] which of late have occupied so much of the attention of the German publicists, and which Prince Metternich has for some time past regarded with much displeasure, if not alarm, I have reason to believe that His Highness found no fitting opportunity as He had expected, for freely discussing this subject with the King. His Majesty, I have been assured, felt that it was a ground

[65] Hermann Ulrich Wilhelm Freiherr von Bülow.

[66] The Cartel Convention of 1833 between Prussia and Russia for the mutual extradition of deserters and criminals was not renewed in 1843.

[67] For the Prussian disputes on mixed marriage and the arrest of the Archbishop of Cologne, cf. pp. 88–91 in Frankfurt section.

too delicate to touch upon under present circumstances.

FO 7/310: Robert Gordon to Earl of Aberdeen, No 17, Vienna, 3 March 1843

Tokay wine as present to the Queen

Having been privately requested by Her Majesty's Master of the Household[68] to make some enquiries here in regard to the possibility of procuring for the use of Her Majesty's table some of the wine called Imperial Tokay, I lately made an application quite of a private nature to Count Czernin, who acts in the capacity of Master of the Household to His Imperial Majesty, asking to be informed if it would be possible for me to purchase some of the same wine which is purchased for the Imperial cellars. The fact of my application to Count Czernin accidentally came to the Emperors' knowledge, I was speedily informed of His Imperial Majesty's desire to send a present to Her Majesty the Queen of some of the best Tokay which His cellar affords, and this day I have received the official notification of His Imperial Majesty's intention through the Chancellor of State, of which I have the honour herewith to enclose a copy to Your Lordship.[69]

FO 7/322: Robert Gordon to Earl of Aberdeen, No 26, Vienna, 17 May 1845

Improved situation of Protestants in Austrian dominions; objections by Catholic hierarchy

It is not unworthy of remark that whilst Her Majesty's Government are occupied with the enactment of measures which should tend to the conciliation of the Roman Catholicks in Ireland and especially whilst their attention is being directed to an improvement in the moral condition of the Roman Catholick Priesthood, the Austrian Government are actually engaged in a plan for placing the Protestant clergy in the Austrian dominions upon the same footing with the Catholick as far as regards their dependence upon the State, at present the maintenance of the Protestant Clergy depends entirely upon the voluntary contributions of their congregations; receiving no provision whatever from the Government, the Protestant faith is consequently merely tolerated and cannot be said to be supported in this Country. Great inconvenience

[68] Charles Augustus Murray.
[69] Enclosure: Copy, Prince Metternich to Robert Gordon, 3 March 1843.

results from the present state of the law, which refuses the establishment of Protestant worship in any district whatever, where one hundred families shall not have applied for it and have bound themselves by contract to provide a suitable subsistence for the officiating Minister.

It but too often happens that this provision is not sufficiently complied with, and generally speaking, with the exception of Hungary where there exist ample endowments of Church property amongst the Protestants, and where in fact they enjoy equal privileges with the Catholicks, it must be admitted that the religious interests of the Protestants in the Austrian dominions are most unjustifiably disregarded.

The Austrian Government moved by a spirit of toleration would desire to improve them, and wishes to provide for the Protestant in the same manner as for the Catholick clergy. When the Emperor Joseph confiscated the whole of the Church property[70] in his Empire he founded a religious fund out of the proceeds of that confiscation from whence the whole Church Establishment has ever since been maintained by the State; but the Protestant confessions in Austria being possessed of no property, no such fund could be established for their maintenance and hence they have hitherto been under the necessity of supporting their own Clergy. It is now contemplated to place in the hands of the Government the amount, which is voluntarily paid by the communes, and which after due augmentation by the State might be regularly paid to a limited number of pastors without exposing them as now to be dependant on the caprice of their communicants.

Whilst Prince Metternich has imparted to me the nature of the plan proposed by the Government in regard to this question, He has not disguised from me that there are strong objections opposed to it by the Catholick Hierarchy, which it may not be easy to overcome.

FO 7/323: Arthur Magenis to Earl of Aberdeen, No 6, Vienna, 12 September 1845

Railroad projects in Austria

The opening of the railroad from Vienna to Prague through Olmütz, by which the Capital of Bohemia is connected with the Imperial Residence, and a communication between the Danube and the Elbe is established, took place on the 20th Ult°. His Imperial Highness the Archduke Francis Charles, Representing on this occasion the Emperor

[70] Based on the decree concerning the dissolution of the monasteries of 12 January 1782, between 700 and 800 monastic houses were secularized in Austria under Joseph II. However, church property was not confiscated in its entirety.

his brother, together with several numbers of the Imperial Family were present at the ceremony.

The various members of the Diplomatick Body at Vienna received invitations to accompany the Train, which I, with several of my Colleagues, thought it right to accept. The reception of His Imperial Highness along the whole line to Prague, a distance of 300 English miles, was most enthusiastick, and on the newly opened portion, from Olmütz to Prague – 165 English miles – it might correctly be termed a popular rejoicing. A deputation from the States of Bohemia awaited His Imperial Highness at the frontier, with an address of congratulation, and on his arrival at Prague the Municipality, through their Burgo-master,[71] presented him with a similar Address. His Imperial Highness was entertained during the two days he stopped at Prague by the Municipality and Commerce of that Capital, and all the persons who had accompanied him from Vienna were invited to those fêtes. The greatest enthusiasm prevailed in all classes, and considerable advantages were anticipated by them from the more easy and increased intercourse between the two Capitals.

This new line of railroad of 165 English miles, has been completed by the Government in less than three years, and the works for continuing it to the Saxon frontier are in progress , and a part of that line is expected to be open in 1848.

The care and anxiety with which the Austrian Government have applied themselves to the formation of Railways, is in accordance with their constant desire to develope the means of internal communication, though it offers a remarkable contrast with their tardiness in adopting improvements in other departments of the Administration, and some allusion to the subject may not be unworthy of Your Lordship's notice.

The first step in this new Line was a privilege which was granted in 1836 to the House of Rothschild[72] to form a Railroad, which after passing through Moravia, was to have branches, one to the frontier of Silesia at Troppau, and another by Cracow to the Salt mines of Bohemia in Galicia. This line has been open for some years as far as Olmütz, from whence the line to Prague commences.

It was, however, enacted by the Imperial Prescript of December 1841, that those Lines whose importance, in a political and commercial point of view, was deemed the greatest, should be distinguished as 'State Railroads', and their execution carried on and completed under direction of the Government, without however entirely excluding private

---

[71] Joseph Ritter von Müller.

[72] On 9 April 1836 Emperor Ferdinand I granted permission for the railway line planned and financed by Salomon von Rothschild to be built as the *Kaiser-Ferdinands-Nord-Bahn*.

contribution. In accordance with that resolution, the lines from Vienna to the Saxon frontier, and to Triest; that from Venice to Milan; and a projected line in the direction of the Bavarian frontier were declared to be 'State Railroads'. Of these lines, that to the Saxon frontier is finished to Prague; that to Triest as far as Grätz, a distance of 112 English miles of Railroad (though the passage of the mountain between Schottwien and Mürzzuschlag is still performed by the ordinary road) and a further portion of 80 miles in the direction of Laybach nearly finished, and the continuation to Triest in progress; while on the line from Venice to Milan the portions at either ends, to Vicenza, and to Monza, are nearly completed, and the intermediate works in progress.

The importance of these labours, whether as means of increased intercourse in time of Peace, or of facilitated communication in time of War, can hardly be too highly appreciated; and great praise is undoubtedly due to the Government and to the Minister of Finance, Baron Kübeck, for the judgement with which they have been selected and the energy with which they have been persecuted.

The Imperial Government, however, have deemed it prudent to set some bounds to the spirit of speculation in Railroads, which prevails here as well as in other countries, and an Imperial Rescript was addressed, the beginning of last month to the Minister of Finance, declaring that no permission to form any new lines of Railroad should be granted till 1850. It is said that the reasons which led to the adoption of this measure were: the apprehensions entertained from the accumulation of workmen, who when the projected Railroads were completed would be left without employment; that the expenses of those Railroads undertaken by the Government were increased by the competition and demands of other Companies; and finally the desire to restrain in some degree the spirit of speculation and jobbing in Railroad shares.

FO 7/323: Arthur Magenis to Earl of Aberdeen, No 21, Vienna, 15 November 1845

Measures to secure supply of essential foodstuffs by stabilizing prices to prevent disturbances

The apprehensions entertained by this Government that the very high prices of all the necessaries of life in this capital might lead to disturbances, has induced the Chief of the Police department[73] to call together the principal Bakers and Butchers resident here, and enquire from them whether they could undertake to supply those necessaries

---

[73] Peter Edler von Muth.

during the Winter months, at such prices as might still be within the means of the poorer inhabitants. The deputation are said to have answered that they could undertake to do so, if it was forbidden to provision the towns and villages in the neighbourhood from the Vienna Market. I understand, however, that as yet, it has not been decided whether such a prohibition shall be issued.

If, as it would appear to be at present, the immediate neighbourhood of Vienna draws any large portion of its sustenance from the Capital, the very fact shows that there must be a great scarcity of provisions, as every article of consumption pays a very heavy retroi on entering the gates, and obtains no drawback on being sent out of them, whereas the import beyond the city is comparatively very light.

I am informed that the Government is not, however, entirely tranquillized by the above assurances, and that a larger portion of the Garrison than is usual, is in consequence held in immediate readiness to repress any disturbance which may arise.

Although the harvest is reported to have been generally below an average one, I am told that no serious fears are entertained of general scarcity, and that at present no measures are likely to be put in force to prohibit the exportation of grain. The Government has also declined a proposal made by the civil administration of Lower Austria to permit the free importation of foreign corn, and to remove for the present the duties payable on articles of consumption at the gates of Towns.

FO 7/328: Arthur Magenis to Earl of Aberdeen, No 9, Vienna, 21 February 1846

State of things at Cracow; conspiracy uncovered; aim of conspiracy

I have the honour to inform your Lordship that in consequence of the inability of the Senate and public authorities of the free City of Cracow, to maintain order, and to protect the lives and properties of the peaceably disposed citizens against the designs of a widely spread conspiracy, and at their request for assistance, that City was occupied on the 18th Instant by an Austrian corps of from 1,000 to 1,200 men from the neighbouring garrison of Podgorze.

Order and tranquillity had been reestablished by the presence of the Austrian troops; no opposition was made by the conspirators to their entrance into the City; and they were welcomed on their arrival by addresses of thanks from the Senate and well disposed inhabitants, and up to the departure of the post of the 18th everything remained quiet.

This conspiracy appears to have been a ramification of a more extensive one which was to have broken out at Posen on the 14th

Instant, but which was completely suppressed by the timely and energetic measures of the Prussian authorities there.[74] The suspicions of the Police had been roused by the arrival of numerous young Poles coming, as was alleged, to be present at a public dinner which was to have been held at the Bazaar on the evening of the 14th, and it was discovered that numerous purchases of arms, powder, ball &c had been made by them. At 2 o'clock on that day, the various Bridges and Gates of the town were occupied by military, all further ingress and egress was stopped, numerous patrols paraded the streets, and several persons were arrested. At the Bazaar was found a box containing letters of credit, bills of exchange, and about 60,000 Thalers in specie, and a Banker of the town was found to be implicated and arrested; and I believe that no doubt is entertained that this conspiracy had been organized and the necessary funds furnished by Poles established in Belgium and France. [...]

The principal object of this conspiracy appears to have been pillage and the overthrow if all constituted authority, and it is fortunate at both places it has been so quickly suppressed.

Prince Metternich does not believe that any Russian Troops will occupy Cracow, and His Highness informs me, that he despatched a Messenger yesterday to London, by way of Paris, to give full explanations of the measures which had led to the temporary occupation of that City.

FO 7/336: Lord Ponsonby to Lord Palmerston, No 53, Vienna, 15 June 1847

Information about Metternich's policy; his views on European politics; wishes and hopes of the inhabitants of the Austrian empire; strong feelings of nationality; question of a representative constitution

With a view to the better execution of your Lordship's directions, I took steps to obtain the means of giving you more certain information respecting the policy of Prince Metternich, than you could find in a report from me, where there might be inaccuracies of recollection on my part or of narration.

The Prince likes to communicate with me by means of what he calls 'Feuilles volantes' I wrote to him and recalling much of what had passed in conversations between us, I added remarks upon the state of

---

[74] Cf. p. 221 in Prussia section. The exposure of the conspiracy in Posen meant that attempted revolutions in Poland failed, even before the 'Polish National Government' in Cracow issued a call for a general uprising on 22 February, one day after this dispatch was written.

affairs, which I hoped would produce a reply and I enclose one which I did receive. I have since its reception had a very long communication with the Prince, in which he referred to his written commutation and confirmed it.

I must request that Your Lordship will consider as strictly confidential that communication. It is not intended for any others than for her Majesty's Government and I should do wrong to make it known elsewhere.

The Prince mistook something I wrote. I did not say that war would arise now between England and France nor that Louis Philippe may not have the Power to delay its coming and the will to do so, nor did I compare the actual power of France to that of the time of Napoleon. I said that the prevailing spirit in the French and what they imagine to be their interest will occasion War, and that too perhaps within no very long period of time: that the predominating feelings in France resembled those which existed when Napoleon governed. I mentioned jealousy, such as one Beauty may have of another, and the fear of English power as stimulating to measures for its reduction.

I think it right to lay before Your Lordship the expression of Prince Metternich's sentiments, respecting a part of the Policy of the British Government, notwithstanding the freedom with which he dissents from and censures it.

Your Lordship has further required, that I should say something respecting the course of Policy pursued or intended to be pursued by Austria, in regard to the various matters which from time to time may occupy the attention of Europe.

It will be necessary that I should speak of many of the European Powers, and I fear I shall be tedious without giving any new information.

The Russian Government and the Austrian are united in opinion on the most important question, namely the political position of France with respect to Europe. I speak of the Emperor of Russia. I know there is a large number of men in Russia, who have a leaning to the French and look to France as being likely to favor their wishes for conquest and its gains.

It is not believed here that the Emperor meditates the incorporation of Poland with his other Sovereignties.[75] It is thought to be already existing and that any further measure is useless, there seems to be some idea that the Russians and the Prussians may have differences, If that should happen, the Austrian Government will do all they can to restore harmony.

The Austrian Government is united with that of Prussia by the strongest interests, and is tremblingly alive to all that passes in Prussia.[76]

[75] Cf. n. 46 in this section.
[76] Cf. pp. 235–241 in Prussia section.

The prevailing opinion is here that The King of Prussia has shewn great weakness and his Ministers extreme want of ability, and there is great fear lest the changes in the Constitution of Prussia should occasion dissensions and give rise to a Party in that Country which may think that it has an interest in a close connection with some Party in France. I have in other Communications stated to Your Lordship that Prince Metternich has not the least idea of interfering with Prussian proceedings. [...]

I have not been long enough in this Country to feel much confidence in any opinions I may form of the wishes and views of the mass of its inhabitants, but I have heard a great deal from various persons upon that subject, and they have generally said that there exists much dissatisfaction with the existing form of government, and that a change in it, is wished for. I have asked in which of the classes of men is the greatest discontent to be found. The replies, I have received from the various persons, to whom I addressed my interrogations, may be stated generally. That the men a lettres, (a determination including a very large number) are the most adverse to the present, & the most anxious for change, though not agreed very much as to what should be established when the desired destruction of what is can be effected. Those who belong to the learned professions, as they are called, partake very much in the feelings and opinions of the men of letters, & have in some ways more influence in as much as they come more in contact with the greater numbers of the people.

The higher members of what is called the Burghers also are said to desire changes.

The artisans also complain, & the lowest class now suffering from high price of food &c is said to attribute to the Government, much of the evil that affects them.

The high nobility has many individuals in its class, much disposed also to depreciate the system, under which they are placed. It appears thus, that dissatisfaction exists in a very large portion of the inhabitants of this Country, & that there may be amongst them a readiness to accept change.

On the other hand there are many, who whilst they feel and admit the faults of the theory and practice of the system of Government, set forth strongly objections to the ideas of the friends of alterations of such magnitude, as are said to be necessary to remedy existing evils, they particularly examine the question of a representative constitution; Is it to be a central and national representation? if so, it must be formed of the representatives from all those kingdoms and principalities &c, which united under one crown make this empire, and of them how are the different and contesting interests to be settled? Is there a chance, that such parties will consent to compromises? Is it to be assumed that a sentiment of nationality will exist amongst Hungarians, Bohemians, Italians, Poles, and all the varieties of nations and tribes, to be represented? Will they unite in one common effort to maintain the rights and honor of the empire against a foreign foe? Will they even be able to understand each other? If not what will happen? May it not be the destruction of the best existing support of German independance, by establishing a perpetual weakness in the Government, and thereby forcing it to submit to foreign superiority? I need not proceed with the reasonings of the persons I speak of.

What I have further to add is, that notwithstanding the prevalence of the dissatisfaction I have stated, it is asserted, that the army is wholly uninfluenced by it, and that the Government may depend upon that, from the General down to the common soldier; for energetic support against any attempts that may be made by the discontented. The Question then will be. Will the Government use the army? If it will, I doubt much if there <u>ought</u> to be a doubt as to the result. What may be thought or said of the local dissatisfaction of Hungary, Bohemia and other members of the existing empire, I cannot learn, so as to report with any sort of satisfaction to Your Lordship. I am however told, that the same opinion and feeling is found in those states and also something of the same notions I have last mentioned of the danger of changes.[77]

---

[77] Enclosure: Copy of reply by Prince Metternich dated 9 June 1847.

ANNOTATED INDEX OF NAMES

Abel, Karl August von (1788–1859), Bavarian statesman. 1809 joined civil service; 1818 town and police commissioner in Bamberg; 1819 appointed *Regierungsrat*, 1827 *Ministerialrat* in Munich. As Bavarian minister of the interior (1837–1847), Abel pursued a strongly anti-protestant and monarchist policy. After his dismissal following the Lola Montez affair, 1847–1850 envoy in Turin and then advisor to King Maximilian II. 90n, 435, 437–438, 440–442, 446, 456, 464–469, 472–473, 476, 480.

Abercromby, Ralph (1803–1868), from 1858 second Baron Dunfermline. British diplomat. 1831–1836 secretary of legation in Prussia; minister resident in Tuscany; 1839 envoy extraordinary and minister plenipotentiary to the German Confederation, 1840–1852 to Sardinia, and 1852–1858 to the Netherlands. xii, *94–96, 131–133, 135–140*

Aberdeen, see **Hamilton-Gordon, George**

Adelaide (1792–1849), Princess of Saxe-Meiningen; from 1830 wife of William IV, King of England. 310n

Adolf (1817–1905), from 1839 Duke of Nassau; his regency ended when the duchy was annexed by Prussia in 1866. 101, 108

Agoult, Hector Philippe, comte de (1782–1856), French diplomat. 1814 secretary at the Spanish embassy, where he at times acted as chargé d'affaires until 1818; then stationed in Hanover, Stockholm and The Hague. 1827–1831 envoy extraordinary and minister plenipotentiary to Berlin. 116

Ahrens, Heinrich (1808–1874); *Habilitation* in 1830 at the University of Göttingen. After the failed uprising in Göttingen in 1831, Ahrens first taught in Paris; 1834 professor of philosophy in Brussels. After the revolution of 1848 deputy in the Frankfurt national assembly. From 1850 professor in Graz, from 1859 in Leipzig. 10

Alban, student; took part in the Storming of the Frankfurt Guard House on 3 April 1833. Managed to escape from prison and avoid legal proceedings, after one failed attempt in 1834. 63n

Albert, (1828–1902), Prince, from 1873 King of Saxony. 332

Albrecht (1817–1895), Archduke of Austria; eldest son of Archduke Karl. 379, 449–450

Albrecht (Friedrich Heinrich Albert) (1809–1872), Prince of Prussia, called Albert, youngest son of Friedrich Wilhelm III. 120

Albrecht, Wilhelm Eduard (1800–1876), professor of law. After *Habilitation*, first professor in Königsberg, then from 1830 in Göttingen. 1837 dismissed by King Ernst August of Hanover as one of the seven Göttingen professors who protested against the repeal of the Basic State Law. Moved to Leipzig, from 1840 professor of German law there; 1848 envoy of Oldenburg, Schwarzburg, and Anhalt at the *Bundestag* in Frankfurt, and at the same time deputy in the Frankfurt national assembly. From 1869 life-long member of the first chamber in Saxony. 162n, 315

Alexander I Pavlovitch (1777–1825), 1801–1825 Emperor of Russia. 168, 510, 513

Alexandra Feodrovna (1798–1860), previously Charlotte, daughter of Prussian King Friedrich Wilhelm III; from 1817 married to Grand Duke Nikolai I Pavlovitch, from 1825 Tsar. 138, 183

Allen, William (1770–1843), Quaker, associate of Elisabeth Fry, prominent campaigner against slavery. 181

Alleye de Ciprey, Jean Baptiste, baron de, French diplomat. 1815–1825 secretary of legation in Frankfurt; 1830–1839 envoy to the German Confederation in Frankfurt; 1839–1846 envoy to Mexico. 69n, 134

Ancillon, Friedrich von (1767–1837), Prussian statesman. 1814 *Geheimer Legationsrat*, and 1818 director of the political department in the foreign ministry; 1817 member of the *Staatsrat*; after the victory of the reactionary forces, he joined the Crown Prince's Party; 1832–1837 Prussian foreign minister. 75, 130, 133–137, 140, 145, 148–151, 154, 160, 427, 504, 507–508

Andrian-Werburg, Ferdinand Freiherr von (1776–1851), jurist in the Bavarian civil service. *Regierungspräsident* of the Bavarian Rhenish Provinces from February to June 1832. After the Hambach Festival transferred to Franconia where he was *Regierungspräsident* in Ansbach until 1848. 360

Anger, Carl Friedrich (1764–1834), Saxon officer. At the end of his career aide-de-camp to the Dresden military governor, Heinrich Adolph von Gablenz. 299

Anton Klemens Theodor (1755–1836), King of Saxony from 1827 to 1836. 120, 293, 296–298, 307, 309–311

Armannsperg, Joseph Ludwig Graf von (1787–1853), Bavarian statesman. 1816–1820 *Regierungsdirektor* in Speyer; 1820–1823 director of the *Oberster Rechnungshof*; 1823 vice president of the government of the Regen district; 1825 second president of the Bavarian chamber of deputies; 1826 interior and finance minister; member of the *Staatsrat*; 1828–1831 foreign minister; 1832 president of the Greek regency council; 1835–1837 chancellor of Greece. 409–411

Arnim-Boitzenburg, Adolf Graf von (1803–1868), Prussian civil servant and politician. 1842–1845 interior minister, then deputy in the United Diet. In March 1848 temporary head of the *Staatsministerium*. 216, 219–220, 240

Arnoldi, Wilhelm (1798–1864), 1842–1864 bishop of Trier; initiated the pilgrimage to the Holy Coat in 1844. 101

Aschbach, Gerhard Adolf (1793–1842), judge and politician. Liberal deputy in the Baden *Landtag* from 1831 to 1841, when the Baden government refused to release him on his appointment as a judge. 383

August (1783–1853), 1829–1853 ruling Grand Duke of Oldenbourg; 1851 general in the royal Prussian infantry regiment. 268

August (1813–1885), Prince of Württemberg. 353

August I (August the Strong) (1670–1733), from 1694 Prince Elector of Saxony; from 1697 also King of Poland. 332n

Backhouse, John (1772–1845), 1827–1843 British under-secretary of state for foreign affairs. *131–132*, 442

Barnard, Charles Townshend, British diplomat. 1824 appointed secretary of legation at Dresden; from 1841 chargé d'affaires at Coburg. *299–302, 307–308*, 326–327, 336

Barrot, Camille Hyacinte Odilon (1791–1837), French statesman and leading politician of the moderate Left. 1831–1847 deputy in the French national assembly; 1848/1849 justice minister.   501

Bauer, Jacob (1787–1854), Bavarian civil servant; 1838–1854 mayor of Munich.   457

Becker, doctor in Berlin, [nothing further could be established].   117

Becker, Nikolaus (1809–1845), court scribe in Geilenkirchen. 1840, influenced by German–French tensions, wrote the poem: *Sie sollen ihn nicht haben, den freien deutschen Rhein* (They shall not have it, the free German Rhine).   439

Behr, Wilhelm Josef (1775–1851), Liberal politician. 1799–1821 professor of public law at the University of Würzburg; 1821 elected mayor of Würzburg for life; 1832 dismissed from office. 1836 sentenced to imprisonment for an unspecified period of time for repeated attempts to commit high treason and lese-majesty; 1839 released on condition that he be detained in Passau, then Regensburg; 1848 permitted to return to Würzburg; deputy for Kronach in the Frankfurt national assembly.   12, 409

Beisler, Hermann von (1790–1859), Bavarian civil servant. 1823 appointed *Regierungsrat*; 1837 *Regierungsdirektor* in upper Bavaria; 1843–1859 president of *Oberster Rechnungshof*; November 1847 to March 1848 justice minister; 1848–1849 deputy in the Frankfurt national assembly.   484

Bem, Jozef (1794–1850), Polish patriot and freedom fighter. Took part in the Polish struggles for independence against Russia in 1812 and 1830/1831 and in the Hungarian Uprising of 1848. After fleeing to the Ottoman Empire, converted to Islam in 1849 and became governor of Aleppo (as Murad Pasha).   301

Benedict XIV (1675–1758), from 1740 Pope. Previously Cardinal Prospero Lambertini.   169

Berks, Franz von (1792–1873), Bavarian civil servant and professor at the University of Würzburg; 1847–1848 minister of the interior.   484n

Bernhard II (1800–1882), from 1803 nominal Duke of Saxe-Meiningen; from 1821 ruling Duke; renounced 1866.   109, 327

Bernstorff, Albrecht Graf von (1809–1873), Prussian diplomat. Stationed in Hamburg, Munich, St Petersburg, Paris and Naples. 1842 *Vortragender Rat* in the political department of the Prussian foreign ministry. 1845 envoy extraordinary and minister plenipotentiary in Munich, 1848 in Vienna, 1851 in Naples and, with an interruption in 1861/1862, when he was Prussian foreign minister, 1855–1873 in London. 477–478, 480

Bernstorff, Christian Günther Graf von (1769–1835) Entered the Danish diplomatic service in 1787; 1800–1810 minister president and foreign minister in Copenhagen; 1811–1817 Danish envoy to Vienna, 1817–1818 to Berlin; 1818 transferred to the Prussian service and took part in the Congress of Aachen; 1818–1832 Prussian foreign minister; represented Prussia at the Carlsbad Congress; his policies were closely modelled on Metternich's principles of restoration. 114, 145–147

Beroldingen, Joseph Ignaz Graf von (1780–1868), Württemberg diplomat and statesman. After a military career, envoy extraordinary and minister plenipotentiary in London (1814) and in St Petersburg (1816). 1823–1848 Württemberg foreign minister. 356, 363, 368, 375–376, 381–382, 392

Berr, Felix (1795–1873), physician; 1838–1847 chief medical officer at the Munich orphanage. 443

Bestelmeyer, Joann Georg (1785–1852), tobacco manufacturer and politican. 1825 moved to Nuremberg, where he was chairman of the *Gemeindekollegium, Magistratsrat*, second mayor and *Landtag* deputy; a keen supporter of the 1848 movement, he gave up the office of second mayor in 1849. 409

Biedermann, Carl (1812–1901), Saxon scholar, writer and politician. 1835 *Privatdozent*; from 1838 until dismissed in 1853, and 1865–1901 professor of philosophy at the University of Leipzig. Published variously from the 1830s onwards. 1845–1848 deputy in the Leipzig *Stadtverordnetenversammlung*; 1848/1849 deputy in the Frankfurt *Vorparlament* and in the Frankfurt national assembly; 1849/1850 and 1869–1876 deputy in the second chamber of the Saxon *Landtag*; 1871–1874 also a *Reichstag* deputy. 338, 340

Binder von Kriegelstein, Franz Freiherr von (1774–1855), Austrian diplomat. By dint of postings to Stockholm in 1801, Berlin in 1803, St Petersburg in 1809, and Kopenhagen in 1810 regarded as a specialist on the political situation in the north. 1812 envoy in Stuttgart;

1813 summoned to the congress in Prague; 1814/1815 took part in the Congress of Vienna; 1815 envoy in The Hague; 1820 in Turin; 1823/1824 special mission in Portugal; 1826 envoy in Bern; 1832–1834 carried out special commissions for the state chancellery, in Berlin and elsewhere. 1837–1843 envoy extraordinary and minister plenipotentiary at the Saxon court in Dresden. 130–131, 315

Bingham, Richard Camden (1801–1872), British diplomat. 1831–1839 secretary of legation in Munich, 1840–1852 in Sardinia, then envoy to Sicily and Naples. *430–432*

Bismark, Friedrich Wilhelm, from 1816 Graf von Bismark (1783–1860), Württemberg diplomat, general, and writer. From 1820 lifelong member of *the Kammer der Standesherren*; envoy to various courts while retaining his command of a cavalry brigade. 1821–1848 accredited in Carlsruhe as legation representative, 1825–1845 envoy extraordinary and minister plenipotentiary in Berlin, Dresden and Hanover. 353

Bligh, John Duncan (1798–1872), British diplomat. 1829–1831 secretary of legation in Tuscany, 1831–1832 in the Netherlands; 1832–1835 minister ad interim in St Petersburg; 1835–1838 minister to Sweden; 1838–1856 envoy extraordinary and minister plenipotentiary at the court of Hanover. *251–287*

Blittersdorf, Friedrich Landolin Karl Freiherr von (1792–1861), diplomat. Initially Baden's chargé d'affaires in St Petersburg, 1821 promoted to the position of envoy to the *Bundestag*. Kept this position until 1835, when appointed minister for foreign affairs in the *Staatsministerium*; November 1843 returned to his position at the *Bundestag*, where he remained until 1848. 3, 6, 22, 29–30, 77–79, 377–379, 385, 388–389, 391–392

Blomberg zu Sylbach, Ludwig August Freiherr von (1790–1858), Württemberg diplomat. 1830–1841 envoy extraordinary and minister plenipotentiary to Vienna; 1846–1848 envoy to the *Bundestag* at Frankfurt. 108

Blücher, Gebhard Leberecht Fürst, from 1814 von Wahlstatt (1742–1819), Prussian field marshal. Distinguished himself in the revolutionary wars; removed from his command in 1811 at Napoleon's insistence; after returning to the army in 1813 assumed supreme command of the Silesian army; contributed to the convincing defeat of the French troops and led his troops to the capture of Paris; after Napoleon's return from Elba in 1815 again supreme commander of the

Prussian army; with Wellington, was crucial in deciding the campaign in favour of the allies at the Battle of Waterloo; 1817 appointed to the *Staatsrat*. 244

Blum, Robert (1807–1848), politician and publicist. From the mid-1830s leading member of the democratic movement in Saxony and Germany. Active in numerous oppositional organizations and associations. 1846 *Stadtverordneter* in Leipzig; 1848 vice-president of the Frankfurt *Vorparlament* and spokesman for the Left in the Frankfurt national assembly. October 1848 took part in the Vienna uprising; in November executed for high treason, having been condemned by an Austrian court martial. 102n, 340

Bodelschwingh, Ernst von (1794–1854), Prussian statesman. Having studied law, entered the Prussian civil service in 1817. 1831–1834 *Regierungspräsident* in Trier; 1834–1842 *Oberpräsident* of the Rhine province; 1842–1844 finance minister; 1844–1845 cabinet minister; 1845–1848 minister of the interior; 1851–1854 *Regierungspräsident* in Arnsberg. 209, 216, 220, 235, 245

Börne, Ludwig (1786–1837), really Juda Löb Baruch, journalist and representative of the political-literary movement *Junges Deutschland*. 1830 moved to Paris, whence he spread the ideas of the revolution of July 1830 to Germany in his *Briefe aus Paris*. 76–77

Bowring, Sir John (1792–1872), British economist, writer, diplomat and MP. Sent by British government on various commercial missions abroad. 1831 secretary to the commission for inspecting the accounts of the United Kingdom; 1831 commissioner to investigate the commercial relations between England and France; 1838 founding member of the Anti-Corn Law League; 1839 deputed to Prussia with the object of inducing the Geman Commercial Union to modify its tariff on English manufactures. The result of his investigations in Berlin was the Report on the Prussian Commercial Union. 1847–1853 consul in Canton/China; 1854–1859 minister plenipotentiary to China, governor, commander-in-chief, and vice-admiral of Hong Kong and its dependencies, and chief superintendent of trade in China. 179–180

Braun, Karl (1807–1868), liberal deputy of the second chamber of the Saxon *Landtag*; 1845 its president. 1848/1849 minister president; then a civil servant in his home town of Plauen. 335, 338

Bray-Steinburg, Otto Camillus Hugo Graf von (1807–1899), Bavarian diplomat and politician. 1841 minister resident in Athens;

1843 chargé d'affaires in St. Petersburg. From early 1846 to February 1847 and again in April 1848 Bavarian foreign minister. 1849 returned to St Petersburg; 1858 envoy extraordinary and minister plenipotentiary in Berlin, 1860 in Vienna; 1870/1871 minister president and foreign minister; returned to his post in Vienna until 1896.   469, 472–474, 476

Brenner, Adolf Freiherr, Austrian diplomat. 1847–1849 chargé d'affaires in Munich while there was no envoy; 1865–1866 envoy extraordinary and minister plenipotentiary to Hesse-Darmstadt.   481

Bresson, Charles Joseph, comte de (1798–1847), French diplomat. 1833–1844 envoy extraordinary and minister plenipotentiary in Berlin.   135, 137, 158, 160, 188–189, 191

Brieglep, Moritz (1809–1872), leading liberal politician in Saxe-Coburg-Gotha. 1848 secretary of the *Vorparlament* in Frankfurt and deputy for Coburg in the Frankfurt national assembly. From 1851 plenipotentiary for the administration of Prince Albert's lands in Germany; from 1862 fufilled the same function for Queen Victoria and for King Leopold I of Belgium. 1871 elected to the German *Reichstag*.   336–337

Broglie, Achille Léonce Victor Charles, duc de (1785–1870), French statesman, diplomat and leader of the moderate liberals after the restoration. Occupied several cabinet posts (1835/1836 premier minister) under King Louis Phillippe; 1847/1848 ambassador to London. After the revolution in February 1848 elected to the French national assembly.   507

Broitzem, Eduard von (*1798), 1844–1855 director of the circle of Leipzig; then *Geheimer Finanzrat* and *Direktor* of the Saxon finance ministry.   333

Büchner, Georg (1813–1837), poet and playwright. As a member of the opposition in Hesse he wrote the influential *Der hessische Landbote*. 1835 fled first to Strasburg, then to Zurich where he lectured in anatomy. Main literary works include *Dantons Tod*, *Woyzceck*, *Leonce und Lena*, and *Lenz*.   307n

Bülow, Heinrich Ulrich Wilhelm Freiherr von (1791–1846), Prussian diplomat and statesman. 1821 *Vortragender Rat* in the foreign ministry; 1827–1841 envoy extraordinary und minister plenipotentiary in London; 1841/1842 Prussian envoy to the *Bundestag* in Frankfurt ;

1842–1845 foreign minister. 17, 149–151, 181, 190–191, 206–207, 209, 214, 216, 219, 523

Bunsen, Christian Karl Josias (from 1856 **Freiherr von**) (1791–1860), diplomat. From 1818 at the Prussian legation in the Vatican, 1827–1838 as minister resident. 1839–1842 envoy extraordinary und minister plenipotentiary in Berne, 1842–1854 in London. Friend of King Friedrich Wilhelm IV and his advisor in religious and political matters. 170, 212, 217, 520

Bunsen, Gustaf (*1804), doctor in Frankfurt. After participating in the Storming of the Frankfurt Guard House on 3 April 1833 Bunsen fled to Texas. No further information available for the period after 1836. 44

Bussche-Ippenburg, Friedrich August Philipp Freiherr von dem (1771–1844), general. Until 1813 in the service of Great Britain and the English-Hanoverian German Legion, after 1813 of the kingdom of Hanover. 11

Cabre, Auguste de, from 1822 to 1840 French envoy extraordinary and minister plenipotentiary in Cassel. 59

Campe, Julius Wilhelm (1792–1867), publisher. Under his control the Hamburg publishing house *Hoffmann & Campe* became closely connected with oppositional literature from all parts of Germany. Even though facing strong censorship was successful in publishing authors of the *Junges Deutschland*. 77n

Canitz und Dallwitz, Julius Freiherr von (1815–1894), Prussian diplomat. Started his career as secretary of legation in Munich. 441

Canitz und Dallwitz, Karl Ernst Wilhelm Freiherr von (1787–1850), Prussian general, diplomat and statesman. Started military career in 1806; 1812 joined York's general staff; 1822 became Prince Wilhelm's adjutant. 1819–1841 envoy extraordinary und minister plenipotentiary in Cassel; 1828/1829 interrupted his activities in Cassel when on a special mission to the Prussian legation in Constantinople and (1831) as an observer in the Russian headquarters during the Polish uprising. From 1833 also envoy extraordinary and minister plenipotentiary in Hanover, 1841–1845 in Vienna. 1845–1848 minister for foreign affairs. 59, 212, 221, 285

Canning, Henry, British diplomat. 1823–1841 consul-general; from 1837 also chargé d'affaires to the Hanse Towns in Hamburg. xxii

Canning, Stratford, from 1852 first Viscount Stratford de Redcliffe (1786–1880), British diplomat. 1807 foreign office official; 1808 legation secretary; 1810–1812 chargé d'affaires at Constantinople; 1814–1820 minister to Switzerland; 1820–1824 minister to the United States; 1825 ambassador to Constantinople, charged with pacifying the situation in Greece and reconciling Turkey and Russia; 1828 returned to London as member of parliament; 1842 ambassador to Constantinople, 1847 to Berne, and 1848–1858 again to Constantinople. 1848 on special mission to Germany. *202, 326, 442–444*

Cappaccini, Francesco (1784–1845), priest and diplomat. 1829 papal nuntio in The Hague, 1830 internuntio in Munich, from 1831 in the curia. 1837 diplomatic missions to Vienna, Berlin and Bonn. Appointed cardinal in 1845, the year of his death. 161–162

Cartwright, Sir Thomas (1795–1850), British diplomat. 1821–1827 secretary of legation in Munich; then secretary of embassy in The Hague and on a special mission in Belgium. 1830–1838 envoy extraordinary and minister plenipotentiary to the German Confederation in Frankfurt, 1838–1850 in Stockholm. x–xi, xiii, xvii–xix, *10–88*, 40n, 69n, 134, 368

Catherine II (1729–1796), as Princess Sophie Frederike Auguste, daughter of the Prussian general Prince Christian August of Anhalt-Zerbst, married the heir to the Russian throne in 1756; after his murder in 1762, Tsarina of Russia as Catherine (the Great). 154

Chad, George William (1784–1849), British diplomat. 1816–1817 chargé d'affaires in the Netherlands, 1817–1824 secretary of embassy there; 1824–1828 envoy extraordinary and minister plenipotentiary to Saxony, 1829–1830 to the Germanic Confederation, 1830–1832 to Prussia. xiv, *43–48, 114–123*

Charles X (1757–1836), King of France (1824–30), Count of Artois. 12n, 186, 361, 408, 492

Christian VIII (1786–1848), 1839–1848 King of Denmark, at the same time Duke of Holstein and Duke of Schleswig. 105n, 470n

Clam-Martinitz, Karl Joseph Graf von (1792–1840), Austrian military officer and statesman. Joined the army in 1809. 1831/1832 Austrian special envoy in Berlin at the congress of the German Confederation's military commision. As the Austrian emperor's adjutant general from 1835, and from 1836 also head of the military section in the Austrian *Staatsrat*, Clam held two of the most important military positions in Austria. He was one of Metternich's party faithfuls. 130

Closen, Karl Ferdinand Freiherr von (1786–1856), Bavarian civil servant; pensioned off in 1825. From 1810 deputy in the second chamber of the Bavarian *Landtag*. 409

Colloredo-Waldsee, Franz de Paula Graf von (1799–1859), Austrian diplomat. Envoy extraordinary and minister plenipotentiary in The Hague (1824), Dresden (1829), Munich (1837), and St Petersburg (1843). From March to May 1848 envoy to the *Bundestag* in Frankfurt; 1852–1856 ambassador in London, then envoy extraordinary and minister plenipotentiary at the Holy See in Rome. 301

Cotta von Cottendorf, Johann Friedrich Freiherr (1764–1832), bookseller and significant German publisher. From 1787 head of *J.G. Cottaschen Buchhandlung*, where he founded the *Allgemeine Zeitung* in 1798. Cotta had contact with almost all the important literary figures of his time and published, among others, the works of Herder, Hölderlin, Kleist and Schiller. 341, 427n

Cotta von Cottendorf, Johann Georg Freiherr von (1796–1863), bookseller, publisher. 1832 took over *J.G. Cottaschen Buchhandlung* from his father, Johann Friedrich Cotta. As chief of the *Allgemeine Zeitung* and founder and editor of the *Deutsche Vierteljahresschrift*, he gained great influence over the political life of his time. 390, 427n

Cowley, see **Wellesley**.

Craven, Augustus Denham (d. 1884), British consul and secretary of legation (during Malet's absence) at Carlsruhe. 398

Czernin, Eugen Graf (1796–1868), head chef of the Imperial Majesty of Austria. 524

Czerski, Johann (1813–1893), liberal theologian. Suspended from the priesthood and left the Catholic church in August 1844. His congregation in Schneidemühl then constituted itself into the *Christlich-apostolisch-katholische Gemeinde*, which in 1845 joined the German Catholic movement initiated by Johannes Ronge. On 12 July 1845 Czerski was excommunicated; in the 1860s he increasingly rejected the Christian faith. 103, 229

Dahlmann, Friedrich Christoph (1785–1860), historian and liberal politician. 1812 professor in Kiel, from 1829 in Göttingen. 1831–1833 deputy in the second chamber of the Hanovarian *Landtag*. In 1837 he led the protest action by the seven professors against King Ernst August's breach of the constitution. After his dismissal, lived first in Jena; 1842 appointed to a chair in Bonn; 1848 deputy in the Frankfurt *Vorparlament* and in the Frankfurt national assembly.   162n, 274, 285n, 315

Degenfeld-Schonburg, Ferdinand Christoph Graf von (1802–1876), Württemberg envoy extraordinary and minister plenipotentiary in Munich 1844–1868.   480

Diepenbrock, Melchior Ferdinand Joseph Freiherr von (1798–1853), Catholic priest. 1824 studied theology and for the priesthood, then *Domkapitular* (1830) and *Generalvikar* (1842) of the Regensburg diocese. 1845 elected prince bishop of Breslau, from 1850 cardinal.   475

Dieskau, Julius Otto Heinrich von (1798–1872), lawyer in Plauen and politician. 1836–1840 liberal deputy in the second chamber of the Saxon *Landtag*. 1848 deputy in the Frankfurt *Vorparlament*, and member of the economic committee of the Frankfurt national assembly.   314

Disbrowe, Edward Cromwell, from 1823 Sir, (1790–1851), British diplomat. 1828–1834 envoy extraordinary and minister plenipoteniary in Stuttgart. 1834 ambassador to Sweden.   *347–368*

Dönhoff, August Hermann Graf von (1797–1874), Prussian diplomat and statesman. After his studies, entered diplomatic service in 1821 and was stationed in Paris, Madrid, and London. 1833 envoy extraordinary and minister plenipotentiary in Munich; 1842–1848 envoy to the *Bundestag* in Frankfurt. In spring 1848 tried in vain to persuade the Prussian government to instigate reforms along the lines of national unity. September–November 1848 Prussian foreign minister. From 1849 member of the first chamber, and after it was transformed in 1854 was given a seat in the Prussian *Herrenhaus*.   431

Droste zu Vischering, Kaspar Maximilian Freiherr von (1770–1846), 1825 elected bishop of Münster.   170

Droste zu Vischering, Clemens August Freiherr von (1773–1845), Catholic priest. 1807 *Koadjutor* of the bishop of Münster, 1810 appointed *Generalvikar*. Because he rejected Hermesianism came into conflict with the Prussian government and tried in vain to make the theology students at the University of Bonn study in Münster. 1820 gave up the office of *Generalvikar*. 1827 appointed suffragan bishop of Münster; 1835 archbishop of Cologne. In 1837, as part of the Cologne church conflict over mixed marriages, was dismissed by the Prussian government and arrested. 1839 released to Münster and withdrew from public life. xx, 88–89, 161–167, 170, 175, 185–186, 196–197, 228, 478, 520

Dunin, Martin von (1774–1842), Catholic priest. After ordination, first *Domherr* in Wraclawek, from 1815 Domkanzler in Gnesen and *Domkapitular* in Posen. 1829 became administrator of Posen-Gnesen; 1831 elected archbishop of Posen at the suggestion of the Prussian government. 185–186

Dusch, Alexander von (1789–1876), Baden diplomat and politician. 1826 Baden chargé d'affaires at the Swiss Confederation, from 1828 as minister resident; 1835 minister resident in Munich; 1838 Baden envoy to the *Bundestag* in Frankfurt ; 1843–1849 head of the ministry of the Grand Duke's house and of foreign affairs; 1851/1852 deputy in the second chamber of the Baden *Landstände*. 93, 392, 396

Duttlinger (also **Dutlinger**), **Johann Georg** (1788–1841), professor and Baden politician. From 1818 professor in Freiburg im Breisgau, from 1819 deputy in the second chamber of the Baden *Landstände*; its president in 1841. 355, 358n

Eberhard, Anton (Bonaventura) (1807–1887), 1838–1841 preacher at the court church of St Michael in Munich. 440

Edgcumbe, George (1800–1882), British military officer and diplomat. 1838–1858 secretary of legation in Hanover. *254–255*

Eichhoff, Peter Joseph Freiherr von (1790–1863), naval officer. 1815–1818 in the Dutch naval service, member of the Rhine Navigation Commission until, as inspector general, took over the direction of matters concerning navigation on the Dutch part of the Rhine. From 1818 was in the service of Austria. In 1821 the Elbe Act, to which Eichhoff had made a substantial contribution, was concluded. In 1824 worked on the revision of the Elbe Navigation Act as a commissar; 1825 *Gubernialrat* and official in charge of commerce and manufacturing in Bohemia; 1829 *Hofrat* in the general *Hofkammer* in Vienna, and 1835 president of this office. 490, 516–517

Eimer, Heinrich (*1811), student in Heidelberg. Took part in the Storming of the Frankfurt Guard House on 3 April 1833. Failed attempt to break out in 1834. 1836 sentenced to life imprisonment. 63n, 83n

Einsiedel, Detlev Graf von (1773–1861), from 1813 cabinet minister in Saxony and secretary of state for home affairs, as well as military and economic matters, and later also for foreign affairs. 1815 followed King Friedrich August to lead the negotiations in Pressburg and in Vienna, ending with his reinstatement. From 1817, after abolishing the *Geheime Consilium*, he concentrated the whole of government power in his own hands; opposed to reform of any sort; brought down during the Dresden riots of 1830.   292, 296, 317

Eisenmann, Gottfried (1795–1867), doctor and politician. 1818 cofounder of the *Burschenschaft* in Würzburg. 1828 founded the *Bayerisches Volksblatt*, a constitutional-monarchist and patriotic journal, which was banned in 1832; arrested because of an article taken from another, censored journal; spent four years on remand; sentenced to an indefinite period in prison for high treason; 1847 pardoned; 1848 deputy in the *Vorparlament* in Frankfurt and the Frankfurt national assembly.   12

Elisabeth Ludovika (1801–1873), daughter of King Maximilian I of Bavaria, in 1823 married Crown Prince Friedrich Wilhelm of Prussia. From 1840 Queen of Prussia.   210–211

Elliot-Murray-Kynynmound, Gilbert, styled Viscount Melgund 1813–1814, second Earl of Minto 1814 (1782–1859), British diplomat. 1832–1834 British envoy extraordinary and minister plenipotentiary to Berlin. 1835 First Lord of the Admiralty. In Lord John Russell's cabinet of 1846 became Lord Privy Seal (1846–1852); 1847/1848 was despatched on an extraordinary mission to Switzerland, Sardinia, Tuscany, the Vatican, and the Two Sicilies.   xiii, xviii, 40n, *123–131, 133–135*, 503

Ende, Karl Heinrich Konstantin von (1784–1845), Saxon *Geheimer Rat* and president of the University of Leipzig.   292

Engelhardt, Frédéric Auguste (1796–1874), French delegate at the Mainz Navigation Commission 1815–1831; then continued as consul in Mainz; 1852 French envoy to Baden.   178

Ernst August (Ernest Augustus) (1771–1851), fifth son of George III. From 1799 Duke of Cumberland and from 1837 King of Hanover.   xv, xxii, 85, 87–88, 91–96, 162–164, 176, 180n, 185, 251–264, 269–277, 279, 283–286, 319–320

Ernst I (1784–1844), from 1806 Duke of Saxe-Coburg, 1826 of Saxe-Coburg-Gotha.   316

Ernst II (1818–1893), from 1844 Duke of Saxe-Coburg-Gotha, brother of Prince Albert. 109, 336–337, 342–343

Erskine, David Montagu, second Baron (1776–1855), British diplomat. 1806 MP for Portsmouth; 1806–1809 envoy extraordinary and minister plenipotentiary to USA, 1825–1828 to Württemberg, 1828–1843 to Bavaria. xiii, 355, *407–414, 416–430, 432–433,* 434, *438–445,* 503

Erskine, James Stuart (1821–1891), son of David Montagu second Baron Erskine; settled in Bavaria and married Wilhelmina Countess Törring-Minucci. 439

Esterházy von Galántha, Paul Anton Fürst von (1786–1866), Austrian diplomat. 1810 envoy to Dresden, later to The Hague, 1814 to Rome; 1815–1841 Austrian ambassador in London; 1848 foreign minister. 492, 513

Ewald, Heinrich (1803–1875), Bible researcher, Orientalist and politician. 1827–1837 professor in Göttingen until his dismissal as one of the seven professors involved in the Hanoverian constitutional dispute. 1838 chair at the University of Tübingen, 1848 returned to Göttingen. 1867 dismissed again after refusing to take the oath of homage to the Prussian King. 1869–1875 deputy in the north German and German *Reichstag* as a member of the opposition Guelph party. 162n, 315

Falkenstein, Gertrude (1803–1882), lover and common-law wife of Friedrich Wilhelm I of Hesse-Cassel. Elevated to Freifrau Schaumburg. 13

Falkenstein, Johann Paul Freiherr von (1801–1882), Saxon statesman. Posts in ministry of justice and interior; from 1835 *Kreisdirektor* in Leipzig; 1844–1848 interior minister; 1853 minister for cultural affairs; 1866–1871 minister president, then minister of the royal house. 329, 335

Fane, John, styled Lord Burghersh, 11th Earl of Westmorland 1841 (1784–1859), British diplomat. 1814–1831 minister to Tuscany; 1841–1851 envoy extraordinary and minister plenipotentiary to Berlin; 1851–1855 ambassador to Vienna. *203–209, 213–221, 223–226, 231–245*

Faraday, Michael (1791–1867), British physicist and chemist. 1821 proved the rotation of an electric conductor round a magnet pole and vice versa; 1824 fellow of the Royal Society; 1825 director of the laboratory of the Royal Institution; 1831 discovered induction; 1833/1834 formulated the basic laws of electro-chemistry named after him and introduced electrochemical nomenclature.   200

Ferdinand (1763–1834), Duke of Württemberg 1806; 1829–1834 governor of the federal fortress in Mainz.   28, 45

Ferdinand I (1793–1875), from 1835 Emperor of Austria. Gave up the throne on 2 December 1848.   138–139, 286, 371–372, 452, 511, 516–519, 524, 526–527

Ferdinande Phillippe Louis (1810–1842), Duke of Orleans, Son of King Louis Phillippe.   161, 167n

Flad, Philipp von (1778–1865), *Geheimer Legationsrat.* Abel's close friend in the Bavarian foreign ministry, retired in 1848.   473

Fontenay, Anne Louis Gabriel, vicomte de (1784–1855), French military officer and diplomat. 1828–1849 envoy extraordinary und minister plenipotentiary in Stuttgart.   370

Forbes, Francis Reginald (1791–1873), British diplomat. 1833–1859 envoy extraordinary and minister plenipotentiary at the Saxon court in Dresden. From 1841 also accredited to the court of Saxe-Coburg-Gotha and from 1847 to the Courts of Saxe-Weimar-Eisenach, Saxe-Altenburg and Saxe-Meiningen.   *302–344*

Fox, Henry Edward (1802–1859), British diplomat. 1835–1836 secretary of embassy and minister plenipotentiary ad interim in Vienna.   *512–514*

Fox-Strangways, William Thomas Horner, fourth Earl of Ilchester 1858 (1795–1865), British diplomat. From 1825 secretary of legation in Tuscany and Naples, 1833 secretary of embassy in Vienna; 1835–1840 parliamentary under secretary for foreign affairs; 1840–1849 envoy extraordinary and minister plenipotentiary to the German Confederation in Frankfurt.   xix, *97–98, 101, 104–110, 510–512*

Franckenberg-Ludwigsdorf, Karl Ludwig von (died 1849), Baden envoy extraordinary and minister plenipotentiary at the Berlin court.   218–219, 394.

Franz I (II) (1768–1835), last Emperor of the Holy Roman Empire as

Franz II 1792–1806, Emperor of Austria as Franz I 1804–1835. 50, 51, 138–139, 371–372, 497, 510–511, 513–517

Franz Karl (1802–1878), Archduke of Austria; son of Emperor Franz I. From 1824 married to Princess Sophie of Bavaria. When his brother Emperor Ferdinand I abdicated in 1848, he gave up his right of succession in favour of his son Franz Joseph. 518–519, 525–526

Fraser, John, member of the British mission in Vienna 1830–1838. 515

Frederik VI (1768–1839), from 1808 King of Denmark, Duke of Schleswig. As Duke of Holstein ruling sovereign of the German Confederation. 85–86

Frederik VII (1808–1863), from 1848 King of Denmark, Duke of Schleswig and of Holstein. 105n

Freitag, August (born between 1795 and 1798), lawyer in Herzberg and Osterode. Went to the USA after the failed uprising in Osterode in 1831; 1848/1849 returned to his hometown of Waake near Göttingen. 10

Freund, Heinrich Joseph (*1814), student in Würzburg; took part in the Storming of the Frankfurt Guard House on 3 April 1833. 1836 sentenced to life imprisonment. 83n

Friederike Karoline Sophie (1778–1841), Princess of Mecklenburg-Strelitz and after her marriage to Ernest Augustus, Duchess of Cumberland; from 1837 Queen of Hanover. 140, 274n

Friedrich August I (1750–1827), as Friedrich August III Prince Elector 1763–1806, King of Saxony from 1806. 152

Friedrich August II (1797–1854), from 1830 co-regent, from 1836 King of Saxony. 291–292, 295–297, 307, 309–311, 318, 320, 324–325, 331–334, 343

Friedrich I (1657–1713), from 1688 Prince Elector of Brandenburg; on 18 January 1701 he crowned himself 'King in Prussia' in Königsberg, with the agreement of Emperor Leopold I. 152n, 184, 190n

Friedrich I Wilhelm Karl (1754–1816). 1797 as Friedrich II Duke of

Württemberg; 1803 prince elector; from 1806 King of Württemberg. 350n

Friedrich II (Frederick the Great) (1712–1786), King in Prussia from 1740, King of Prussia from 1772. 152n, 154, 165–166, 168, 191, 200

Friedrich Wilhelm (1802–1875), co-regent of Hesse-Cassel 1831, prince elector from 1847 until electoral Hesse was annexed by Prussia in 1866. 13, 14, 58n

Friedrich Wilhelm III (1770–1840), King of Prussia from 1797. xv, 114–116, 119–121, 130, 138–139, 145, 148–149, 153, 155, 157, 160–162, 166, 170–172, 174, 182–185, 187, 191, 194–195, 201, 213, 215, 228, 236, 239, 274n, 291, 310, 351, 477, 497, 503, 520–521

Friedrich Wilhelm IV (1795–1861), from 1840 King of Prussia. xv, 100, 147–148, 157, 164, 171–172, 174, 182–197, 199–206, 208, 210–213, 215, 217–226, 228, 230, 235–247, 256, 271, 274, 286, 343–344, 379, 387–389, 399, 440, 477, 522–523, 531

Fries, Eduard (*1811), student in Heidelberg. Took part in the Storming of the Frankfurt Guard House on 3 April 1833. 1836 sentenced to life imprisonment. Escaped from Frankfurt jail on 10 January 1837. 83n, 84n

Fritsch, Karl Wilhelm Freiherr von (1769–1850), Saxon-Weimar statesman. 1791 member of the *Generalpolizeidirektion* in Weimar, from 1805 its head; 1793 appointed *Regierungsrat*; 1811 member of the *Geheimes Consilium*; 1815–1848 *Wirklicher Geheimer Rat* and *Staatsminister*; 1819 represented Weimar at the Carlsbad Congress; 1833/1834 represented the whole Saxon-Ernestine house at the conference of ministers in Vienna. 109

Fry, Elizabeth (1780–1845), Quaker and influential co-founder of the Association for the Improvement of the Female Prisoners in Newgate. Her work for the welfare and health system was acknowledged by Queen Victoria. 181–182

Fürstenberg, Karl Egon Fürst zu (1796–1854), governing prince of the principality of Fürstenberg, mediatized in; 1818 married Amalie von Baden; from 1819 member of the first chamber of Baden. 347

Gablenz, Heinrich Adolf Freiherr von (1764–1843), Saxon general and military governor of Dresden. 299

Gebsattel, Lothar Anselm von (1761–1846), archbishop of Munich-Freising. Initially bishop of the diocese of Würzburg, then designated first archbishop of Munich-Freising; confirmed by the Pope in 1818, consecrated in 1821; advocated a fundamental restoration of ecclesiastical discipline and religiosity. 441

Geiger, Johann, prison warder in Frankfurt. Helped those who took part in the Storming of the Frankfurt Guard House to escape from Frankfurt prison on 10 January 1837. 84

Georg (1819–1878), son of Ernst August of Cumberland, from 1837 crown prince of Hanover. Despite being blind, ruled as King Georg V of Hanover from 1851 until Hanover was annexed by Prussia in 1866. 268–269, 275, 279, 285–286

George IV (1762–1830), from 1811 prince regent, from 1820 King of England. 4, 86–87

Gervinus, Georg Gottfried (1805–1871), historian and publicist. From 1830 *Privatdozent*, from 1835 professor at the University of Heidelberg, 1836 at the University of Göttingen. In December 1837 dismissed from the university as one of the seven professors who protested against the breach of the constitution by Ernst August. Became honorary professor in Heidelberg; 1847 editor-in-chief of the newly-founded liberal-constitutional *Deutsche Zeitung*; 1848 deputy in the Frankfurt national assembly, but returned his mandate as early as July 1848 owing to political disappointment with Prussia's ruling elite. His magnum opus is the eight-volume *Geschichte des neunzehnten Jahrhunderts*. 162n, 315

Gevers, J.C., Dutch minister resident in Munich and Stuttgart. 478, 480

Gise, August Friedrich Freiherr (1783–1860), really von Koch auf Teublitz, Bavarian diplomat and politician. After postings as envoy extraordinary and minister plenipotentiary to The Hague (1815) and to St Petersburg (1824), 1831–1846 Bavarian foreign minister. During his time as foreign minister he supported the idea of Bavarian independence. 412, 416–418, 421, 427–428, 430, 433–434, 441, 458, 468

Gneisenau, August Wilhelm Anton Graf (from 1814) Neidhardt von (1760–1831), Prussian army leader. From 1785 officer in the Prussian service; apart from Scharnhorst, he was the most significant person in the Prussian army reform; during the wars of liberation, he was Blücher's quartermaster general; 1825 field marshal; 1831 commander-in-chief of four army corps in the east during the Polish revolt.   119

Gordon, Sir Robert (1791–1847), British diplomat. 1810 appointed attaché to the British embassy in Persia; 1813–1815 secretary to the embassy at The Hague, and 1815–1826 Vienna; 1826–1828 envoy extraordinary and minister plenipotentiary in Brazil; 1828–1831 in Constantinople; 1841–1846 ambassador to Vienna.   *522–525*

Görres, Joseph von (1776–1848). Inspired by the ideas of the French Revolution, Görres became the spokesman and leader of a republican club in Koblenz in 1793; 1799–1800 represented his home town in Paris, thereupon retired from active politics in 1800; from 1806 lectured at the University of Heidelberg. Became a romantic and published *Die teutschen Volksbücher* in 1807, returning to Koblenz in 1808. In 1814–1815 was director of public education for the Middle Rhine, and founded the *Rheinische Merkur*. In 1819 fled from the forces of reaction to French Strasbourg; here he returned to Catholicism, and became a pioneer of Catholic journalism in Germany; 1827–1848 professor of history and literary history at the University of Munich. His magnum opus was the *Christliche Mystik*.   431–432

Grabbe, Christian Dietrich (1801–1836), German poet. His most important works include the dramas *Napoleon oder die hundert Tage* (1831), *Hannibal* (1835) and *Hermannschlacht* (1836).   76

Graefe (also **Graeffe**), **Karl Ferdinand von** (1787–1840), surgeon and ophthalmologist. From 1810 professor in Berlin.   268

Grandaur, Bernhard Ritter von (1776–1838), Bavarian civil servant. 1806 district judge, and 1826 in the ministry of the interior; from 1828 *Kabinettssekretär*, in which position he supported Ludwig I's actions against the liberal movement in Bavaria.   413

Granville see **Leveson-Gower**

Gregor XVI (1765–1846), from 1831 Pope. Previously Cardinal Bartolomeo Alberto Cappellari.   16n, 175–176, 521

Grimm, Jacob (1785–1863), philologist. After studying law, started career as a librarian in Kassel; 1830 moved to Göttingen as librarian and professor. Dismissed from the university as a co-signatory to the letter of protest against the breach of the constitution by Ernst August. 1840 appointed to the acadamy of sciences in Berlin. 1848/1849 deputy in the Frankfurt national assembly, belonging to the 'centre right'. Most famous for publishing, with his brother Wilhelm, a collection of fairytales, *Kinder und Hausmärchen*, and for the German dictionary project. 162n, 285n, 315

Grimm, Wilhelm (1786–1859), philologist. After studying law, he worked with his older brother as librarian in Hesse-Kassel from 1815; 1830 moved to Göttingen as librarian; appointed professor in 1831. Dismissed from the university on 14 December 1837 as a co-signatory to the letter of protest against the breach of the constitution by Ernst August. 1840 appointed to the academy of sciences in Berlin. 162n, 285n, 315

Grollmann, Karl Wilhelm Georg (1777–1843), Prussian general. 1791 joined the Prussian army; 1809 served in the Austrian army in the war against France; 1810 joined the Spanish army; 1813 major in the Prussian general staff during the wars of liberation. After the war helped to organize general conscription and the reorganization of the general staff. In 1819 resigned in protest against the onset of reaction; resumed service in 1825 as lieutenant general and in 1832 became commanding general in Posen. 193, 521

Gruben, Peter Joseph Freiherr von (1773–1851), diplomat. 1817 *Kammerherr* and *Geheimer Referendar* at the *Staatsministerium* in the Grand Duchy of Hesse; 1820 *Geheimer Staatsrat*; 1822 envoy extraordinary and minister plenipotentiary at the court of the Duke of Nassau; 1823–1836 and 1846–1848 envoy and minister plenipotentiary at the Bavarian court and envoy of the Grand Duchy of Hesse to the *Bundestag*; 1826 *wirklicher Geheimer Rat*; 1829–1847 life member of the first chamber of the Estates; 1829 its second president; 1834 plenipotentiary at the Vienna conferences. 93, 104

Guaita, Friedrich von (1772–1851), from 1807 member of the Senate of the city of Frankfurt. All in all Guaitia took on the office of senior mayor on six occasions. 41, 43–47, 51, 74–75

Gumppenberg, Anton Freiherr von (1787–1855), Bavarian officer. From 1810 adjutant and travelling companion of crown prince Ludwig. 1839–1847 war minister. 472, 475

Gurney, Joseph (1788–1848), brother of Elizabeth Fry and like her a

Quaker involved in various philanthropic projects. Author of numerous books on religion and morals.   181

Gustav II Adolf (1594–1632), King of Sweden from 1611.   228n

Gutzkow, Karl Ferdinand (1811–1878), journalist and author. While studying at Berlin, Jena and Heidelberg he was a member of the secret *Burschenschaft*. Editor and contributor to numerous liberal periodicals and newspapers. Sentenced to two and a half months imprisonment because of his novel *Wally, die Zweiflerin*, published in 1835. He and the other members of the political-literary movement *Junges Deutschland* were banned from writing and publishing in the states of the German Confederation. 1847–1850 artistic and literary director of the Dresden court theatre; after 1850 published other novels and engaged in diverse literary and journalistic activities.   77, 188n

Halkett, Hugh Freiherr von (1783–1863), Hanoverian infantry general.   260

Hamilton, Sir George Baille, British diplomat. Secretary of legation in Berlin 1836–1846.   *161–162, 171–172, 177–178, 210–213*

Hamilton-Gordon, George (1784–1860), 1791–1801 styled Lord Haddo; 1801 fourth Earl of Aberdeen. 1813–1814 ambassador to Austria; 1828–1830 and 1841–1846 foreign secretary. 1852 appointed First Lord of the Treasury.   *3–9, 98–105, 113–114, 197–201, 203–223,* 231, *273–283, 291–297, 321–339, 347–348, 384–398, 407–408, 441–442,* 443, *444–470, 489–492, 522–529*

Handel, Paul Anton Freiherr (1776–1847), Austrian diplomat; 1810 *kaiserlich-königlicher Regierungsrat;* 1815 *wirklicher Geheimer Rat,* took part in the territorial negotiations in Frankfurt; 1816–1834 *Bundeskanzleidirektor* in Frankfurt ; at the same time Austrian minister resident for the free cities of Frankfurt, Hessen, Nassau, and Hamburg.   50–51

Handschuh, Hermann Friedrich (*1812), student in Erlangen; took part in the Storming of the Frankfurt Guard House on 3 April 1833. Failed attempt to break out in 1834. 1836 sentenced to life imprisonment. Escaped from Frankfurt jail on 10 January 1837.   63n, 83n, 84n

Hardenberg, Karl August Freiherr von (1750–1822), Prussian statesman. From 1790 in the service of Prussia in Ansbach and Bayreuth. In 1798 transferred to Berlin, where he was charged with part of the business of the ministry for foreign affairs. In 1806 dismissed on

Napoleon's orders, reinstated as minister in 1807, but dismissed again after the Peace of Tilsit. On the instructions of Friedrich Wilhelm III, wrote a memorandum on reform and restructuring the Prussian state. In 1810 was appointed chancellor of Prussia, took over the direction of financial, domestic and foreign policy, and continued Stein's reforms. At the Congress of Vienna in 1814–1815 ensured that Prussia gained a considerable amount of territory, and restructured the administration of this enlarged Prussia after 1815. When Prussia joined Metternich's system of restoration, his influence decreased.   160n, 184

Harleß, Adolph von (1806–1879), Protestant theologian and politician. 1825–1845 professor at the University of Erlangen. From 1840 represented the University of Erlangen in the first chamber of the Bavarian *Landtag*, where he was a firm opponent of Abel's religious policy. In order to prevent his further involvement in politics, was appointed *Konsistorialrath* and transferred to Bayreuth in 1845.   435

Hartmann, Otto Emil von, until 1843 resident for Prussia in the Free City of Cracow.   141, 143

Hassenpflug, Ludwig (1794–1862), from 1821 *Obergerichtsrat* at the court of appeal in Cassel. Head of the government of electoral Hesse from 1832 until he resigned in 1837. Before returning to electoral Hesse where he was interior and justice minister from 1850 to 1855, first head of the administration of Hohenzollern-Sigmaringen, 1839 civilian governor of Luxemburg, 1841 *Obertribunalrat* at the *Kammergericht* in Berlin and from 1846 president of the supreme court of appeal in Greifswald.   58–59

Hecker, Friedrich (1811–1881), politician, deputy in the second chamber in Baden. At the beginning of the 1848 revolution pleaded for a German republic at the Heidelberg assembly; in April 1848 failed with a republican uprising in Constance. Fled to Switzerland and emigrated to the USA. 1861–1864 took part in the American Civil War as a colonel in the union army.   218–220, 394–395

Hegel, Georg Wilhelm Friedrich (1770–1831), German philosopher and professor in Heidelberg (1816) and Berlin (1818).   xxi, 119

Heine, Heinrich (1797–1856), German poet and most prominent representative of the political-literary movement *Junges Deutschland*. From 1831 correspondent for the *Allgemeine Zeitung* in Paris. His most well known works include *Buch der Lieder*, *Deutschland ein Wintermärchen* and *Atta Troll*.   76, 77n

Heinrich (1473–1541), Duke of Saxony, called the Pious. In 1536 introduced the Reformation in Freiberg and Wolkenstein. In 1539, after the death of his brother Georg who was ruling there, he also introduced it in Albertine Saxony.   318

Heinzen, Karl Peter (1809–1880), radical publicist. After military service and work as a Prussian civil servant, published various pieces criticizing Prussia's social order, i.a. *Die preussische Bürokratie* (1844/1845). 1844 fled to Belgium and then Switzerland, where he continued his career as a publicist. During the revolution of 1848, returned to Germany after a short stay in the USA. 1849 again moved to Switzerland; rejected from there and returned via London to the USA, where he was the editor of various German-language newspapers, most of them short-lived.   404

Helene Luise Elisabeth (1814–1858), daughter of the Arch Grand Duke of Mecklenburg-Schwerin. 1837 married Ferdinande Phillippe Louis, Duke of Orleans.   161, 167n

Henkell, Adam (1801–1866), wine merchant from Mayence.   24

Henry, see **Heinrich**

Hepp, Phillipp (1797–1867), doctor in Neustadt. As a member of the *Press- und Vaterlandsverein* gave the opening speech at the Hambach Festival in 1832, then briefly imprisoned. 1833/1834 arrested on suspicion of having taken part in the Storming of the Frankfurt Guard House. From 1840 deputy in the second chamber of Bavaria. During the revolution of 1848/1849 member of the provisional government. After the failed uprising in the Palatinate in 1849, fled to Switzerland. 1865 returned to Germany after an anmesty.   25

Herdegen, Johann Christoph von (1787–1861), Württemberg civil servant and politican. After working as a community scribe, appointed to the ministry of finance in 1817; 1821–1832 became an extraordinary member of the *Geheimer Rat*, and then a regular member (1831–1832). 1832–1844 and 1849–1850 minister of finance. From 1850 head of the statistics office in Stuttgart.   390

Heres, Friedrich Ritter von, Bavarian civil servant and finance minister from November 1847 to March 1848.   484n

Hermes, Georg (1775–1831), Catholic theologian. From 1807 professor of dogmatics in Münster, from 1820 in Bonn; he developed the theology of Hermesianism. 1825 became a member of the *Domkapitel* in Cologne. 161–162

Herschel, Sir John (1792–1871), astronomer and private teacher, son of the astronomer Sir William Herschel. 200

Hertling, Friedrich Freiherr von (1781–1850), Bavarian officer. Took part in all Bavarian campaigns between 1800 and 1815; 1831 major general and brigadier; 1839 represented the Bavarian war minister for six months; 1840 lieutenant general. 453

Hertzberg, Ewald Friedrich Graf von (1725–1795), Prussian statesman and cabinet minister. 155

Herwegh, Georg (1817–1875), poet and publicist; known for demanding freedom and national unity for Germany. 1842 expelled from Prussia because of a letter of protest to the Prussian King; emigrated to Switzerland, and in 1844 to Paris. In 1848 took an active part in the Baden uprising and when it was defeated returned to Paris. From 1851 worked for various newspapers in Zurich; returned to Germany in 1866 following an amnesty. 100, 204, 387–388

Hess, Heinrich Freiherr von (1788–1870), Austrian military officer. 1839–1860 head of the *Generalquartiermeisterstab*; during the Crimean War of 1854/1855 occupied the Danube principalities. 1859 took part in the campaign in Italy; 1860 captain of the *Hofburgwache* in Vienna. 438

Hildegard (1825–1864), Princess of Bavaria, daughter of Ludwig I; 1844 married Archduke Albrecht of Austria. 449

Hodges, Sir George Floyd (1792–1862), British chargé d'affaires and consul general to the Hanse Towns 1841–1860. xxii

Hoffmann, Ernst Emil (1785–1847), liberal politician in Hesse-Darmstadt. In 1820 played a crucial role in bringing about the Hessian constitution; 1826 elected to the second chamber of the Hessian *Landtag*. Until 1829 prevented from taking up his mandate by the Hessian government; in 1835 it was withdrawn from him altogether. 1832–1842 *Gemeinderat* in Darmstadt. 355

Hofstätter, Heinrich von (1805–1875), Catholic priest. From 1839 to 1875 bishop of Passau. 448

Hohenhausen, Leonhard Freiherr von (1788–1872), Bavarian military officer. After the wars of 1805–1815 continued his military career while at the same time tutor to the crown prince, later King Maximilian I; 1847/1848 minister of war; 1848 lieutenant general and divisional commander.   476, 484

Hohenthal, Peter Wilhelm Graf von (1799–1859), Saxon civil servant and until 1831 member of the old Saxon *Landtag*.   302

Hommer, Joseph von (1760–1836), Catholic priest; 1822–1836 bishop of Trier.   170

Hornthal, Franz Ludwig (from 1815) von (1760 or 1763–1833), jurist and liberal politician in Bamberg. Elected mayor of Bamberg and a deputy in the second chamber, drew attention to himself by supporting the idea that the army should take a constitutional oath, and by signing a petition against the Carlsbad decrees. In 1831 prevented from taking up his *Landtag* mandate by the Bavarian government.   409

Howard, Sir Henry Francis (1809–1898), British diplomat. 1832 started his diplomatic career as secretary of legation in Munich and Berlin. 1855–1859 envoy extraordinary and minister plenipotentiary to Lisbon, 1859–1866 to Hanover, and 1866–1872 to Munich.   *202–203, 222–223, 227–231, 245–248, 414–415*

Hübler, Carl Balthasar (1788–1866), jurist and mayor. From 1820 member of Dresden city council. In 1832 became the first elected mayor of Dresden after the introduction of the *Allgemeine Städteordnung*. Resigned in 1846 for health reasons.   330

Hügel, Ernst Eugen Freiherr von (1774–1849), Wurtemberg minister of war 1829–1842.   356

Humboldt, Alexander Freiherr von (1769–1859), naturalist and geographer. After studying science and mining, worked from 1792 to 1796 as a junior mining official in the Prussian civil service; 1799–1804 expedition to south and central America; after his return lived mainly in Paris. He used the results of his journey to produce a work, published from 1805 to 1834, which established him as an internationally respected natural scientist in a number of areas; 1827 returned to Berlin; 1829, on the suggestion of the Tsar, undertook an expedition to Asiatic Russia which also produced a travel account (1837–1842); 1830 in Berlin; his last work in four volumes, *Kosmos* (1845–1858), is an encylopaedic attempt infused with the spirit of classicism and has been translated into all major languages.   182

Isabella II (1830–1904), from 1833–1868 Queen of Spain.   107n, 196

Itzstein, Johann Adam von (1775–1855), Baden politician. From the 1820s leading representative of the liberal-democratic opposition in Baden. His vineyard in Hallgarten became a meeting-place for the opposition in south-west Germany in the 1830s and 1840s. 1822–1823 and 1831–1849 deputy in the second chamber of the Baden *Landtag*; 1848 deputy and second vice president of the Frankfurt *Vorparlament*.   25, 218–220, 358, 384, 394–395

Jacobi, Friedrich (1780–1844), jurist and civil servant in Stade and Hanover. Deputy and president of the second chamber of the Hanoverian *Landtag* during the constitutional dispute (1838–1840).   255

Jarcke, Karl Ernst (1801–1852), jurist and Catholic publicist.   76

Johann (1801–1873), brother of King Friedrich August, from 1854 King of Saxony.   309, 314, 331–333, 336

Jordan, Johann Ludwig von (1773–1848), Prussian diplomat and statesman. 1799 joined the ministry of foreign affairs; 1802 appointed *Kriegsrat*; 1806–1807, and thereafter involved in negotiations with the French, and 1809, as *Geheimer Kriegsrat*, headed the second section of the ministry of foreign affairs. 1810 promoted to *Staatsrat*. During the campaigns of 1813–1814, and at the Congress of Vienna, assisted Hardenberg. 1814 appointed chief of the second, then the second and third sections in the foreign ministry. 1819–1848 minister plenipotentiary to the court of the King of Saxony, and also accredited in the duchies of Saxony, Schwarzburg, and Reuß.   301, 303

Jordan, resident banker at Coblenz, applied for the post of British consul in the Rhineland.   178

Jordan, Sylvester (1792–1861), jurist and politician. 1820–1822 *Privatdozent* and supernuminary professor at the University of Heidelberg; 1822–1839 professor at the University of Marburg. 1830–1832 and 1848–1849 deputy in the diet of Electoral Hesse. April–July 1848 envoy of electoral Hesse to the *Bundestag* in Frankfurt; at the same time deputy in the Frankfurt *Vorparlament* and then in the Frankfurt national assembly. In the Erfurt Union of 1849/1850 member of the arbitration tribunal.   25

Joseph II (1741–1790), from 1764 German Emperor; also co-regent of the Habsburg hereditary territories. From 1780 King of Bohemia and Hungary. 525

Kapff, Sixt Eberhard von (1774–1851), Württemberg civil servant and politician. From 3 January 1831 until 3 April 1832 interior minister. 356

Kappes, Johannes (1773–1837), member of the senate of the Free City of Frankfurt ; 1833 junior mayor. 42, 44–45, 51

Karl (1771–1847), Archduke of Austria; third son of Emperor Leopold II. 450

Karl (1785–1837), Duke of Mecklenburg-Strelitz. In the Prussian military service from 1799; 1817 member of the *Staatsrat*; 1827 its president; main defender of the principle of restoration, whose influence was growing, especially after Hardenberg's death; during Lottum's ministry (from 1823), he was considered the leading statesman. 171

Karl (1823–1891), Crown Prince of Württemberg, from 1864 Karl I, King of Württemberg. 398n, 403

Karl (Friedrich Karl Alexander) (1801–1883), Prince of Prussia, third son of King Friedrich Wilhelm III. 171

Karl Friedrich (1783–1853), from 1828 Grand Duke of Saxe-Weimar-Eisenach, married Maria Pavlovna (1786–1859), daughter of Tsar Paul I of Russia. 327

Karl II (1804–1873), Duke of Brunswick and Lüneburg, regent 1823–1831; after he was deposed, lived in Spain, England, and France. 3–8, 86–87

Karl Theodor Maximilian (1795–1875), Prince of Bavaria, second son of King Max I Joseph of Bavaria; Bavarian general. 408, 429n, 436, 441

Karoline (1776–1841), Queen of Bavaria, daughter of Hereditary Prince Karl Ludwig of Baden, married Maximilian Joseph of Bavaria in 1797. 426, 440–442, 477

Karoline Auguste Charlotte (1792–1873), daughter of King Maximilian I of Bavaria, fourth wife of the Austrian Emperor Francis I. 515, 518

Künßberg, Karl Konstantin Freiherr von, 1835–1848 director of the circle of Zwickau; previously *Kreishauptmann* of the Circle of Erzgebirge.   322

Kuper, Henry George, British diplomat. Appointed to the Frankfurt mission in 1836; chargé d'affaires 1838 and 1842/1843.   *88–93, 98–101*

Lafayette, Marie-Joseph-Paul-Yves-Roch-Gilbert du Motier, marquis de (1757–1834), Liberal French politician and general. After travelling to America in 1777, deeply influenced by American ideas, institutions, and individuals, especially by George Washington; in France, advocated a constitutional monarchy; member of the assembly of notables in 1787; took a leading role in the oppositional conspiracies of the early 1820s.   26, 501

Lamb, Frederick James, third Viscount Melbourne, Baron Beauvale (1782–1853), British diplomat. 1811 secretary of legation; 1812 minister plenipotentiary ad interim at the court of the Two Sicilies; 1813 secretary of legation at Vienna, in August minister plenipotentiary ad interim; 1815–1820 minister plenipotentiary at Munich; 1817, 1820–1824 at the German Confederation in Frankfurt; 1822 sworn into the privy council; 1827 nominated a civil GCB; 1825–1827 minister plenipotentiary to Spain; 1827 ambassador to Lisbon; 1831–1841 ambassador to the court of Vienna.   ix, xiii, 40n, 64, 363, *493–510, 515–522*

Lambton, John George, Earl of Durham (1792–1840), British politician and diplomat. 1813–1828 MP in the House of Commons. Then Lord Privy Seal in the Wellington and Grey governments until 1833. 1835–1837 envoy extraordinary and minister plenipotentiary in St Petersburg. 1838 appointed governor general of Canada.   140n, 145

Lamenais, Hugues-Félicité-Robert de (1782–1854), French priest and political publicist. His attempts to combine liberal and democratic ideas with Catholicism led to conflict with the official Catholic church and to a papal ban in 1834.   432n

Lang, Friedrich (1779–1859), lawyer and politician from Hanover. City magistrate in Verden and deputy in the second chamber of the Hanoverian *Landtag*. In 1839, during the constitutional conflict, resigned his seat as a deputy.   262

Langenn, Friedrich Albert von (1798–1868), Saxon jurist and historian. Appointed to the court of appeal, the highest Saxon court, in 1828. 1829 entered the Saxon government as a privy counsellor and counsellor of justice. 1835–1845 tutor to the eldest son of Prince Johann. 309

Lasaulx, Ernst von (1805–1861), professor of philosophy, 1835 at Würzburg, 1844 at Munich. 1847 temporarily suspended from office because of his part in the Lola Montez affair. 1848 deputy in the Frankfurt national assembly; 1849 deputy in the Bavarian *Landtag*. 476

Ledebur, Friedrich Clemens Freiherr von (1770–1841), priest from 1795, 1825–1841 bishop of Paderborn. 170

Leiningen-Westerburg, Graf Victor von (1821–1863), officer in the Austrian army; 1844–1847 president of the *Texasverein*. 109

Leopold (1790–1852), from 1830 Grand Duke of Baden. 78, 348–351, 354, 358–359, 361, 383, 385–386, 388–389, 391–392, 398

Lepel, Georg Ferdinand Freiherr von (1779–1873), from 1798 in the diplomatic service of the Electoral Principality of Hesse-Kassel. 1816 envoy extraordinary and minister plenipotentiary in Vienna; 1817–1823 envoy from Electoral Hesse to the *Bundestag* in Frankfurt ; at the same time, 1821–1823, chargé d'affaires in Munich. 1836 minister of the house of the Prince Elector and foreign minister; 1840–1846 leading minister in Saxe-Coburg-Gotha. 326, 327

Lerchenfeld, Maximilian Freiherr von (1778–1843), Bavarian diplomat and statesman. 1803, after studying law, entered Bavarian civil service; after the fall of Montgelas, 1817–1825 finance minister; 1825–1833 envoy to the *Bundestag*; 1833–1834 finance minister again; 1835–1842 envoy extraordinary and minister plenipotentiary to Vienna; 1842–1843 envoy to the *Bundestag* again. 3, 29, 33, 41–43, 53, 420

Leveson-Gower, Granville, first Viscount Granville 1815, first Earl Granville 1833 (1773–1846), British diplomat. 1798 special mission to Prussia; 1804 appointed ambassador in St Petersburg; 1805 returned to England; July–October 1809 secretary at war; 1824–1847 ambassador in Paris, reappointed ambassador in Paris by Earl Grey, with a brief interval in 1834, until 1841. 192, 507

Liegnitz, Auguste Fürstin von (1800–1873), morganatic wife of Frederick William III. 139, 184.

Liehmann, 1836 resident for Austria in the Free City of Cracow [nothing further could be established]. 141, 143

Lindau, Wilhelm Adolf (1774–1849), writer and journalist. After studying jurisprudence, worked as a police inspector in Dresden from 1806. 1832 moved to Leipzig, where he edited the *Conversations-Lexikon der neuesten Zeit und Literatur*, published by Brockhaus, and the newspaper *Leipziger Allgemeine Zeitung.* 315

Lindenau, Bernhard August von (1779–1854), Saxon statesman. 1798 *Assessor* in Altenburg; 1801 councillor at the *Kammerkollegium*; 1804 director of the observatory in Gotha; 1820 took over the Gotha ministry; 1827 transferred to the Saxon civil service, initially spending two years as envoy to the *Bundestag*; 1829 director of the *Landesökonomiekollegium* and the deputation for manufacturing and commerce, and supervisor of the art and science collections; 1830 leading cabinet minister; 1831–1843 chair of the *Gesamtministerium*, 1831–1834 also minister for the interior. 1832–1848 member of the *Landtag* of the Duchy of Saxe-Altenburg, 1848 deputy in the Frankfurt national assembly. 296, 302, 305, 311, 332

Lindner, Friedrich Ludwig (1772–1845), writer and journalist. Began working as a journalist in Vienna in 1803, from 1809 in Weimar; 1813–1814 professor of philosophy at Jena; 1817 again editor in Weimar; from 1818 in Stuttgart as editor of *Europäische Annalen*; in 1819 was also given the editorship of the newspaper *Tribüne*, another Cotta publication. In 1825 moved to Augsburg, and in 1827 to Munich, where he continued to edit *Europäische Annalen*. 1832 was appointed editor of the official Bavarian state newspaper. 415

List, Friedrich (1789–1846), German economist. 1817 professor of state administration at Tübingen; 1819 founded the *Deutsche Handels-und Gewerbeverein* to promote a customs union in Germany; for this reason dismissed from the service of the state. As a deputy for Württemberg calling for administrative reforms, was sentenced to prison in 1822 for sedition, and released in return for promising to migrate to America; 1832 returned to Germany, where he continued to work for a German customs union and the establishment of a railway network. 1831–1833 American consul in Baden, 1834–1837 in Saxony and 1845 in Württemberg. His *magnum opus*, *Das Nationale System der Politischen Ökonomie*, was published in 1841. 100n, 342, 390

Livesy, British messenger from Vienna [nothing further could be established]. 492

Loechner, *Königlich Württembergischer Obersteuerat* and Württemberg commissioner to the Commercial Union Congress at Berlin 1846. 397

Luther, Martin (1483–1546), reforming theologian. 291, 318

Luxburg, Friedrich Graf von (1783–1856), Bavarian diplomat. 1803 attached to the legation in Switzerland; 1806 secretary of legation in Switzerland, 1808 in St Petersburg and 1810 in Paris; 1813 envoy extraordinary and minister plenipotentiary to the imperial Westphalian court in Kassel; 1813 escaped from Kassel when the legation archive was burned; temporary retirement in 1814; 1816 envoy extraordinary and minister plenipotentiary in Dresden; 1826 also envoy extraordinary in Berlin; 1830–1846 envoy extraordinary and minister plenipotentiary in Paris, 1847–1849 in Vienna. 353

Mackenna, British subject [nothing further could be established]. 53

Magenis, Sir Arthur Charles (1801–1867), British diplomat. Attached to mission in Berlin, 26 August 1825; 1830–1838 attaché in St Petersburg; 1838–1844 secretary of legation in Switzerland; 1844–1851 secretary of embassy in Austria; 1851 minister plenipotentiary to the Swiss Confederation; 1852 envoy extraordinary and minister plenipotentiary to Stuttgart, 1854 to Sweden and Norway, and 1859–1866 to Lisbon. *525–529*

Malet, Sir Alexander Charles, second baronet (1800–1886), British diplomat. 1824 attaché in St Peterburg, 1827 in Paris, 1833 in Lisbon; 1835 secretary of legation in Sardinia, 1836 in The Hague. 1843 secretary of embassy in Vienna; 1845 envoy extraordinary and minister plenipotentiary in Stuttgart and Carlsruhe, and 1852–1866 at the German Confederation in Frankfurt. *393–400*, 402

Maltzahn, Mortimer Graf von (1793–1843), Prussian diplomat. 1822–1824 chargé d'affaires in Paris, 1826 in Darmstadt; from 1830 envoy extraordinary and minister plenipotentiary in The Hague, 1834–1841 in Vienna. 1841–1842 Prussian foreign minister. 188, 520

Manteuffel, Georg August Ernst von (1765–1842), Saxon statesman and diplomat. 1791 entered electoral Saxony's civil service; 1809 and 1813 member of the *Immediatskommission*, which carried out government during the King's absence; after the King's return, member of the *Geheime Consilium*; 1820 *Wirklicher Geheimrat* and president of the *Geheime Finanzcollegium*; 1828 *Konferenzminister*; 1830–1840 envoy to the *Bundestag* in Frankfurt. 3, 14–15, 46, 53, 95, 202

Maria Anna (1803–1884), daughter of King Victor Emanuel of

Sardinian Piedmont. 1831 married the successor to the Austrian throne, Ferdinand; from 1835 Empress of Austria. 515, 518

Maria Leopoldine (1803–1877), daughter of the Bavarian king, Maximilian I Joseph. 1833 married Crown Prince Friedrich August of Saxony; from 1836 Queen of Saxony. 310

Maria Theresia (1717–1780), Archduchess of Austria. From 1737 Grand Duchess of Tuscany, from 1740 Queen of Hungary and Bohemia, from 1745 Empress. 152

Marie (1825–1889), Princess of Prussia, daughter of Prince Wilhelm. 1842 married Prince Maximilian of Bavaria; after 1848 Queen of Bavaria. 444–445

Marie Alexandrine (1818–1907), daughter of ruling Duke Joseph of Saxe-Altenburg. 1843 married Georg von Cumberland, Crown Prince of Hanover, from 1851 Queen of Hanover. 279

Marie Luise Viktoria (1786–1861), Princess of Saxe-Coburg. Wife of Edward Duke of Kent, who died in 1820, and mother of Victoria, successor to the British throne. 310n

Marschall von Bieberstein, Ernst Freiherr (1770–1836), state minister of Hesse-Nassau from 1806–1836. 27

Marx, Karl (1818–1883), German philosopher. 100n

Matthiae, Ernst (1812–1837), student at Heidelberg. Took part in the Storming of the Frankfurt Guard House on 3 April 1833; 1836 sentenced to life imprisonment; 10 January 1837 escaped from Frankfurt prison. 83n, 84n

Maucler, Paul Friedrich Theodor Eugen Freiherr von (1783–1859), Württemberg statesman. 1806 member of the *Oberjustizkollegium*; 1808 *Kreishauptmann* in Ludwigsburg; 1810 *Obertribunalrat* in Tübingen; 1811 *Landvogt* in Calw; 1812 director of the *Criminaltribunal* in Eßlingen; 1816 *Hofkammerpräsident*; entered government after the change of sovereign, 1817 as privy councillor; from 1818 minister of justice; 1831–1848 president of the privy council; forced to resign by the revolution, but remained a member of the first chamber until his death. 368

Mauguin, Francois (1785–1854), French politician; from 1827 opposition deputy. After the July revolution of 1830, first a member of the provisional government, then again a member of the opposition.   501

Maurer, Georg Ludwig Ritter von (1790–1872), legal historian and statesman. From 1826 professor of civil law and the history of law at the University of Munich; 1829 member of the Council of State and *Geheimer Hofrat*; 1831 became lifetime member of the first chamber of the Bavarian *Landtag*. 1832–1834 member of the regency council for King Otto of Greece; 1847 became justice minister and foreign minister.   472, 476, 480

Maximilian (1759–1838), Prince of Saxony.   296

Maximilian I Joseph (1756–1825), 1795 Duke of Pfalz-Zweibrücken, 1799 Elector and 1806 King of Bavaria.   421

Maximilian II (1811–1864), King of Bavaria after the abdication of his father, Ludwig I, in 1848.   429n, 436–437, 441, 444, 458, 468, 477–478

Mazzini, Giuseppe (1805–1872), Italian revolutionary and republican. 1831 set up the secret organization, Young Italy; 1834, in Switzerland, whence he had fled after the failure of a plot, called on like-minded Europeans to join Young Europe, and to establish national secret organizations. In the same year went into exile in London. 1848 returned to Italy, only to flee abroad again after the collapse of the revolution. Subsequently took part in unsuccessful uprisings in Mantua (1852), Milan (1853), and Piedmont (1858). On Garibaldi's side in the struggle for Italian unification.   72

Mehmet Ali (1769–1849), from 1805 Ottoman Governor of Egypt. In 1841 he made the position of governor hereditary.   181n, 188n

Meidinger, Herrman (died 1898), bookseller. He was appointed at the Hambach Festival to superintend the revolutionary interest in Frankfurt and the duchy of Nassau.   24

Melanchton, Philipp (1497–1560), German humanist, reforming theologian and first systematizer of Lutheranism; author of fundamental confessions of faith.   222

Merkel, mayor and deputy of the city of Dassel and Duchy of Hohstein in second chamber of the Hanoverian *Landtag*. Resigned his seat in 1839 during the constitutional conflict.   262

Metternich, Clemens Wenzel Fürst von (1773–1859), Austrian statesman. 1809 foreign minister, 1821 *Haus-, Hof-* and *Staatskanzler*; from 1826 head of the ministry for home affairs, thus effectively head of state. Created and directed the German Confederation as a defence against moves towards a national state; supported the principle of restoration. This also meant re-establishing dispossessed ruling families as heads of state and securing the re-established order against aggression and revolution. As a reactionary, he had to flee to England in 1848. ix, x, 50, 120, 126n, 130–131, 136–137, 165, 169, 175, 188, 194–195, 204, 215, 284–285, 306n, 380, 402, 479, 481, 491–508, 510–514, 516–525, 529–531

Meyer, Joel Wolff, trader in Berlin [nothing further could be established]. 148

Mieg, Arnold Ritter von (1778–1842), Bavarian civil servant, politician and diplomat. 1823 *Ministerialrat* in the ministry of the interior, from 1826 *Generalkommissär* of the Rezat circle in Ansbach. 1832–1833 as finance minister was one of the driving forces behind the creation of the German Customs Union. From his resignation in April 1833 until his death, envoy to the German *Bundestag* in Frankfurt. 85, 93, 413, 421, 428

Mieroslawski, Ludwik (1814–1878), Polish writer and revolutionary who lived in France from 1832 after the failure of the November uprising. 1845 went to Posen to unleash a pan-European uprising; 1846 arrested, 1847 condemned to death in Berlin, pardoned in 1848 during the revolution; 1849 took part in the Italian war of independence; from the end of 1849 – with one break in 1863 – in Parisian exile again. 221

Milbanke, Sir John Ralph (1800–1868), British diplomat. 1823 clerk in the foreign office; 1826 secretary of legation at Frankfurt; 1835 secretary of embassy in St Petersburg, and 1838 in Vienna; 1843 envoy extraordinary and minister plenipotentiary in Munich and 1862 in The Hague. xii, xiv, 9, 447–450, 454, 455–485

Minckwitz, Johannes von (1787–1857), 1819–1822 minister of state in the kingdom of Saxony and envoy in Berlin; 1830–1843 foreign minister of the kingdom of Saxony. 293, 303, 305

Minto, Earl of see **Elliot**

Molé, Louis-Mathieu, comte de (1780–1855), French politician and prime minister 1836–1839. 161, 176

Molyneux, Francis George, British secretary of legation at the German Confederation in Frankfurt 1835–1847. xx, *84–85, 93–94, 96–97, 102–104, 108*

Montez, Lola (1818–1861), real name Marie Dolores Gilbert, dancer. Her relationship with the Bavarian king, Ludwig I, who made her Countess of Landsfeld, precipitated a government crisis in Bavaria in 1847. February 1848 she fled to Switzerland, thereafter touring Europe and North America where she settled permanently in 1852. 472–474

Montgelas, Maximilian Josef Graf von (1759–1838), most important statesman of enlightened absolutism in Bavaria. 1799 responsible for Bavaria's domestic and foreign policy as *Geheimer Staats- und Konferenzminister* under Maximilian I Joseph; 1803–1806 and 1809–1817 also finance minister; from 1806 minister of home affairs and cultural affairs; removed from office in 1817 while preparing the new constitution. 431

Moore, Thomas (1779–1852), Irish poet. After publishing *A Selection of Irish Melodies* (1808–1834), a collection which drew on old Irish melodies, he was celebrated as the 'Irish bard'. 200

Moré, Hermann Friedrich (*1814), student at Heidelberg. Took part in the Storming of the Frankfurt Guard House on 3 April 1833; sentenced to life imprisonment in 1836. 83n

Moßdorf, Bernhard (1802–1833), after studying at Leipzig, lawyer in Dresden. Leader of the *Bürgerverein*, established in December 1830. After his arrest on 18 April 1832, sentenced to fifteen years' imprisonment. 299–300

Motz, Gerhard Heinrich (1776–1868), finance minister in electoral Hesse. 1798 entered the service of the Landgraviate of Hesse-Kassel; 1821 *Vortragender Ministerialrat* in the Kassel ministry of state; 1831 finance minister; temporarily also filled the posts of justice minister and foreign minister; retired in 1848. Contributed substantially to the fact that electoral Hesse sought a compromise with Prussia and entered the Customs Union in 1831. 59

Müller, Heinrich Moritz, merchant, leading member of the Dresden *Bürgerverein.* 299

Müller, Joseph (from 1845 Ritter von) (1792–1862), from 1817 member of the Prague municipal council; mayor from 1839 to 1848. 1848 resigned for political reasons, and subsequently became Moravian-

Silesian *Appellationsrat*, later *Hofrat* at the highest law court in Vienna. 526

Münch-Bellinghausen, Joachim Graf von (1786–1866), Austrian civil servant. 1815 sent to France as *Gouvernementscommissär* for the *départements* of l'Ain and Montblanc; 1819 captain of town militia in Prague, then *Hofrat* with the ministry for foreign affairs; 1822–1848 minister plenipotentiary and presidential envoy at *Bundestag* in Frankfurt; 1831 elevated to Austrian nobility; 1841 appointed minister of state; 1861 named lifelong member of Austrian upper chamber. 3, 6, 12, 18–19, 28, 30–35, 38–40, 66n, 69, 71n, 76, 94–95, 97, 106, 108, 416, 493, 500, 502

Münchhausen, Börries Wilhelm von (1794–1849), Hanoverian diplomat. From 1831 envoy extraordinary and minister plenipotentiary at the Prussian and Saxon courts, 1837–1840 in London. 123

Münster, Ernst Friedrich Herbert Graf von (1766–1839), Hanoverian statesman. 1801–1804 envoy to St Petersburg; minister of state and cabinet minister of the English King in Hanover; dismissed as a leading minister after protests against the old feudal system in Hanover 1830/31. 4

Mundt, Theodor (1808–1881), poet, historian and member of the political-literary movement, *Junges Deutschland*; became professor at Breslau (1848) and Berlin (1850). 76

Murray, Charles Augustus (1806–1895), British diplomat and writer. 1838 appointed Her Majesty's Master of the Household; 1844 secretary of legation at Naples; 1846 consul general in Egypt; 1853 British envoy in Switzerland; 1854 envoy to Tehran; 1859 envoy in Saxony; 1866 envoy to Denmark, and 1867 to Portugal. 524

Muth, Peter Edler von (1784–1855), Austrian official. 1817 commissioner of police in Brno, 1835 in Prague; 1845–1848 chief commissioner of police in Vienna. 527

Nagler, Karl Ferdinand Friedrich von (1770–1846), Prussian diplomat and statesman, in the service of the Margrave of Ansbach and Bayreuth. 1809 deputy post-master general, then *Geheimer Staatsrat*; 1821 president of the general post office, 1823 post-master general, also elevated to nobility; 1824–1834 envoy to the *Bundestag* (Federal Diet); 1836 appointed *Geheimer Staatsminister*. 3, 6, 21, 27, 66, 68, 71

Palmerston see **Temple**, Henry John

Pechlin von Löwenbach, Friedrich Christian Freiherr (1789–1863), Danish envoy for the Duchies of Holstein and Lauenburg at the *Bundestag* in Frankfurt, 1825–1839 and 1846–1848. 51, 52

Peel, Sir Robert (1788–1850), British politician. 1821–1827 home secretary in the Liverpool cabinet and under Wellington in 1828–1830. After his first term as prime minister, from November 1834 to April 1835, Peel attempted to reorganize the Tory party. 1841–1846 again headed the government. As an advocate of free trade, abolished the Corn Laws in 1846. Rejection of the Irish Bill precipitated his resignation on 29 June 1846. 206n, 220–221, 342, 397, 427n

Perier, Casimir Pierre (1777–1832), French statesman. Under King Louis Philippe he was minister without portfolio in 1830, and prime minister in 1831. 356

Peter, Joseph Ignatz (1789–1872), civil servant and politician in Baden. 1845–1849 deputy in the second chamber of the Baden *Landtag*; 1841 could not take his seat as the Baden government refused to grant him leave from his position as *Oberhofgerichtsrat* in Mannheim. April 1848 took part in the first Baden uprising; thereafter deputy in the *Vorparlament* and the national assembly in Frankfurt. During the second Baden uprising from May to June 1849, headed the ministry of justice, was a member of the provisional government, and a member of the secret war commission. Fled to Switzerland in July 1849; later condemned to twenty years imprisonment for high treason; amnestied in 1862. 383

Petersen (Peterson), Francis Henry British vice-consul at Schwerin 1834–1848. 227

Pfeiffer, Burkhard Wilhelm (1777–1852), jurist, archivist and politican, from 1803 in the service of electoral Hesse. 1831 deputy and president of the diet of electoral Hesse, and after it was dissolved in 1843, chairman of the permanent committee. 25

Pfizer, Paul Achatius (1801–1867), jurist and politician. 1823 entered the service of the state of Württemberg; expelled in 1831. 1831–1848 leader of the liberal opposition, until 1838 deputy in the second chamber of the Württemberg estates, and contributor to various newspapers, including *Der Freisinnige*. 1848–1849 deputy in the *Vorparlament* in Frankfurt and the national assembly; 1848 headed the Württemberg ministry of culture, education and church affairs; 1848–1850 member of the supreme court; 1851–1858 *Oberjustizrat* in Tübingen.   355

Philippi, Karl Ferdinand (1795–1852), journalist and publisher of numerous literary and political journals in Grimma (Saxony).   302

Piret de Bihain, Ludwig Freiherr von (1783–1862), Austrian general. From 1833 commander of the federal troops in the free city of Frankfurt; later commander of the Hungarian fortress at Temesvar.   64

Pius VIII (1761–1830), real name Francesco Saverio Castiglioni; elected Pope in 1829.   169–170

Platen-Hallermund, Karl Graf von (1810–1887), estate owner, chamberlain at the Hanoverian court. Member of the first chamber of the Hanoverian *Landtag*, and its president during the Hanoverian constitutional conflict (1838–1840).   255

Platen-Hallermund, Gustav Graf von (1814–1889), Hanoverian officer.   283

Ponsonby, John (1770–1855), second Baron Ponsonby 1806, Viscount Ponsonby 1839, British diplomat. 1826–1828 envoy to the Argentine Republic, 1828–1829 to Brazil; 1830–1831 joint commissioner from the conference of London to Belgium; 1832–1833 minister plenipotentiary to the Two Sicilies; 1832–1841 ambassador to Turkey, 1846–1850 to Austria.   *529–532*

Quante, Andreas, from Würzburg, legal adviser to Baron von Frankenstein [nothing further could be established].   42

Radowitz, Joseph Maria von (1797–1853), Prussian officer and diplomat. From 1812 pursued a military career in Westphalia, electoral Hesse and Prussia, where, in 1828, he became a major on the general staff in Berlin. Co-founder and contributor to the weekly *Berliner politisches Wochenblatt.* 1836–1848 Prussian military plenipotentiary at the *Bundestag* in Frankfurt ; 1842–1848 also envoy extraordinary and minister plenipotentiary in Karlsruhe. In 1848–1849 deputy in the Frankfurt national assembly, where he joined the extreme right. From September to November 1850 he was briefly Prussian foreign minister.   166, 212, 389, 438

Rätzsch, Friedrich August (died 1848), community judge in Dresden.   294n

Rauch, Christian Daniel (1777–1857), sculptor. Received commissions from all over Europe, and his equestrian statue of Friedrich II (1851) was the most significant large piece of sculpture in nineteenth-century Berlin. As the founder of the Berlin School of Sculpture, he was at the centre of Berlin's artistic life in his lifetime. 184

Rauschenplatt, Ernst Johann Hermann von (1807–1868), lawer, qualified to teach at a German university in 1830 at the University of Göttingen. After the failed uprising in Göttingen in 1831, initially remained in contact with the opposition movement in Germany and Europe. 1840 switched political camps, joining Metternich's secret police in Strasburg. 1848 worked against the Baden revolutionaries, and returned to Hanover in 1851. 10, 44

Rechberg, Graf Ludwig von, *aide de camp* to Ludwig I, King of Bavaria. 441

Reichenbach, Emilie Gräfin (1791–1843), originally Emilie Ortlöpp, daughter of a businessman from Berlin. From 1820 had a relationship with Crown Prince Wilhelm of Hesse-Kassel, who, after acceding to the throne in 1821 as Prince Elector Wilhelm II, elevated her to the rank of countess, and, in 1841, after the death of the Princess Elector Auguste, married her (morganatically). 13

Reitzenstein, Sigismund Freiherr von (1766–1847), statesman from Baden. 1788 entered the service of the state of Baden; in 1803 ambassador to Paris, where he successfully pursued the enlargement of Baden. As minister of state, he devoted himself in 1809–1810 to building up a centralized administration on the French model. After his appointment to a second term in 1813 Reitzenstein secured Baden's territorial status quo in an international treaty with Austria. His third period of office, 1832–1842, was determined by the policy of the restoration. 359, 363

Renouard de Bussière, Jules Edmond Louis, baron (1804–1888), from 1836 to 1845 French envoy extraordinary and minister plenipotentiary at the Saxon court in Dresden. 310

Rey, Lucien (*1805), French advocate and politician. Took part in the Hambach Festival in 1832 as the representative of the Straburg association *Amis du Peuples*. 23n

Richarz, Johann Peter von (1781–1855), Catholic priest. 1835–1836 bishop of Speyer; from 1836 bishop of Augsburg. 442, 475

Riedel, Valentin von (1802–1857), Catholic priest. 1842–1857 bishop of Regensburg. 448

Rochau, August Ludwig von (1810–1873), jurist. As a student, took part in the Storming of the Frankfurt Guard House on 3 April 1833; 1836 sentenced to life imprisonment. One day after the publication of his sentence, escaped from prison in Frankfurt and fled to France. Returned to Germany in 1848; 1870–1873 deputy in the *Reichstag*. 83–84

Rödinger, Johann Friedrich (1800–1868), jurist and journalist. After legal studies, judge 1826–1828, legal adviser in Stuttgart 1828–1853. From 1830 published and co-edited the newspaper *Der Hochwächter*; 1833 faced criminal proceedings for breaking the censorship laws. 1831 was prevented from taking his seat in the Württemberg chamber of deputies because of a past prison sentence; 1848–1849 deputy in the Frankfurt *Vorparlament* and national assembly; 1848–1868 deputy in the Württemberg second chamber, while also working as a journalist in Stuttgart. 354

Rönne, Friedrich Ludwig von (1798–1865), diplomat, Prussian politician. 1820 entered the Prussian legal service; 1834–1843 resident minister in Washington; 1843 president of the trade office in Berlin and member of council of state; 1848 elected to the Frankfurt national assembly, chairing the political economy committee; 1848–1857 extraordinary ambassador in Washington; 1859–1865 seat in the Prussian house of deputies as a Liberal, from 1861 as a member of the *Fortschrittspartei* (Progress Party). 208, 227

Ronge, Johannes (1813–1887), theologian and leader of the *Deutschkatholiken* (German Catholics). After completing his studies, curate from 1840, admonished by the official Catholic Church in 1841 for freethinking doctrines, and suspended in 1843 for publishing an article in the *Sächsiche Vaterlandsblätter*. 1844 excommunicated for an open letter to the bishop of Trier in which he argued against exhibiting the Holy Garment in Trier; 1845 founded the *Deutsch-Katholische Kirche* in Breslau. 1848 joined the political left in in Frankfurt; 1849 fled to England. 1861 returned to Germany; 1863 founded the *Religiöse Reformverein zum Kampf gegen Pfaffentum* (religious reform association to combat papacy). 102–103, 229, 328n, 333, 394n

Rother, Christian (von) (1778–1849), Prussian statesman. 1810 appointed to the state chancellery by Hardenberg; from then on one of his most loyal colleagues, involved in finance reforms and work on general constitutional questions; 1817 member of the council of state; 1820 president of the new administration of the national debt, and president of the independent *Seehandlung* bank; influential in matters of state debts and credits; 1835–1837 head of the trade office; 1836 *Geheimer Staatsminister*, 1837 also head of the *Preußische Bank*; remained in this position under Friedrich Wilhelm IV until dismissed in March 1848. 217, 223–224

Rothschild, Amschel Mayer Freiherr von (1773–1855), private banker in Frankfurt. 51, 447

Rothschild, Salomon Mayer Freiherr von (1774–1855), private banker, from 1816 in Vienna. 526n

Rotteck, Karl Rodecker von (1775–1840), historian, political scientist, liberal journalist, politician. 1798 professor of world history, from 1818 professor of political science, of 'natural, private, public, and international law' at the University of Freiburg im Breisgau and the university's deputy in the first chamber of the Baden *Landtag*; 1831–1840 deputy in the second chamber; from 1832 professorship suspended; from 1834 edited the *Staats-Lexikon oder Encyclopaedie der Staatswissenschaften* with Karl Theodor Welcker, his colleague from Freiburg. 25, 78, 358n

Rubner (died 1834), student from Wunsiedel. Took part in the Storming of the Frankfurt Guard House; died while attempting to escape from prison in Frankfurt. 63n

Rüdt von Collenberg-Bödigheim, Ludwig Freiherr (1799–1885), Baden diplomat. Began his diplomatic career in 1826 at the Baden mission to the German *Bundestag* in Frankfurt; 1834–1843 envoy extraordinary and minister plenipotentiary in Stuttgart, from 1838 also in Berne; 1843–1848 minister resident in Munich; 1849–1856 Baden's foreign minister; 1856–1861 envoy extraordinary and minister plenipotentiary in Vienna. 384, 480

Rüdt von Collenberg-Eberstadt, Franz Freiherr (1789–1860), Baden statesman. Official in the ministry of the interior from 1824, 1838–1844 minister of the interior. 384

Rumann, Wilhelm (1784–1857), Hanoverian politician. After studying at Göttingen, entered the Hanoverian civil service. 1824 became *Stadtdirektor* of Hanover, suspended in 1838 in the course of the Hanoverian constitutional conflict, and pensioned off in 1841. 1826 elected to the second chamber of the *Landtag*, 1831 became its president and headed the parliamentary commission to prepare the new state basic law. Reelected to the second chamber in 1848. 259–261, 276–277

Rupp, Julius (1809–1845), Protestant theologian and lecturer at the University of Königsberg. Most significant philosopher of the free-thinking movement. After being dismissed from his office as a clergyman in 1845, founded the *Königsberger Freigemeinde*, the first religious community to opt out of the Prussian system of a state church. 229–230

Russell, Lord George William (1790–1846), after a military career, British diplomat from 1831. 1834 envoy extraordinary and minister plenipotentiary to Stuttgart, 1835–1841 to Berlin. *140–170, 172–177, 179–198, 370–374,* 427

Rust, Johann Nepomuk (1775–1840), surgeon and ophthamologist. 1803 professor at the University of Cracow; 1812 chief surgeon at the *Allgemeine Krankenhaus* (general hospital) in Vienna; 1816 head of the newly established surgical ophthamological clinic in the *Charité* hospital; 1822 major general of the army's medical corps; 1824 professor at the University of Berlin; from 1831 he studied and fought the cholera that was spreading from Russia to Prussia; 1837 *Wirklicher Geheimer Obermedicinalrat.* 115

Sainte Aulaire, Louis Clair, comte de (1778–1854), French politician, writer and diplomat. Ambassador in Rome 1831, in Vienna 1833 and in London 1841–1847. From 1841 member of the *Academie Française.* 137, 509

Sandizell, Cajetan Graf von und zu (1782–1863), hereditary *Reichsrat* of the Bavarian Crown, *Obersthofmeister* and *Oberst-Ceremonienmeister* of the King. 410

Satori, Ignatz (*1811), student in Würzburg. Took part in the Storming of the Frankfurt Guard House on 3 April 1833. 1836 sentenced to life imprisonment; escaped from Frankfurt jail on 10 January 1837. 83n, 84n

Sauerwein, Johann Wilhelm (1803–1847), writer and journalist. Studied theology, then from late 1820s journalist in Frankfurt. Co-founder and editor of various oppositional periodicals. 1834 fled to Switzerland, 1835 to France where he taught German and English at a grammar school until 1844. 24

Savoye, Joseph (1802–1869), lawyer at the court of appeal in Zweibrücken. Co-founder of the *Press- und Vaterlandsverein*. Took part in the Hambach Festival. Thereafter fled to France. 26

Sayn-Wittgenstein-Hohenstein, Wilhelm Ludwig Georg Graf (from 1804) Fürst zu (1770–1851), Prussian official and statesmen. 1797–1805 Queen's *Oberhofmeister*; 1812 *Geheimer Staatsrat* in charge of the police; 1814–1819 minister for the police; 1819–1851 minister of the royal house; supported reactionary trends. 160, 174, 183–184, 194

Schaf, farmer, deputy representing the farmers of Calenberg in the second chamber of the Hanoverian *Landtag*. Resigned his seat in 1839 during the constitutional conflict. 262

Schaffrath, Wilhelm Michael (1814–1893), jurist and Saxon politician. Deputy in the Saxon *Landtag* 1845–1849 and 1871–1875. 1848/49 deputy in the *Vorparlament* and the Frankfurt national asssembly; 1867–1869, 1871–1874 and 1878/79 deputy in the *Reichstag*. 338, 340

Schele zu Schelenburg, Georg Victor Freiherr von (1771–1844), Hanoverian statesman and politician. As a deputy representing the knights of Osnabrück in the Hanoverian *Landtag*, in 1818 successfully called for the reintroduction of the provincial diets and the bicameral constitution in the new Hanoverian constitution (1819). 1820 president of the *Obersteuer- und Schatzkollegiums*; 1822 member of the *Geheime Rat*; from 1833 member of the first chamber of the Hanoverian *Landtag*. 1837–1844 cabinet minister and foreign minister under King Ernst August. 257, 262, 272, 274

Schenk, Eduard von (1788–1841), Bavarian statesman. From 1818 official in the Bavarian Ministry of Justice; switched to the ministry of the interior 1825; 1828 minister of the interior. After his resignation in 1831, *Generalkommissär* and *Regierungspräsident* of the Regen circle; 1838 also member of the council of state. In addition to his political work, a writer and poet; for a time Ludwig I's closest adviser on culture policy. 415

Schlöffel, Friedrich Wilhelm, factory owner and journalist in Hirschberg, Silesia. Because of his commitment to the lower classes, Schlöffel was suspected by the Prussian government of having been one of the initiators of the Silesian weavers' uprising in 1844; 1846 he was cleared of all accusations. 214

Schön, Heinrich Theodor von (1773–1856), Prussian civil servant. 1813 appointed governor of the *Länder* between the Russian border and the Vistula; in 1816 *Oberpräsident* of the new province of West Prussia, seat in Danzig. After unification of the two Prussias to form the province of Prussia, *Oberpräsident* in Königsberg (until 1842). 190, 195, 196

Schönburg-Hartenstein, Heinrich Eduard Fürst zu (1787–1872), Austrian envoy extraordinary and minister plenipotentiary in Stuttgart 1825–1837. 492–493

Schönlein, Johann Lukas (1793–1864), medical doctor and professor in Würzburg (1825–1832), Zurich, and Berlin (1840–1859), where he was also personal physician to the Prussian king, Friedrich Wilhelm IV. 387–388

Schramm, Karl Friedrich Wilhelm, merchant, leading member of the Dresden *Bürgerverein*. 299

Schreder, Andrej Andrejewitsch (*1783), Russian diplomat; envoy extraordinary and minister plenipotentiary in Dresden 1829–1859, simultaneously accredited to Hanover until 1847. 301, 314

Schrenck von Notzing, Karl Freiherr von (1806–1884), Bavarian diplomat and politician. From 1834 official in the ministry of the interior; 1845 president of the administrative district of the Palatinate; 1846 succeeded his father as justice minister; December 1846 until his resignation in March 1847 also head of the minstry for church affairs. 1847 president of the administrative district of Upper Palatinate and Regensburg; 1848 deputy in the Frankfurt national assembly; 1848–1850 president of the administrative district of Lower Bavaria; 1851–1859 and 1864–1866 envoy to the German *Bundestag* in Frankfurt; 1859–1864 foreign minister and head of the council of ministers; 1870–1871 envoy extraordinary and minister plenipotentiary in Vienna; 1872 president of the first chamber of the Bavarian *Landtag*, of which he was a member from 1866 to 1884. 469, 472

Schrenck von Notzing, Sebastian Freiherr von (1774–1848), jurist. Studied law at the University of Ingolstadt until 1792; from 1796 in the judicial service. 1811 *Oberappellationsgerichtsrat* in Munich; 1819 deputy in the second chamber of the *Landtag* and its president until 1837; 1820 *Ministerialrat* in justice ministry; 1827 president of the court of appeal for Regensburg administrative distict in Amberg; 1832–1846 minister of state for justice. 468–469

Schulz, Carl Gustav (died 1856), Prussian military officer, writer and journalist. 1832–1838 editor of the Berlin *Politisches Wochenblatt*. 172

Schuster, Theodor (*1808), jurist and physician. 1830 *Habilitation* at the University of Göttingen. After the failure of the Göttingen uprising in 1831, fled to France where achieved a leading position in the *Bund* *der Deutschen.* Studied medicine in Paris, and lived there until 1866.   10

Schwanthaler, Ludwig von (1802–1848), Bavarian sculptor and graphic artist.   439

Seinsheim, Karl August Graf von (1784–1864), Bavarian statesman. 1832–1840 president of the administrative district of Upper Bavaria; 1827–1843 deputy in the second chamber; 1840–1843 its president; 1840–1847 Bavarian finance minister in Abel's cabinet.   472, 479

Senckendorff-Gutend, Theodor Graf von (1802–1858), Prussian diplomat. 1841 envoy extraordinary and minister plenipotentiary in Hanover, 1847 in Brussels, 1852 in Stuttgart and 1858 in Munich.   275, 277

Senfft von Pilsach, Friedrich Christian Ludwig Graf (1774–1853), diplomat. Electoral Saxony's ambassador to Paris in 1806, and subsequently, on Napoleon's request, Saxon foreign minister. 1814–1815 transferred to the Austrian civil service; from 1826 in Turin as Austrian envoy extraordinary and minister plenipotentiary; from 1832 in Florence; from 1837 in The Hague and 1843–1847 in Munich.   448, 470, 480

Seuffert, Johann Adam von (1794–1857), jurist and politician. 1819 professor at the University of Würzburg; 1831 delegated to the Bavarian *Landtag* by the university; 1832 tranferred to Straubing for disciplinary reasons because of his democratic attitude as a judge, and relieved of his teaching post. 1839 gave up his job for health reasons, and worked as a journalist in Munich.   41

Shee, Sir George (1784–1870), British diplomat. 1830–1834 undersecretary of state in the Foreign Office, 1836–1844 envoy extraordinary and minister plenipotentiary in Stuttgart.   *374–376, 379–387,* 388, *391–393*

Siebenpfeiffer, Philipp Jakob (1789–1845), jurist and journalist; co-initiator of the Hambach Festival in 1832. Arrested 1832, fled to Switzerland in 1833, where he became a professor of criminal law at Berne.   21–22, 25

Sieveking, Karl (1787–1847), Hamburg diplomat. 1819–1821 minister resident in St Petersburg; from 1820 head diplomat of the Free City of Hamburg; 1831–1838 and 1841–1844 envoy to the German *Bundestag* in Frankfurt.   15–17

Smidt, Johann (1773–1857), statesman from Bremen, member of the Bremen senate from 1800. 1814–1815 took part in the Congress of Vienna; from 1816 envoy from the Hanse town Bremen to the German Confederation; 1821 became second mayor of Bremen.   51

Solms-Braunfels, Karl Wilhelm Bernhard Prinz zu (1800–1868), son of Queen Frederike of Hanover by her first marriage. 1839 appointed president of the council of Hanover.   140, 235, 256

Speßhardt, Haubold Hans Carl von (1797–1860), deputy in the *Landtag* of Saxe-Coburg-Gotha. 1834–1839 and 1844–1848 director of the *Landtag*; 1848 minister in Saxe-Meiningen, thereafter colonel and aide-de-camp to the Duke of Meiningen.   337

Spiegel zum Desenberg, Ferdinand August Graf (1764–1835), Catholic priest. 1813 bishop of Münster; 1817 member of council of state; 1819 *wirklicher Geheimer Rat*; 1824 archbishop of Cologne.   169–170

Stein, Dietrich Carl August Freiherr von (1793–1867), from 1835 member of the executive committee of the government of the Duchy of Saxe-Coburg-Gotha. January–October 1840 and 1846–1849 headed the ministry of state.   343

Steinsdorf, Kaspar von (1797–1879). After a career in the Bavarian justice service, became Munich's second mayor in 1837, and from 1854 to 1870 first mayor of Munich.   457

Stephan, Martin (1777–1846), theologian. From 1810, as pastor to the Bohemian community in Dresden, advocated extreme Lutheran doctrine. 1838 emigrated to the USA with 700 supporters, and allowed himself to be made bishop of his community there; deposed in 1839 for sexual immorality and embezzlement.   317, 331

Stralenheim, Karl Friedrich Freiherr von (1777–1848), Hanoverian diplomat. 1817–1842 envoy extraordinary and minister plenipotentiary to the Free City of Frankfurt; at the same time, 1827–1843, envoy to the German *Bundestag* in Frankfurt, and accredited in Munich and Württemberg 1832–1838.   3–4, 6, 10, 85, 92, 261

Strohmeyer, clerk, and 1838–1839 deputy representing the landowners of Grubenhagen in second chamber of the Hanover *Landtag*.   257

Stüve, Johann Carl Betram (1798–1872), jurist and politician. From

1824 deputy in Hanover's second chamber; 1833 mayor of Osnabrück; 1837 stood out because of his resistance to the repeal of the basic law to whose drafting he had contributed; 1848 minister for the interior, but resistance from conservatives forced him to resign in 1850; mayor of Osnabrück again 1852–1864. 260

Sulivan, Stephen Henry (1812–1857), British diplomat, secretary of legation in Munich 1839–1840. *433–437, 445–447, 450–455*

Tafel, Johann Friedrich Gottlob (1801–1874), jurist and politician. After studying law, legal consultant in Stuttgart 1826–1874. 1830–1864 publisher and co-editor of the newspaper *Der Hochwächter* (from 1833 *Der Beobachter*). 1831 not permitted to take his seat in the Württemberg chamber of deputies because of a past prison sentence; 1848–1849 deputy in the Frankfurt *Vorparlament* and national assembly; 1848–1849, 1851–1855 and 1864–1868 deputy in the Württemberg second chamber; 1868–1871 deputy in the *Reichstag*. 354

Tauffkirchen-Kleberg, Leopold Ernst Graf von, Bavarian major general and deputy in the Bavarian second chamber. 409

Taylor, Sir Brook (1776–1846), British diplomat. Envoy extraordinary and minister plenipotentiary in Stuttgart (1814–1820), Munich (1820–1828), and Berlin (1828–1831). *113–114*

Temple, Henry John (1784–1865), British statesman. Became third Viscount Palmerston in 1802; secretary at war 1809–1828. Secretary of state for foreign affairs in the Whig cabinets led by Earl Grey (1830–1834), Viscount Melbourne (1835– 1841) and Lord John Russell (1846–1851). 1851 home secretary in Lord Aberdeen's coalition cabinet; 1855–1858 and 1859–1865 prime minister. ix, x, xi, xiii, *10–74, 76–98, 105–110, 114–131, 133–138, 139–197, 223–248, 251–273, 283–287, 297–320, 339–344, 348–370, 372–384, 398–404, 408–422, 424–440,* 442, *470–485, 492–522, 529–532*

Therese Charlotte Luise, (1792–1854), daughter of Duke Friedrich zu Sachsen-Hildburghausen. Married Crown Prince Ludwig of Bavaria in 1810; from 1825 Queen of Bavaria. 440, 442

Thielau, Friedrich Erdmann August von (1792–1848), deputy in the Saxon second chamber; 1847 vice president. 319, 338

Thiers, Adolphe (1797–1877), French politician. 1832–1834 minister of the interior, president of the council of ministers for short spells in

1836 and 1840. 1848 elected to the national assembly and became leader of the 'party of order'. As an opponent of Louis-Napoleon's *coup d'état*, banished from France until the summer of 1852; returned to political life in 1863 as deputy in the national assembly for Paris; 1871–1873 president of the Republic. 181, 193, 380

Thomas, Gerhard (1785–1838), senior mayor of Frankfurt in 1832, 1835 and 1838. 74

Todt, Carl Gottlob (1803–1852), mayor and city judge in Adorf (Vogtland); from 1836 deputy in the second chamber of the Saxon *Landtag*; considered as the father of liberalism in Saxony. 338

Trautmannsdorff-Weinsberg, Joseph Graf von (1788–1870), Austrian diplomat. 1815 envoy extraordinary and minister plenipotentiary in Karlsruhe, 1818 in Stuttgart, 1820 in Munich and 1827–1849 in Berlin. 1861 made a lifetime member of the upper chamber of the Austrian *Reichsrat*. 130

Trott zu Solz, August Heinrich Freiherr von (1783–1840). Subprefect of the new kingdom of Westphalia in Eschwege in 1808; 1809 prefect of the Harz department, in the same year transferred to Marburg; 1818 *geheimer Legationsrat* in foreign ministry in Stuttgart; 1819–1820 took part in the Vienna conferences at which the Final Act was constituted; 1821 appointed *Staatsrat* and on 1 May 1824 envoy to the *Bundestag*; attended its deliberations until his death. 93, 368

Tschech, Heinrich Ludwig (1789–1844), mayor of Storkow in the Brandenburg Marches. Executed in December 1844 because of an assassination attempt on King Friedrich Wilhelm IV. 210

Ungern-Sternberg, Ernst Wilhelm Rembert Freiherr von (1794–1879), Russian diplomat. After a military career, from 1823 secretary of legation with postings to Madrid, London and Berlin. 1834–1847 resident in the Republic of Cracow; 1847 Russian ambassador in Stockholm; 1860 at the German *Bundestag* in Frankfurt; from 1866 in Dresden. 141, 143

Varnbüler von und zu Hemmingen, Karl Eberhard Friedrich Freiherr von (1776–1832), one of the pioneers of modern agriculture in south Germany; 1827–1832 Württemberg's finance minister. 356

Vayhinger, *Finanzrat* and Württemberg commissioner to the Commercial Union Congress at Carlsruhe, October 1845. [nothing further could be established]. 396

Viale-Prelà, Michele (1798–1860), papal diplomat. 1838–1845 nuncio in Munich, 1845–1855 in Vienna; 1841–1853 titular archbishop of Carthage; Cardinal in 1853; from 1855 archbishop of Bologna. 441, 448

Victoria (1819–1901), Queen of England (1837) and Empress of India (1876). 187, 310n, 524

Voltz, Ludwig Friedrich von (1791–1872), Bavarian official and politician. *Ministerialrat* in the Bavarian ministry of the interior 1836–1849; *Regierungspräsident* of Middle Franconia 1849–1853; council of state 1853. 456

Waldkirch, Klemens August Graf von (1806–1858), Bavarian diplomat. After studying law, initially secretary of legation in Berlin 1835; 1837–1841 chargé d'affaires in Athens; 1841–1845 envoy extraordinary and minister plenipotentiary in Dresden and Weimar, and 1845–1847 in Karlsruhe. In March and April 1848 briefly head of the Bavarian foreign ministry. 331

Wallerstein see **Oettingen-Wallerstein**

Wangenheim, Karl August Freiherr von (1773–1850), Württemberg diplomat and statesman. From 1806 in the service of the Württemberg King as president of the *Oberfinanzkammer*. 1811 president of the *Obertribunal* and *Kurator* of the University of Tübingen; 1816–1817 minister for cultural affairs; 1818–1823 Württemberg's envoy to the *Bundestag* in Frankfurt, where he opposed Metternich's policies and advocated a German customs union. Deputy of the Württemberg second chamber. 354–355

Ward, Edward Michael (1789–1832), British diplomat. 1816–1823 secretary of legation and chargé d'affaires in Lisbon; 1824–1825 secretary of embassy in St Petersburg; 1828–1832 envoy extraordinary and minister plenipotentiary in Dresden. *291–299*

Watzdorf, Otto Friedrich von (1801–1860), jurist and landowner. Member of the old Saxon *Landtag* (Diet) 1830–1831; 1839–1843 deputy in the second chamber; 1844–1850 in the first chamber of the Saxon *Landtag*; 1848 deputy in the Frankfurt *Vorparlament*. 302

Wellesley, Sir Henry, 1828 first Baron Cowley (1773–1847), British diplomat; brother of Duke of Wellington. Began his diplomatic career in Stockholm as secretary of legation; 1807 MP; 1808–1809 one of the secretaries to the Treasury; 1809 sworn into the privy council; 1809 secretary to the embassy in Spain, later envoy extraordinary, 1811 appointed ambassador; 1812 knighted; 1815 created GCB; 1823–1831 ambassador to Vienna; 1835 ambassador to Paris. *489–492*

Wellington see **Wellesley**, Arthur

Werther, Heinrich August Alexander Wilhelm Freiherr von (1772–1859), Prussian diplomat. 1810 entered the diplomatic service after serving in the Prussian army and as Friedrich Wilhelm III's *Kammerherr*; nominally Prussian minister plenipotentiary in Madrid, but stayed on in Berlin; 1821–1824 envoy extraordinary and minister plenipotentiary in London, then in Paris until 1837; 1837–1841 cabinet minister for foreign affairs. 176, 181, 188, 190, 217

Westmorland, see **Fane**

Westphalen, Otto Graf (1807–1856), Prussian diplomat. Ambassador in Oldenburg 1847–1848 after being rejected as the ambassador to the Hanoverian court because of his conversion to Catholicism. 1854–1857 envoy extraordinary and minister plenipotentiary in Stockholm. 285–286

Wheaton, Henry (1785–1848), American envoy to Berlin from 1836 to 1846. 173

Wienbarg, Ludolf (1802–1872), writer and philosopher. After studying at Kiel, Bonn and Marburg, *Habilitation* at the University of Kiel in 1833. He dedicated his lectures on *Ästhetische Feldzüge* (Aesthetic campaigns) (1834) to the literary-political movement *Junges Deutschland* (Young Germany). From 1835 co-editor of *Deutsche Revue* in Frankfurt; from 1842 Hamburg editor of *Börsenhalle*. 77

Wiesend, Anton, *Stadtkommissar* and censor in Würzburg. Wiesend was dismissed as censor in June 1838 as a result of Prussian protests against the anti-Prussian articles in the *Neue Würzburger Zeitung*. 53

Wietersheim, Carl August Wilhelm Eduard von (1787–1865), Saxon official and statesman. After taking part in the Wars of Liberation, Wietersheim was first *Justitzrat* in Dresden and 1827–1828 *Kreishauptmann* in Plauen and Zwickau; 1831 president of the *Landesdirektion*; 1835

Kreisdirektor in Dresden and the leading official in the ministry of the interior; 1840–1848 member of Julius von Könneritz's conservative cabinet as Saxon minister of culture.   329

Wigard, Franz Jakob (1807–1885), politician and stenographer. In addition to working as the stenographer for the second chamber of the Saxon *Landtag* he was, from 1839, director of the Stenography Institute in Dresden and founder and chair of the German Catholic community in Dresden. 1847 the Saxon government prevented him from taking his seat in the Dresden municipal council, of which he was a member 1849–1852, 1864–1874, and 1881–1882; 1848–1849 deputy in the Frankfurt *Vorparlament* and in the national assembly. 1850 removed from his positions as stenographer for the *Landtag* and director of the Stenography Institute; thereafter, he studied medicine. From 1858 he practised as a doctor. In 1850 and 1869–1872 he was a deputy in the second chamber of the Saxon *Landtag*; in 1867–1873 a deputy in the *Reichstag*.   328–329

Wilhelm (1783–1851), Prince of Prussia, brother of Friedrich Wilhelm III; 1824 governor of the federal fortress in Mainz, 1830–1831 governor general on the Lower Rhine.   120, 171

Wilhelm (1797–1888), Prince of Prussia, second son of King Friedrich Wilhelm III. 1858 took over the regency from his brother Friedrich Wilhelm IV; 1871 proclaimed German Emperor in Versailles.   138, 171–172, 202, 212, 215–217, 258, 400

Wilhelm (1806–1884), governing Duke in Brunswick from 1830–1831, after the overthrow of his brother, Duke Karl II.   7, 101

Wilhelm (August Heinrich Belgicus) (1792–1839), Duke of Nassau, regent from 1816.   14–15, 60

Wilhelm I (1781–1864), from 1816 King of Württemberg.   108, 347, 349–350, 353–354, 356, 360, 362–364, 368–369, 372–374, 376–377, 379–382, 388, 393, 397–399, 402–404, 452, 481, 492–493

Wilhelm II (1777–1847), Prince Elector of Hesse-Cassel 1821–1847.   9, 13–14, 58, 120

Wilhelm, Philipp (1798–1840), medical doctor. After a brief period as lecturer at Würzburg, from 1824 professor of surgery at Munich.   426

Wilkens, Karl Friedrich (from 1825) von Hohenau (*1792), diplomat. 1821–1842 envoy extraordinary and minister plenipotentiary of Electoral

Hesse in Berlin, 1842–1851 in Vienna and 1853–1861 again in Berlin. 353

Willem I (1772–1843), regent from 1802, 1815–1840 King of the Netherlands; gave up the throne in 1840. 186

Willers, mayor of Burgdorf and deputy representing the town in the second chamber of the Hanoverian *Landtag*. Resigned his seat in 1839 during the constitutional conflict. 256

William IV (1765–1837), younger brother of George IV, Duke of Clarence; from 1830 King of England and Hanover. xv, xxii, 4, 10, 149–150, 251n, 264, 284, 286, 310n, 411

Willich, Friedrich Justus, lawyer in the Bavarian Palatinate and deputy in the second chamber of the Bavarian *Landtag*. 464

Winter, Ludwig Georg (1778–1838), Baden statesman. Studied law, then entered Baden civil service in 1800. 1815 *Ministerialrat* in the ministry of the interior, from 1830 minister of the interior. His reform policy included such areas as freedom of trade and of the press, the introduction of public proceedings in trials by jury and modern community regulations, and the promotion of education and transport. 359, 363

Wirschinger, Ludwig von (1781–1840), Bavarian politician. After studying law, entered the civil service in 1805. 1823 in charge of matters relating to the Catholic church in the ministry of the interior. Under Ludwig I his first responsibilities were customs and representing the government in the *Landtag*. From 1828, as general customs administrator, he supported the German Customs Union in the finance ministry; from 1835 council of state and minister of finance. 437

Wirth, Johann Georg August (1798–1848), after studying law at Erlangen and Halle, intially embarked upon a legal career. From 1830 worked as a journalist. 1832 moved to the Bavarian Palatinate in order to benefit from the milder exercise of censorship there, but immediately fell foul of the censor again. At the Hambach Festival in April 1832 Wirth, as one of the main speakers, called for a new order in Europe on the basis of liberal democracy. After serving the prison term to which he was sentenced in 1833, Wirth remained under police surveillance until he fled to France in 1836. 1848 returned to Germany, and was a deputy in the Frankfurt national assembly until his death in July. 19n, 21–22, 25–26, 501

Wislicensus, Gustav Adolf (1803–1875), Protestant theologian. In 1834 pastor in Klein-Echstedt near Querfurt, 1841 in Halle; 1845 removed from office because he participated in a meeting of the free-thinking movement; 1848 deputy in the Frankfurt *Vorparlament* and chair of the Democratic Association in Halle; 1853 sentenced to two years' imprisonment for his Bible criticism. Thereafter emigrated, first to the USA, later to Switzerland, where he spent the rest of his life writing and lecturing. 229

Wittgenstein, see **Sayn-Wittgenstein-Hohenstein**

Witzleben, Karl Ernst Job (Hiob) von (1783–1837), 1815 appointed chief of general staff in Prussian general command; 1816 in war ministry; 1817 head of military cabinet; 1818 adjutant general; 1831 royal Prussian lieutenant general; 1833 temporary war minister; 1834–1837 minister of state and war minister. 160, 174

Wrede, Karl Philipp (from 1814) Fürst von (1767–1838), Bavarian officer and diplomat. Gave up career in the civil service when entered the Bavarian army in 1801. 1804 lieutenant general; 1812 led Bavarian troops of the Great Army; 1813 concluded Treaty of Ried; 1814 field marshal; 1814–1815 Bavaria's representative at Congress of Vienna; 1822–1829 commander-in-chief of the Bavarian army. 1832, as extraordinary *Hofkommissär*, he was responsible for the liberation of the Palatinate after the Hambach Festival, and in 1835 headed the *Kronrat.* 306n, 416, 429

Wrede, Karl Theodor Fürst von (1797–1871), 1837–1845 *Regierungspräsident* of the Rhine administrative district in Bavaria; member of the first chamber. 465–466

Yorck von Wartenburg, Hans David Ludwig (1759–1830), Prussian officer. On 30 December 1812, as commander of the Prussian auxiliary corps in Napoleon I's Russian campaign, he concluded a neutrality convention with Russia on his own authority. With the Silesian army under General Blücher, he fought for the Elbe crossing at Wartenburg in 1813. 165

Zehler, Wilhelm (*1811), student at Würzburg. Took part in the Storming of the Frankfurt Guard House on 3 April 1833; 1836 sentenced to life imprisonment; escaped from Frankfurt jail on 10 January 1837. 83n, 84n

Zenetti, Johann Baptist (from 1837 Ritter von) (1785–1856), Bavarian official and politician. 1832–1837 *Regierungsdirektor* in the Lower Danube administrative district in Passau; 1837–1846 *Ministerialrat* in the Bavarian ministry of the interior; 1846–1847 *Regierungspräsident* of Lower Bavaria; 1847 council of state and *Ministerverweser* in the Bavarian ministry of the interior; 1848 deputy in the Frankfurt national assembly. 1849–1850 *Regierungspräsident* of the Palatinate. 476

Zeschau, Heinrich Anton von (1789–1870), Saxon politician. *Geheimer sächsischer Finanzrat* in 1822; 1829 envoy to the *Bundestag* (Federal Diet); 1830 *wirklicher Geheimrat* and *Oberconsistorialpräsident* in Dresden; 1831 president of the *Geheime Finanzkollegium* and finance minister; 1835–1848 additionally foreign minister; played an important part in the negotiations concerning the German Customs Union; reformed the Saxon taxation system in Saxony; 1849 *Ordenskanzler*; 1851 additionally minister of the royal house and supervised the king's private fortune. 121–122, 302, 308–309, 316, 320, 331, 334–335

Zu Rhein, Friedrich August von (1802–1870), Bavarian statesman and official. Interrupting his term as minster president and *Verweser* of the justice and finance ministry in 1847, 1841–1849 *Regierungspräsident* of the Upper Palatinate and Regensburg; thereafter until 1868 *Regierungspräsident* of Lower Franconia. 475–476

Zu Rhein, Maximilian Joseph von (1780–1832), statesman and official. After studying law, entered the civil service of Bavaria and Württemberg. From 1817 first vice president, and from 1826 *Regierungspräsident* of Lower Franconia. Bavarian minister for justice 1832. 413

SUBJECT INDEX